I0606236

Inscriptions: Architecture Before Speech

K. Michael Hays
Andrew Holder

Distributed by Harvard University Press
Cambridge, Massachusetts and London, England

$-S$	Transcendental Originals	Labyrinths Eidetic Houses Booleans
$\overline{S}$	Revealed Originals	Superimpositions Revelations Slack Collections Scatters, Remnants
S	Immanent Originals	Dirt, Earth, and Rocks Trabeated Stacks First Houses Seven Wonders
$-\overline{S}$	Encountered Originals	Monoliths Anamorphic Figures The Creaturely

i Table of Contents

Table of Contents

1 Prelude

Andrew Holder
Inscriptions; or, Plurality by Design

> *In posing the problem of an "origin," we presuppose the discovery of a* final *point of arrival: a destination point that* explains *everything, that causes a given "truth," a primary value, to burst forth from the encounter with its originary ancestor. . . . To avoid the chimera of origin, the genealogist must avoid all notions of linear causality. He thus exposes himself to a risk, provoked by the shocks and accidents, by the weak point or points of resistance that history itself presents.*
> —Manfredo Tafuri, "The Historical 'Project'"

Against the popular characterization of contemporary architecture as a centerless field where anything goes and everything is possible, this book aims to show that much recent work belongs to a collective undertaking of *inscriptions*. Yes, at the level of individual projects the work collected here looks mixed, if not willfully, kaleidoscopically disparate. Underneath this, though, there is a shared mechanism, an agreement about how architectural objects emerge from the procedures of design. This conjecture emerged in the last days of 2017 as the editors of this volume collaborated to mount a survey exhibition of contemporary architecture and noticed a pattern. It was not the unearthing of similar forms exactly but rather the insistent flash of recognition itself that gave the discovery of each project a quality of confirmation, of underscoring premonitory knowledge. What did we see? Outsized fragments of infrastructure, stacked to afford box-like shelter but teetering at the outer limits of structural and aesthetical precariousness. Structurally stable, conventionally built constructions of plywood designed to afford shelter in the manner of haphazard stacks. Concrete columns and slabs so relentlessly trabeated—horizontal, vertical, horizontal, vertical—that the homogeneity of concrete atomized visually into a basic grammar of discrete parts, turning building envelopes into stacks of niches. Parts accumulated in vast, haphazard arrays submitted as designs for the most programmatically and technically determined environments like gyms and amphitheaters. Masses of parts bundled into tidy sets so that cutting or joining rooms, roofs, or walls becomes push-button simple Boolean arithmetic. Arrays of rooms stretching horizontally to labyrinthine extremes of repetition, suggesting a life lived navigating unending interiors, all within the tiny footprints of shotgun houses or patches of exhibition space. Interiors formed by the press and cluster of creatures around empty living spaces. Living spaces of another kind, replete with furniture, doors, pianos, and every accoutrement of convention, all decoded as clearings from a tangle of marks on cubes or spheres drawn in multiple projections. Projections that limn the edges of cubic agglomerations, finding, tracing, and cutting thicknesses that capture and store the heat of the sun in blunt stacks of oversized blocks. Rocks.

Box, stack, array, set, maze, body, mark, block, rock: at first glance it is an almost nursery-rhyme survey of objects in an untidy room. But that's just it. The logic of the list is the thing-by-thing recitation of fundamentals. Each form, each operation, is known, emphatically familiar, even ancient. What are we to make of this? Should we find in it a nostalgic safe harbor at a moment of maximal global insecurity, a return to certainties achieved long ago? The impulse, in Tafuri's words, "to regain the innocence of archetypal symbols; the pyramid, the sphere, the circle, the ellipse, and the labyrinth"?[1] An urge to pour the comforting fictions of durable truths and enduring social compacts into the molds of past forms in order to mass-produce a familiar New Civic Architecture with just enough aesthetic untidiness to impart a whiff of belonging to the present? Not the pristine neoclassicism implied by Tafuri's circles and ellipses but the long-awaited neo-not-modernism that, just as we thought, would look something like a cartoon of prehistory—caves, mounds, and all? Is the future to be housed in some new primitive hut? A hut not of logs shaped into a temple but an agglomeration of late capitalism's "garbage and throwaways,"[2] massed jauntily into a pyramid and platted out in something like the suburbs, as though such a form could secure meaning and permanence for refuse?

No, the significance of this body of work lies not in its value as a cultural symptom of withdrawal from societal turmoil into the safety of an imagined past, nor in the projection of that past forward into a reactionary version of the future. Inscriptions do not offer stability per se. Although known in the sense of being immediately ascertainable, the objects at play in this book are not drawn from an historically definite past, or even a past at all. Some are ancient (pyramids), some not so ancient (ranch houses), and others do not belong to real time (giant creatures). And many of these objects are present as an *emptiness*. Infrastructural elements stack *around* a box; creaturely skins huddle *toward* a hut: for all their definiteness, the box and the hut are vacant armatures on which works are constructed.[3] If we have indeed entered an architectural moment characterized by recognition, then, it is not one stabilized by backward glances or reassuring presences. By foregoing these reassurances, however, we can begin to identify kernels of truth in the structural logic of the otherwise cynical rumination above. The symbolic grandeur of pyramids set against the illogic and technical difficulty of construction from remnants is a handy image of inscription. Architects pitch design against—or rather *inscribe* it onto—the emptiness that we would call an original (more on that word later) such that the original persists as a regulating substrate even while it is overwritten by the accumulation of architectural activity reforming its surface. This is not an analogy to writing; it is a constructive act. No matter how abstract or technically specialized the work may be, the stacking, blocking, marking, and set making of the projects in this volume can be regarded after the fact as having come into being through a kind of manual cognition.

Again, though, there is the question of cultural significance. What are we to make of these strange familiarities and recurrences? We propose two different but complementary answers to this question. At the end of the book, K. Michael Hays proposes inscriptions as a progression in the history of architecture and subject formation. This architecture is nothing less than a way of hailing a new version of us, of calling out newly minted capacities to understand the built environment. Charting the emergence of this new subject out of older models in language and psychoanalysis, he offers inscription as a way for architects to work in definite, even figural terms, and to do so with ethical clarity long after the collapse of master codes of meaning and virtuous action.

In this essay I offer a converse but compatible view. Instead of beginning with differences between projects that are resolved through a model of the subject, I stress a consistent mechanism operating across projects that forms groups and we-constructions filled with difference. The claim is this: inscriptions gather things and people around a shared architectural endeavor. Let's call this *plurality formation*. Admittedly, the phrase requires some shoring-up in order to convey the meaning I intend. In the shadow of the postmodern delight in samples and fragments drawn from everywhere, the term *plurality* comes to us now as a limp category roughly equivalent to "whatever." The tradition of pluralism as it arises from politics and philosophy, though, is anything but passive acceptance. Pluralism entails reckoning with the fact that "the immense, contradictory, and varying flow of human life renders it irreducible and unaccountable from the perspective of one single outlook."[4] The brutality of this realization makes for two halves of the pluralist project (if the word is to be used as an agenda rather than a passive descriptor). First, there is the task of merely admitting and naming the irreconcilable differences evident in an empirical survey of the world. The products of this work in philosophy go by names like "value pluralism," "sphere fragmentation," and the "polytheism of values" that liken the contest of viewpoints to warring gods.[5] Second, there is the implicit expectation that pluralists offer some common venue where these differences can make contact without lapsing into hostility, schism, or all-out collapse. Democracy was thought to be one such structure, and ideas about how pluralities might coexist within it are at the crux of exchanges between early 20th-century political theorists.[6] The problem, and the point of contention, was *how* to live pluralism as a social and political experience. To say that inscriptions form pluralities is to claim nothing less than this at the scale of buildings. They produce gatherings open to difference while also cohering around a shared sense of architecture—temporary and jittery with divergent interests, at once caring about and indifferent to the discipline, filled with doubt and arriving on the scene with wildly varying degrees of knowledge. The rest of this essay will trace the mechanics of this process in four parts: first, how individuals can come to understand themselves as belonging to a plural “we-construction” gathered around a work of architecture; second, how coalescing these pluralities preserves an essential doubt that allows them to dissolve and re-form according to other impulses of configuration; third, how this process has already enlisted architectural history as a means of expanding the materials, aesthetics, and populations that might congregate in an architectural plurality; and fourth, how inscriptions, by deliberately incorporating the “shocks” and “ruptures” of these expansions, offer a model for structuring a coherent architectural discourse at a moment when the only durable fact seems to be the shattering of the field into incommensurable fragments.

Subtending this move toward plurality, charging it with a political fervor, is architecture’s present reckoning with how to open itself up to difference. Every architectural act is newly met by the questions “by whom?” and “for whom?”: Who made it? Who are the ranks of our practitioners? And for whom did we make it? Do we serve those who are like us? Or the egalitarian version of us we aspire to be? As part of this struggle, we may wish to describe the artifacts produced by our discipline as evidence of letting “one hundred flowers blossom,” as if providing a visual index of progress made toward openings into other spheres. But this is not the case. In fact, a broad swath of work we are producing today betrays an emergence from some origin, signaling underlying accord. This is perhaps not so much a judgment on the failure of our efforts to open ourselves up as it is a signal that some additional, as-yet unarticulated process is in play. New practitioners and new clients, after all, do not guarantee a parallel opening in aesthetics, nor do they necessarily make for better professional ethics. As a complement to the model of separate spheres (practitioners, clients, buildings) linked by processes of representation (the characteristics of the client reproduced in the characteristics of the practitioner), inscriptions propose the centrality of the architectural object as a common plane of interaction on which to gather difference.

Imagining oneself or one's work as a participant on this plane is not to subordinate architecture to a master narrative of progress but rather to build a shared model of practice that offers purchase for alternative futures—a collectively held image that is subject to critique and modification.[7] At some other moment in architectural history we may have referred to this activity as theory. At present let us simply say inscriptions are effective.

First Office, PS1 Dolmen, model, 2016.

1. Forms of Gathering

Take, as a first example, First Office's PS1 Dolmen. It offers one of the more obvious invitations to think of architecture as an accumulation of marks on a substrate: an ancient megalith, pocked and speckled with little dents, screw heads, plywood seams, and water stain rivulets—all signs of design and construction happening atop *something*. This *something* is both less and more than it would initially appear to be. Less in the sense that the dolmen has been emptied of historical specificity. The title promises a dolmen at the Museum of Modern Art outpost in Queens, and that's basically what is delivered, though the question remains: which dolmen and what's it doing in New York? Is this a copy of a dolmen with some particular significance? Digging through the firm's history unearths a long-held fascination with neolithic stone constructions, an interest in the photographs of the naturalist Eugène Trutat, and at least three projects similar to the PS1 Dolmen, but no clues as to its particular form. The PS1 Dolmen is a historical blank. The underlying *something* is also less as a result of the geometric system First Office uses to describe it. The geometric vocabulary is confined to boxes that substitute for the traditional lithic structures, as if to trace the shape of rocks with such coarse fidelity that each becomes a six-sided polygon. The coarse and speckly elevations of rocks are emptied out to the point of being simply indicated by a rectangular plane—a blank picture

Eugène Trutat, *Dolmen de Cap del Pouech*, photograph, 1859–1910.

plane maybe, with the implicit suggestion that something might eventually fill it in. The crenellated edges of the rocks are eradicated too as all lines trace straight paths to meet at 90-degree intersections. All that's left after these formal erasures are the rotations of one volume against another, along with the props and wedges required to keep these balanced in a state of poise. Far from being the residual afterthought that their small size and scattered distribution might imply, these little crutches are required to fix in place the *real physics of an emptiness* imported from some other set of gravitational conditions (a Trutat photograph perhaps) into those that obtain in the Museum of Modern Art PS1 courtyard. The panels of the box volumes are built outward from these fixed points at the interstices—not stacked up as we would understand the construction of a dolmen pictured by Trutat but rather measured from the air around it.

This is where the less of historical evacuation and the less of formal erasure add up to more. The rotations, the cants measured in half-degrees, the precarious balance: the construction is definite, present, and happening in the now. The effect of this—the specificity of the dolmen form without a definite historical or representational antecedent—is to deliver a promise to the audience gathered in the courtyard.[8] First Office places "dolmen" in the public domain as a term held in common, making it shared knowledge, no matter how much or how little one knows about the word. And not only *a* dolmen passes from the architect to the audience, but *that* dolmen. The question—which dolmen, and why?—shifts to a collective declaration: *We're doing that*. The audience–architect relationship flattens into something more like the we-construction of plurality.

The firm's design work happens atop this newly shared term, inscribed on its surface with all those little screws, pocks, dents, and seams. There is a blunt literalism to this, in the sense that the substrate "dolmen" participates materially as an underlying limit or support for an accretion that proceeds from the fixed points of rotation that pin each volume in place: standard wood-stud construction describes the edges of the voided dolmen rocks, plywood sheathing encloses these as hollow volumes, dottings of screws secure the panels to the studs in legible but irregular patterns, and everything is washed in a grayish stain to fill, or rather to hold and stabilize, the otherwise empty elevations.[9] Instead of accruing toward complexity or inscrutability, each of these inscriptive marks opens the project up to possible readings. At each stop along the scalar hierarchy emerges a new analytical point of view, as well as a new task that might be undertaken with one's hands—either literally through the group-sourcing of labor or via the ease of imaginatively projecting oneself as a participant in the construction. The scope of the we-construction grows with the addition of each analytical frame while the

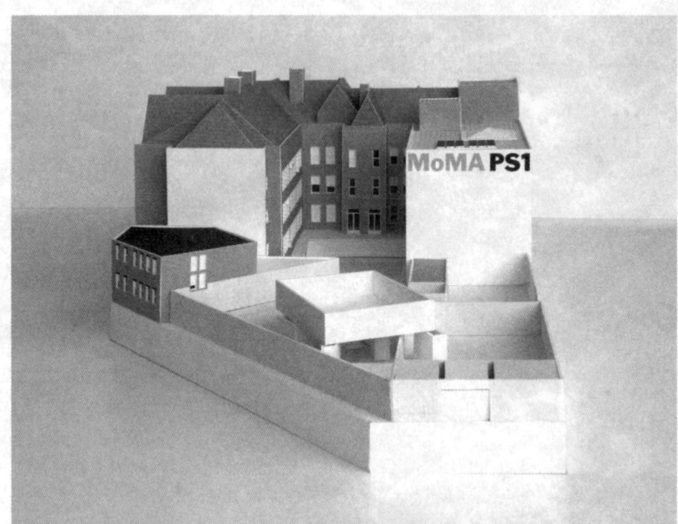

First Office, PS1 Dolmen, model, 2016.

constant meter of physical inscription furnishes a plane of contact between them. Close up, in surface effect: the gray color of the stain and the sparkly albedo of the screw heads take what would in quarried rock be a unitary optical phenomenon and mimic it uncannily with heterogeneous elements. The screws glitter dimly against the flat gray, obviously the result of drill and paintbrush work but no less striking for it, just experientially split between screw and stain, so that the enjoyment of optical sensuality happens through the physical mechanics of inscription. At the next scale, plywood sheets are laid out in symmetrical paneling patterns on the dolmen feet to stabilize what would otherwise be picturesquely irregular forms into cruciform shapes and centered grids. The genre expectations of architectural drawing, with its straight lines and regular orderings, are superimposed, with the help of butt joints, on the areas of the dolmen that would normally borrow the conventions of landscape painting. At the level of volumetric logic, the wall cavities of Type V construction turn solid rocks into hollow rooms but distribute them according to the foot-and-top-plate logic of simple statics. Finally, in the realm of labor and visual effects that exceed the scale of the solitary dolmen, construction conforms to expedient, widely available standards while at the same time elevating the finished result to the level of a logistical miracle. How did something so big and ungainly make it inside the courtyard? How is it hovering over the wall so excruciatingly close without touching it? Read in reverse order, as list of analytical positions taken up *through* the physical performance of the task at hand, it's phenomenology by screw gun, art history through plywood layups, formal analysis through hollow-wall construction, and connoisseurship through the trade of rough carpentry.

While the marks and scratches on the PS1 Dolmen are particularly vivid inscriptions, the project exemplifies a pattern found across all of the work in this volume. Even in the

Ensamble Studio, The Truffle, 2010.

case of projects that do begin with historical inquiry or a dig into the ground, the familiarity at the center of each work is not the uncovering of an "origin," a first "linear cause," or an invitation to "find the murderer."[10] Instead, a figure is emptied and put forward as a term held in common that initiates the manual task of inscription.[11] Like First Office, architects use form to point—*See? We're doing that*—and then proceed with the task of inscribing the hollowness designated by "that." Ensamble Studio's Truffle begins with a literal hole, hay, and concrete, promising to make a rock. JaJa Co's project Scoring, Building, begins with the edges of a four-sided polygon, light-gauge studs, and a schedule, promising to make a room. Paul Preissner Architects' Yeoui Naru Ferry Terminal begins with an ovoid patch of water, to which he brings tranches of building materials—decking, a steel grid, stubby towers—promising, in effect, that the deliberately ad hoc collection of stuff will float, so long as the architect sediments it skillfully enough in a series of layers atop the plan of the egg-shaped site.

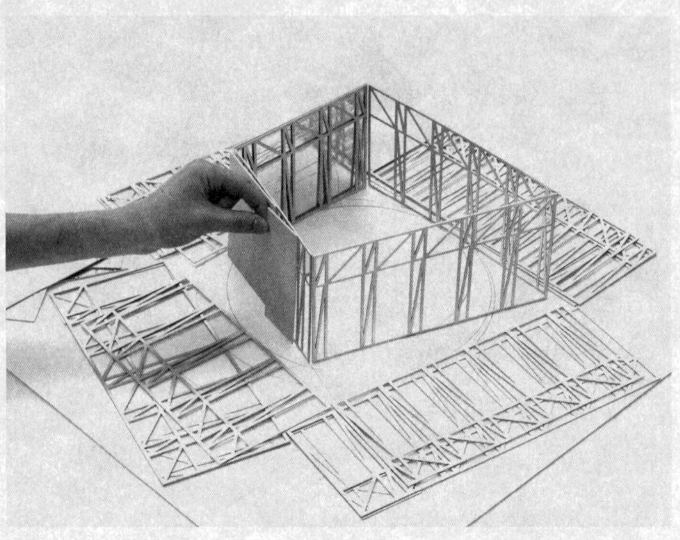

JaJa Co, Scoring, Building, model, 2020.

What is this term at the center of these other projects? The equivalent of the word *dolmen* that makes them known in advance? Yes, a prior lurks in these projects. But as with the dolmen that comes from some foggy prehistory, each of these examples is chronologically nonspecific, more out of place than some antecedent that actually came before. Taking this quality of anachronism together with their function as compacts with an audience, we call these forms "originals," but not in the way Tafuri meant. Yes, they may involve a model or even a basis from which to start, but they are invoked inside the space of a project and must be conjured anew with each one. My use of the word is meant to emphasize the characterological individuality (a "real original") of something that is distinctively legible but not a generic from which multiples are reproduced. As such, originals cannot be reduced to the concepts that architectural history

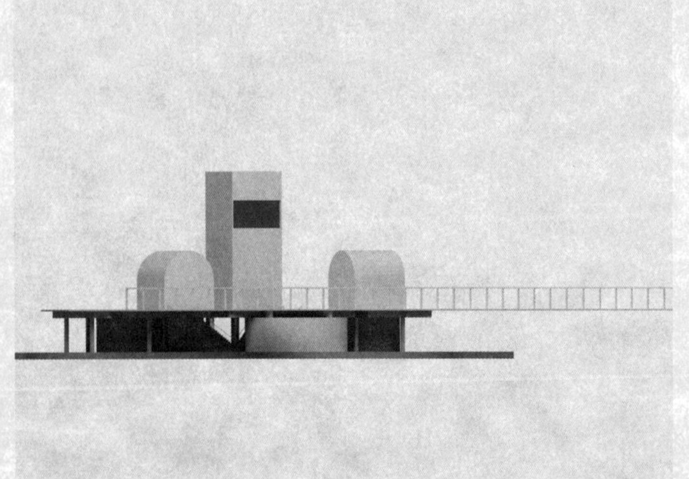

Paul Preissner Architects, Yeoui Naru Ferry Terminal, rendering, 2017.

has used to describe things that persist outside the bounds of a particular project. Originals are not *beginnings*; they do not set in motion linear causation that can be evaluated on the basis of its fidelity to the point of origin. Originals are not *primitives*.[12] Information and detail do not progress from blank to fully formed—neither in the manner of Leonardo da Vinci's sketches of ideal churches, which begin with circles and squares and then mature in a miraculous projection from plan to section through the orders, nor as in the metaphor of biological development from embryo to fetus. They are not *types*, although the structuralist use of this word comes closest to describing originals as a measure that indexes ensuing architectural acts.[13] But if the idea of type that was theorized by J. N. L. Durand, Aldo Rossi, and Rafael Moneo suggests a durable model that unites the logic of forms with cultural significance or programmatic effectivity, then originals tend toward the opposite. The contemporary impulse seems rather to counter-inscribe—sepulchral ziggurats into houses (Medium Office's Stack Villas or d.esk's Ziggurhut), haphazard structural arrays into museums (Preston Scott Cohen, Inc.'s Eyebeam Atelier Museum or Mack Scogin Merrill Elam Architects' Kaohsiung Cultural and Popular Music Center), or monumental towers into concert halls (Endemic Architecture's Music Hall for Golden Gate Park)—all in a knowing unconcern for typological unity. Whereas types require radical abstraction and the fabrication of long-term continuities to arrive at unification, originals are transient but still structurally (metrically) effective; they find their place in specific instances of somatic cognition.

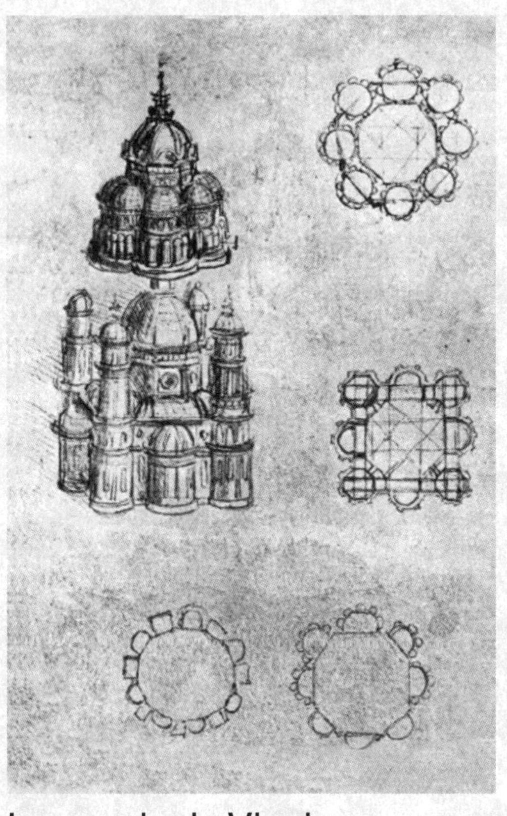

Leonardo da Vinci, *Two Churches and Plans (Codex B)*, drawing, 1492.

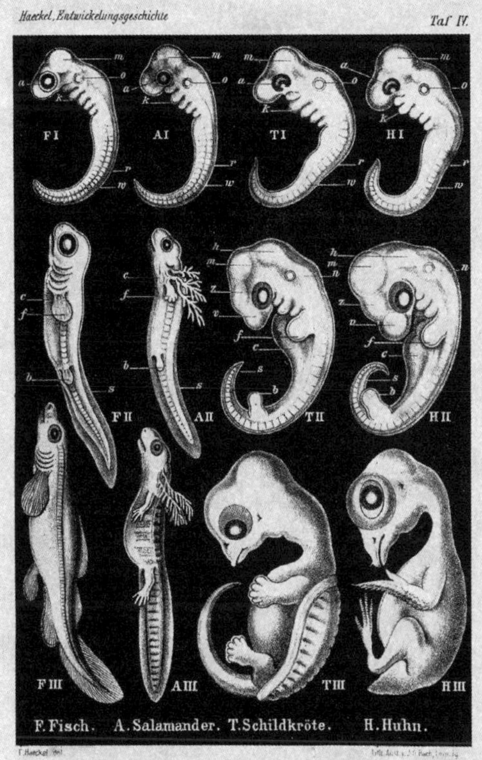

Ernst Haeckel, *Anthropogenie (Fish, Salamander, Turtle, Chicken)*, drawing, 1874.

Like types, primitives, and beginnings, though, the original at the center of each inscription works as the hinge that connects the individual project with a larger conception of whom the project is for and who is implicated or touched by the presence of the finished product. Up to this point, *gathering* and *audience* have been the words used to describe this move from singular project to larger we-constructions, but this deserves further specification. First, inscriptions emerge from an imagination of the task to be done.[14] This is an invitation to deliberately conflate the manual work of the task with a point of view, in the way that the screws and stain of the dolmen are an opening for the phenomenologically minded to enjoy sensation *through* the artifacts of screwing and staining. This goes for other modes of architectural analysis familiar to academic practitioners, but it works in other registers too. JaJa Co's project Scoring, Building, comes close to collapsing the task of inscribing a square into the actual act of construction. The project operates as a graphic set of instructions for building around a polygon, almost to the point of handing over a construction technique so nonprofessionals can take on the task of building as if it were a barn raising. The Truffle perhaps comes even closer to this possibility by suggesting buildings are immanent in the dirt all around—all anyone needs is a shovel, the project seems to promise. Program too can be opened as a function of the task set by the original. The interior of the Truffle remaps sleeping and living arrangements onto the increment of the hay bale falsework inside the cast. Paul Preissner Architects' Yeoui Naru Ferry Terminal does something like this by treating departures, arrivals, and waiting in strata, as though organization were coincident with the task of laying down parts in layers that float.

Second, the original—the object at the center of the agreement—refuses to be completely determined by the process of design. It is never fully in play and cannot be plastically deformed into something else. Instead, architecture arrives as the fulfillment of an already disclosed agreement when the inscription of the original is itself the objective. This obdurate quality is fundamentally unlike a postmodern reworking of classical organizations into contemporary building types, or the deformation of a geometric primitive into a commodious form. With inscriptions an intervening layer of symbolic conversion or plastic force modifies the project to render it credible for its audience. This removal of intervening authority—symbolic, authorial, or otherwise—means that the social or political import of these projects resides in the gatherings they coalesce and the durability of the object as a point of gathering. Third, the original provides a form of reassurance to the points of view it gathers: it is a measure by which to index change. Sometimes these are quantitative like the number of steps in a ziggurat, the potential energy locked in a mound's angle of repose, or the volume of dirt removed from hole; alternatively, the standard may be norms of deportment. Whether buried or scattered by these works, rocks are engaged with landscape, for example, while monuments stand atop it. Taken together, these aspects of gathering form the rudiments of a pluralistic compact: to include, to resist change, and to evidence the change that does occur. It promises nothing more or less than the possibility of convening mutually incomprehensible positions around an object.

2. Forms of Doubt

But gatherings around permanent certainties are not pluralities. By definition, pluralities do not relinquish their points of view or values when brought together. Instead, they contest. Structures that hold them together need to be elastic enough to absorb and encourage these reconfigurations as pluralities to not only increase or decrease in size but also form and reform themselves around shifting reasons for getting together. Correspondingly, inscriptions not only furnish stabilities but also have two ways of building doubts into them as a kind of happy guarantee of failure.

First, inscriptions encourage reforming according to new terms by reconfiguring what is meant by the word *design* and the role of the person we call "architect." Both are pulled away a little from total identification with the building and become freer to enter into different relationships with their audience. Silver House Studio, by Current Interests, provides a useful example. The "studio" is the original, and it sets the terms of the task. It is like the dolmen in the sense of furnishing a term in common, except that "studio" refers to the Angeleno habit of constructing an accessory building alongside a house (there's even an accessory building provision in the municipal code). In Current Interests' version of this almost ubiquitous act, dangling sheets of insulation and weatherproofing hang from the studio's outer limits, and a structural frame marks out the same volume from its lodgment inside—so that the empty shape of the studio original is described from both within and without. These acts of draping and propping aren't measurable on a spectrum from authored design to unauthored emergence. They can't be attributed to the machinations of an architect-genius or to an autonomous cultural or formal procedure managed by the architect-technician, nor really to any other role that would assign degrees of responsibility to a generating hand.

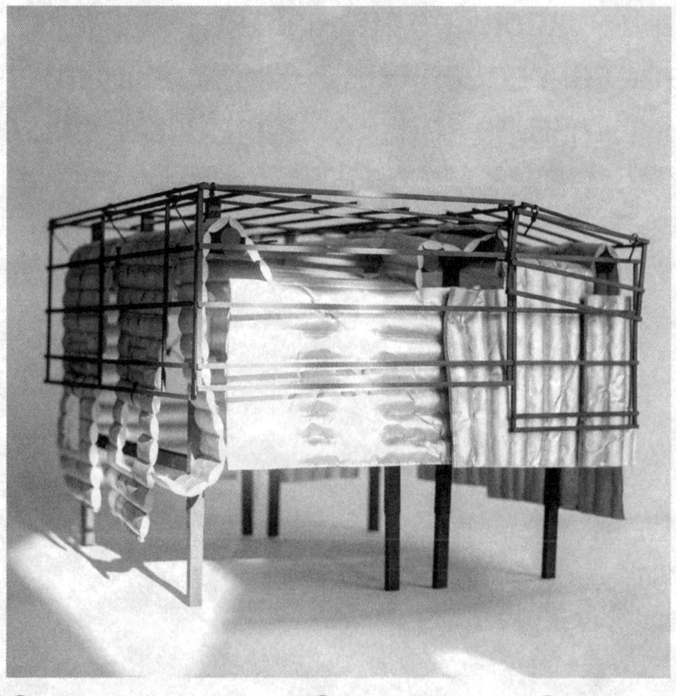

Current Interests, Silver House Studio, model, in progress.

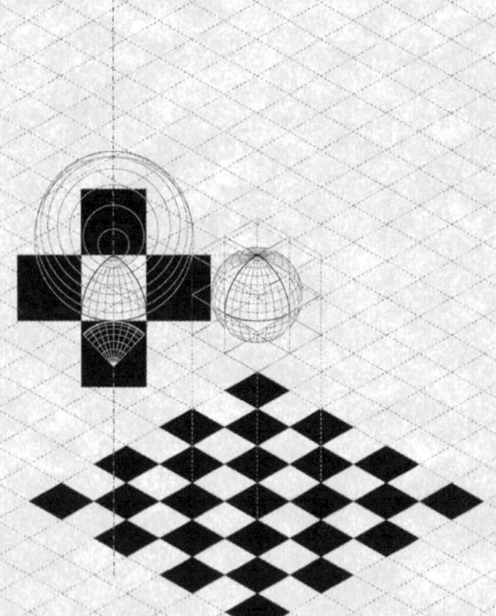

JaJa Co, Hat to Home; or, Dome to Domus, drawing, 2015.

In fact, it's not at all clear that the architect's role is to design the studio in the usual sense. Instead, we think of Current Interests' design act as a *physical mode of address*. It's a theatrical *apostrophe*, an exclamatory address to an inanimate object. Current Interests comes at the studio like a tailor to a dress form before a crowd of onlookers: *Oh, here you go, let's pin this here, and that there.* Design happens around and on the prefigured form of the studio in a way that constantly includes the audience (the client, or neighbors, or City administrators) without addressing them directly. The beauty of Silver House Studio therefore lies in the architect's invitation to approach and consume the work with a DIY frame of mind, as though it were always open to the reconfiguration of roles that would happen if someone made a suggestion to drape differently. The dishevelment of hanging insulation isn't messy; rather, it's the beauty of a system of authorship that can, despite a high degree of formal determination and aesthetic control, be undertaken by anyone in a casual aside.

While the plurality gathered around Silver House Studio reforms easily when someone else steps up to redrape or rescaffold the original, other modes of address can be more intensely personal and consequently imply the possibility of more dramatic dissolutions. JaJa Co's Hat to Home and FreelandBuck's "drawing objects" perform the inscription of inside-the-discipline projection techniques like spherical drawing or anamorphosis. These projects form pluralities around the charismatic allure of a mediumistic practice that purports to convey something from sphere, something not seen by the audience but nonetheless desired. The viewer sees the results of the drawing techniques (like views of ceilings that miraculously resolve the appearance of full spatial depth from

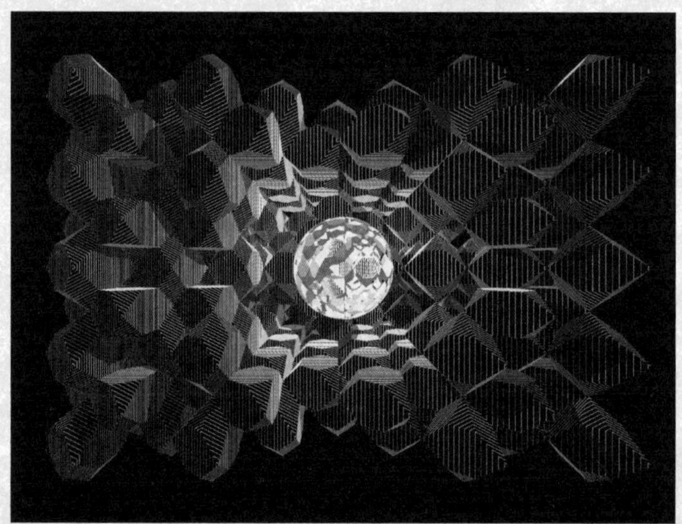

FreelandBuck, Objective Perspective (Interior Volume Mapped to Ball), 2015.

d.esk, Ziggurhut, 2018.

certain vantages in FreelandBuck's work) but has to rely on secret activities undertaken by the architect. Observers can't know the mechanism used by the architect to map her spheres and shapes—knowing would spoil the pleasure of spectating. And in fact, the original state of the spheres and shapes remains a secret too. The audience can only take the architect's word for it that some original is being interpreted and recorded. Through all this the person of the architect remains a central figure of fascination, which risks the total collapse and reformation of the audience as its desire finds other targets. The possibility of this collapse is essential: it has to be risked so the audience can dissolve and reform in a different configuration.

Architects can also address the original in a representative mode, inscribing the client brief on the figure of the original. Both d.esk and Medium Office do this with houses inscribed into the figure of a ziggurat. In these instances, it's not that the ziggurat is an especially good or bad form for a house; the ziggurat is there as the foil against which the client's interests are advocated by the architect-representative. The pleasure comes from the surprise of seeing the architect's advocacy pay off against all odds, as windows and doors are rescaled and reoriented in blocky increments that constantly shift the relationship of plan to building envelope. Of course, there's also the very real risk (again, essential to the formation of pluralities) that the gambit strains credulity and the architect fails to "win" the battle with the figure.

The apostrophe, the architect-medium, and the architect-representative: these three modes of address—just three instances drawn from reservoirs of possibility in theater, hermeticism, and politics—can be thought of as configurations that sow doubt. Each mode of address fixes in place for a moment a relation of architect, design, original, and audience, but at the same time imbues it with both a small jitter of

Medium Office, Stack Villa 4, 2019.

possible role shuffling and a greater risk of collapse as participants decamp for some other mode.

If this first kind of doubt engendered by inscriptions is about configuration, then there is a second kind concerning knowledge. Inscriptions undercut the "known" qualities that accompany ziggurats, rocks, stacks, and creatures and induce a renewed sense of skepticism. While the form of the original may resist plastic deformation, *knowledge* of it is modified by the mode of address. There is an intercalibration of the original against the inscription that makes a new coherence, marked by reciprocal adjustments to convention. The PS1 Dolmen, for instance, is marked by intercalibration of rock stacking against panelization—those symmetrical cross-patterns of seams breaking the surface of otherwise rough and shaky blocks. The hollow-wall construction, likewise, turns the spatial order from a trabeated capstone and columns into a hollow plenum resting above little rooms. "The inner chamber can't be occupied in any way we know how to live," say the architects—in other words, mission accomplished. The same claim could be made for Silver House Studio. Draped building materials stop short of touching the ground, as if a skirt lifted to allow egress and light underneath, rather than the accessory building's usual structural perimeter, fortified at the base by a concrete stem wall. A humdrum architectural task like insulating a wall ends up provoking skeptical reflection on architecture's usual means of getting in and looking out. We are no longer certain of architecture's conventions. But unlike the iconoclastic ambitions of past avant-garde proposals, these critical reflections can be undertaken from a point of relative security and calm: adjustments may be radical while avoiding disruptions to habitation as it currently exists. There is no great anxiety about the status of the whole thing. It's not a representation of internal conflict; it's a stable form of doubt.

This consolidation of knowing and doubt—both in the configuration of pluralities and the security of their knowledge—resolves longstanding oppositions between theories of architecture's audience that revolve around questions of how much its members can or should know and how secure or unstable they will feel as a result of this knowledge. On one side, easy forms of knowing mobilize audiences without allowing doubt to enter. Robert E. Somol's essay "Green Dots 101" epitomizes this position, advocating for shapes and logos as easy, legible vehicles for convening audiences around the projection of new futures.[15] Logos are, in a word, known. Their virtue is to signal and deliver on a promise, all in the space of an acquisition. Everybody "gets it," so long as they can get one. On the other side, opposed to this more scrutable formalism, Tafuri calls for architects to embed themselves in systems of architecture's production, in a sense withdrawing from audiences by turning attention to rarified or hidden knowledge. The architect is to become a "'new technician' immersed within those organizations which determine the capitalistic management of building and regional planning."[16] While this technocratic immersion may give architects more direct access to the machinery of capital, it is a withdrawal from common knowledge. Audiences, or at least the kind that might freely crowd around a project, are not given the equipment to take a view of form, to look and position themselves in the built world.

The revolution may or may not arrive—either via the logo's quickening of our current system of production and consumption or Tafuri's anticipation of its overthrow—but architecture has already evolved a more flexible and sensitive formal apparatus that can both rally an audience and disabuse it of ideological adherence to a singular outcome. Inscriptions relocate form to a space between architecture and observer, making it the site for agreement and gathering. The tasks to be performed are neither marketed publicly nor secreted away in the machinery of technical bureaucracies. Tasks are executed under the terms of an agreement that convenes gatherings, but accord does not arrive, exhausted, as the satiation of demand. Both the objects and the means of design are adjusted, displaced from their respective conventions. Inscriptions, then, mobilize gatherings in doubt and enchantment.

3. The Empirical Eye

Plurality formation does not result in a neutral politics. It does not simply reiterate the "whatever" of the postmodern visual field through the ranks of viewpoints gathered around architecture. Instead, pluralities tend toward progressivism, continually confronting our discipline with expanded notions of who gathers in a plurality and the kinds of forms around which they assemble. This political significance is accomplished by allying the practice of history with the practice of design. They now share an *empirical eye*.[17] In both architectural history and architectural design, the empirical eye scans "an entire production cycle rather than a single work," seeking to identify "material constraints which determine the production cycle itself."[18] In practice these material constraints are essentially "facts," atomic units of observation reiterating the world as seen. The interest in "mundane matter" taken up by many historians—things like "food, bodies, housing, markets, cities, and culture"[19]—suggests a mode of analysis that views the world "as it is" in material terms, but so does stock-a-studio's shopping from catalogs, Common Accounts' reuse of found digital models, and T+E+A+M's construction of a pillow fort–like house from construction bric-a-brac.

The empirical eye is directed; it seeks a specific sensation. That is to say, Tafuri's taste for how critical historical practice should feel—delivering "shocks" to the continuity of the present, "deconstructing" ideal models, uncovering the hidden "intertwining of phenomena"—can apply not only to the historian's task but also to the architect's.[20] For both, the delivery of shock to the discipline is in fact the signal of a system working as intended to preempt or disable the development of higher-order systems of classification that architecture uses to describe itself and to replace these with other narratives of measure and order that hew closer to facticity.[21] Form might at first seem to be a casualty of this process, insofar as form is exactly about holding boundaries to make possible the discernment of one architectural thing from another. But everywhere form is eclipsed, the stage is also being set for its return in the pattern of an original waiting to be taken up by processes of inscription. We can see this in two recent instances of the empirical eye at work, an exhibition and a book.

Fulfilled, a 2020 exhibition curated by Ashley Bigham and designed by Outpost Office, displayed artifacts from contemporary architectural practices (many of them represented in this book) alongside the USPS Large Flat Rate boxes in which they were shipped.[22] The "fact" of the exhibition—the measurable commonality among submissions—was a 12¼" × 12¼" × 6" cardboard container, conveyed over a certain distance with something packed inside, serving in the gallery as an index of distributional logistics and fulfillment networks. The myth of exhibitions as the conveyance of an architect's ideas via models and drawings gave way to a beautiful scene of cardboard samples, as if a butterfly collection, in various states of unfolding and disgorging. Who cares what anyone actually submitted to the show? Little of that was memorable. The value lay elsewhere: the shock of puncturing the myth of exhibition became the delight of realizing, and realizing again with every displayed submission, the vast potentiality of the box. It was a manufacture of material inputs for inscriptions. The cubic volume of the box was hollowed out, emptied of its obligation to carry models. So was the volume of the exhibition space, and in a larger sense the orbiting networks of truck routes, which no longer carried messages from studios. Each of these became an original awaiting uptake. And at the same time, the exhibition reproposed the box and the material that could be put to work enclosing these newfound figures. All that folded cardboard from all those places. Fold it

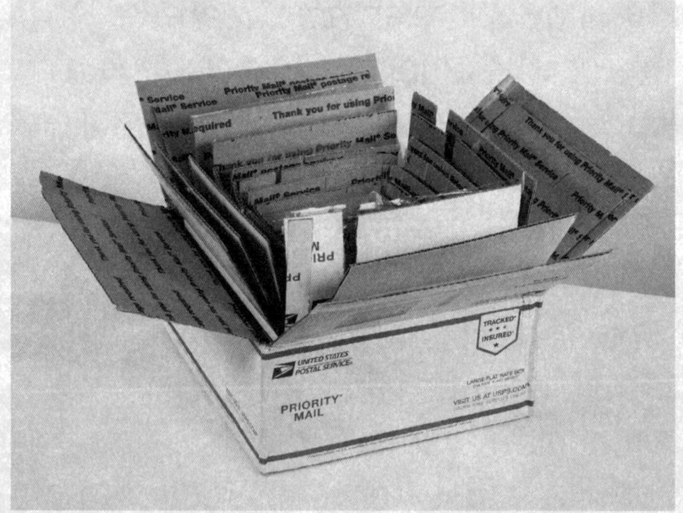

Medium Office, Submission to *Fulfilled*, 2020.

around. Pack it alongside. Wrap it. Unbox it. Send it on a trip.

In her book *Kinesthetic Knowing*, Zeynep Çelik Alexander recounts and deconstructs a founding myth of German aesthetic theory—namely, that there is a bodily sort of intellection capable of apprehending the world of forms through feeling and sensation. (Think of Heinrich Wölfflin's claims of the body's ability to feel directly, unmediated by the mind, the mass and movement of baroque facades.) There is in fact an entire history of psychoaesthetician failing to find, through experimental methods, the causal links between sensation, cognition, and the apprehension of form. In one such "peculiar experiment": "a German schoolteacher by the name of Rudolf Schulze gathered a group of children in the courtyard of an elementary school in Leipzig" and exposed them to a series of images, photographing and documenting their smiles and frowns as proof of the "immediacy between form and affect".[23] It was as though a field of pictures could produce a map of almost programmatic stimulus-response mechanisms traceable to individual pictures like a crucifixion, outputting an index of form-induced feeling not unlike Jean-Jacques Lequeu's portraits of facial passions. As with *Fulfilled*, where attention shifts from architectural models to shipping boxes, the narration of experimental failure punctures the myths of aesthetic discourse by tending to the material conditions of Schulze's experiment. What about the classroom setting? Or the expectant presence of the experimenter among a group of young girls? One could add to this list the content of the images themselves, the camera, the presence of other adults, and so on until the expanding field of causes and effects leaves the relation between form and sensation assumed by the experimenters not so much disproved

Welche Stimmung zeigen die Kinder?

Reagent A: „Schon daß man selbst mitlachen muß, wenn man die Kinder hier sieht, das sagt genug. Sie zeigen ein Bild ausgelassener Heiterkeit, es ist ein herziges Sichauslachen. Der Gegenstand des Bildes liegt sicher ganz im Interessenkreise der Kinder, es sind ganz vertraute Gestalten. Ganz eigenartig ist, wie die Kleineren mehr aus sich herausgehen, während die Ältere (Kupfer, in der Bildmitte) sich schon etwas zurückhält. Sie scheint zu sagen: Du bist eigentlich schon drüber naus. — Vielleicht ist es eins der Casparischen Bilder."

Nach Vorlegung der zwölf Steinzeichnungen: Welches Bild entspricht am meisten der Stimmung der Kinder?

„Caspari, die Nimmersatten".

1 2 3 4 5 6 7 8 9 10 11 12

Die Nimmersatten.

Rudolf Schulze, *Die Mimik Der Kinder Beim Künstlerischen Geniessen*, 1906.

Jean-Jacques Lequeu, *Il tire la langue and L'homme à la lippe*, drawings, 1757–1826.

as stranded, unimportant in a much more interesting and finely structured array. The empirical eye empties the experimental apparatus. In place of a truth-testing device, it leaves the scenario of the affinity test as an original to be taken up, with cameras and pictures as the materials with which to inscribe it. A field of pictures shown to a crowd in exchange for their expressions: could architecture be this spare? This severe in its formal scheme and yet wildly generative in terms of output quantity and range of affective responses?

Medium Office, A+D Assembly 2, 2018.

It already is. The scene of the affinity test has been taken up as an original by EXTENTS, stock-a-studio, and T+E+A+M in their proposals for parks and gyms where people cluster around arrays of images, props, and material swatches.[24] The *Fulfilled* boxes become the materials Medium Office uses in the task of draping its *shelving*. Anthony Titus Studio uses both the material of the box and the newly empty cubic void to give ground-hugging pictures the task of folding up toward space-displacing volumes, as though attempting to enclose the newly empty void. Arresting the process midway, Titus's work falls between picture-making and *architecture*. MIRACLES Architecture's drawing projections do something like the reverse, peeling back from a cubic enclosure to invest the flat picture plane with multiple suggestions of how it might come together again to make an *envelope*.[25] In each case, the empirical eye begets the precursors to inscription by recounting the world "as it is." Glimpses of new architectures come from collective tasks addressed to artifacts from a kind of past—artifacts that have been selected to shock, rupture, and open up the present. Put another way, desiring audiences come together with ease, but now around the difficult and unstable materials of Tafuri's history.

Anthony Titus Studio, The Light in the Window is a Crack in the Sky, 2008.

Effecting the full promise of this relationship requires a new discourse. The task is to align architecture's texts with the formation of pluralities that emanate from architecture's artifacts and patterns of work: to accept the impermanence of topics that form the basis of agreement, as well as the excessive, unaccountable remainder of any attempt to organize and structure the field of conversation: to make discourse—discourses—plural.

4. How to Read this Book

Curation is perhaps the ideal test bed for this ambition to align discourse with architecture's artifacts. How can projects be collected and organized to persuade an audience to gather around a single point of view, while at the same time anticipating the dissolution of that agreement, even the repurposing of the evidence in support of other arguments, arrangements, and ways of hanging one picture next to another? Further, how is this procedure to retain an integrity as the curation changes format from exhibition to lecture to catalog and so on? These translations arrive as a series of imperatives to perform a physical task: sort images, hang a show, fill a book. Our response to this problem, and in a way our prescription for discourse more broadly, is to accept each of these as an original, in our own parlance. Each was an empty figure waiting to have its surface manually overwritten with our collection of projects. Discourse and cognition would begin with constructional operations around a waiting figure before the arrival of language on the scene.

MIRACLES Architecture, Poppy Red, 2019.

A diagram was our first attempt to arrange the body of work onto a set of graphic conventions, a project undertaken at the end of 2017, as the first body of work was assembled for the gallery show at the Harvard University Graduate School of Design. We borrowed the semiotic square developed by A. J. Greimas. In a proper structuralist

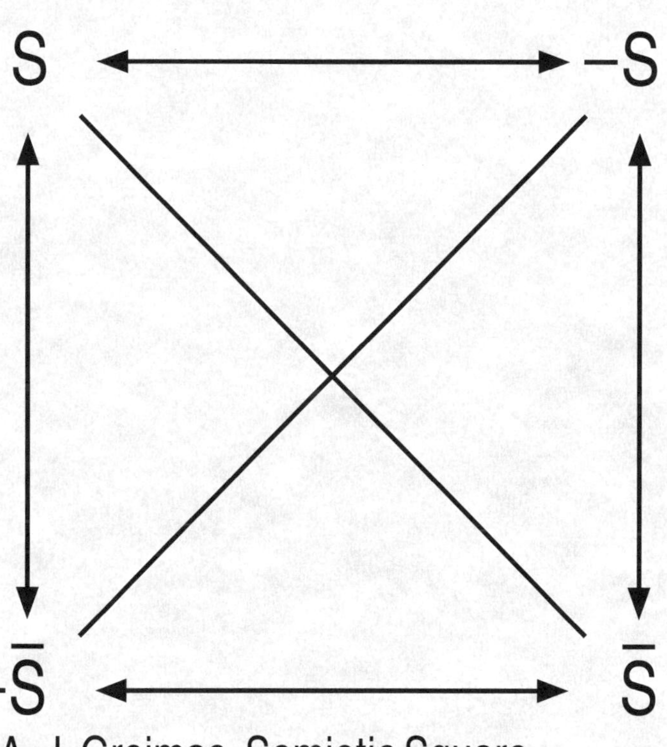

A. J. Greimas, Semiotic Square.

mode, completing the four corners of the square would begin the process of "exhausting" logical positions. It would produce, like a kind of machine, the language that anticipates the thinkable range of work. We instead thought of the square as a map with ordinal directions but a completely blank terrain. Projects fill in this blank space, encrusting the surface of the square with work and a geographic coherence. Placing a project near one of the corners was like saying "you go over there," as in that is where you *go* but also that is the region we can imagine you coming *from*. *Immanent originals*, in the upper right corner (like an arrow pointing "immanent originals this way"), come from the here and now; these projects use the woods, muds, and gravities of the world around us to execute a task and establish what is at stake. They can use real precariousness to evidence worldly physics, as in the tenuous cantilever and counterbalance arrangements of Ensamble Studio's Hemeroscopium House, or an intellectual projection of manual tasks, like the giant compositions of Toshiko Mori Architect's Thread Artists' Residency and Cultural Center, which seem beyond the scale of the individual laborer. *Transcendental originals*, our second category, emerge from the opposite kind of space, nonphysical but still real, where things like ideals, types, and virtual entities reside. Constructional labor is supplanted by logical and mathematical operations—no less manual, but performed by a different part of the body, let's say. *Revealed originals* arise from a not-immanent third space in the field. These are apparitions descried by the architect through accumulations of marks and then read back to an audience, not unlike a medium deciphering otherwise inscrutable signs. Preston Scott Cohen, Inc.'s early drawings for Cornered House use this practice, superimposing a three-part order over a thicket of descriptive lines to interject the mass of a modified ranch-style home. And while we use the word *medium* to suggest access to such spaces by practices of divination, it is also to draw attention to the way they become visible through media that index or render their processes. *Encountered originals* emerge from the last kind of space, where buildings are positioned as coequals to their human observers. They enter discourse through analyses of their subjecthood, rather than as objects. This kind of inanimate subjecthood is made possible by the generation of "life effects" latent at the limits of modern art making, where qualities of the object overwhelm more familiar efforts

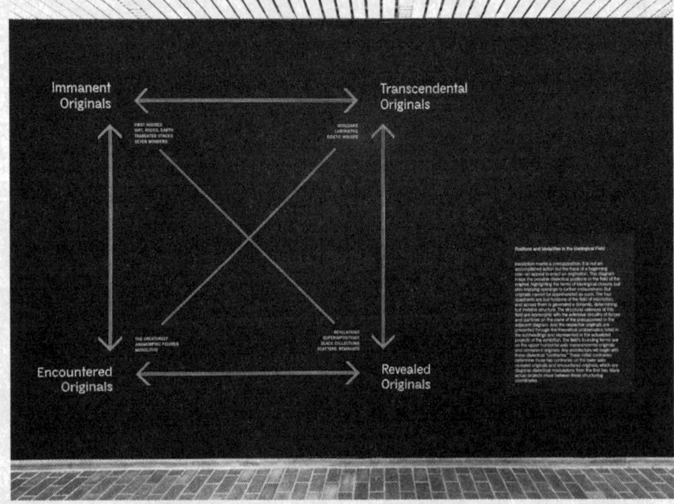

Inscriptions Greimas Square.

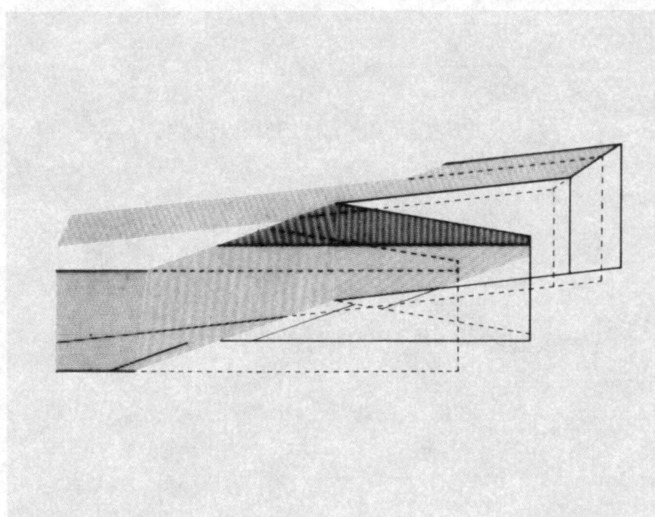

Preston Scott Cohen, Inc., Cornered House, drawing, 1992.

to engage problems of representation or medium. In these works, hollow, surficial form creates a theatrical experience of being "distanced, or crowded, by the silent presence of another *person*."[26] Or in other instances, repetitions of autonomous formal systems give artifacts a lifelike ability to propagate; or in yet others, the mimesis of body forms moves artifacts from the domain of building to that of encounter with another being.

From the organization of the diagram, the field of projects underwent a second reworking onto the conventions of an exhibition wall. Whereas the square worked as map of almost unlimited size, pulling apart dissimilarities of spatial origin among the projects, hanging work on a single wall meant accepting both finite space and a linear organization. The task was conceived as a manual unfurling. We snipped the compact ordination of the square, pulling a z-shaped string of relations between its corners into a straight line, and hung the contents salon style in the Harvard GSD's Druker Design Gallery. Fixing the string of projects to particular locations—*hang it here, next to this one*—allowed project-to-project affinities to dominate. Correspondences, clots, and clusters of similar projects began to read more strongly than the four big regions that belonged to the corners of the square. The diagram's organization of places where things reside—transcendental, revealed, immanent, encountered—now read, left to right, as a teeming gradation of artifacts native to each of those places. We named these in fourteen bands of affinity: labyrinths; Booleans; eidetic houses; superimpositions; revelations, slack collections; scatters, remnants; dirt, rocks, and earth; first houses; trabeated stacks; seven wonders; monoliths; anamorphic figures; and the creaturely. These were meant to be evocative and not exclusive names. Visual rhymes and little "slides" between the end of one section and the beginning of another made it possible to see several seven wonders as trabeated stacks, and vice versa. This is the happy result

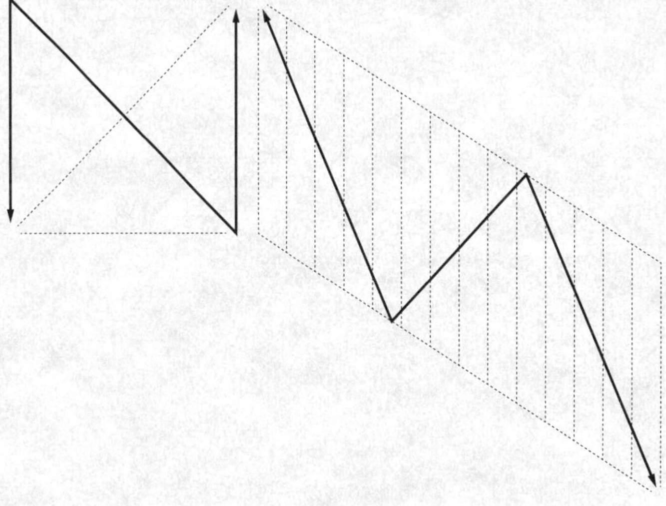

Greimas Square unrolled to salon wall.

of approaching curatorial design as a series of manual transformations that leaves a trail of unaccountable excess.

From diagram to exhibition, the field of work now undergoes a third, final transformation into the pages and chapters of this book. Just as the reworking of projects from diagram to wall was taken as a task of manually unrolling and hanging one onto the other, we took the task of the book as a charge to accept the salon wall as given and manually paginate it. Unlike the diagram, though, the salon wall introduced two sets of physical properties to contend with. It was both linear and view dependent, in the sense that one could walk along the wall left to right but also get closer or farther away to bracket different scales of view, from several hundred projects to just one.

View of 2018 exhibition.

The book's chapters are organized around these "zooms-in," the experience of moving from a view of several hundred images all at once to a few dozen at a time to ten, two, and finally just to one seen at nose-length. We start from the greatest distance, with the entirety of the collection as an alphabetized *field* of thumbnails, corresponding to the present essay as an introduction and my own position as an architect-generalist. Moving one step closer, in "Pattern Recognition: Scanning Inscriptions," Stan Allen revisits his longstanding interest in fields of relationships by tracing objects that persist over long periods of time and undergo shifting significance. These objects may begin their lives as technological marvels and—like the manual calculator that first appeared as an astounding instrument and endures today, alongside digital computers, as a kind of talisman—eventually become sites around which aesthetic subcultures gather. We call this scale the *category*. Surveying more finely grained groups and clusters, Lucia Allais asks whether a term like *cohort* is still a useful way to think about a group of architects as a discourse-producing unit. Age, geography, and education, she finds, converge around a group she calls "Screen Graspers," bent on

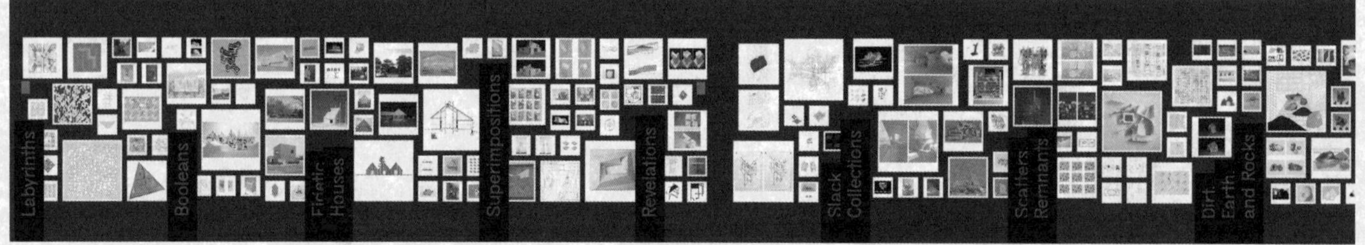

2018 Exhibition salon wall.

reclaiming the manual operations of architecture through the various screens on which immaterial computation is displayed. At the scale of the *pair*, Sylvia Lavin confronts architecture's crisis of methodology: are the analytical methods of the recent past still useful? In "Next Slide Please: Media History and the Archive of Everything Architectural," Lavin first interrogates and then rehabilitates the use of pairs of images as a rhetorical and analytical strategy in architectural lectures. Finally, at the scale of the single *project*, twelve individual works are described by their authors.

The linear, left-to-right array is used to lay out images in the category, cohort, and pair chapters, where the scales of view correspond to what can be seen and absorbed by an embodied observer. Each of these proceeds in order through the same fourteen bands of affinity listed above, which are introduced in each chapter with short texts that focus on a particular aspect of inscriptions: the manual tasks it entails, the figure of the original, or the effects of an inscriptive architecture on its audience. Occasionally there are further intensifications around key ideas, addressed by contributing authors in this book's *interludes*. In "Cotton Mather Engraved and Ungraved," Edward Eigen trades our concept of inscription for that of engraving to open up a terrible history of attempts at possession involving a Puritan minister and his human property. Eigen reminds us that inscription is implicated in the formation no less of subjects than of objects. Catherine Ingraham, in "Sites of Inscriptions," pitches inscription against site and play—two ideas foundational to a mechanics of audience that includes but also extends beyond the examples of theater discussed in this essay—and points us to where we can expect inscriptions to leave marks on the discipline. Marrikka Trotter's "Blanks, Dents, Casts, and Other Forms of Negative Architecture" revisits Sir John Soane's long affair with geology to unearth an ideology of noninvention and sampling by plaster cast that undergirds the sunken, inverted forms of his oeuvre. In "Field Notes on the Creaturely (from the Monstrous to the Cute)," Phillip Denny charts the return and re-return of the creaturely impulse in architecture, which, in the course of its clockwork reemergence in offices as disparate as Mack Scogin Merrill Elam Architects and Greg Lynn Form, also calls upon a range of representational techniques and engenders a variety of affective responses

in its audiences. In "Archetype, Ornament, and the Subversion of Architectural Categories," Antoine Picon locates the place at which archetype encounters ornament and discusses how this meeting destabilizes long-held definitions of architecture's elements.

With each of these reconfigurations—diagram, exhibition, book—exceptions burst forth and threaten to overwhelm the scheme. How is it, after all, that we find Sylvia Lavin and Lucia Allais here in a book that argues on behalf of form's centrality to the discipline, when the most recent work by both thinkers is aimed at uncovering the material practice of architecture exactly against the aesthetic autonomy of its outcomes? How is it that d.esk's Column and Canopy series of digital experiments with synthetic scales and unearthly simulations of gravity could appear next to Studio Anna Heringer's Three Bamboo Hostels, which are demonstrations of local craft expertise aimed at lifting the economic condition of impoverished communities? Any anxiety about these tensions is the residue of an antiquated form of architectural progressivism. If only we could get on the right side of ideology and finally see our way to the correct method, these anxieties whisper. If only we could find a just way of working and an accurate way of seeing, then we would finally know what architecture is supposed to do and how it is supposed to look. This is the promise of a class consciousness handed down from Walter Benjamin's "author as producer" and Tafuri's "architect as producer," the promise of a new awareness of subjugation.[27] But these promises ignore the evidence of the present moment. Ideologies are now too easy to form—each around mutually unintelligible sets of "facts" that produce Others in their remainders and residues—and too difficult to disband. Architecture's role in any one of them—whether as Trumpian Federalist style or some new new urbanism—is merely the aesthetic index of belief, as opposed to the real inheritance waiting to be grasped: the assumption of powers to form, convene, dissolve, and reform as a response to our perpetually jolting recognitions that injustices exist and Others await inclusion.

The exceptions and jitters of this book, our setting into orbit authors and schemes around ideas that are foreign to their professed positions, is itself a demonstration of an alternative political commitment. Our translation of the gallery wall into the pagination of theme and the zoom in to chapter divisions does not guarantee a consensus, but the book form does provide a prospect from which multiple critical vantages can be joined in a collective exactly around the subject matter of their doubt. This is inscription's promise: first, the ability to gather, disperse, and regather in the mode of doubt, for which knowing and familiarity are not signifiers of retrograde nostalgia but indications that stable forms of agreement can be made without surrender to unseeing belief; second, that the practice of architectural history can reform a relation with architectural futurity by allowing design to convert shocks and blind spots into the raw materials of mobilization; and finally, a transition in discourse from subject formation to plurality formation, from the private encounter of reader with text to the projection of new multitudes around design's forms in common—an architecture before speech.

1 Manfredo Tafuri, "The Historical 'Project,'" *in The Sphere and the Labyrinth: Avant-Gardes and Architecture from Piranesi to the 1970s*, trans. Pellegrino d'Acierno and Robert Connolly (Cambridge, MA: MIT Press, 1987), 6.

2 Manfredo Tafuri, "'L'architecture dans le boudoir': The Language of Criticism and the Criticism of Language," trans. Victor Caliandro, in *Oppositions Reader*, ed. K. Michael Hays (New York: Princeton Architectural Press, 1998), 292.

3 To say buildings are constructed around emptiness has the sound of something oblique. This is not meant to be the case. In the simplest scenario, the boxes, rocks, and bodies so evident in the work of this group are a kind of falsework that defines the figure of the interior.

4 Carla Yumatle, "Pluralism," in *The Encyclopedia of Political Thought*, ed. Michael T. Gibbons (Hoboken, NJ: Wiley & Sons, 2015), 9.

5 See, for instance, Isaiah Berlin, "The Pursuit of the Ideal," in *The Crooked Timbers of Humanity: Chapters in the History of Ideas*, ed. Henry Hardy (New York: Alfred Knopf, 1991), and Max Weber, "Science as a Vocation," in *From Max Weber: Essays in Sociology*, ed. and trans. H. H. Gerth and C. Wright Mills (New York: Oxford University Press, 1946).

6 Perhaps less well known than the philosophical strain of pluralism, at least to architectural audiences, is the work of American political theorists who emphasized group formation and collective political advocacy as essential mechanisms for accommodating pluralism in the functioning of representative democracy. Mary Parker Follett—who was posthumously designated a pluralist political thinker, although she saw herself as both admirer and critic of those who more self-consciously adopted the term in early 20th-century America—built a model of the state from elective participation in local groups, while Harold Laski founded his advocacy for the fragmentation of the state on the idea that groups will form, persist, and contest one another's interests. See Mary Parker Follet, *The New State: Group Organization the Solution of Popular Government* (New York: Longmans, Green, 1918), and Harold Laski, *Studies in the Problem of Sovereignty* (New Haven: Yale University Press, 1917). Both Follet and Laski make extensive reference to William James and the fluid movement of his thought between "all-forms" and "each-forms" epitomized by the axiom, "Things are 'with' each other in many ways, but nothing includes everything, or dominates over everything." William James, *A Pluralistic Universe* (New York: Longmans, Green, 1909), 321.

7 While discourse in this vein has recently been greeted with skepticism in architecture, if not hostility, other disciplines claim the imaginary without embarrassment as instrumental. One need look no further than the title of Benedict Anderson's *Imagined Communities* or C. Wright Mills's *The Sociological Imagination* to see the role of imagination at the center of real movements of nations, people, and capital.

8 "Gathering" in this essay refers to inscriptions' offers of participation. These are offers of being seen in a way that is compatible with already-formed points of view, as in analytic approaches that architects and critics use to approach built work, but also offers of literal participation. People can build inscriptions, or can at least imagine doing so. "Audience" is the whole range of people who receive such an offer to gather. Like the subject, the audience is a theoretical construction that anticipates a group that may or may not arrive. My concern is with the mechanics of this anticipation and the degree to which it is open or closed to various kinds of participation. This notion of gathering and

audience is distinct from a countable crowd that is physically managed by architecture that aids or impedes assembly. One sense of the word stresses how the audience comes to imagine itself as a coherent unit through the encounter with architecture, while the other stresses architecture as an instrument of control. These of course are not exclusive, as architecture's spur to imagination always exerts control of some kind when it is actualized in the world, and conversely an instrument of control can produce an awareness of belonging to a class. The distinction here can be thought as chronological: a choice to begin with the imagination of belonging, or to begin with the instrument of management. For a discussion of architecture's role in the latter, see Sarah Whiting's "Quiet Riot (Protest Space: When Speech is Zoned, is it Free?)," *Wired*, vol. 11, no. 6 (June 2003): 145.

9 That the dolmen is a void at the center of the construction makes it no less material. See the postlude to this volume, by K. Michael Hays, for an extended analysis of how emptiness can work as a substrate for the architecture that surrounds and encloses it.

10 Tafuri, "The Historical 'Project,'" 3. While First Office's PS1 Dolmen ostensibly begins with a dolmen pictured in a Eugène Trutat photograph, it is cut off from this point of origin by its unfaithful retracing in boxes. Similarly, d.esk's Colossal Paper is based on a Maxime Du Camp photograph of Egyptian ruins, but approximations of stone in a digital simulation of paper leave intact only a grammar of prepositions that regulate what leans against or sits on. The symbolic head at the center of the photograph is copied as a heightfield using tone values from the photograph, losing the figural representation of the head altogether in the lumpiness of the computer's sampling pattern—it's just a chunk on a sheet.

11 The word *task* is used intentionally instead of *labor*. The latter word has received a great deal of contemporary attention as the discipline recons with its working conditions and hiring practices. Labor also belongs to a wage economy that privileges money over any particular output. Labor in this sense is flexible and to some extent agnostic about its ends, focusing instead on remuneration and the conditions under which it performed. Tasks are defined first by their outputs: *what* is being done is paramount. Choosing a task means choosing it as an intrinsically valuable way to spend time apart from the wage economy. It opens the possibility of making more deliberate decisions about the ethics and value of what is produced: Do I want this thing? And do I believe in it?

12 For a recent description of architecture that inherits the idea of a plastically deformable primitive, see Bryony Roberts, "Beyond the 'Querelle,'" *Log* 31 (Spring/Summer 2014): 15. Roberts, examining contemporary architecture circa 2014, also notices a tendency for practitioners to invoke ancient antecedents cagily, working "with facility across the empirical realms of material and digital experimentation" while remaining "in dialogue with scholarly histories of techniques and precedents."

13 Tafuri cites Emilio Garroni's understanding of typological models as capable of "defining a series of structural constants to form a base upon which to measure the degree of innovation in each architectural experiment." While innovation is not a concern of this essay, the measurement of design operations against structural features of an original is a useful parallel to inscriptions. See Tafuri, "L'architecture dans le boudoir," 42.

14 Buildings of course exist en bloc in the present, but inscriptions offer a foothold to think of the project as expanded in time, coming into being in stepwise as the execution of a task that arrives the present—first this, then that, and so on.

15 In describing the powers of logo as an architectural category, Somol happily shrugs, “They don't represent anything . . . but they might, under certain circumstances, do something. It's like the big, yellow smiley face the Smithsons once associated with Mies—and that 2x4 later proposed for OMA's IIT Student Center—a prescription of graphic Prozac. No deep, tragic truths, just potential felicities, in Austin's sense. Go graphic and get happy.” R. E. Somol, “Green Dots 101,” *Hunch* 11 (2007): 37.

16 Tafuri, “L'architecture dans le boudoir,” 311.

17 See the discussion of Paul de Man's “*material* vision,” in Hays's postlude to this volume.

18 Tafuri, “L'architecture dans le boudoir,” 311.

19 See, for instance, the Aggregate Architectural History Collaborative's description of their book *Governing by Design: Architecture, Economy, and Politics in the Twentieth Century* (Pittsburgh: University of Pittsburgh Press, 2012).

20 Taken together, there is not only a consistent method to these fact-finding projects but something like a theory of facticity consistent with the philosophical projects of Giorgio Agamben, Quentin Meillassoux, and others. Meillassoux defines facticity as “the absence of reason for any reality; in other words, the impossibility of providing an ultimate ground of existence of any being.” Meillassoux, “Time without Being” (lecture, Middlesex University, 2008).

21 About the hypertrophy of this tendency Bryan Norwood comments, “This seems to be precisely what postcritical architectural theory was looking for in its most radical form—a completely contingent practice in which the exploration of the medium itself is entirely immanent and empirical.” Bryan Norwood, “Metaphors for Nothing,” *Log* 33 (Winter 2015): 118.

22 *Fulfilled* was exhibited at the Ohio State University Knowlton School of Architecture, February 10–27, 2020.

23 Zeynep Çelik Alexander, *Kinaesthetic Knowing: Aesthetics, Epistemology, Modern Design* (Chicago: University of Chicago Press, 2017), 4.

24 These are not causal relations in the sense that Çelik Alexander's work preceded T+E+A+M's. The potential of these “facts” is discovered simultaneously in both architectural and historical domains.

25 This is not to claim that the *Fulfilled* show is the “cause” of design in the manner of a cardboard box. Rather, it is to remark that the “discovery” of the box in the show is more or less coincident with the appearance, across the field of contemporary architecture, of a “discovered” or found form.

26 Michael Fried, “Art and Objecthood,” in *Art and Objecthood: Essays and Reviews* (Chicago: University of Chicago Press, 1998), 155.

27 Tafuri, “L'architecture dans le boudoir,” 57, and Walter Benjamin, “The Author as Producer,” in *Walter Benjamin: Selected Writings*, ed. Michael W. Jennings, Howard Eiland, and Gary Smith, vol. 2, pt. 2 (Cambridge, MA: Belknap, 1999), 768–82.

Viola Ago and Hans Tursack	Thick Skin, 2018	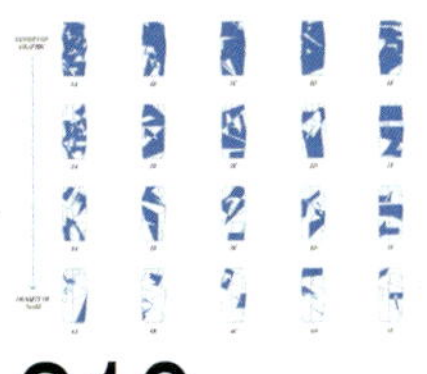 310
	Understorey, 2019	 189  189 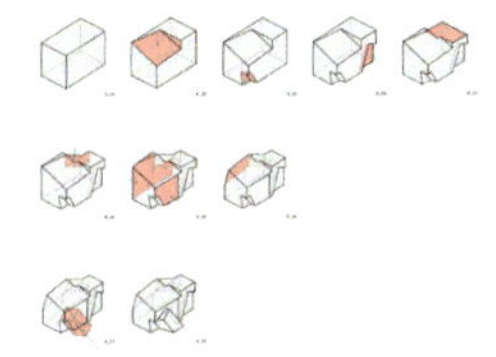 189
Alam/Profeta (Maya Alam and Daniele Profeta)	Casa Zwei, 2019	 213
Volkan Alkanoglu	Cloud Scape, 2018	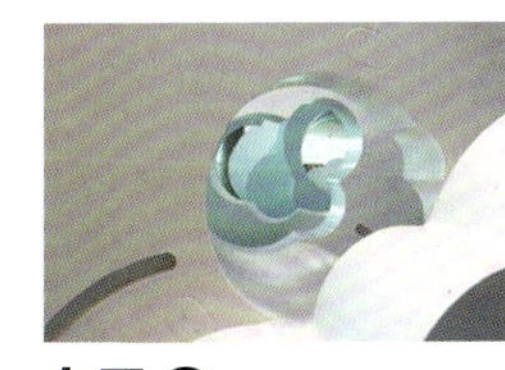 153

Architect	Project	Images
Amélia e Rodrigo (Amélia Brandão Costa and Rodrigo da Costa Lima)	Building Stories, Garagem CCB Lisboa, 2018	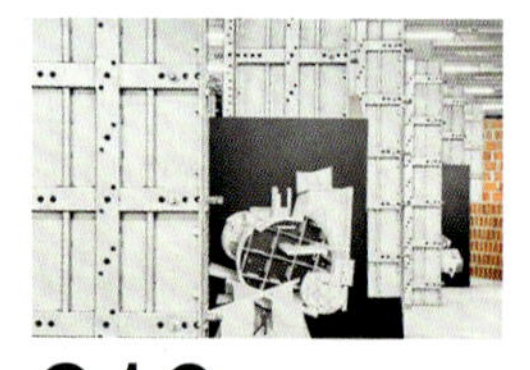 216 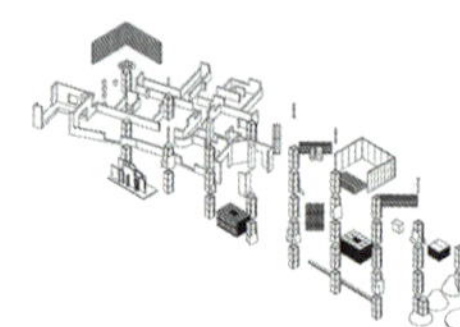 221  245
Paul Anderson and Paul Preissner	Summer Vault, 2015	 257
Andy and Dave (Andrew Miller and David Ruperti)	Function Agnostic Courtyard, 2018	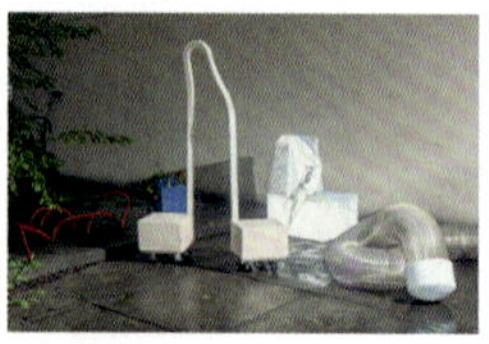 197
	Precarious Mass, 2019	 217
	Wanna go there! (Partition), and Where is this? (Bench), 2018	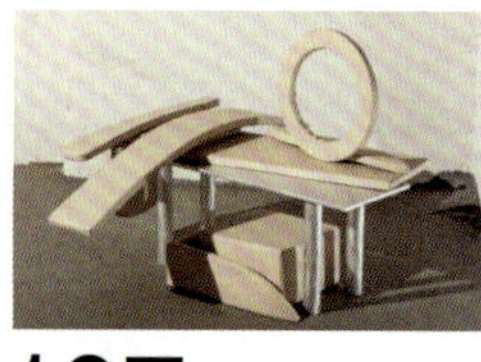 197 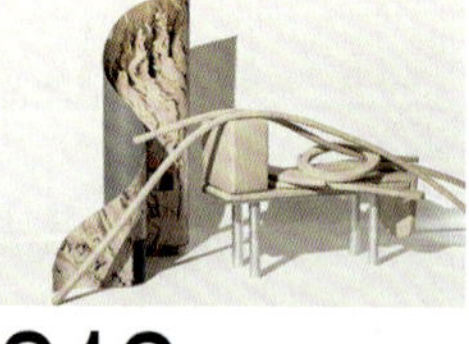 312

Anthony Titus Studio

Landing, 2012

208

The Light in the Window is a Crack in the Sky, 2008

183

199

318

Wish Well, 2012

206

Architecture Office (Jonathan Louie and Nicole McIntosh)

House in House, 2016

160

160

161

294

Architecture Office

Parti Wall, 2014

196

196

BairBalliet (Kelly Bair and Kristy Balliet)

Loud Lines, 2018

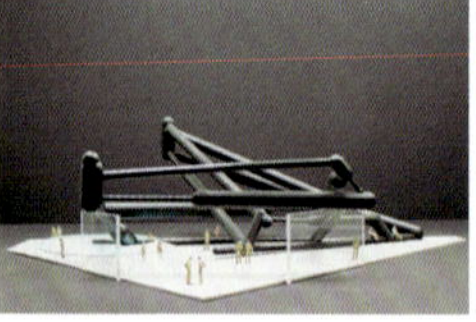
183

252

258

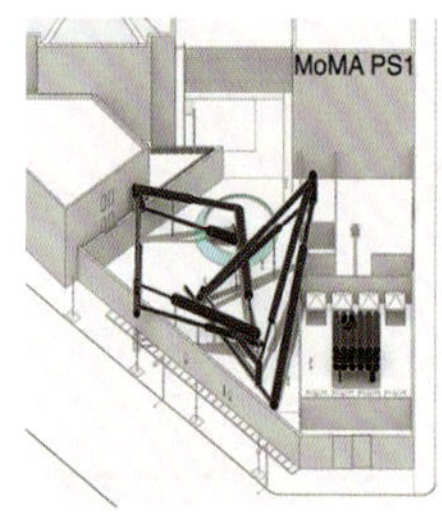

307

Low Volumes, 2017

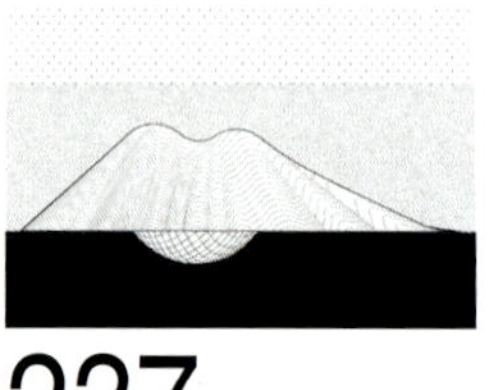
237

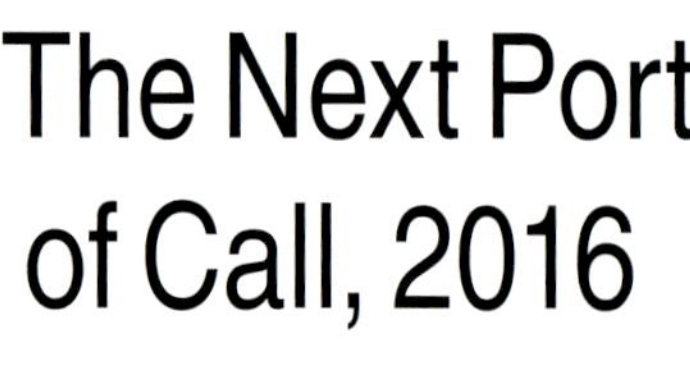
The Next Port of Call, 2016

260

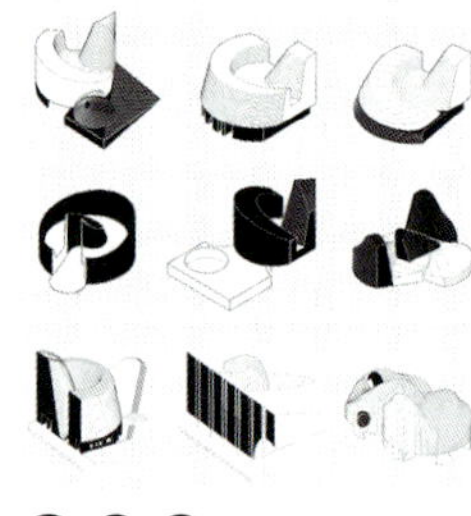
260

542

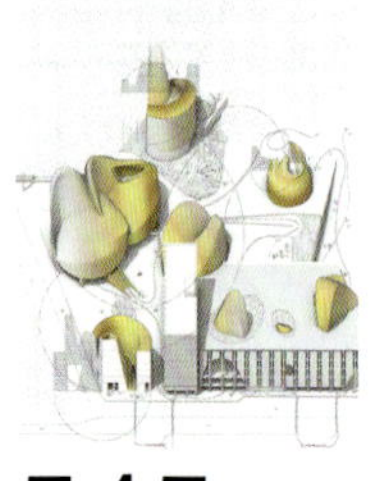
545

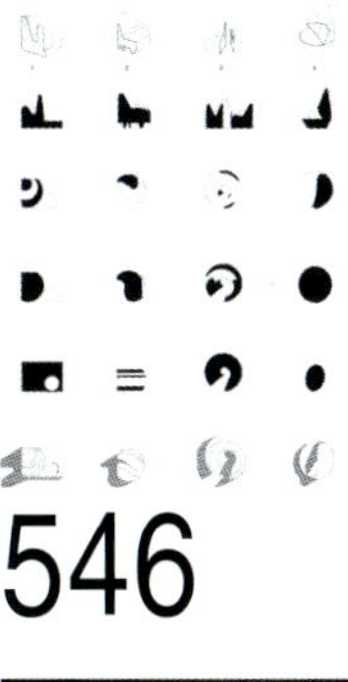

546

No Middle Midrise, 2016

260

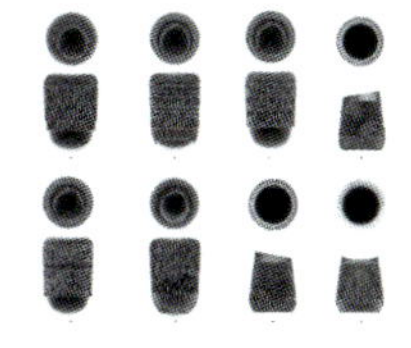

260

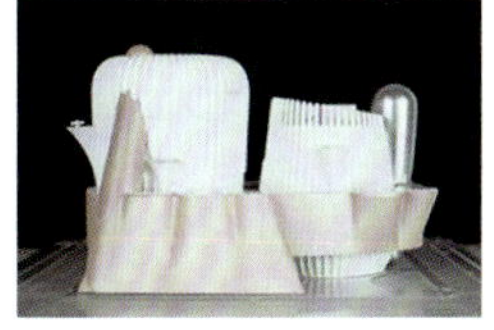

345

Kristy Balliet

Beyond Volume, 2014

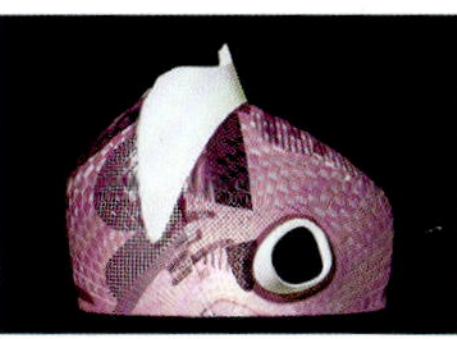

186

188

Block (Refiguring the Typology of the Typical Berlin Block), 2014

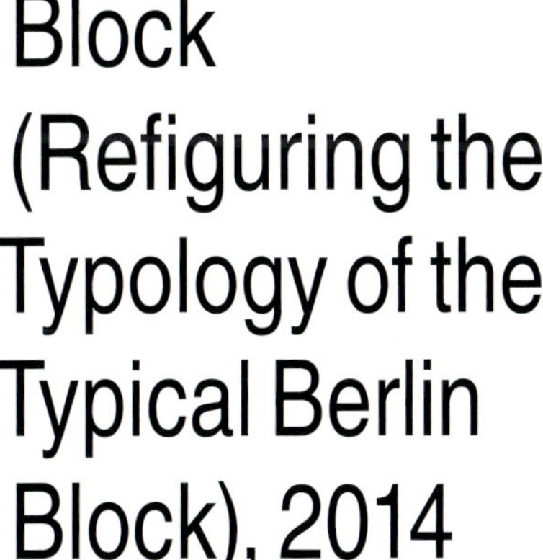

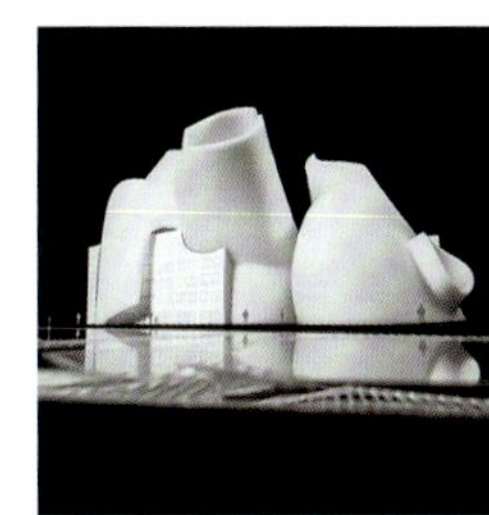

265

Kristy Balliet

Elbows (A Mini Golf Proposal), 2015

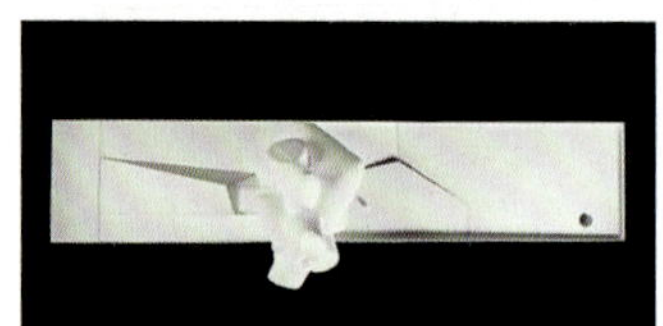
258

Inverted Icon, 2013

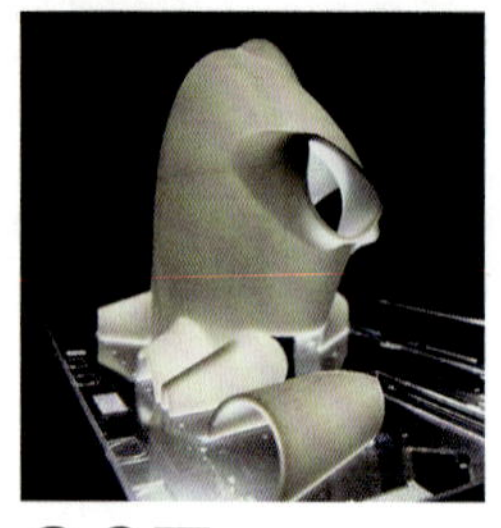
267

Besler & Sons (Erin Besler and Ian Besler)

Cabins, 2016

166

The Entire Situation, 2014

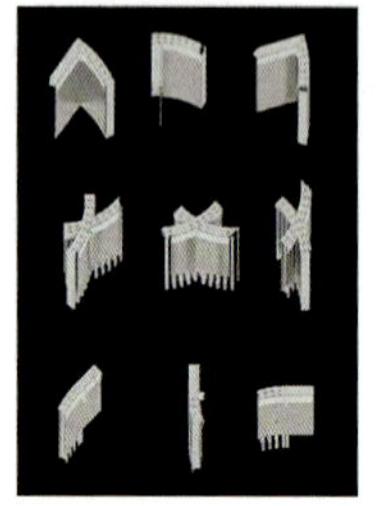
185

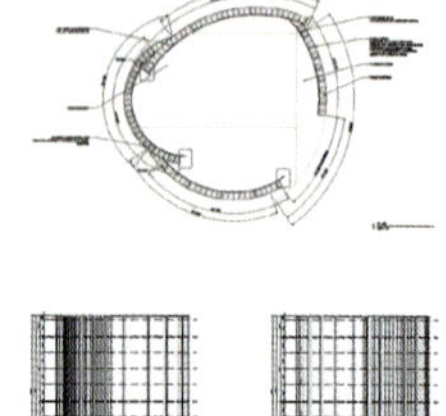
185

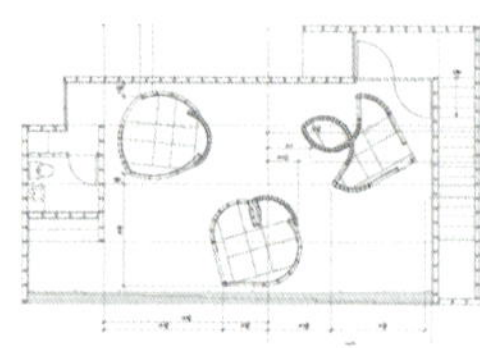
193

Props, in progress

213

321

	Roof Deck at MoMA PS1, 2015	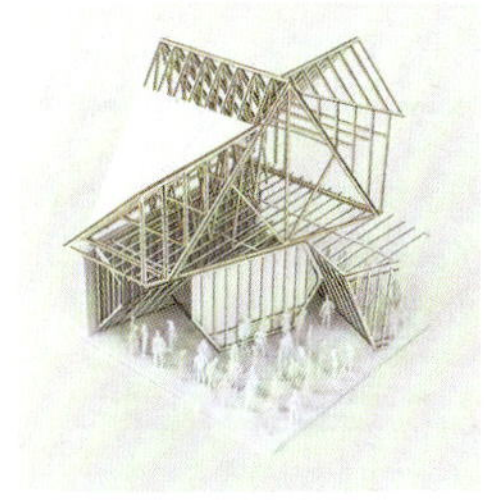 165	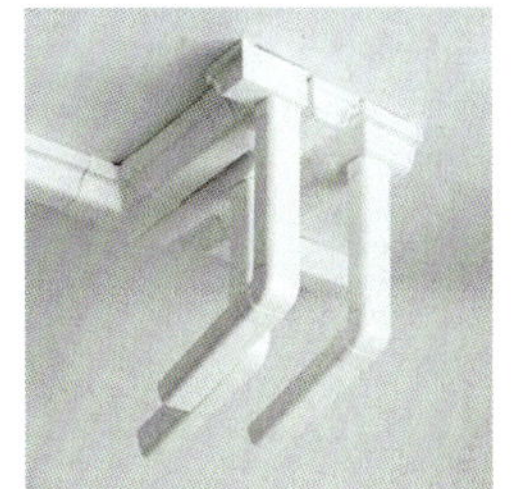 255
	Storage Ensemble, 2016	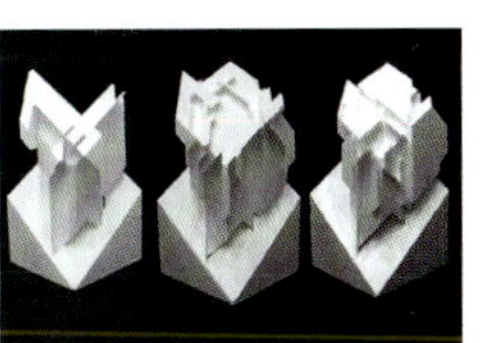 229	
Erin Besler	Low Fidelity, 2012	 181	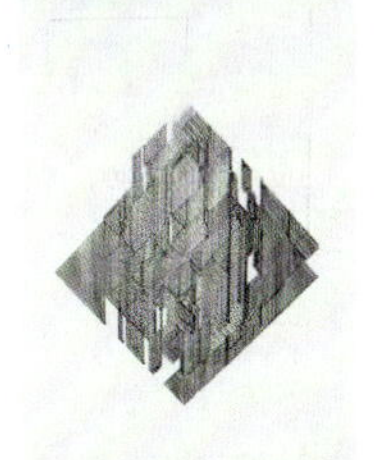 187
		 310	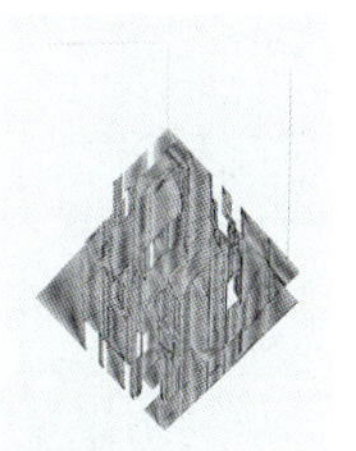 471
		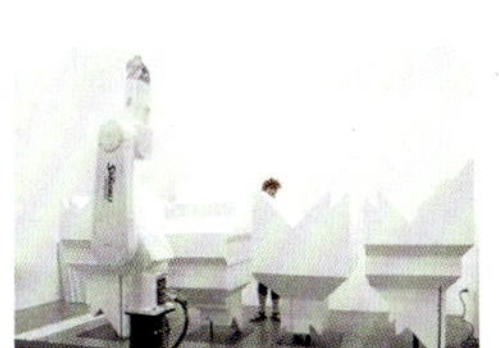 472	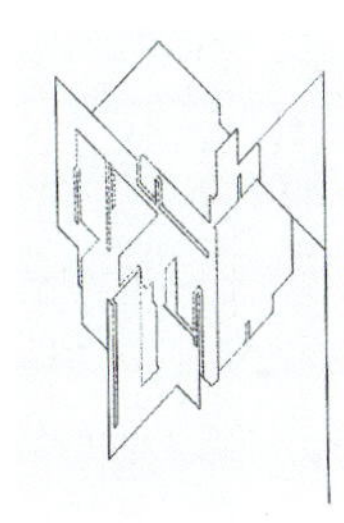 473
		 474	474

The Bittertang Farm (Michael Loverich and Antonio Torres)

Bessie, 2014

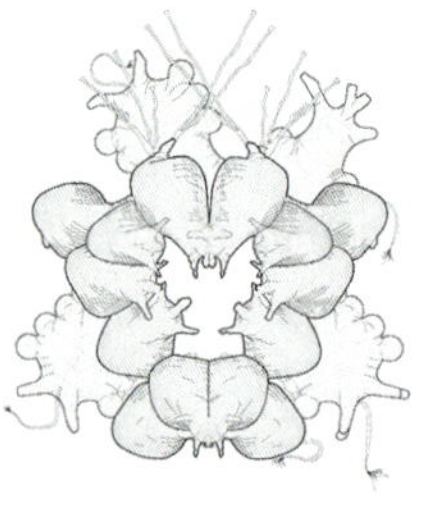

262

347

Bookshelf, 2016

259

Brood of Fluffy, 2018

263

Buru Buru, 2014

263

346

Gels, 2015

262

Workout Bench, 2016

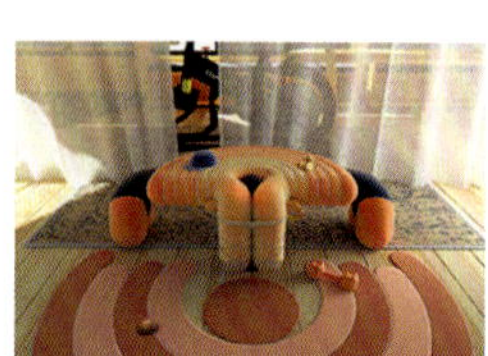

415

Lluís Alexandre Casanovas Blanco with María Luisa Blanco

Real Estate Boom House, Dynemaa Bobbin Lace Curtain Prototype #1, 2018

196

314

Jackilin Hah Bloom and Florencia Pita

The New Zocalo, 2016

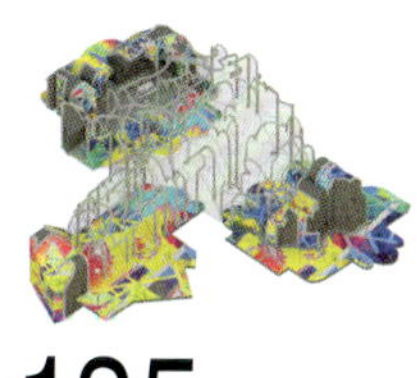

185

Bureau Spectacular (Jimenez Lai)

The Future Archaeologist, 2019

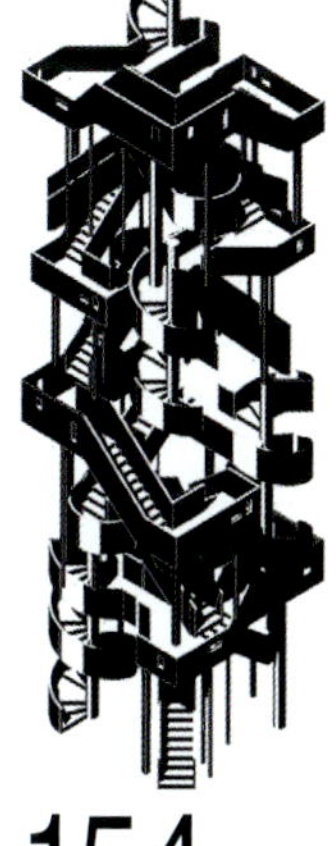

154

Ghosted Drawing Series, 2015

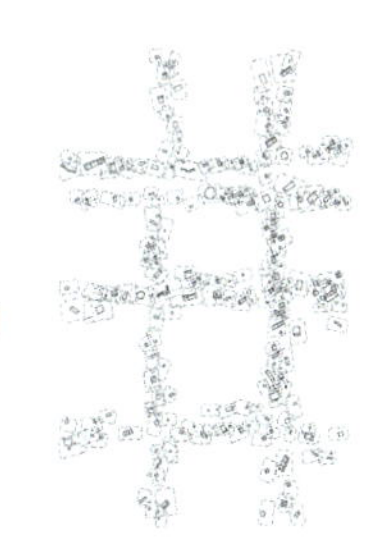

187

308

Bureau Spectacular	Inside Outside Between Beyond, 2017	 180	
	Lost and Found (Studies), 2015	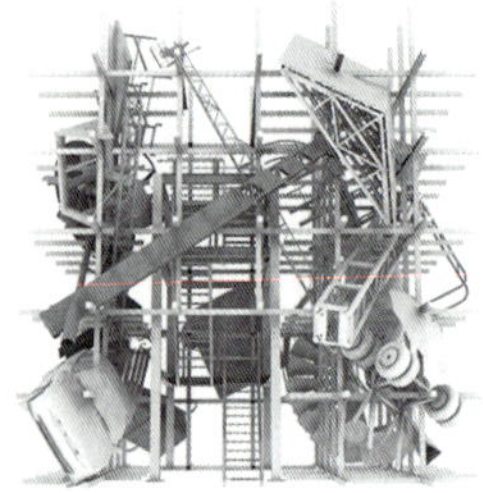 195	
	Maison Bande Dessinée, 2019	 171	 298
		 298	
Central Standard Office of Design (Kelly Bair)	The Cat that Ate the Canary, 2015	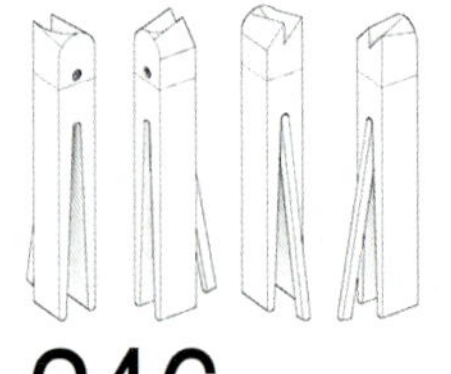 246	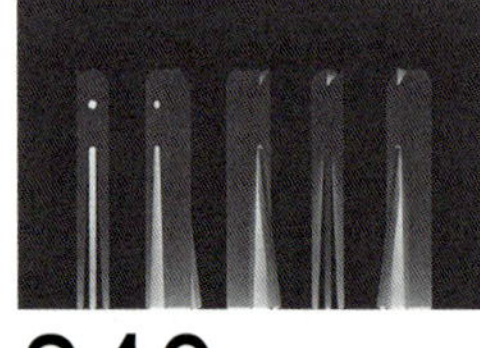 340
	Pyramid Scheme House, 2015	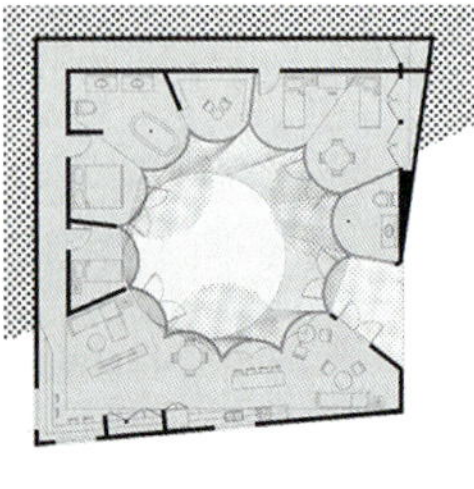 240	 242

Christ & Gantenbein (Emanuel Christ and Christoph Gantenbein)	Harris Island, 2013	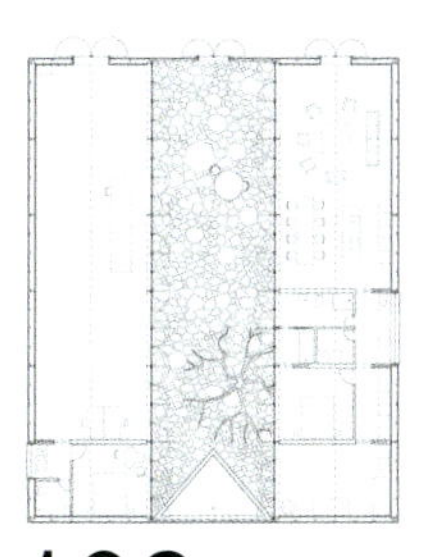 162, 163
	Lindt Home of Chocolate, 2020	 153,  153
	Maniera 12–Athens Series, 2017	 246
	 Zurich University Hospital USZ, 2019–	 224
CO-G (Kyle Coburn and Elle Gerdeman)	Plum Island House, 2017	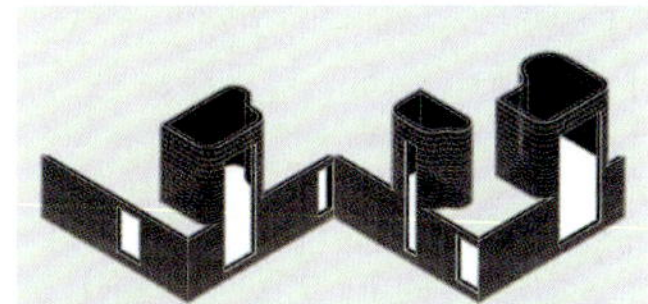 168, 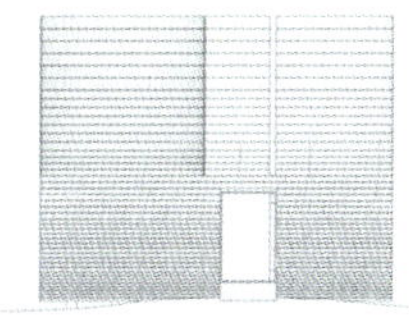 248, 339

Cobalt Office (Robert Booth and Andrew Colopy)	Tumble, 2016	 183	
Collective-LOK (Michael Kubo, Jon Lott, and William O'Brien Jr.)	Heart of Hearts, 2016	233	
	Mappa Mundi, 2015	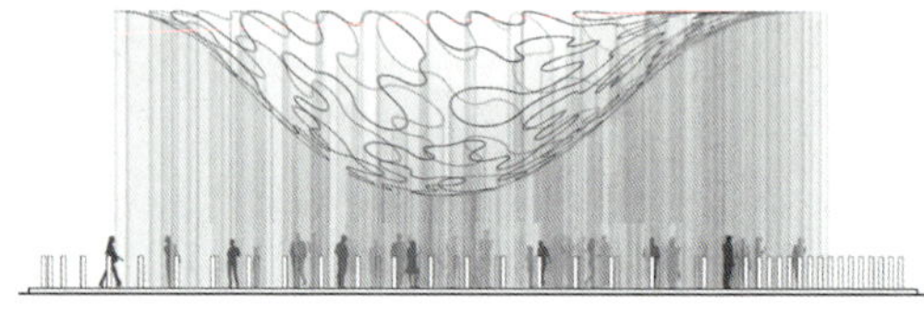 151	
Common Accounts (Igor Bragado and Miles Gertler)	Going Fluid: Cozy Crusade, 2019	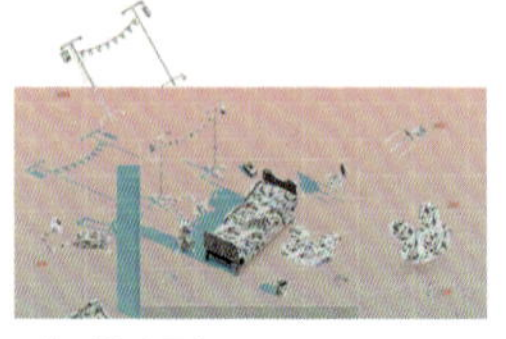 197	
	Itaewon Chair, 2019	 258	
	Refresh, Renew Pavilion, 2019	 195	 396

Three Ordinary Funerals, 2018

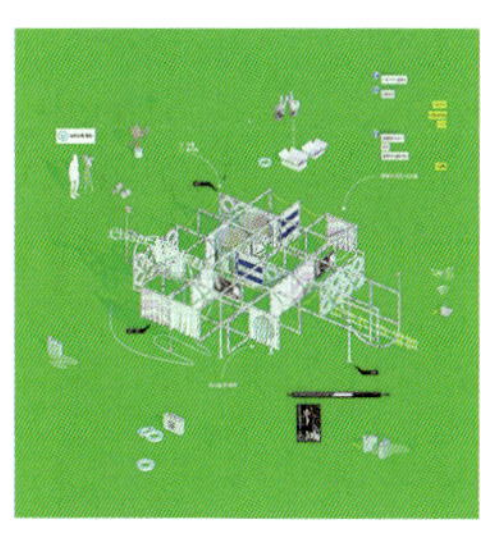

195

Current Interests (Matthew Au and Mira Henry)

Eave House, 2016 (Mira Henry)

251

Hedges of the World: Folio Edition, 2018

230

Silver House Studio, in progress

225

330

406

The View Inside, 2016 (Mira Henry)

176

176

d.esk (David Eskenazi)

Colossal Paper, 2019

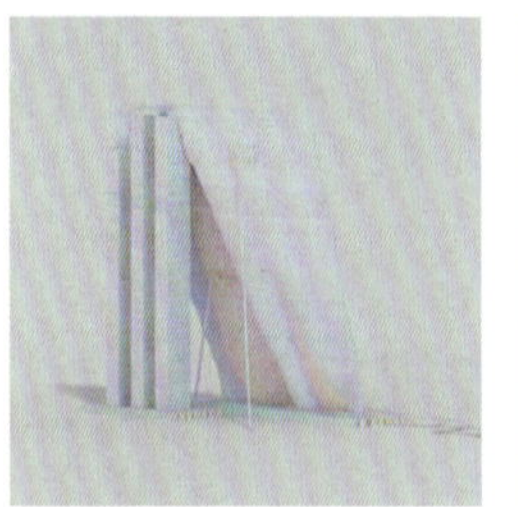
229

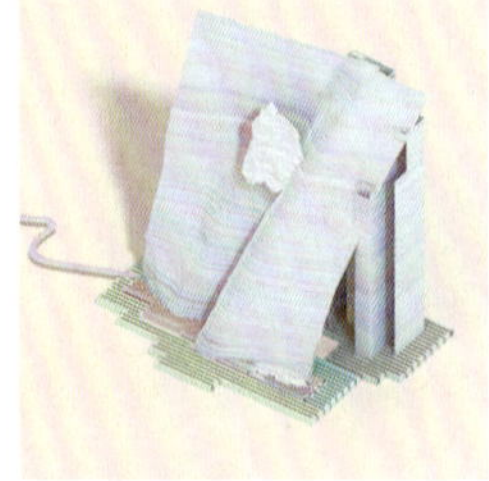
407

Column & Canopy, 2016

200

202

228

316

Paperweight, 2013

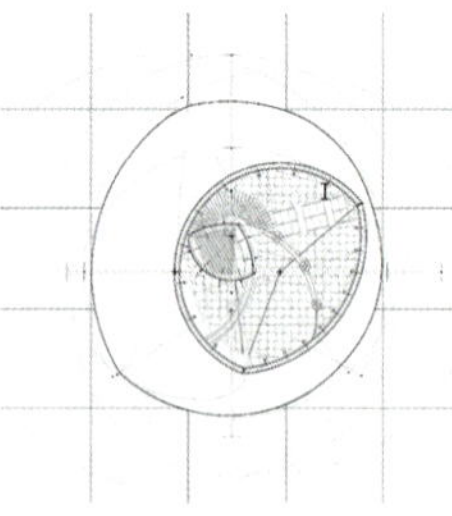
178

207

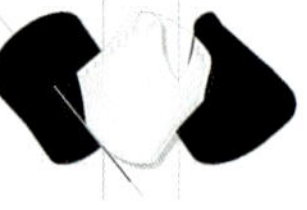
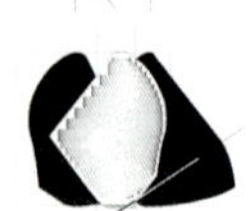
207

322

Slump Model, 2019

188

262

344

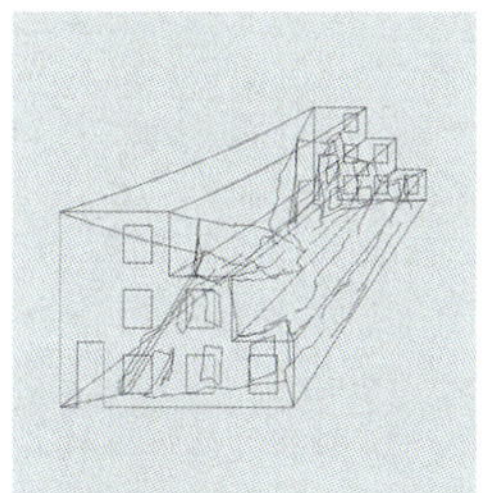
395

Training Wheels, 2015

194

195

201

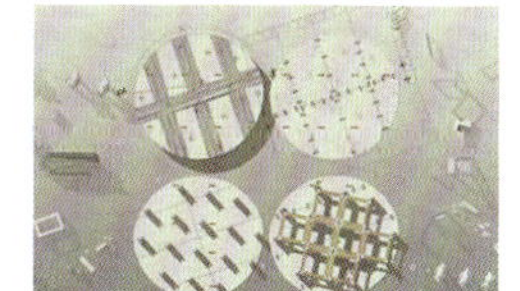
317

Two Scrolls, 2019

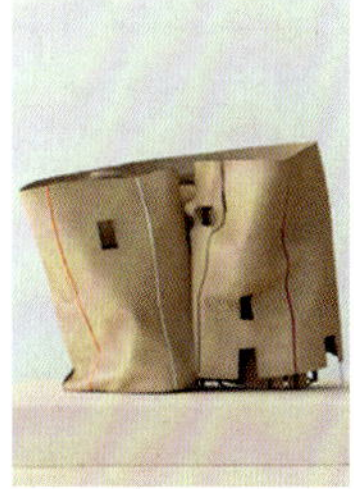
229

Ziggurhut, 2018

242

335

Tom de Paor

4am, 2010

239

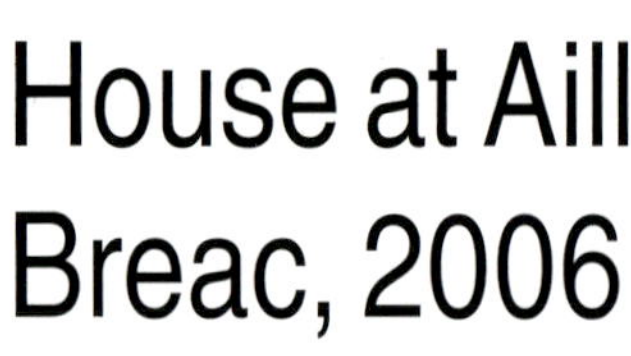

House at Aill Breac, 2006

162

Descriptive Services (Gabriel Fries-Briggs)

10 Casts, 2016

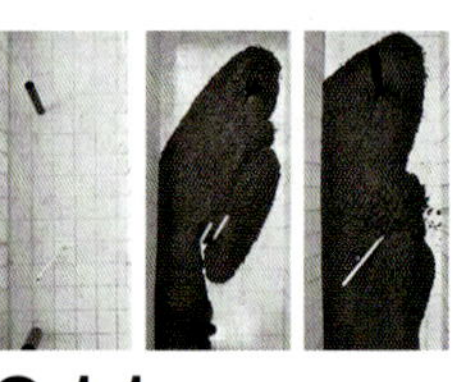

211

212

401

Counting Bricks, 2012

210

Drawing In-Painting, 2018

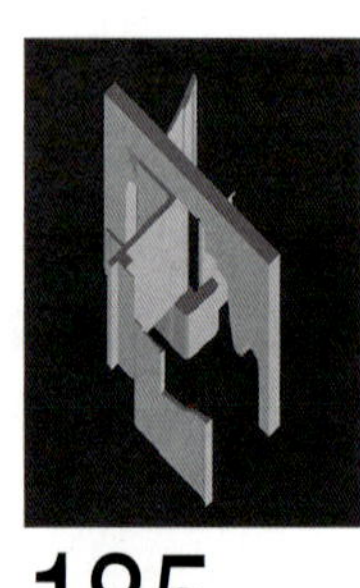

185

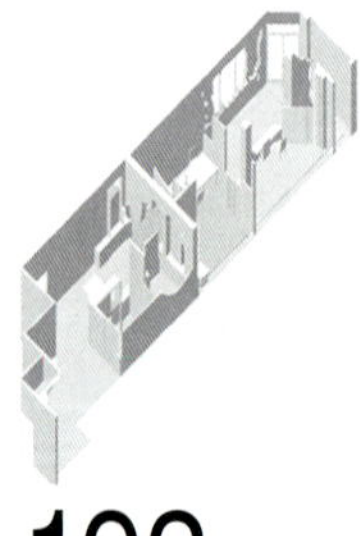

192

315

Design Earth (Rania Ghosn and El Hadi Jazairy)	Julia: The Submerged Volcano, 2019	 214
	Of Oil and Ice, 2017	 234
	Trash Peaks, 2017	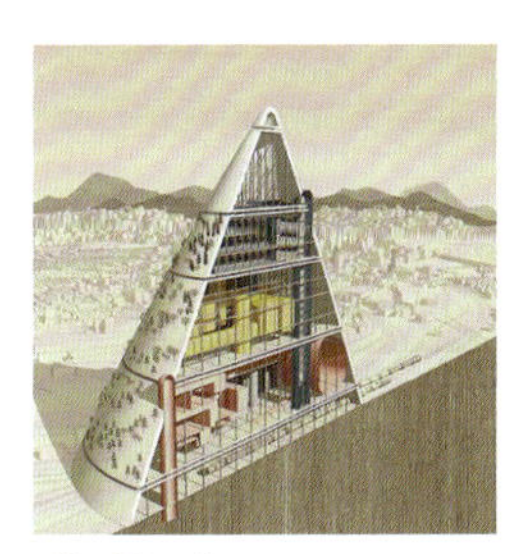 234 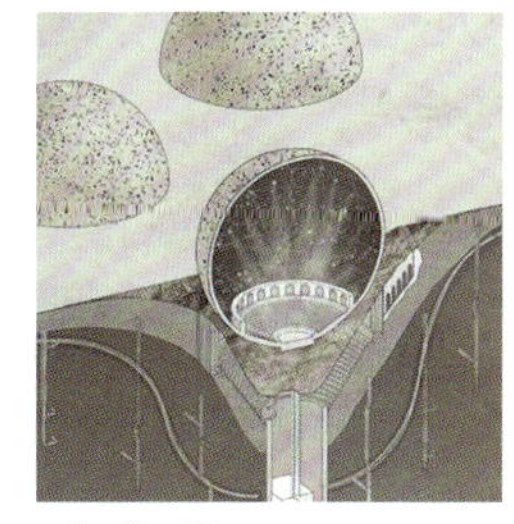 409
Design with Company (Stewart Hicks and Allison Newmeyer)	Character Buildings (Deskasaur), 2012	 250
	Chicago Reframed, 2017	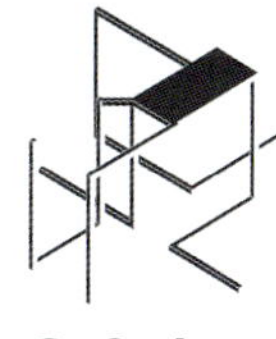 261

Design with Company	Talent Pool, 2016	255	
	A Zinery and Ziggurats, 2013	249	
EADO (Ellie Abrons)	Inside Things, 2016	264	264
		346	
(with Adam Fure)	Mirror Mirror, 2013	212	
(with Adam Fure)	Pup Huddle, 2013	262	

Endemic Architecture

Three-One Rooms, 2016

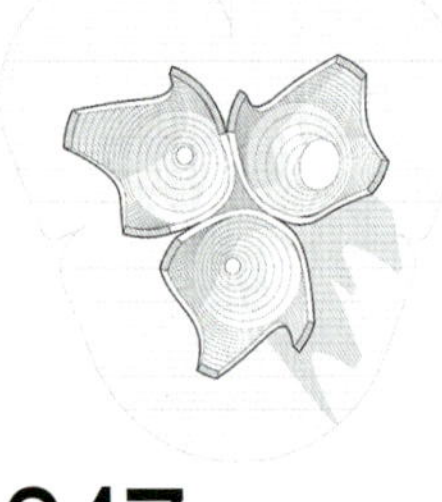

247 247

Mircea Eni

Don't Mind the Rock, 2017

208

Ensamble Studio (Antón García-Abril and Débora Mesa)

Big Bang Towers, 2013

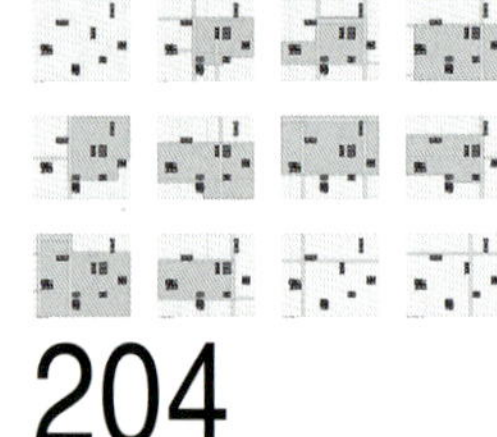

204

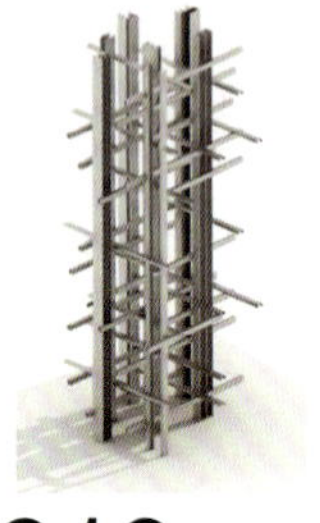

320

219

Hemeroscopium House, 2008

218 218

327 494

494

495

495

497

Musical Studies Centre, 2002

224

Structures of Landscape, Inverted Portal, 2016

210

Tabula Acustica, 2016

212

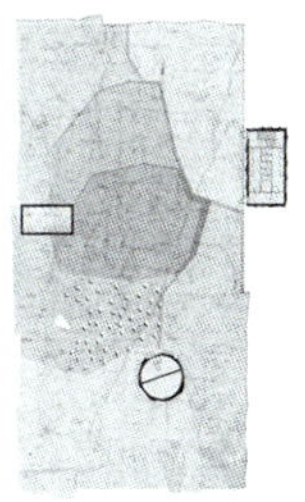
213

322

Towers of Landscape, 2017

247

Ensamble Studio	The Truffle, 2010	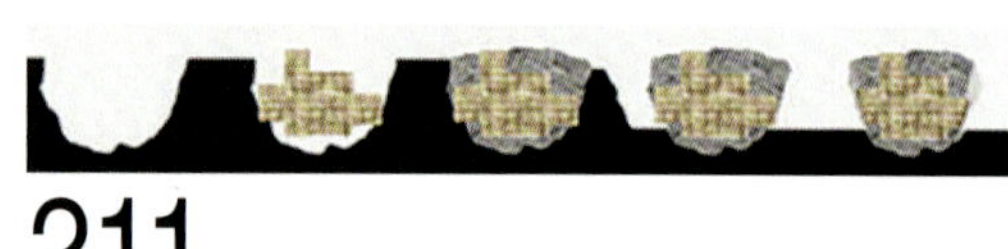 211  212  400
EXTENTS (McLain Clutter and Cyrus Peñarroyo)	Hedgehog House, 2009 (McLain Clutter)	 166
	House UU, 2017 (Cyrus Peñarroyo)	 157 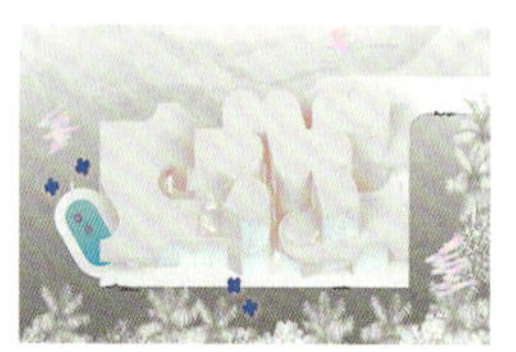 342
	Just Looking, 2019 (Cyrus Peñarroyo)	 218
(with stock-a-studio)	nude, 2018	 200

318

SRFC_PLAY, 2017 (Cyrus Peñarroyo)

200

201

318

The Thrill of the Threshold, or Circle, Jerk, 2018

238

Farshid Moussavi Architecture

Folie Divine, 2017

177

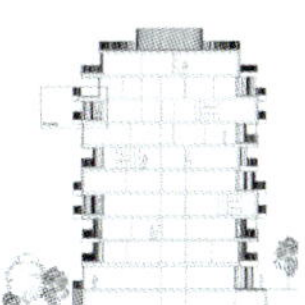
218

245

338

Farshid Moussavi Architecture	Folie Divine, 2017	 405
Farzin Farzin (Farzin Lotfi-Jam)	Consuming Cute™, the Taj, 2015	 220
	Consuming Cute™, the Pisa, the Eiffel, the Parthenon, the Sydney, 2015	  266
Fievre + Jones (Alain Fievre and Victor Jones)	Bywater Artist Residence I, in progress (Victor Jones)	 182  190 306

First Office (Andrew Atwood and Anna Niemark)

Battleship House, 2020

505

505

506

509

509

510

513

513

514

Blocks of blabla, 2016

231

Circle, 2017

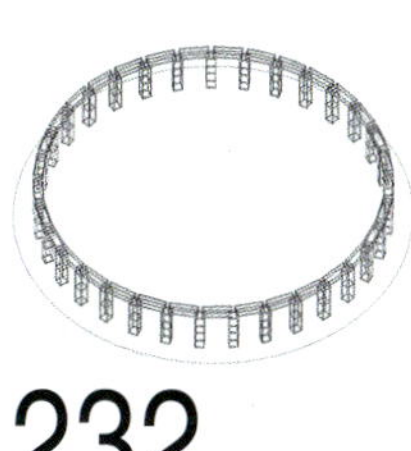

232

First Office

Circle, 2017

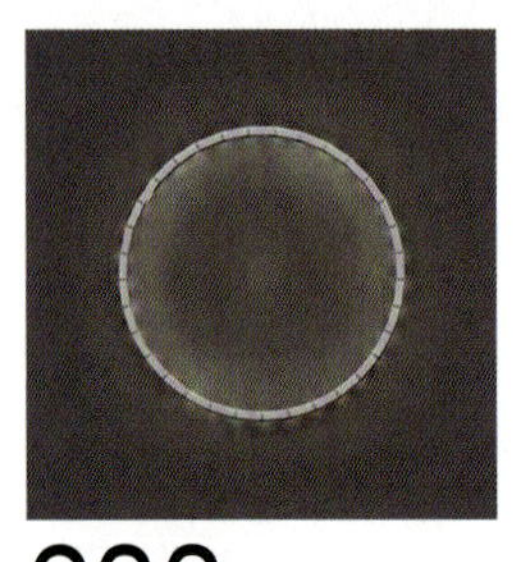
233

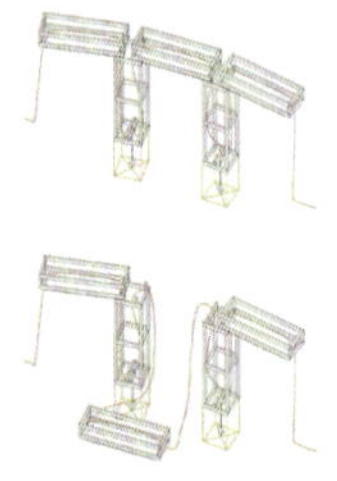
251

City Render, 2017

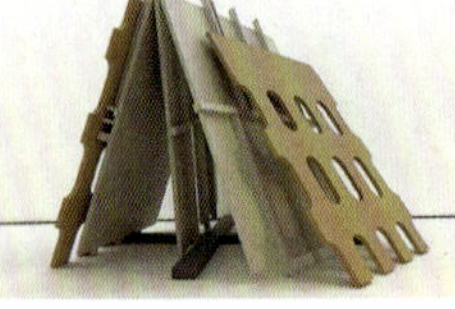
228

Monument, 2011

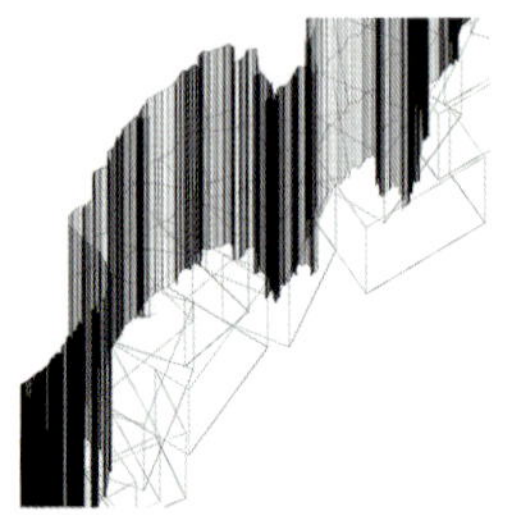
184

Mountain House, 2013

186

Possible Table, 2014

189

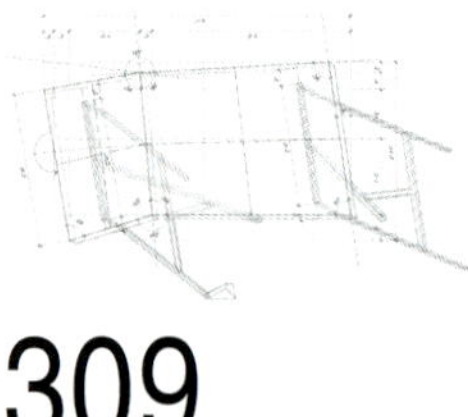
309

PS1 Dolmen, 2016

231

231

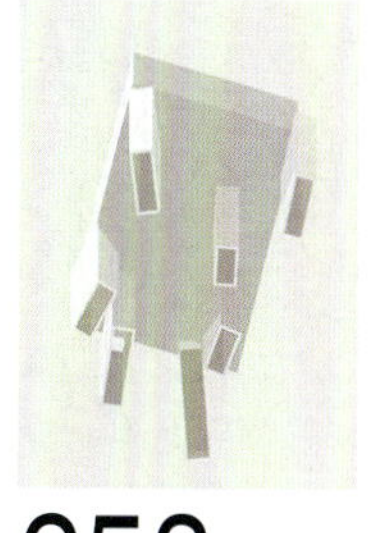
258

Rude forms among us, 2020

231

Shotgun House, 2014

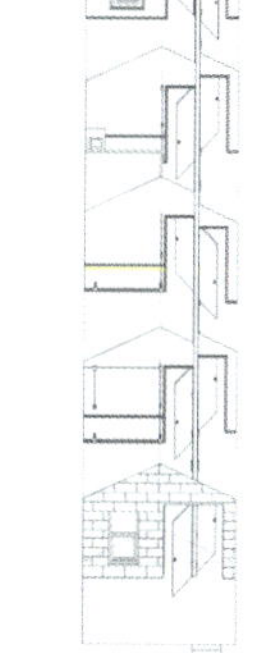
158

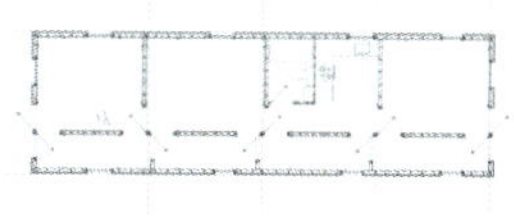
292

293

Studio for Art, 2017

230

331

FORMA (Miroslava Brooks and Daniel Markiewicz)

Imigongo Chapel, 2019

157

Field	Project	Images	
FORMA	Windsor Residence, 2018	 194	 257
FreelandBuck (David Freeland and Brennan Buck)	Hungry Man Production Offices, 2017	 172	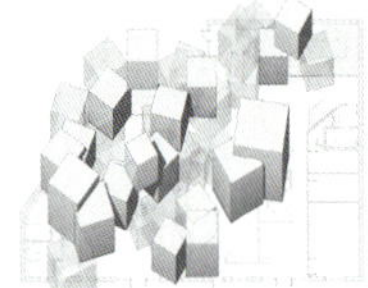 173
	Mountain View House, 2019	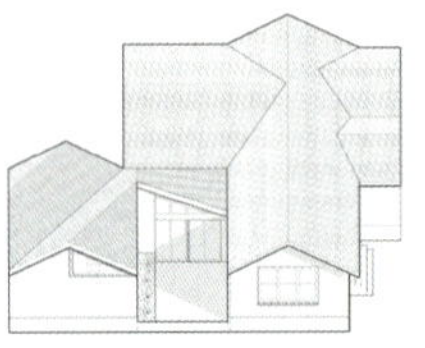 163	
	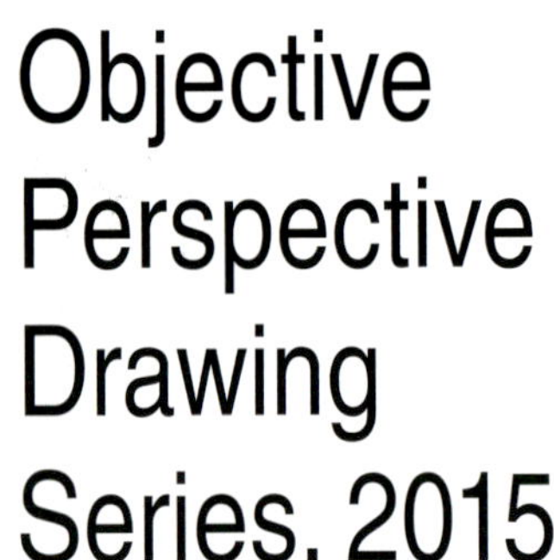 Objective Perspective Drawing Series, 2015	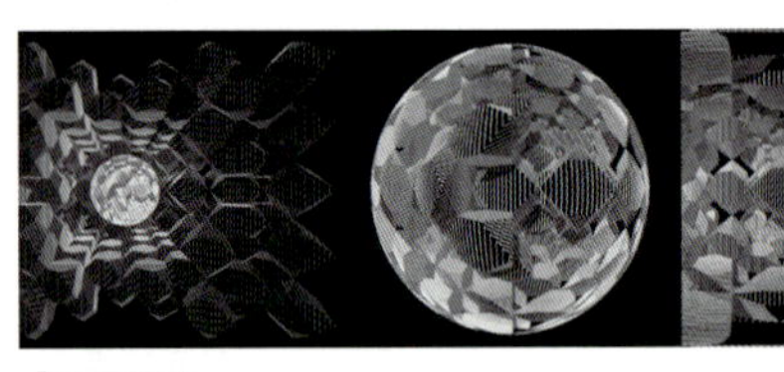 177	
		 186	
	Second House, 2018	 181	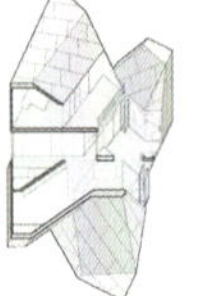 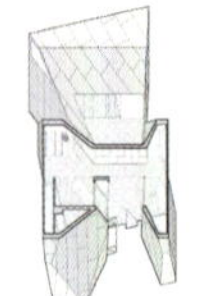 191
	Stack House, 2018	 172	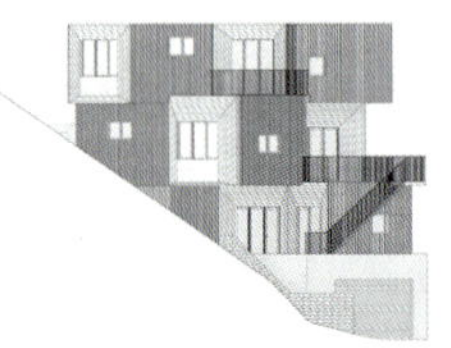 220

French 2D (Anda French and Jenny French)	Outlier Lofts, 2018	162
Adam Fure	The Force of Things, 2016	226
(with EADO)	Mirror Mirror, 2013	212
(with EADO)	Pup Huddle, 2013	262
	Rocks, 2014	 209, 325
	Tap, 2016	210

Höweler + Yoon (Eric Höweler and J. Meejin Yoon)			
	Collier Memorial, 2015	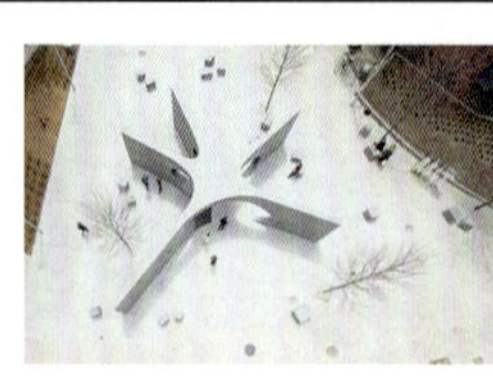 157	
	DDP Kiosk, 2016	 169	
	Float Lab, 2021	 233	
	Lithos Wellness Center, 2021	 169	391
	Shanghai Expo Park: Viewfinder Bridge, 2018	 256	 343
	UVA Memorial to Enslaved Laborers, 2020	 233	

Hume Coover Studio (Abigail Coover Hume and Nathan Hume)

Black Sheep, 2015

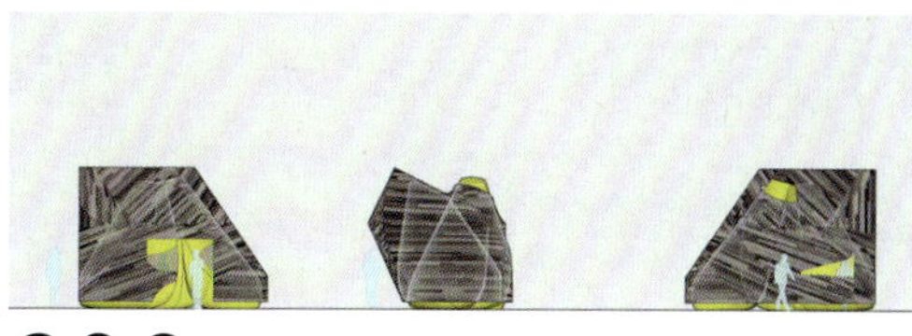
206

208

Down by the River, 2015

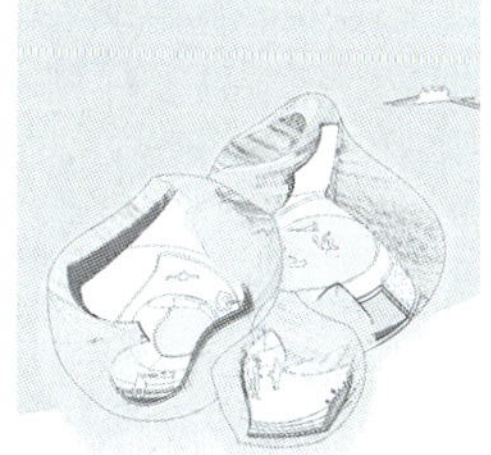
207

324

Lake Baths, 2015

263

Re-Make/Re-Model, 2018

167

Husos Architects (Diego Barajas and Camilo García)

MULTI-SPECIES REFUGE, and Responsible Micro-landscaping Actions with Hummingbirds as Trojan Horses and Other Allies, 2013

231

Independent Architecture (Paul Anderson)

Catamount Dormitory, 2016

255

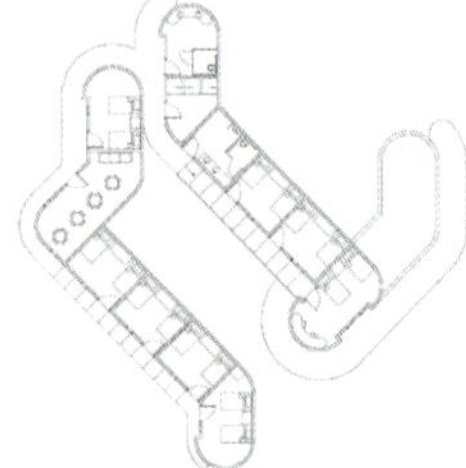
255

342

Emerald Workshops, 2020

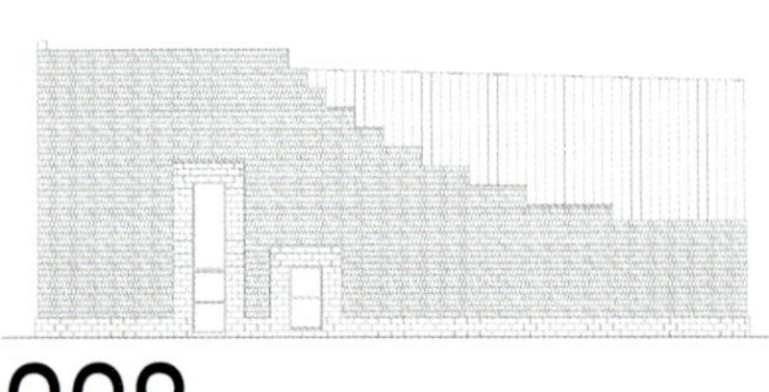
228

Motherhouse, 2019

162

294

is-office (Jeff Mikolajewski and Kyle Reynolds)

Bad Lines, 2013

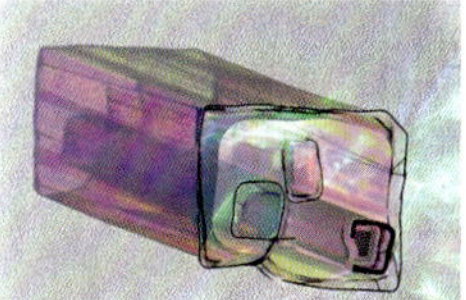
190

192

Crowns, 2015

150

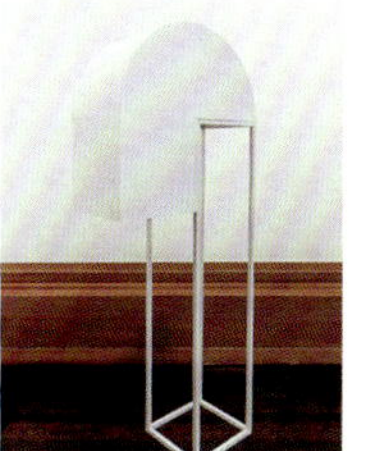
250

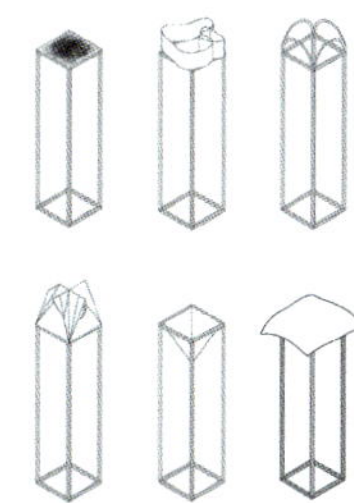
253

JaJa Co (Michelle Chang)

Hat to Home; or, Dome to Domus, 2014

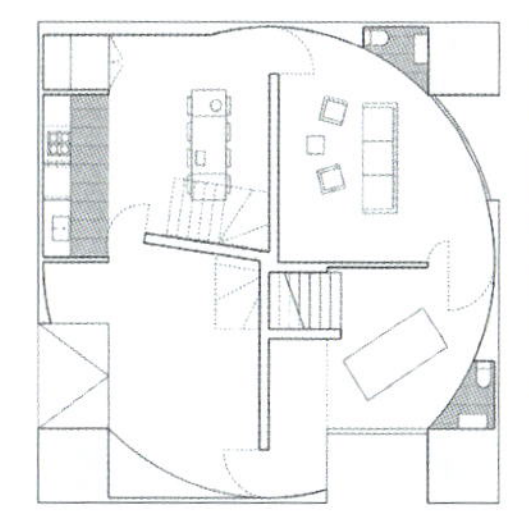
177

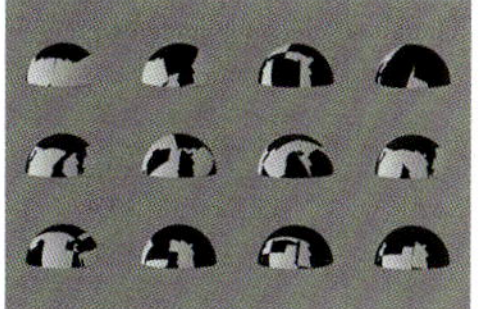
179

JaJa Co

Hat to Home; or, Dome to Domus, 2014

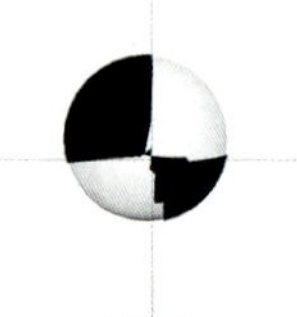

179

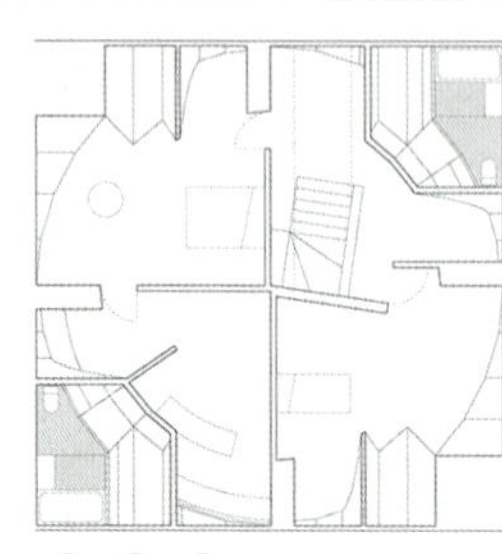

392

A Hole in the Wall, 2019

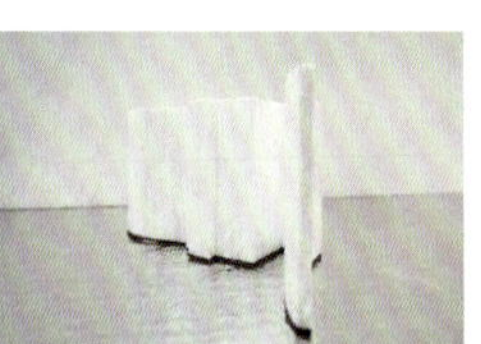

184

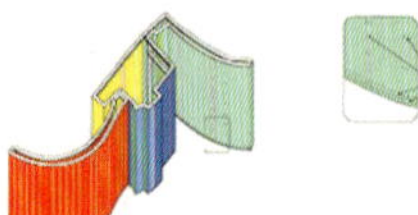

185

Millefeuille, 2020

156

Noise, Pt. 3, 2016

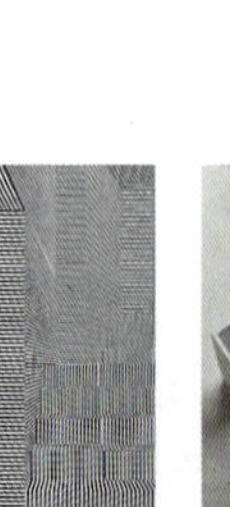

174

176

181

Scoring, Building, 2020

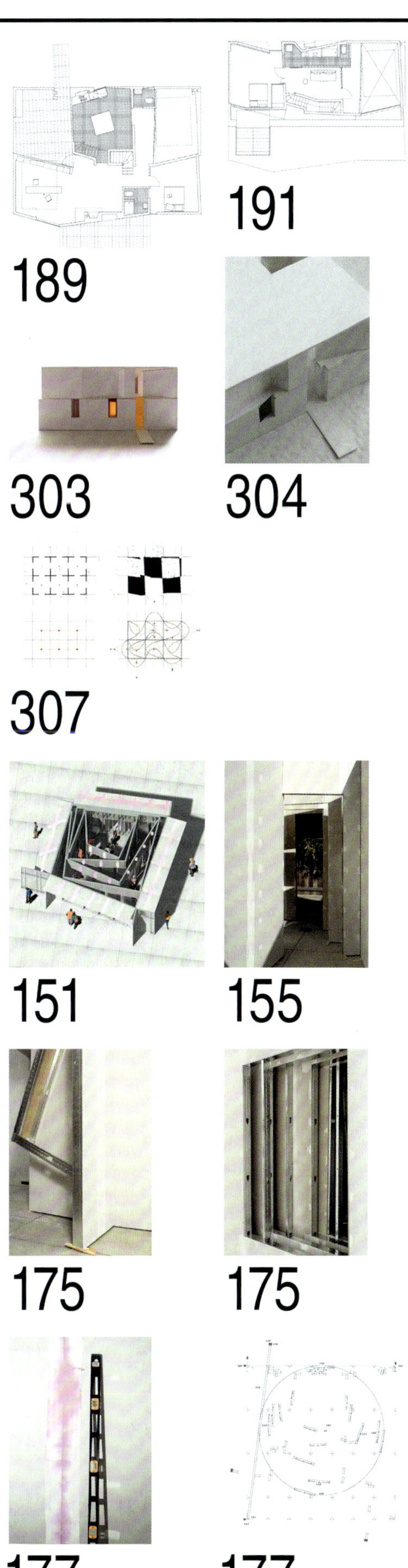
189 191 303 304 307 151 155 175 175 177 177

JaJa Co

Scoring, Building, 2020

454

457

458

459

460

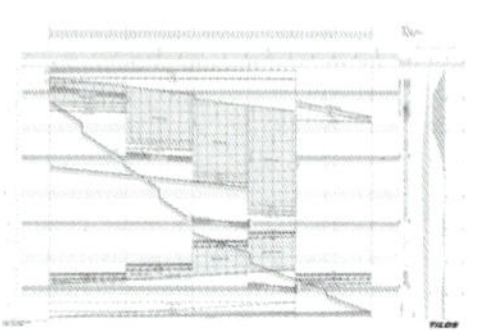
460

Studio-Gallery, in progress

230

Ania Jaworska

Entrance Installation, 2017

257

Gated Area, 2015

254

	Set / Unit 3 (Side Credenza), 2016	 258
	Set / Unit 6 (Armchair), 2016	 259
Johnston Marklee (Sharon Johnston and Mark Lee)	1787, Shenzhen and Hong Kong Bi-City Biennale 2011, 2011	 222
	Grand Traiano Art Complex, 2009	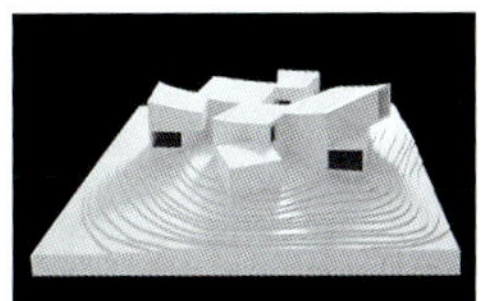 172
	Hut House, 2014	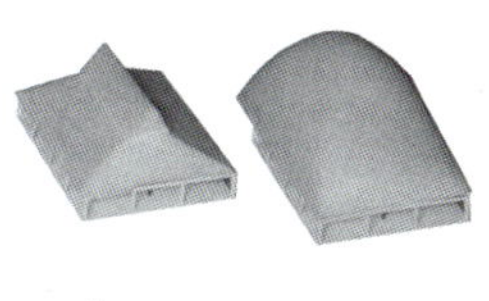  161 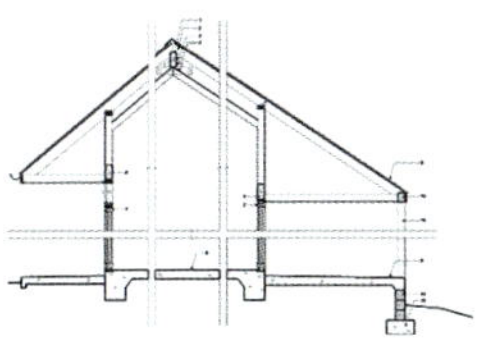 161 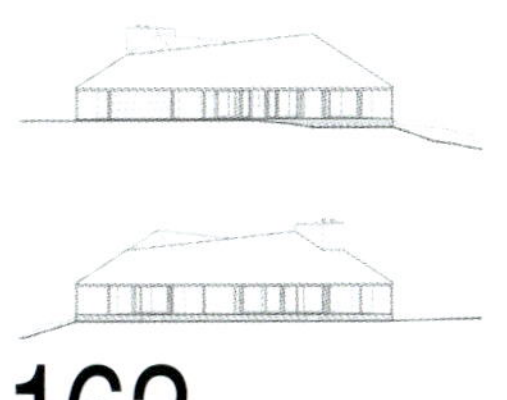 162  175

Johnston Marklee	Hut House, 2014	305
	Vault House, 2013	 171; 390
	View House, 2009	 254
Karamuk Kuo (Ünal Karamuk and Jeannette Kuo)	Augusta Raurica Archaeological Center, in progress	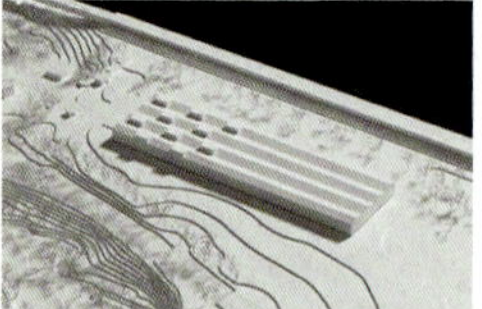 160;  295
	Campus-Ruetli Sports Hall, 2009	 222
	Chillon Castle Visitor Center, 2013	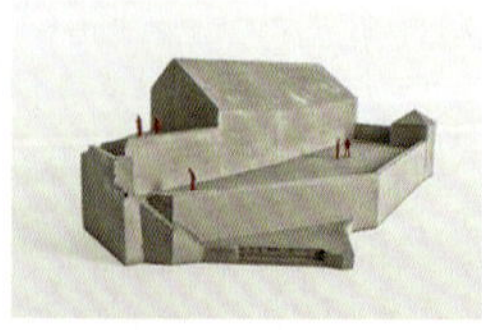 164;  164

Christoph a. Kumpusch	Temple, 2017	 240
The LADG (Claus Benjamin Freyinger and Andrew Holder)	Cast of Things: Van Buren and Federal, 2017	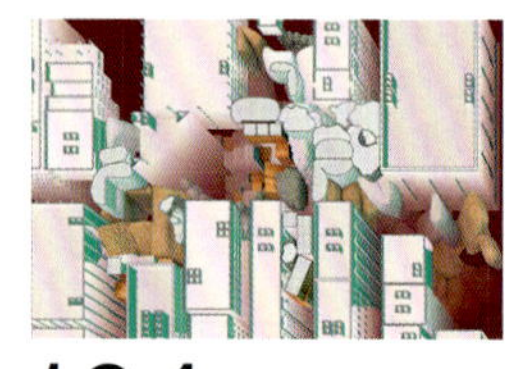  194  194
	House in Los Angeles 1, 2016	 165  193  518  518  521  522 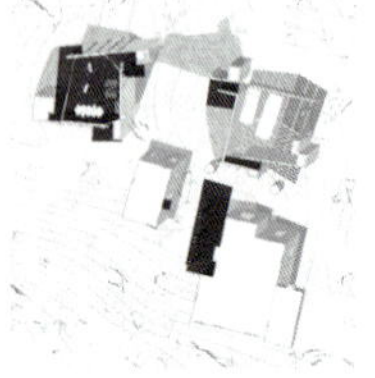 525

The Kid Gets out of the Picture, 2016

198

198

227

228

313

332

Pillow Babies, 2014

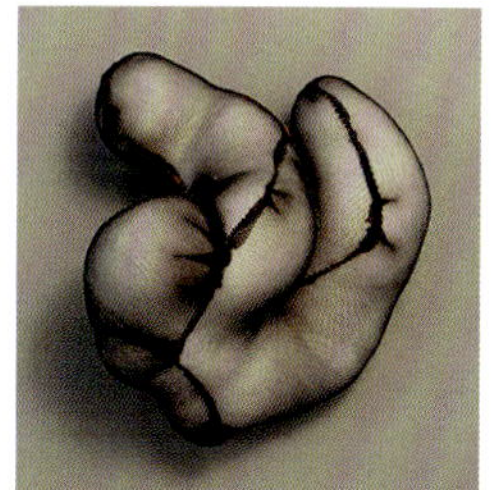
266

347

Tchotchke, 2016

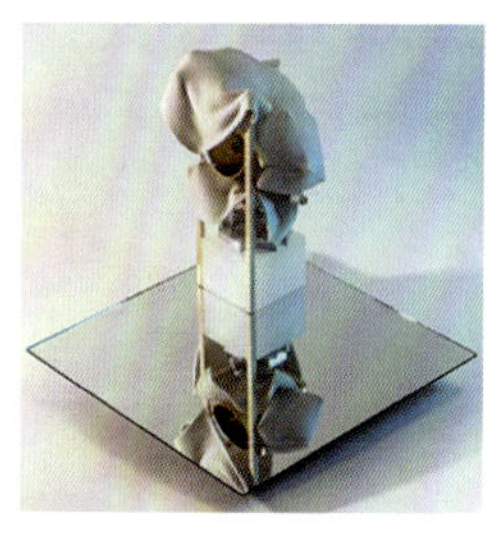
197

LAMAS (Vivian Lee and James Macgillivray)

Bright Street, 2016

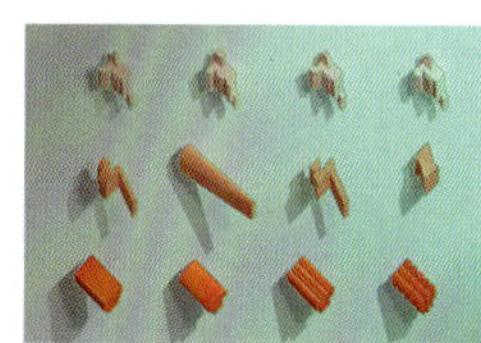
253

LAMAS

Delirious Facade, 2017–

175

Film to Wit, 2012

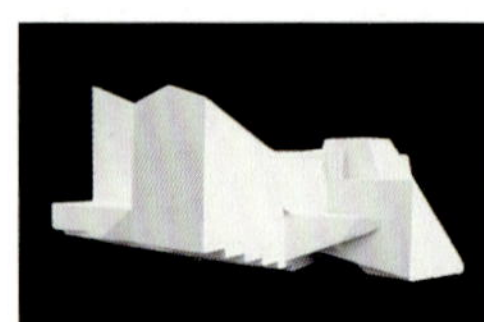
181 237

Hats, Ceilings, and Rooms, 2017

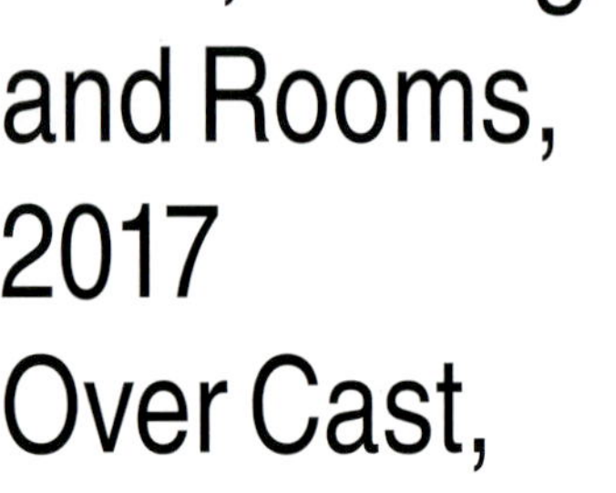

168

Over Cast, 2015

221

329

Tattoo Architecture, 2014–

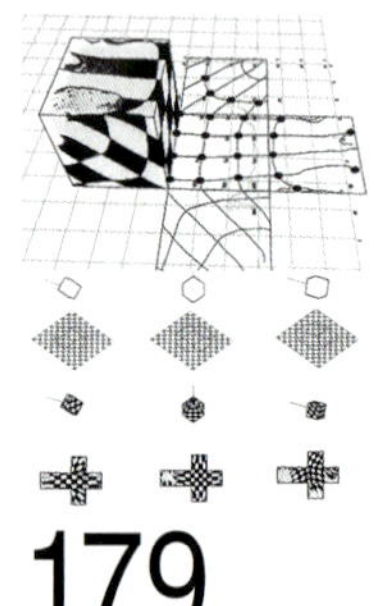
179

Townships Farmhouse, 2017

159

164

295

Alex Lehnerer	The Second Sun, 2010	 243	 243
Mack Scogin Merrill Elam Architects	The Atlanta Pavilion, 2005	 227	 331
	House above the Bug Line, 1993	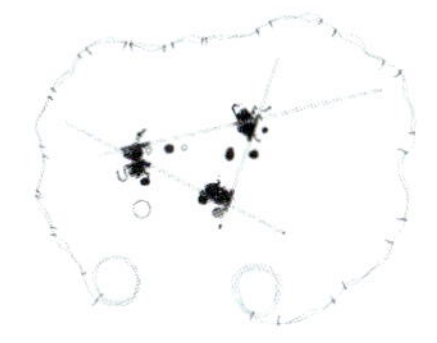 192	 193
	Kaohsiung Maritime Cultural & Popular Music Center, 2004	 193	

Mack Scogin Merrill Elam Architects

Laban Centre for Movement and Dance Invited Competition, 1997

190

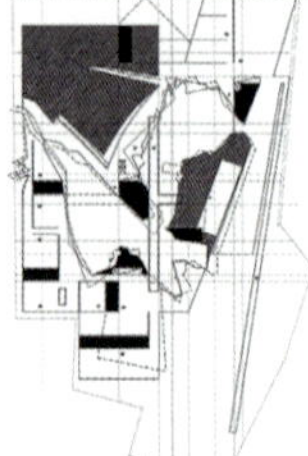

190

Wolfsburg Science Center, 1999

261

Zhongkai Sheshan Villas, 2005

191

MALL (Jennifer Bonner)

Best Sandwiches, 2016

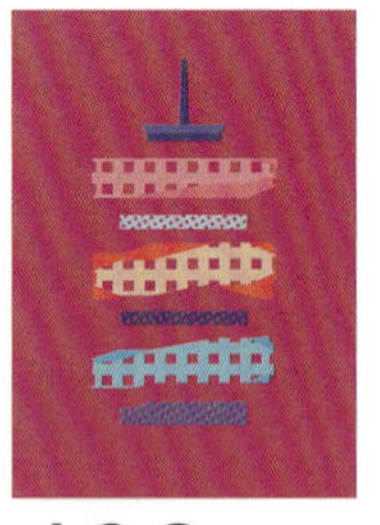

403

BLT (Bacon, Lettuce, Tomato); Best Sandwiches, 2016

220

Domestic Hats, 2014

162

182

180

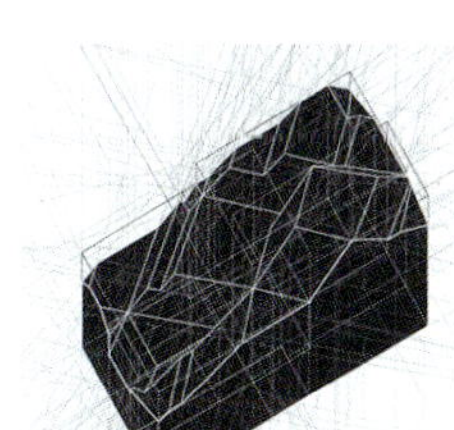

187

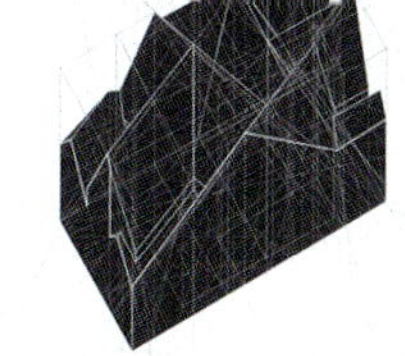

394

Haus Gables, 2018

181

Office Stack, 2018

498

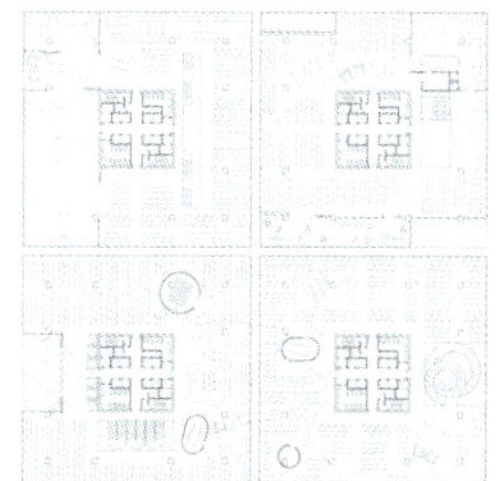

501

501

MAIO (Maria Charneco, Alfredo Lérida, Guillermo López, and Anna Puigjaner)

110 Rooms, 2016

251

Exhibition at MACBA, 2014

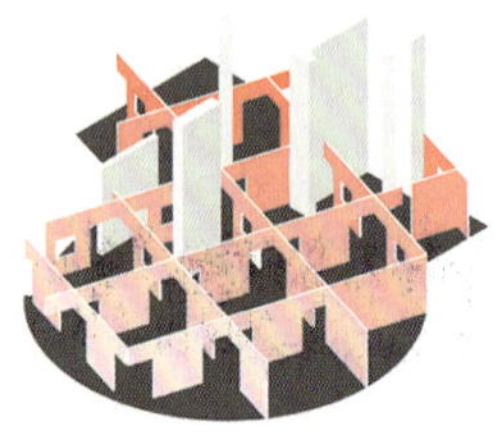

291

The Grand Interior, Chicago Architecture Biennial 2017, 2017

203

Ajay Manthripragada

Laurent House, 2019

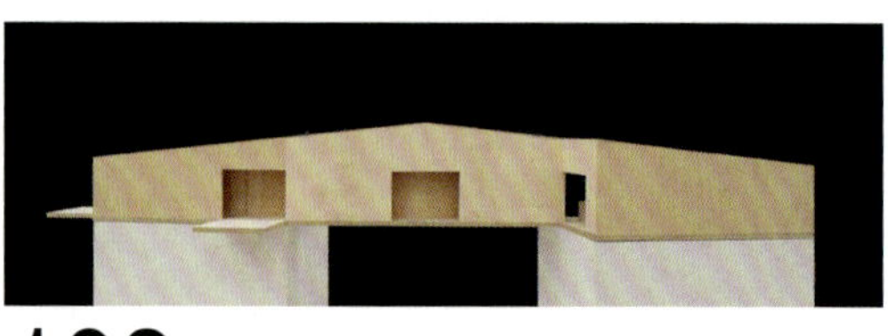

163

Page House and Gallery, 2017

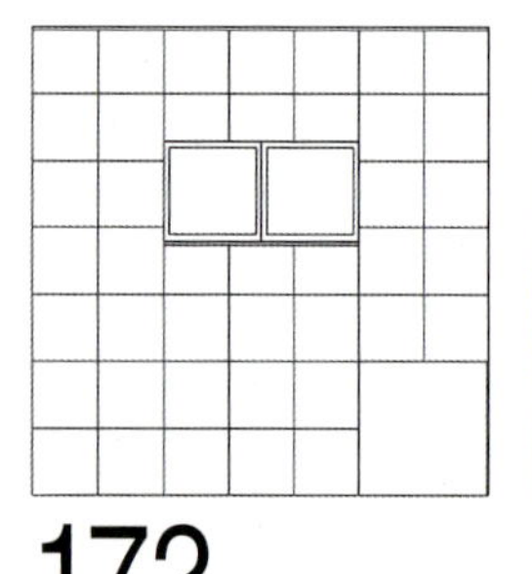

172 173

Marshall Brown Projects

Ziggurat, 2016

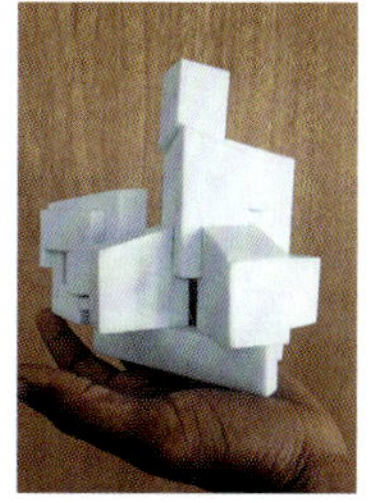
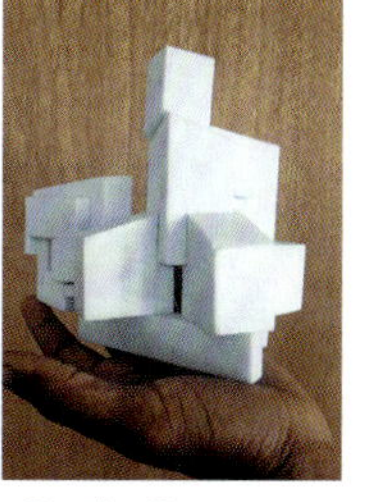
216

217

534

536

537

539

539

Matter Design (Brandon Clifford, Johanna Lobdell, and Wes McGee) (with CEMEX Global R&D)

Buoy Stone, 2016

266

Cannibal's Bath, 2019

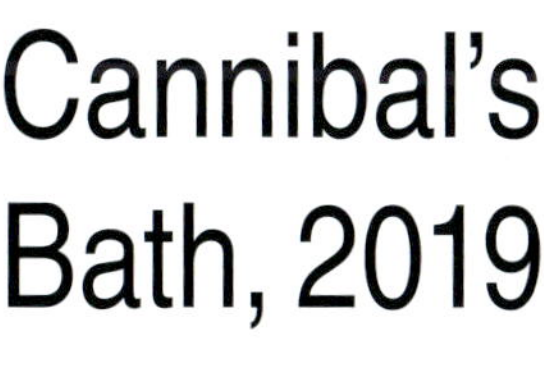

218

264

Matter Design

McKnelly Megalith, 2018

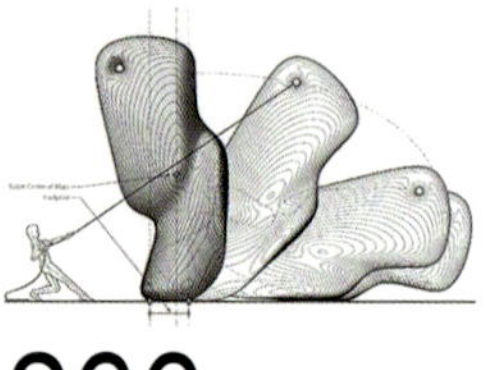

266

267

(with CEMEX Global R&D)

Walking Assembly, 2019

214

249

324

413

Kyle May

Extent, 2018

196

Alex Maymind

Proposal for a Vertical Office Block, 2012

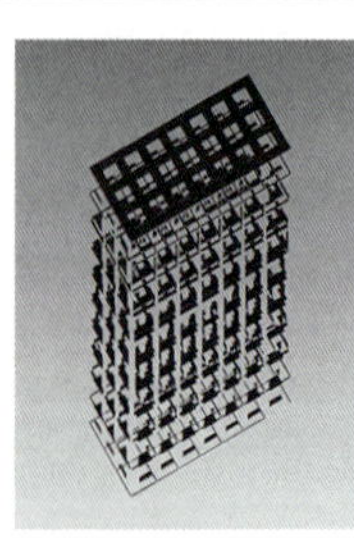

223

	Shoots and Ladders, No. 27, 2013	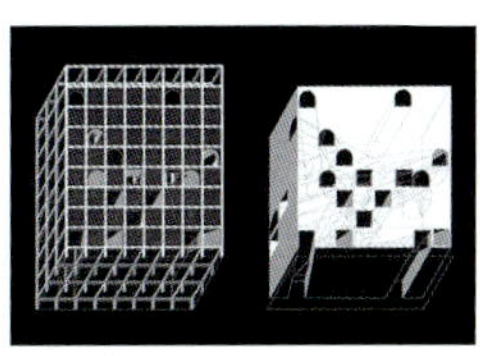 302
	Shoots and Lattices, No. 19, 2013	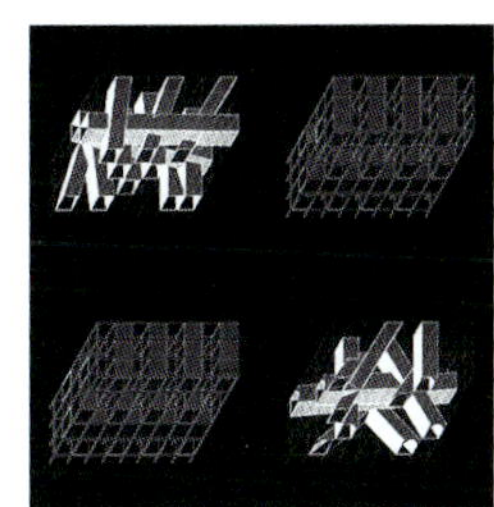 171
	Sixteen Four-, Nine-, and Sixteen-Square Variations on OMU's Residential Blocks, 2013 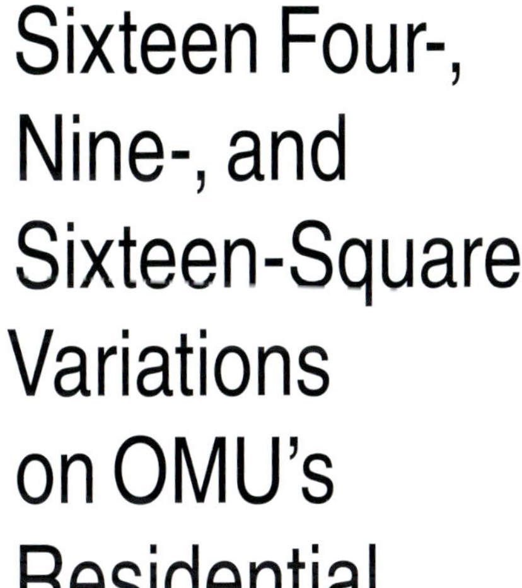	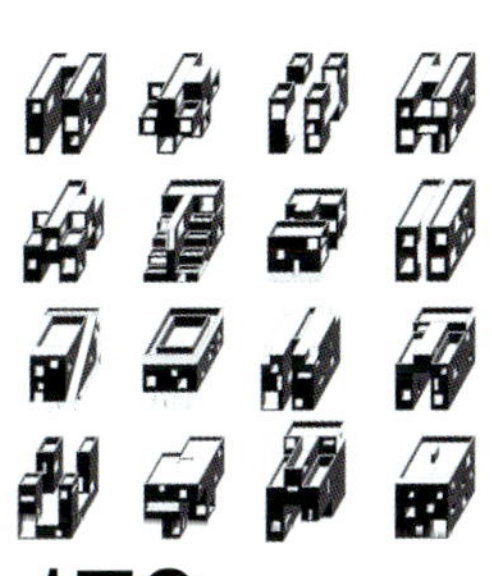 173
Medium Office (Alfie Koetter and Emmett Zeifman)	Frame Tower, 2016	 219 328
	Sienna, Detroit (2015), and Framing Folly (2019)	 217  217

	Stack Villa 4, 2019	 235	
Kyle Miller	Other Ways to Make an Entrance, 2019	  238	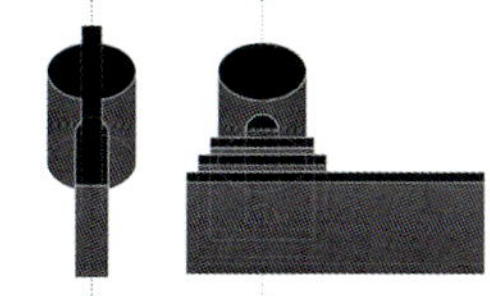 239
	The Plan is the Generator, 2016	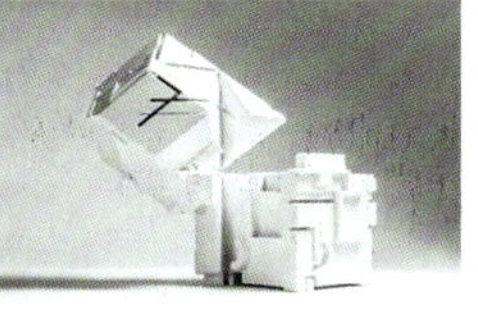 180	
Miller Moran (Meredith Miller and Thom Moran)	Between You & Me, 2015	 264	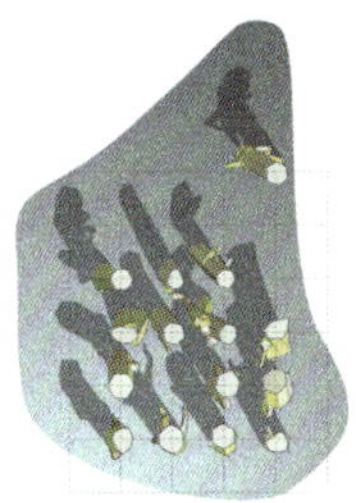 264
	Fort Blanket, 2015	 227	
	Plastic Sunrise, 2015	 254	

Miller Moran	Post Rock, 2016	 211	
MILLIØNS (Zeina Koreitem and John May)	Bathing, Again, 2018	 478	 478
		 481	 481
		 482	
	Beirut Rooftop, 2014	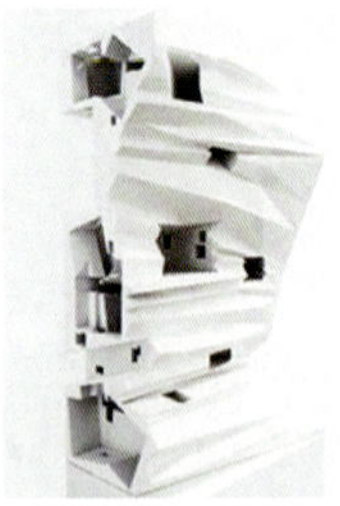 170	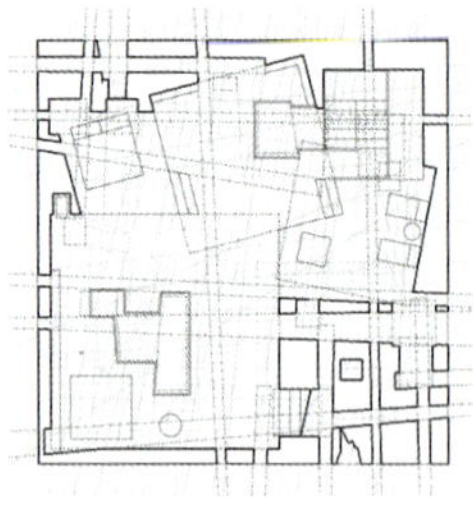 171
		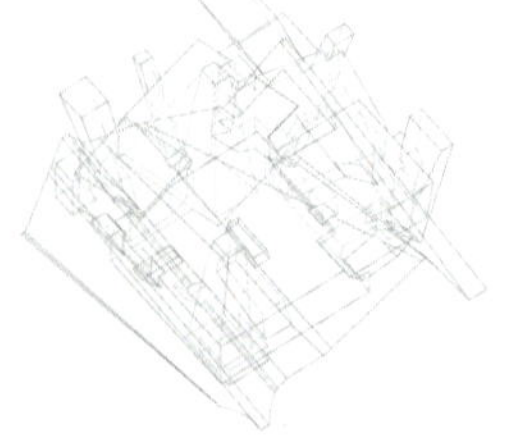 311	

Collectives I, 2014

153

170

186

Collectives II, 2016

156

301

301

MIRACLES Architecture (Viola Ago)

Pink Box, 2017–

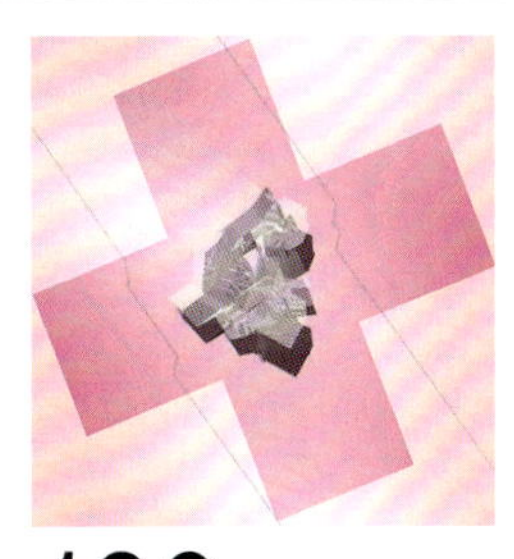
186

MIRACLES Architecture	Poppy Red, 2019	188
MoDus-Architects (Matteo Scagnol)	Mountain Lodge, Ponte di Ghiaccio, 2017	231
Kiel Moe	Longhouse, 2015	173
Kiel Moe and Ron Mason	Stackhouse, 2008	173
Thom Moran	Tables and Chairs, 2010	 235  336

MOS (Michael Meredith and Hilary Sample)	Community Center No. 3 (Lali Gurans Orphanage), in progress	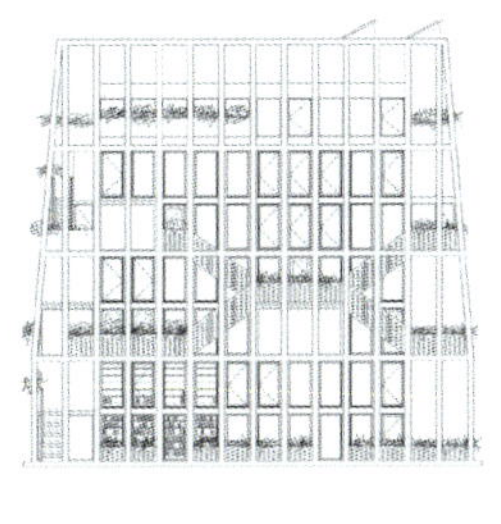 236	 333
	Currently Untitled, in progress	 230	
	House No. 10 (House with Courtyard), 2015–18	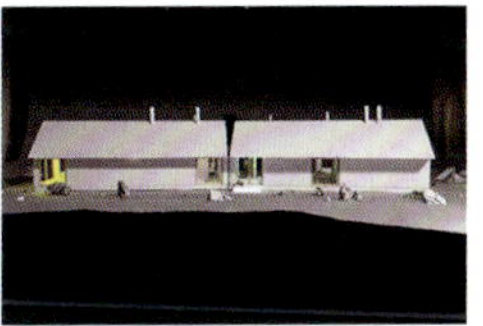 165	 389
	Installation No. 8 (Pile), 2009	 228	
	Installation No. 9 (Rainbow Vomit), 2010	 214	
	Mixed Use No. 3 (Housing and Art Foundation), 2014	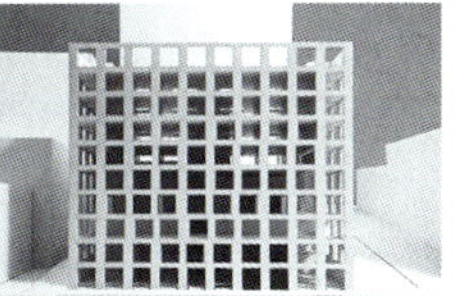 224	

MOS	Rock, in progress	 211	 325
MR Studio (Emily Mohr and Jonathan Reike)	Serendipitous Formalism, 2018	 198	
	Teh Developed Srf, 2019	 197	315
nARCHITECTS (Eric Bunge and Mimi Hoang)	NY State Equal Rights Heritage Center, 2018	 173	 175
NEMESTUDIO (Neyran Turan)	Manual of Instructions, 2019	 230	
	Museum of Lost Volumes, 2015	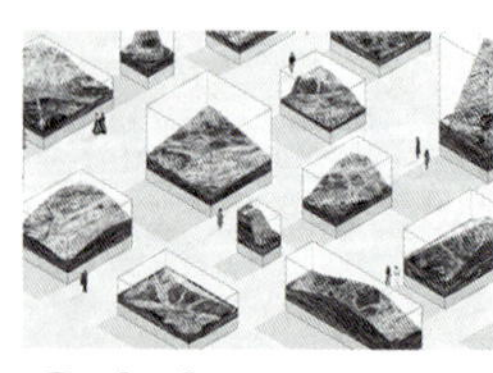 214	 234

408

New Cadavre Exquis, 2017

202

205

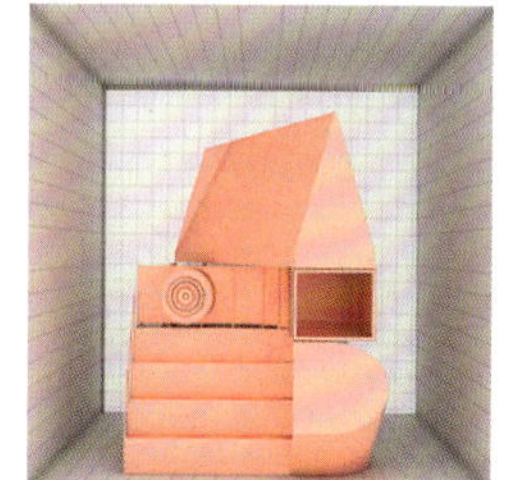
250

Our Junk, Their Ruin, 2018

229

313

New Affiliates (Ivi Diamantopoulou and Jaffer Kolb) (with Sam Stewart-Halevy)

Farmstead Retreat: Event Venue, 2020

163

Testbeds, in progress

216

New Affiliates

Tunbridge Winter Cabin, 2017

154

163

182

Owen Nichols

Hats Drawing Series, 2019

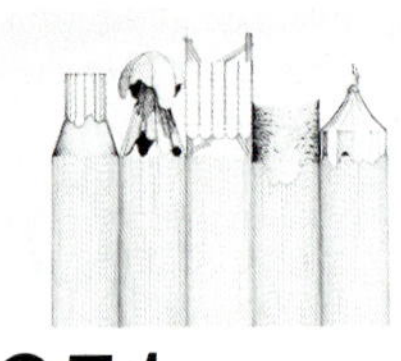
251

iffy architecture, 2018

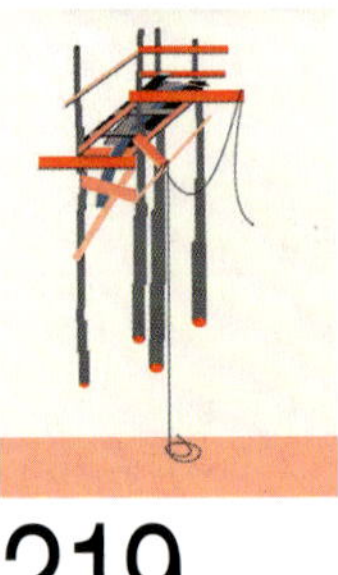
219

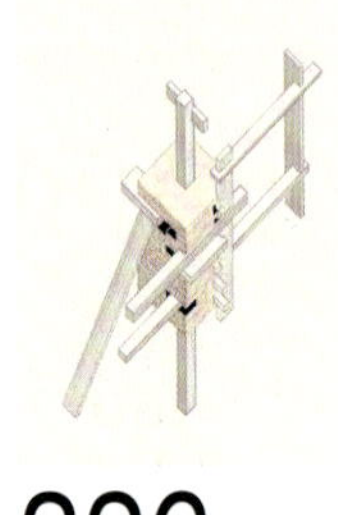
326

Owen Nichols, John Yurchyk, and Marc Acciari

A Garden Theater, 2019

241

NILE
(Nile
Greenberg)

4 Modernist
Corners, 2017

219

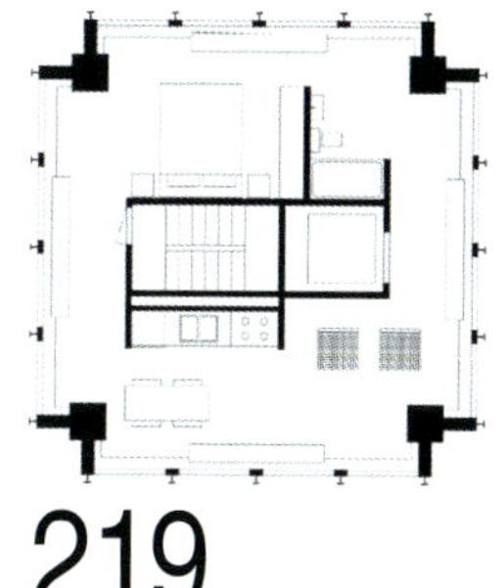
219

Dear Landlord,
2016

170

The Other
House, 2019

228

Our House,
2018

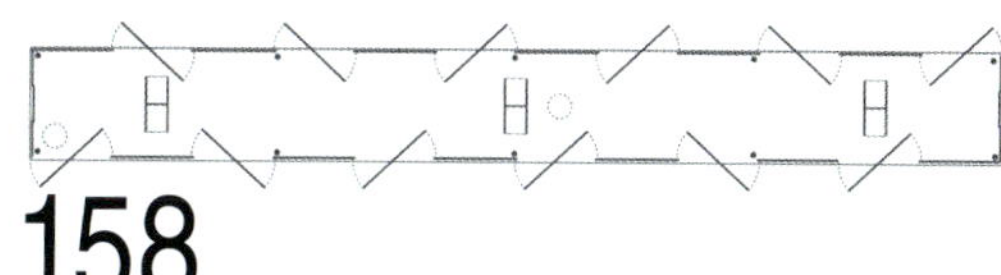
158

Norman Kelley
(Carrie Norman
and Thomas
Kelley)

Lincoln Log
Cabin, 2014

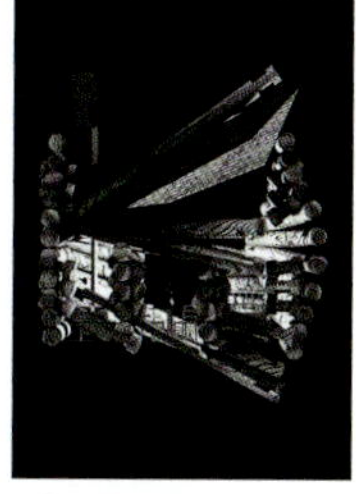
226

Wrong Chairs,
2014

259

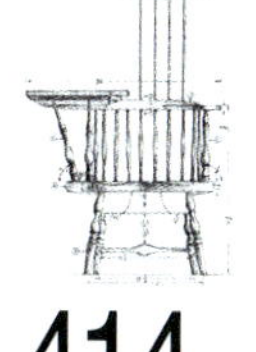
414

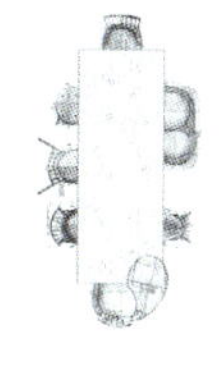

Now Here (Katy Barkan)

1/2 House, 2017

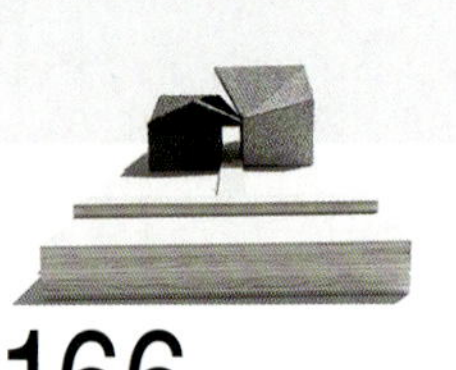
166

166

3 Stairs, 2019

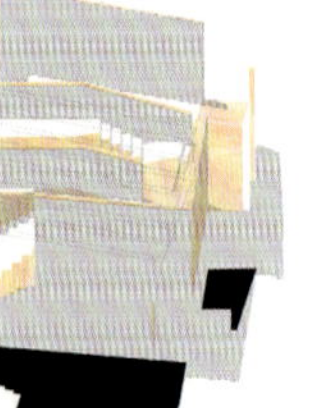
156

176

190

6 Work Surfaces, 2019

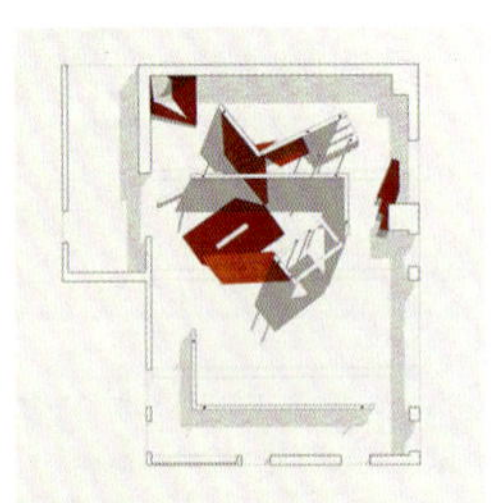
191

Office III (Sean Canty, Ryan Golenberg, and Stephanie Lin)

Open Your Heart, 2019

256

OFFICE Kersten Geers David Van Severen

Hatlehol Church, 2008

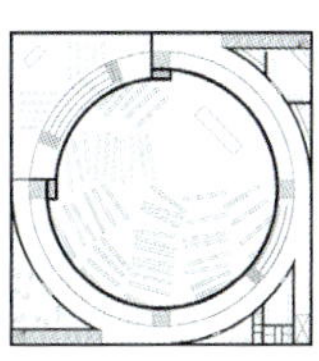
152

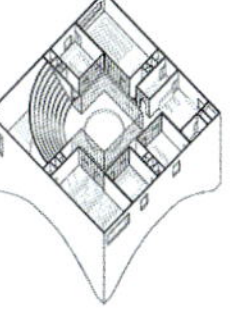
291

OFFICE 49: Water Tower, 2008

218

327

OFFICE 51: 25 Rooms, 2009

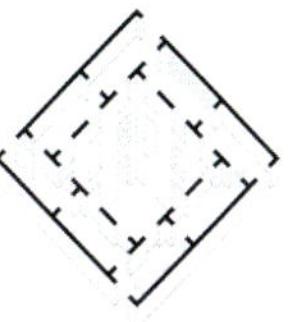
240

OFFICE 162: New NCCA, 2014

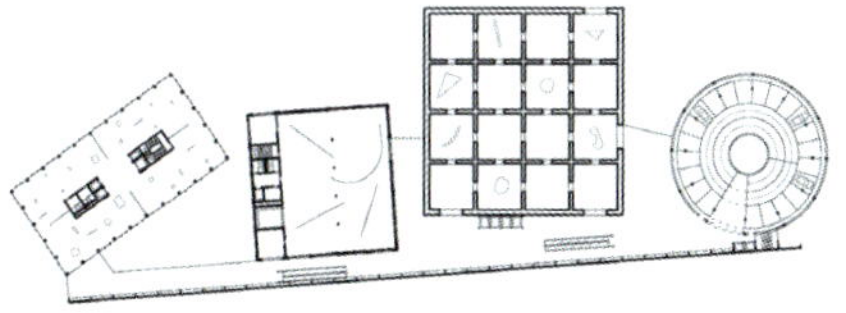
244

244

338

OFFICE 171: Arvo Pärt Center, 2014

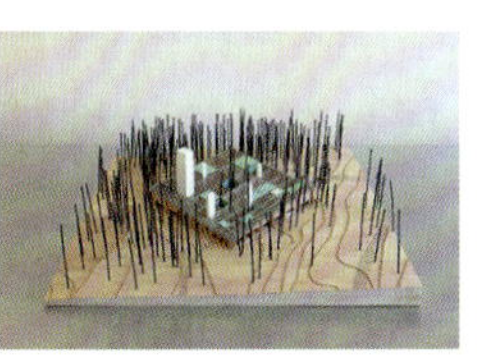
151

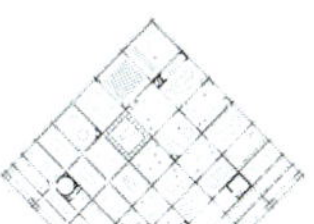
291

OFFICE 184: Radio & Television (VRT), 2015

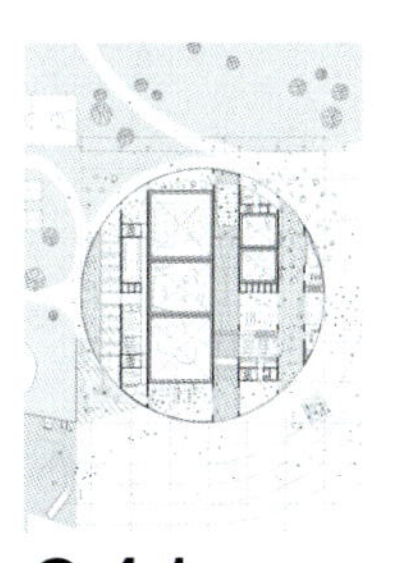
241

244

New Investigations in Collective Form, 2018

214

Scaffoldia, 2016

235

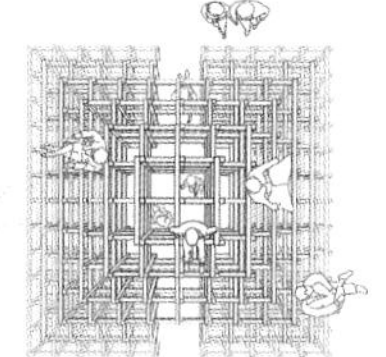
236

335

Varna Public Library and Archive, 2015

201

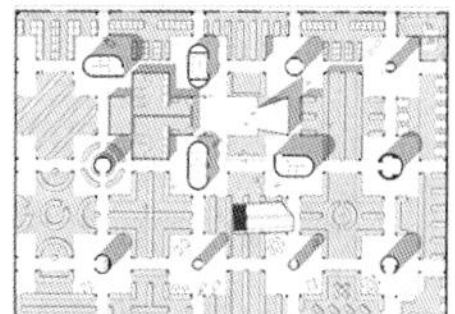
203

215

Outpost Office (Ashley Bigham and Erik Herrmann)

Another Digital, 2017

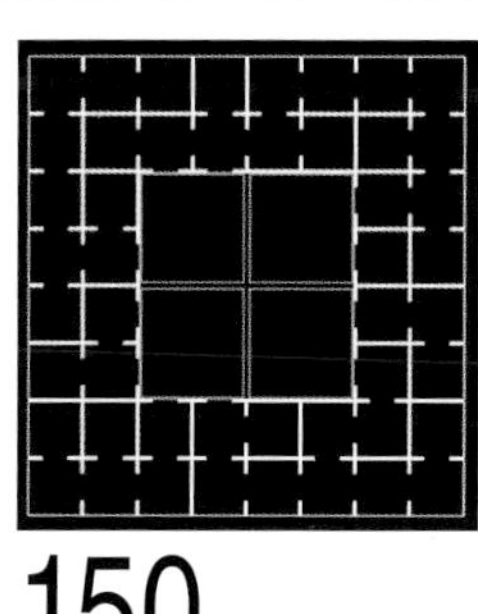
150

Outpost Office

Color Block, 2019

216

216

Computer-architektur No. 4, 2016

386

Computer-architektur No. 5, 2016

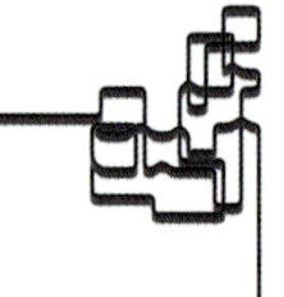
261

348

Ground Game, 2018

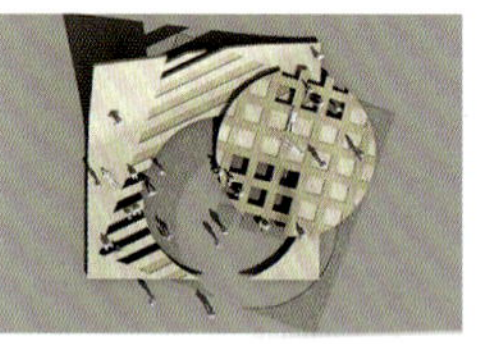
199

201

Labyrinth Tower, 2016

260

A Long House, 2020

164

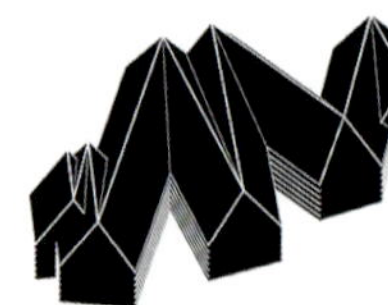
168

Open/Work, 2019

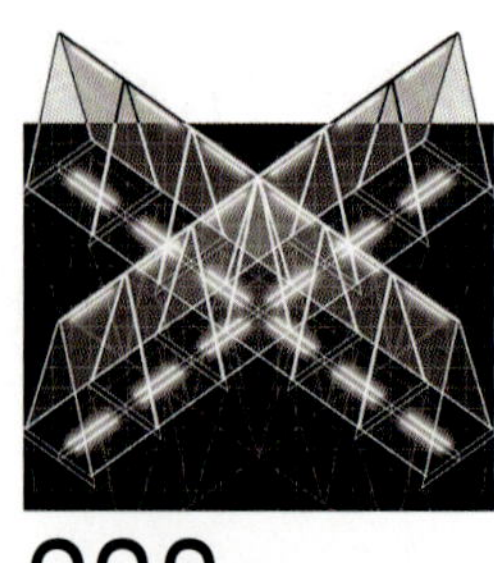
238

Primitive Villa, 2017

168

Twins, 2019

250

Upstate House, 2017

166

Villa Shotgun, 2017

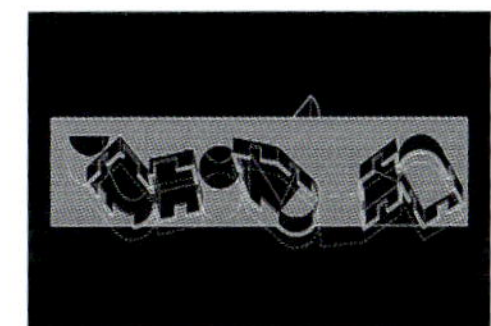

299

299

PARA Project (Jon Lott)

Crawford Attic Writing Room, 2010

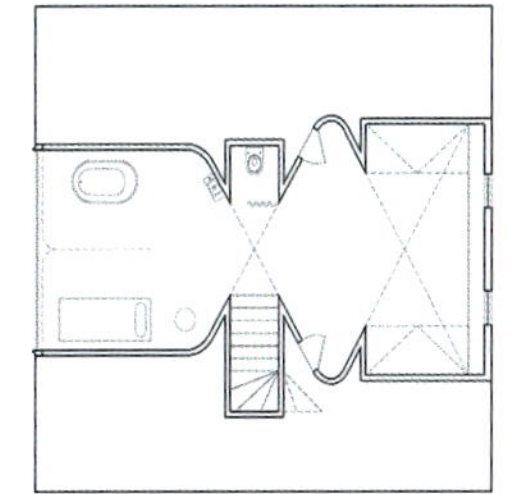

170

297

Open Fort, 2009

334

PARA Project

Pioneertown House, 2018

202

529

529

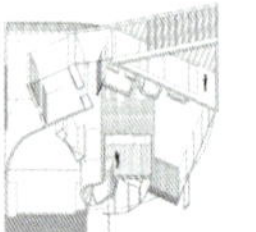

530

531

532

Roche Dinkeloo Double, 2018

236

240

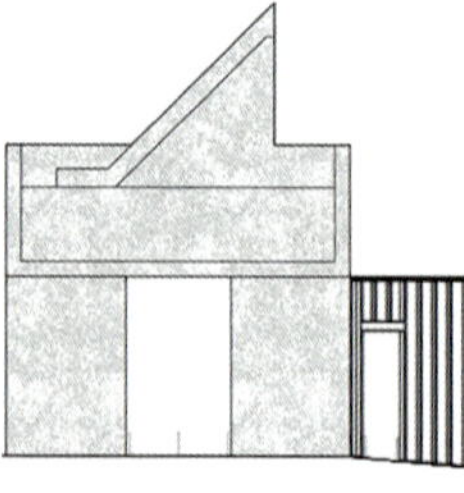
240

Stump House, 2019–

165

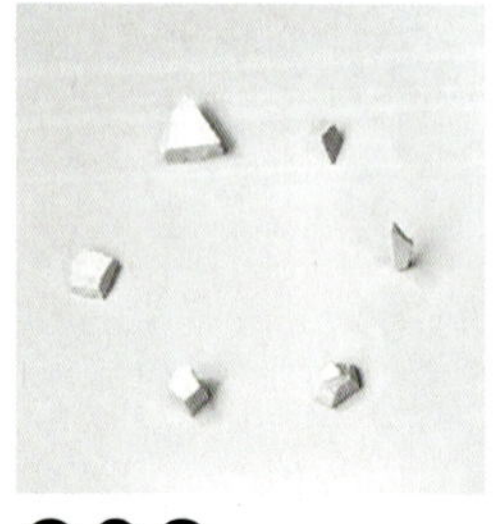
203

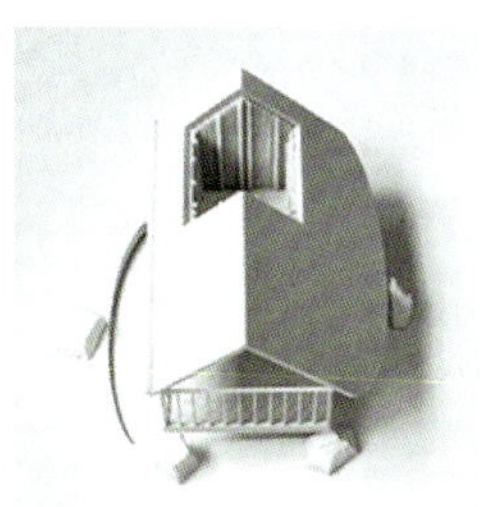
226
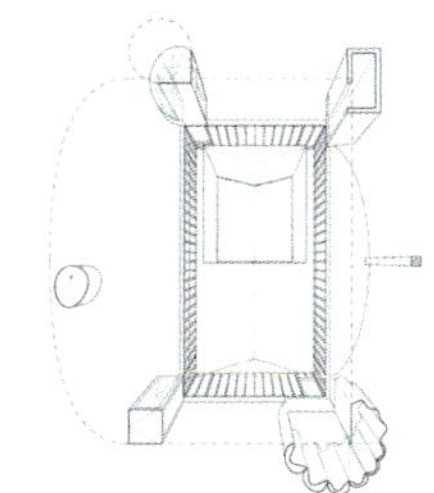
257

294

Paul Preissner Architects

Beer Sheeba Daycare, 2013

205

Five Rooms, 2017

249

House in Oregon, Illinois, 2018
161

Port of Kinmen Passenger Ferry Terminal, 2014

205

235

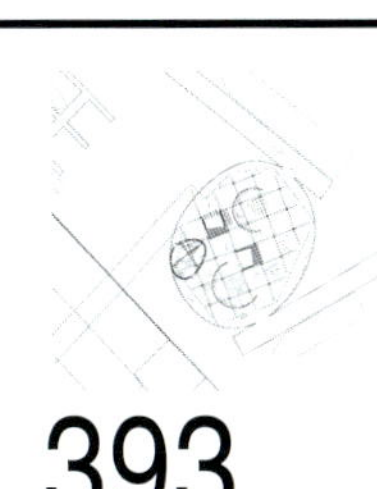
393

Pezo von Ellrichshausen (Mauricio Pezo and Sofia von Ellrichshausen)

Bell Pavilion, 2017

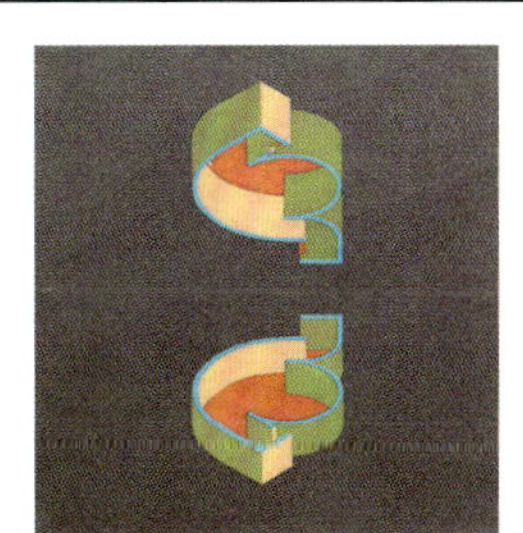
257

341

Crux Pavilion, 2013

238

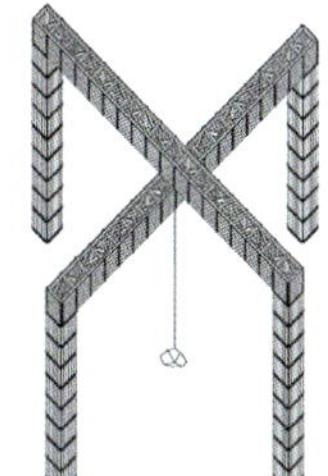
238

239

Guna House, 2015

240

Meri House, 2014

154

155

Pezo von Ellrichshausen

Meri House, 2014

155 290

Mine Pavilion, 2014

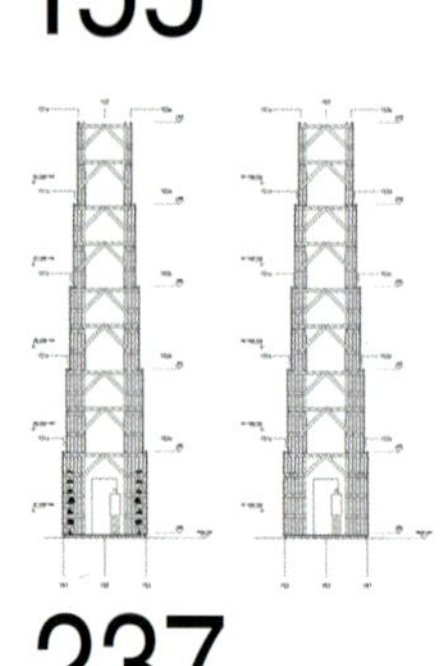

237

334

Nida House, 2016

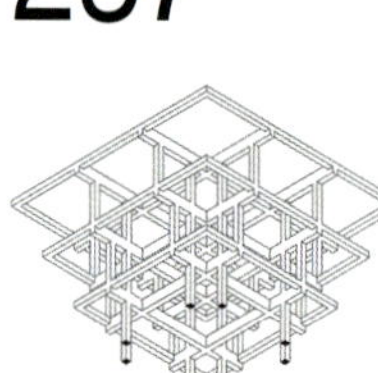

222

222

Vara Pavilion, 2016

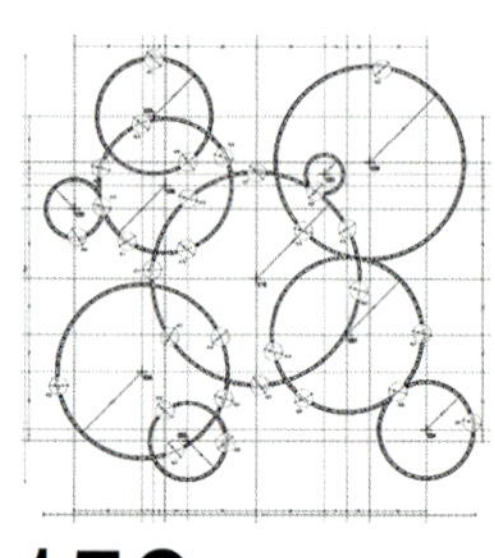

152 152

Preston Scott Cohen, Inc.

Cornered House, 1992

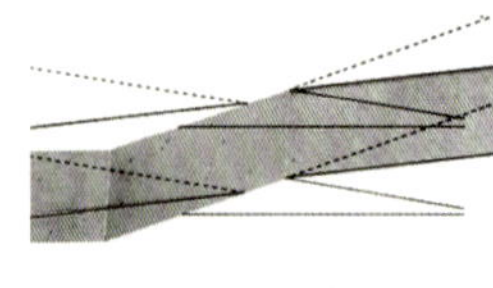

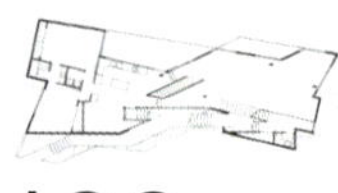

188

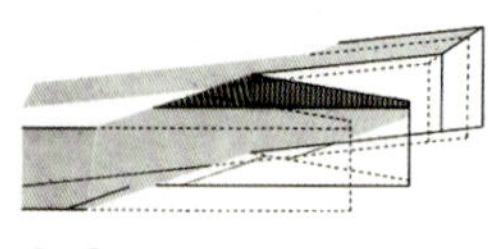

182

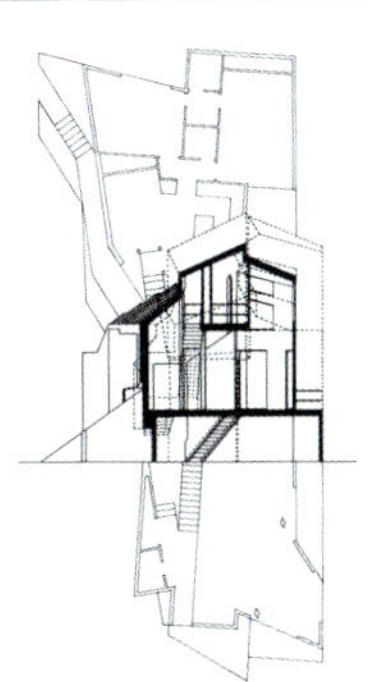

191

304

Eyebeam Atelier Museum, 2001

192

198

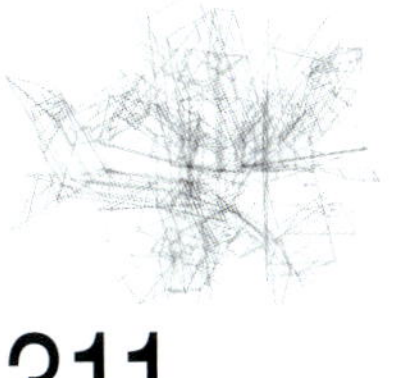

311

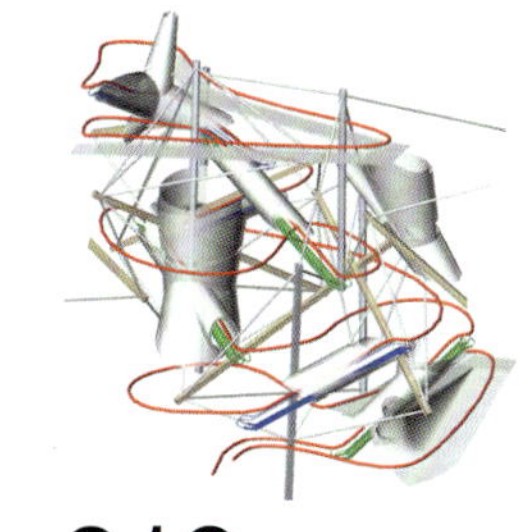

313

Goodman House, 2004

160

Head Start, 1996

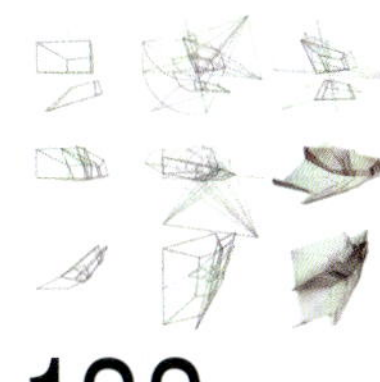

188

Teopanzolco Cultural Center, 2017

236

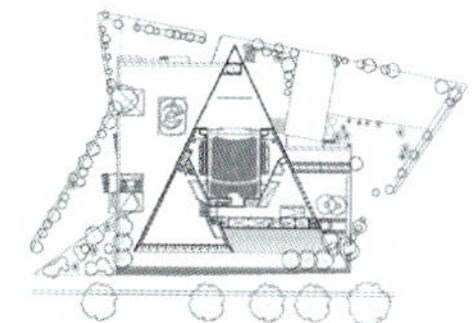
236

237

Curtis Roth

100% Sunshine, 2017

217

Decorating Villa Wolf, 2016

155

201

319

Instrument 3: The Mesh, 2016

398

Curtis Roth	Instrument 10: The Exhibition, 2017	 176
	Past Perfect, 2013	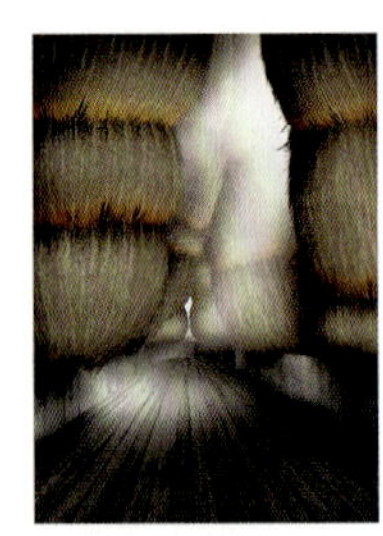 263
Nick Safley	Huflor, 2013	 262
SCHAUM/ SHIEH (Troy Schaum and Rosalyn Shieh)	Slider Tower, 2012	 153 246
	Sponge Urbanism, 2011	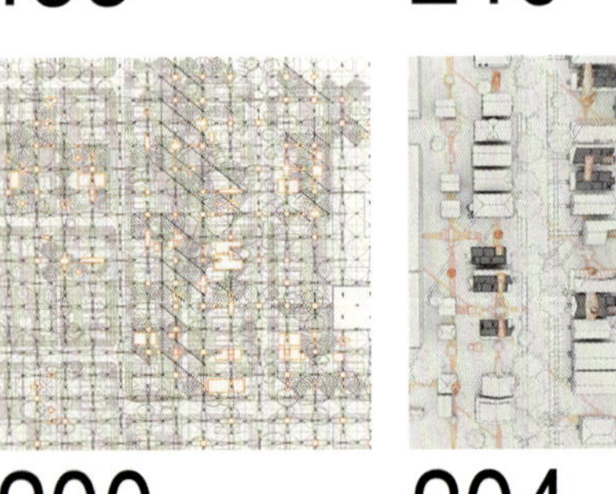 200 204

	Virginia House, 2015 Model, 2021 Building	 167
Somewhere Studio (Jessica Colangelo and Charles Sharpless)	Familiar Exceptions, 2017	 162   163
	Frame for Books, 2018	168
SpinaGu (Jia Yi Gu and Maxi Spina)	Other Turns, 2016	 253
	Soft Service, 2019	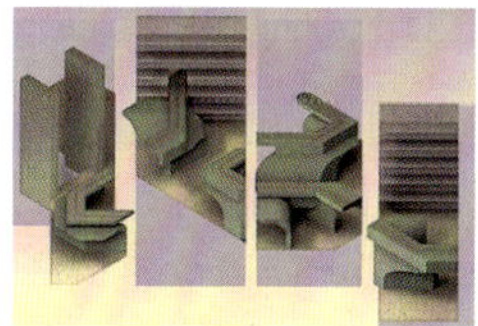 256
	Thick, 2017	 180 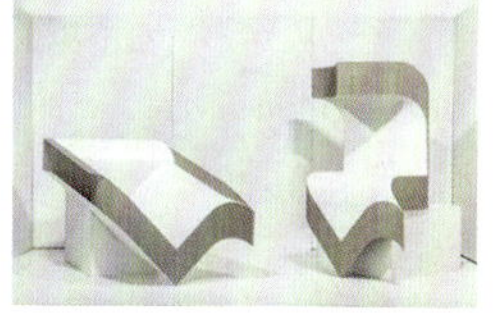 252

SPORTS (Greg Corso and Molly Hunker)

City Thread, 2018

261

Hearts of Gold–Buttonwillow Rest Area, 2018

170

Myth, 2014

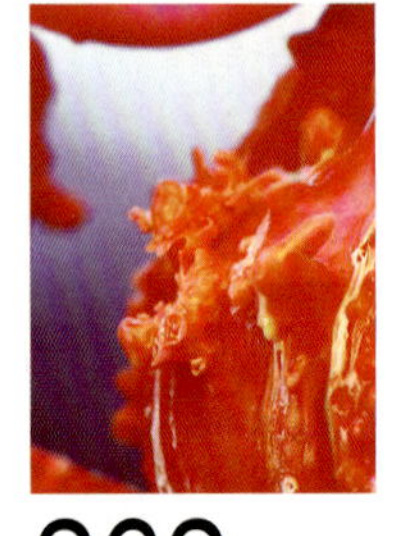

262

265

Rounds, 2016

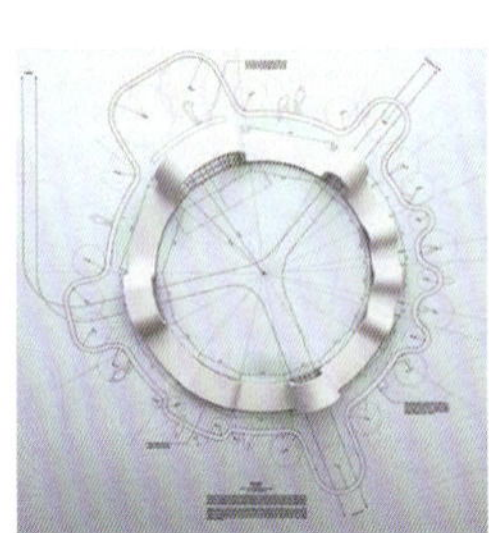

232

Runaway, 2017

187

Some Kind of Kinda, 2019

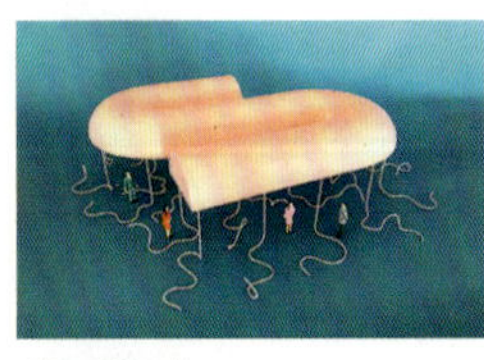

261

The Sweetness, 2014

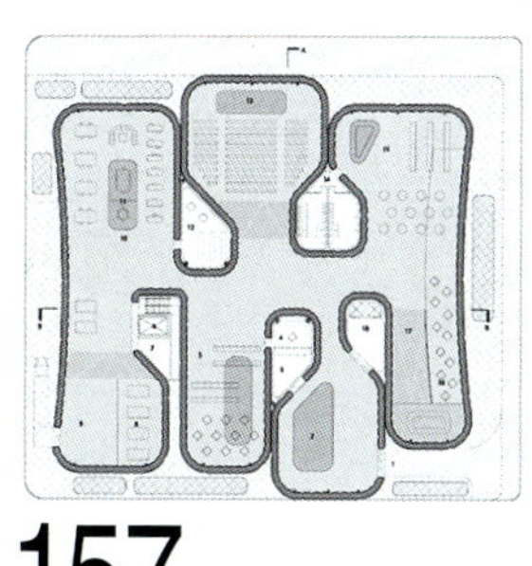

157

stock-a-studio (Laida Aguirre)

[a kit of these some parts] x budget gym], 2019

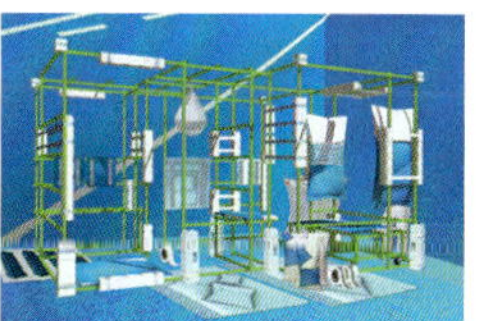

195

195

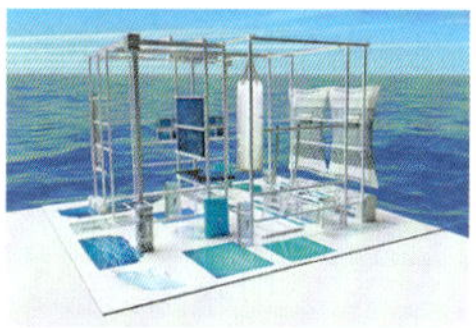

397

all out of this one rock, 2017

323

arlington audit, 2014

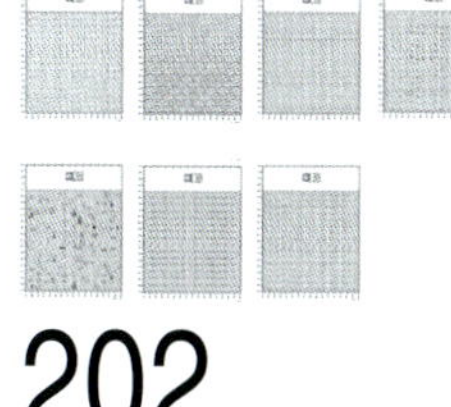

202

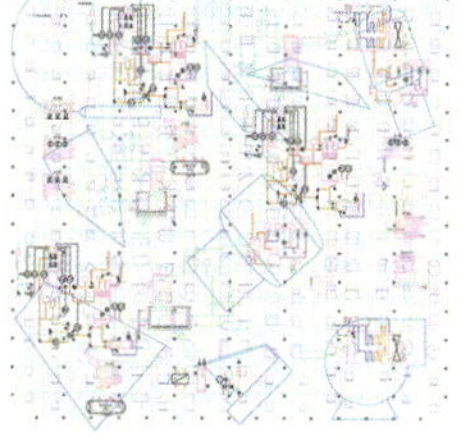

203

concrete pavers in room, 2017

215

stock-a-studio (with EXTENTS)

neighbor neighbor, 2019

200

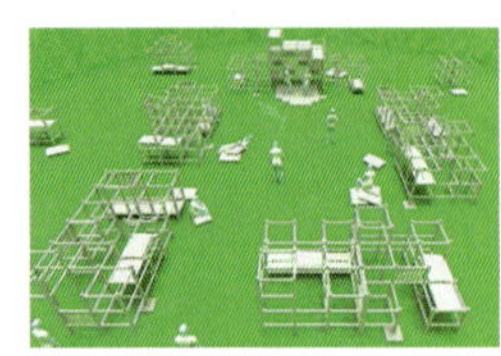
317

nude, 2018

200

318

rocks on grid, 2017

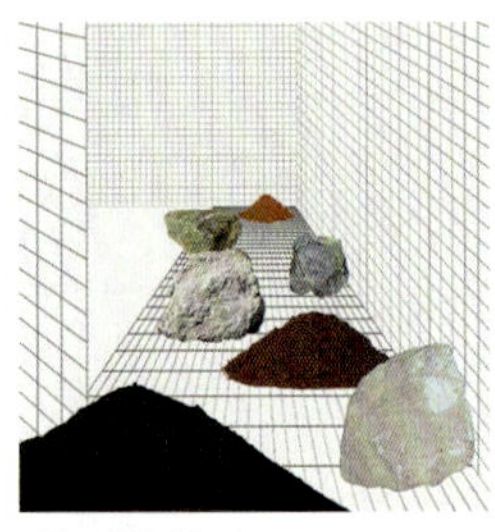
209

rocks on plinths, 2017

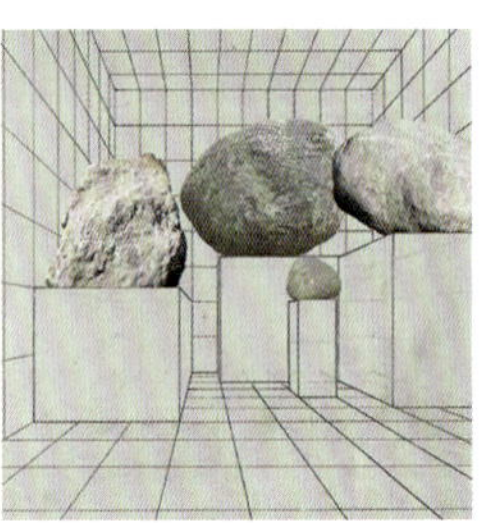
207

xs to xl, 2017

245

Studio Sean Canty

Figure-Ground Studies, 2019

157

House with a Void, 2016

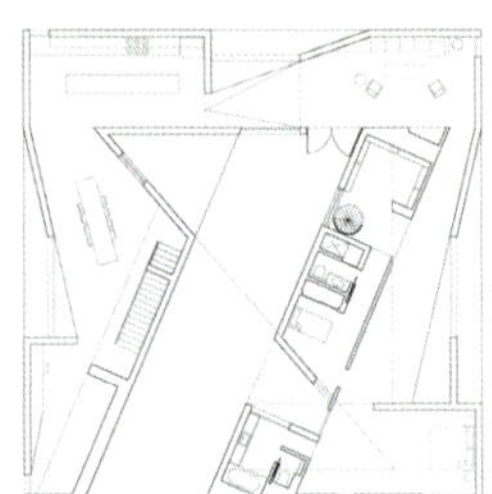

178

178

305

Irregular Infills, 2019

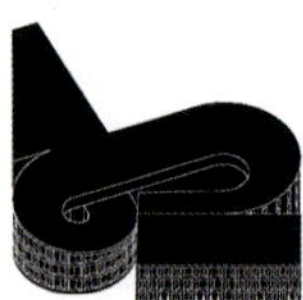

256

343

Janus House, 2019

164

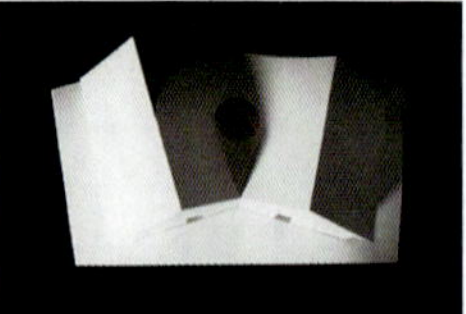

388

462

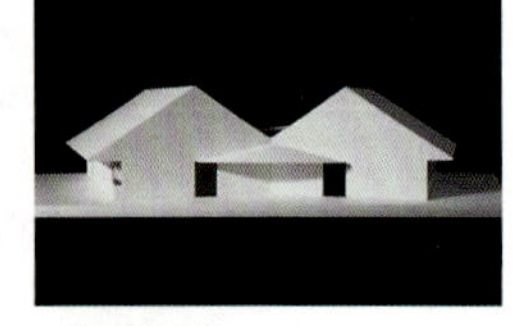

462

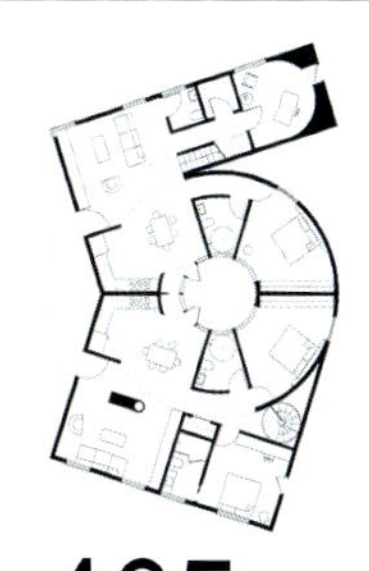
465

466

studioPM (Megan Panzano)

Not-So-Still Life, 2018

187

194

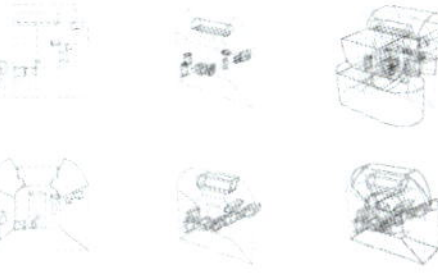
309

Stowaway House, 2016

164

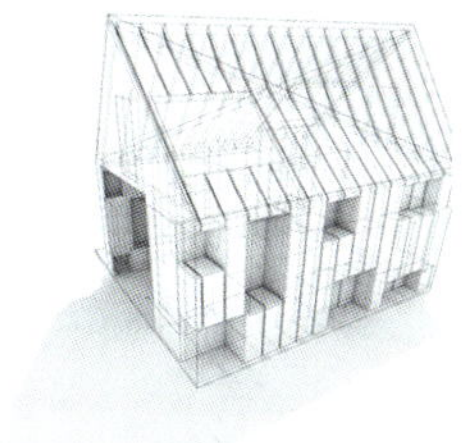
165

T+E+A+M (Ellie Abrons, Adam Fure, Meredith Miller, and Thom Moran)

Clastic Order, 2017

210

Detroit Reassembly Plant, 2016

208

T+E+A+M

Detroit Reassembly Plant, 2016

208

209

209

234

242

484

487

488

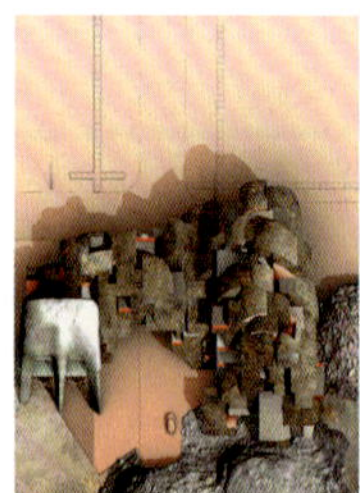
490

491

A Range Life, 2017

225

226

226

331

Team B (David Corns, Quinn Kummer, and John Stoughton)

Children's Park Restroom, 2017

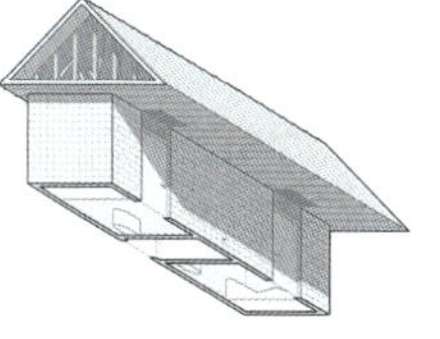
159

Ragdale Ring: Framed Follies, 2017

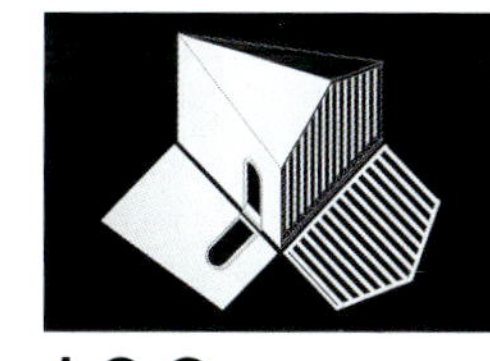
166

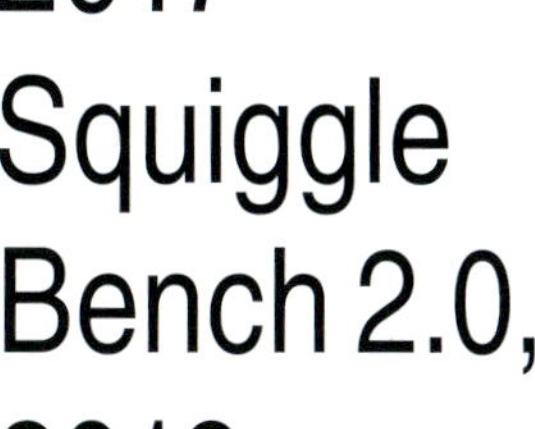
Squiggle Bench 2.0, 2019

257

Filip Tejchman

Motivational Rock, 2019

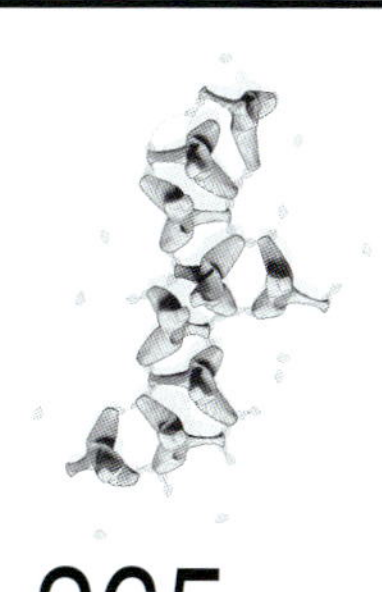
265

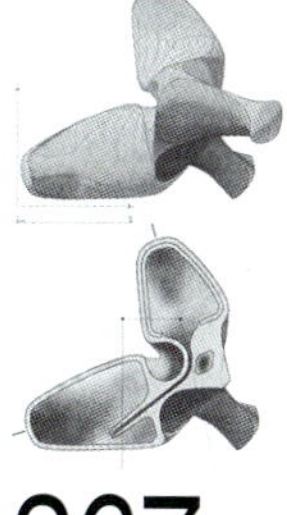
267

Architect	Project	Images	
Toshiko Mori Architect (with Tei Carpenter)	Dialogue in the Details, Venice Biennale 2012, 2012	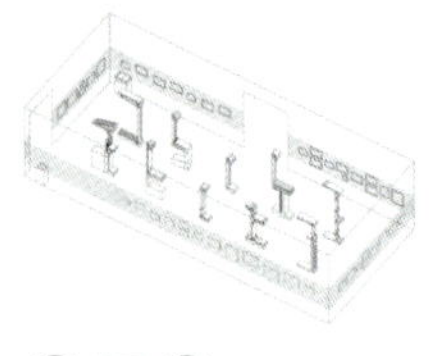 253	 253
Toshiko Mori Architect 	Ordos Villa 64, 2009	 172	
	Thread Artists' Residency and Cultural Center, 2015	 227	
		 229	
		332	

Architect	Project	Images
Hans Tursack	Graphic Fields, Composition VI, 2015	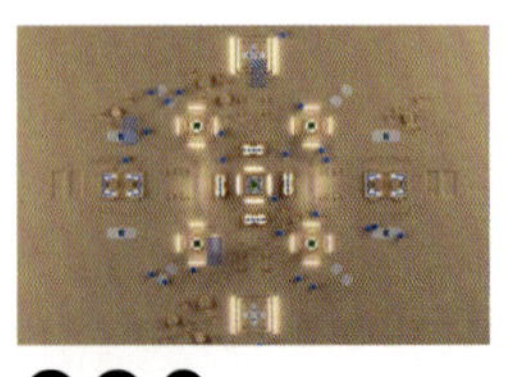 320
	Graphic Fields, Composition VII, 2015	 200

Graphic Fields, Composition VIII, 2015

203

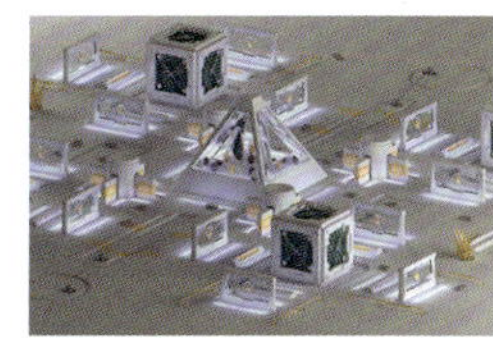

399

Precarious House, 2020

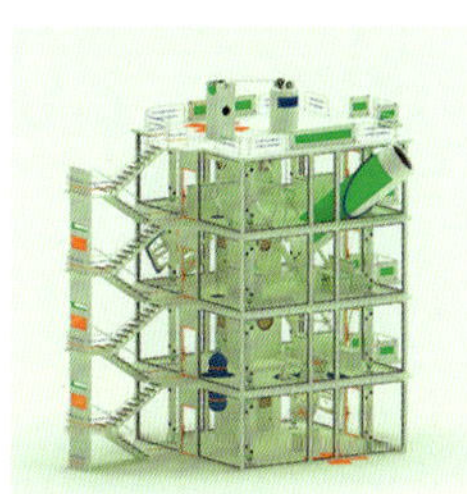

192

Ultramoderne (Aaron Forrest and Yasmin Vobis)

Chicago Horizon, 2015

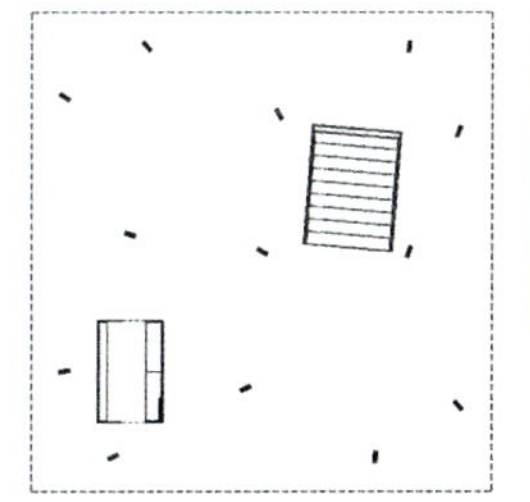

204

221

Escape, 2017

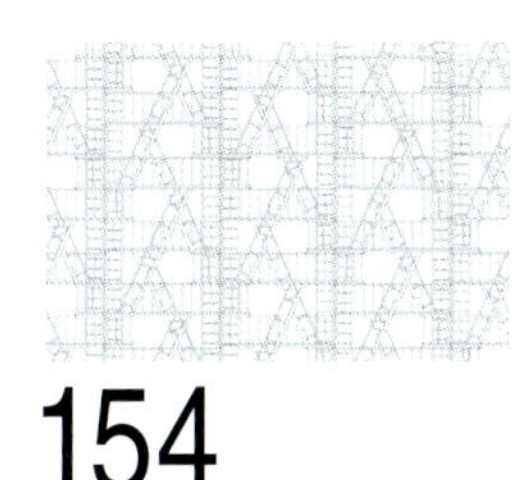

154

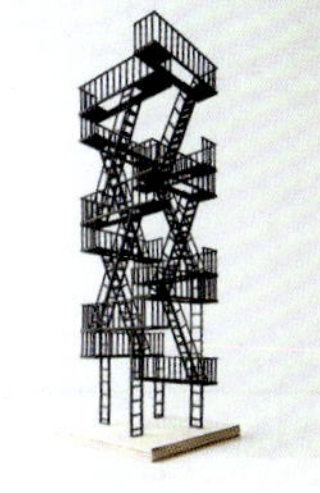

220

Four Corners, 2014

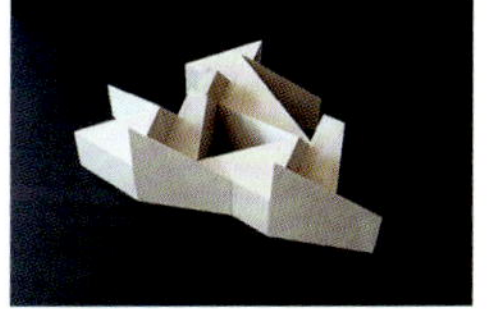

180

306

Framework, 2018

222

Ultramoderne	Recess PS1, 2016	 241
(with RISD Architecture)	Southlight, 2016	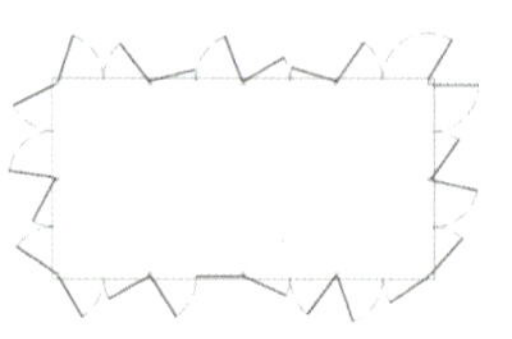 158  245  292
	Southside Cultural Center, in progress	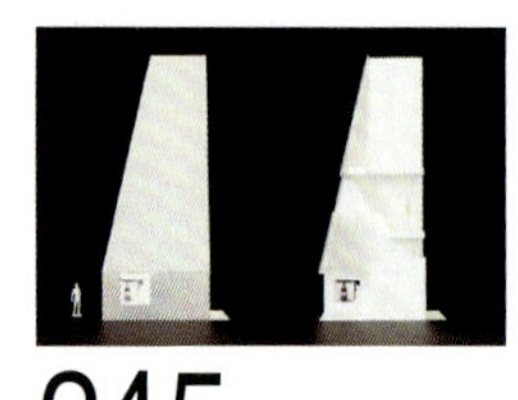 245

Jesús Vassallo	Aalto's Ghost, 2015	 235
	Timber Towers, 2015	 248 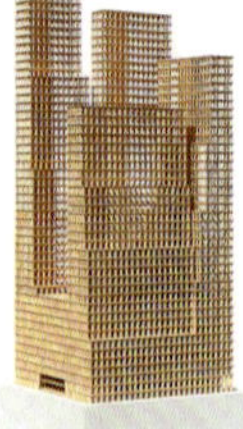 339

Water Towers, 2017

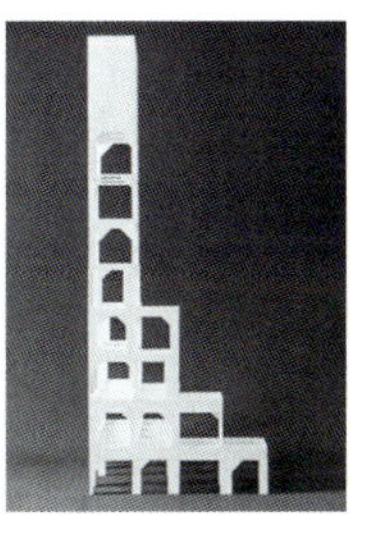
248

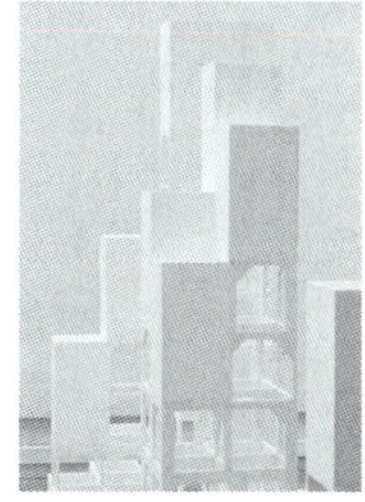
248

339

410

Welcome Projects (Laurel Consuelo Broughton)

Retrospective City, 2014

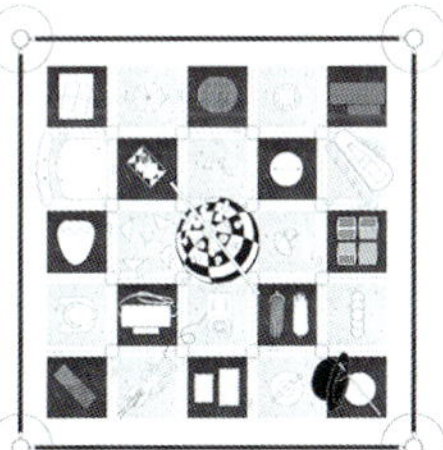
196

314

WOJR (William O'Brien Jr.)

Church, 2014

243

Dwelling, in progress

154

160

WOJR

Dwelling, in progress

296

Études, 2015

250

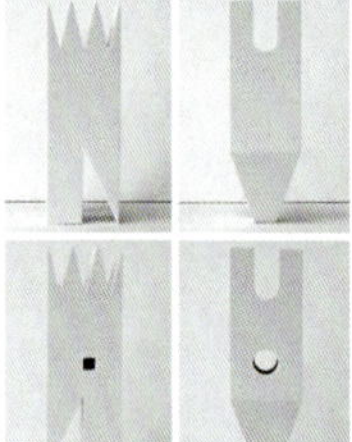

251

412

Ghosts, 2012

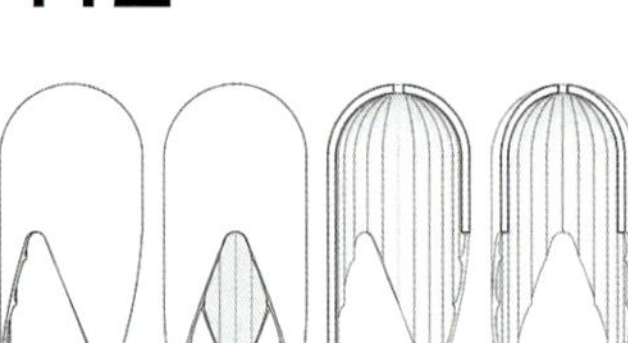

247

House of Horns, in progress

169

300

300

House of the Woodland, 2019

161

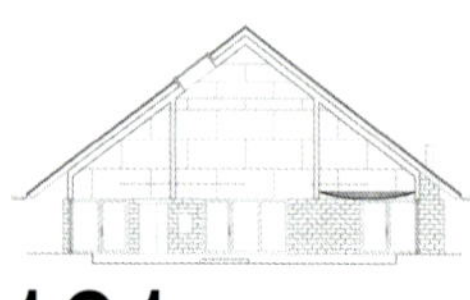

161

296

Hut, 2014

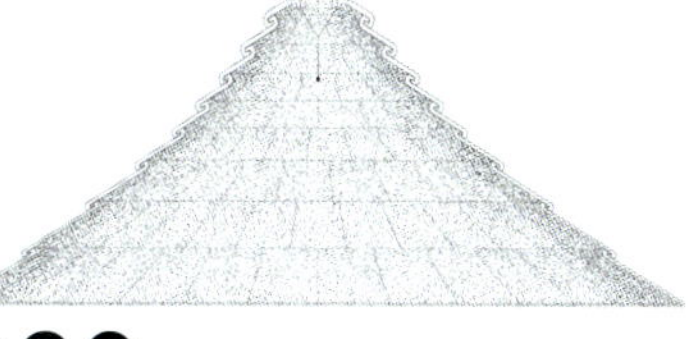

229

Labyrinth, 2013

152

169

Non-Labyrinths, 2014

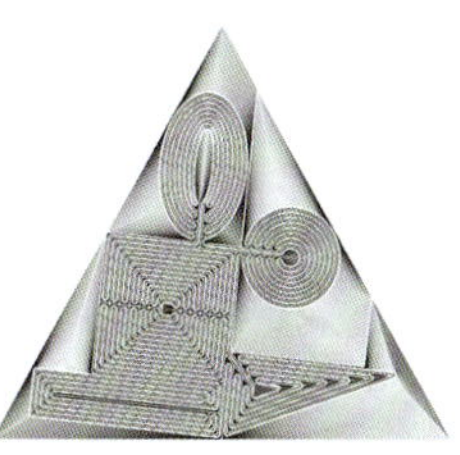

152

Other Masks, 2017

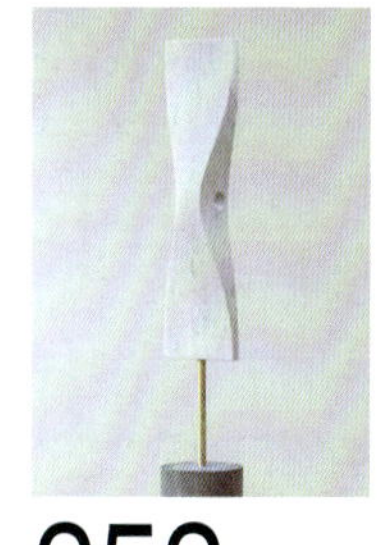

252

252

Young & Ayata (Kutan Ayata and Michael Young)

Base Flowers, 2015

265

Bauhaus Museum Dessau, 2015

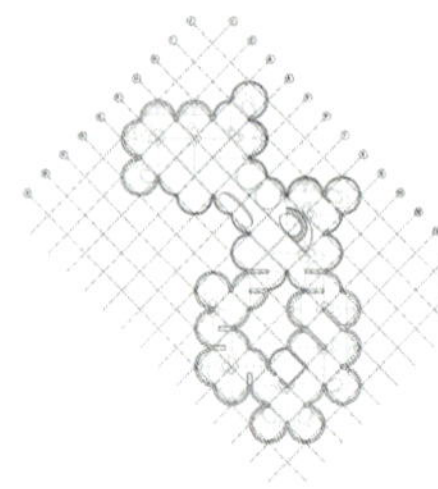
152

263

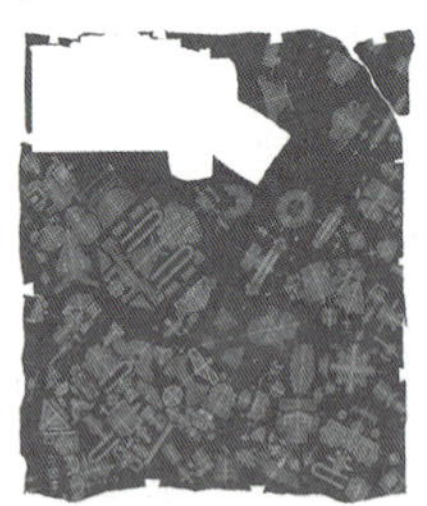
345

Campo Field Entourage, 2019

205

Guggenheim Museum Helsinki, 2014

267

LIMA-MALI-AMIL-ILAM, 2016

156

387

Catherine Ingraham
Sites of Inscription

New creative work in architecture, like all creative work, often seeks something like a clean or innocent beginning, unpolluted by former ideas and aesthetic regimes. Upon arrival, however, we always already know too much. As many have said in different ways, new ideas arise in the presence of givens—precedents—rather than starting afresh as if just born. This dependency (Harold Bloom's "anxiety of influence") is what supports the seesaw of Hegelian dialectics, Michel Foucault's tables of operation, and Jacques Derrida's linguistic and philosophical concept of play. What is given of course shifts from generation to generation. In Western architectural contexts, modernism is still with us, as is surrealism, neoclassicism, postmodernism, and other coalescences that inform us lightly and heavily as we create new frameworks. Perhaps this is what is meant by one of the curator's remarks in the pamphlet that accompanied the 2018 *Inscriptions* exhibition at the Harvard GSD: "We still believe in the Project," this curator wrote, "but not in its truth."[1]

I am not sure which Project this remark specifically refers to, but even without knowing this I somehow understand what this phrase means. Achieving an alliance with one's zeitgeist is a questionable, and probably unreachable, goal since we only synthesize the character of a zeitgeist once it is over. But there is plenty of evidence—as serendipitous and clear as the fall of the Berlin Wall—that history is on the move every nanosecond, and it is entirely possible that a Project (any Project) could remain useful but lose its truth. How a Project endures without its truth is an interesting question. And how much can we bend it slightly this way or that before we are the ones who are bent by it, yet again?

I was invited here to reflect on Mack Scogin and Merrill Elam's well-known 1999 competition entry for a science center in Wolfsburg, Germany, with a specific focus on the subject of figuration. Most would generally agree that Scogin and Elam's proposal is a figural building. What does this mean in this context, as well as in larger contexts? In a conversation with a colleague, I once glibly defined *figuration* as a reference to living forms—animal, human, botanical. This definition was not quite accurate. It is less the organic than the dynamic features of living forms (as well as other objects) that figuration—a form of representation—tries to capture. The Wolfsburg Science Center project references, among other things, its site: a transportation hub and modern industrial complex. This project is not a literal figuration of tentacles, transportation passageways, or cables and piping, although the site might well have conjured up an alliance between these things. It is instead a refiguration, or translation, of these things into tendrils that support a box-like structure in the air. Traveling through this tendril system reveals how the center is held up, such that the tendrils bring the center of the architectural project into play.[2] To be sure, the project refers to "human or animal figures" by proposing a system of squid-like legs,[3] but its goal is to solve some part of a dynamic relationship between "Big Science" and "Big Architecture." While there will not be enough room here to do justice to this process, I think this competition project was itself part of Scogin and Elam's rich laboratory of experiments. Their design for the Ohio State University Knowlton School of Architecture comes to mind as an analog to Wolfsburg. A later, built project, it also has a box volume held up by very tall *pilotis*, now straight but indexical in the same way.

One of the synonyms *Merriam-Webster's Collegiate Dictionary* gives for *figural* is "extended."[4] In literature, figures of speech or figurative speech is a way of extending

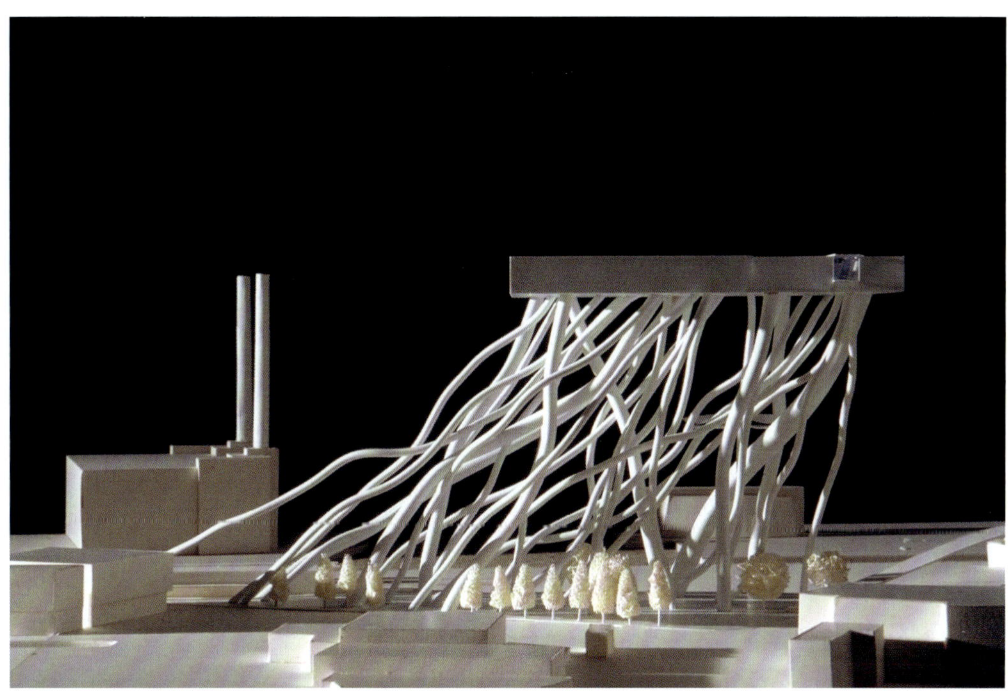

Mack Scogin Merrill Elam Architects, Wolfsburg Science Center Invited Competition, physical model, 1999.

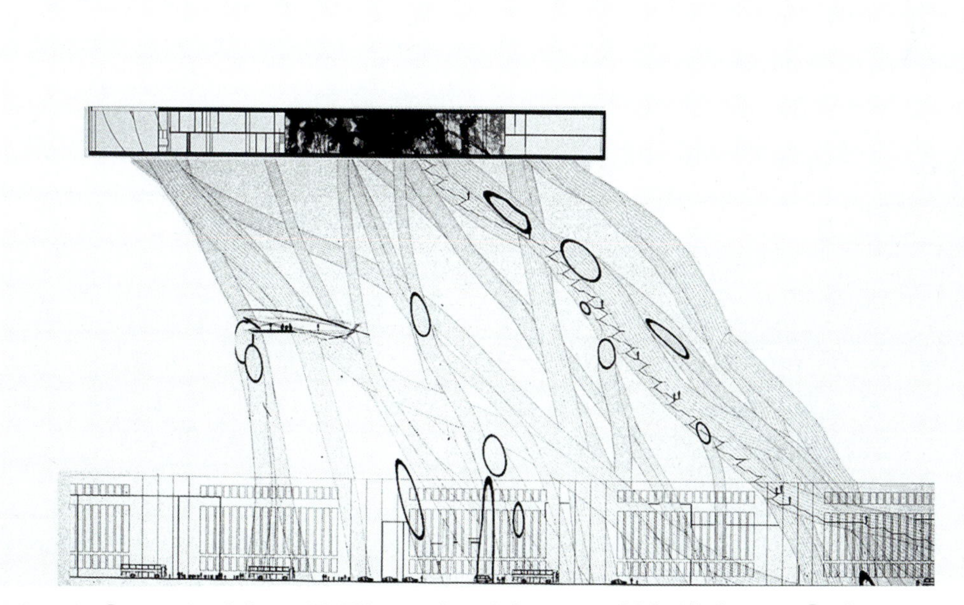

Mack Scogin Merrill Elam Architects, Wolfsburg Science Center Invited Competition, drawing, 1999.

Mack Scogin Merrill Elam Architects, Wolfsburg Science Center Invited Competition, physical model, 1999.

Mack Scogin Merrill Elam Architects, The Ohio State University Austin E. Knowlton School of Architecture, 2004.

meaning to the physical world and its infinity of things through allegories, similes, and metaphors. Metaphors, contrary to their intent, often impoverish the scene or thing that is meant to be enhanced (extended) by comparison. Metaphor can deflect rather than extend. Metonymic relations, unlike metaphors, force comparison to stay close to its referent. Metonymy develops part of the whole to which it refers.

In order to gesture more directly toward the *Inscriptions* project, I want to adopt Francis Bacon's distinction (and Deleuze's interpretation of that distinction) between figuration and the figure. Bacon's paintings battle against figuration, which he regards as a representational technique that is no longer relevant to modern life. Instead, he pursues the figure as an athleticism of the body that seeks to escape itself. This figure reveals a modern crisis and a necessity that requires "attendants" and fields of operation. To oversimplify, 19th-century portraiture (John Singer Sargent's, for example) sought to represent—to illustrate and document, in Deleuze's terms—the relatively stable outside appearance of a body.[5] Bacon tries to make visible *inside* forces that are imminent to the formation of a figure. In this context, figuration is an expansion of meaning that stills the body in order to characterize or make known its appearance. In painting, from which architecture has learned so much, figuration is generally defined as that which is always representational, or as some definitions say, "clearly derived from real objects."[6] But once figuration is scrubbed (Bacon's word) as in impressionism, or rendered latent, as in surrealism, or disappeared, as in modernist painting, the reality of objects is thrown into question. Bacon's paintings—insofar as they are figural, "relating to human and animal figures"—present human figures as contorted bodies at the mercy of animal and psychic impulses that are often contextualized in calm and even pretty spaces with windows and curtains or pools of light. Both forms of portraiture, old and new, claim to be capturing a dynamic reality. The relation of representation to the real, needless to say, is a project in Western cultures that has been, and still is, about theories of truth.

In regard to Scogin and Elam's proposal for the Wolfsburg Science Center, which, as they write, "involves rigorous research, informal experimentation, large proportions of play," I would argue that they are engaged not merely in general play but in *figural* play, which is related to Bacon's reconfiguration of figuration.[7] I have been interested for some time in Scogin and Elam's extraordinary willingness to venture into multiple experiments—both conceptual and material—and their expert management of what they then pursue. They consciously take these risks *in search* of architecture. I do not think they believe that architecture is ready to hand or that an architectural career leads automatically to architectural work.[8] In this work, the elusiveness of architecture does not render it fantastical or in any sense outside the normative constructions that architects are engaged with, although imagination plays a central role.[9] The figural appears, in the context of the Wolfsburg Center, as a probative reconfiguration of givens (such as support structures). This disturbs the whole apparatus and brings the demure box on top of a scramble of legs into play. The figural plays with what is known or expected—precedents—but feels free to contest the truth and reality of precedents and alter the rules.

Architectural precedents are already configured elements, real objects that are open to reconfiguration. We turn to precedents for diverse reasons: perhaps we need a historical referent to buttress our argument, or we want reminding about how a certain spatial or structural amalgam works, or we need to incorporate concepts that we do not yet dare throw away. Precedent is treated as a given set of possibilities, but it can be reshuffled into almost anything we need or want it to be.

To understand more about the kind of play I am referring to, we need to pick up the concept of "transcendental originals" from *Inscriptions*.[10] This term refers to the diverse set of projects in the exhibition that claim to be, and seem to be, avoiding idealism (and its associated iconography) but still work under the umbrella of the Project, which now appears to be the canon of precedents selected by and for this generation of faculty and students. The Project (whose truth is in question) does not hinder originality, but it does add a transcendental element. Kant's transcendental idealism (loitering in the wings here) was challenged by Derrida on the grounds that transcendental anything relies on placing its center *out of play*.[11] This center is unreachable and/or off-limits, and only as such can it exercise authority over the system that it runs. Derrida's point, in philosophical terms, is that the transcendental (even in a secular context) is made possible by types of authority that are absolutist in nature, essentially theological. Kant's transcendental idealism grants, for example, an *a priori* and universalist status to human faculties of reasoning and perception. These faculties are the only realities for Kant; things-in-themselves remain unknown. This *a priori* is synonymous with what is given. Given by whom or what? one might ask, to which one might point to yet another well-known project, this time about epistemic and ontological theories of human knowledge, perception, and being. *Inscriptions* generally borrows Kant's transcendental format, rather than the content, of the *a priori* to describe the work in the exhibition as "anterior to meaning . . . prior to phenomena, performance, themes, theses, tropes of discourse," and "prior to speech."[12] The removal of critical analysis from this work in effect suggests that while the work is, of course, originated through thought, it can only be seen as something that is not created in the presence of precedents. It is either archaic— temporally both very old and after the fact—or, less clearly, very innocent, very young. Figural play without the known. A paradise of omnipotence.

Transcendental originations—again in reference to the *Inscriptions*—"work through" the site of inscription with diverse forms of agency. This work is like Kant's faculties in a world that has come alive through late 20th-century concepts of emergence, agency, and virtuality. It is clear that we are meant to leave behind the conceits of philosophy and history in order to understand this. This might also imply the abandonment of totalizing "centers," although I would be reluctant to agree to this since the context within which the work happens is not nothing. It is a school, an institution, a set of multiple voices, opinions, points of view. An archaic object, in architecture, still carries the powers of the unformed and yet is also, because of its essentialist character, but one micro-thought away from the classical. It is not grounded in givens because it is seen as the first given. The archaic is, by definition, not in figural play with the known, nor is it in figural play with its essentialist center. The Wolfsburg project seems far from archaic, and with few exceptions most of the projects in the *Inscriptions* exhibition do not seem archaic either. If not from the archaic, then, where do these awkward amalgams and forms—"hysterias of meaning," "shocks of pleasure," and "jouissance"—come from?[13]

We are left with innocence, it seems, or rather a recovery of innocence, since the work is done by adults. At a lecture in 2019, Andrew Holder suggested that the void produced by the suspension of iconography made room for an influx of questions about identity—a striking comment that I have been turning over for some time.[14] In peculiar ways, this is an anti-Lacanian position, insofar as identity comes about, for Jacques Lacan, through gradual exposures to iconic meanings of the self. And yet Lacan is pointedly in the air of *Inscriptions*. Questions of identity recall theories of identity formation. In talking about figural play, are we talking about the mirror stage? Late Lacan (RSI and the symptom)? Child's play? Derridean play (which reveals the powers of the center)? To all three possibilities, I would say not quite. Instead, I think it might be Winnicott's play.

Douglas Winnicott was a contemporary of Jacques Lacan, both students of Sigmund Freud. The difference between these two psychoanalysts lies in how they understood the scenography of mirroring. In Lacan's mirror stage, the child's image is reflected back to her or him from afar, thus simultaneously opening the world and establishing the ground for a yet-to-be-formed autonomous self. This pre-speech mirroring sets the stage for social relations essential to human development. It is no different for Winnicott, except for one thing. Winnicott argues that it is not only the reflection of a child mirrored in the eyes of the parent (the mirroring agent) that is returned to the child but also, along the same path, the facial expression and composure of the parent or caretaker. In effect, the reflection of the child is accompanied or framed by expressions that are incorporated into its development of self-realization. This is how the "already known" enters the picture. Objects play a particular role in this relationship. Winnicott's theory of the "transitional object" adds what he calls a third step, "between inner psychic reality and the actual world in which the individual lives."[15] This third step is what Winnicott calls an "environmental" space of play—a space between subjective object and the object objectively perceived—which expands into the general creativity of life and "into the whole cultural life" of humans.[16] Transitional objects are playful objects over which a child is allowed to imagine she or he has total (if illusory) control and is thus able to create symbolic meanings of the object apart from its given meaning. How this play succeeds or fails, as a way of transitioning to the autonomy of the self, depends on whether the child is given a full opportunity to play in this way. Winnicott credits this play with the location of the beginning of cultural life in general, not just artistic or architectural creativity but also the ways in which we create, and cultivate for ourselves, the creative process of living.[17] I want to align this developmental sense of play with the kind of figural play that manipulates what is known (fields of operations, precedents) in search of architecture.

As adults, we understand that our autonomy is limited and there is no going back to our prespeech period, although the potential of spaces to afford creative acts influences every aspect of our lives. Winnicott's claim is that the childhood experience of play with transitional objects is essential to development because it allows an experimental period in which the figural character (of objects) is malleable.[18] It is not pinned down by proper usage or other strictures and yet it is not entirely free of tradition either. It is paradoxical.[19] As in surrealism or the baroque, distortion upsets the value of objects and disturbs the categories of things, but it does not distort the object out of recognition. Impressionism and surrealism, for their part, both preserve and allude to perspectival representation. The crooked leg of the Wolfsburg Science Center appears to be an unwieldy support, but it remains leg-like. Sites of inscription could be understood, then, as spaces for figural play between givens and transitional objects. Jennifer Bonner of MALL, for example, acknowledges the neighborhoods and places from which she selects rooftops but then freely models these "domestic hats" as figural objects liberated from their contexts. First Office, alternatively, maintains the structural integrity of the dolmen, but freely operates on its architectural context. This is to say that transitional objects and figural play do not disappear when we develop into social beings ("after speech," so to speak). While the rule sets of precedents are never totally abandoned in the architectural experiments now underway, it is clear that this work is both testing and forging new epistemological frameworks.

1 Exhibition pamphlet for *Inscriptions: Architecture Before Speech*, Druker Design Gallery, Harvard University Graduate School of Design (Cambridge, MA: Harvard University Graduate School of Design, 2018), 6.

2 "What we also know is that the architecture will be ever changing with the atmosphere and the climatic effects, as well as with the direction and speed of approach; that the science center will fascinate and captivate the imagination; and that as an object of interest it will be a clue to the curious wonders of the science within. The ride up the inclined lift, snaking through the tendrils, the jungle of supports, is enough to warrant a visit. . . . Discovering how the lift works, how the center actually stands up, how the center is heated and cooled, and how it captures the wind and lighting may even become a part of the visit. A small introduction to the world of science and invention. A big discovery of the City of Wolfsburg." Wolfsburg Science Center Invited Competition project description, Mack Scogin Merrill Elam Architects website, http://msmearch.com/type/museums-and-galleries/wolfsburg-science-center-invited-competition.

3 *Merriam-Webster* defines *figuration* as "an act or instance of representation in figures and shapes" and *figural* as "of, relating to, or consisting of human or animal figures." *Merriam-Webster*, s.v. "figuration (*n.*)" and "figural (*adj.*)," https://www.merriam-webster.com.

4 *Merriam-Webster*, s.v. "figural," https://www.merriam-webster.com/dictionary/figural.

5 Gilles Deleuze, *Francis Bacon: The Logic of Sensation*, trans. Daniel W. Smith (Minneapolis: University of Minnesota Press, 2004), 9.

6 Wikipedia, s.v. "Figurative Art," https://en.wikipedia.org/wiki/Figurative_art.

7 Mack Scogin Merrill Elam Architects, Wolfsburg Science Center project description.

8 Conversations with Mack Scogin during Spring 2020 final reviews at the Harvard GSD, and with Mack Scogin and Merrill Elam during Spring 2019 final reviews at Pratt Institute.

9 Mack Scogin Merrill Elam Architects, Wolfsburg Science Center project description.

10 Exhibition pamphlet for *Inscriptions*, 4.

11 Jacques Derrida, "The Parergon," in *The Truth in Painting*, trans. Geoff Bennington and Ian McLeod (Chicago: University of Chicago Press, 1987), 37–82.

12 Exhibition pamphlet for *Inscriptions*, 2.

13 Ibid., 7.

14 Andrew Holder and Preston Scott Cohen, "Five on Five," Harvard University Graduate School of Design, January 23, 2018, March 27, 2019, video, 1:32:07, 1:33:49, https://www.gsd.harvard.edu/event/five-on-five-books-looks.

15 D. W. Winnicott, *Playing and Reality* (London: Routledge, 2005), 2–4.

16 Ibid., 138–48.

17 One could point to autopoietic systems by which all organisms abide. These systems are internally organized yet externally energized (requiring air, water, and nutrients from outside their specific organization as an organism). They are thus required to construct an environment

in which these two components are operative.

18 Sigmund Freud, *Beyond the Pleasure Principle*, trans. James Strachey (New York: Norton, 1990). Freud's original 1915 lectures, published in this book, included his remarks on *fort/da*, an account of his nephew's use of an object to master the absence of the mother, which influenced Winnicott, Lacan, and Melanie Klein, among others.

19 Winnicott, *Playing and Reality*, xv–xvi.

Stan Allen
Pattern Recognition: Scanning Inscriptions

> Fully imagined cultural futures were the luxury of another day, one in which "now" was of some greater duration. For us, of course, things can change so abruptly, so violently, so profoundly, that futures like our grandparents' have insufficient "now" to stand on. We have no future because our present is too volatile.
> — William Gibson, *Pattern Recognition* (2003)

1

Favored by aviators and rally drivers, the Curta is a compact, beautifully designed mechanical calculator. It was manufactured in Liechtenstein from 1947 until 1972, when the widespread availability of inexpensive electronic calculators rendered it obsolete. Today they are sought-after collector's items, subjects of an elaborate subculture tracking serial numbers, manufacturing variations, and condition.[1] But the Curta also has a fraught backstory that goes to the heart of the 20th century's complex web of history, geopolitics, and military technology. The design of the Curta was finalized in the Buchenwald concentration camp. Before the war, Curt Herzstark, son of a Jewish father and a Catholic mother, was the technical director of his family's business in Vienna, the *Rechenmaschinefabrik der Austria Erstanden Compagnie* (Austrian Calculating Machine Manufacturing Company). He had already filed patents that covered the primary technical innovations of what would become the Curta. In 1943 he was arrested and sent to Buchenwald.[2] His expertise in precision toolmaking saved him from forced labor (and likely death), and he became a supervisor at the adjacent machine works. There he was encouraged to perfect the design of his calculating machine, and after liberation he managed to have three working prototypes fabricated in Weimar. Fearing that the Soviets would appropriate his invention (as the Nazis had threatened to), he smuggled the dismantled prototypes through

Curt Herzstark, Curta Model 1 Rotary Calculator, 1948–1972.

occupied Czechoslovakia to Austria. In Vienna, his brother had taken over the management of the factory. Determined to see his calculator project through on his own terms, Herzstark settled in Liechtenstein, financed by Prince Franz Josef II, who sought to build up a precision-manufacturing base there after the war.

The Curta is one of a number of iconic 20th-century objects that appear in William Gibson's 2003 novel *Pattern Recognition*. Gibson is the science fiction writer who coined the term "cyberspace." His 1984 novel *Neuromancer* became a touchstone for imaginative speculation on the interpersonal, urban, and architectural consequences of the digital future.[3] *Pattern Recognition* was written in the wake of September 11, 2001, and it is the first of his novels to be set in the present day. For Gibson, this was a logical progression: "I found the material of the actual 21st century richer, stranger, more multiplex than any imaginary 21st century could ever have been. And it could be unpacked with the toolkit of science fiction."[4] *Pattern Recognition* was followed by *Spook Country* (2007) and *Zero History* (2010), all three set in the present. Advertising, fashion, underground marketing, internet subcultures, industrial espionage, mercenaries, hacker culture, rogue CIA agents, Russian oligarchs, Cuban exiles, and the shadowy workings of international capital are among the subjects of these novels. Locations continually shift, from global cities such as London, Tokyo, New York, and Vancouver to post-Soviet Russia and Eastern Europe. Science fiction, it seems, no longer needs the future; the protocols of the genre map seamlessly onto the complex realities of the present. Gibson's future is now, and the earth, as J. G. Ballard says, really *is* an alien planet.

Alongside a realization of the imaginary futures of the late 20th century, another theme in Gibson's fictional universe is a new sense of history. Linear progression is replaced by a temporality marked simultaneously by rapid, catastrophic change and by slow, cyclical duration: "This perpetual toggling between nothing being new, under the sun, and everything having very recently changed, absolutely, is perhaps the central driving tension of my work."[5] Gibson's novels provoke a rethinking of what it means to be modern, when modernity itself has become a relic of the past. His books are littered with the detritus of obsolete technologies of the first modernity. In addition to the Curta, they include a buried Stuka bomber, the iconic MA-1 flight jacket, and a ZX81 computer: relics of 20th-century modernity that have a strange afterlife as objects of desire in the present. These technologies were the engines that undergirded the modernist aesthetic revolution: a hundred-year-old revolution that increasingly appears opaque and distant today. It is at once all too familiar—no longer radically other—and at the same time remote and inaccessible. The "modern" takes on a paradoxical character:

still imbued with optimism and progressive values, but reduced to an echo of a now obsolete past. Today's recycled modernity is a modernity detached from its newness value, which allows it to become a free-floating aesthetic category, freely mixed with other categories. And with this comes a narrative of loss. The distance from the present to this first modernity is underscored, which allows what was once radically other to become pure atmosphere.

The best known of these recycled icons of the 20th century that appear in Gibson's books is the MA-1 flight jacket originally made by the United States military for Air Force and Navy pilots in the 1950s. Cayce Pollard, the central character in *Pattern Recognition*, wears a black MA-1 from Buzz Rickson's, a Japanese company that makes obsessively crafted reproductions of vintage military clothing.[6] "The MA-1," Gibson writes, "is a very complexly iconic garment, having manifested in a number of subcultures since its initial military issue in the '50s. A tiny cult of proto-Mods favored it [in] early-sixties Soho, skinheads made it a part of their intensely narrow dress code (often in burgundy, which the USAF never issued either), it was part of a certain gay uniform, goths wore it (always in black)."[7] Gibson leverages this fluid referentiality throughout the novel, in particular the culture of the reproduction. The digital turn of the late 20th century has at once reinforced and complicated the narrative of technological progress. It has made available new technologies that flatten the landscape of history and engender a culture of sampling and copies: "History erased via the substitution of an identical object."[8]

This form of fluid and open-ended referentiality, moving seamlessly between pop culture and high culture, between history and present-day technology, between the archaic and the new, pervades the work in *Inscriptions*. In fact, it's hard to know exactly where to start, or how to organize the field. There are established offices with significant built work and recent graduates just starting out; there is excessive materiality and stripped-down minimalism; there is shape, there are stacks, there are formless piles, and there are field-like arrays. Vernacular allusions mix with knowing disciplinary quotation, low-tech and DIY alongside sophisticated digital fabrication. The overriding impression is of the energy and freshness of a younger generation, but there are present and former Harvard Graduate School of Design chairs represented. Most teach. Acronyms, initials,

Miriam Mibao, MA-1 Flight Jacket, 2016.

and UPPERCASE firm names suggest tongue-in-cheek branding. Some appear multiple times in different guises (the members of T+E+A+M, for example). There is Office, First Office, Small Office, Medium Office, and Outpost Office. There are friends and colleagues, practices that I admire and practices that I identify with, and former students (I count at least 12). There are also many names I had to look up. So any kind of critical objectivity is clearly impossible here.

Ever since the 1979 publication of Rosalind Krauss's "Sculpture in the Expanded Field," the preferred device for organizing an unruly field has been the semiotic square, and the curators propose four diagrams that organize the work according to variations on the question of the original: transcendental originals, immanent originals, encountered originals, and revealed originals. This is supplemented by two additional diagrams, organized as gradated scales, that signify the variability of the work exhibited, but also begin to suggest the limitations of the diagram. In part, this is the crux of the argument. It is not so much that the work falls neatly into categories, the curators suggest, as that it maps at variable scales, and onto multiple diagrams. There is no overarching schema to organize cultural production today, and no single diagram will ever be adequate. We need new tools to map the field. What *Pattern Recognition* offers—both as upper-case cultural reference and as lower-case operational strategy—is an approach to the complex field of *Inscriptions*. It seems to me that some version of Gibson's nonsequential historical temporality is present in almost all of the work in the exhibition, and that the only possible approach to the proliferation of work and approaches in the exhibition is to begin, tentatively and provisionally, to tease out patterns—patterns that will be more local than global, micro instead of macro, patterns in time as much as patterns in space.

In *Pattern Recognition*, Cayce Pollard is employed as a "cool hunter," spotting and tracking fashion trends. It is her job to see an emerging pattern before it is visible to others. And those patterns are fleeting; fashion moves at lightning speed from the margin to the mainstream. In the novel's construct, it is not accidental that Cayce's expertise equips her perfectly to track what may (or may not) be an elaborate conspiracy of industrial espionage that unfolds throughout the book. Multiple and overlapping patterns emerge from the profusion of projects and perspectives in *Inscriptions*: there are generational mappings, formal mappings, procedural mappings, and mappings of affect; diagrams of influence, and diagrams of affiliation. There are subcultures of technique, subcultures of material, and subcultures of reference. This collection could in turn be mapped onto other recent publications and exhibitions, where there is significant overlap.[9] All of these patterns shift over time and coalesce only momentarily. None of the maps or diagrams will ever be definitive, and, like a moiré, new patterns appear when they are overlapped and compared.

The curators have already mapped out many of these patterns, with considerable intellectual subtlety. I am not interested in adding to or contesting their categories. But from the point of view of technique, it is worth pointing out that this particular cross section of contemporary production also tracks a broad shift in the field today: from drawing to modeling (and graphics) as conceptual templates for design operations. It is not simply that models proliferate in the work of the architects exhibited; the foregrounding of the model as display strategy marks a conceptual shift in design thinking.[10] Drawings and models signify differently: drawings demand to be read and imply projection and translation; models are immediate and present. And, with a few significant exceptions, nearly all of the two-dimensional representations collected together here are derived from models: photographs of physical models or the graphic output of a computer model.[11]

Architectural models are inherently object-like. A model is a thing you can pick up, hold in your hands, and manipulate directly; it has an immediate relationship to the body. For this reason, models are often associated with materiality and tactility, and an improvisational design method. I want to argue the counterintuitive case, and insist that the model is actually one of the architect's most abstract design tools. Scalar reduction erases detail and renders the model intrinsically diagrammatic. Its compaction is the compaction of an idea or phenomenon made immediately visible in simplified form.[12] This is the instrumentality of the model in scientific culture, where complex systems are "modeled," typically as data-driven computer simulations. The category "model" today needs to encompass GIFs and 3D computer models, as well as complex data sets. The model is, in this sense, related to the diagram, but distinct. Where a scientific model is a dynamic construct, an architectural model is insistently object-like, but it retains the conceptual power of the scientific model—that is, the ability to figure and fix future forms and patterns. Models toggle insistently between real and abstract; they are the ideal avatars for the concept of *inscription* advanced here, as the point of inflection between "pure potential and expression, between force and form."[13]

The models shown here are also, for the most part, not constructed: they are output—that is to say, monolithic and singular. This is true, for example, even of a handmade model such as Ensamble Studio's cast concrete roof: the ubiquity of the computer model, and the inevitable intercession of photography, has retooled the character of the physical model. In a culture of drawing, an imagined (but not-yet-existing) form is described through a series of two-dimensional representations. Each drawing is partial; as the object becomes

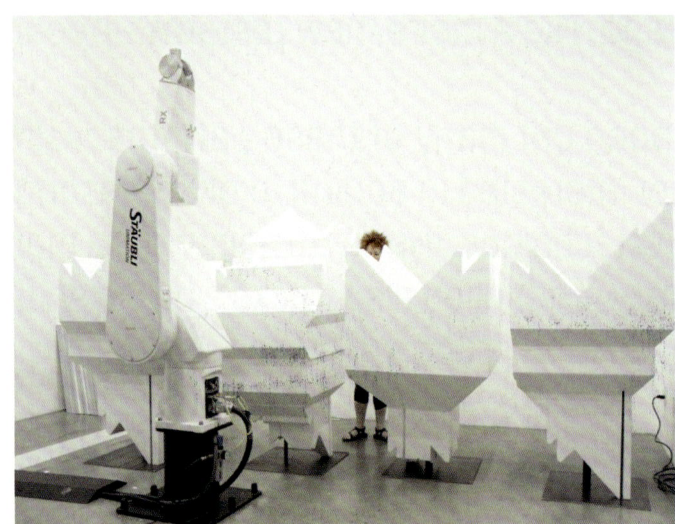

Erin Besler, Low Fidelity, physical model, 2012.

more complex, more drawings are required. Projection, construction, and assemblage are the key operations. As Robin Evans has described in both historical and operational detail, it is projection that enables this translation, a process that architects over time have internalized as a conceptual template deeply embedded in the culture of the discipline.[14] For Evans, and for a close reader of Evans such as Preston Scott Cohen, the architectural imagination operates in this space of translation between the measurable two-dimensional plane of the page (or the screen) and three-dimensional form, built or projected.

The comprehensive move to 3D modeling in design practice means that an architectural project is now studied, visualized, and developed almost exclusively through the slow build-up of an abstract computer model situated in boundless space. Even as it extends and internalizes the workflow, the computer model collapses the space of projection; it becomes more direct and immediate. Operations of transcoding and transposition displace translation, with its inevitable linguistic overtones. And among the work exhibited, there is a clear preference for mass and surface—the properties of the model—over plane and line, the stuff of drawings. The aesthetics of disjunction and fragmentation, complex curvilinearity, intricacy, and assemblage are almost completely absent. This effect is visible across a wide swath of the work exhibited. The immediacy and "presentness" of the model informs the work of WOJR, Collective-LOK, Studio Sean Canty, the LADG, Paul Preissner Architects, JaJa Co, and Outpost Office, among others. The spatial logics of design procedures associated with computer modeling, such as Boolean operations, render this work more plastic than geometric: the computer allows the designer to work with form as if it is *already* matter—mass that can be molded or carved, as in Erin Besler's Low Fidelity.[15]

formlessfinder, Tent Pile, photograph, 2013.

T+E+A+M, Detroit Reassembly Plant, rendering, 2016.

Drawing has historically been concerned with precise description and close formal control. In any number of practices represented here (MOS, formlessfinder, Hans Tursack, Outpost Office), form-finding software has been repurposed to simulate material behaviors: heaps, piles, draped blankets, stacks, and arrays that calculate their own angles of repose, indifferent to meaning. The Bittertang Farm works directly with living organic materials, replacing conventional design techniques with operations of cultivation and stewardship, leaving "traces of frothy matter in various disciplines." T+E+A+M's Detroit Reassembly Plant is at once concerned with the visceral effects of lumpen materiality, represented through intentionally awkward models, and at the same time a graphic translation that flattens and schematizes the work, reinscribing brute matter into the logic of the image.

The "shape" phenomenon identified by Robert Somol, and associated with practices such as Bureau Spectacular and Kyle Reynolds of is-office, could also be seen as a transposition of the logics of modeling. The suppression of detail and the immediacy of the form associated with shape aligns architecture with graphics and modeling rather than the culture of drawing, which tends toward the accumulation of detail, layering, and intricacy. Here the immediacy of communication—a building like a logo—serves to short-circuit linguistic analysis. In their diminutive scale and abstraction, models are also almost toy-like: the figures of the hobbyist and the doll house are never too far away from the model. Those projects identified by Andrew Holder as the creaturely could be usefully analyzed under the aesthetic categories proposed by Sianne Ngai: zany, cute, and interesting. Following Walter Benjamin's remarks on toys and dolls, Ngai identifies "cuteness" in particular with the simplified anthropomorphic figure.[16] And finally, in their flatness, reduction, and lack of detail, drawings produced by OFFICE Kersten

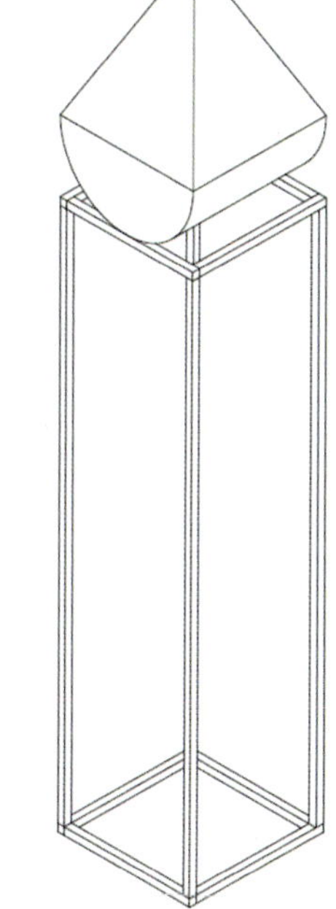
is-office, Crowns, drawing, 2015.

Geers David Van Severen, among many others, reflect the logic of modeling back onto the conventions of drawing itself. Less images of buildings, they are depictions of iconic, modeled forms sitting on an abstract ground against a colored backdrop.

> I am not alone in having been born backward into an incoherent realm of texts, products, and images, the commercial and cultural environment with which we've both supplemented and blotted out our natural world. I can no more claim it as "mine" than the sidewalks and forests of the world, yet I do dwell in it, and for me to stand a chance as an artist or citizen, I'd probably better be permitted to name it.
> — Jonathan Lethem, "The Ecstasy of Influence" (2007)

2

For an earlier generation of architects, "expanding" the field meant recognizing a limit and transgressing it; there was a center and margin, established variously by mainstream practice, the academy, or canonical disciplinary history. Today both center and margin have been dissolved and dispersed, and the visual field is oversaturated. This is a generation that has traded the "anxiety of influence" for the "ecstasy of influence." Like Lethem, their frame of reference mixes high and low, popular culture and historical reference. This opens up a rich and varied field of reference and affiliation at the same time as it presents a dizzying array of possibilities, at once liberating and potentially paralyzing. For Lethem, it is a matter of finding a way to work effectively within the "vastly expanded and recombinant toolbox of strategies, tones, traditions, genres, and forms that a legacy of modernist-style experimentation, as well as a general disintegration of boundaries (between traditions, tones, etc.), has made available to a writer, or to any kind of artist."[17] Note that Lethem's catalog includes both modernist and postmodern tropes: experimentation, but also the dissolution of fixed points of reference. The modern and the postmodern both belong to history today.

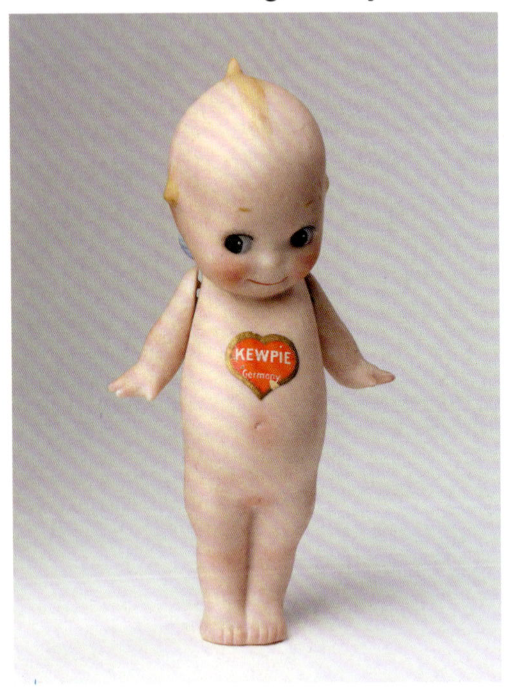

Rose O'Neill, Kewpie Doll, bisque figurine, 1913.

The curators of *Inscriptions* refuse to accept the double bind that haunts the critic and practitioner alike today: either enter into this expanded field and compete at the level of spectacle with ever more iconic and brash forms, or retreat into silence and negation. They have opted instead for inclusion, creating an expansive, figured field and proposing new categories that can help to order that field. But *Inscriptions* also maps the dilemma of the exhibition curator when practice itself has become a form of curation.[18] For many younger architects, including some represented in this publication, design is reconceived as an operation of selecting, sorting, and editing. Their ambition is not to bring new forms into being; rather, they settle for reworking existing forms, without anxiety or a sense of loss. They are in conversation simultaneously with the history of the discipline—the vast catalog of past forms—but also with the world at large, from media to fashion, art, and the image culture of the global city.

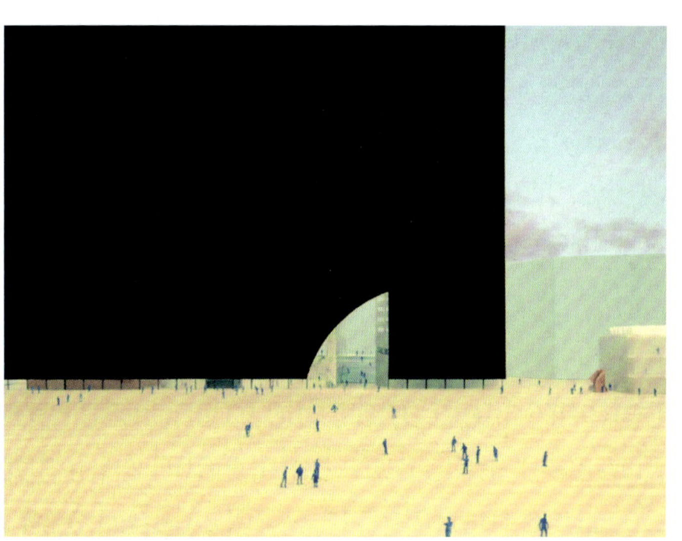

OFFICE Kersten Geers David Van Severen, OFFICE 162: New NCCA, collage, 2014.

Collecting and curating are forms of pattern making, and subcultures of collecting play a key role in *Pattern Recognition*. Editing and sorting involve not just seeing patterns among the profusion of images and objects but also creating new patterns, new connections, and new contexts. The Curta calculator, for example, is connected to a 20th-century history that includes mass killing and slave labor, but it is also an enigmatic object that circulates in a contemporary economy of collecting and trading. Seeing a number of Curtas nestled in the trunk of a car, Cayce Pollard mistakes them for grenades. The Curta is also a beautifully made object that reminds us that the digital culture of the present emerges from a history of mechanical computing that includes Charles Babbage's Difference Engine, the Stepped Reckoner of Gottfried Leibniz, or the Jacquard Loom. It is precisely that sense of layered, embedded meaning that makes it an object of desire. An allusive atmosphere surrounds the object. It is a question less of authenticity (although authenticity matters to collectors) than of the capacity to elicit complex histories, associations, and affiliations.

Hans Tursack, Graphic Fields, Composition VII, light box, 2015.

The best of the work in *Inscriptions* operates in a similar multivalent space of meaning. This is in part what the curators mean when they speak of architecture as an "act before speech" that exceeds the "structural and semiotic propositions of the 20th century." "Before" speech preempts the insistent parade of "post-" phenomena that mark the discipline: postmodernism, postcritical, postmedium, post-digital, and others that repeatedly consign the new to a dependency on that which it follows. For the curators of *Inscriptions*, this is a vicious cycle that constrains both architect and critic to endless repetition and minor variations. Architecture always stands both before and after speech. Buildings live in the world, and they produce meaning in complicated and indirect ways, bound up with materiality, shifting social context, and subjective experience. But architecture will never arrive at the transparency of discursive language. Meanings change and evolve over time, and the preferred mode of signification among this generation is layered, multiple, and differential. These works are never mute, nor do they allude to anything specific and recognizable; they are something in between—oblique and suggestive, without ever settling into a single register.

This form of free-floating reference has long been associated with postmodernism, but there are important differences. Postmodernism defined itself as that which followed and replaced a late and exhausted modernism; in so doing, it still operated according to a modernist logic of succession. And if architecture's past is something remote, positioned on the far side of the modernist rupture, it can only ever be signified, never alive in the present. Irony and distance were fundamental tropes in postmodern architecture, and postmodernism operated, of necessity, in the semiotic register.

The curators of *Inscriptions* understand very well that multiplicity, in and of itself, is not enough. Repetition, multiplication, and excess—the "incoherent realm of texts, products, and images" identified by Lethem—have become the banal realities of everyday experience. The media machine is so powerful and ubiquitous that modernist strategies of negation are easily co-opted. Broken as it is, the culture of the image is the only tool we have. And so, in place of the semiotic register associated with postmodernism, the curators detect a pattern of reference that is more tonal and atmospheric, antecedent instead of "post-." By introducing expansive constructs such as transcendence and immanence, they push back on the idea that architecture today is all surface and image. A significant work of architecture always gestures back in time to an original—found, revealed, or instaurated. Though they are fully aware that such historical grounding can be suspect today, they nevertheless insist that architecture needs to be grounded, even if only provisionally. So they look deep into architecture's

Thomas Ruff, *W.H.S. 10*, chromogenic print, 1988.

past, to archetypal forms and patterns, while at the same time functioning, of necessity, in a contemporary media landscape. Historical time is simultaneously compressed and extended.

There is a photograph by Thomas Ruff that performs an analogous operation of temporal estrangement.[19] For the 2001 exhibition *Mies in Berlin* at the Museum of Modern Art in New York, Ruff was commissioned to rephotograph the buildings that Ludwig Mies van der Rohe designed in Germany before his departure for the United States in 1937. How to see again these canonical and overfamiliar works? How to represent this work, which belongs to a fraught and now distant German history, in the present? The false color and blurred registration of Ruff's photograph *W.H.S. 10* ostensibly distance the image from photography's traditional documentary value and declare it to be a constructed artifact, made in the present. Detail is suppressed, which aligns it with the uncanny real/unreal character of works by his peer Thomas Demand. The blurred image of Mies's 1927 housing block in the *Weissenhofsiedlung* suggests something caught in motion, an object that resists specific location in time and space. The photograph oscillates between historical past and the present, never settling comfortably into either register. The progressive optimism of the modernist project is confronted with, and overlaid onto, more recent memories of the complex and fraught realities of the 20th century.

The blur has the effect of a partial erasure. Everything in the photograph is derived from reality ("stenciled off the real," to use Susan Sontag's memorable phrase), and yet it belongs assertively to the culture of the image. It is simultaneously slow and fast. There are no markers of scale or context; the tree, the lawn, and the railing are all now indistinct. And it cannot be accidental that it looks more like a photograph of a model than a photograph of a

Christ & Gantenbein, Triptych, physical model, 2015.

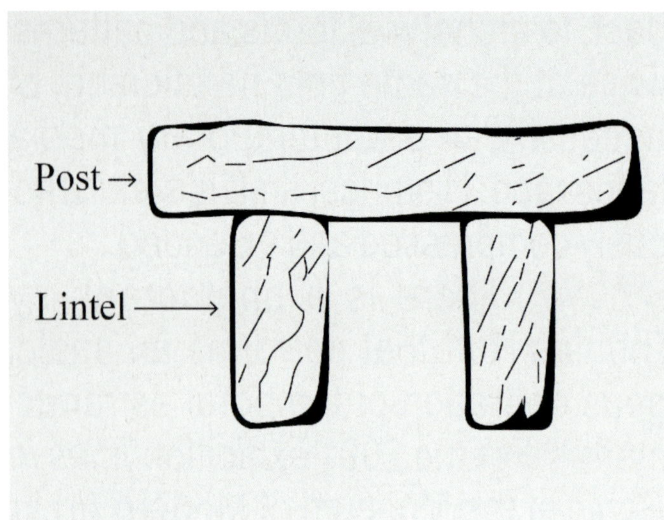

Post-and-lintel diagram.

building. The image no longer functions as the record of a monumental building in a specific place. By representing the building as model, it diminishes and abstracts the architecture to a repeatable idea, at once more and less than the original.

Andrew Holder has used the phrase "presencing of the available," by which I think he means architecture's capacity to operate within the culture of the "available"—the collective reservoir of shared images and references, both inside and outside the discipline, past and present—but also the ability to pull an image out of the flow, to make it present and real, in ways that other image technologies cannot.[20] Among the works exhibited, this is evident in the appeals to the archaic and to archetypal forms deeply embedded in shared cultural memory. In works by Jennifer Bonner and MALL, Christ & Gantenbein, Johnston Marklee, and EXTENTS, archetypal pitched roofs recall vernacular sheds and suburban houses but also classical pediments and the primitive hut. At the same time, it's just geometry, at once familiar and, in its repetition, deformation, and intersections, strange. The flat roof was a signifier of modernity; the pitched roof, of domesticity. But here, an insistent abstraction renders the familiar unfamiliar. These projects resonate with Sianne Ngai's evocation of "aesthetic experiences grounded in equivocal affects," which "index situations of suspended agency." She speaks of irritation as opposed to anger, which in turn maps onto Holder's notion of "flat affect."[21] First Office's Dolmens, for example, are intentionally awkward and weirdly scaled. If they reenact archetypal post-and-lintel tectonics, they also suggest child's blocks casually piled up. The "original" implied here is less something deep in history or authentically present than it is something immediate and available. The pitched roof and the trabeated frame are elemental forms that belong not only to the culture of the discipline but also to a larger collective consciousness, and that intersection is

First Office, PS1 Dolmen, physical model, 2016.

fundamental to architecture's political task. Architecture in this sense is always both more and less than a culture of images.

> If I were a writer . . . how I would enjoy being told the novel is dead. How liberating, to work in the margins, outside a central perception.
> — Don DeLillo, *The Names* (1989)

3

Perfect Acts of Architecture was an exhibition curated by Jeffery Kipnis and originally shown at the Wexner Center for the Arts in 2001. While two of the projects shown (Morphosis's Sixth Street House and Peter Eisenman's House VI) were constructed, the exhibition located the "perfect" act of architecture in the realm of drawing: a site of pure possibility and imagined futures. Kipnis's thesis highlighted architecture's ability to expand the horizon of the possible through the speculative project, and the drawing "as an end in itself, as a fully realized, self-sufficient work of architecture rather than a subordinate representation." Kipnis described an emerging ethos in the wake of the upheavals of 1968 that culminated in the "conviction that the bankrupt heritage—and its collaborating architecture—would soon, and easily, be replaced by a more radical, democratic, free, uninhibited world."[22] Recalling the quotation from William Gibson that opens this essay, the works in *Perfect Acts* could credibly be described as "fully imagined cultural futures." Projects such as Daniel Libeskind's Micromegas, Bernard Tschumi's Manhattan Transcripts, or OMA and Rem Koolhaas's Exodus described alternative futures and imagined new roles for architecture. Operating on the more familiar territory of the detached house, Morphosis and Eisenman, in different ways, also sought to reinvest architecture with cultural significance and reinvigorate an exhausted modernist project.

The chronological window of *Perfect Acts* (1972–1987) coincided with the rise and fall of postmodernism and the recession of the late 1970s. In the imperfect world of the late 20th century, and in the face of the economic marginalization of architecture, Kipnis argues that the speculative project is architecture's best chance to recuperate a legitimate cultural space. But also perhaps its last. *Inscriptions* documents the evolution of the discipline in the two decades since *Perfect Acts* while also recording the effects of accumulating historical distance. The 50-year interval that separated the architects of the 1970s from the heroic modernism of the 1920s now separates the present from the postmodernism of the 1970s.[23] These younger architects operate in an entirely distinct cultural space, aspiring not to "perfect acts" but situating their work, for better or worse, in an imperfect world. Having lived through 9/11, the financial collapse of 2008, and now COVID-19, #MeToo, and Black Lives Matter, they are acutely aware of the fragility and volatility of the now. A fully formed imagined future is, to them, suspect—not out of cynicism but rather as the result of a legitimate suspicion of predictive claims in general, on both aesthetic and political grounds. They are skeptical of the big project and the grand cultural narrative. Prospects for future practice are almost by definition diffuse, experimental, and interdisciplinary. These young architects accept the reality that an ever-stricter regulatory environment, a more fluid and interconnected cultural realm and its entanglement with markets, publicity, and social media have eroded the traditional agency of architecture.

For these younger architects, the inherent slowness of architecture is neither to be celebrated nor resisted. Acutely aware that architecture today needs to compete for attention with faster and more agile mediums, they know that the cultural project of architecture has become increasingly marginalized, at the very same time that architecture is more visible than ever. But in different ways, at least for the cross section of the field represented in this exhibition, there is also a new sense of freedom and possibility, as described by DeLillo: "How liberating, to work in the margins, outside a central perception." If both center and margin have today been dispersed and dissolved, it opens space for new work, and new thoughts. This is a generation that has inherited a different sense of history, more attuned to Gibson's nonsequential temporality, to Lethem's ecstasy of influence, or to Ruff's temporal estrangement. For these architects—and for the curators of *Inscriptions*—architectural knowledge is cumulative, not progressive. Ideas from across the spectrum of history are available to architects in the present. The address to the past is less linear, less specific, and more open. The curators of *Inscriptions* are not invested in a "recovery of history" but rather in coming to terms with the flattened historical landscape of the present: a moment in which history is not so much located on the other side of the modernist rupture, but where all histories (modernist history included) are equally distant yet also equally available.

1 See "The CURTA Calculator Page," The Calculator Reference, last modified September 20, 2019, http://www.vcalc.net/cu.htm.

2 Curt Herzstark, interview by Erwin Tomash, September 10–11, 1987, Nendeln, Liechtenstein, translated transcript, OH 140, Charles Babbage Institute at the Center for the History of Information Processing, University of Minnesota, Minneapolis, http://www.vcalc.net/OralHistoryEnglish.pdf. It seems likely that Herzstark was arrested on a pretext, in order to gain control of his technical expertise; his brother, who was also half-Jewish, was allowed to remain free and operate the factory in Vienna, which had itself been co-opted into the Nazi war effort.

3 Gibson participated in the first ANY conference in 1991, a marker of the interest in his work among architectural circles at the time.

4 William Gibson, "Talk for Book Expo, New York" (2010), in *Distrust That Particular Flavor* (New York: Berkley Books, 2012), 46.

5 Gibson, "Dead Man Sings" (1998), in *Distrust That Particular Flavor*, 52.

6 The brand takes its name from Steve McQueen's character in the 1961 film, *The War Lover*. In Gibson's description, the temporal slippage, and blurring of original and copy is made explicit: "Cayce knows, for instance, that the characteristically wrinkled seams down either arm were originally the result of sewing with prewar industrial machines that rebelled against the slippery new material, nylon. The makers of Rickson's have exaggerated this, but only very slightly, and done a hundred other things, tiny things, as well, so that their product has become, in some very Japanese way, the result of an act of worship. It is an imitation more real somehow than that which it emulates." *Pattern Recognition* (New York: Berkley Books, 2003), 11.

7 William Gibson, "Buzz in Black," blog, December 31, 2005, http://williamgibsonblog.blogspot.com/2005_12_01_archive.html. See also Joe Clark, "'PR'-Otaku: Logging and Annotating William Gibson's *Pattern Recognition*," fawny.org, last updated August 13, 2007, https://fawny.org/pr.

8 Gibson, *Pattern Recognition*, 194.

9 Among others, the exhibition and book *Possible Mediums* (2018); the 15th issue of *PRAXIS*, "Bad Architectures" (2019); Michael Meredith's *44 Houses* exhibition at Princeton (2018); Johnston Marklee's 2017 Chicago Biennial, *Make New History*; or the 14-part Treatise publication project (2015–), edited by Jimenez Lai.

10 See Stan Allen, "Thinking in Models," *Log* 50: "Model Behavior" (Fall 2020): 17–27.

11 See John May, "Everything Is Already an Image," *Log* 40 (Spring/Summer 2017): 9–26. May's insights are useful, but in my view, he elides the model too quickly with the image and pays insufficient attention to the variety of drawing types and their distinct agencies. Architectural drawings were part of an image culture long before the computer, and the instrumentality of orthographic drawing persists in the computational realm (and is baked into graphic software). The most consequential software development in practice today is building information modeling, which operates according to a data-driven modeling logic, not an image logic.

12 See the catalog *Idea as Model*, ed. Kenneth Frampton and Silvia Kolbowski (New York: Rizzoli, 1981).

13 K. Michael Hays and Andrew Holder, "*Architecture before Speech*: A Conversation," *Inscriptions* exhibition lecture, Harvard University Graduate School of Design, January 23, 2018, video, 1:32:07, https://www.gsd.harvard.edu/event/k-michael-hays-and-andrew-holder-exhibition-lecture-inscriptions.

14 "Projection could be considered the universal ether of constructability." Robin Evans, *The Projective Cast* (Cambridge, MA: MIT Press, 1995), 357.

15 I originally introduced this distinction, between the plastic and the geometric, in Stan Allen, "Nothing But Architecture: John Hejduk," in *Hejduk's Chronotopes*, ed. K. Michael Hays (New York: Princeton Architectural Press, 1996), 79–97. It seems to me that, as a formal reference for this generation, Hejduk is more significant than Eisenman.

16 Sianne Ngai, *Our Aesthetic Categories: Zany, Cute, Interesting* (Cambridge, MA: Harvard University Press, 2012), 73.

17 Jonathan Lethem, "Postmodernism as Liberty Valance," in *The Ecstasy of Influence: Nonfictions, Etc.* (New York: Vintage, 2012), 81–82.

18 "Once the operations of collection and curation are understood as an extension of the architect's toolkit, I think we will be able to reassert a sense of agency for the discipline, to reclaim a kind of disciplinary specificity that seems to have been otherwise lost in the stockpile." Michael Meredith, "One Thing Leads to Another," in *Under the Influence*, ed. Ana Miljacki and Amanda Reeser Lawrence (Cambridge, MA: SA+P Press, 2014), 71–72.

19 Jesús Vassallo (whose architectural work is also represented in the exhibition) has written insightfully on contemporary architecture's dialogue with photographic practice. See his *Seamless: Digital Collage and Dirty Realism in Contemporary Architecture* (Zurich: Park Books, 2016), and *Epics in the Everyday: Photography, Architecture, and the Problem of Realism* (Zurich: Park Books, 2019).

20 Andrew Holder, in conversation with the author, April 2020.

21 Sianne Ngai, "Our Aesthetic Categories: The Cute, the Interesting, and the Zany," interview by Adam Jasper, *Cabinet* 43 (Fall 2011).

22 Jeffery Kipnis, "An Introduction to a Perfect Act," in *Perfect Acts of Architecture* (New York: Museum of Modern Art, 2001), 12.

23 Gibson—through the voice of his fictional character Hubertus Bigend—identifies the "fully imagined cultural future" with the generation of our grandparents; this actually maps pretty well onto the generational schema of the present exhibition. For the bulk of the younger generation represented in *Inscriptions*, Eisenman et al. would indeed correspond to their grandparents. For the most part, these architects were taught not by the generation of *Perfect Acts* but by students of the generation represented in *Perfect Acts*: figures like Preston Scott Cohen, Jesse Reiser, Andrew Zago, Robert Somol, Greg Lynn, Sarah Whiting, Sylvia Lavin, and myself.

Category

Labyrinths
Eidetic Houses
Booleans
Superimpositions
Revelations
Slack Collections
Scatters, Remnants
Dirt, Earth, and Rocks
Trabeated Stacks
First Houses
Seven Wonders
Monoliths
Anamorphic Figures
The Creaturely

Labyrinths

One has heard the characterization of the recent generation of work as neo-postmodern. The assumption behind this label is twofold: first, that postmodern architecture sought, through index or metaphor, to reference specific and multiple historical precedents, and second, that certain contemporary practices, because they can't fathom any way forward, *reference that referencing* in a Möbius strip–like bending back—the eternal return of the same. Might it be suspected, then, that the category of labyrinth might signal a retreat to old certainties? We see the situation differently. If the ancient labyrinth was supposed to contain the path to wisdom and freedom, then the contemporary labyrinth signals the acceptance of the failure of a universal language, the failure to complete the Tower of Babel. Jacques Derrida recognized this. As he said in a 1986 interview with Eva Meyer, "Only the *incompletion* of the tower makes it possible for architecture as well as the multitude of languages to have a history." By identifying a transcendental dimension to certain contemporary architecture projects, we do not intend to refer to an idealist imposition of predetermined and invariant forms on a range of similar objects. Rather, transcending is a working through toward a newly actualized architectural object. Yet once a "transcendental original" project is actualized, it appears that it was always already there, just waiting to be put to use. Thus certain unprecedented and eidetic images like the labyrinths presented here strike us as uncannily resonant and contemporary yet at the same time enigmatic and archaic. They must be understood as inscriptions anterior to any reference, as material potential for new organizations, not to be discovered but to be created.

is-office, Crowns, 2015

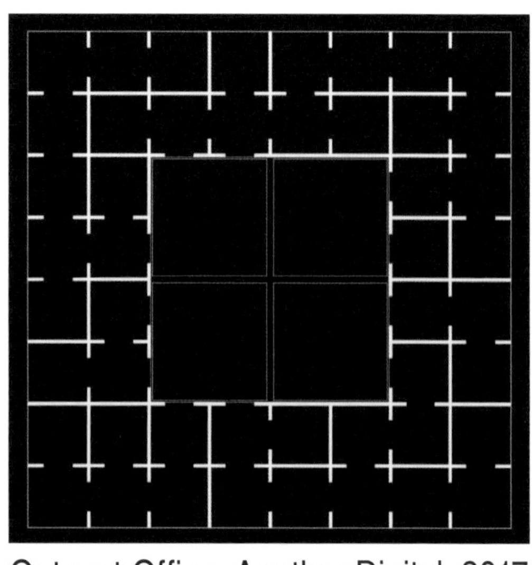

Outpost Office, Another Digital, 2017

Collective-LOK, Mappa Mundi, 2015

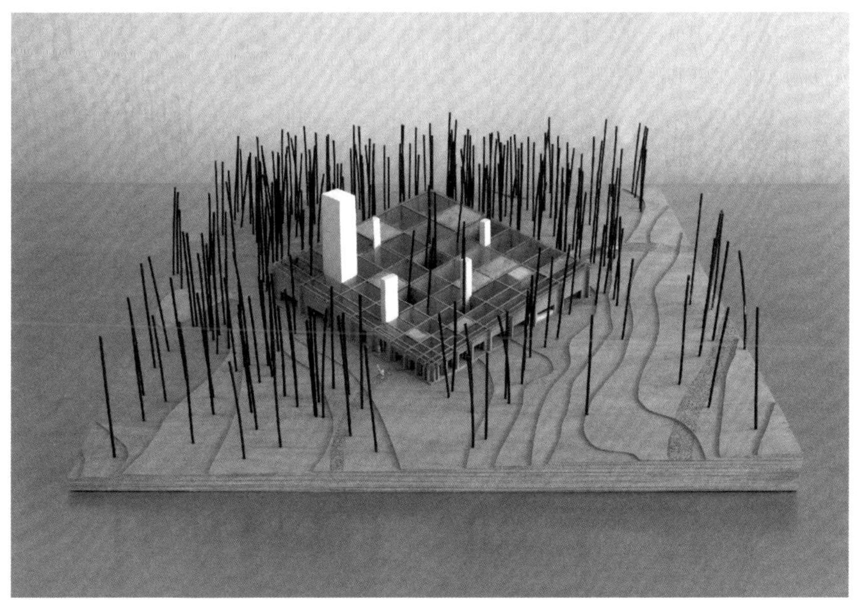

OFFICE Kersten Geers David Van Severen, OFFICE 171: Arvo Pärt Center, 2014

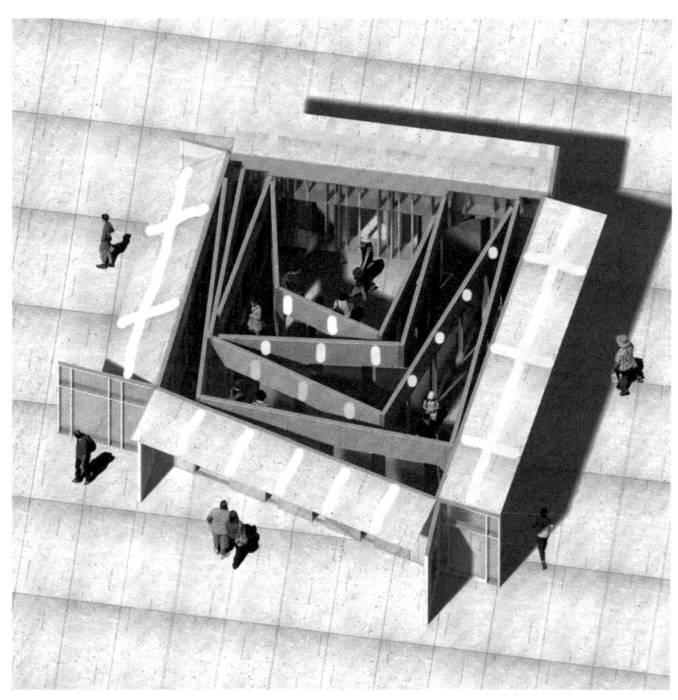

JaJa Co, Scoring, Building, 2020

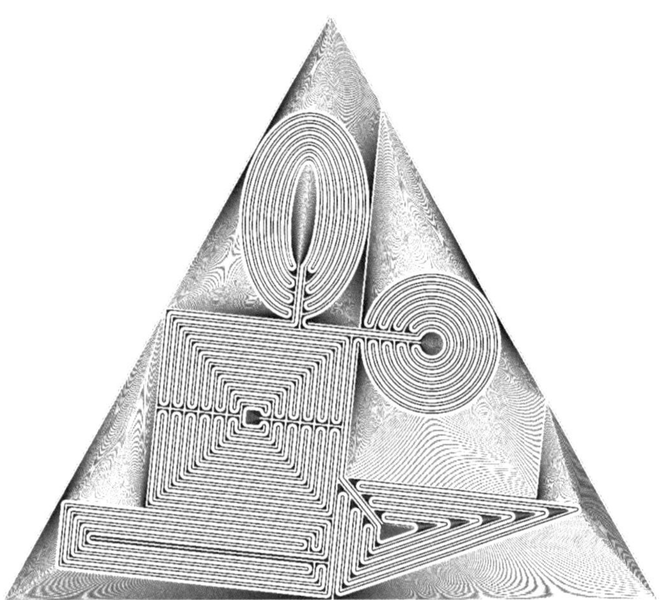
WOJR, Non-Labyrinths, 2014

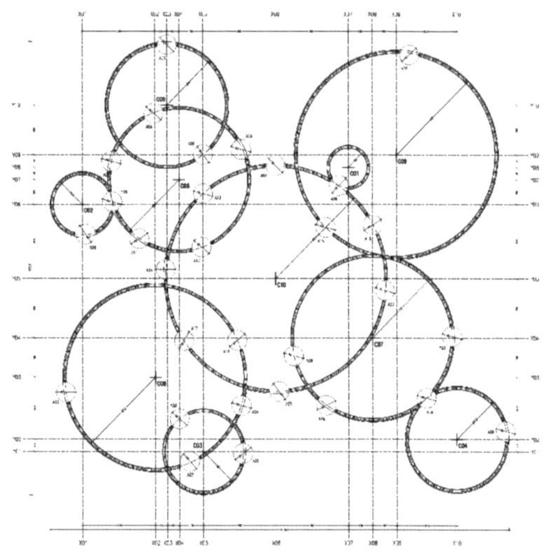
Pezo von Ellrichshausen, Vara Pavilion, 2016

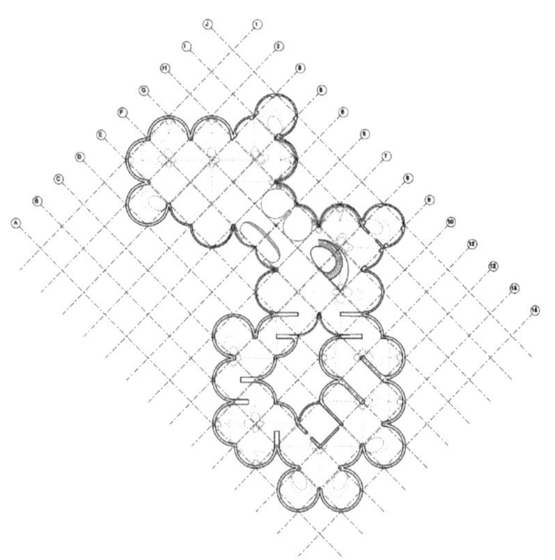
Young & Ayata, Bauhaus Museum Dessau, 2015

WOJR, Labyrinth, 2013

Pezo von Ellrichshausen, Vara Pavilion, 2016

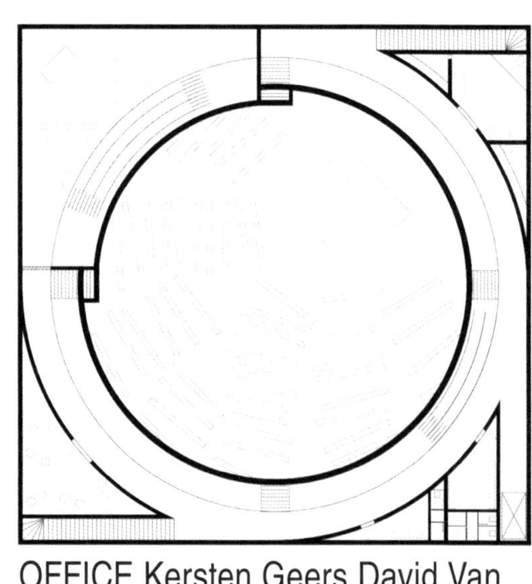
OFFICE Kersten Geers David Van Severen, Hatlehol Church, 2008

MILLIØNS, Collectives I, 2014

Christ & Gantenbein, Lindt Home of Chocolate, 2020

SCHAUM/SHIEH, Slider Tower, 2012

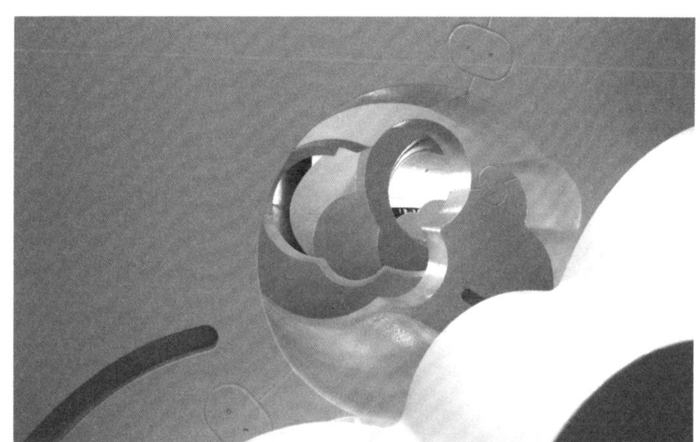
Volkan Alkanoglu, Cloud Scape, 2018

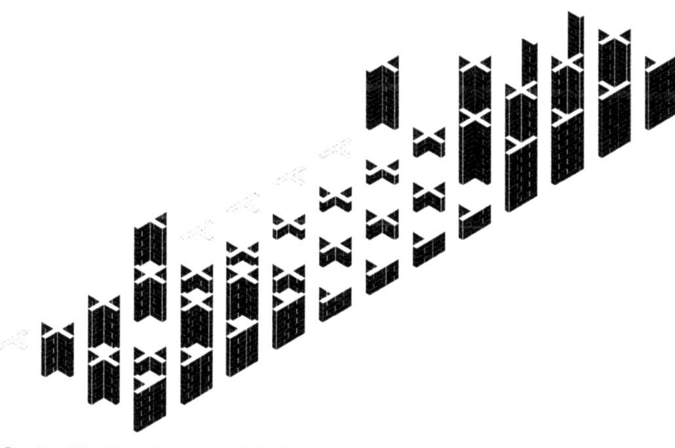
Only If, Performa Hub, 2015

Christ & Gantenbein, Lindt Home of Chocolate, 2020

New Affiliates, Tunbridge Winter Cabin, 2017

WOJR, Dwelling, in progress

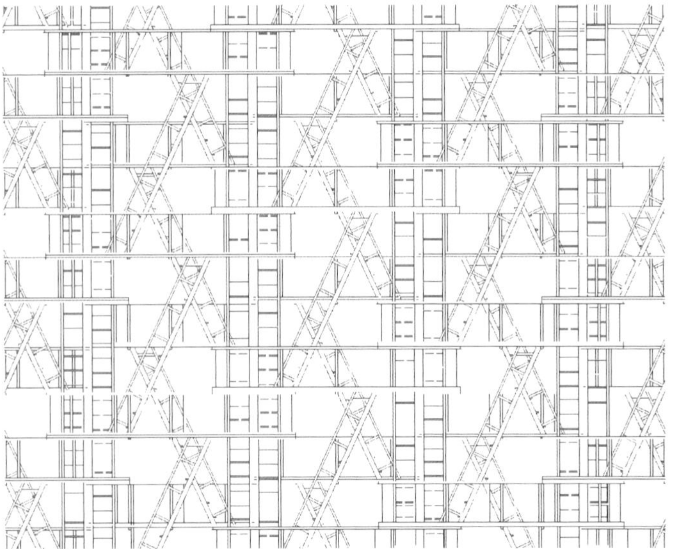
Ultramoderne, Escape, 2017

Pezo Von Ellrichshausen, Meri House, 2014

Bureau Spectacular, The Future Archaeologist, 2019

Pezo Von Ellrichshausen, Meri House, 2014

JaJa Co, Scoring, Building, 2020

Pezo Von Ellrichshausen, Meri House, 2014

Curtis Roth, Decorating Villa Wolf, 2016

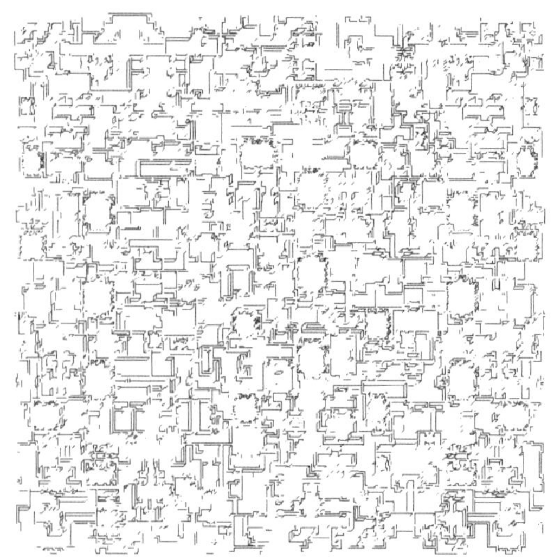
Young & Ayata, LIMA-MALI-AMIL-ILAM, 2016

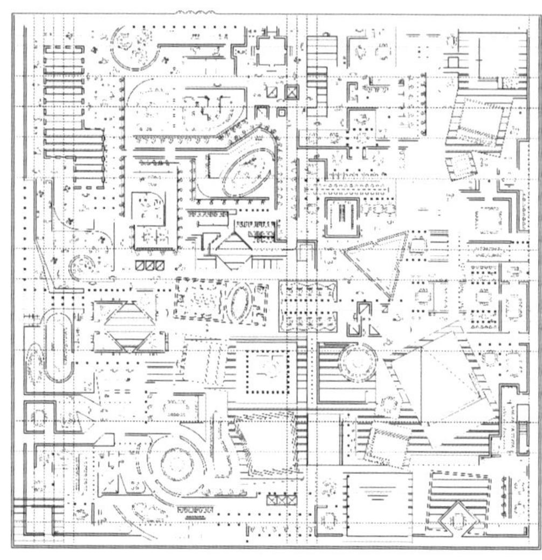
Endemic Architecture, Tech Plan No. 3: Contained Corridor vs. Enfilade, 2018

Now Here, 3 Stairs, 2019

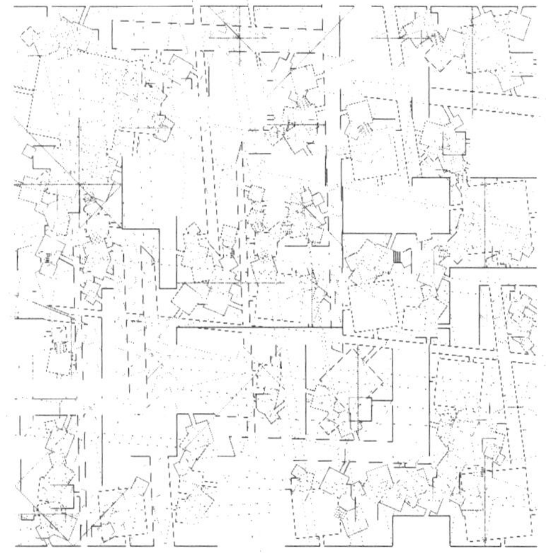
MILLIØNS, Collectives II, 2016

JaJa Co, Millefeuille, 2020

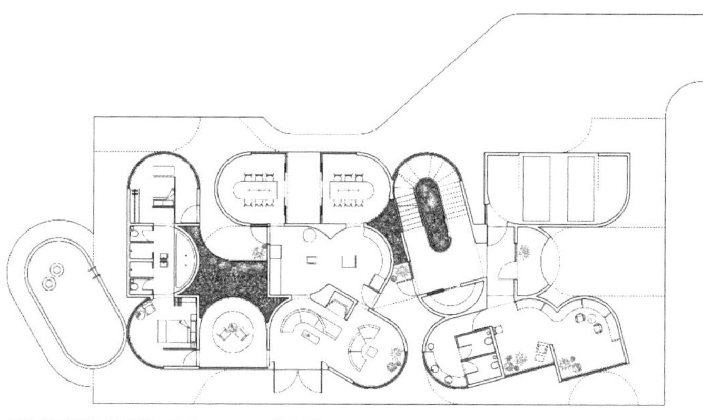

EXTENTS, House UU, 2017

Studio Sean Canty, Figure-Ground Studies, 2019

FORMA, Imigongo Chapel, 2019

Höweler + Yoon, Collier Memorial, 2015

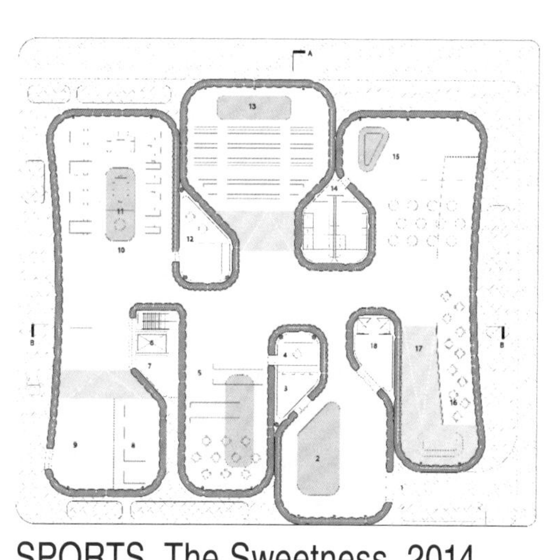

SPORTS, The Sweetness, 2014

Labyrinths

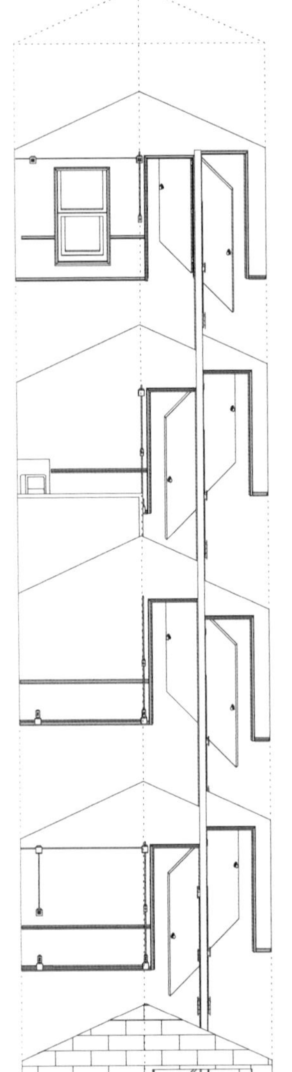

First Office, Shotgun House, 2014

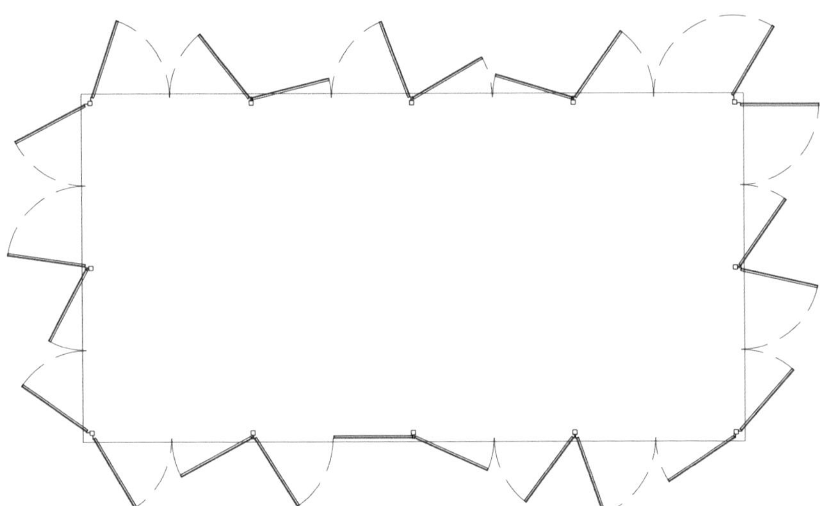

Ultramoderne, Southlight, 2016

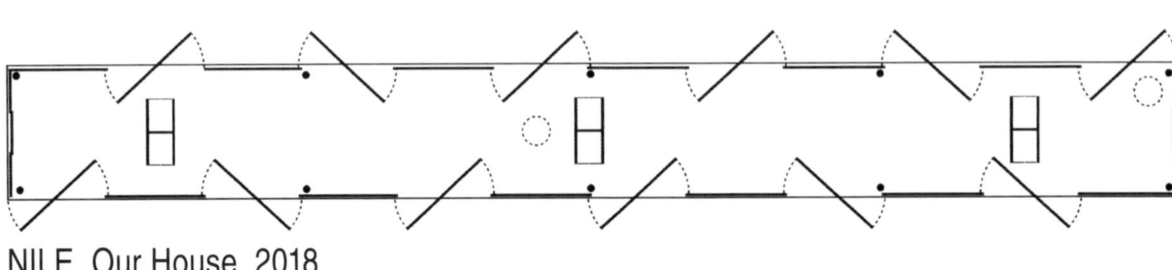

NILE, Our House, 2018

Eidetic Houses

When a building conforms so much to the expected image of a building that the two cannot be distinguished, we call this eidetic. Instead of being boring, this architecture scintillates with the freshness of just-as-I-thought details drawn from memory but also appearing right there—directly traced, as it were, marked in the flesh. The counterintuitive effect of this is to pull apart familiarity from the reassurances of continuity, historical and otherwise. Details may be expected, remembered, but from where exactly? Searches for origins vanish in the deserts of primitive-hut fantasies or numb repetitions of alpine building techniques. Eidetic houses do not emerge in response to the particularities of environment or context. Rather, they *appear*, in the two senses of that word: they arrive all at once without evident cause and do so with a seemingly deliberate gravity. Freed from the obligation to justify or evidence how they came into being, eidetic houses perform as future-facing set pieces. They support the choreography of plots: subjects are set loose in time against building organization. Domesticity in these is not a comforting mood but a brute configuration of possibility, as though all of life at home is the unfolding of transactions between walls, a roof, and a body.

LAMAS, Townships Farmhouse, 2017

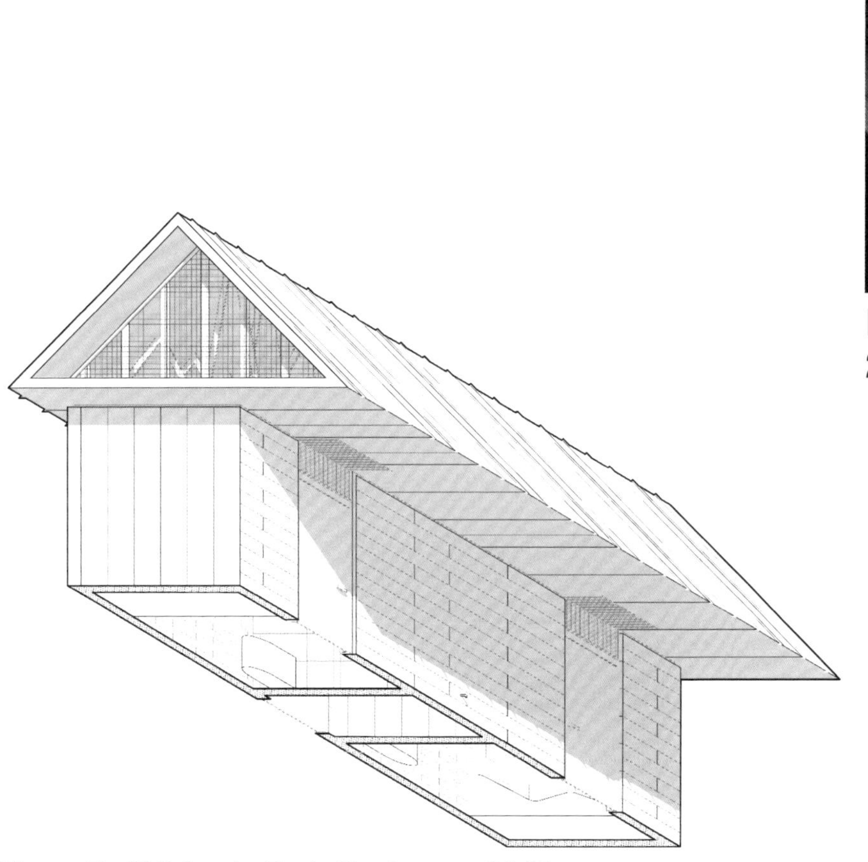

Team B, Children's Park Restroom, 2017

WOJR, Dwelling, in progress

Preston Scott Cohen, Inc., Goodman House, 2004

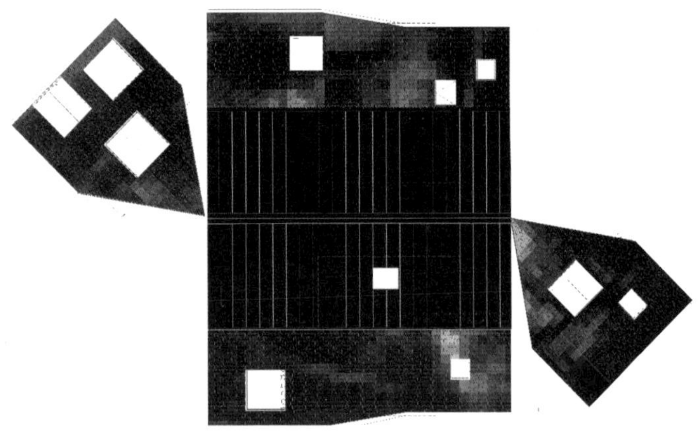
Architecture Office, House in House, 2016

Architecture Office, House in House, 2016

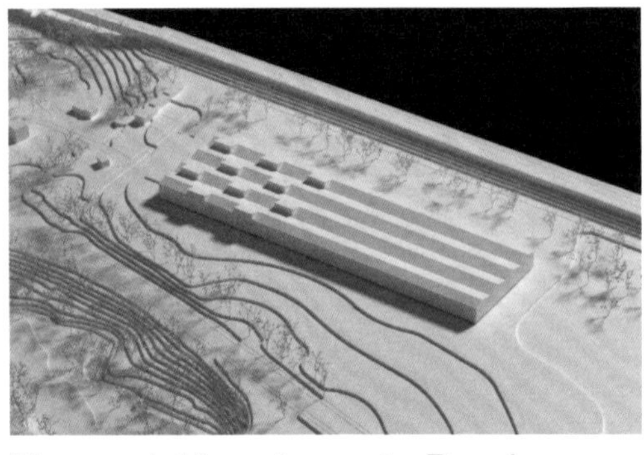
Karamuk Kuo, Augusta Raurica Archaeological Center, in progress

Studio Offshore, Lakeshore Hut, 2016

WOJR, House of the Woodland, 2019

Paul Preissner Architects, House in Oregon, Illinois, 2018

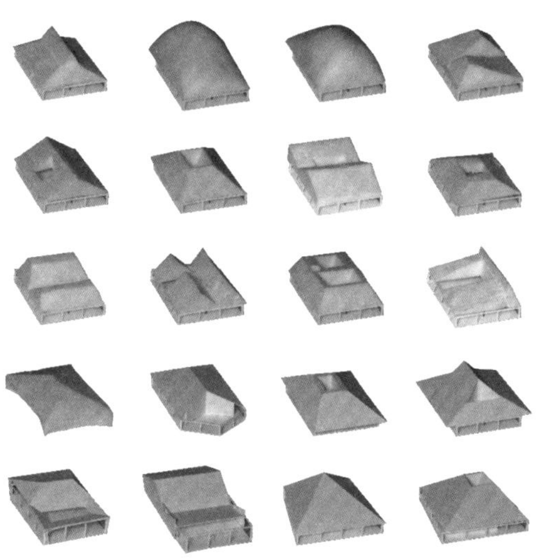
Johnston Marklee, Hut House, 2014

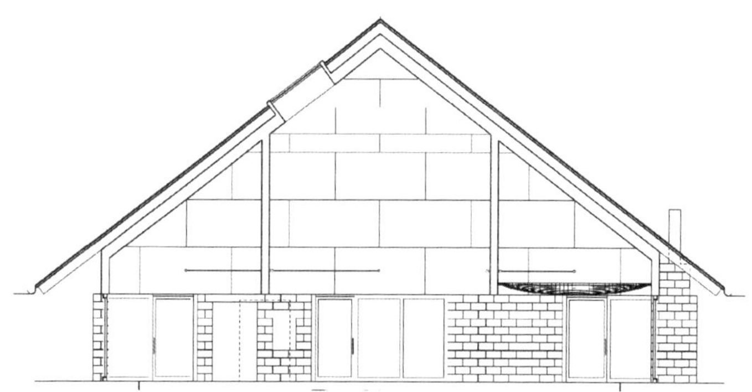
WOJR, House of the Woodland, 2019

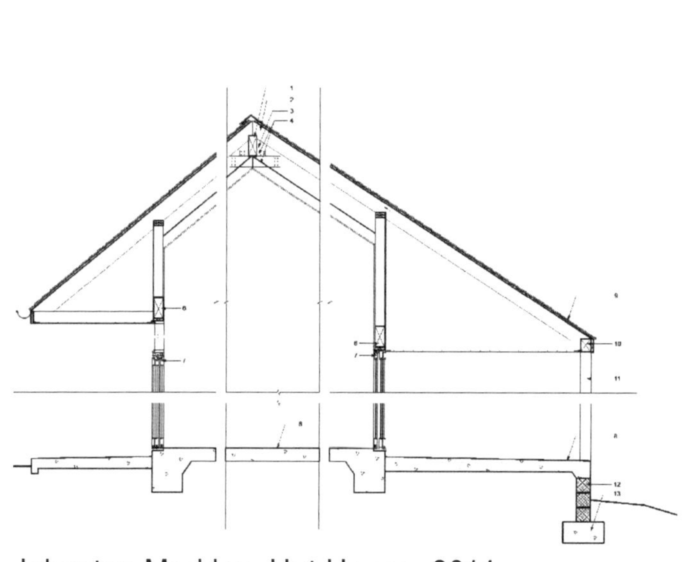
Johnston Marklee, Hut House, 2014

Architecture Office, House in House, 2016

Eidetic Houses

Independent Architecture, Motherhouse, 2019

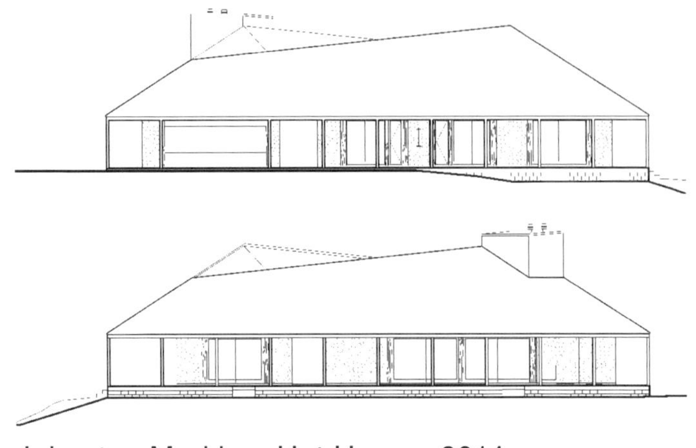
Johnston Marklee, Hut House, 2014

French 2D, Outlier Lofts, 2018

Tom de Paor, House at Aill Breac, 2006

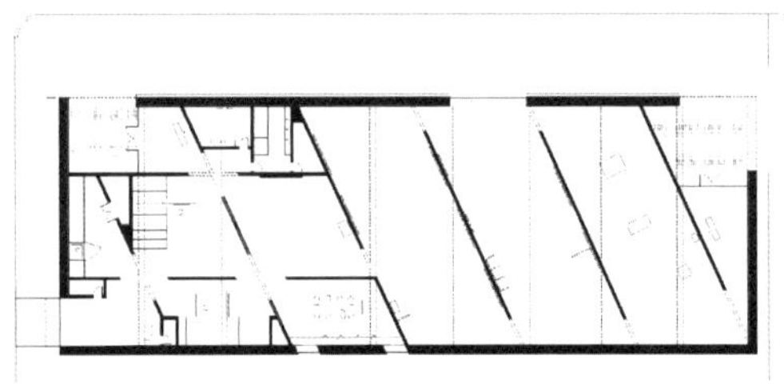
Somewhere Studio, Familiar Exceptions, 2017

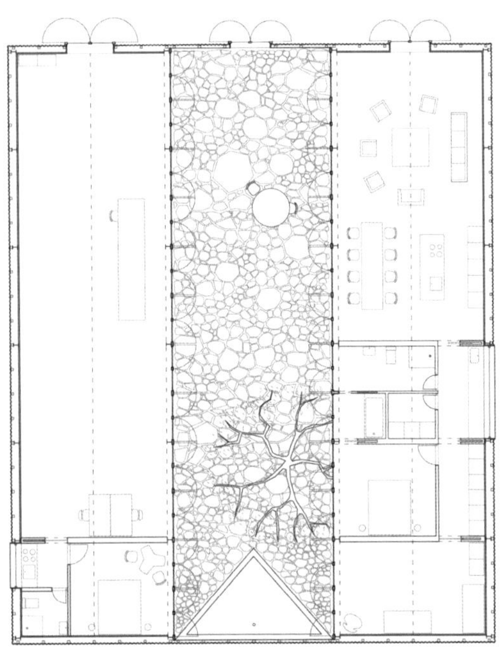
Christ & Gantenbein, Harris Island, 2013

MALL, Domestic Hats, 2014

Ajay Manthripragada, Laurent House, 2019

Somewhere Studio, Familiar Exceptions, 2017

New Affiliates, Farmstead Retreat: Event Venue, 2020

FreelandBuck, Mountain View House, 2019

New Affiliates, Tunbridge Winter Cabin, 2017

Christ & Gantenbein, Harris Island, 2013

Eidetic Houses

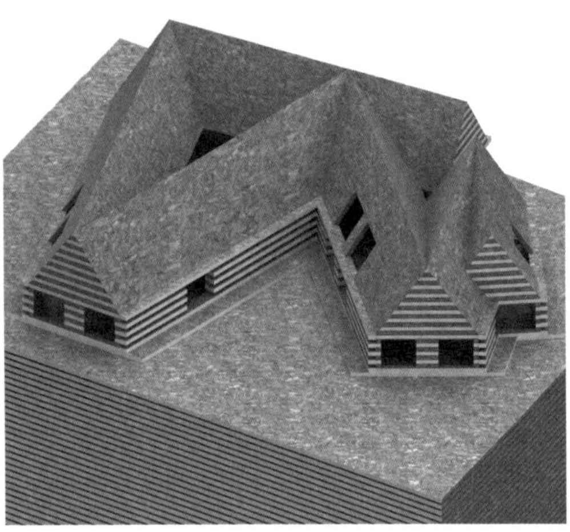

Outpost Office, A Long House, 2020

Studio Sean Canty, Janus House, 2019

Karamuk Kuo, Chillon Castle Visitor Center, 2013

LAMAS, Townships Farmhouse, 2017

studioPM, Stowaway House, 2016

Karamuk Kuo, Chillon Castle Visitor Center, 2013

The LADG, House in Los Angeles 1, 2016

PARA Project, Stump House, 2019–

Besler & Sons, Roof Deck at MoMA PS1, 2015

studioPM, Stowaway House, 2016

MOS, House No. 10 (House with Courtyard), 2015–18

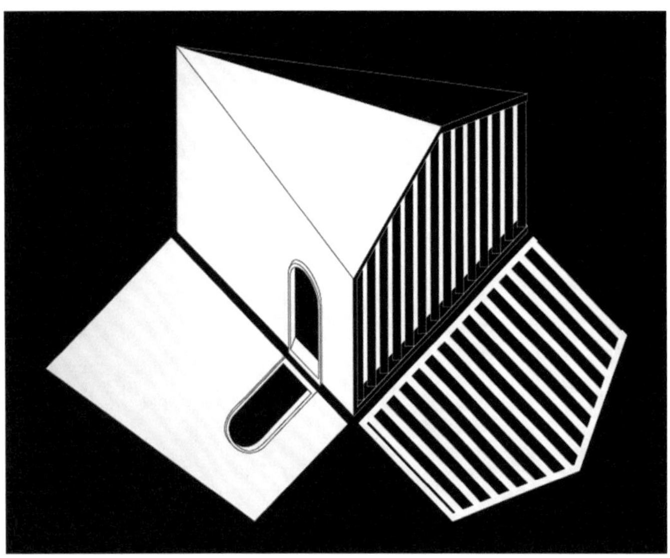
Team B, Ragdale Ring: Framed Follies, 2017

Now Here, 1/2 House, 2017

Outpost Office, Upstate House, 2017

Now Here, 1/2 House, 2017

EXTENTS, Hedgehog House, 2009

Besler & Sons, Cabins, 2016

Booleans

By ignoring the Vitruvian truism that architecture is made of parts, design can work at higher levels of abstraction. An unruly array—of people, lumber, everything in a wall, everything to be walked on, or everything except glass—can be imagined as a set, held tight enough inside a declaration of similarity that heterogeneous elements behave as a homogeneous chunk. Architecture imagined in this way works through an arithmetic of things. Operators like *and*, *or*, and *not* commingle groups of things at overlaps, join them, and remove them in bites, one taken out of the other. Eventually, though, the tidy homogeneity of a set will be overwhelmed by differences between its constituent pieces: even if the designer refuses to admit the fragility of abstraction in the course of design, it will emerge in construction when a truck pulls up to the job site loaded with materials for a wall: studs, plywood, nails, drywall, tape, mudding, paint. The marks of Boolean architecture emerge at this moment, when homogeneous wholes are threatened by the multitudes that comprise them and architects must intervene to manage the excess. Because they occur at the moment where logic is overrun from below, these marks toy with the apprehension of effects that are first promised by simple arithmetic and then are complicated, frustrated, inverted, or redoubled at various levels of realization. In the end, even Duchamp's door at 11 rue Larrey, perhaps the most absolute attempt to make architecture a pure logical operation between one room and another, must make use of a tiny decorative sign to show where an opening's jamb becomes the wall of the neighboring room.

SCHAUM/SHIEH, Virginia House, 2015 Model, 2021 Building

Hume Coover Studio, Re-Make/Re-Model, 2018

Karamuk Kuo, Crematorium in Thun, 2016

Booleans

Outpost Office, A Long House, 2020

Studio Anna Heringer, Traunstein
Forum Internat, in progress

LAMAS, Hats, Ceilings, and Rooms, 2017

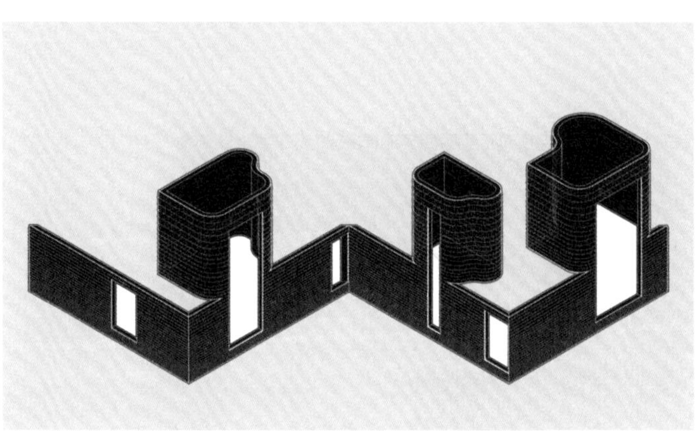

CO-G, Plum Island House, 2017

Outpost Office, Primitive Villa, 2017

Somewhere Studio, Frame for Books, 2018

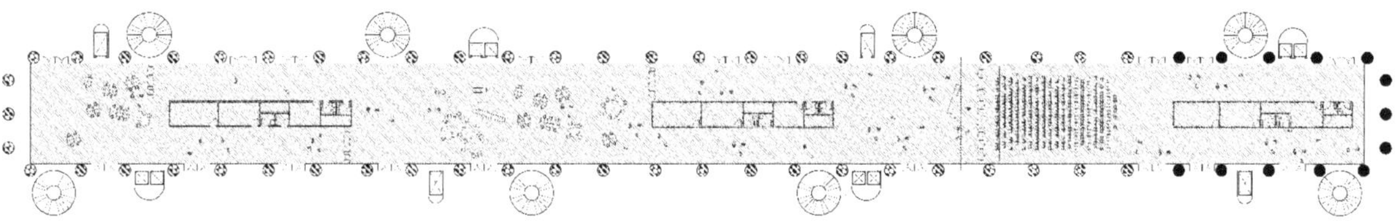

Paul Preissner Architects, Tripoli Special Economic Zone, 2019

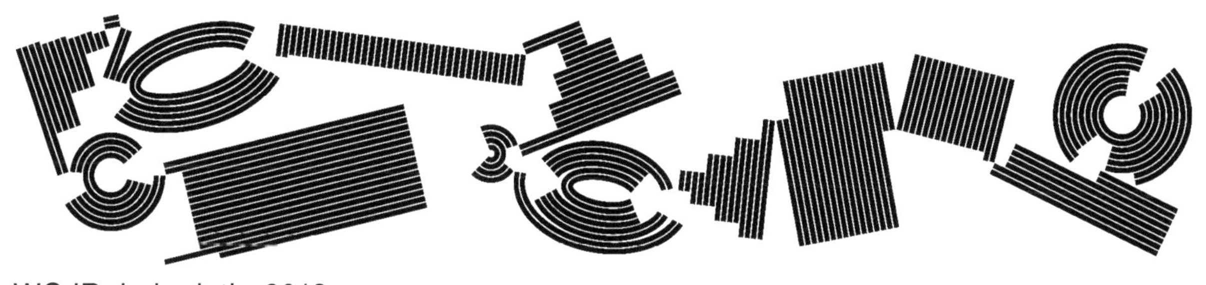

WOJR, Labyrinth, 2013

Höweler + Yoon, Lithos Wellness Center, 2021

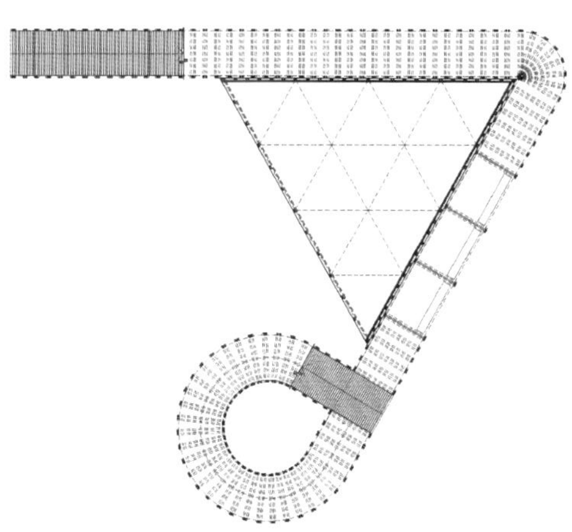

PRODUCTORA, Pavilion on the Zocalo, 2014

WOJR, House of Horns, in progress

Höweler + Yoon, DDP Kiosk, 2016

NILE, Dear Landlord, 2016

MILLIØNS, Collectives I, 2014

SPORTS, Hearts of Gold–Buttonwillow Rest Area, 2018

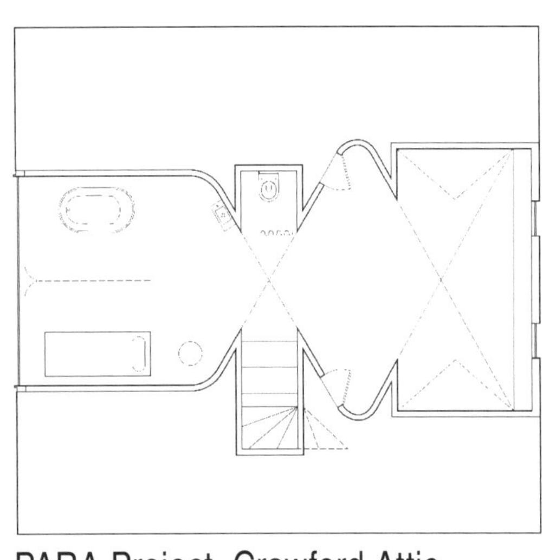
PARA Project, Crawford Attic Writing Room, 2010

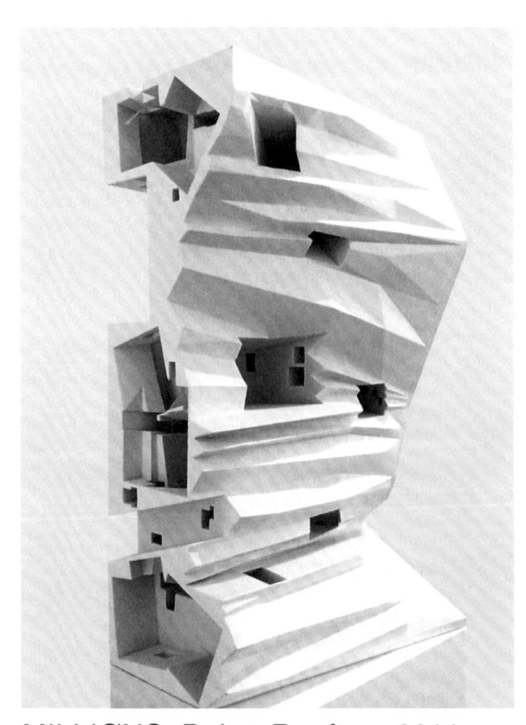
MILLIØNS, Beirut Rooftop, 2014

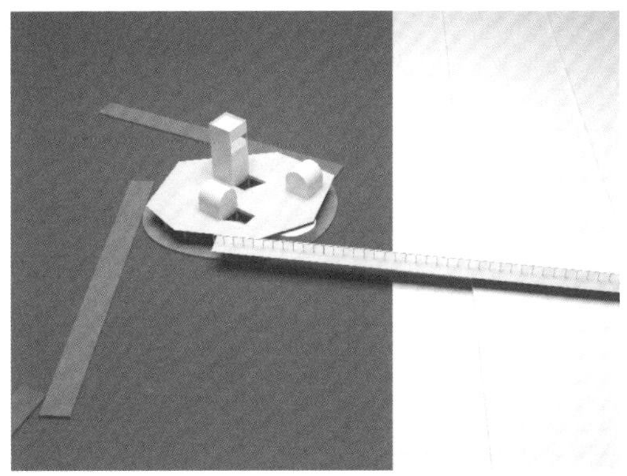
Paul Preissner Architects, Yeoui Naru Ferry Terminal, 2017

Johnston Marklee, Vault House, 2013

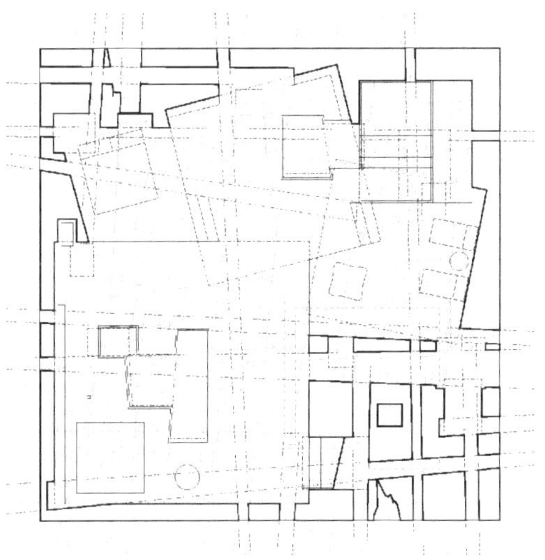
MILLIØNS, Beirut Rooftop, 2014

Bureau Spectacular, Maison Bande Dessinée, 2019

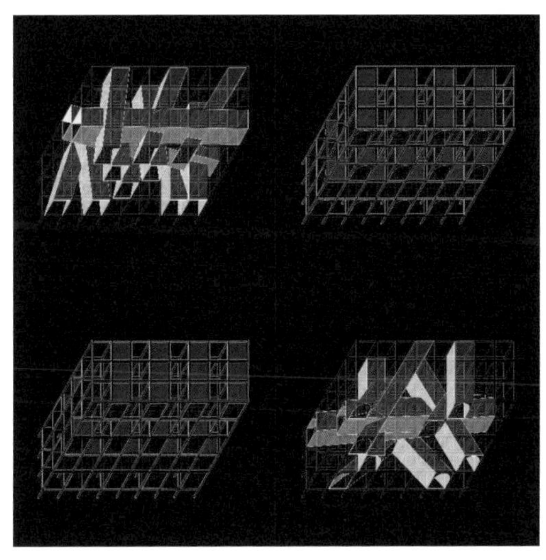
Alex Maymind, Shoots and Lattices, No. 19, 2013

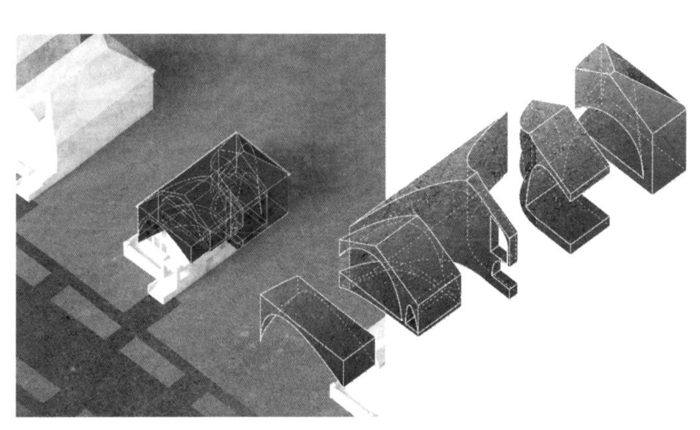
Jaffer Kolb, Form in Form, 2015

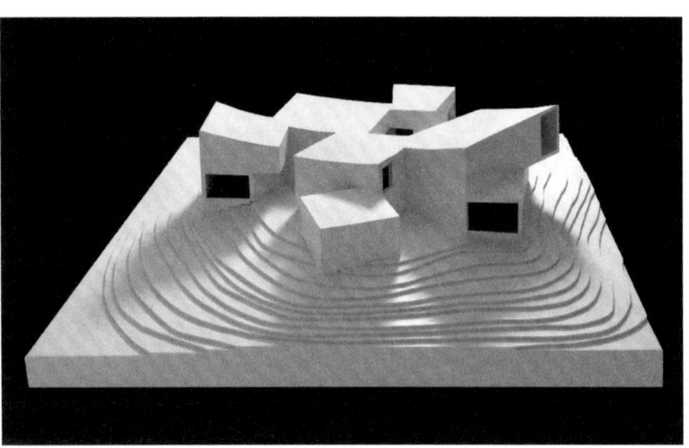
Johnston Marklee, Grand Traiano Art Complex, 2009

Toshiko Mori Architect, Ordos Villa 64, 2009

FreelandBuck, Hungry Man Production Offices, 2017

Only If, House 1 and House 2, 2014

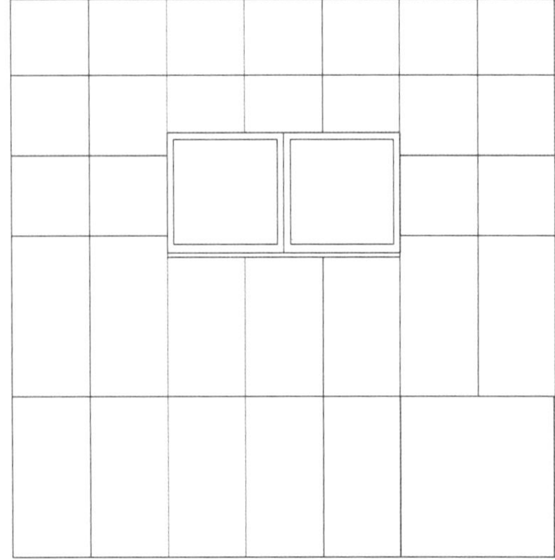
Ajay Manthripragada, Page House and Gallery, 2017

FreelandBuck, Stack House, 2018

Ajay Manthripragada, Page House and Gallery, 2017

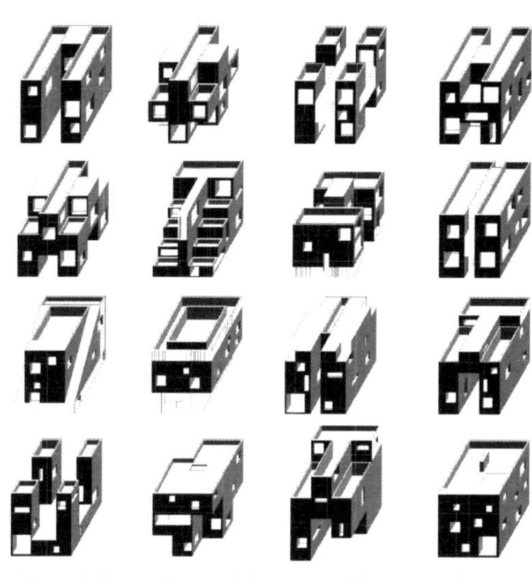

Alex Maymind, Sixteen Four-, Nine-, and Sixteen-Square Variations on OMU's Residential Blocks, 2013

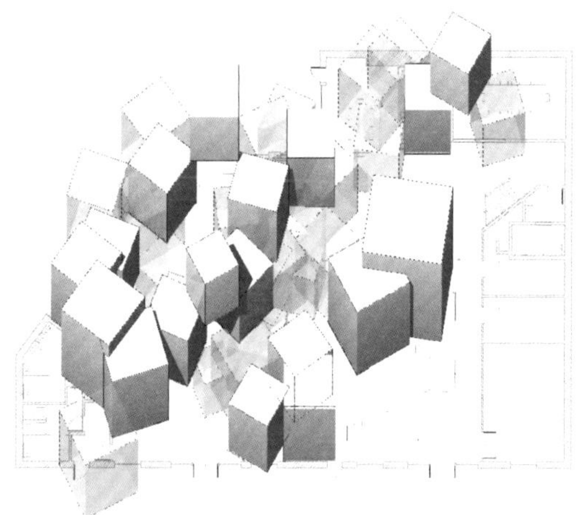

FreelandBuck, Hungry Man Production Offices, 2017

Kiel Moe, Longhouse, 2015

nARCHITECTS, NY State Equal Rights Heritage Center, 2018

Kiel Moe and Ron Mason, Stackhouse, 2008

Superimpositions

Not long after the invention of photography, enterprising con artists discovered that superimposed exposures could be used to produce "spirit photographs," introducing images of the dead in photographic negatives alongside the subjects who sat for the photographs. While in one sense the technique produced "lies"—for two separate figures were not actually present at the sitting, and in fact could never occupy the same space any more than a living person could wander the afterlife—there was nevertheless some truth to spirit photography, from the perspective of medium. Photography's use of light to create an image through exposure meant that living and dead people were both, from the perspective of photosensitivity, equally present and in communication with one another. Superimpositions trade on this switch, between, on the one hand, the incommensurability of figures that emerge from different geometrical or cultural spaces and, on the other, the tendency of these figures to collapse into a form of communication with one another when drawn or built in a shared constructive system. But collapse is the wrong word—too negative—because the figures are not erased. Rather, at any given point in the building, it is necessary to specify not only which figure will be expressed but also how it will be marked and inflected by and in the latent presence of the other. A new hierarchy comes into play where figures take turns being seen *through* the properties of each other. This seeing through can occur in almost any register of observation. In the case of plan geometry, for instance, a square envelope in JaJa Co's Hat to Home; or, Dome to Domus, seems to jut outward in centripetal arms from the points of tangency with the circle inscribed inside it. If we read the View Inside by Current Interests through the genre of fixtures, the wall behind a Roman shade becomes the surface of cheap space, like a generic office or budget hotel. In the purely figurative experiments of Preston Scott Cohen, Inc.'s Cornered House drawings, the triangle above a continuous base is read, through the classical lexicon, as a pediment.

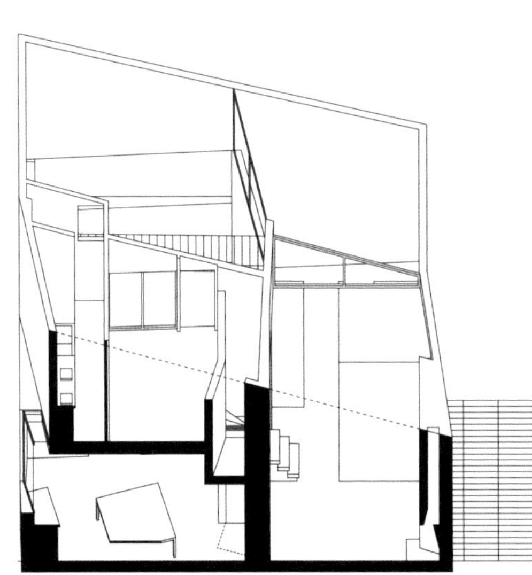

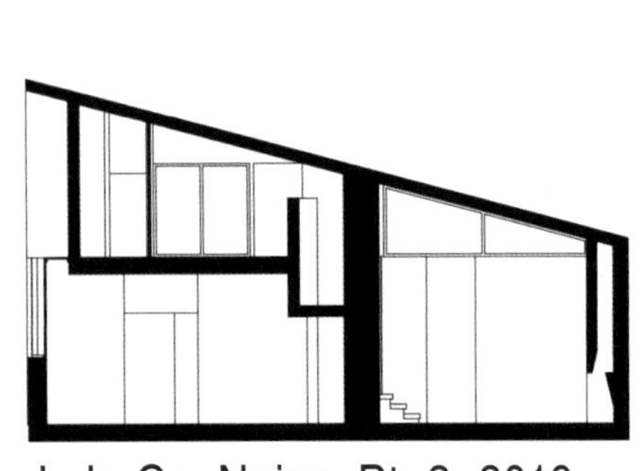

JaJa Co, Noise, Pt. 3, 2016

JaJa Co, Scoring, Building, 2020

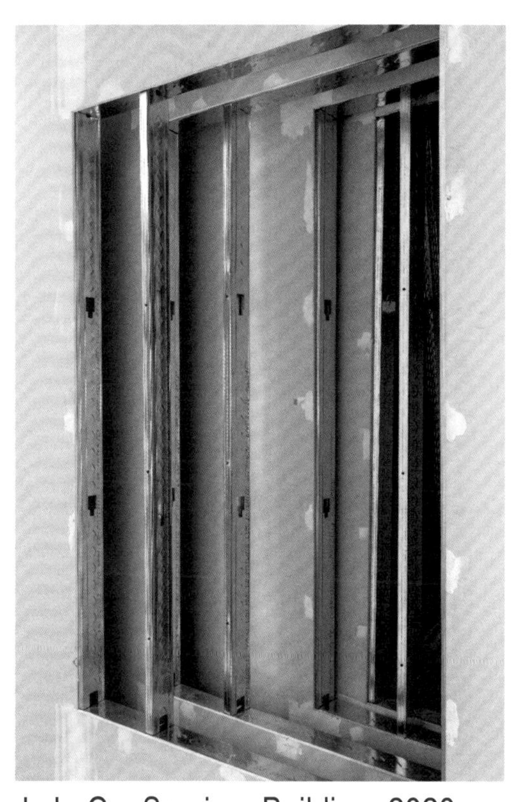

JaJa Co, Scoring, Building, 2020

nARCHITECTS, NY State Equal Rights Heritage Center, 2018

LAMAS, Delirious Facade, 2017–

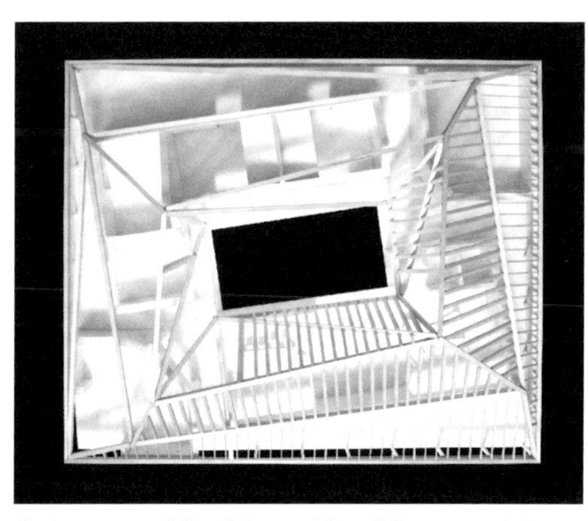

Johnston Marklee, Hut House, 2014

Superimpositions

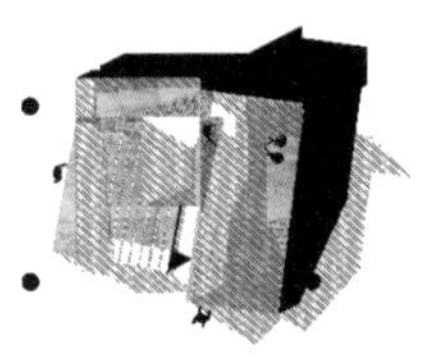

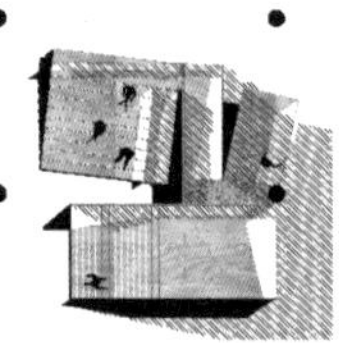

Now Here, 3 Stairs, 2019

JaJa Co, Noise, Pt. 3, 2016

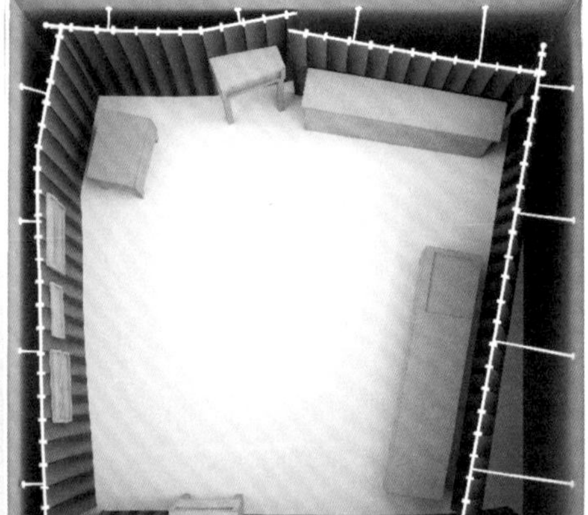

Current Interests, The View Inside, 2016

Current Interests, The View Inside, 2016

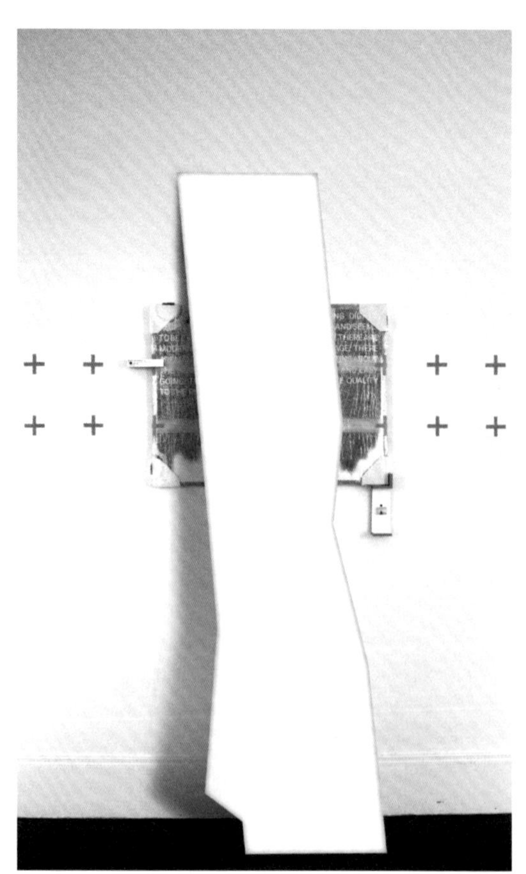

Curtis Roth, Instrument 10: The Exhibition, 2017

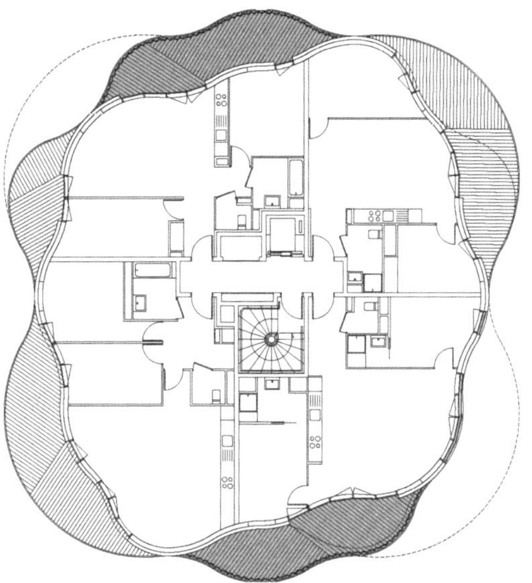

Farshid Moussavi Architecture, Folie Divine, 2017

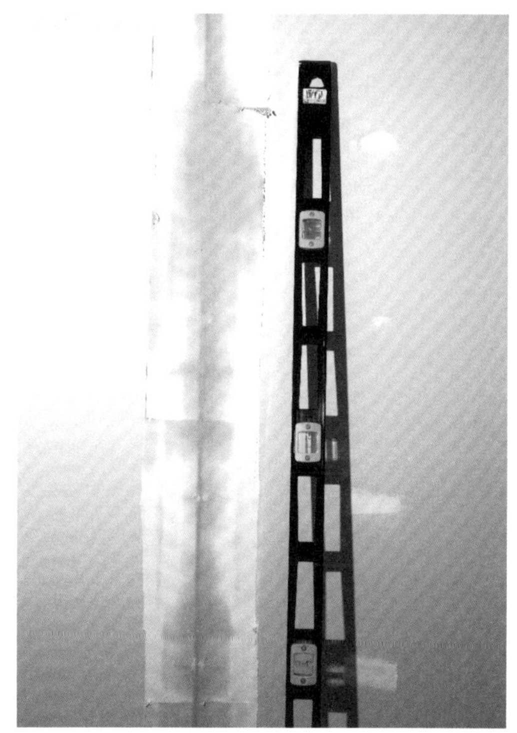

JaJa Co, Scoring, Building, 2020

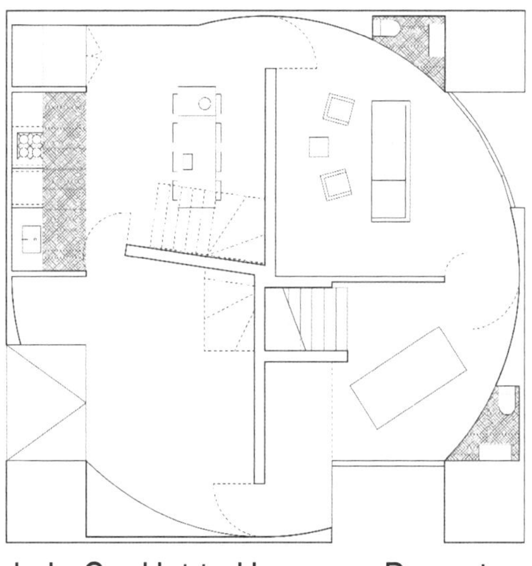

JaJa Co, Hat to Home; or, Dome to Domus, 2014

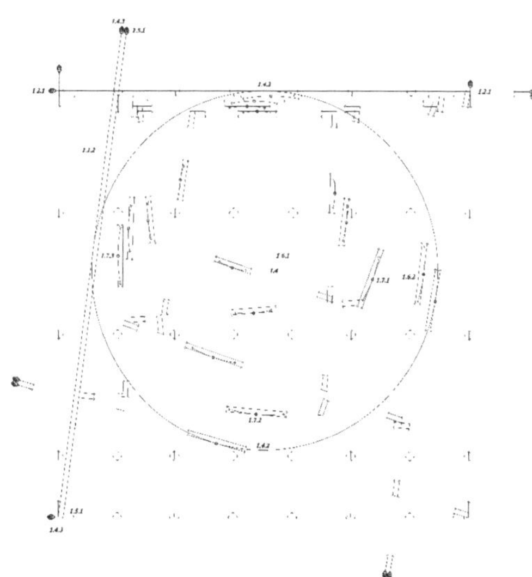

JaJa Co, Scoring, Building, 2020

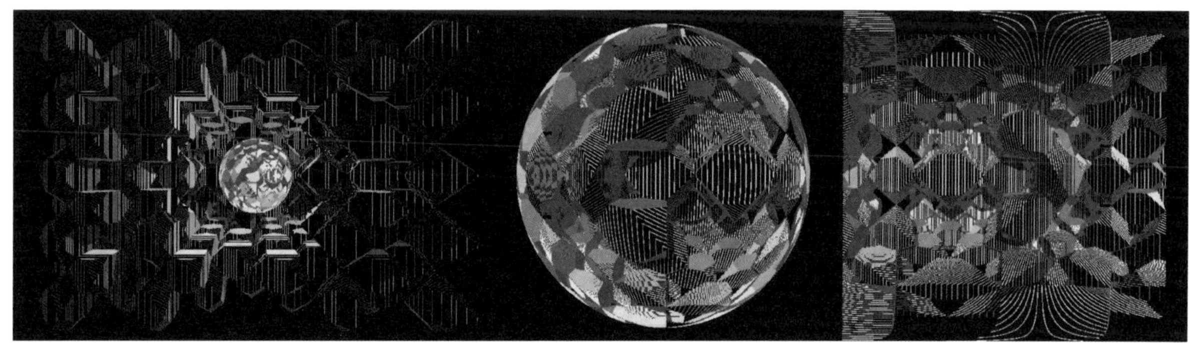

FreelandBuck, Objective Perspective Drawing Series, 2015

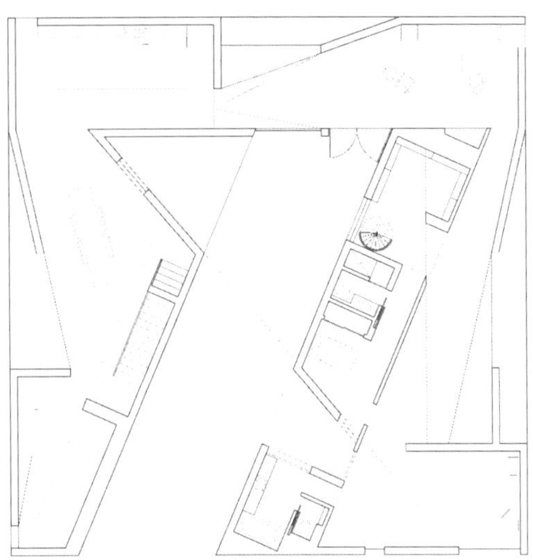

Studio Sean Canty, House with a Void, 2016

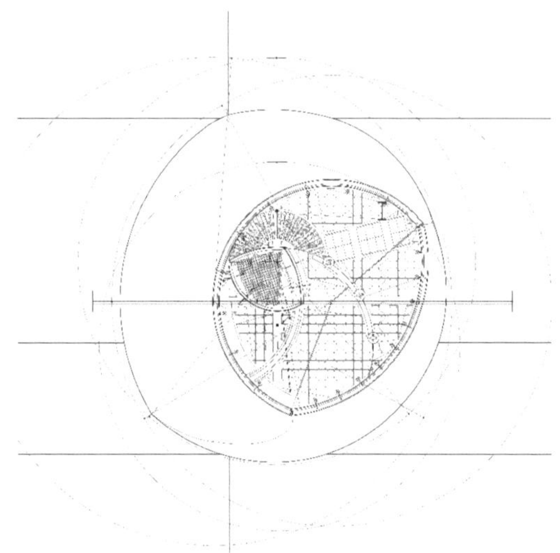

d.esk, Paperweight, 2013

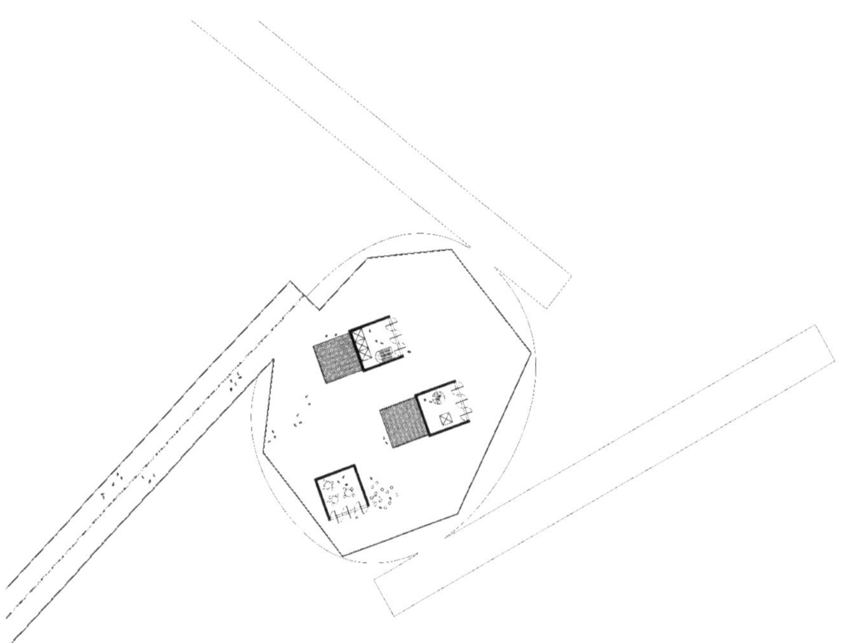

Paul Preissner Architects, Yeoui Naru Ferry Terminal, 2017

Studio Sean Canty, House with a Void, 2016

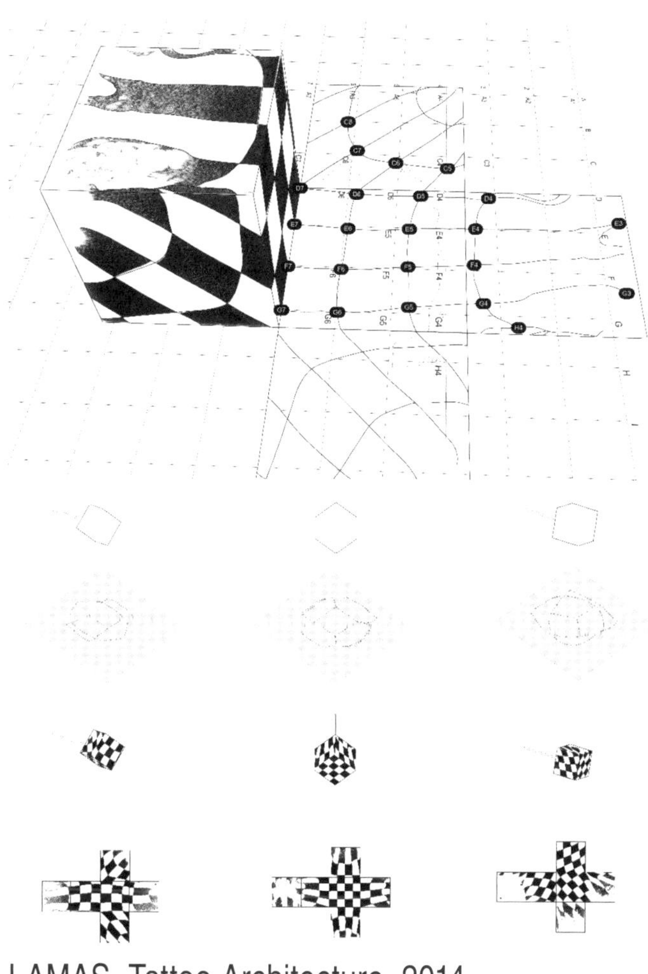

LAMAS, Tattoo Architecture, 2014–

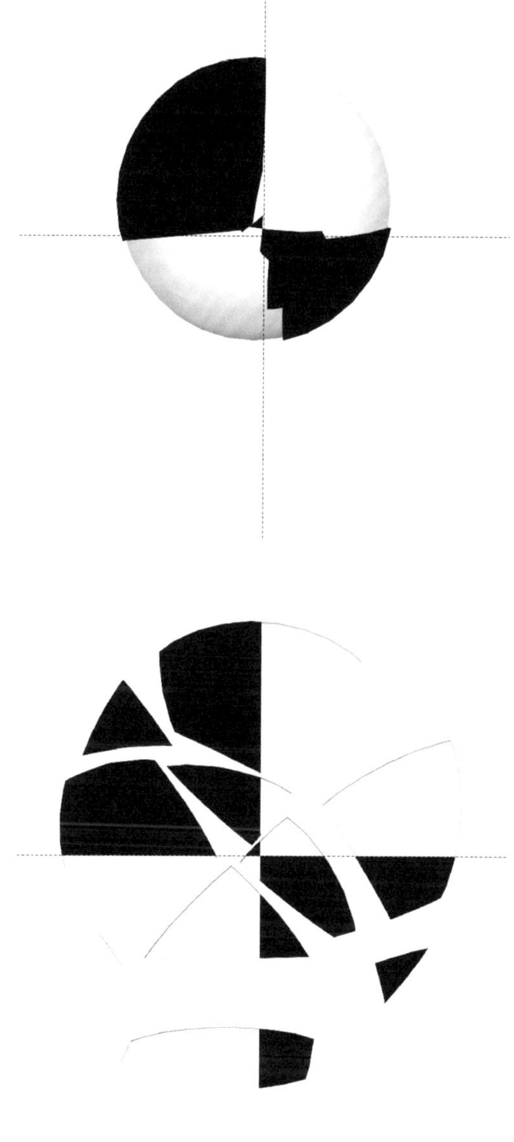

JaJa Co, Hat to Home; or, Dome to Domus, 2014

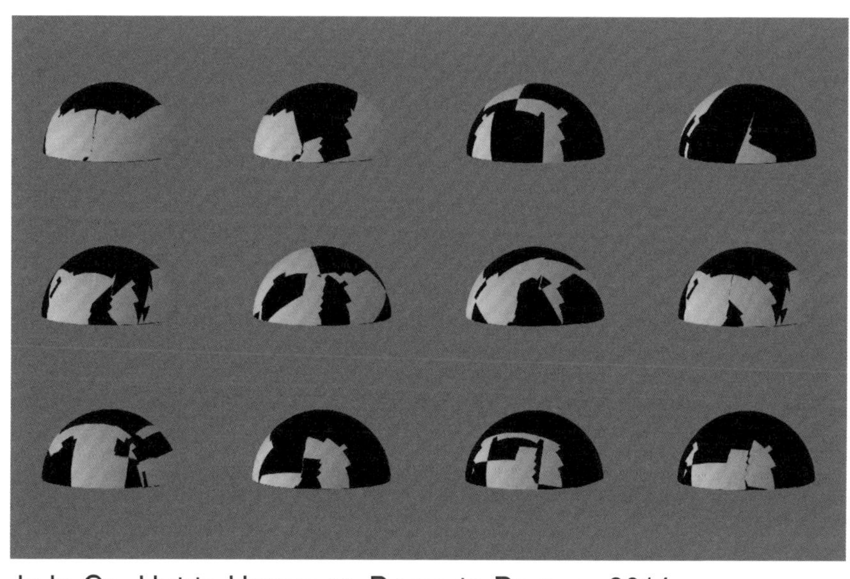

JaJa Co, Hat to Home; or, Dome to Domus, 2014

Superimpositions

SpinaGu, Thick, 2017

Kyle Miller, The Plan is the Generator, 2016

Ultramoderne, Four Corners, 2014

MALL, Domestic Hats, 2014

Bureau Spectacular, Inside Outside Between Beyond, 2017

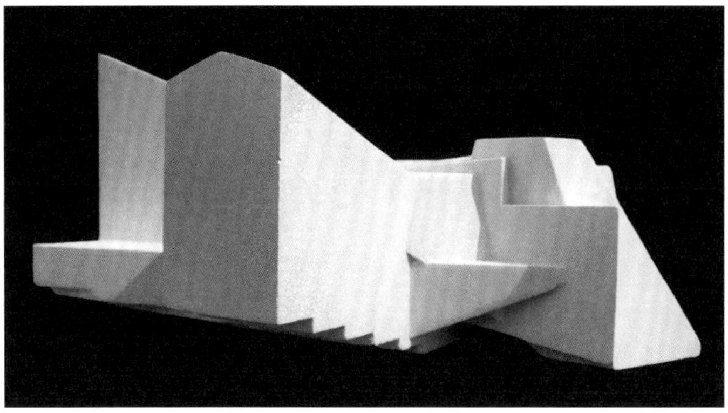

LAMAS, Film to Wit, 2012

JaJa Co, Noise, Pt. 3, 2016

FreelandBuck, Second House, 2018

MALL, Haus Gables, 2018

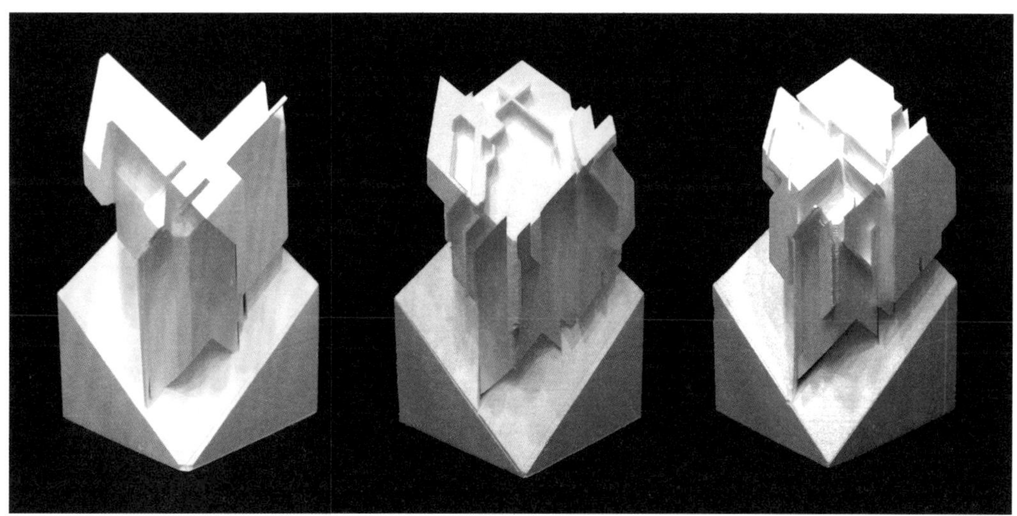

Erin Besler, Low Fidelity, 2012

Superimpositions

Fievre + Jones, Bywater Artist Residence I, in progress

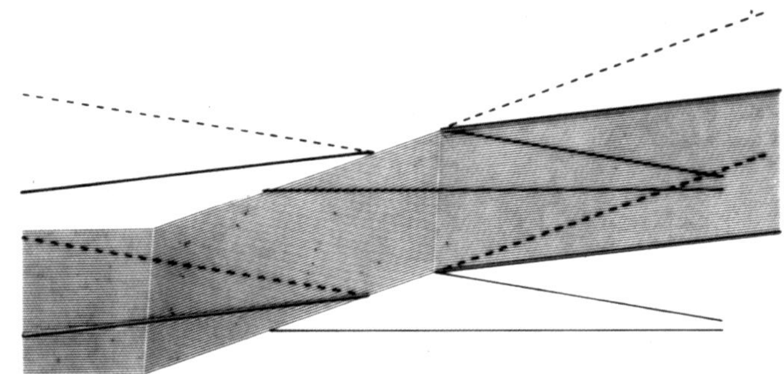
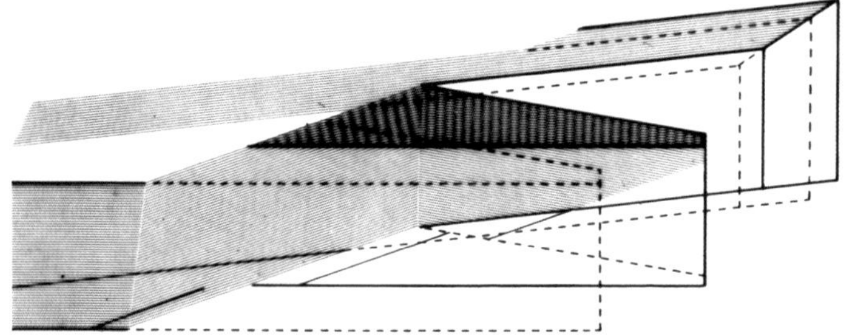
Preston Scott Cohen, Inc., Cornered House, 1992

New Affiliates, Tunbridge Winter Cabin, 2017

MALL, Domestic Hats, 2014

Anthony Titus Studio, The Light in the Window is a Crack in the Sky, 2008

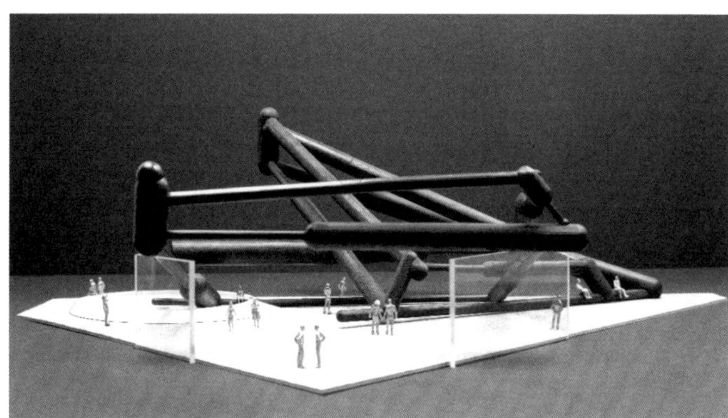

BairBalliet, Loud Lines, 2018

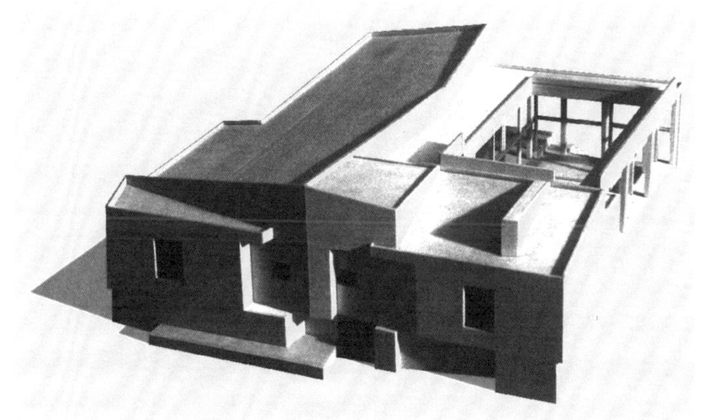

Preston Scott Cohen, Inc., House on Longboat Key, 1992

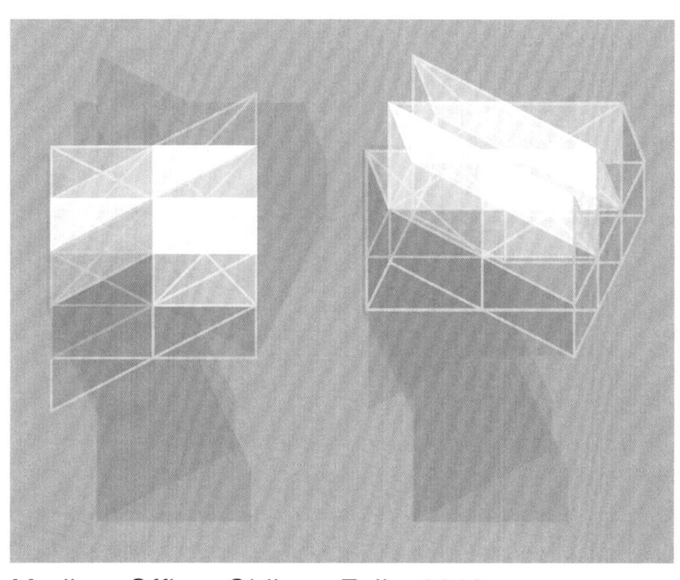

Medium Office, Oblique Folly, 2016

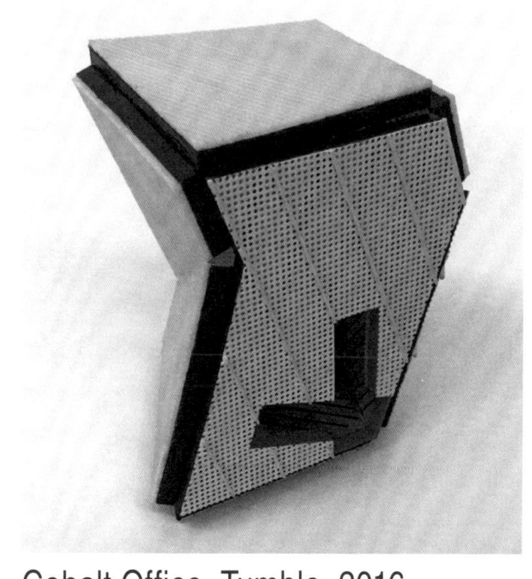

Cobalt Office, Tumble, 2016

Let's say we still believe in "the Project" but not in its truth. The Project is architecture's perennial pursuit of the origin—the One, the Thing, and the answer to the question, what does the discipline want? No longer expecting to actually find the answer, we can now enjoy the pursuit itself and, just as important, the sheer artifice of our discipline-driven machinations. The formal results of this project will be complicated: traces of unthinkably complex stochastic processes or the reiterative impulses that eventually produce architectural effects like nesting, buckling, slumping, and pleating (all of which are modes of inscription). Certain constitutive concepts of architecture—orthogonality, symmetry, seriality, and the distinction between interior and exterior (or skin and body cavity)—are produced not as actual substance but rather by implication, read through obscuring operations instead of being precisely specified as definite results. Unlike the immanent tents and huts, which coincide with the natural rhythms of the site and building materials, the revealed project is both compulsive and compelling, and often divorced from the organically regulated frames and cycles of the "immanent originals." On the other hand, the drive toward revelation still unleashes a quasisomatic force on the viewer. In our insistent and unnatural logics, we see the physical, haptic traces of our medial projection that *this* is what Architecture demands.

JaJa Co, A Hole in the Wall, 2019

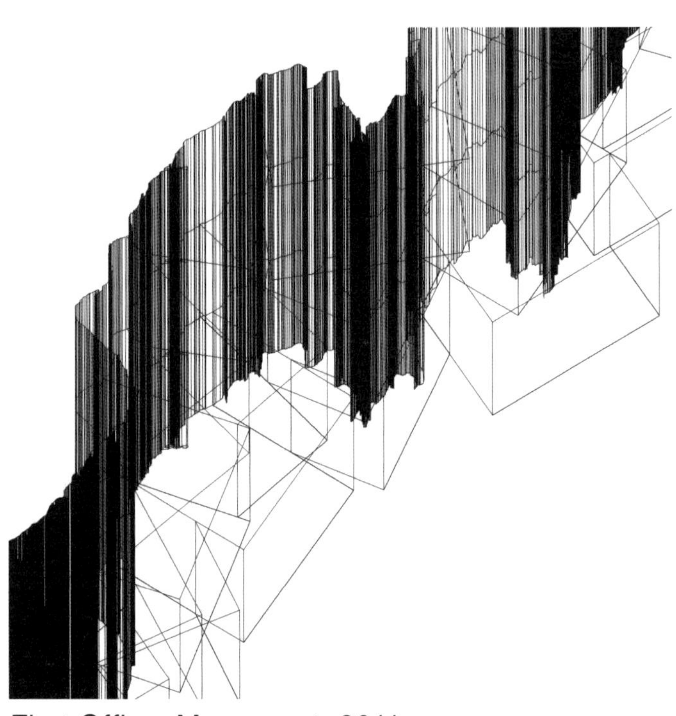

First Office, Monument, 2011

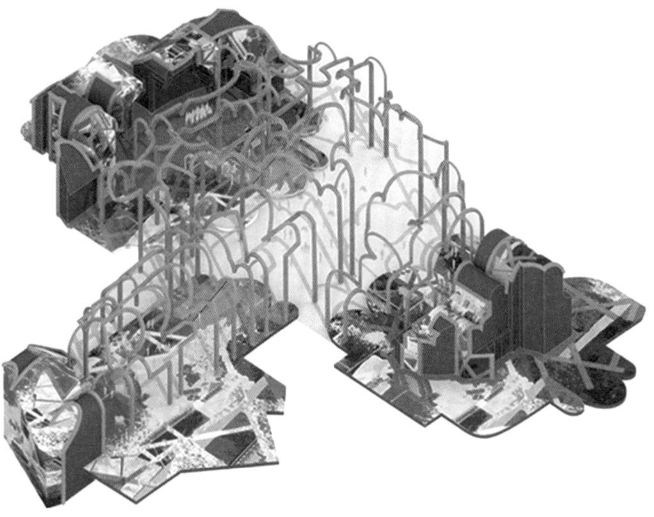

Jackilin Hah Bloom and Florencia Pita, The New Zocalo, 2016

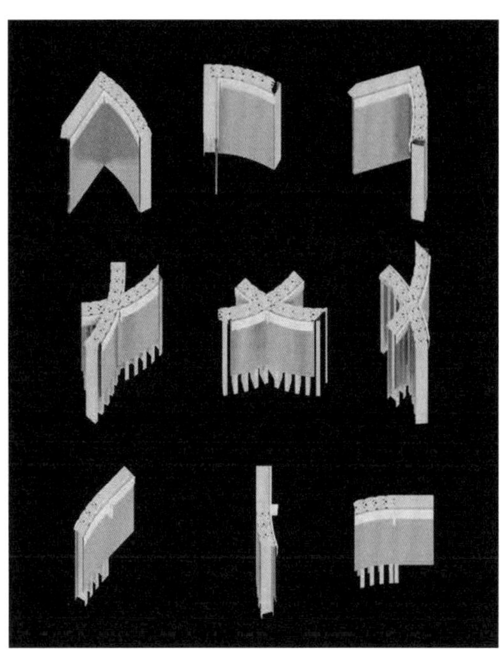

Besler & Sons, The Entire Situation, 2014

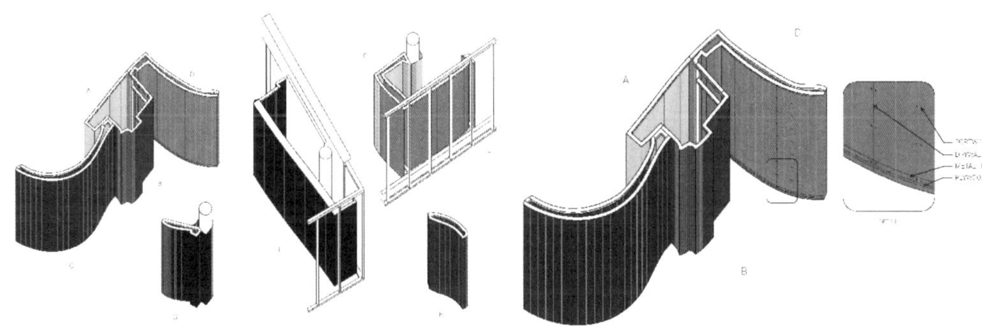

JaJa Co, A Hole in the Wall, 2019

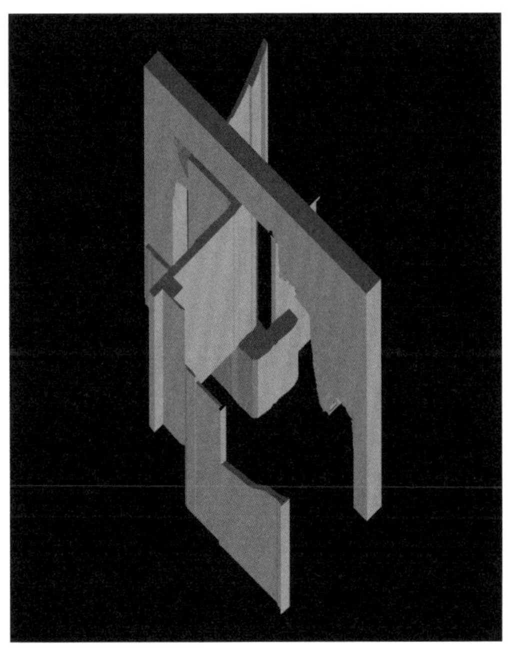

Descriptive Services, Drawing In-Painting, 2018

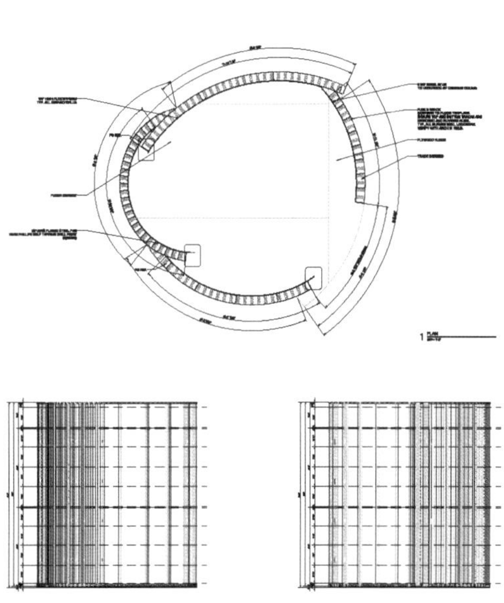

Besler & Sons, The Entire Situation, 2014

FreelandBuck, Objective Perspective Drawing Series, 2015

First Office, Mountain House, 2013

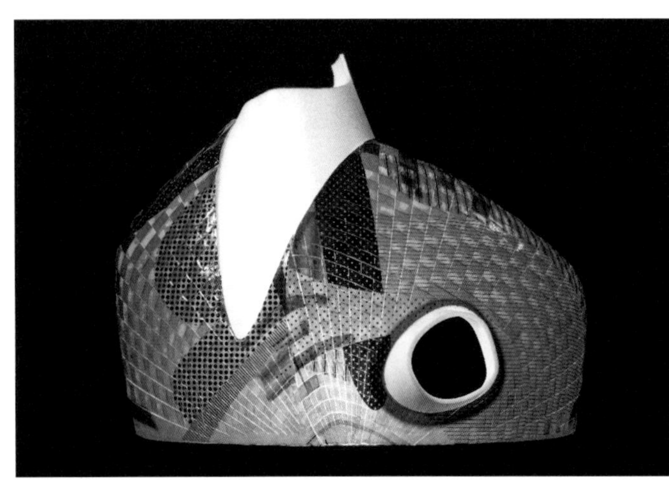

Kristy Balliet, Beyond Volume, 2014

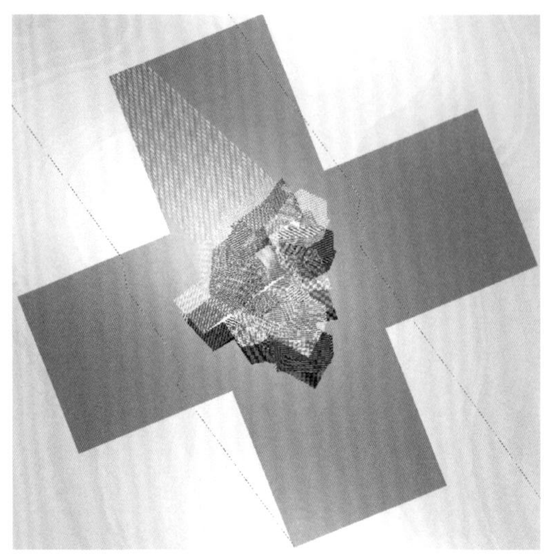

MIRACLES Architecture, Pink Box, 2017–

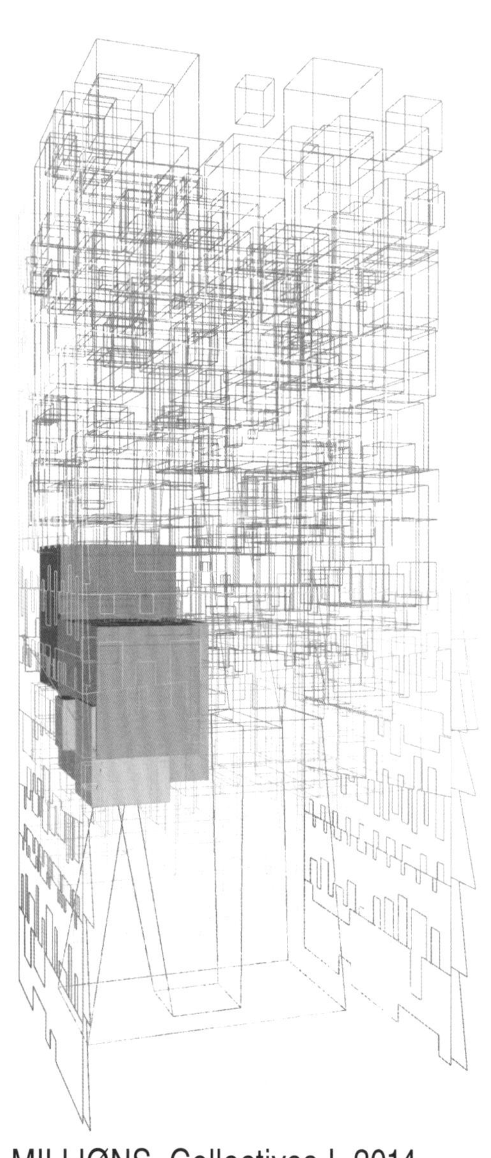

MILLIØNS, Collectives I, 2014

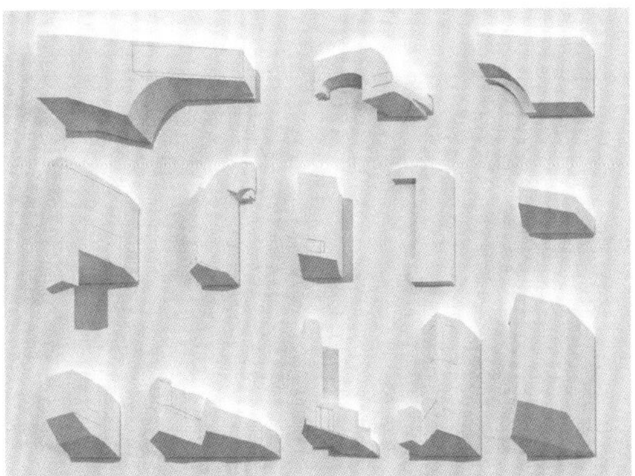

studioPM, Not-So-Still Life, 2018

SPORTS, Runaway, 2017

Erin Besler, Low Fidelity, 2012

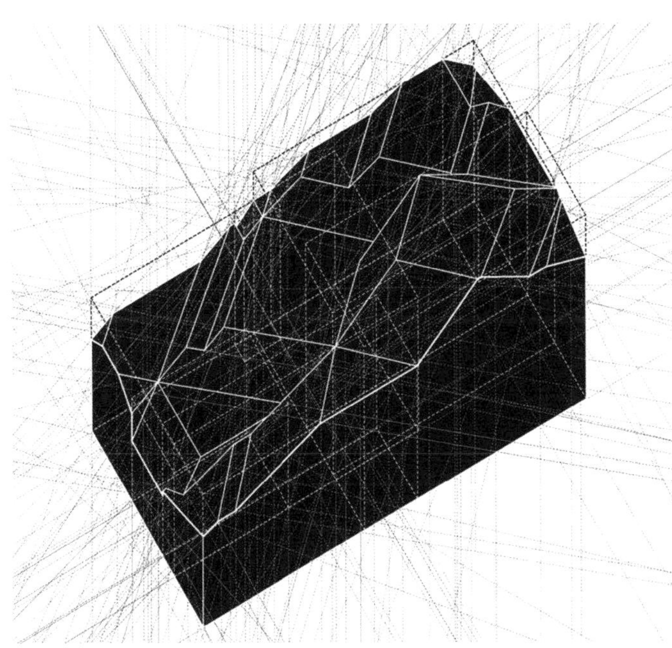

MALL, Domestic Hats, 2014

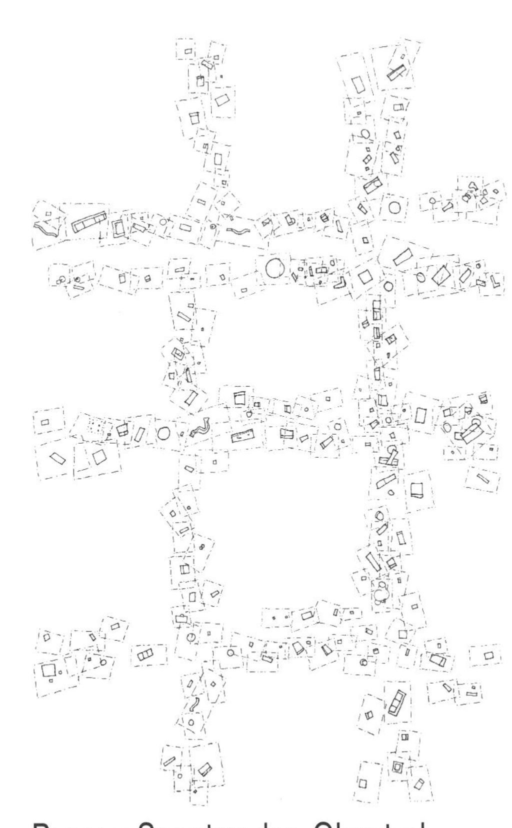

Bureau Spectacular, Ghosted Drawing Series, 2015

d.esk, Slump Model, 2019

Kristy Balliet, Beyond Volume, 2014

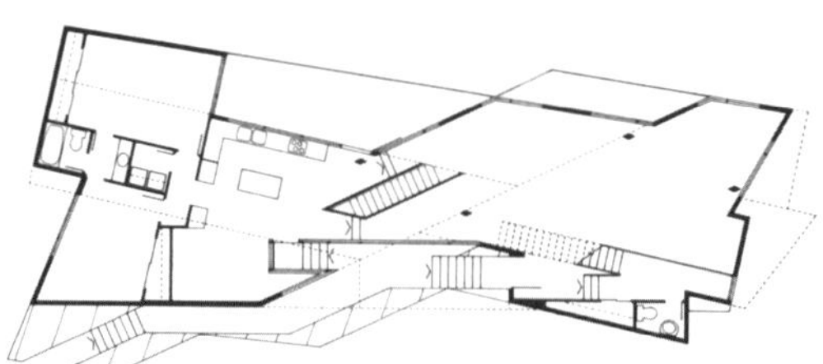
Preston Scott Cohen, Inc., Cornered House, 1992

MIRACLES Architecture, Poppy Red, 2019

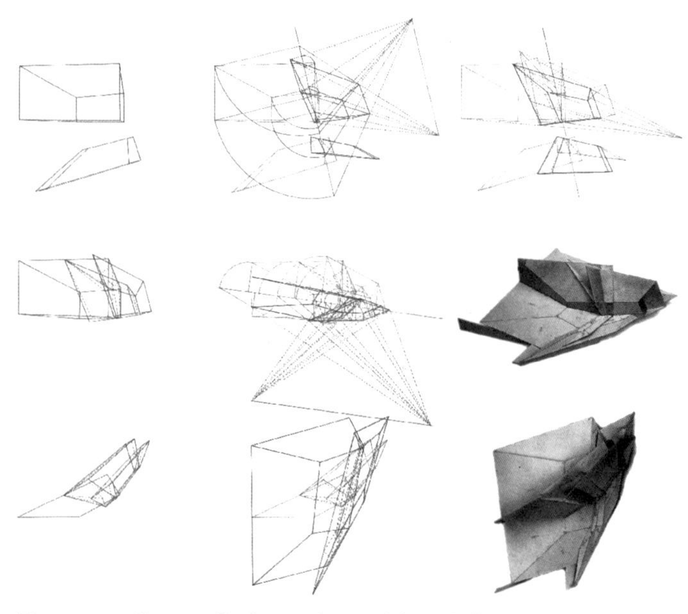
Preston Scott Cohen, Inc., Head Start, 1996

Viola Ago and Hans Tursack, Understorey, 2019

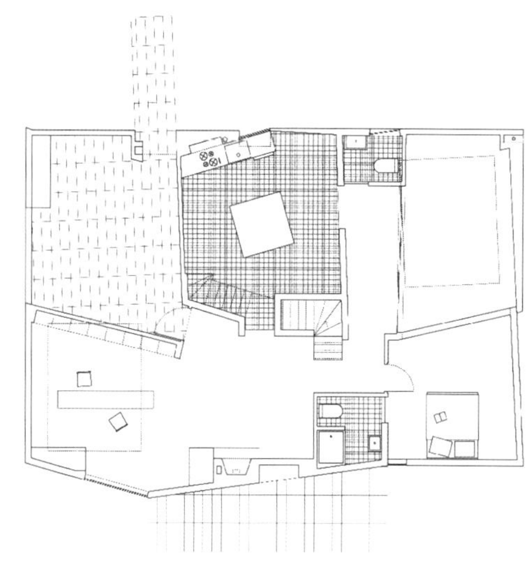

JaJa Co, Noise, Pt. 3, 2016

Viola Ago and Hans Tursack, Understorey, 2019

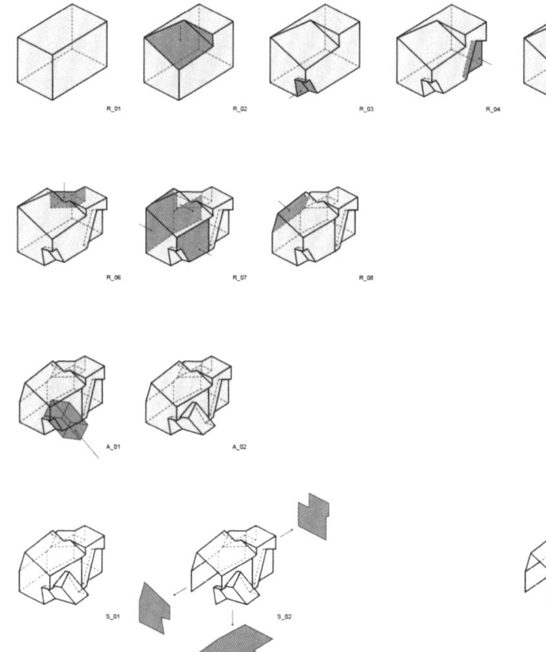

Viola Ago and Hans Tursack, Understorey, 2019

First Office, Possible Table, 2014

Mack Scogin Merrill Elam Architects, Laban Centre for Movement and Dance Invited Competition, 1997

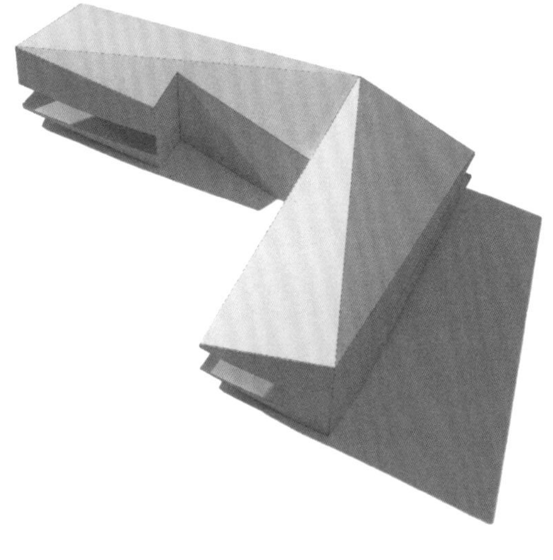

Fievre + Jones, Bywater Artist Residence I, in progress

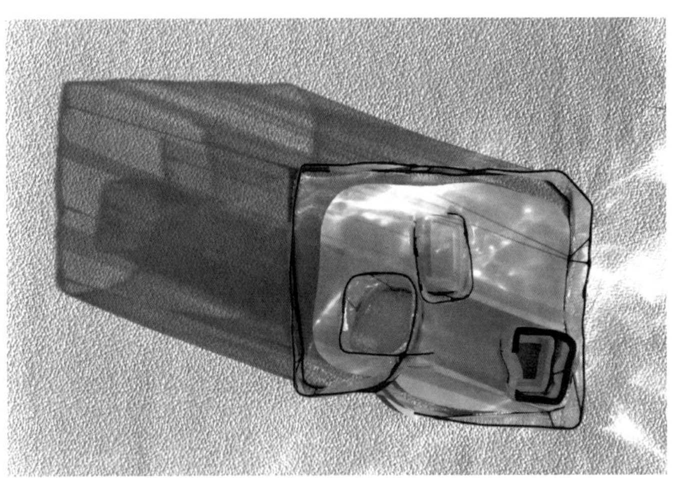

is-office, Bad Lines, 2013

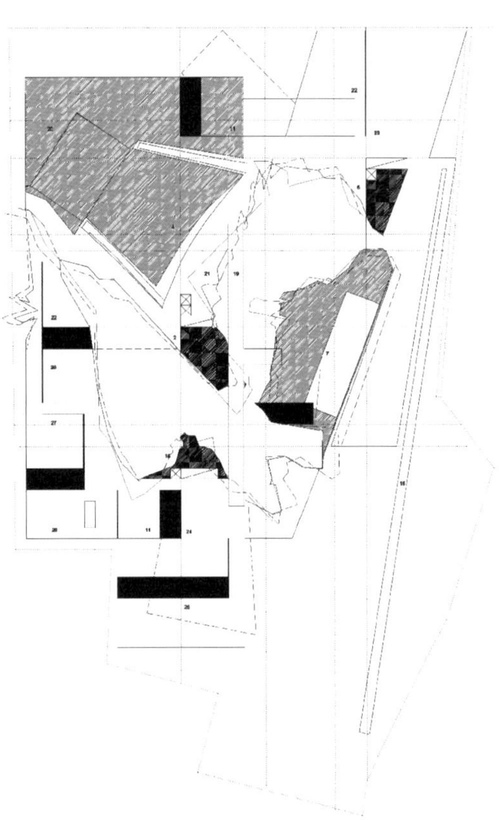

Mack Scogin Merrill Elam Architects, Laban Centre for Movement and Dance Invited Competition, 1997

Now Here, 3 Stairs, 2019

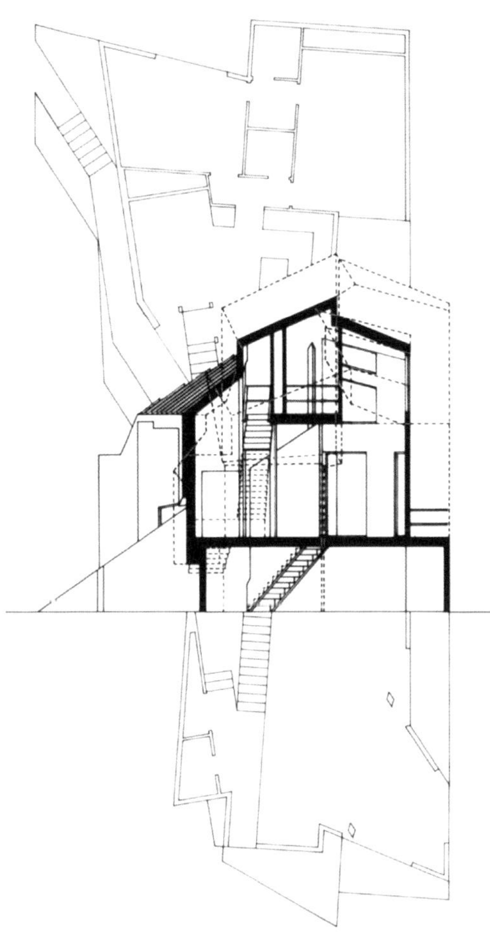

Preston Scott Cohen, Inc.,
Cornered House, 1992

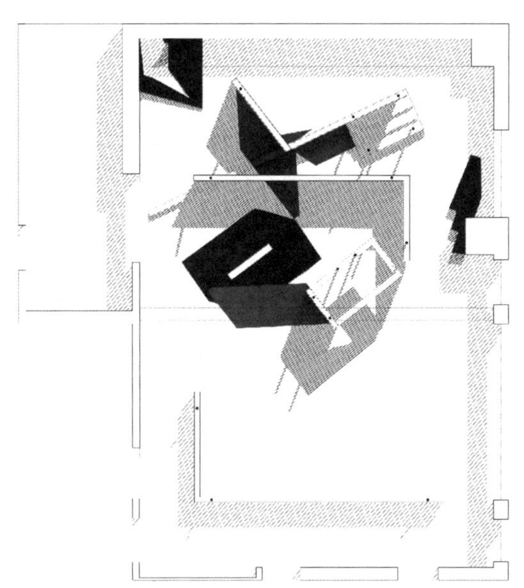

Now Here, 6 Work Surfaces, 2019

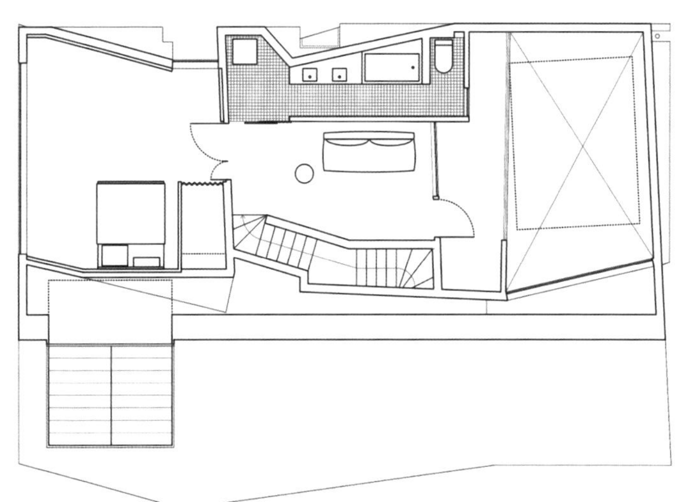

JaJa Co, Noise, Pt. 3, 2016

Mack Scogin Merrill Elam Architects,
Zhongkai Sheshan Villas, 2005

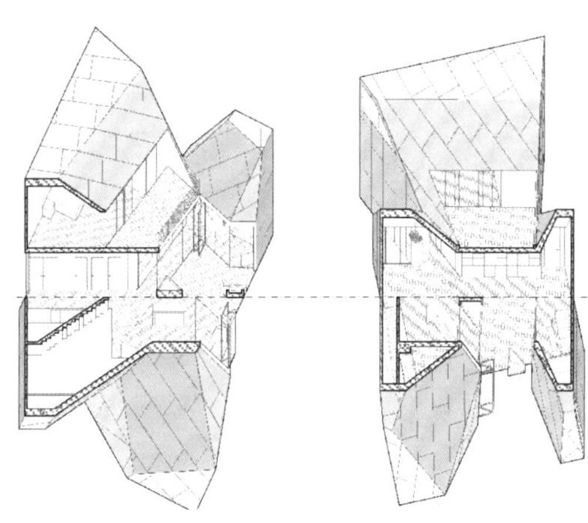

FreelandBuck, Second House, 2018

Slack Collections

The baroque court, Walter Benjamin observed, was "subject to the law of 'dispersal' and 'collectedness.' Things are assembled according to their significance; indifference to their existence allowed them to be dispersed again. . . . The fanaticism of the process of collection is balanced by the slackness with which the objects are arranged." Slack collections are gatherings of objects under a descriptor that seems reasonable enough, like "components of a tensegrity structure" or "workout equipment." For all their reasonableness and apparent logics of similarity, though, the collections are not finite, nor are they arrayed according to a master logic like a catalog or encyclopedia. Objects in slack collections are not selected as representatives of a class in some ordering table, nor for the way they evince the breadth of possibility within a designated schema. Instead, they are gathered around an idea by dint of sheer adjacency. Consequently, the collection is always on the verge of falling apart, imperiled by the inclusion of too many things or else by the addition of one particular thing that disturbs the apparent coherence of the assembly. This decay is forestalled by assigning jobs and roles. Common Accounts and stock-a-studio erect scaffolds for objects to hang within; Preston Scott Cohen, Inc., stacks floor slabs to give a tensegrity something to support—again, not as a tabular system that specifies a necessary location, but to draw a loose perimeter and give a medium in which to disperse and do work: punching bags hang from, mats unroll on, plates rest atop, escalators trace lines of tension. These labors inscribe the rudiments of order: edge, center, neighbors. Evidence of authorship occurs at the joints and interfaces where objects are lashed, strung together, glued, or hung.

Hans Tursack, Precarious House, 2020

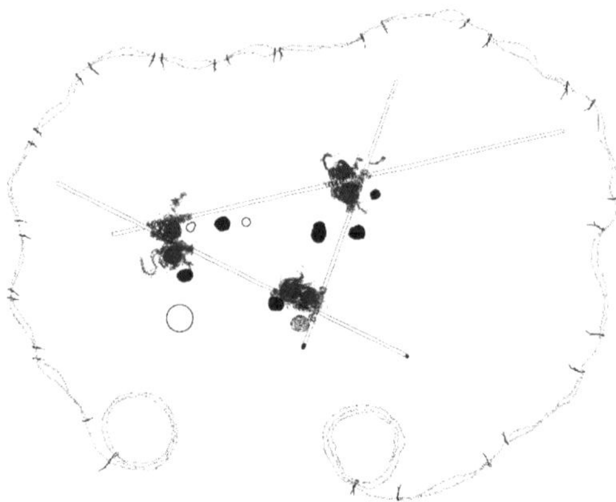

Mack Scogin Merrill Elam Architects, House above the Bug Line, 1993

Preston Scott Cohen, Inc., Eyebeam Atelier Museum, 2001

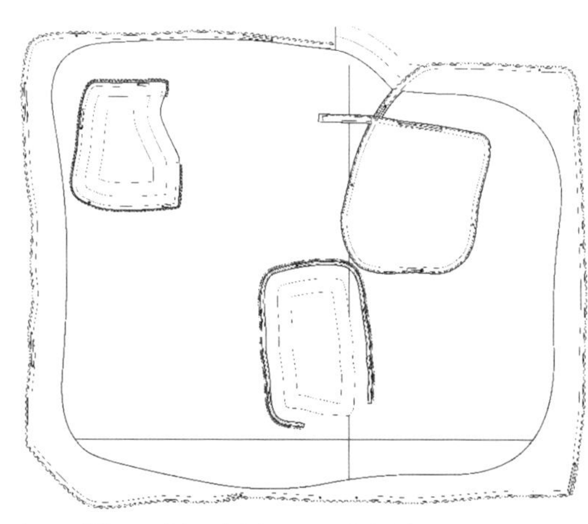

is-office, Bad Lines, 2013

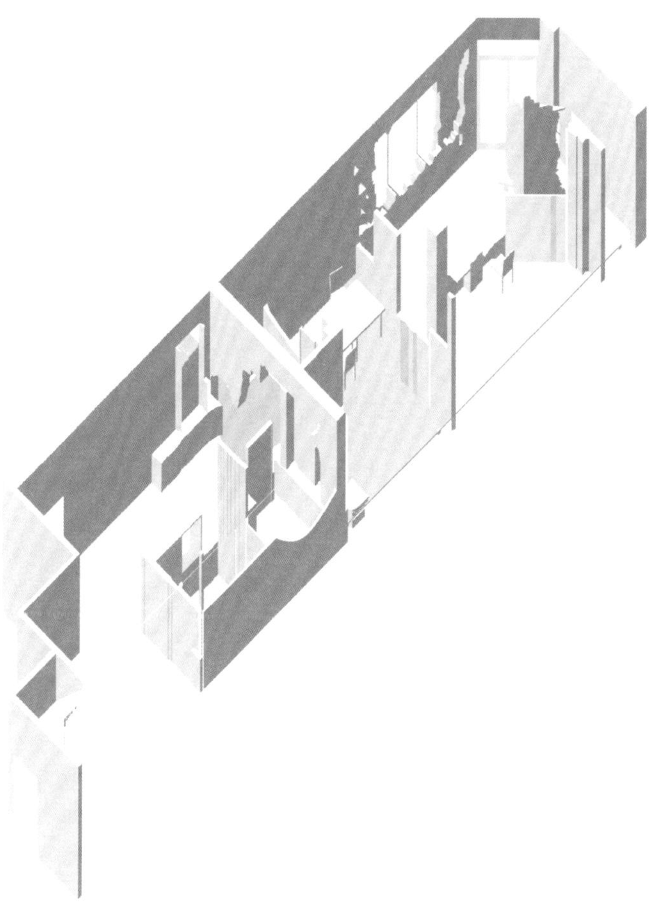

Descriptive Services, Drawing In-Painting, 2018

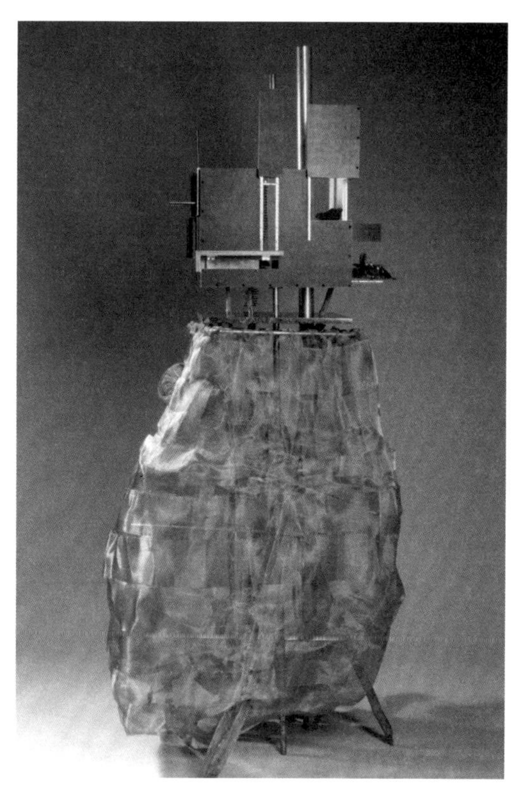

Mack Scogin Merrill Elam Architects, House above the Bug Line, 1993

Mack Scogin Merrill Elam Architects, Kaohsiung Maritime Cultural & Popular Music Center, 2004

The LADG, House in Los Angeles 1, 2016

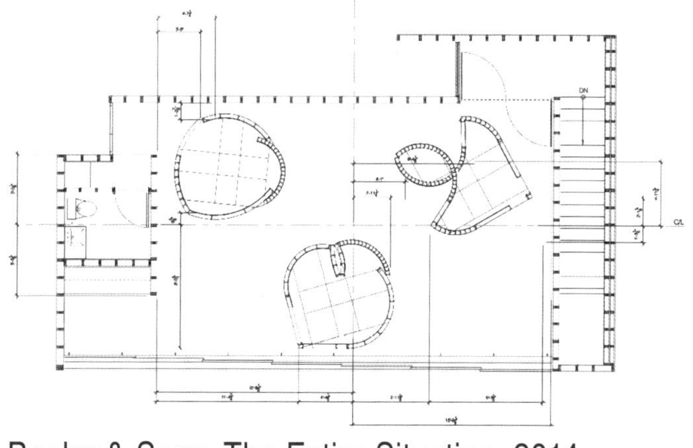

Besler & Sons, The Entire Situation, 2014

studioPM, Not-So-Still Life, 2018

FORMA, Windsor Residence, 2018

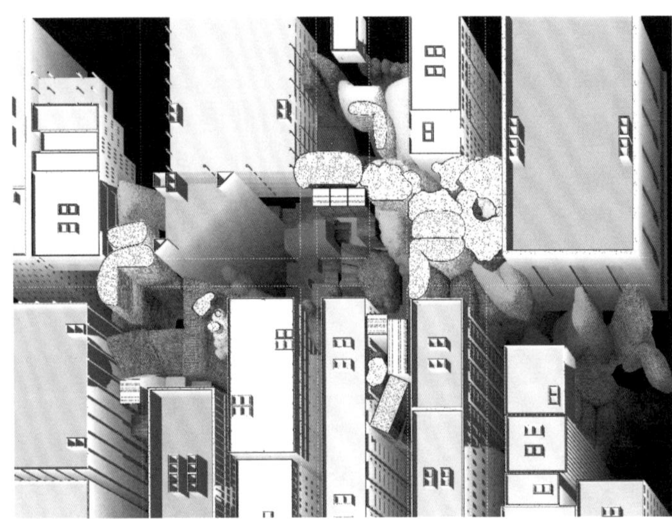
The LADG, Cast of Things: Van Buren and Federal, 2017

d.esk, Training Wheels, 2015

The LADG, Cast of Things: Van Buren and Federal, 2017

Slack Collections

Common Accounts, Refresh, Renew Pavilion, 2019

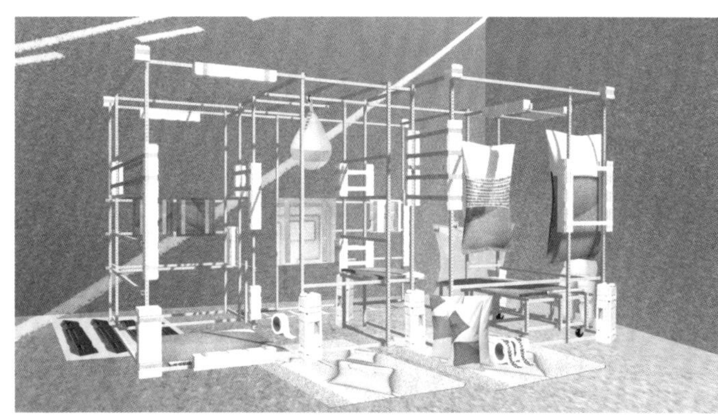

stock-a-studio, [a kit of these some parts] x budget gym], 2019

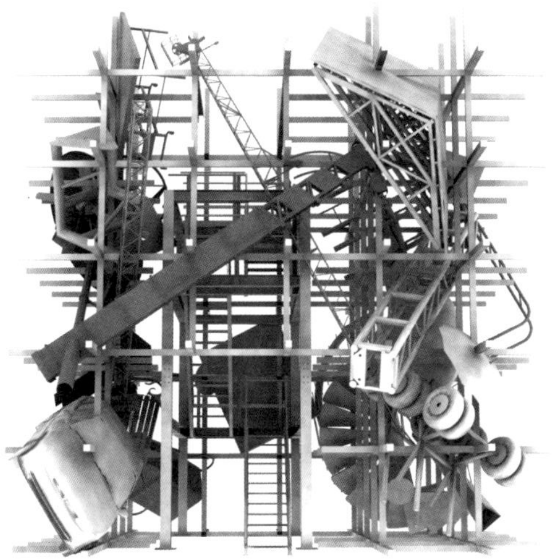

Bureau Spectacular, Lost and Found (Studies), 2015

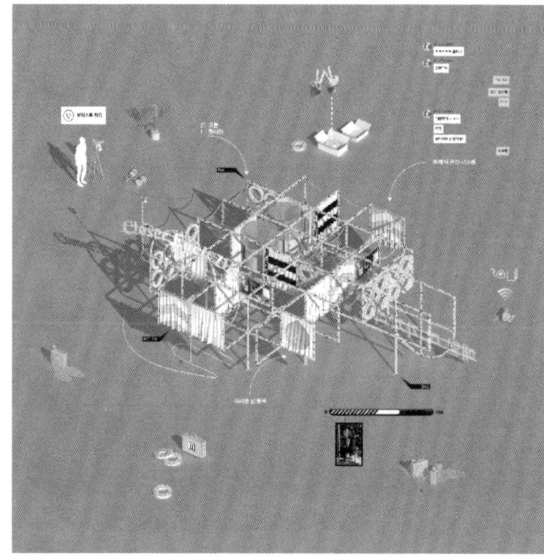

Common Accounts, Three Ordinary Funerals, 2018

stock-a-studio, [a kit of these some parts] x budget gym], 2019

d.esk, Training Wheels, 2015

Slack Collections

Architecture Office, Parti Wall, 2014

Kyle May, Extent, 2018

Lluís Alexandre Casanovas Blanco with María Luisa Blanco, Real Estate Boom House, Dynemaa Bobbin Lace Curtain Prototype #1, 2018

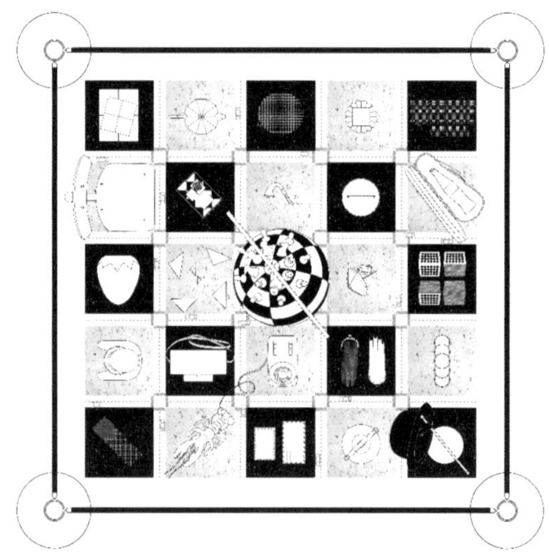

Welcome Projects, Retrospective City, 2014

Architecture Office, Parti Wall, 2014

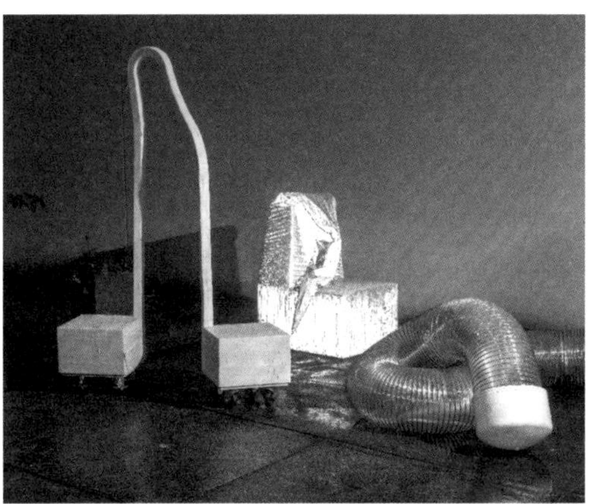
Andy and Dave, Function Agnostic Courtyard, 2018

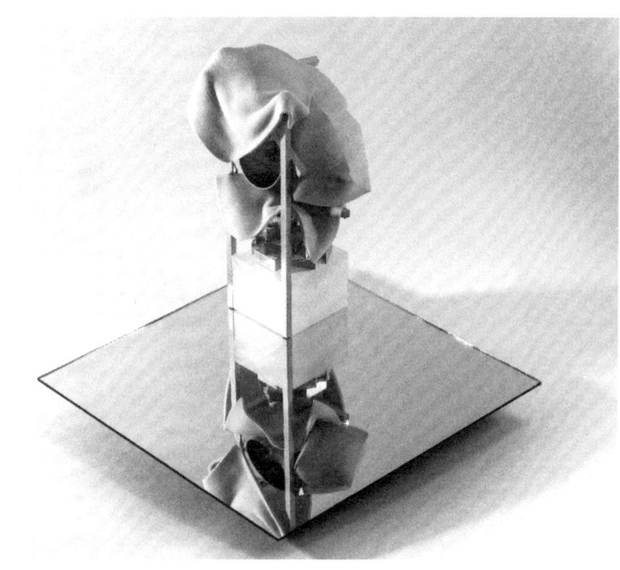
The LADG, Tchotchke, 2016

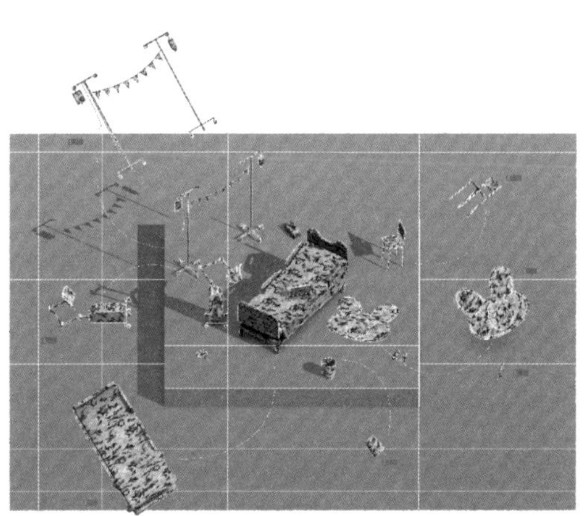
Common Accounts, Going Fluid: Cozy Crusade, 2019

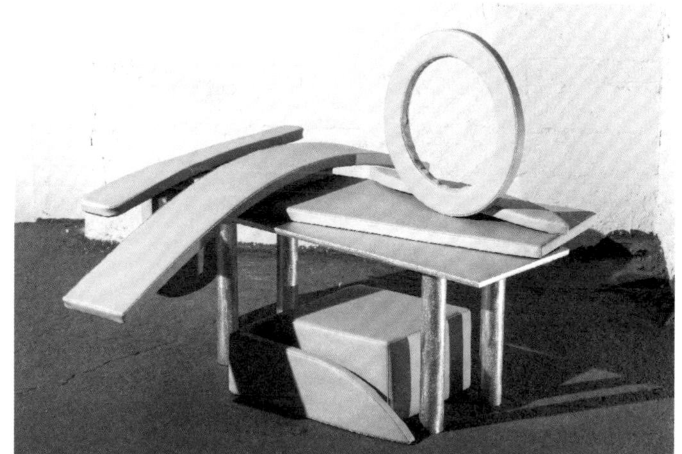
Andy and Dave, Wanna go there! (Partition), and Where is this? (Bench), 2018

MR Studio, Teh Developed Srf, 2019

The LADG, The Kid Gets out of the Picture, 2016

The LADG, The Kid Gets out of the Picture, 2016

MR Studio, Serendipitous Formalism, 2018

Preston Scott Cohen, Inc., Eyebeam Atelier Museum, 2001

Scatters, Remnants

A plane strewn with debris suggests the aftermath of god-like action from above. Whatever happened here has not only left physical objects scattered in its wake (tracks of uncertain origin) but has also charged the air with a physics of attraction and repulsion. Together these gestures become evidence that can be used to reconstruct the event. In scenes by Outpost Office and EXTENTS, paper-thin planes rain from a cutting machine, collecting in laminar piles, hinging and dangling from edges still partially stuck together. In another by Hans Tursack, bits and parts are sorted into tidy piles, placed in alignment with the elevations of half-built constructions in spots marked out by an unfolded drawing, as though waiting to be hoisted into place. In both cases, habitation invades and enlists the remnants left by the event to discharge a programmatic responsibility. The landscape of laminar planes is an amphitheater in the round. Overlapping cuts and punches are hinged and rotated, then used as depressions for seating, allowing a civically scaled space to both accommodate large crowds and retain the intimacy of a living room. Or even more intimate: crowds accumulate in the space of a craft project. At Tursack's composed construction site, the intimation of an urban grid distributes what appear as streets and buildings among stacks of parts. The incipient acts of lifting and hauling synchronize the routines of urban life with the choreography of building. The states that shape the organization of a city—flow and repose, equipment in use and equipment available for use—are cued by the logic of a building in progress that distinguishes assembly from completion, things in place from things out of place.

Outpost Office, Ground Game, 2018

Anthony Titus Studio, The Light in the Window is a Crack in the Sky, 2008

stock-a-studio, neighbor neighbor, 2019

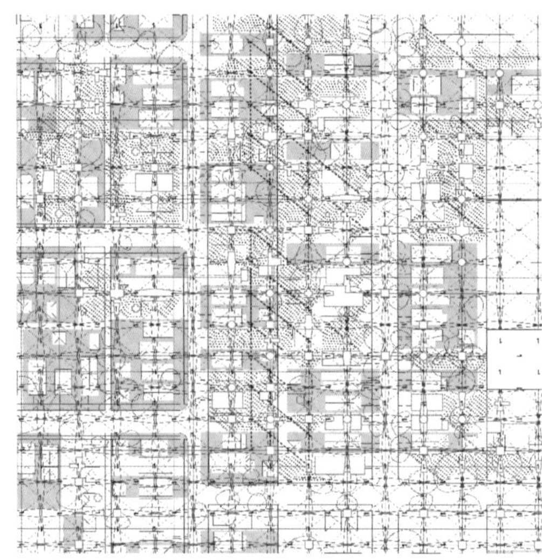

SCHAUM/SHIEH, Sponge Urbanism, 2011

EXTENTS, SRFC_PLAY, 2017

stock-a-studio and EXTENTS, nude, 2018

d.esk, Column & Canopy, 2016

Hans Tursack, Graphic Fields, Composition VII, 2015

Outpost Office, Ground Game, 2018

Curtis Roth, Decorating Villa Wolf, 2016

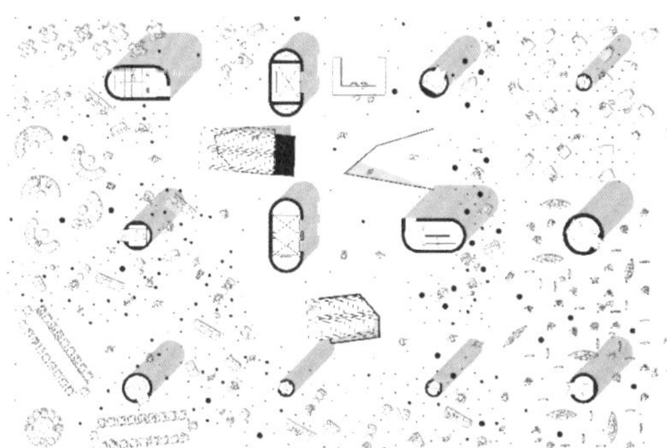
The Open Workshop, Varna Public Library and Archive, 2015

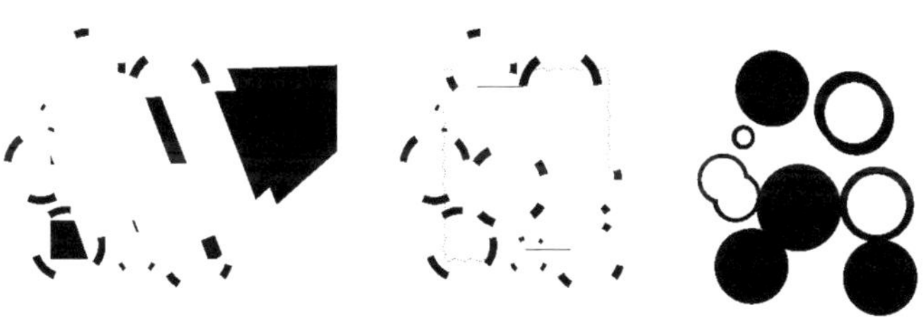
Endemic Architecture, A Music Hall for Golden Gate Park, 2018

EXTENTS, SRFC_PLAY, 2017

d.esk, Training Wheels, 2015

PARA Project, Pioneertown House, 2018

NEMESTUDIO, New Cadavre Exquis, 2017

d.esk, Column & Canopy, 2016

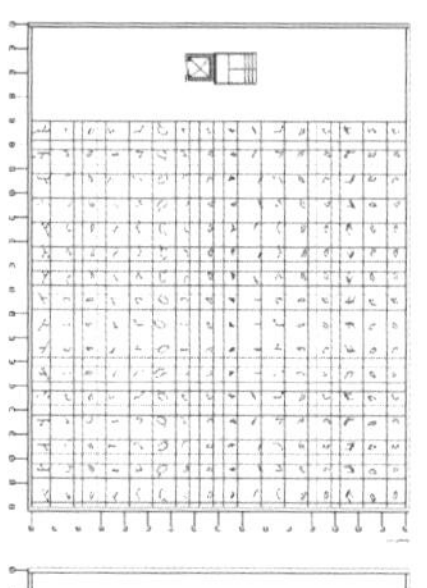

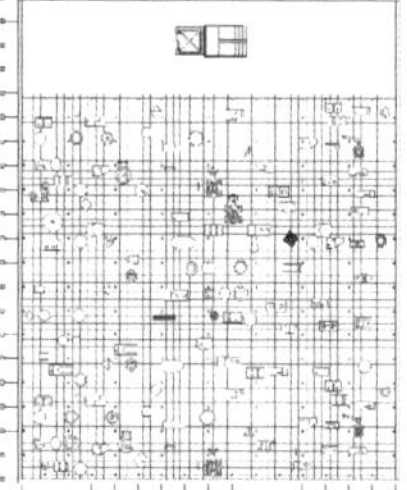

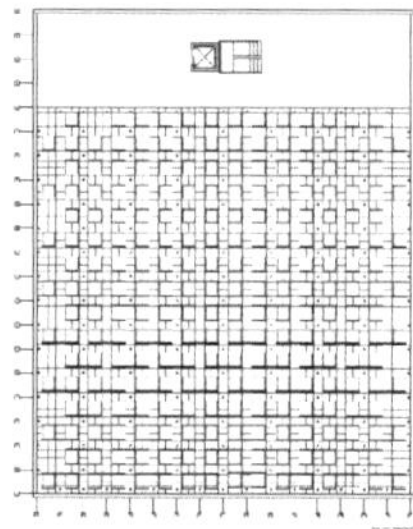

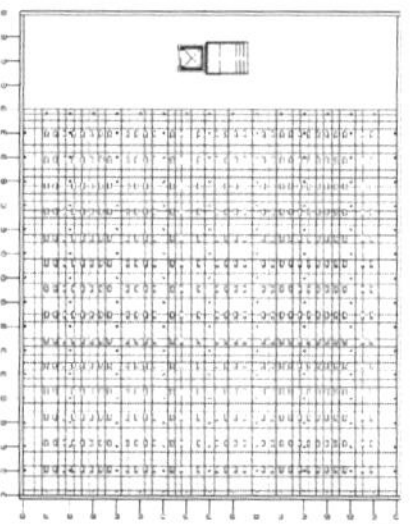

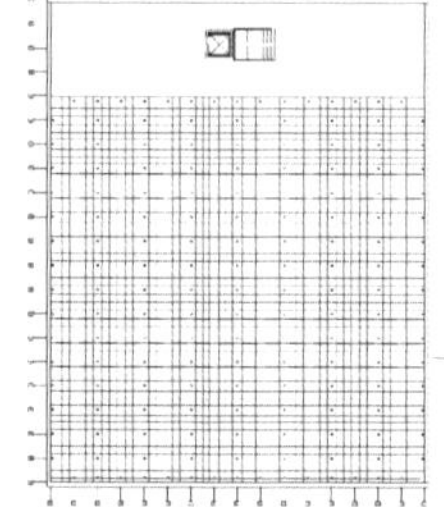

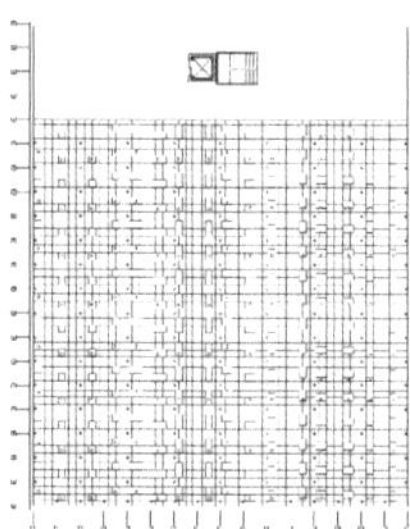

stock-a-studio, arlington audit, 2014

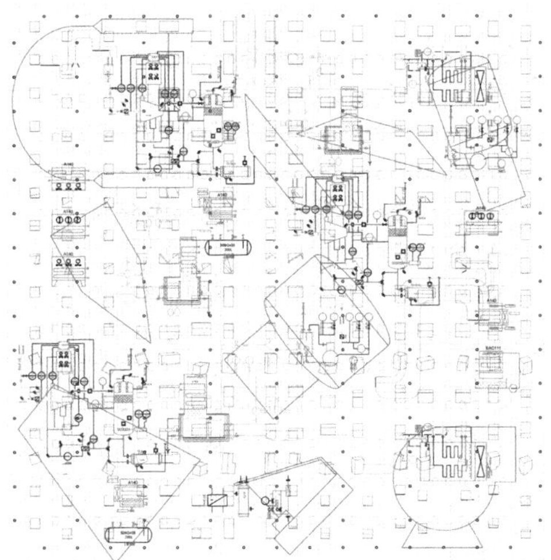

stock-a-studio, arlington audit, 2014

MAIO, The Grand Interior, Chicago Architecture Biennial 2017, 2017

PARA Project, Stump House, 2019–

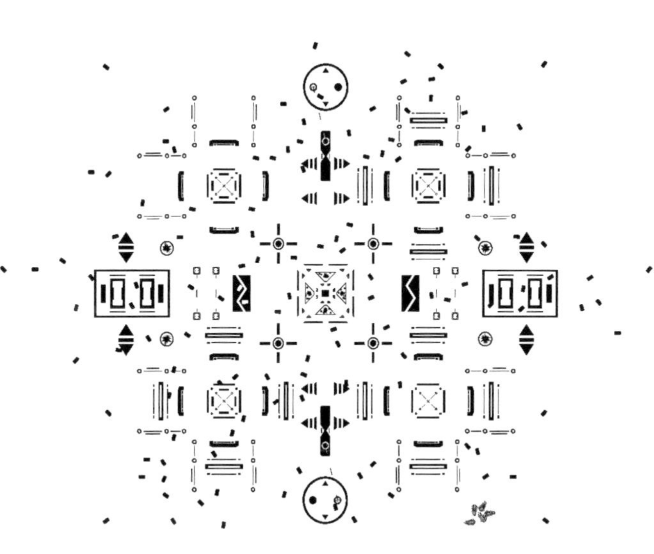

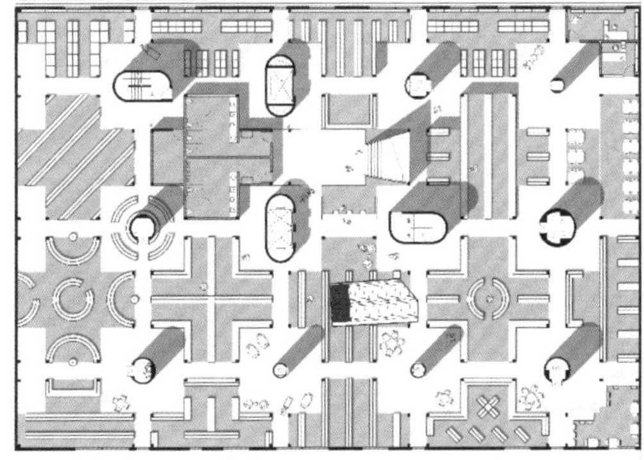

The Open Workshop, Varna Public Library and Archive, 2015

Hans Tursack, Graphic Fields, Composition VIII, 2015

Scatters, Remnants

Paul Preissner Architects, Pyeongchang-dong Art Complex, 2017

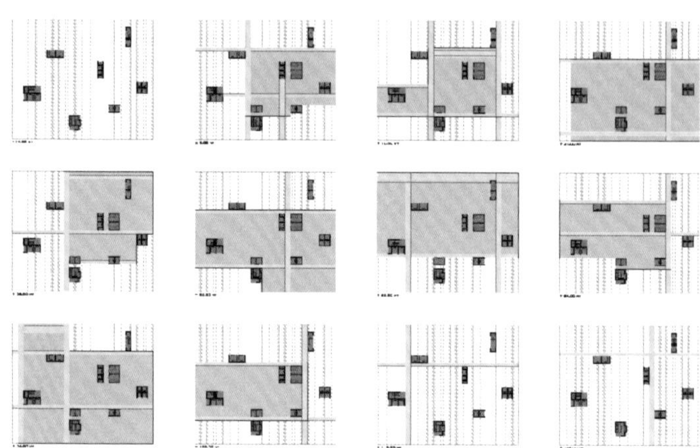

Ensamble Studio, Big Bang Towers, 2013

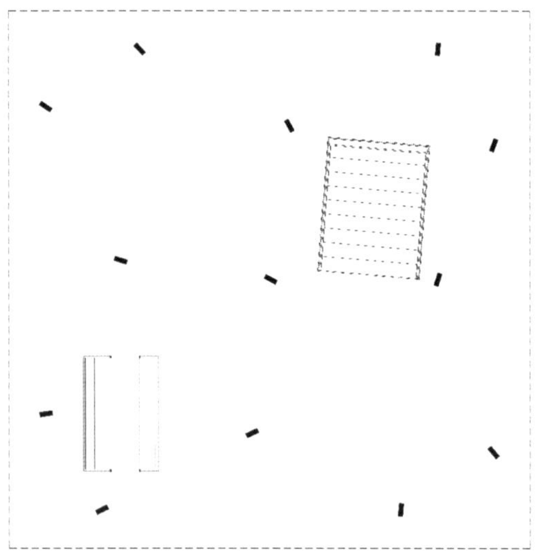

Ultramoderne, Chicago Horizon, 2015

SCHAUM/SHIEH, Sponge Urbanism, 2011

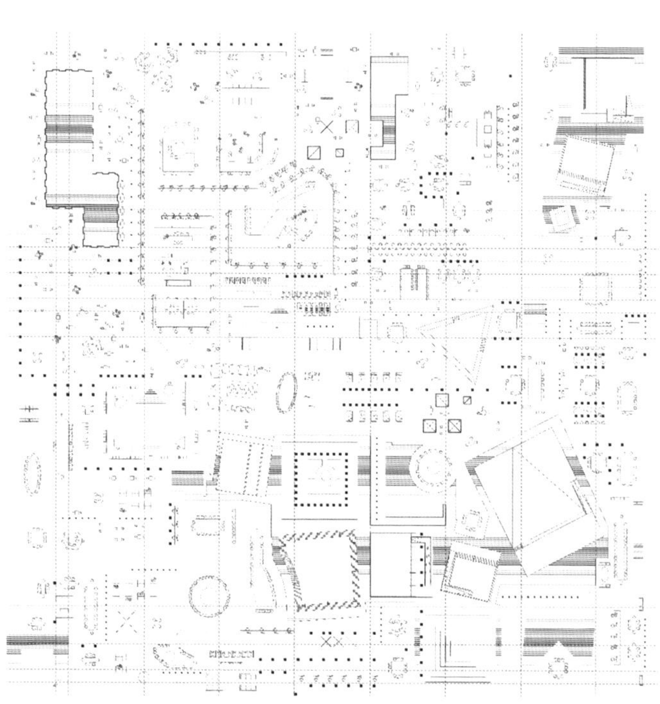

Endemic Architecture, Tech Plan No. 3: Field of Figures and Filigree, 2018

Paul Preissner Architects, Beer Sheeba Daycare, 2013

Young & Ayata, Campo Field Entourage, 2019

NEMESTUDIO, New Cadavre Exquis, 2017

Paul Preissner Architects, Port of Kinmen Passenger Ferry Terminal, 2014

Dirt, Earth, and Rocks

Architecture is again in the business of rocks. Geological surfaces are fabricated out of foam, concrete, and plastic, rocks are arranged in place of walls, and building elements are scattered in picturesque arrays that recall eroding hills. This mimetic exercise is not the expression of a taste or genre, however; it is a reappraisal of architecture's techniques of measure. When applied to objects of such apparent homogeneity, these tend to fragment and expand into elaborate recipes. To be measured, earth and rocks have to be dislodged from the continuous geological field of which they are a part; they have to be moved, rotated, and sometimes broken. In reproducing them, vantage points and degrees of fidelity are set to determine how much detail to reinscribe, and what kind. Replicating just one attribute—for instance, the casual disposition of rocks in a pile—might entail creating a block-like substitution for the rock, contriving a simulated gravity, arresting it, and then inventing details to create the appearance of accumulation in static repose. The effect of these expanded recipes is to turn measure from passive information capture into a tectonic or even organizational system. The puzzled-together fragments of a rock measured from several vantages become the projections of orthographic elevations. The molds used to transfer shape and texture reestablish orientation with the level lines of seams. Reproductions of the careless press of things in piles become openings, stairs, and furniture-scaled niches for people and things.

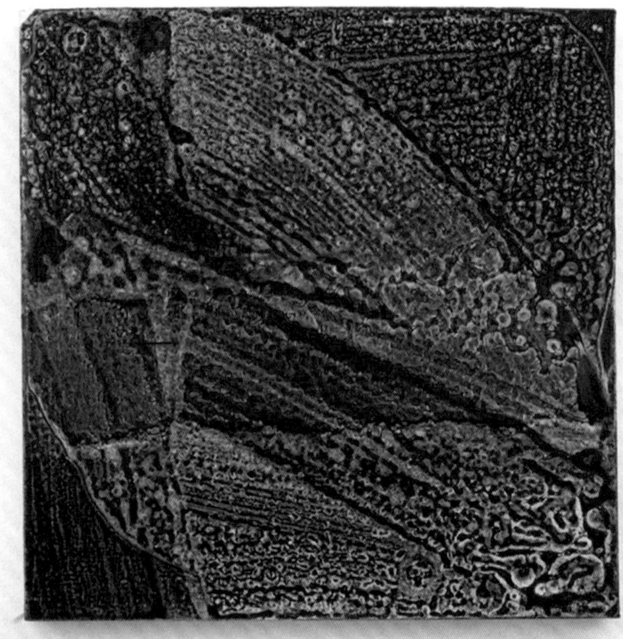

Anthony Titus Studio, Wish Well, 2012

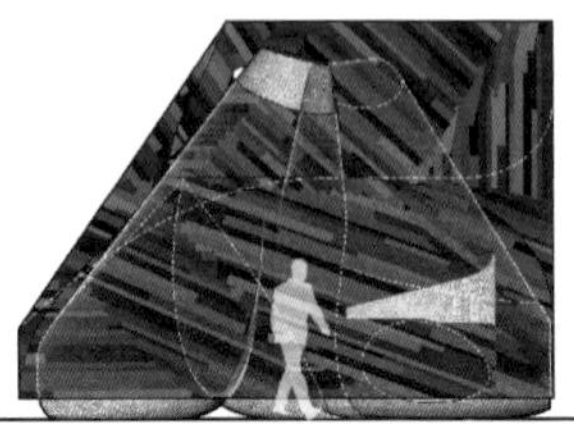

Hume Coover Studio, Black Sheep, 2015

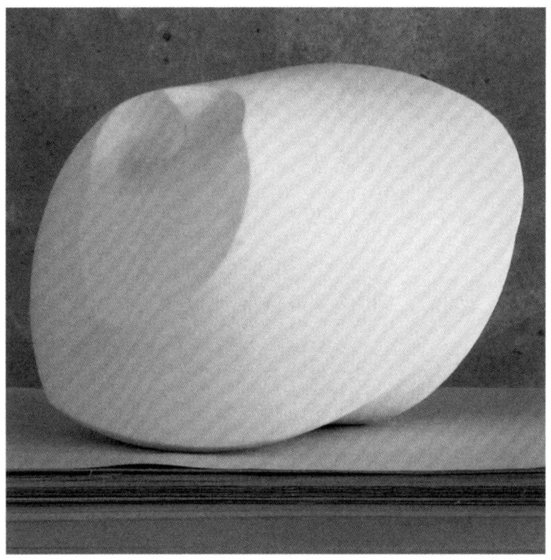

d.esk, Paperweight, 2013

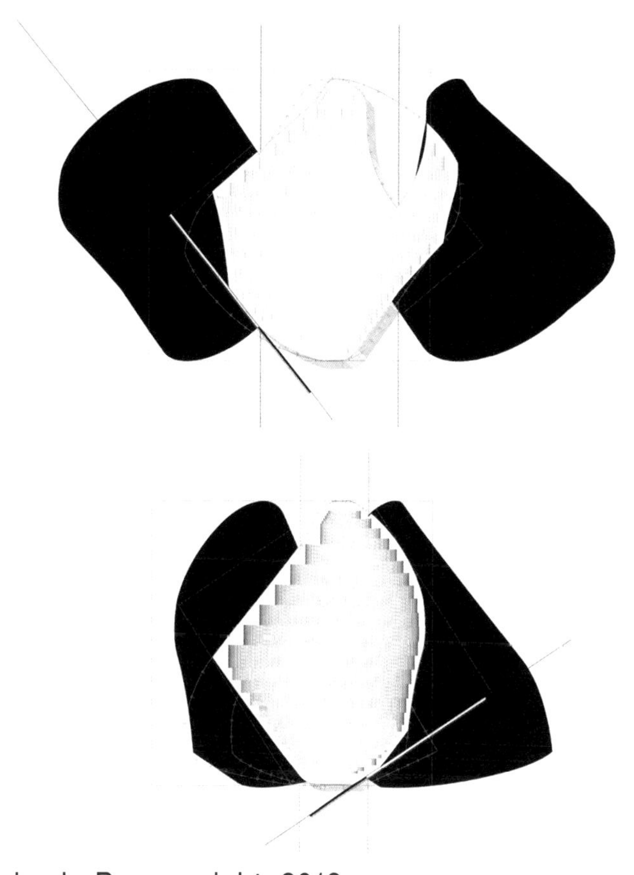

d.esk, Paperweight, 2013

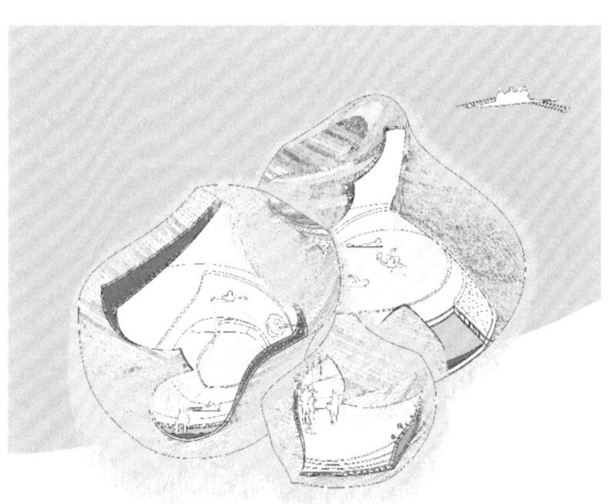

Hume Coover Studio, Down by the River, 2015

stock-a-studio, rocks on plinths, 2017

T+E+A+M, Detroit Reassembly Plant, 2016

T+E+A+M, Detroit Reassembly Plant, 2016

Mircea Eni, Don't Mind the Rock, 2017

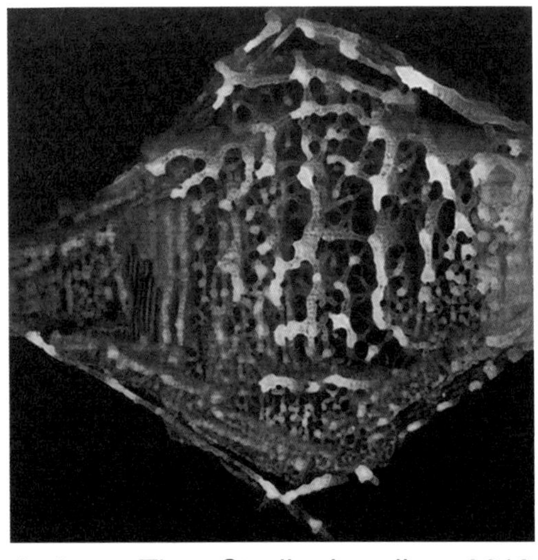

Anthony Titus Studio, Landing, 2012

Hume Coover Studio, Black Sheep, 2015

stock-a-studio, rocks on grid, 2017

T+E+A+M, Detroit Reassembly Plant, 2016

T+E+A+M, Detroit Reassembly Plant, 2016

Adam Fure, Rocks, 2014

Dirt, Earth, and Rocks

T+E+A+M, Clastic Order, 2017

Descriptive Services, Counting Bricks, 2012

Ensamble Studio, Structures of Landscape, Inverted Portal, 2016

Adam Fure, Tap, 2016

Ensamble Studio, The Truffle, 2010

MOS, Rock, in progress

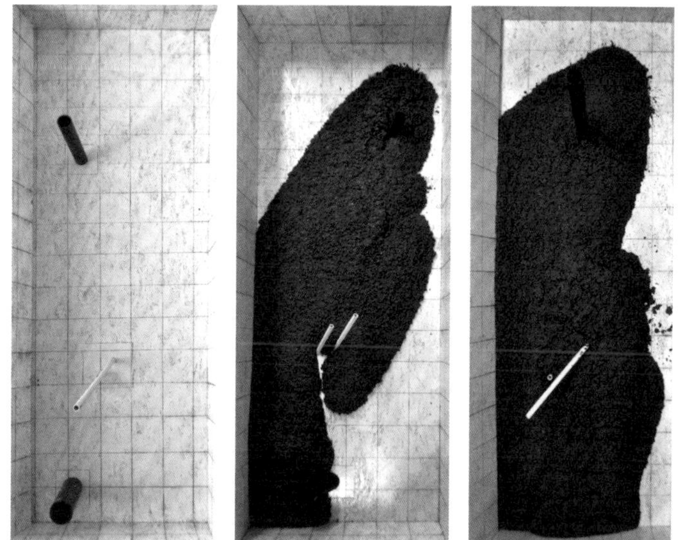

Descriptive Services, 10 Casts, 2016

Miller Moran, Post Rock, 2016

Descriptive Services, 10 Casts, 2016

Ensamble Studio, The Truffle, 2010

Adam Fure and EADO, Mirror Mirror, 2013

Ensamble Studio, Tabula Acustica, 2016

Jaffer Kolb, Form in Form, 2015

Besler & Sons, Props, in progress

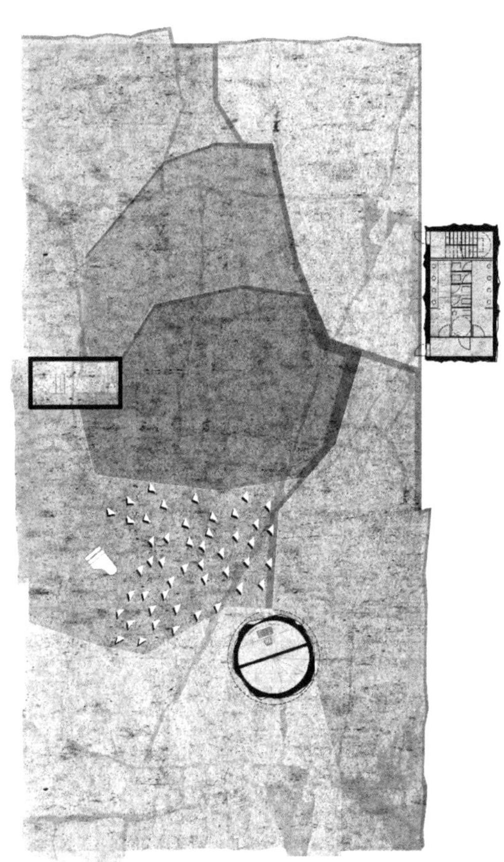
Ensamble Studio, Tabula Acustica, 2016

Alam/Profeta, Casa Zwei, 2019

MOS, Installation No. 9 (Rainbow Vomit), 2010

The Open Workshop, New Investigations in Collective Form, 2018

NEMESTUDIO, Museum of Lost Volumes, 2015

Matter Design, Walking Assembly, 2019

Design Earth, Julia: The Submerged Volcano, 2019

Trabeated Stacks

Objecthood stands against the fungibility of all things, against the idea that atoms, heat, and bacteria move freely, indifferent to name, location, or significance. Trabeated stacks mark out and maintain discreteness while allowing objects to accumulate. As a first rule of trabeation, objects are unaffected by their positionality. The forces of accumulation vanish as they pass through the surface of each body, circulating inside, unseen, and redelivered at the moment of contact with the object on the other side as if by a shock of static electricity. This indifference to position can be reinforced by variations in shape, or by undercuts at the surfaces of contact between objects that throw entire assemblies into the realm of transience and chance. Motion literalizes the separateness that shape only implies, seesawing one part atop another or else by creating the apparent risk of toppling over, with cantilevers and counterbalances that test the extreme limits of static engineering. While some notions of trabeation enforce only separateness in the realm of immanent physical properties, others work in the registers of signification and convention. Substitution—swapping out one thing for another—helps resist the systematic anonymity of bricks. Analogies sometimes underwrite these substitutions, likening buildings to other kinds of heterogeneous wholes that, like sandwiches and Neapolitan desserts, permit non sequiturs within naturally elastic categories. These discontinuities are in some instances made even more extreme by a double separation, as in the case of Water Tower by OFFICE Kersten Geers David Van Severen: building elements differentiate by doing what they are supposed to do—verticals support and horizontals span—yet are also modeled to serve some other purpose, such as storing grain or water.

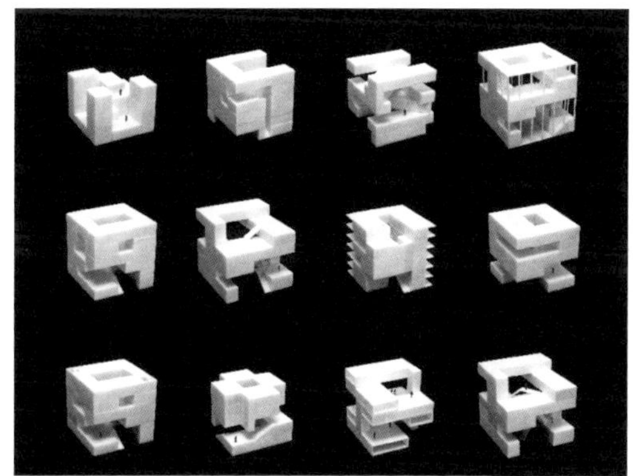

Karamuk Kuo, International Sports Sciences Institute, 2018

The Open Workshop, Varna Public Library and Archive, 2015

stock-a-studio, concrete pavers in room, 2017

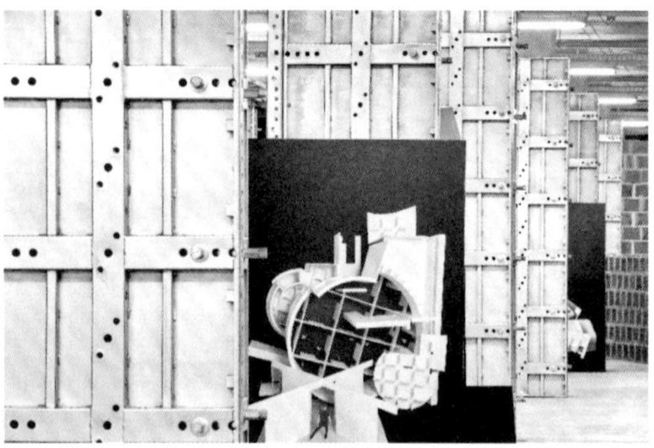

Amélia e Rodrigo, Building Stories, Garagem CCB Lisboa, 2018

Outpost Office, Color Block, 2019

Marshall Brown Projects, Ziggurat, 2016

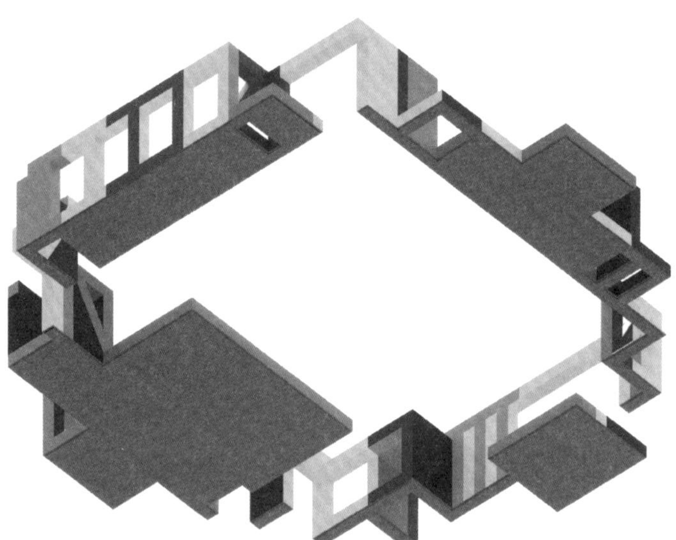

Outpost Office, Color Block, 2019

New Affiliates, Testbeds, in progress

Curtis Roth, 100% Sunshine, 2017

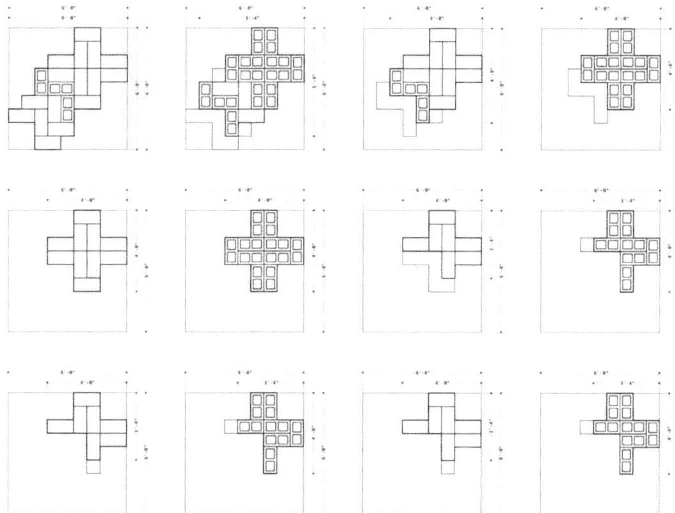
Medium Office, Sienna, Detroit, 2015

Medium Office, Sienna, Detroit (2015), and Framing Folly (2019)

Andy and Dave, Precarious Mass, 2019

Medium Office, Sienna, Detroit (2015), and Framing Folly (2019)

Marshall Brown Projects, Ziggurat, 2016

Trabeated Stacks

EXTENTS, Just Looking, 2019

Matter Design, Cannibal's Bath, 2019

OFFICE Kersten Geers David Van Severen, OFFICE 49: Water Tower, 2008

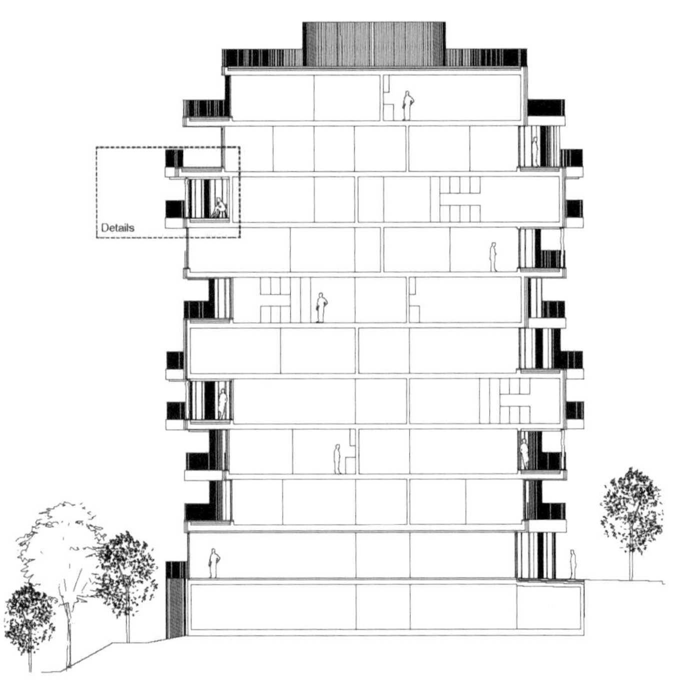

Farshid Moussavi Architecture, Folie Divine, 2017

Ensamble Studio, Hemeroscopium House, 2008

Ensamble Studio, Hemeroscopium House, 2008

Karamuk Kuo, International Sports Sciences Institute, 2018

NILE, 4 Modernist Corners, 2017

Medium Office, Frame Tower, 2016

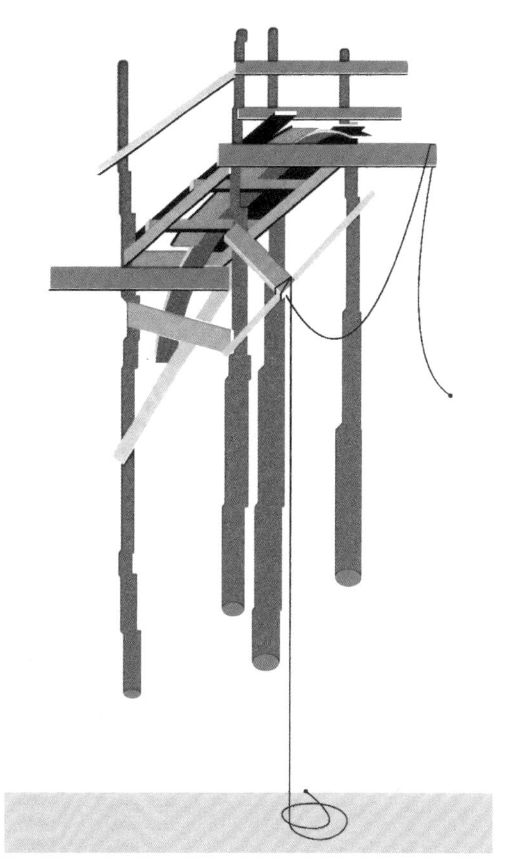

Owen Nichols, iffy architecture, 2018

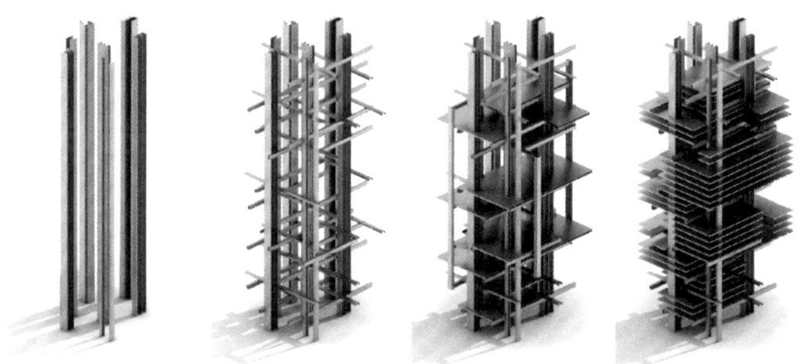

Ensamble Studio, Big Bang Towers, 2013

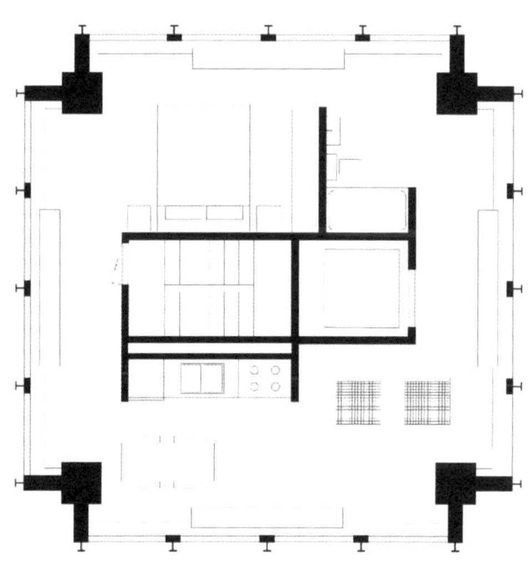

NILE, 4 Modernist Corners, 2017

Trabeated Stacks

FreelandBuck, Stack House, 2018

Ultramoderne, Escape, 2017

MALL, BLT (Bacon, Lettuce, Tomato); Best Sandwiches, 2016

Farzin Farzin, Consuming Cute™, the Taj, 2015

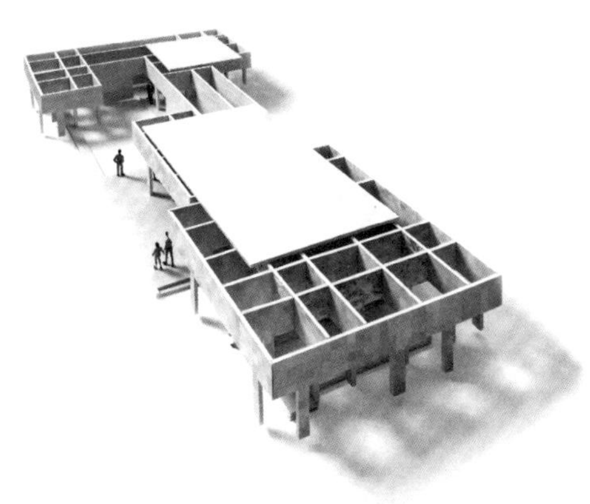

Ultramoderne, Chicago Horizon, 2015

Medium Office, Misreading Barcelona, 2017

LAMAS, Over Cast, 2015

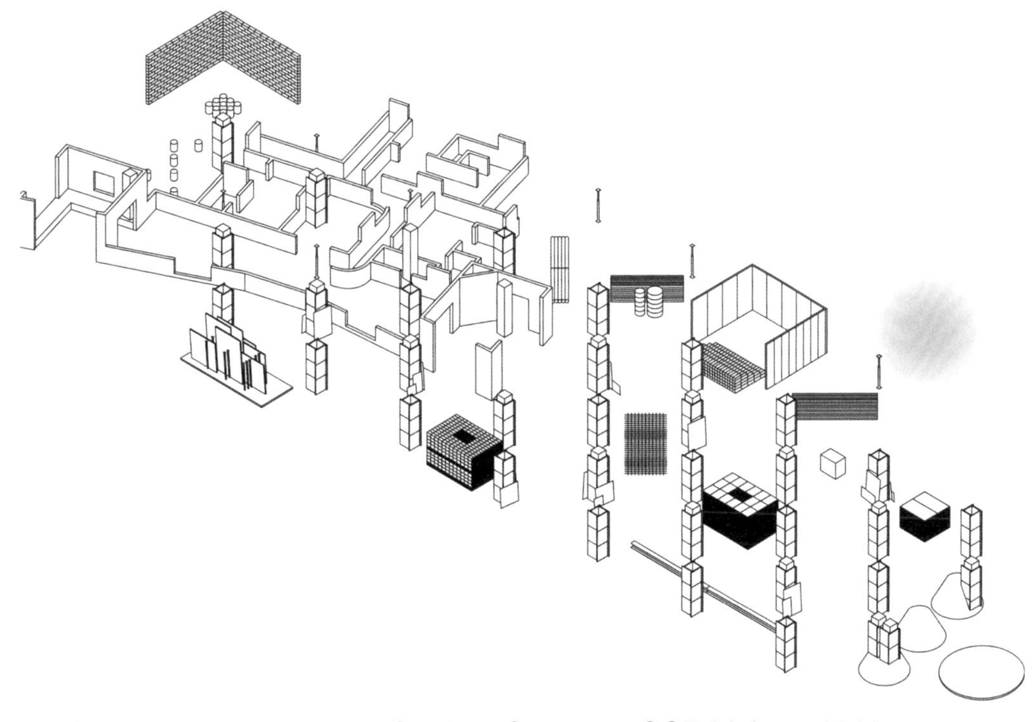

Amélia e Rodrigo, Building Stories, Garagem CCB Lisboa, 2018

Karamuk Kuo, Campus-Ruetli Sports Hall, 2009

Johnston Marklee, 1787, Shenzhen and Hong Kong Bi-City Biennale 2011, 2011

Ultramoderne, Framework, 2018

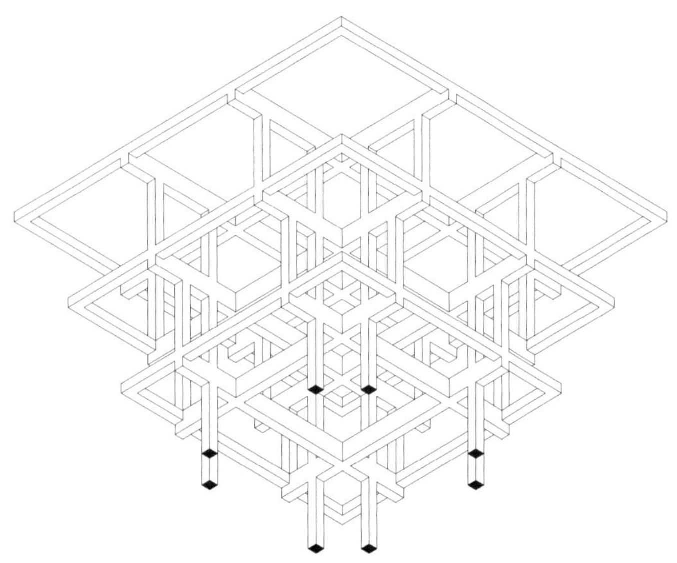

Pezo von Ellrichshausen, Nida House, 2016

Pezo von Ellrichshausen, Nida House, 2016

Alex Maymind, Proposal for a Vertical Office Block, 2012

Paul Preissner Architects, Ring of Hope, 2017–

Karamuk Kuo, International Sports Sciences Institute, 2018

Paul Preissner Architects, Tripoli Special Economic Zone, 2019

Only If, Narrow House, 2020

Christ & Gantenbein, Zurich University Hospital USZ, 2019–

MOS, Mixed Use No. 3 (Housing and Art Foundation), 2014

Ensamble Studio, Musical Studies Centre, 2002

If the Enlightenment idea of the primitive hut loosed fantasies of the first shelter into the architectural imagination, it did so within a rigorous and confining logic of correspondence. Whatever cave, tent, or lean-to the mind might invent as humankind's original architecture had to be plausible as a past that would naturally evolve toward the present. This relation was frequently maintained by a conservation of elements, such that columns stayed columns and roofs roofs, even as materials and construction techniques changed. Contemporary first houses begin instead with plurality. The problem of finding a minimum condition for shelter at maximum economy is transformed into that of deriving the minimum condition for shelter from any given material or logic of assembly—how, basically, to wrangle the universe of available stuff around an empty place where someone could hang out. Reframing the problem in this way entails a shift from mimesis to inscription and from trope to performance. It also entails a problem of selection—where to begin, and with what—that has, in response, prompted everything from monomaniacal experiments in single materials to collections with vague rubrics like "kinds of cheap cladding." No matter the initiating conditions, the economy to which first houses must conform is a theater of self-evidence. Constructions must show obvious, almost inevitable logics of assembly. Or to put it more abstractly, the process of coming into being must be arrested as potential energy and made visible in the jittery misalignment of foam blocks around a hollow or in the lean of found fragments into an A-frame. Architecture's elements become plastic when subordinated to this pressure of arrangement, transgressing basic categories of performance, use, and even naming. Blankets become roofs, roof waterproofing becomes walls, purely digital simulations of paper become tents. The resulting houses invite counterfactual histories of the material traditions that produced them. D.esk's stripey lean-to could belong to the deposition logics of a 3D printer or the colorways produced by a loom. What would Gottfried Semper say? Are the origins of the contemporary tent to be found in the rendered surfaces of a digital obsessive?

T+E+A+M, A Range Life, 2017

Current Interests, Silver House Studio, in progress

Adam Fure, The Force of Things, 2016

Medium Office, Silverlake Pool House, 2017

T+E+A+M, A Range Life, 2017

Norman Kelley, Lincoln Log Cabin, 2014

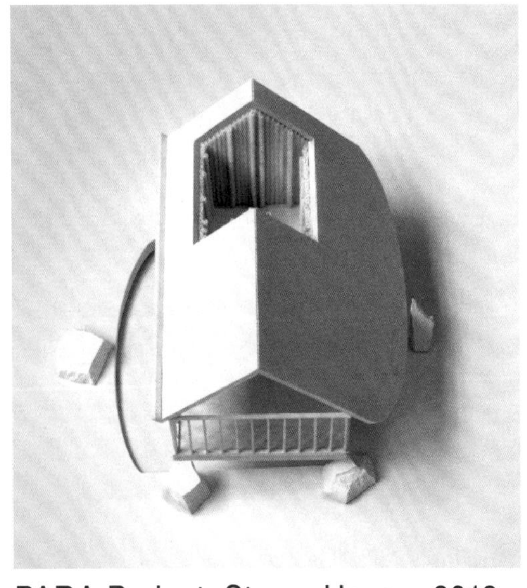
PARA Project, Stump House, 2019–

T+E+A+M, A Range Life, 2017

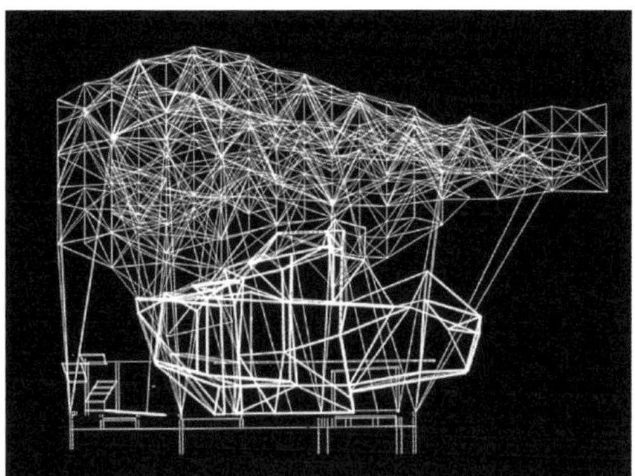
Mack Scogin Merrill Elam Architects, The Atlanta Pavilion, 2005

Studio Anna Heringer, Three Bamboo Hostels, 2016

Toshiko Mori Architect, Thread Artists' Residency and Cultural Center, 2015

Miller Moran, Fort Blanket, 2015

Karamuk Kuo, House on a Slope (Apartments), 2020

The LADG, The Kid Gets out of the Picture, 2016

NILE, The Other House, 2019

MOS, Installation No. 8 (Pile), 2009

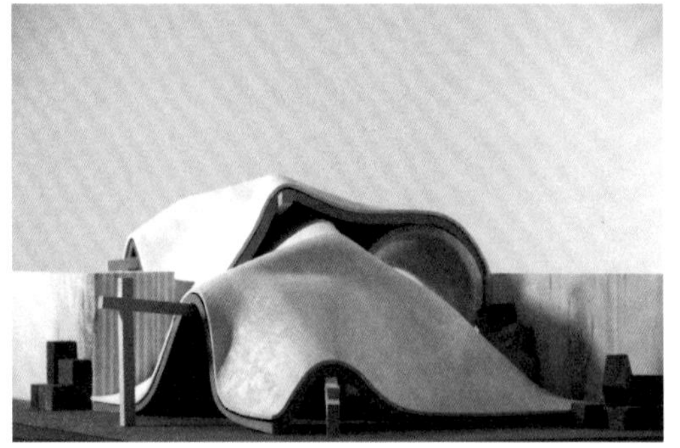

The LADG, The Kid Gets out of the Picture, 2016

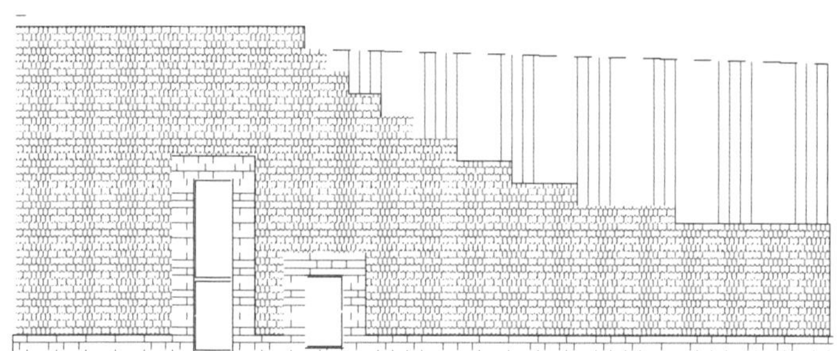

Independent Architecture, Emerald Workshops, 2020

d.esk, Column & Canopy, 2016

First Office, City Render, 2017

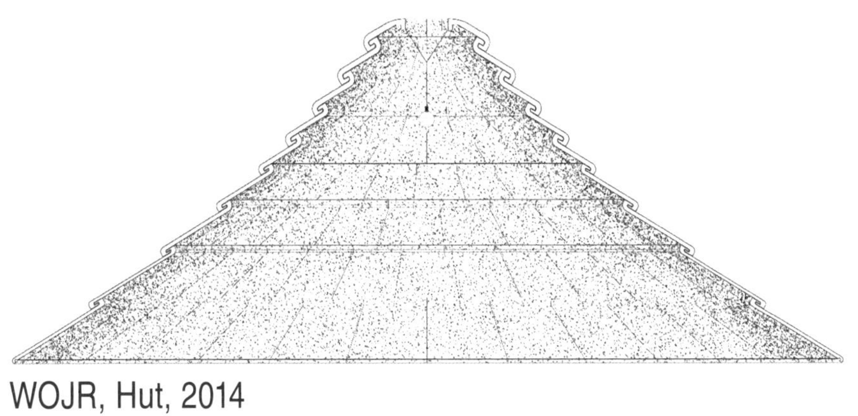
WOJR, Hut, 2014

Besler & Sons, Storage Ensemble, 2016

d.esk, Colossal Paper, 2019

Toshiko Mori Architect, Thread Artists' Residency and Cultural Center, 2015

NEMESTUDIO, Our Junk, Their Ruin, 2018

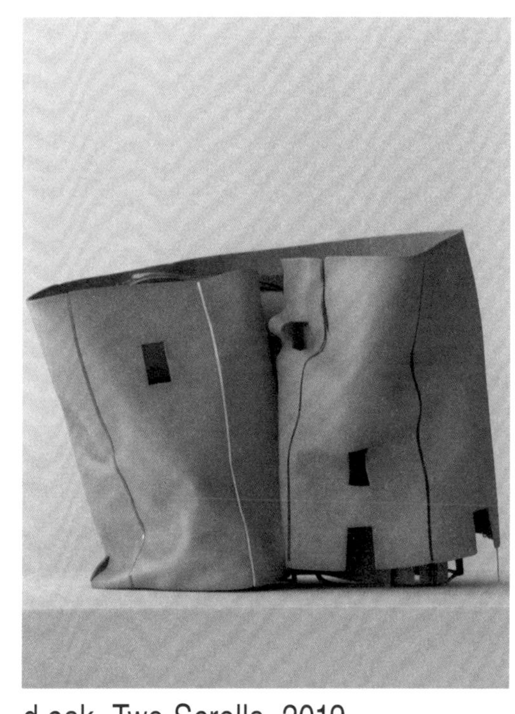
d.esk, Two Scrolls, 2019

JaJa Co, Studio-Gallery, in progress

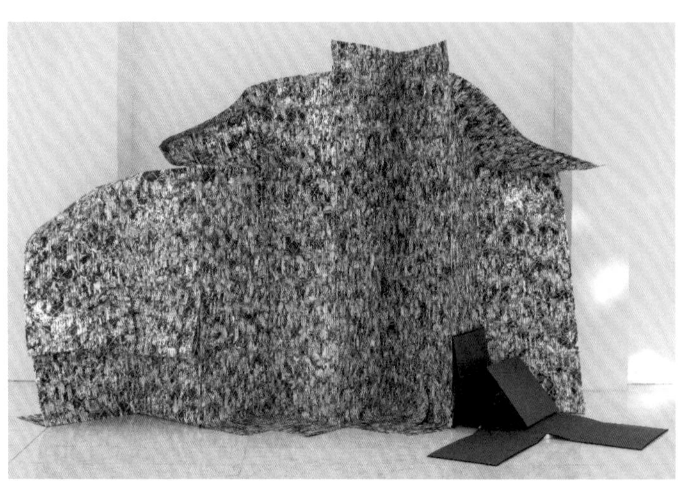
Current Interests, Hedges of the World: Folio Edition, 2018

MOS, Currently Untitled, in progress

NEMESTUDIO, Manual of Instructions, 2019

PRODUCTORA, Housing Prototype in Apan, 2019

First Office, Studio for Art, 2017

First Office, Rude forms among us, 2020

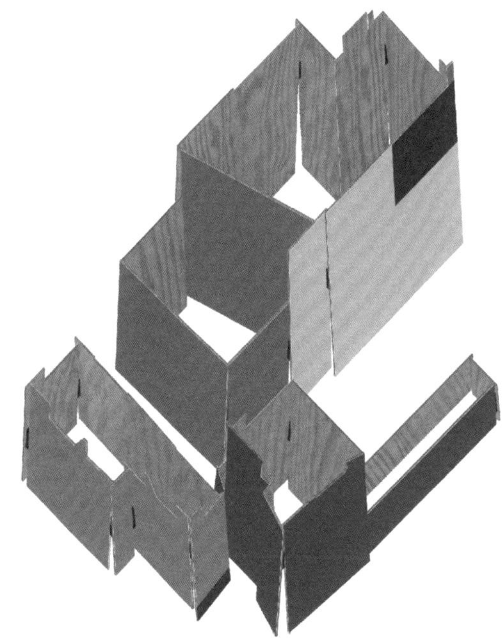

First Office, Blocks of blabla, 2016

Husos Architects, MULTISPECIES REFUGE, and Responsible Microlandscaping Actions with Hummingbirds as Trojan Horses and Other Allies, 2013

First Office, PS1 Dolmen, 2016

First Office, PS1 Dolmen, 2016

MoDusArchitects, Mountain Lodge, Ponte di Ghiaccio, 2017

Seven Wonders

Whether we are speaking of height, mass, material, shape, or subject, absolutes don't make marvels. It is rather the mark of exertion set to an audacious task that provokes wonderment. *They did what with what?* The impulse for ziggurats, towers, pyramids, and monumental stairs in stock dimensional lumber pitches material poverty against a strenuous choreography of the job site. All those sticks hammered by all those hands! As the anonymous author of the *Biblical Antiquities* wrote, "The onlooker, transfixed in admiration" of the Colossus at Rhodes, "can only doubt that such vast masses of bronze could have been melted down and cast, wonder by what clamps they have been held, to what kind of blows they have been subjected, and what strenuous exertions have brought them into being." The visible, public evidence of the task accomplished stands apart, not quite pure shape and not entirely plausible as a building. The evident concentration of expended effort detaches the object from its surroundings: a pile or stack perhaps made of mere ground becomes distinctive by dint of the index of exertion. Effort becomes the terrain where program plays out, and this is audacity too. Wonders defy most systems of judgment, for they can be bad and still succeed. We forgive the results for the pleasure of thinking back on the collective task and bending ourselves to its products. Ramps and stairs may stretch to monumental lengths, windows may reach to absurd heights along the kitchen wall, and a forest of timber joints may become a children's playground, all so long as the disturbance of our contact with these constructions is attended by the thrill of beholding the results of collective enterprise.

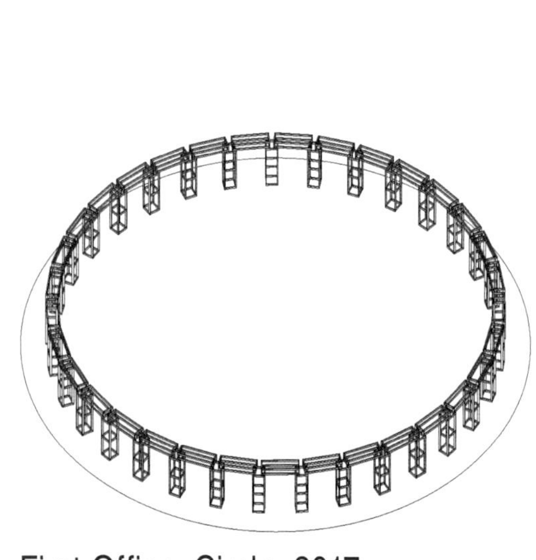

First Office, Circle, 2017

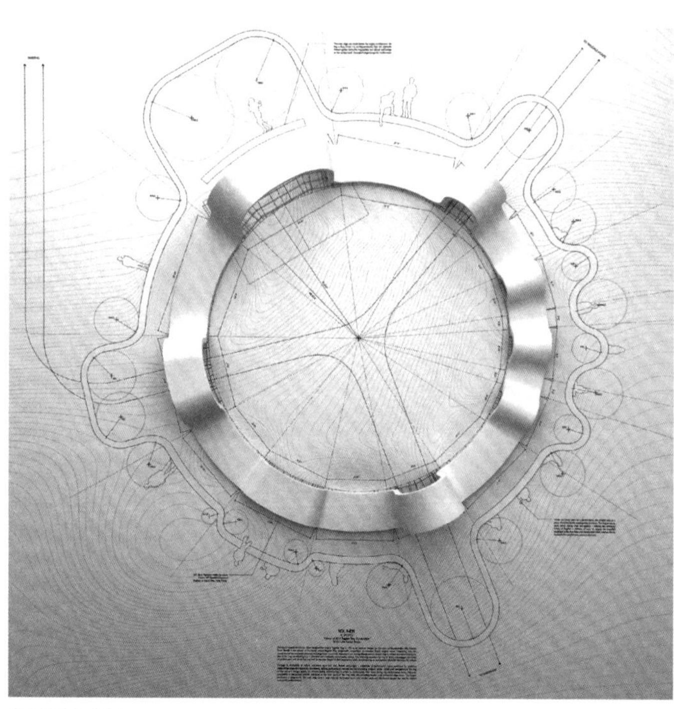

SPORTS, Rounds, 2016

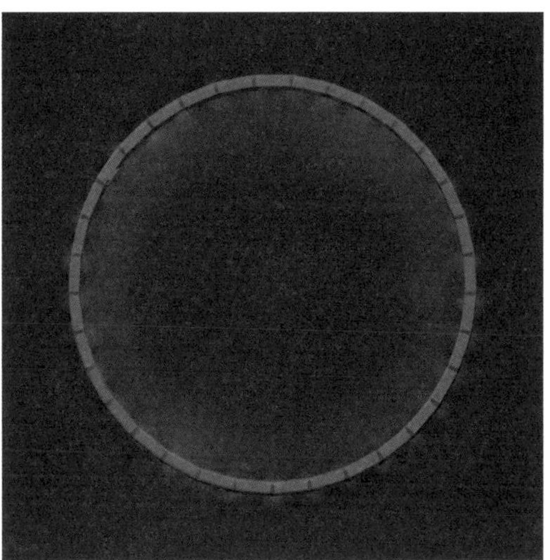

First Office, Circle, 2017

The Open Workshop, Depth of Field House, 2017–

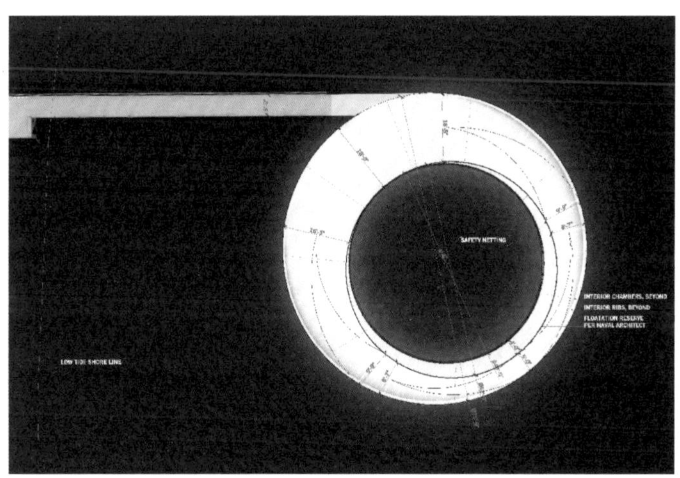

Höweler + Yoon, Float Lab, 2021

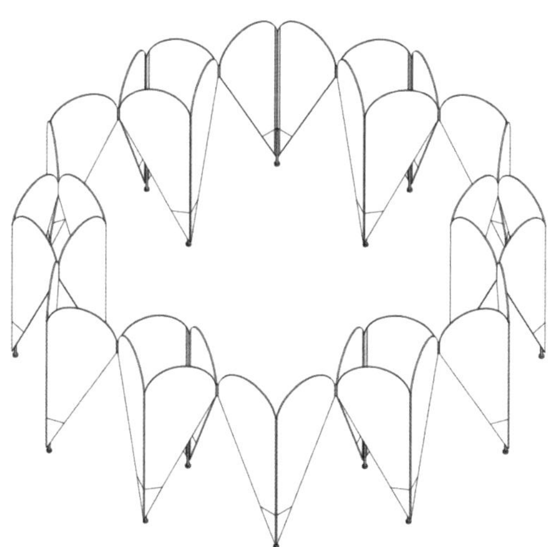

Collective-LOK, Heart of Hearts, 2016

Höweler + Yoon, UVA Memorial to Enslaved Laborers, 2020

Design Earth, Of Oil and Ice, 2017

T+E+A+M, Detroit Reassembly Plant, 2016

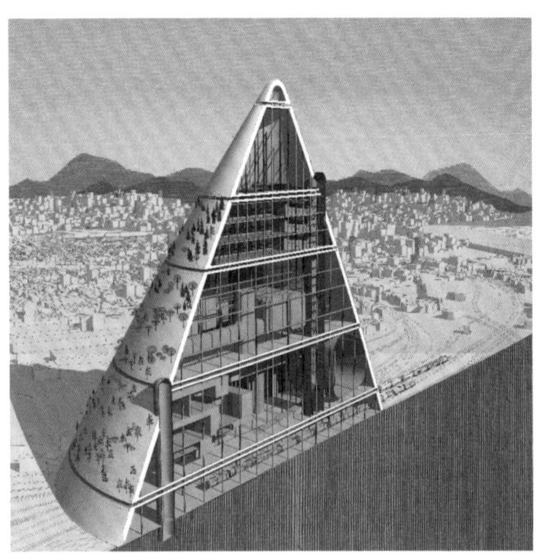
Design Earth, Trash Peaks, 2017

Studio Anna Heringer, METI School, 2006

NEMESTUDIO, Museum of Lost Volumes, 2015

Jesús Vassallo, Aalto's Ghost, 2015

Paul Preissner Architects, Port of Kinmen Passenger Ferry Terminal, 2014

Medium Office, Stack Villa 4, 2019

The Open Workshop, Scaffoldia, 2016

Thom Moran, Tables and Chairs, 2010

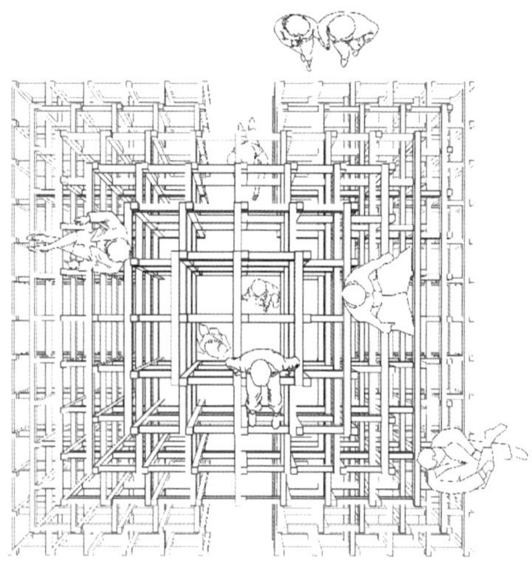

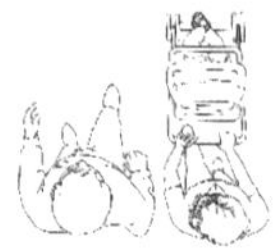

The Open Workshop, Scaffoldia, 2016

PARA Project, Roche Dinkeloo Double, 2018

PRODUCTORA, Teopanzolco Cultural Center, 2017

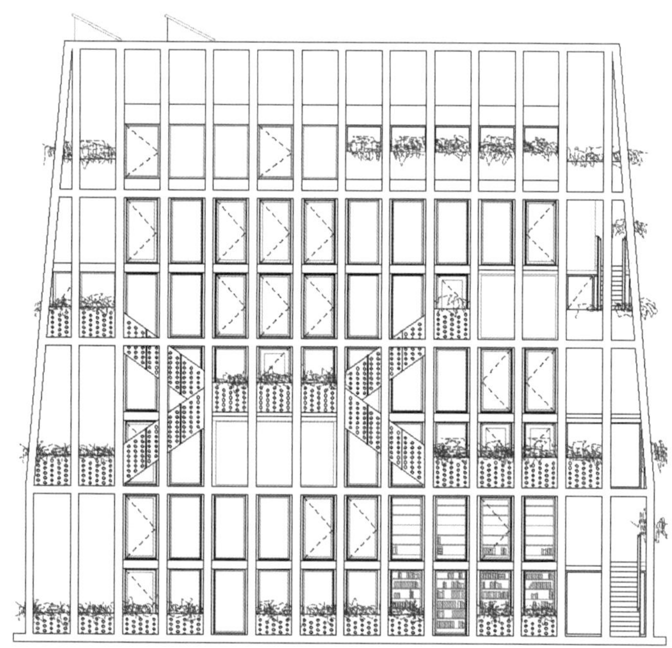

MOS, Community Center No. 3 (Lali Gurans Orphanage), in progress

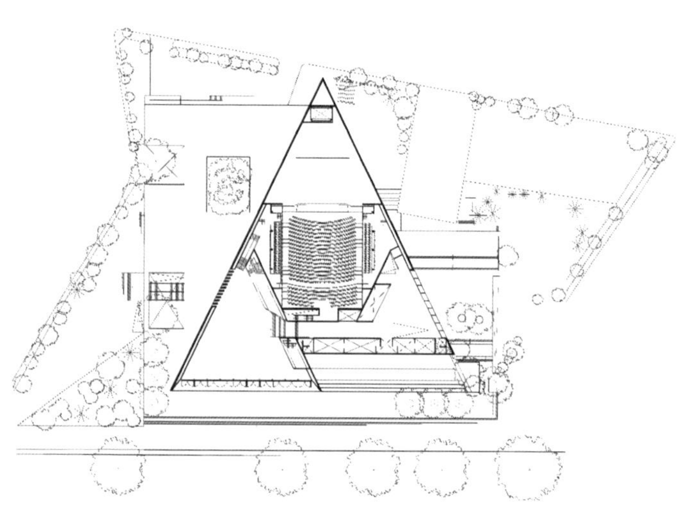

PRODUCTORA, Teopanzolco Cultural Center, 2017

LAMAS, Film to Wit, 2012

BairBalliet, Low Volumes, 2017

PRODUCTORA, Teopanzolco Cultural Center, 2017

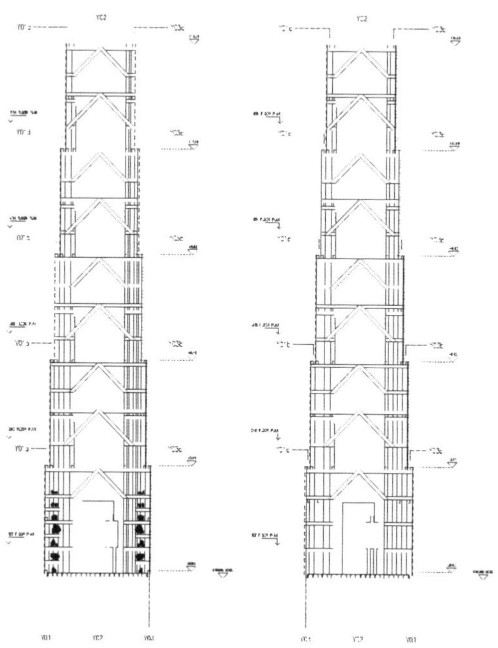
Pezo von Ellrichshausen, Mine Pavilion, 2014

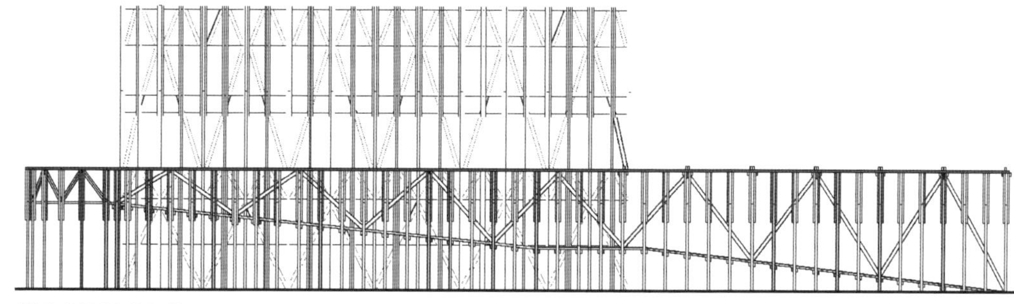
PRODUCTORA, Pavilion on the Zocalo, 2014

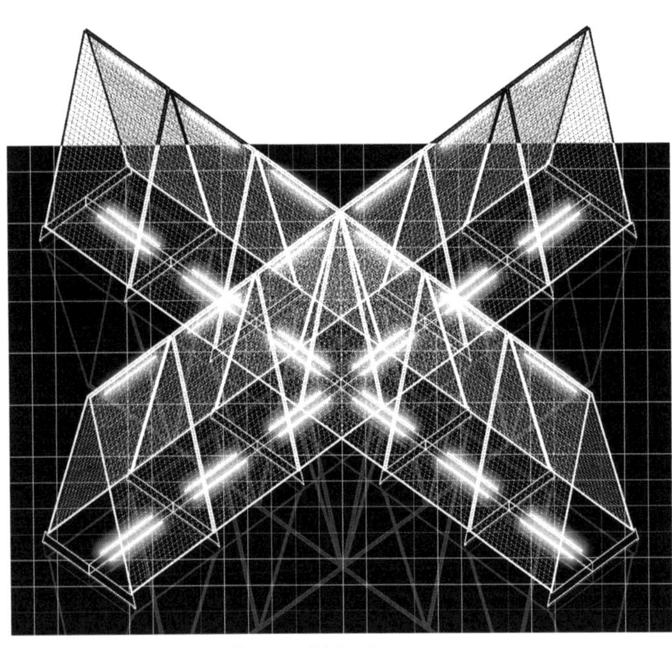

Outpost Office, Open/Work, 2019

Pezo von Ellrichshausen, Crux Pavilion, 2013

Kyle Miller, Other Ways to Make an Entrance, 2019

Pezo von Ellrichshausen, Crux Pavilion, 2013

EXTENTS, The Thrill of the Threshold, or Circle, Jerk, 2018

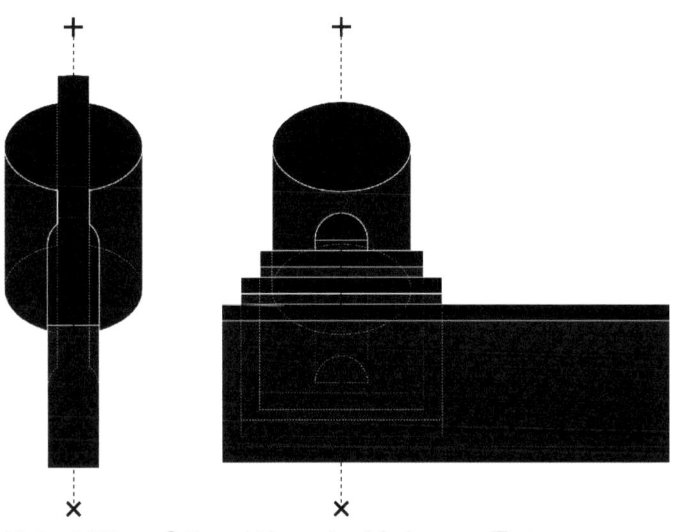

Kyle Miller, Other Ways to Make an Entrance, 2019

Tom de Paor, 4am, 2010

Pezo von Ellrichshausen, Crux Pavilion, 2013

PRODUCTORA, Pavilion on the Zocalo, 2014

The Open Workshop, Garden of New Worlds, 2017–

Christoph a. Kumpusch, Temple, 2017

Pezo von Ellrichshausen, Guna House, 2015

PARA Project, Roche Dinkeloo Double, 2018

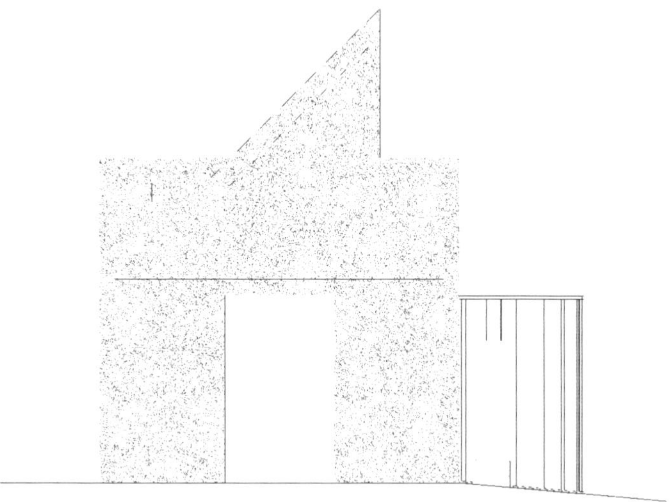

PARA Project, Roche Dinkeloo Double, 2018

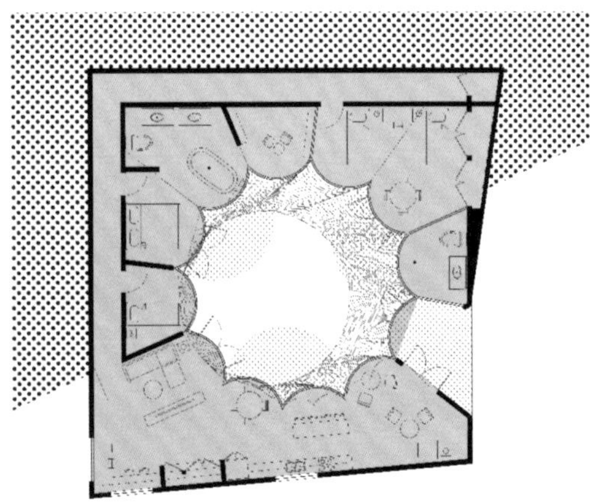

Central Standard Office of Design, Pyramid Scheme House, 2015

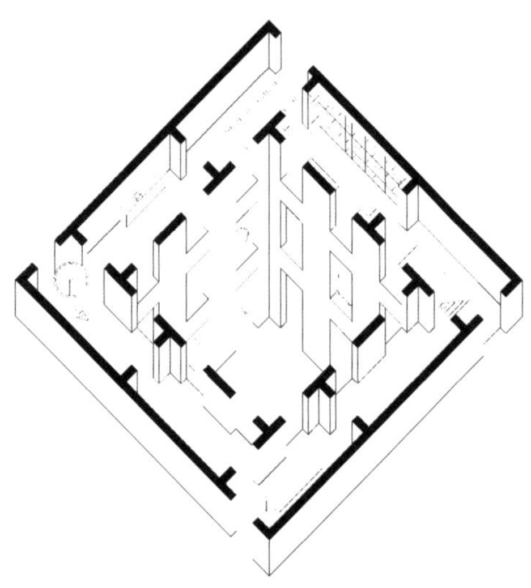

OFFICE Kersten Geers David Van Severen, OFFICE 51: 25 Rooms, 2009

Ultramoderne, Recess PS1, 2016

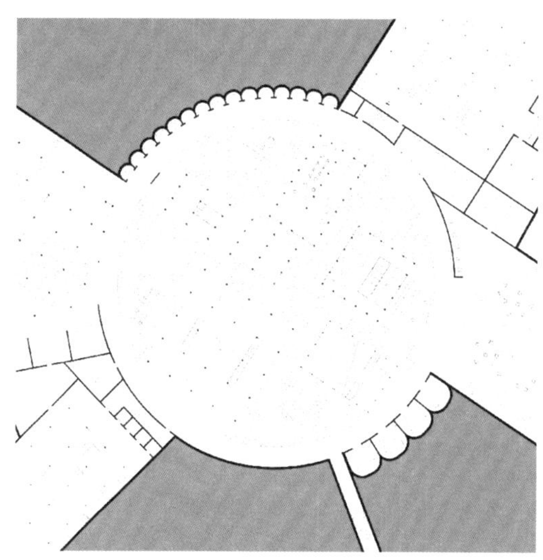

PRODUCTORA, Aalto University Campus, 2012

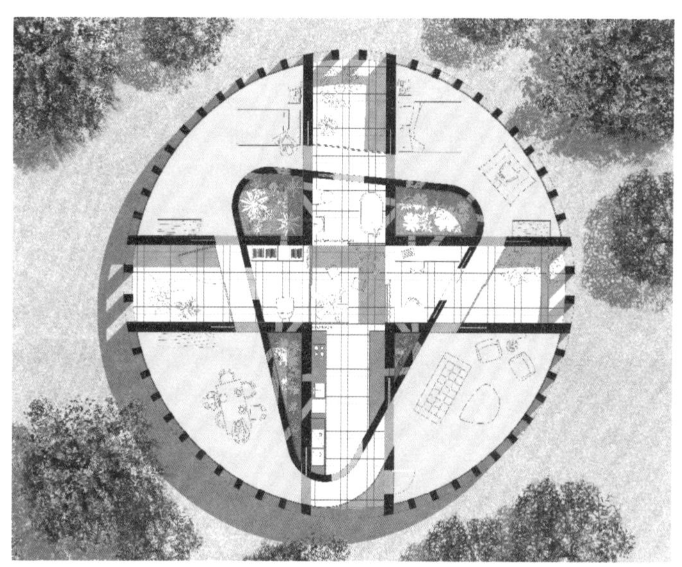

The Open Workshop, Depth of Field House, 2017–

OFFICE Kersten Geers David Van Severen, OFFICE 184: Radio & Television (VRT), 2015

Owen Nichols, John Yurchyk, Mark Acciari, A Garden Theater, 2019

T+E+A+M, Detroit Reassembly Plant, 2016

Medium Office, New New Whitney, 2016

Central Standard Office of Design,
Pyramid Scheme House, 2015

d.esk, Ziggurhut, 2018

Monoliths

Some buildings are designed expressly to stand. This posture, concealing itself in humble structural necessity (everything's gotta stand up, right?), dominates relations to ground, site, and ecology, so that any question of exchange between architecture and the world outside comes down to the distance enforced by its standing apart or atop. From a strictly materialist point of view, structures that stand on the landscape as objects apart—towers, columns, and triumphal solids—fascinate because the discreteness of this standing belies their continuity with forces beyond the visual field. It produces something like the figure of prosopopoeia, not as lyricism but as technique, giving architectural voice to what is fundamentally just "fact." Monoliths are the visible expression of vast machineries of real estate speculation, data circulation, and utility networks. Likewise, the sealed wholeness of these buildings—their indivisibility, their subordination of part to giant, their unitary surfaces wrapped around vacant interiors—is enabled by hidden circulations. While the possibility of a secret life lived inside the hollowness of a Robert Morris sculpture was merely Michael Fried's paranoid suspicion, monoliths literalize this fantasy. Standing alongside them is to find oneself distanced by their standing and to be set, even captured, by something like another being in a situation that unfolds over time. If monoliths are not alive, then they generate life-effects.

WOJR, Church, 2014

Alex Lehnerer, The Second Sun, 2010

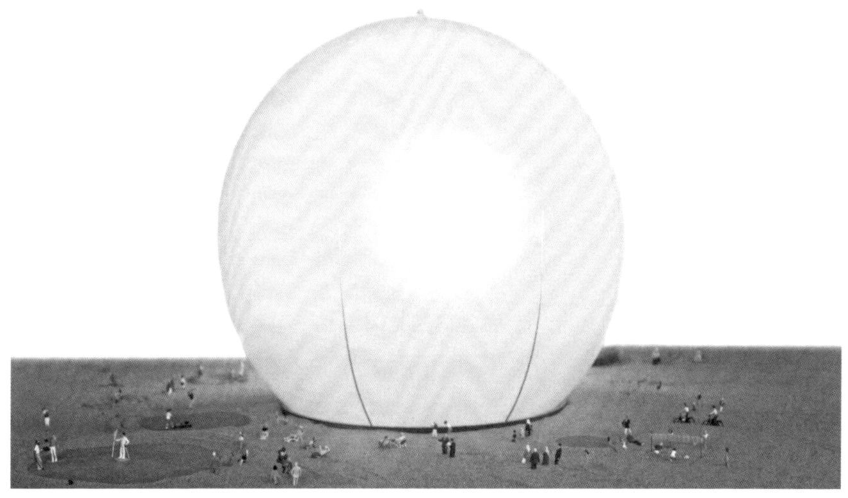

Alex Lehnerer, The Second Sun, 2010

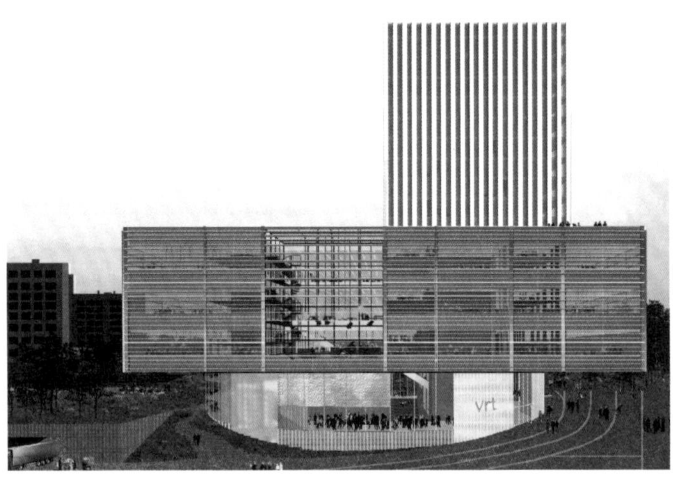

OFFICE Kersten Geers David Van Severen, OFFICE 184: Radio & Television (VRT), 2015

PRODUCTORA, Aalto University Campus, 2012

OFFICE Kersten Geers David Van Severen, OFFICE 162: New NCCA, 2014

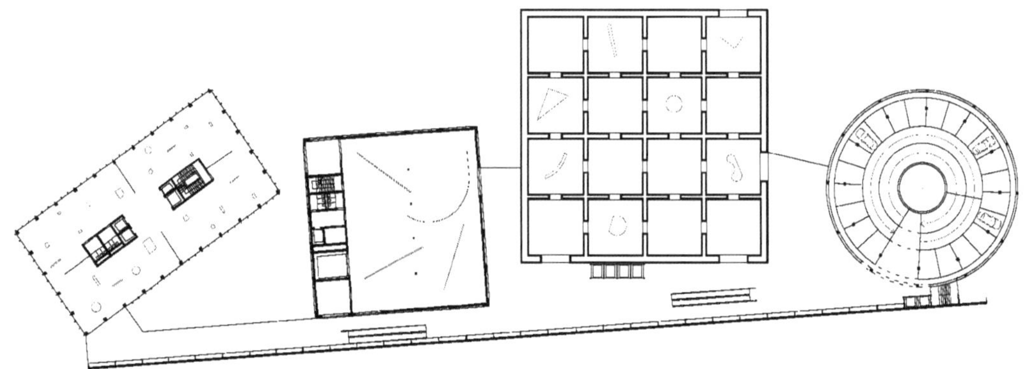
OFFICE Kersten Geers David Van Severen, OFFICE 162: New NCCA, 2014

Farshid Moussavi Architecture, Folie Divine, 2017

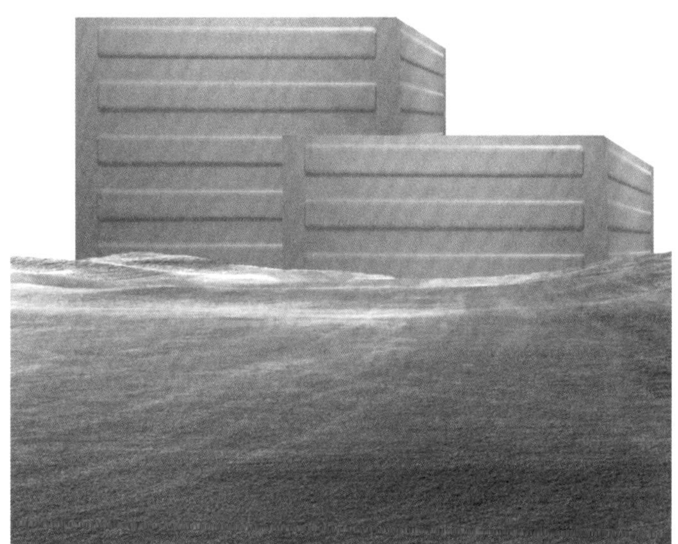

stock-a-studio, xs to xl, 2017

Ultramoderne, Southside Cultural Center, in progress

Ultramoderne, Southlight, 2016

Amélia e Rodrigo, Building Stories, Garagem CCB Lisboa, 2018

Central Standard Office of Design, The Cat that Ate the Canary, 2015

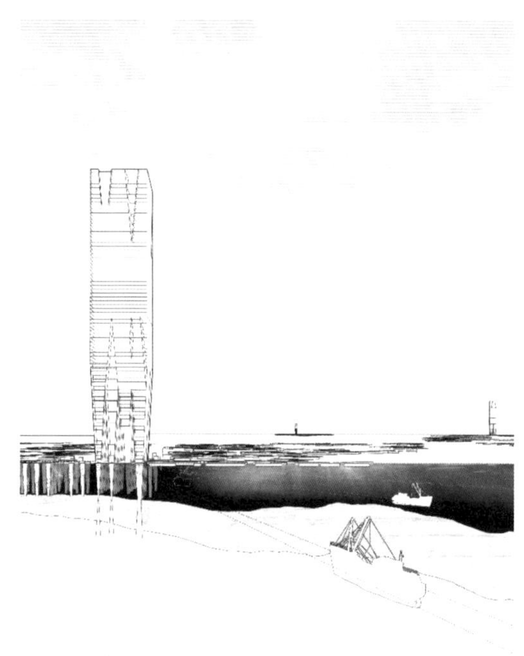

SCHAUM/SHIEH, Slider Tower, 2012

Endemic Architecture, San Francisco Music Hall, 2018

Christ & Gantenbein, Maniera 12–Athens Series, 2017

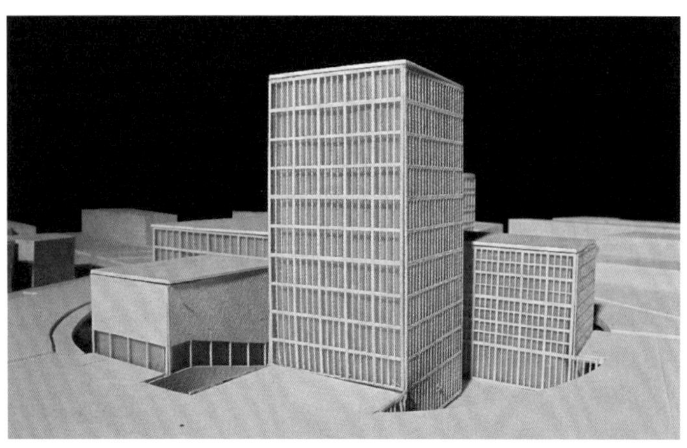

PRODUCTORA, Aalto University Campus, 2012

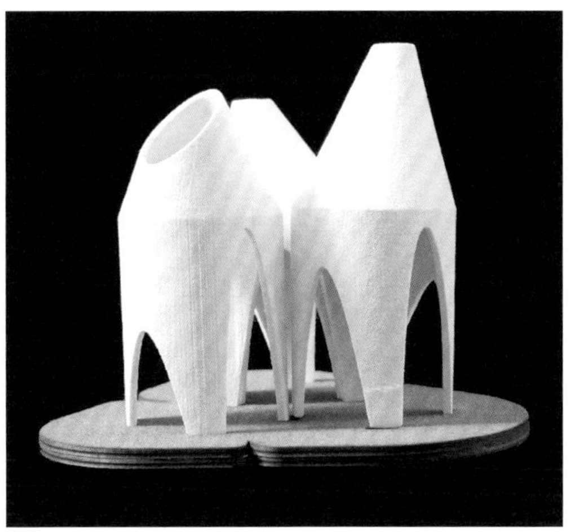

Endemic Architecture, Three-One Rooms, 2016

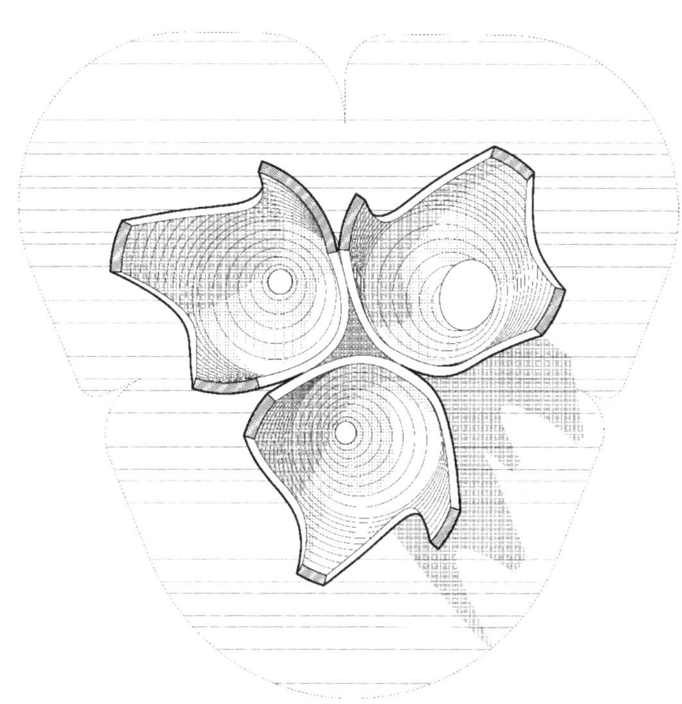

Endemic Architecture, Three-One Rooms, 2016

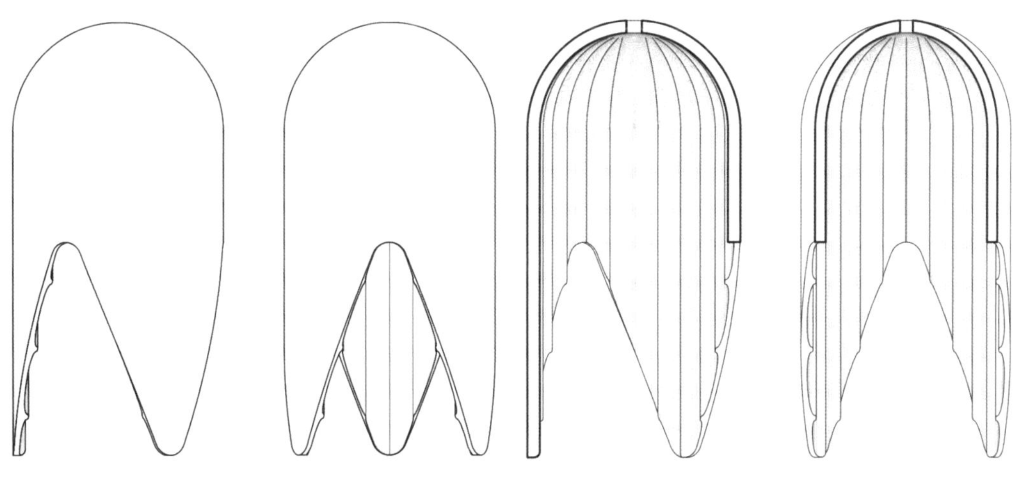

WOJR, Ghosts, 2012

Ensamble Studio, Towers of Landscape, 2017

Jesús Vassallo, Water Towers, 2017

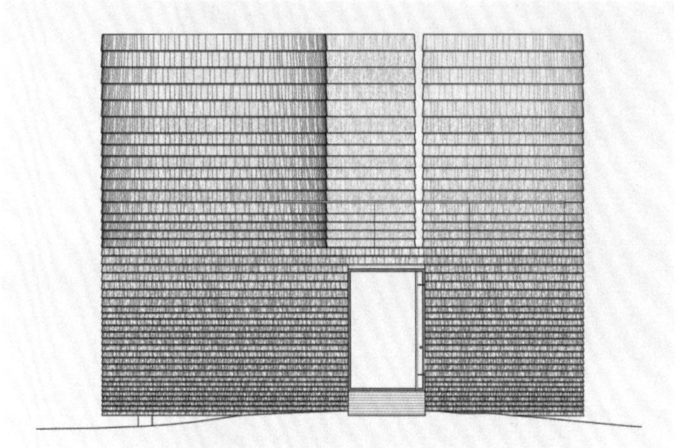
CO-G, Plum Island House, 2017

Jesús Vassallo, Water Towers, 2017

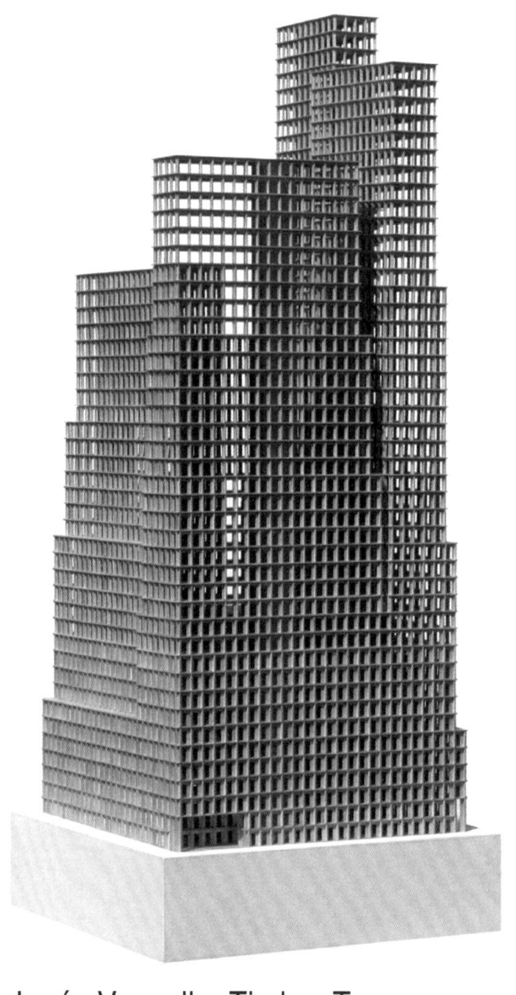
Jesús Vassallo, Timber Towers, 2015

Anamorphic Figures

When Paul de Man speaks of the "uncontrollable power of the letter as inscription," he uses *letter* in the Lacanian sense of a socially inscribed mark, the same sense in which we here use the term *figure*. Letter as figure and figure as letter open onto the material base and disruptive deferring function of inscription. For the letter derives from the dismemberment of language (from sentence to word and finally to letter), and the figure from a progressive disarticulation of architecture to a metonymy of glyphs. The repetition of figures and figural parts then produces a kind of visual assonance of images emptied of meaning. As for *anamorphosis*, we use the term here to designate the tendency of the projects in this category to fold their parts (mostly volumes and skins) into configurations that produce a doubled or oblique vision. Anamorphosis reframes a reality we thought we already knew (modernist architectural composition, for example), forcing us to see it again, to look at it awry. Finally, while the encounter with the anamorphic figure does bend vision, it can also be perceived as quite prosaic and flat. This is due to the blunt facticity of the figure, different from the signifier. Whereas the signifier derives support from the symbolic Other to authorize its signification, the anamorphic figure is self-referential and self-identical, without reference to an Other, and thereby reduces any meaning effects to a gesture. What is more, it does not have the thingy corporeality of the creaturely (though the colors of flesh are oddly popular in this category). In the encounter, the creaturely sees you; the anamorphic figure does not look back. To read these projects as anamorphosis is to see the way in which they present, alternately and simultaneously, an objective self-reflexivity so intense as not only to achieve a state Michael Fried calls "absorptive"—one in which the object is engrossed in a set of figural logics disengaged from its presentation to an audience—but also to withdraw into a stylized but banal signifier-in-isolation whose signification is utterly blank.

Matter Design, Walking Assembly, 2019

Design with Company, A Zinery and Ziggurats, 2013

Paul Preissner Architects, Five Rooms, 2017

Design with Company, Character Buildings (Deskasaur), 2012

Outpost Office, Twins, 2019

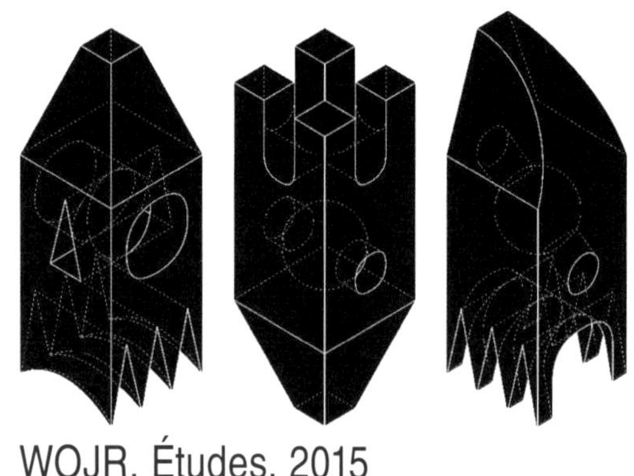

WOJR, Études, 2015

NEMESTUDIO, New Cadavre Exquis, 2017

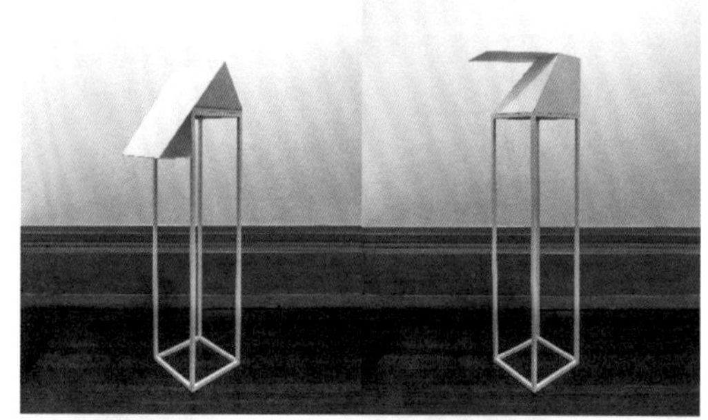

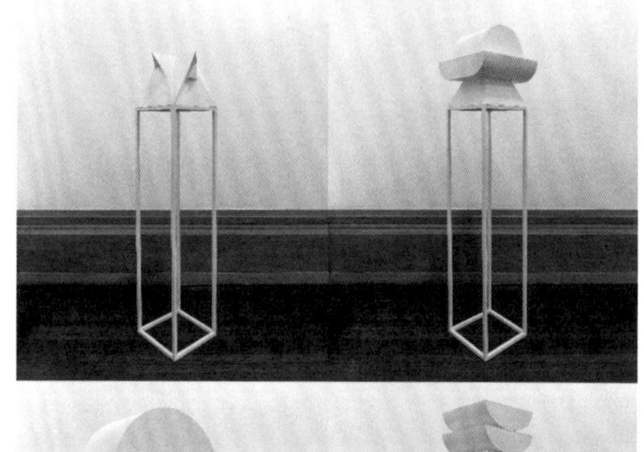

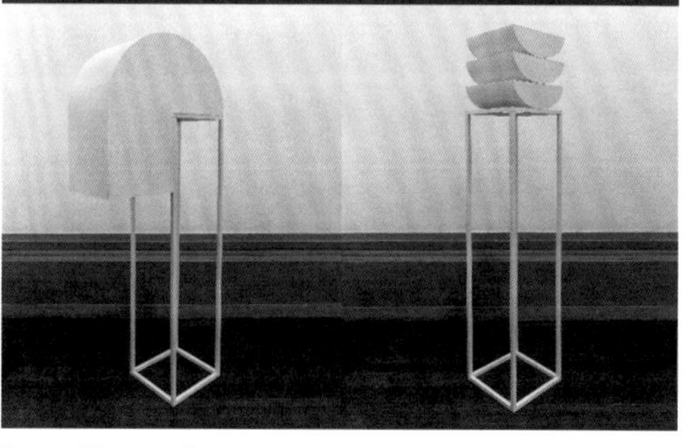

is-office, Crowns, 2015

MAIO, 110 Rooms, 2016

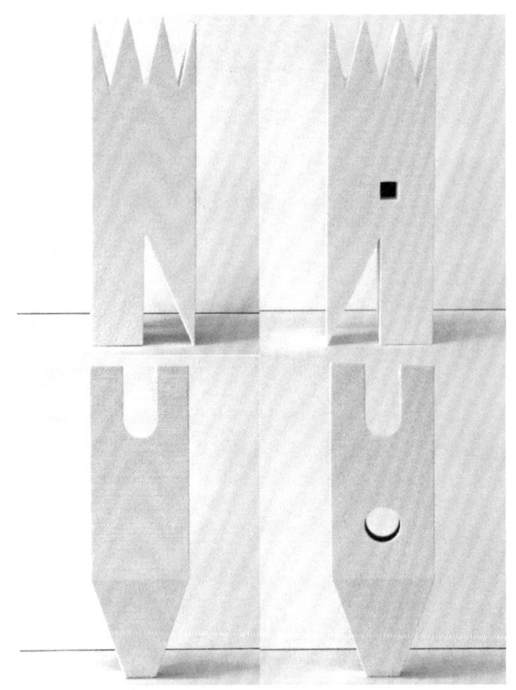

WOJR, Études, 2015

Current Interests, Eave House, 2016

First Office, Circle, 2017

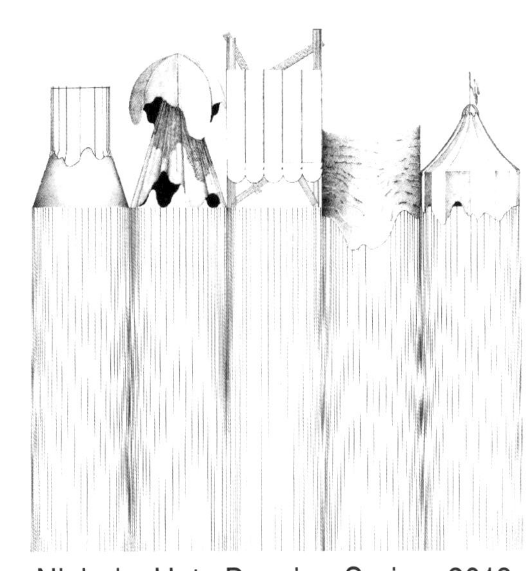

Owen Nichols, Hats Drawing Series, 2019

Anamorphic Figures

BairBalliet, Loud Lines, 2018

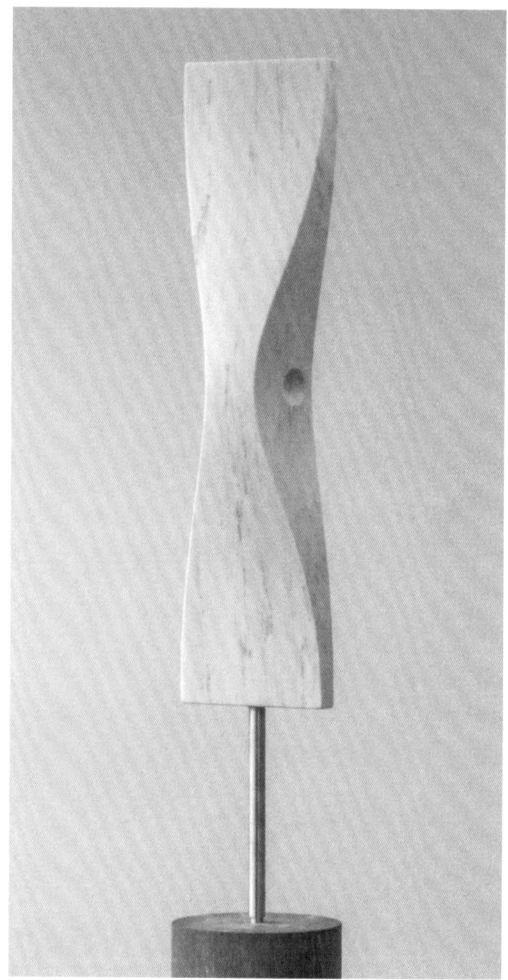

WOJR, Other Masks, 2017

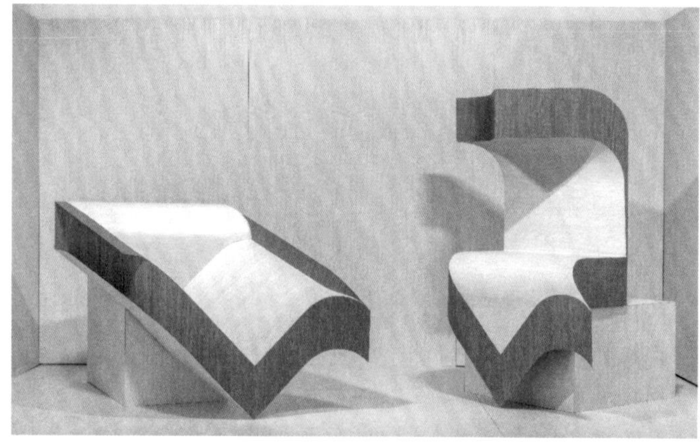

SpinaGu, Thick, 2017

WOJR, Other Masks, 2017

LAMAS, Bright Street, 2016

Toshiko Mori Architect, Dialogue in the Details, Venice Biennale 2012, 2012

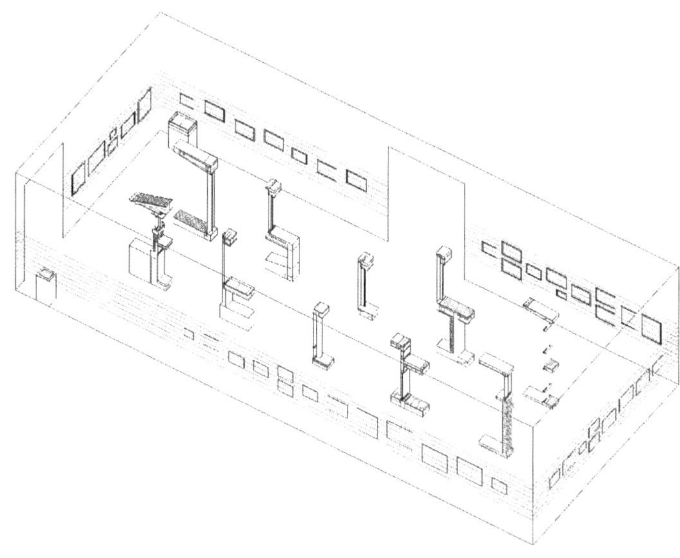

Toshiko Mori Architect, Dialogue in the Details, Venice Biennale 2012, 2012

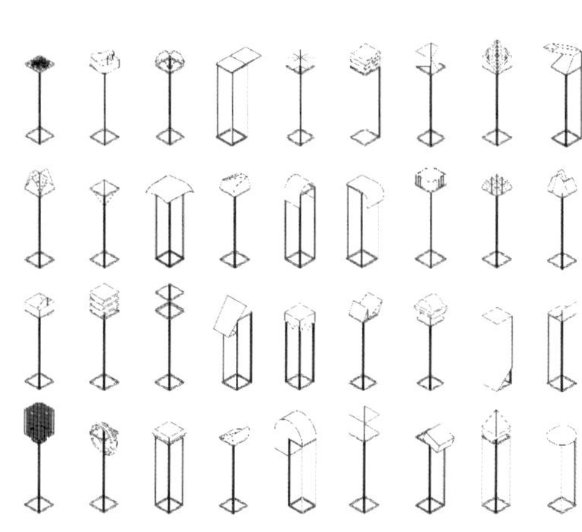

is-office, Crowns, 2015

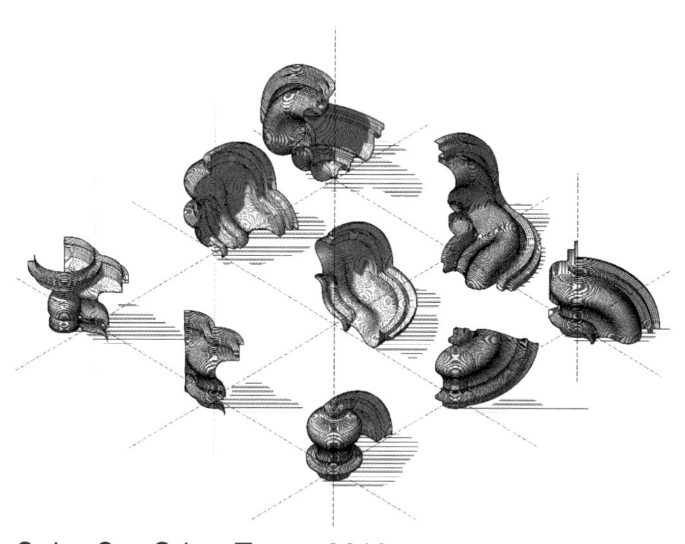

SpinaGu, Other Turns, 2016

Anamorphic Figures

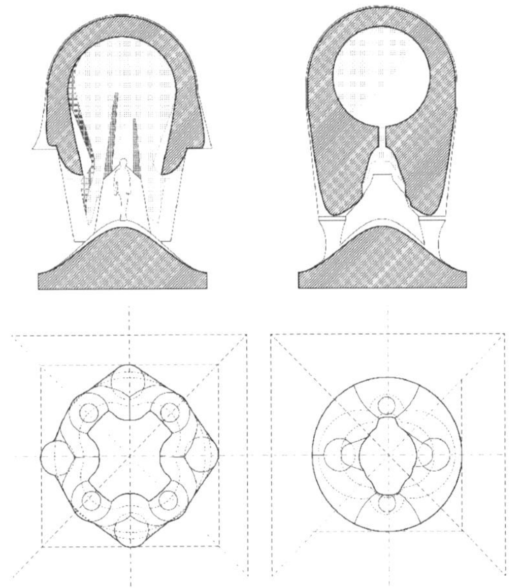

Endemic Architecture, A Project
Four Domes, 2015

Ania Jaworska, Gated Area, 2015

Medium Office, Solid and Striped, 2018

Miller Moran, Plastic Sunrise, 2015

Johnston Marklee, View House, 2009

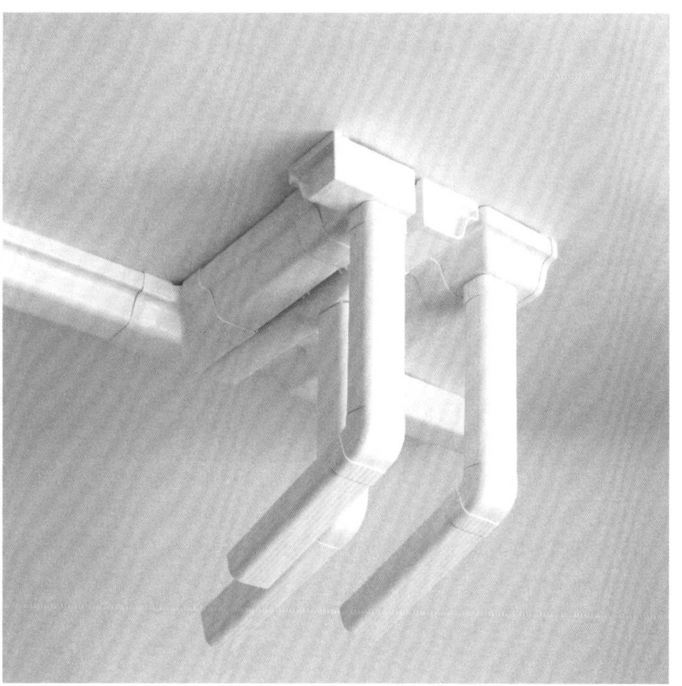

Besler & Sons, Roof Deck at MoMA PS1, 2015

Independent Architecture, Catamount Dormitory, 2016

Design with Company, Talent Pool, 2016

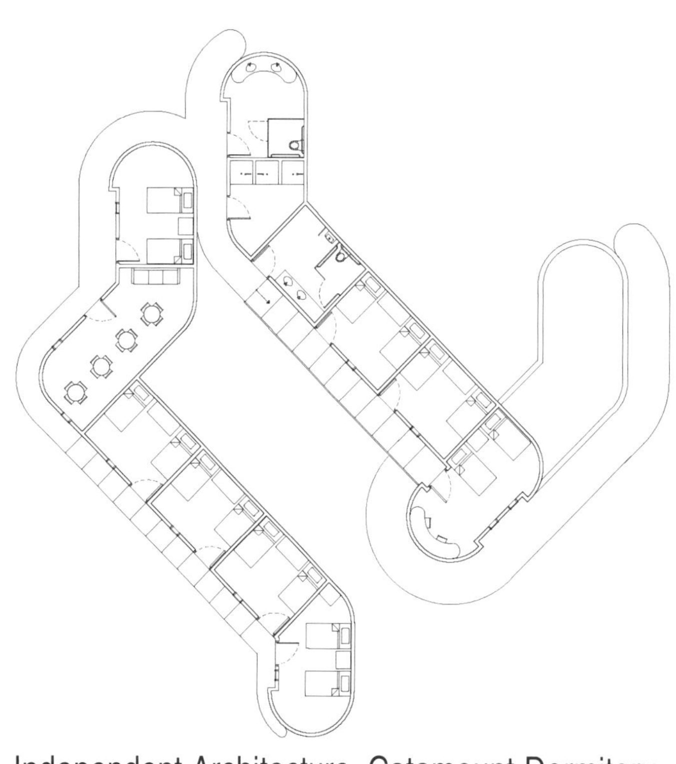

Independent Architecture, Catamount Dormitory, 2016

Anamorphic Figures

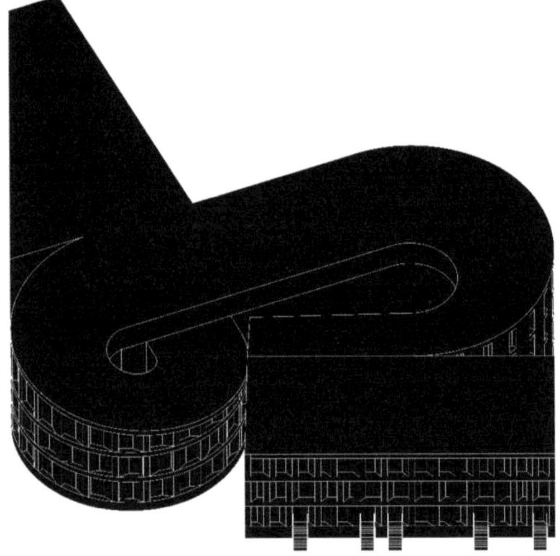

Studio Sean Canty, Irregular Infills, 2019

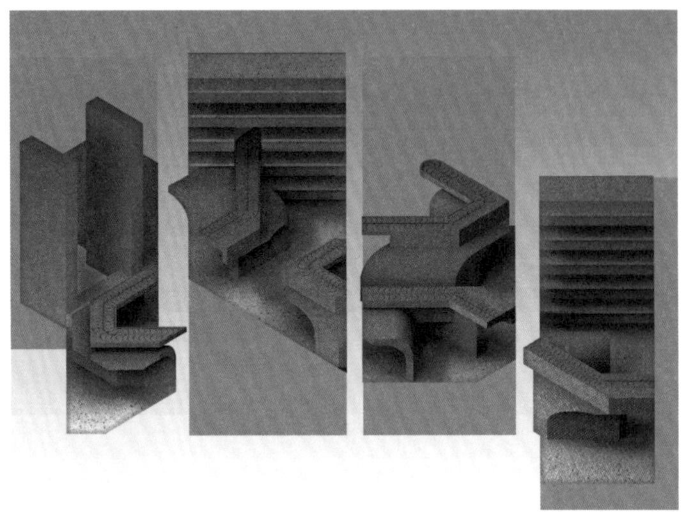

SpinaGu, Soft Service, 2019

Höweler + Yoon, Shanghai Expo Park: Viewfinder Bridge, 2018

Office III, Open Your Heart, 2019

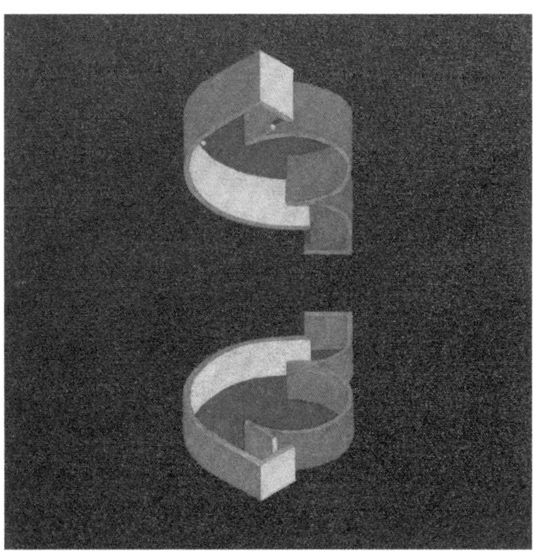

Pezo von Ellrichshausen, Bell Pavilion, 2017

Ania Jaworska, Entrance Installation, 2017

Team B, Squiggle Bench 2.0, 2019

Paul Anderson and Paul Preissner, Summer Vault, 2015

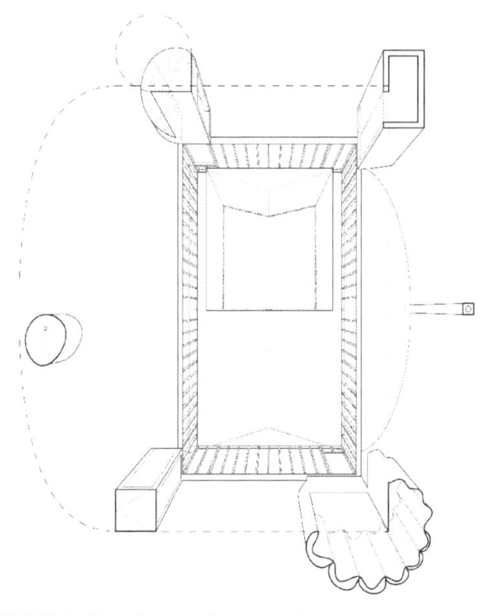

PARA Project, Stump House, 2019–

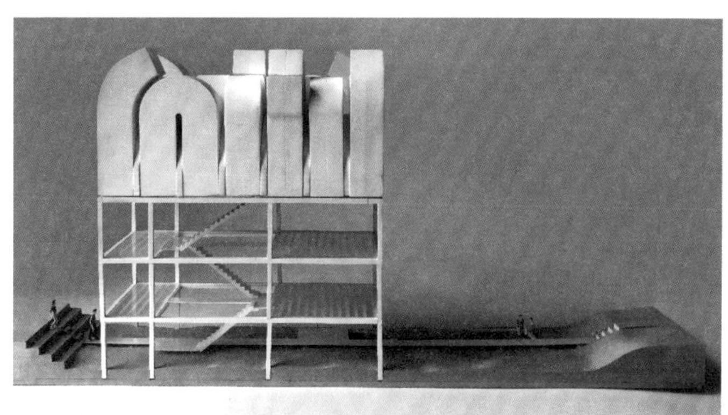

FORMA, Windsor Residence, 2018

Anamorphic Figures

Ania Jaworska, Set / Unit 3 (Side Credenza), 2016

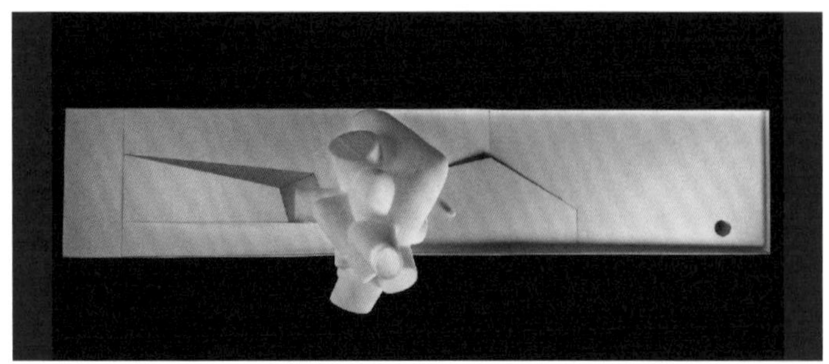

Kristy Balliet, Elbows (A Mini Golf Proposal), 2015

Common Accounts, Itaewon Chair, 2019

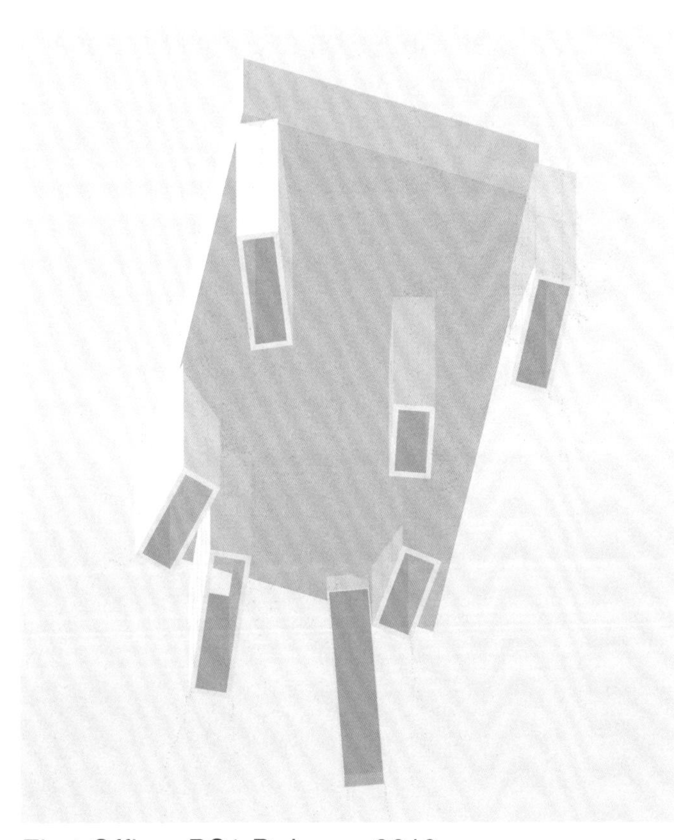

First Office, PS1 Dolmen, 2016

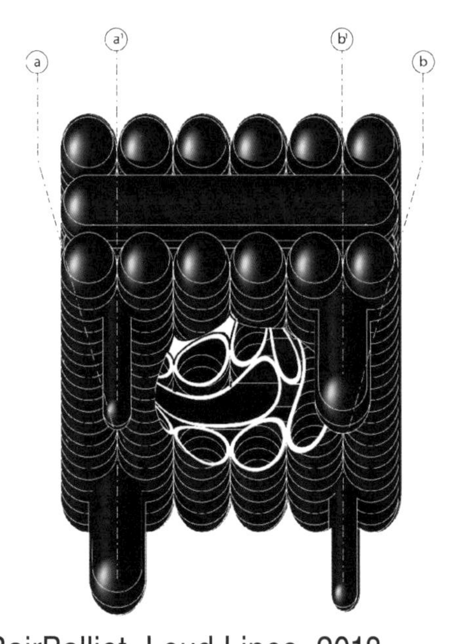

BairBalliet, Loud Lines, 2018

The Creaturely

If the architectural subject is to construct responses to contemporary anomie and escape those modes and relations that have become dominant and cliche (but without losing the specificity of architectural thought), how is it to be configured? Certain projects in this category suggest that what is needed is a new kind of mimesis—materialist rather than idealist, figural rather than representational. These responses involve a new relationship to the body and to materiality that we call the creaturely. The creaturely introduces a mimesis whose proximity to the human body produces anxiety, mainly because the inscription of the body into architecture seems both symptomatic (it is a reflex of contemporary "bare life" and the urgent need to imagine alternatives) and autonomous (we humans don't control it). It is the golem arrived, unsummoned. The relation between the creaturely and the more general domain of nonhuman things produces an openness to transience and discontinuity—an openness to other art practices, including performance and installation—and an immersion in experimentation. At the same time, these prehistorical, preverbal, preoedipal architectural creatures seem to have been exhumed from the most primitive and originary recesses of the architectural psyche.

The Bittertang Farm, Bookshelf, 2016

Ania Jaworska, Set / Unit 6 (Armchair), 2016

Norman Kelley, Wrong Chairs, 2014

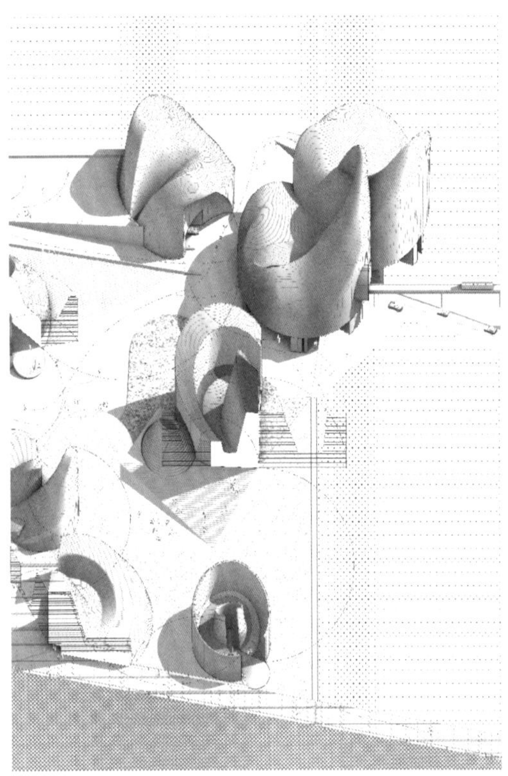
BairBalliet, The Next Port of Call, 2016

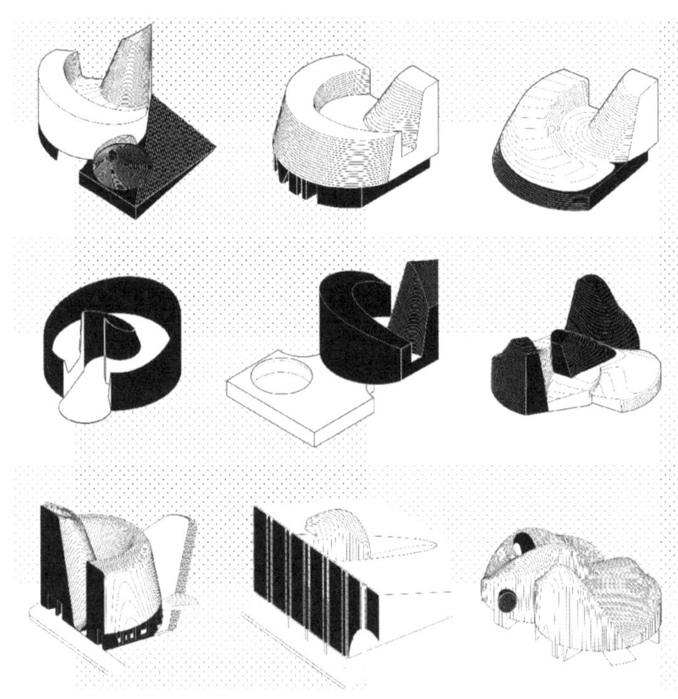
BairBalliet, The Next Port of Call, 2016

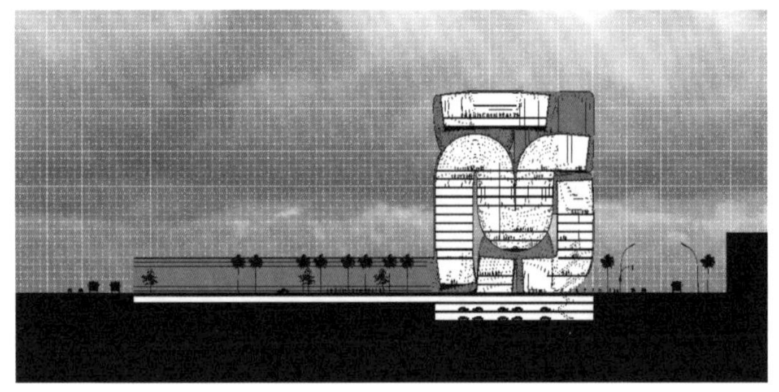
Outpost Office, Labyrinth Tower, 2016

BairBalliet, No Middle Midrise, 2016

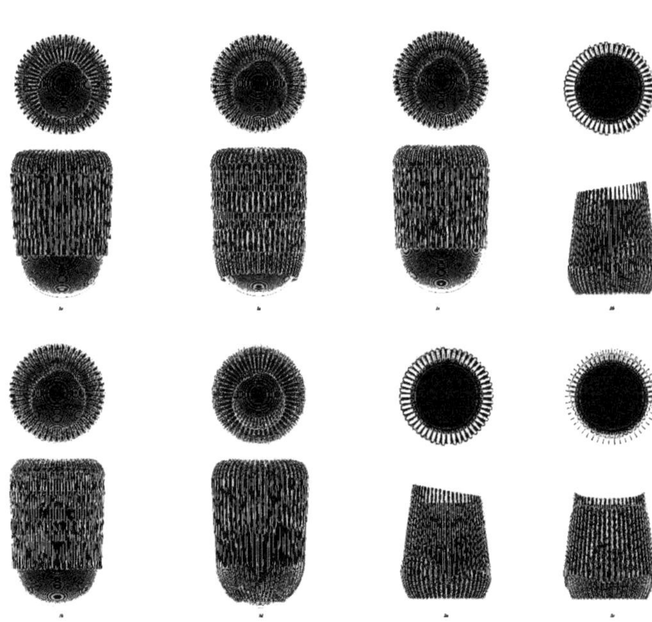
BairBalliet, No Middle Midrise, 2016

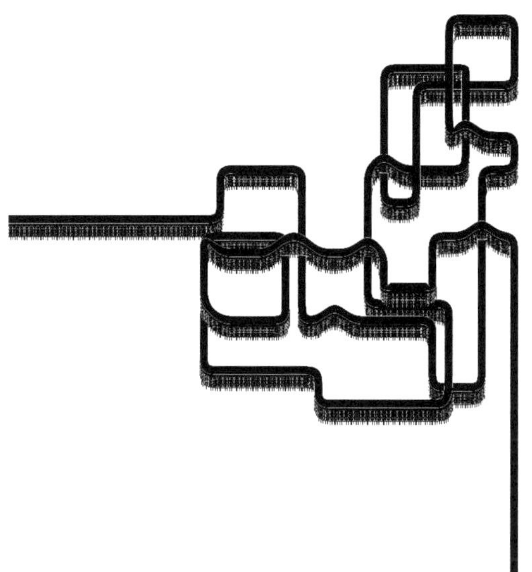

Outpost Office, Computerarchitektur No. 5, 2016

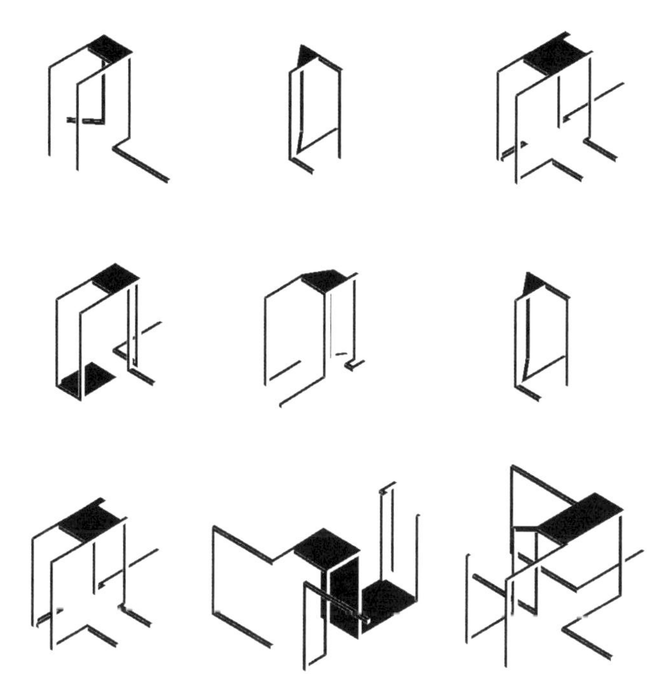

Design with Company, Chicago Reframed, 2017

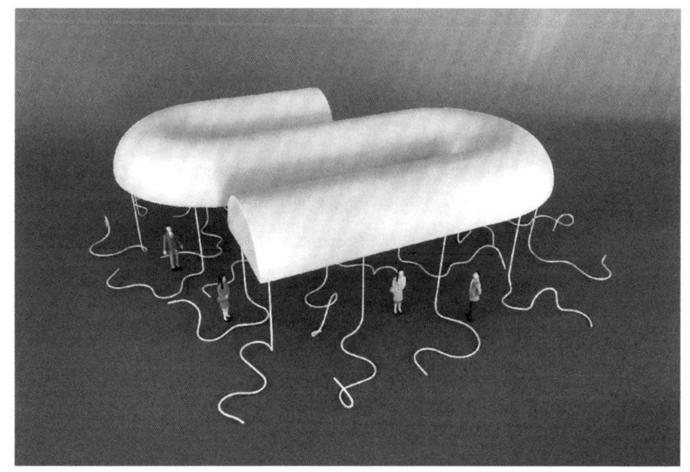

SPORTS, Some Kind of Kinda, 2019

SPORTS, City Thread, 2018

Mack Scogin Merrill Elam Architects, Wolfsburg Science Center, 1999

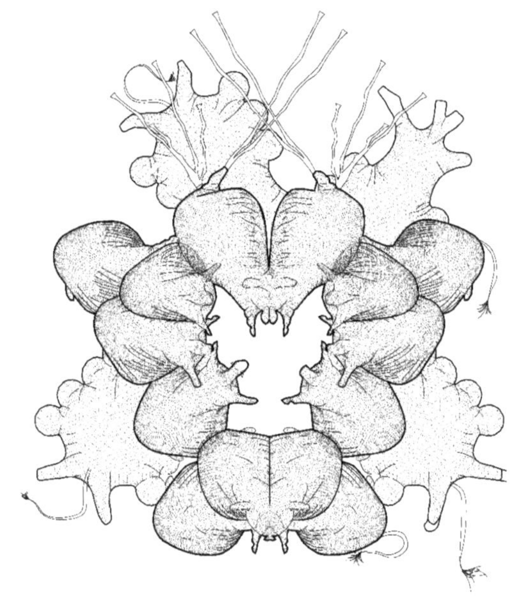

The Bittertang Farm, Bessie, 2014

The Bittertang Farm, Gels, 2015

Adam Fure and EADO, Pup Huddle, 2013

SPORTS, Myth, 2014

Nick Safley, Huflor, 2013

The Bittertang Farm, Brood of Fluffy, 2018

Curtis Roth, Past Perfect, 2013

Hume Coover Studio, Lake Baths, 2015

Young & Ayata, Bauhaus Museum Dessau, 2015

The Bittertang Farm, Buru Buru, 2014

Miller Moran, Between You & Me, 2015

EADO, Inside Things, 2016

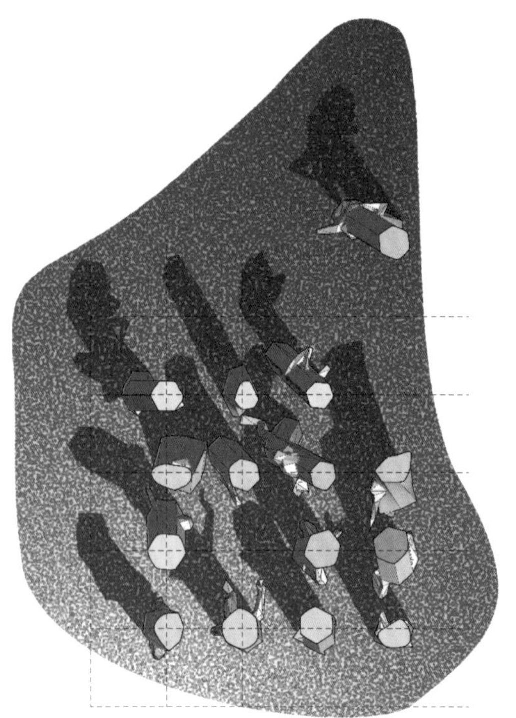

Miller Moran, Between You & Me, 2015

Matter Design, Cannibal's Bath, 2019

EADO, Inside Things, 2016

Kristy Balliet, Block (Refiguring the Typology of the Typical Berlin Block), 2014

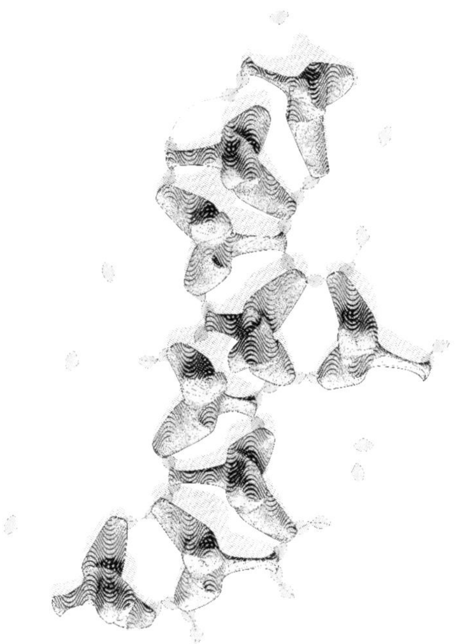

Filip Tejchman, Motivational Rock, 2019

Studio Anna Heringer, Kindergarten for the Permaculture Community PORET Zimbabwe, 2014

Young & Ayata, Base Flowers, 2015

SPORTS, Myth, 2014

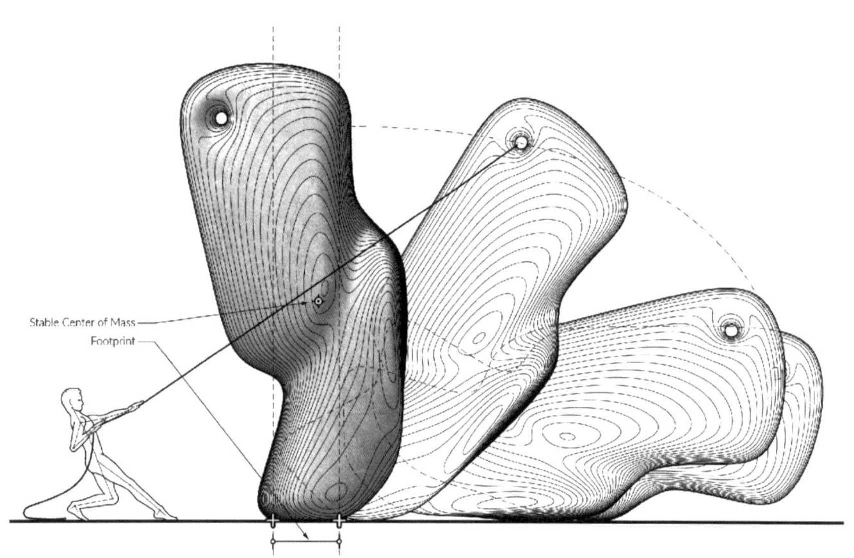

Matter Design, McKnelly Megalith, 2018

Matter Design, Buoy Stone, 2016

Farzin Farzin, Consuming Cute™, the Pisa, the Eiffel, the Parthenon, the Sydney, 2015

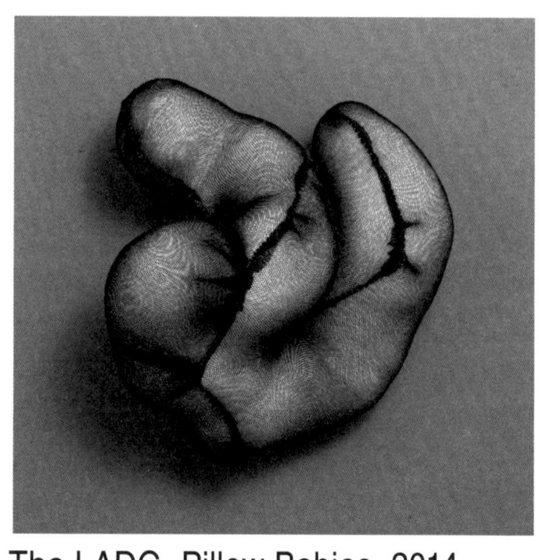

The LADG, Pillow Babies, 2014

Young & Ayata, Guggenheim Museum Helsinki, 2014

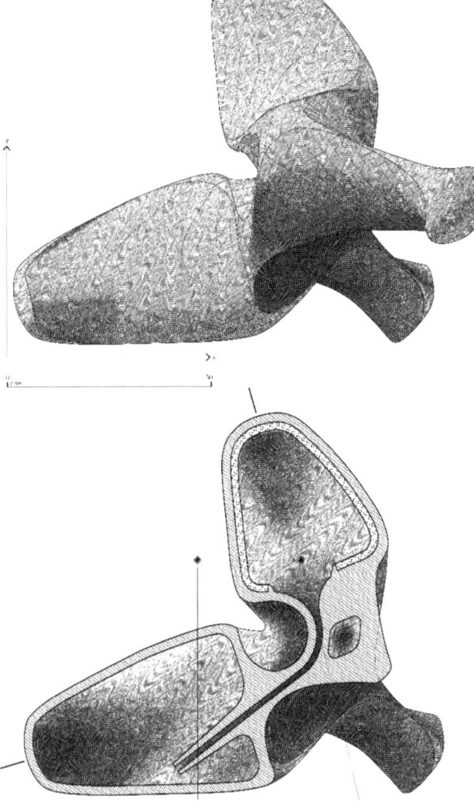

Filip Tejchman, Motivational Rock, 2019

Matter Design, McKnelly Megalith, 2018

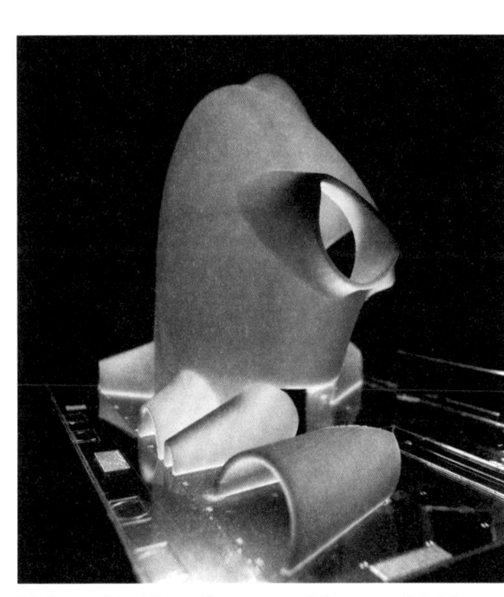

Kristy Balliet, Inverted Icon, 2013

Antoine Picon

Archetype, Ornament, and the Subversion of Architectural Categories

Architectural history is full of types, often associated with specific programs like the Parisian Haussmannian apartment building or, its contemporary, the railway station. Archetypes are far less numerous. They are associated with the notion of an almost direct translation of some kind of need—be it religious or secular, political or economic—into built form. In canonical accounts of the origins of the Western architectural tradition, the Greek temple appears as an archetype. So does the late 19th-century American tall office building, characterized by Louis Sullivan as a "sterile pile," a "crude, harsh, brutal agglomeration" of floors in dire need of architectural treatment.[1]

The archetype points toward a prearchitectural necessity. Because of this, it appears as primitive and above all simple, insofar as it is supposed to predate any architectural operation, beginning with composition. Yet a closer examination of some of the most important archetypes of the past reveals cascading complexities.

To begin with, despite its seemingly straightforward character, the archetype possesses a dual structure. It is produced by the association between a diagrammatic principle and a built form that transposes the diagram. For instance, it is not the Greek temple per se that is an archetype but the association between the primitive hut, often interpreted as its source of inspiration (think of Vitruvius and especially Marc-Antoine Laugier), and the temple. Similarly, it is the diagrammatic stacking of floors, this "crude, harsh, brutal agglomeration," that gives the tall office building its archetypal status.

Not in fact simple, the archetype is a compound. This initial tension between diagram and built form is at the origin of the multiple contradictions generated by attempts to mobilize archetypes past their initial emergence. Jacques-Germain Soufflot's Sainte-Geneviève church, with its disconcerting association between Greek and Gothic, offers a striking example. Rather than adapt the Greek temple's overall organization to 18th-century religious architecture, as Laugier advocated, Soufflot proposed a hybrid that juxtaposes Greco-Roman ordinance and Gothic-like flying buttresses.[2] Sullivan's attempts to civilize the tall office building are by no means less ambiguous, with their references to Florentine Renaissance palazzi or 19th-century neo-Romanesque warehouses and the license they take in the expression of the steel structure, not to mention their sprawling decor.[3]

The archetypal is often rooted in a desire to escape the arbitrariness of design by returning to fundamentals that are supposed to predate architecture, such as the need to shelter human activities. But archetypes cannot truly exist before architecture. Indeed, it is only through the lens of the discipline that a diagram and a built form become associated. Thus, the archetype jeopardizes the very possibility of an objective foundation for architecture, while at the same time pretending to look for it. Le Corbusier's famous attempt at presenting a new archetype with his Dom-Ino structure illustrates this incapacity. For the archetype always already belongs to the architectural realm, despite its claim to be anterior to it.[4]

Another way to put it would be to observe that an archetype is not actually an object but a relation between a virtual object—the diagram—and a built one; or, to be still more

Charles Eisen, Frontispiece of Marc-Antoine Laugier, *Essai sur l'architecture,* 2nd ed., engraving, 1755.

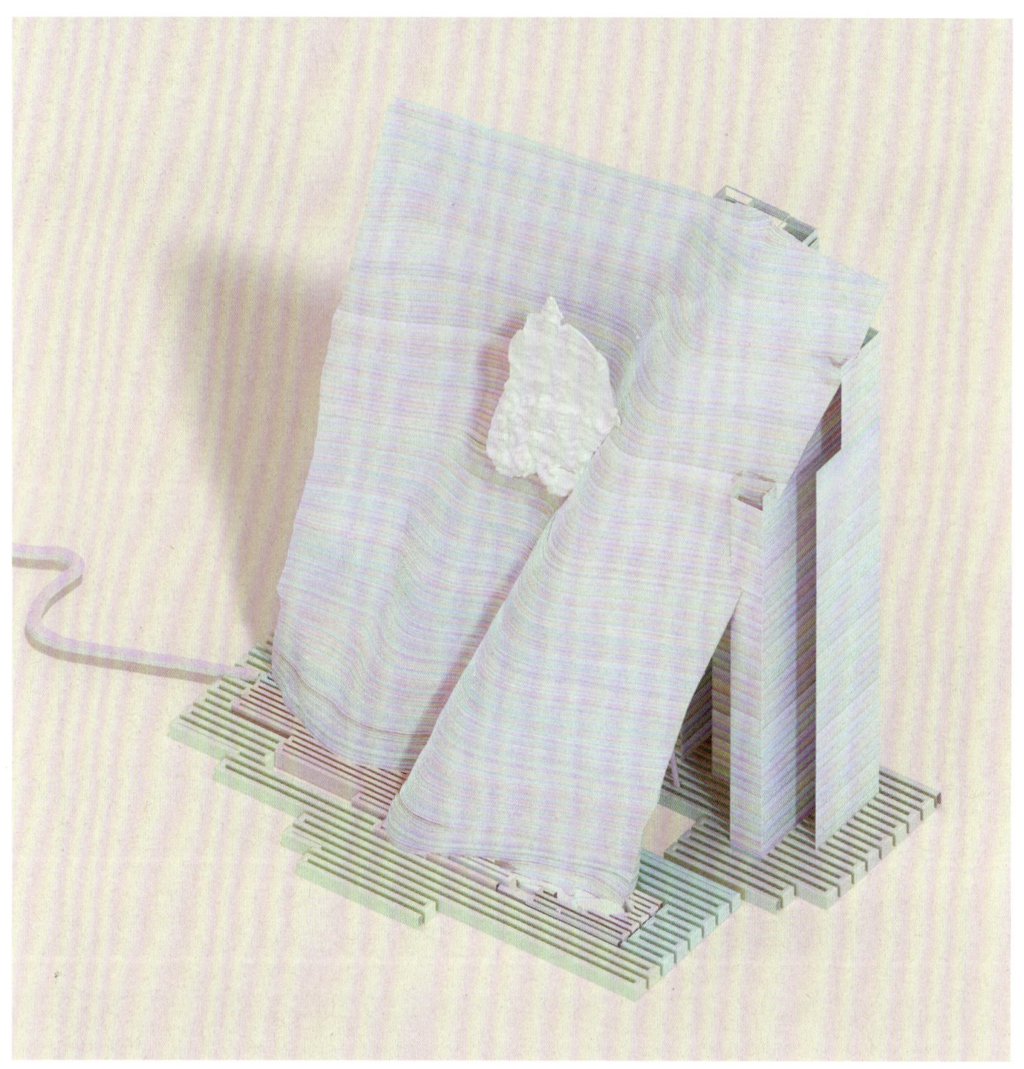

d.esk, Colossal Paper, physical model, 2019.

Dankmar Adler and Louis Sullivan, Wainwright Building, 1891.

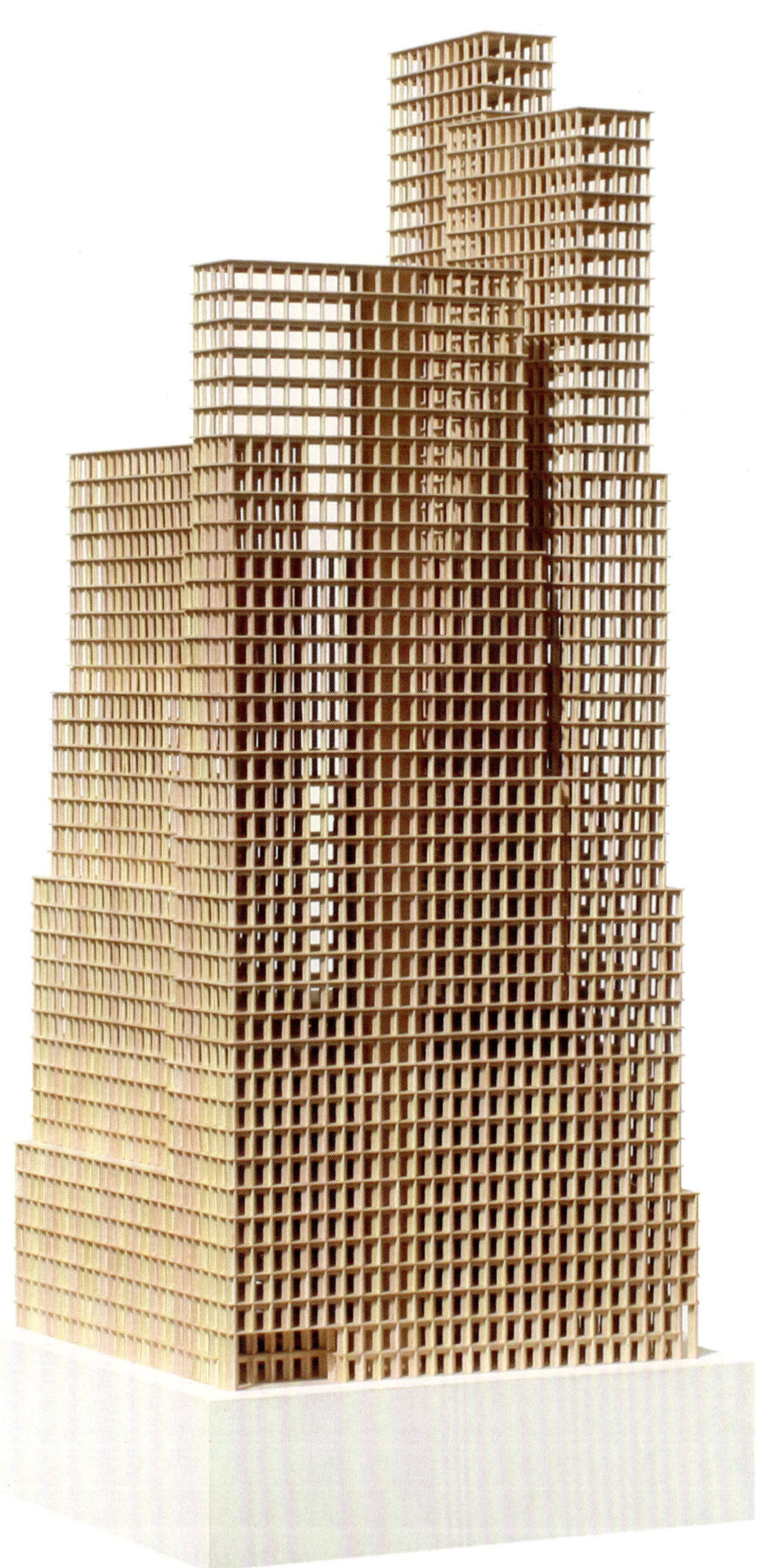

Jesús Vassallo, Timber Towers, physical model, 2015.

accurate, it is an operator that connects the two. Its highly subversive mode of existence (epitomizing the desire for a foundation and ultimately disproving its very possibility) finds a counterpoint in the equally subversive power, albeit in the opposite direction, of the traditional architectural ornament.

Like archetypes, ornaments are not defined through their belonging to a fixed set of objects or elements. Almost anything can acquire an ornamental character. Is a column part of the fabric of the building, or is it an ornament? From Alberti onward, the impossibility of settling this point once and for all is revealing. Any ornament in the ordinary sense is produced by an operator that distinguishes between a background and a foreground, between the fabric and any addition to it, and from the late 18th century on between structure and decor.

While an archetype questions the very possibility of an origin or foundation, ornament challenges the hierarchy between the deep and the superficial, the essential and the accidental. Ornament, at least in its traditional sense, was both essential and added, circumstantial and the bearer of a dynamic order of things that unfolded through architecture. Ornament was like the sort of mask that reveals the wearer more surely than could their naked face. Ornament suggested that architecture was like makeup applied to the skin of the building. A reminder that *cosmos* and *cosmetics* share an etymological origin in ancient Greek, this applied makeup was understood to be in tune with some secret rhythm of the universe that could be conveyed only through architectural means.[5]

The archetypal and the ornamental dimension have returned in recent architectural research, as the present publication makes evident, even if they are approached from very different perspectives than they were before. Archetype has kept its connection with the question of the origin (immanent, transcendent, revealed, or encountered), but its presence is often manifested through an extreme fragmentation, in complete contrast to the simplicity that was once attached to it. Simultaneously, ornament is no longer circumstantial and applied; on the contrary, it appears as a pervasive condition. What has not changed, however, is the ambition to mobilize archetype and ornament to probe the limits of established architectural categories.

1 Louis Sullivan, "The Tall Office Building Artistically Considered," *Lippincott's Magazine* 57 (March 1896): 403–9.

2 Cf. Barry Bergdoll, ed., *Le Panthéon: Symbole des Révolutions* (Paris: Caisse nationale des monuments historiques et des sites, Picard, 1989).

3 William Jordy, "The Tall Buildings," in *Louis Sullivan: The Function of Ornament*, ed. Wim de Witt (New York: W. W. Norton, 1986), 65–157.

4 Peter Eisenman, "Aspects of Modernism: Maison Dom-Ino and the Self-Referential Sign," *Oppositions* 15/16 (Winter/Spring 1979): 118–28; Antoine Picon, "Dom-Ino: Archetype and Fiction," *Log* 30 (Winter 2014): 169–76.

5 Antoine Picon, *Ornament: The Politics of Architecture and Subjectivity* (Chichester, UK: Wiley, 2013).

Lucia Allais
Screen Graspers

Inscriptions is one among several recent exhibitions that have announced the arrival on the American architectural scene of a new, millennial generation of digital designers. Curators K. Michael Hays and Andrew Holder invited me to write an essay identifying several "cohorts" among the architects who took part, but there is here, arguably, only one new cohort to speak of. Most of the participants were born between 1970 and 1990; the majority between 1975 and 1985. All graduated from one of 25 architecture schools, where many now teach. What most of these designers have in common is that they attended architecture school after it had become mandatory to learn to design by computer. This requirement had been a long time coming. The National Architectural Accreditation Board, NAAB, began requiring that schools teach their students familiarity with computing tools in 1983.[1] The first computer labs devoted to "paperless studios" were developed with great fanfare at the Graduate School of Architecture, Planning, and Preservation at Columbia University in 1994.[2] By the turn of the millennium, computer-based design tools had proliferated. Yet even as computation diversified internally, externally its effects on architectural pedagogy were relatively consistent: a wholesale transformation swept through American architecture schools around the year 2000, turning the spaces of the design studio from an open plan of horizontal drafting desks to a grid of vertical workstations. The designers featured in *Inscriptions* arrived to graduate school during or after this conversion. Unlike their teachers, who had *chosen* to be digital, they no longer had to leave the studio and spend time in a darkened computer lab in order to learn the computational ways of the day. They were installed at a fully networked desk where they could sit, upright, looking at a screen. They are, broadly speaking, American architecture's first screen-based cohort.

So, what does it mean to have had a screen systematically interposed between you and your design? Without reducing the architectural projects in

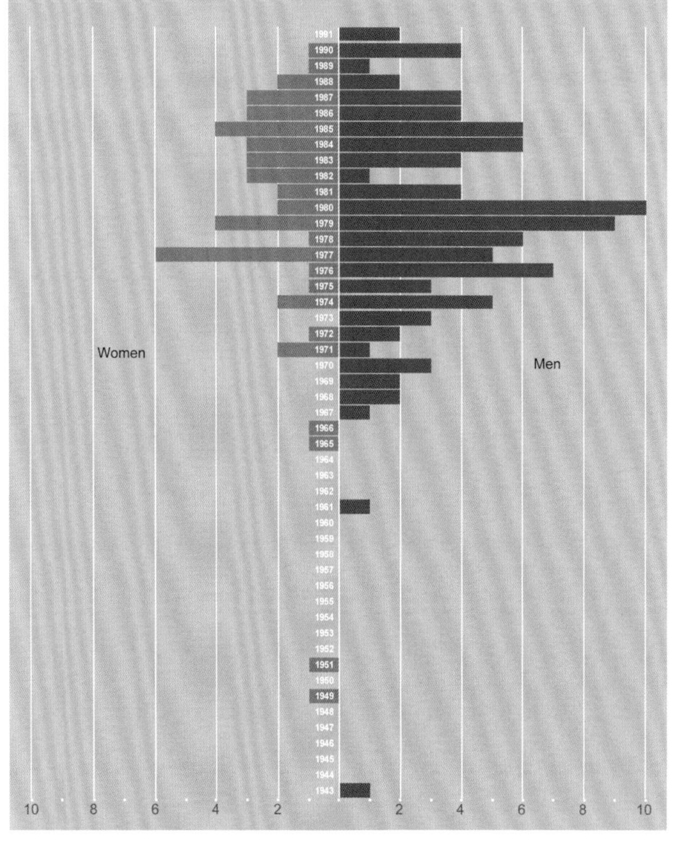

Lucia Allais, Number of Architects by Gender and Birth Year, graph, 2020.

Inscriptions to the computing setup that was used to design them, we can learn a lot by watching these architects negotiate their screens—and especially by noting they all reject the older, humanist understanding of the computer screen as merely a kind of virtual "window."

In this repudiation of the window metaphor, the designers in *Inscriptions* are in agreement with media theorists who have shown that the screen, as a spatial medium, has always delimited space as much as it has opened onto it.[3] These new media archaeologies reach back to antiquity, when the screen was understood as distinct from the wall, in that it could partition space but didn't have to bear a load. In the early modern period, they continue, the screen served as an element used for worship, for hunting, or for war, and as such it shielded its users in two ways: first, it protected them physically from a projectile or metaphysically from the eye of divinities; second, it allowed them to hide rather than reveal their presence and their intentions, offering a surface for visual diversion and representation. This representational opportunity became a dominant feature of the screen, then, when it became a surface for projecting an image mechanically, and later electro-mechanically, in the 19th century and thereafter. The vast entertainment apparatuses that make up the screen's ubiquity today—the cinema, television, the desktop computer, the portable phone—were born from this spatial and discursive delay. In a phenomenon Friedrich Kittler has called "implementation," a screen-based medium periodically becomes naturalized, offering immersive experiences, and the screen becomes the outward-facing component of a media apparatus that relies on a complex and hidden computing network. (A complicated spatial web lies behind a radar screen, for instance, or ties us to a mobile device.) Cinema is a case in point: as a medium it became more autonomous and ubiquitous at the same time, and its screen remained equal parts wall and canvas as the popular entertainment became experimental art form and aesthetic institution. "Implementation" may sound like a purely technical principle, but its aesthetic stakes are high. It leads to a revisionist account of the history of perspective, for instance. For Kittler, the architect Leon Battista Alberti "implemented" perspective vision by inventing a gridded "projection screen" that totally transformed print and painting. Partition, protection, projection, implementation—the point is that the screen is defined by media theorists not as a passive framing device, but through a set of operations.

The "protective" function of the screen, for instance, helps us understand these millennial American architects as fundamentally strategic. The first digital generation of architects was earnest in their engagement with designing machines. Think of Greg Lynn, Morphosis, MVRDV, Reiser + Umemoto, Bernard

PHOTO EDITOR — MELISSA CHEUNG
Construction continues on the new "Paperless Design Studio," which is scheduled to open Monday in Avery Hall. Aspiring architects will soon be using state-of-the-art computer systems.

Avery gets $1.4M computer labs

Photo by Melissa Chung for Bari Meltzer, "Avery Gets $1.4M Computer Labs," *Columbia Daily Spectator*, volume CXVII, no. 78 (September 8, 1995).

Cache, R&Sie, and FOA, to name only a few—all wanted to convince us of their mastery over their tools, the veracity of their calculations, the precision of their analyses. The *Inscriptions* group is more circumspect. When talking about their designs, they speak the language of description. Even when their forms are meant to be aleatory, their images are staged and produced. They don't "show their work"— they want to show that work has occurred. Specifically: they want us to know that a deliberate decision has been made about what to show, and that this decision was not based on the default suggestions of software. Their images often look like screenshots—which is to say, like pictures of a found state—but they are the opposite: they are highly produced selections.

If I had to name one gesture that seems consistently operative across these designers' work, I would call it screen-grasping. These architects try to comprehend and manipulate a world or a reality outside of themselves, but they also accept that something has come to interpose itself between us and this reality. And the only way we will hold, understand, or indeed design anything is first to grasp at it as if through a scrim: with limited senses, using only a restricted tool set, via mediated or transmedial perception, through an imposed color palette, etc. It is not only a question of representing form but of form-making.

The inventions in *Inscriptions* come about specifically when trying bridge this technological divide. Sometimes architecture is obscured by noise—especially ideal geometries, which only ever appear as surrounded by accidental ones (see Medium Office). Sometimes a grasping hand appears to have left marks on forms as they were created, as with fingers crumpling a plane (see d.esk, Meredith Miller, formlessfinder) or squeezing a balloon (see BairBalliet). Sometimes the ill-fit between a geometry and its chosen material creates a material surplus—an oozing or gooping (see the LADG, Andy and Dave). Sometimes the constraints are normative and the game is to show glitches in an auto-correcting architectural planning process (see the door swings of First Office and Ultramoderne, the "wrong chairs" of Norman Kelley, the diameters of Besler & Sons, the shading diagrams of MILLIØNS). At times the technical determinants of the screen, especially its strident colors, have imprinted themselves literally on the architecture's surfaces (see Ania Jarwoska). Many projects assume a screen-based perceiver, and play off the estrangement of presenting real objects as a kind of trompe l'oeil (see FreelandBuck, MR Studio). Even when the forms of the buildings are more or less familiar (as with the pitched roofs and gothic arches that have returned *en masse* in these architects' repertoire), they are transformed into ready-mades, as if a button signifying "building" had been found, then hacked.

By allowing the technical constraints of digital media to imprint themselves onto their designs, these architects show they feel they are extracting their objects from the digital universe in which they originate, and that this gesture of extraction is itself worth designing. Grasping is not a sign of naivete; it is a knowing gesture that defines the reality being grasped.

It may seem strange to talk about reality when discussing design work that embraces an aesthetics of artificiality so wholeheartedly, whether in the name of whimsy or difficulty. After all, these projects are still supposed to wow or seduce us with their spectacular prowess, minimalist beauty, maximalist lust, and so on. But the "real" of which I am speaking is not the opposite of the virtual, the fantastical, or the fictional, not even the utopian. The real is that which is given. The definition of realism that has most relevance for this group may well be Bruno Latour's discussion of the "reality demonstrations" that give scientific statements their authenticity and their political value.[4] Like the scientist who kicks a rock or the politician who bangs a fist on a table, millennial architects use digital media to "add reality" to their designs. Certainly, a scientific imaginary pervades the catalog of screen-grasping gestures I have just sketched out. Some designers are inspired by geology—hence the proliferation of rocks, stones, mounds (see Mircea Eni, Filip Tejchman)—and others by ethnographers and prehistorians who find and draw roughly made things (see Matter Design). Others look at architecture's more traditional scientific allies, such as geometers and mathematicians, for whom a perfect square exists amidst an infinity of non-square variations (see Karamuk Kuo and many others). There are also

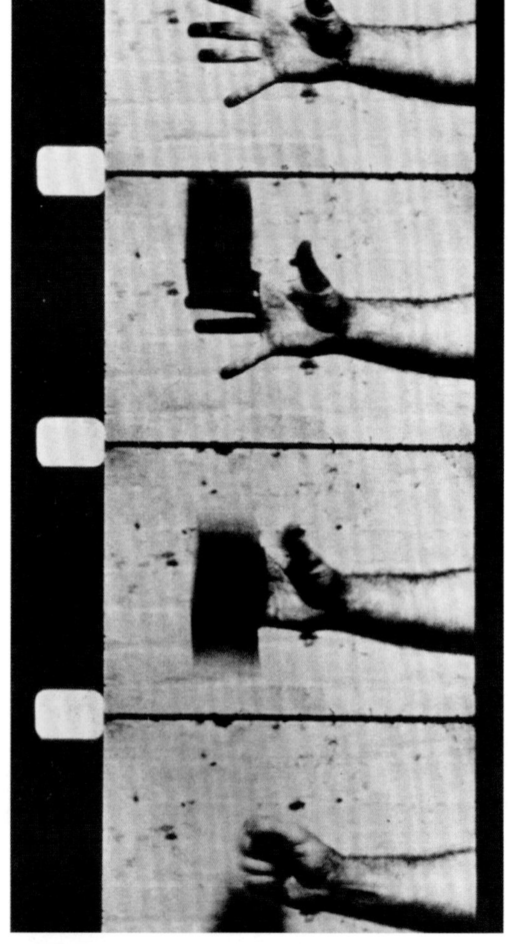

Richard Serra, *Hand Catching Lead*, film stills, 1968.

natural scientists, who classify and categorize the world by shape and type (see NEMESTUDIO, New Affiliates); there are chemists who experiment with states of matter (see stock-a-studio, Adam Fure); and material scientists looking to synthesize a new substance (see EADO).

These acts of digital empiricism are not all performed the same way, however. Broadly speaking there are two strategies: one that records a process of grasping "at" something ineluctably physical, but with a fundamentally unsuitable tool—as if the hand in Richard Serra's 1968 piece, *Hand Catching Lead*, was made of software. The other is to reach for a real that has already been digitized, as data has become a second nature, and attempt to "grasp" its meaning by using it to shape a physical thing. Here, imagine a version of Marcel Duchamp's 1913–1914 *3 Standard Stoppages*, which would take not the meter but a digital set of quantities as its test unit.

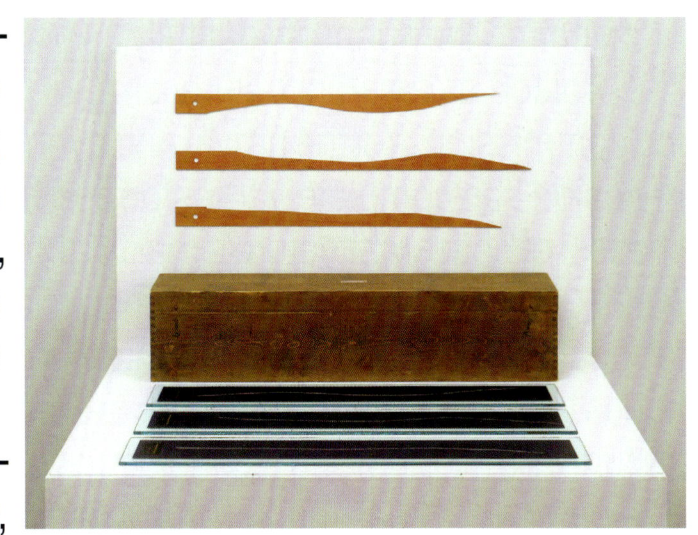

Marcel Duchamp, *3 Standard Stoppages*, sculpture, 1913–1914.

Despite borrowing the realist stance of the expanded artist-designer-scientist, however, few of the architects in this exhibition seem interested in elevating their findings to an objective principle, or deriving from them a political agenda. The ethical and epistemic stakes of their grasping seem constrained, less by computational limits than by disciplinary ones. The relevant legacy from the early 2000s is, this time, discursive. Even as screens and partitions were quietly being installed in the studios of American architecture schools, debates between "theory" and "practice" were raging in its seminar rooms and auditoria, polarizing the field. This so-called practice turn in American architecture (fueled in part by a backlash against the unlikely success of Deconstructivist architecture, with its exuberant buildings and inscrutable texts), hoped to veer architecture away from the literary, the critical, and the theoretical, by calling for a return to the "practical," even "pragmatism." This was of course a false dichotomy, taking place largely among academics who write more than they build.

Inscriptions's millennial cohort has fully internalized the anxieties of these earlier debates, and landed squarely on the side of "practice." They present themselves as ready to build. Many have adopted variations of the word "Office," "Practice," "Firm." Even though some speak very eloquently and write very insightfully about digital media, art history, and other cultural issues, when it comes to architecture they perform dutifully as practitioners. Even without clients, all accept "the project" as an architectural unit, in the sense of a singular, place-based, building commission. Yet the arrival and eventual dominance of the computer as a force in design has completely transformed the value of such posturing, on both sides. The test of both architecture's reality *and* its cultural purchase became not whether a design was practical, but rather how it might be technically reproduced, scaled, fabricated—in a word, implemented. In response to this, this group forcefully critiques the myth of generative form or smooth fabrication by calling attention to architecture as a medium and technology, in tool-based investigations that are not driven by a particular client, market, public program, or even a social vision. Their political paralysis (for some) or evasion (for others) is surely a result of being pulled in these two directions: whether to challenge architecture as a profession, or as a medium.

Many designers have reached for social relevance in other ways. Some "learn from" software, as if it was a new architectural vernacular. Others focus on housing typologies, and hide geometric play in their facade designs (see LAMAS, Paul Preissner Architects). Those who reinvent pre- and proto-historical forms like caverns and piles retrofit them with stacked floors, to gesture at normality (see PARA Project, Ensamble Studio) or grand spaces, for a hint of utopia. Those who confront the demands of fabrication offer media-materiality as a way out of a post-Fordist economy (see T+E+A+M). In all cases, the onus for applicability of any idea is placed entirely on the forms themselves.

But the most consistent test of buildability over the last 15 years has come from the exhibitionary complex. Strange and scaleless digital objects can be exported as gallery-sized installations, sometimes only minimally weightier than the screen-based experiments from which they came. This too has fostered cohort cohesion: being thrust as co-exhibitors in a growing circuit of architectural exhibitions, fairs, biennials, and festivals, where architects are asked to construct things that are less building mock-ups than proofs of concept. And the galleries of American architecture schools have played a critical role in offering students and faculty an entry into this circuit. Every pedagogical initiative now terminates in an exhibition. Thus, the resurgence of the architecture school gallery has been integral to the "implementation" of computing technology in architecture that began in the 2000s and has unfolded since. It is now 2020 and the professional design school has reinstitutionalized itself around its digital technologies, becoming a media apparatus whose entire gallery acts as a "screen": a visual space where resolved propositions are projected while much else remains hidden from view.

This brings me back, in closing, to *Inscriptions* and its curation and design. The exhibition was installed to give visitors the impression of having wandered to

Inscriptions: Architecture Before Speech, exhibition. Cambridge, MA: Druker Design Gallery, Harvard University Graduate School of Design, 2018.

the other side of an architect's computer screen. The long back wall of the gallery had been painted deep-space black. A paper-thin collection of unframed view ports had been pinned to this wall in square, social-media-friendly proportions. Whether they were plans, elevations, or perspective views, these drawings showed structures floating in digital color *vacui*. Effectively, this was a drywall-and-paper mock-ups of a computer screen. The physical models that had been assembled on stands in the gallery facing this wall, in contrast, looked like they had been yanked directly out of a rendering engine. They bore proud traces of their own fabrication, whether manual or digital. Some retained their digital facture: shapes made with foam cutters, routers, laser cutters, and 3D printers. At the other extreme, hyper-specific materials like gravel, mesh, concrete, and even bird carcasses had been laid down and arranged just so, as if waiting for a high-resolution photo shoot. At the back of the gallery, the title wall had also been painted black, this time to serve as an immersive backdrop for Hays and Holder's diagrams and texts, set in an oversize technical font and unchanging line weight. If you stepped close enough to the wall, this screenly treatment seemed a fitting illustration of Hays's longstanding interest in the seductive abstraction of the architectural surface. But stepping back a few feet, with discourse rendered as a wire frame, even theory seemed ready to come life as a fully reified, three-dimensional object.

Why grant these screen-grasping experiments an apparent objectifying power, almost an autonomy? Of what do we make a blank slate when we call architects' computer printouts "pre-verbal," and display them in frames and on pedestals, as the curators have done? Far from "preceding speech," the screen is the terminal outlet of a vast babbling enterprise where all ideas, including architectural ones, have come to circulate and deteriorate. Not only software but screen culture at large has affected how architecture is designed and how architects influence one another. A massive shift in collective learning occurred when the screen entered the architecture studio, bringing with it all of web 2.0—that distributed, amorphous, and chaotic source of content. It was no longer only by looking over one's shoulder at the project on the neighboring desk, or by watching reviews at the end of the semester, that architecture students could see what others were doing. It was by engorging a daily feed of images produced by designers and marketers far away. With no one in particular in charge, peer pressure went global. One of the first skills this cohort acquired, then, was to survive as visual producers in a crowded and rapidly evolving image ecology.

This near-native digital literacy helps to explain the recent return of hyper-specific geometric forms to the center of the architectural scene. Every time a student-architect designs anything, she can run a quick search for comparands on the web. It is arguably against this veritable avalanche of preformed architectural ideas that young architects are protecting themselves behind their screens today. Leaving things rough, engaging with algorithmic aesthetics, tightly controlling geometry, pushing the boundaries of taste and gravity, insisting on exquisite details—all of these are symptoms of grasping for originality.

But if we look *inside* these architects' images, we can see an entirely different narrative about architecture's capacity to individuate. In these architectural spaces we find an almost complete disappearance of the partition, of the wall as purely spatial divider. Despite the fact that they express their agency by designing objects that are laboriously extracted from being on the other side of a screen, these architects are depicting, inside their projects, the consequences of the implementation of the computer as technology, which is to say the total irrelevance of the screen *qua* architectural surface. Spaces are made by disposing objects—furniture, almost-sculptures, shed roofs, service cores. Even facades can rarely be straightforwardly read as partitioning an inside from an outside. Although they insist that we pay attention to the fact that they are stuck behind a partition, their architecture depicts a state where the partitioning function of architecture has become obsolete. A radically Kittlerian reading of this compulsion would say that these designers are depicting the obsolescence of the designer—if the designer is that agent who sits behind a screen. This would be confirmed by the way in which the scale figures in these renderings are still drawn and disposed as highly individuated persons and groups, as if they were separated by invisible partitions. Almost ornamental, human subjects are purely "fictional" and created at will, not based on data. When given freedom, these architects design human individuation; when following a technical logic they demonstrate that architecture is no longer capable of individuating subjects, only of producing strange semi-living objects. A more generous reading, then, would see their paralysis not as political but as metaphysical. Like organs that no longer serve a purpose, the architectural things in the *Inscriptions* show not architecture before speech, but post-design. Shapes that are strange not because they are primordial, but rather vestigial.

Postscript

Exhibitions like *Inscriptions* are so accomplished and image-dense that they have the power to convince us that architecture's only claim to the real lies in its projecting powers. But as I write this conclusion, a veritable social upheaval has come to upend what it means to learn from the image's reality in a digital age. A pandemic has forced the highly wired architectural community to have screens-only interaction. In America, one of the most thoughtful and well-read protest movements in history, Black Lives Matter, has exploded into a mass movement with global repercussions, first through marching in the streets, and then by setting off a wave of self-education for "unlearning whiteness," both phases buttressed indispensably by social media. This has transformed what it means to perpetuate the Western tradition, including that of Alberti. What's more, it has been a millennial revolution, fueled by the energies of a generation once derided for being too narcissistic to act, and too solipsistic to educate. This revolution has included many architects, some even involved in the *Inscriptions* show, who are leveraging the powers of image-diffusion to provoke change, and promote the cause of justice. Will they also change their guarded attitude towards the architectural real? Will their tool-sharpening exercises become meaningful architectural statements, or remain resistance graffiti on the walls of a pedagogical cave? This may depend on whether the media apparatus that is the architecture school is able to expand its powers of public persuasion farther afield than by publishing the work of its own graduating cohorts. Or, it is possible that these architects will leap out of the gallery and the school, and begin grasping for the unspeakable realities that have suddenly materialized before all of our eyes, bursting through our windows, our screens. The medium may be the message, but this message has, for once, the capacity fundamentally to change the medium.

1 See “Implications of NAAB Evaluation Criteria to the Educational Practice of CAD” in *ACADIA* 4, no. 1 (1985): 15–16.

2 Bari Meltzer, “Avery Gets $1.4M Computer Labs,” *Columbia Daily Spectator*, volume CXVII, no. 78 (September 8, 1995).

3 This cursory overview draws from the following: Erkki Huhtamo, “Elements of Screenology: Toward an Archaeology of the Screen,” *Iconics* 7 (2004): 31–82. Craig Buckley, Rüdiger Campe, Francesco Casetti, eds., *Screen Genealogies: From Optical Device to Environmental Medium* (Amsterdam: Amsterdam University Press, 2019), especially Rüdiger Campe, “‘Schutz und Schirm’: Screening in German During Early Modern Times,” 51–72, and Noam M. Elcott, “Material. Human. Divine. Notes on the Vertical Screen,” 295–319; Friedrich Kittler, “The perspective of print,” in *Configurations* 10, no. 1 (Winter 2002) 37–44; Campe, “Kittler’s Humanities: On Implementation,” in *The Technological Introject*, Jeffrey Champlin and Antje Pfannkuchen (New York: Fordham University Press, 2018), 9–26; Bernhard Siegert, “After the Wall: Interferences Among Grids and Veils,” in *GAM: Graz Architektur Magazin* 9 (2013): 18–33; and Noam M. Elcott, *Artificial Darkness: An Obscure History of Modern Art and Media* (Chicago: University of Chicago Press, 2018), 84–86.

4 Bruno Latour, “Why has Critique Run Out of Steam? From Matters of Fact to Matters of Concern,” in *Critical Inquiry* 30 (Winter 2004), 225–48.

Labyrinths
Eidetic Houses
Booleans
Superimpositions
Revelations
Slack Collections
Scatters, Remnants
Dirt, Earth, and Rocks
Trabeated Stacks
First Houses
Seven Wonders
Monoliths
Anamorphic Figures
The Creaturely

Labyrinths

The labyrinth is a structure of holes and lines, thresholds and intervals—a scattering of multiple centers connected by paths. Some of the projects in this cohort are loose aggregates with particular, local connections; others have precise geometric grids whose parts remain porous and interstices active. But neither type should be read part by part. The presentation of a labyrinth implies the preexistence of a matrix or energy field that generates its singular becoming. In some examples of this cohort, every room of the labyrinth is a different size or shape. In others, every room is the same, but the many possible paths through them produce circulatory paradoxes such that precisely repeated squares or even a single volume can produce a maze effect. In all cases, what Stan Allen calls "field conditions" predominate, redefining relations between figure and ground. The figure is not a marked object read against a neutral and stable field but a specific effect emerging from the field itself. Waves of intensity flow across local moments of the array while the overall form is treated with indifference. Ariadne's thread becomes knotted, and the knots join into a weave.

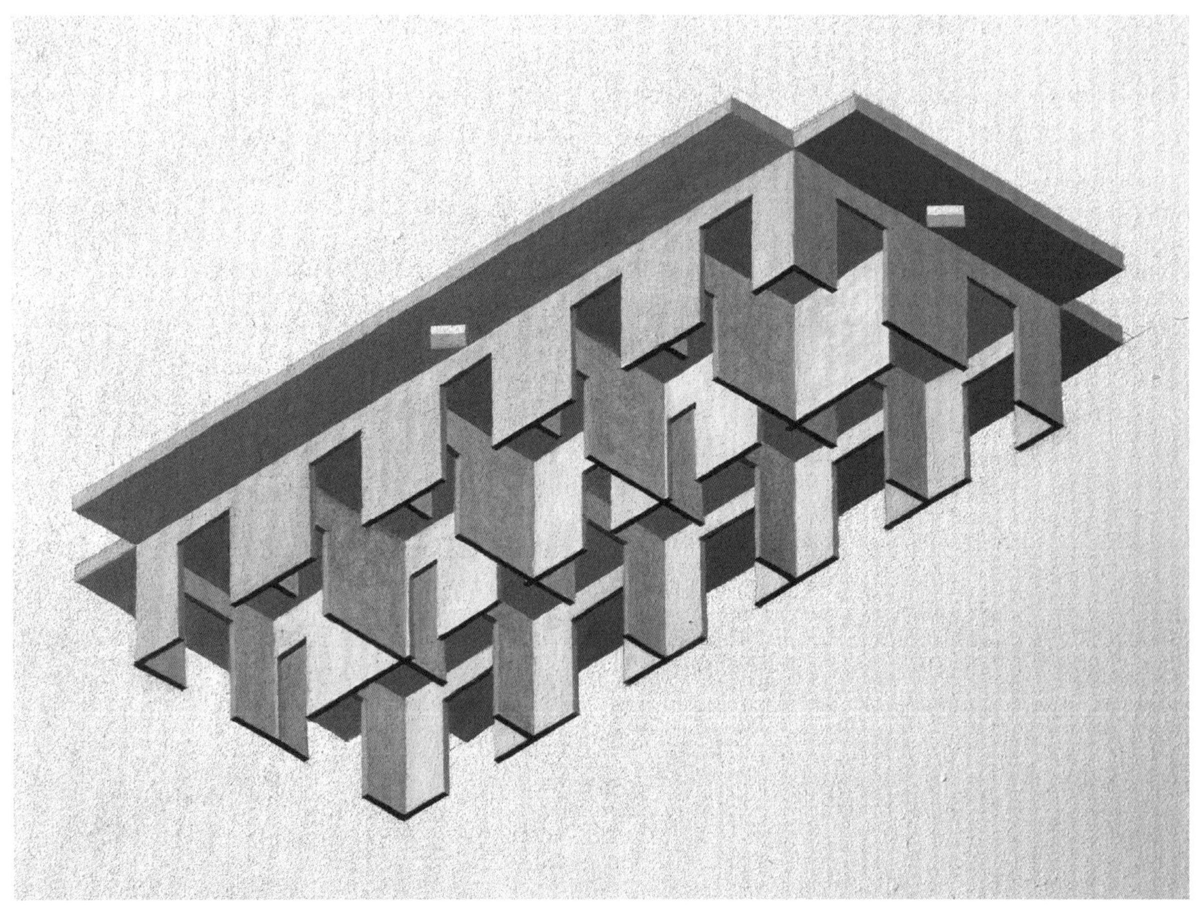

Pezo von Ellrichshausen, Meri House, 2014

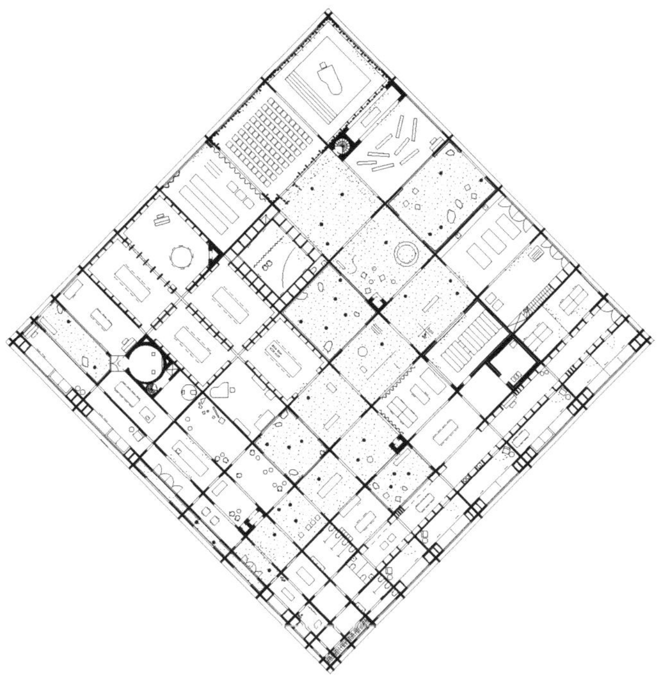

OFFICE Kersten Geers David Van Severen, OFFICE 171: Arvo Pärt Center, 2014

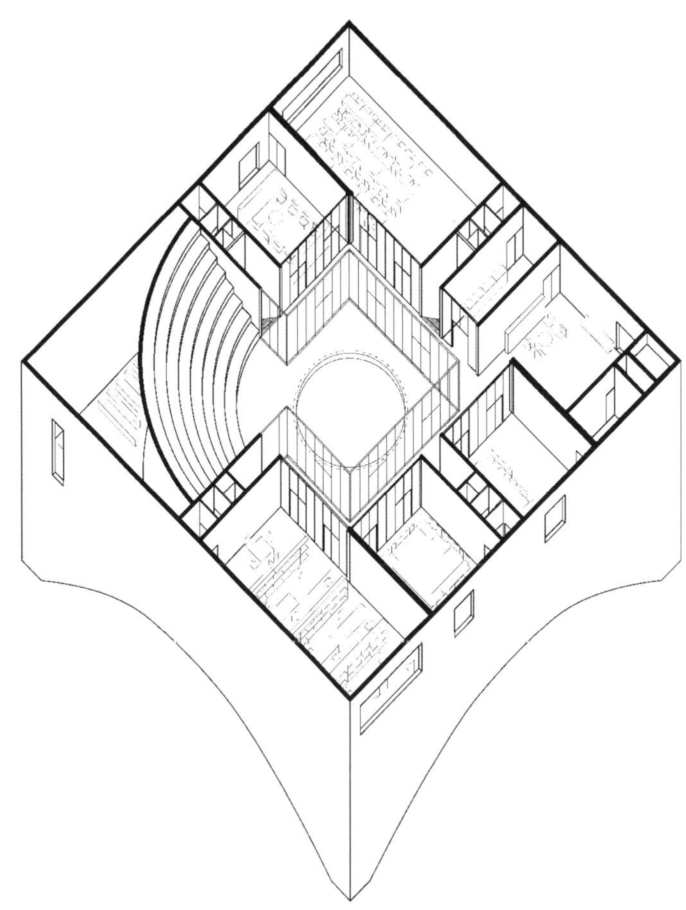

OFFICE Kersten Geers David Van Severen, Hatlehol Church, 2008

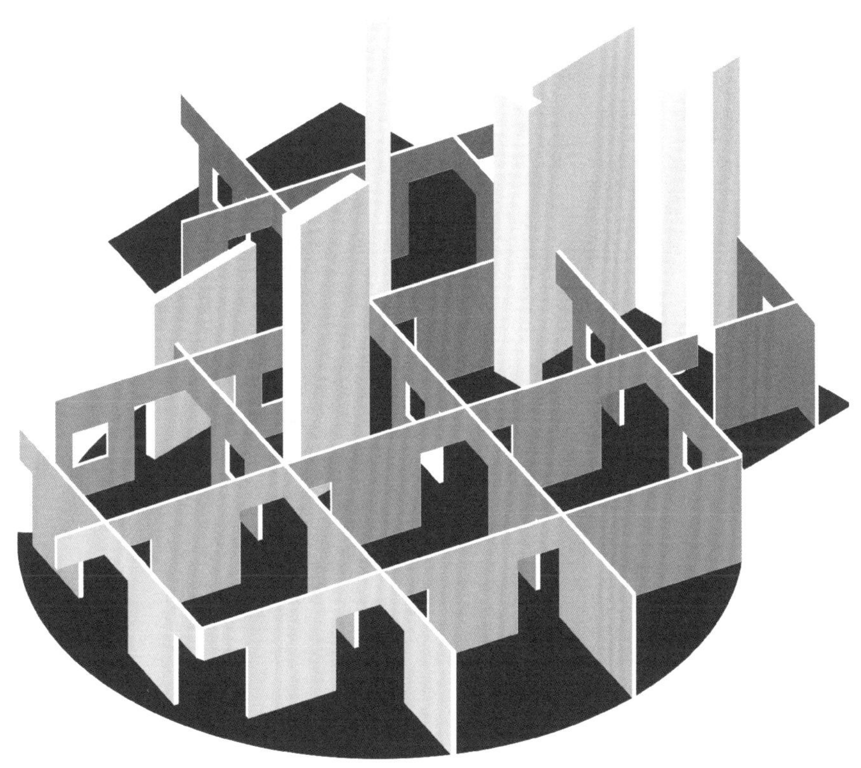

MAIO, Exhibition at MACBA, 2014

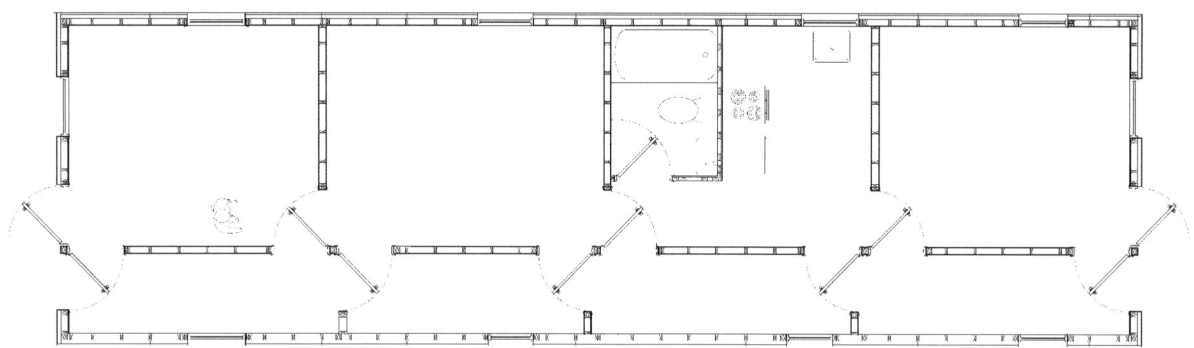

First Office, Shotgun House, 2014

Ultramoderne, Southlight, 2016

The zero-degree formula of the eidetic—"a house is a house"—gives each building element a twofold transparency. They are, first, glimpses into the building's configurative logic (the system that governs what goes where), and because the eidetic offers no space between image and actuality, they also foreshadow the forms of life that unfold inside that configuration. Not to be confused with the "machine for living" that separates the spheres of devices and people, the declaration "this is a house," then, can also be read, "these are the people" and "this is how they live." Architecture, that is, marks the imagination of human affairs in these houses so emphatically that the language used to designate elements and their arrangement is the same language that specifies people and their relations to each other. The holed-up someone under WOJR's big roof may occasionally become visible as they peer out from circular attic window, while the deck-traipsers and loungers below promenade and recline beside the lower glass box. Choosey ruminators ponder the options for opening and closing doors and windows that look like doors in First Office's Shotgun House, while the indifferent opener of an Independent Architecture door gives no thought to which of the four identical choices happen to deliver her onto roughly equal versions of the same patio—it's all, equally, ok.

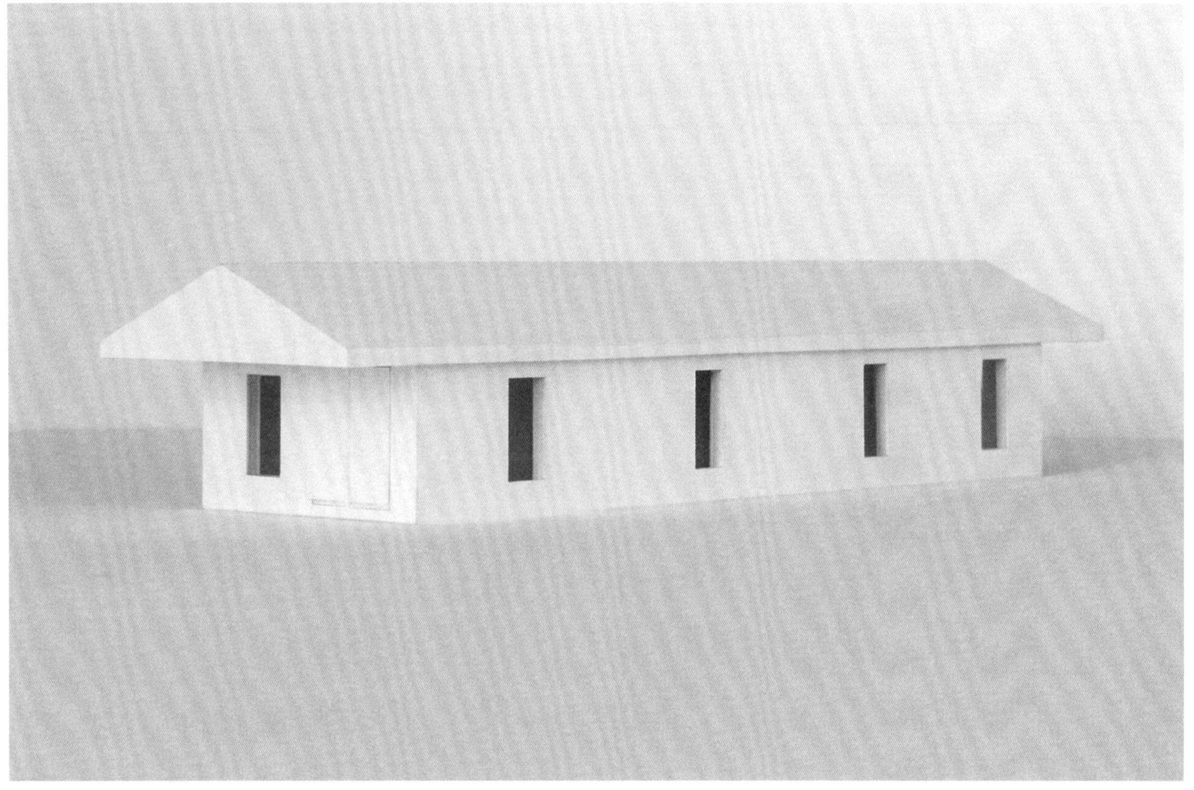

First Office, Shotgun House, 2014

PARA Project, Stump House, 2019–

Architecture Office, House in House, 2016

Independent Architecture, Motherhouse, 2019

LAMAS, Townships Farmhouse, 2017

Karamuk Kuo, Augusta Raurica Archaeological Center, in progress

WOJR, House of the Woodland, 2019

WOJR, Dwelling, in progress

Booleans

Having elected to gather the unruly componentry of architecture in higher-order sets, Boolean architecture keeps records of the arithmetic of things in pairs and multiples. Houses are drawn from above and below, modeled inside and outside, or rendered as solids and then as hollow volumes. The apparent symmetry of accounting—things in this drawing perfectly corresponding to those things in that drawing—allows drastically different sets of things to deliver effects to each other through the shifting vantages of representation. A solid cast of the walls, then another of the room: as though the space one occupies in a plan is pushed into place by the contents of walls. A bird's-eye view of the roof from above, then a worm's-eye looking up at the eaves: the shapes of skylights seen by a passing helicopter are the qualities of sunlit rooms for the wanderer below.

PARA Project, Crawford Attic Writing Room, 2010

Bureau Spectacular, Maison Bande Dessinée, 2019

Bureau Spectacular, Maison Bande Dessinée, 2019

Outpost Office, Villa Shotgun, 2017

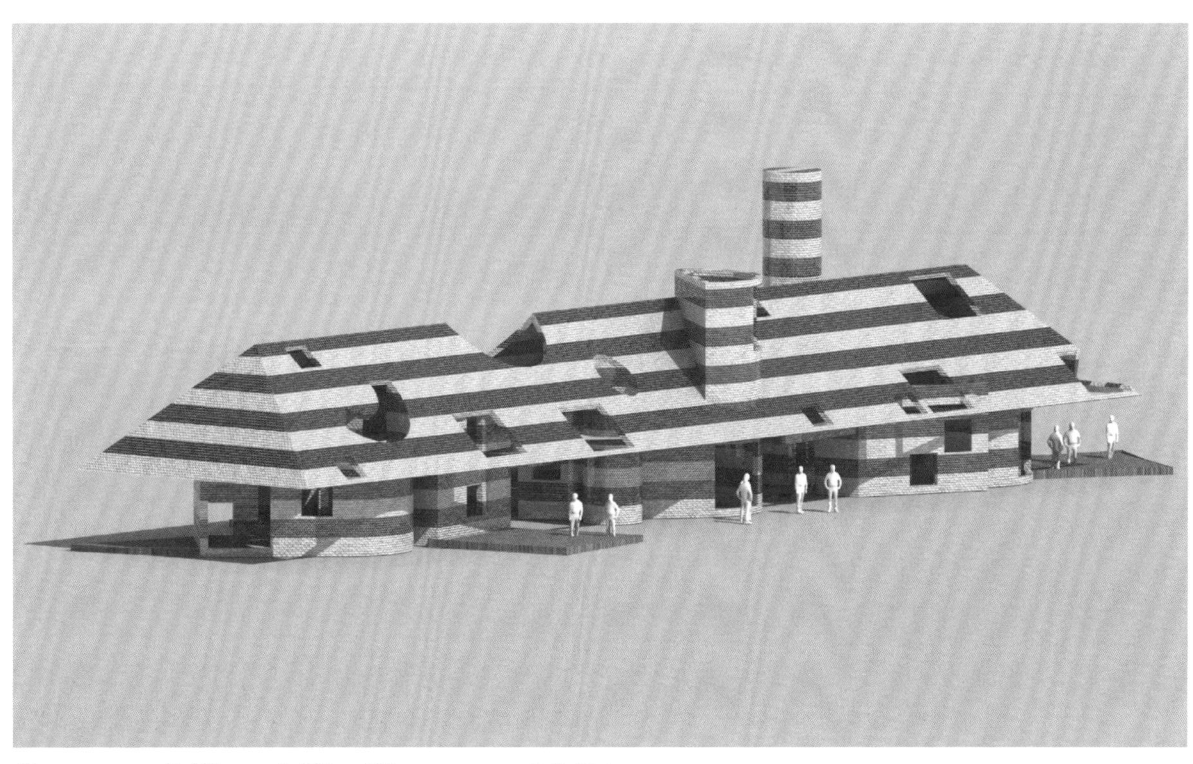

Outpost Office, Villa Shotgun, 2017

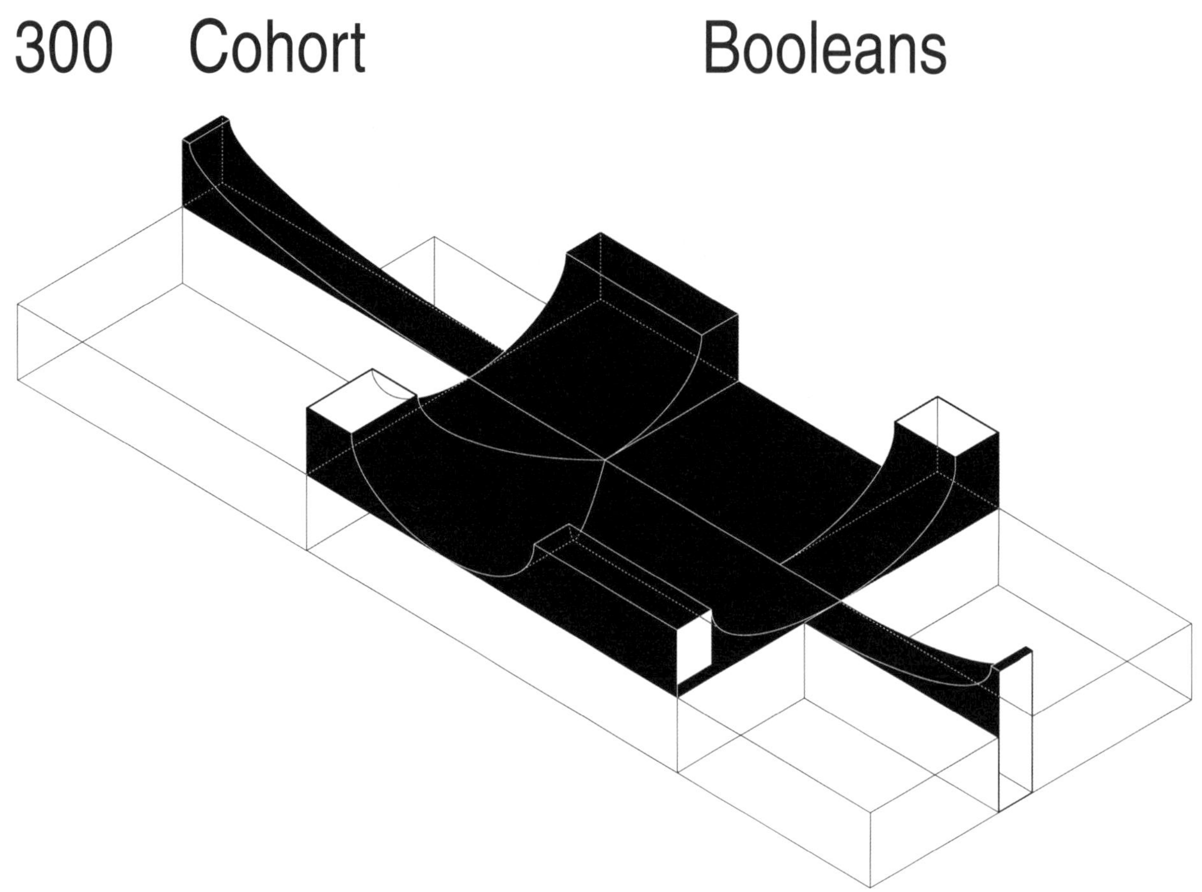

WOJR, House of Horns, in progress

WOJR, House of Horns, in progress

MILLIØNS, Collectives II, 2016

MILLIØNS, Collectives II, 2016

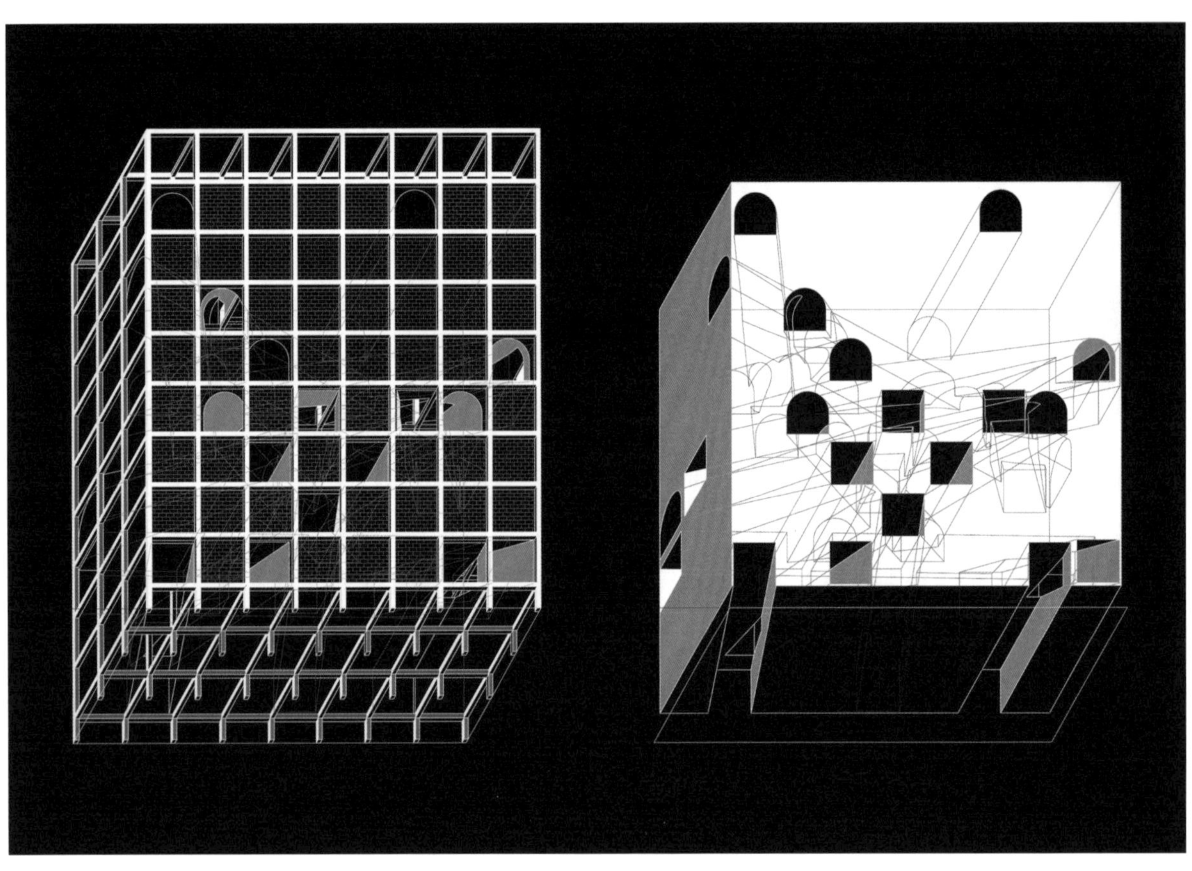

Alex Maymind, Shoots and Ladders, No. 27, 2013

The house-on-house and shape-on-shape strategies of this group generate near doublings of rooms, walls, and scenes that, while they are duplicates in terms of appearance, disagree on basic obligations like carrying load, providing egress, or affording shelter. For instance, one pitched elevation of Fièvre + Jones's Bywater Artist Residence fronts a house volume as expected, while the other is partially a house front and partially a courtyard wall—the result of bending and superimposing a bar-shaped house onto a much larger hipped-roof volume, which is half hollowed out as a consequence. These repetitions of appearance that shift architectural performance have split subjects: a person approaching the Bywater Residence facade may be at once a neighbor calling over the garden wall and a lurker at the rear window. The effect is to allow subjects to be visited by displaced versions of themselves, shifted in position, mood, or time, but in otherwise apparently identical settings. Courtyards and voids play a key role, allowing one part of the building to regard itself from another and to contemplate the strangeness of a literal encounter with the question of an alternate self. What if I were over there, or were to work down the hall tomorrow, or under the influence of a different roof, or . . . ?

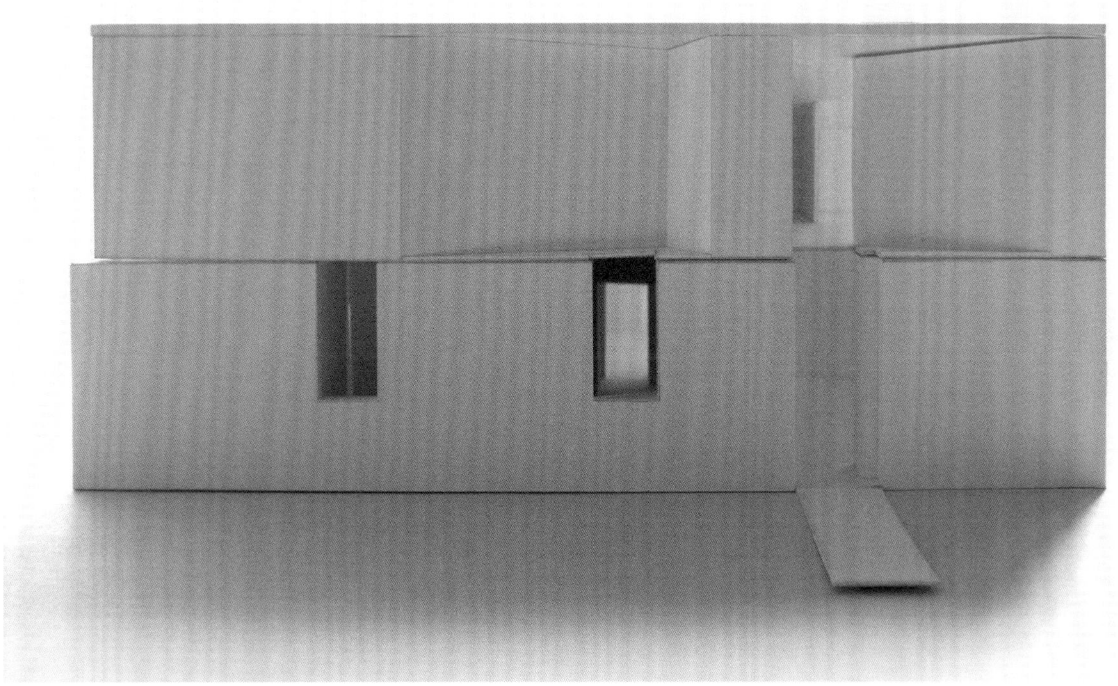

JaJa Co, Noise, Pt. 3, 2016

JaJa Co, Noise, Pt. 3, 2016

Preston Scott Cohen, Inc., Cornered House, 1992

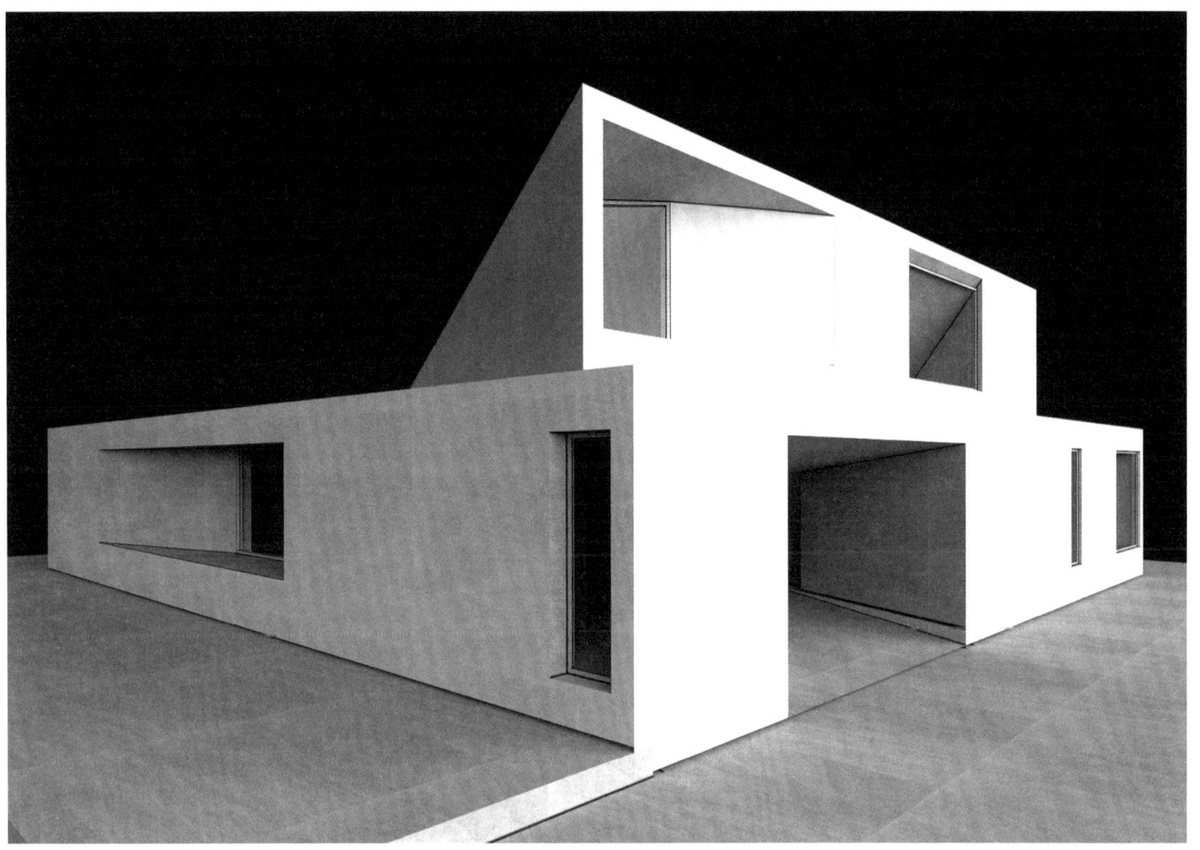

Studio Sean Canty, House with a Void, 2016

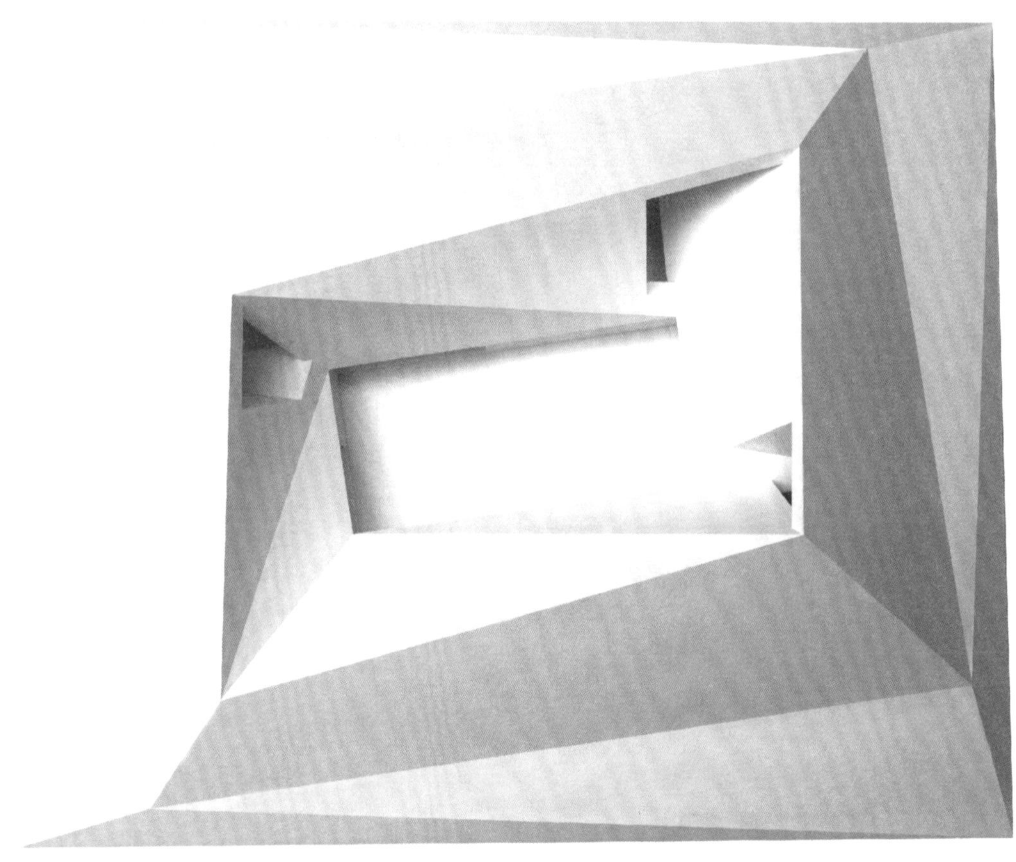

Johnston Marklee, Hut House, 2014

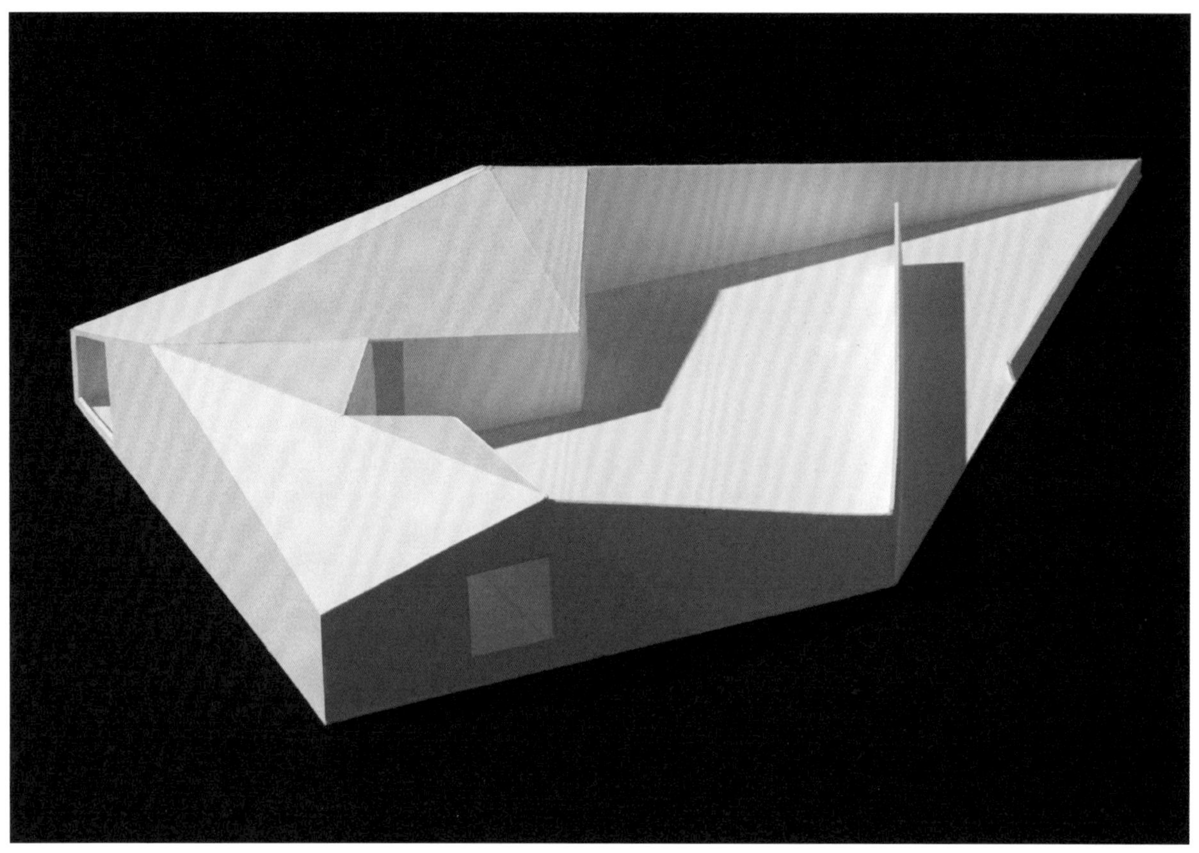

Fievre + Jones, Bywater Artist Residence I, in progress

Ultramoderne, Four Corners, 2014

Superimpositions

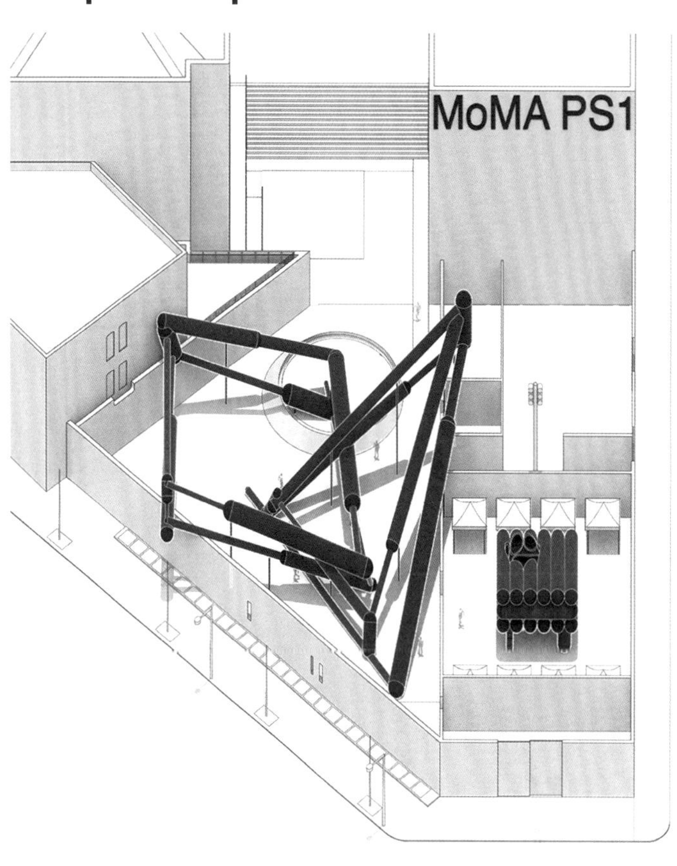

BairBalliet, Loud Lines, 2018

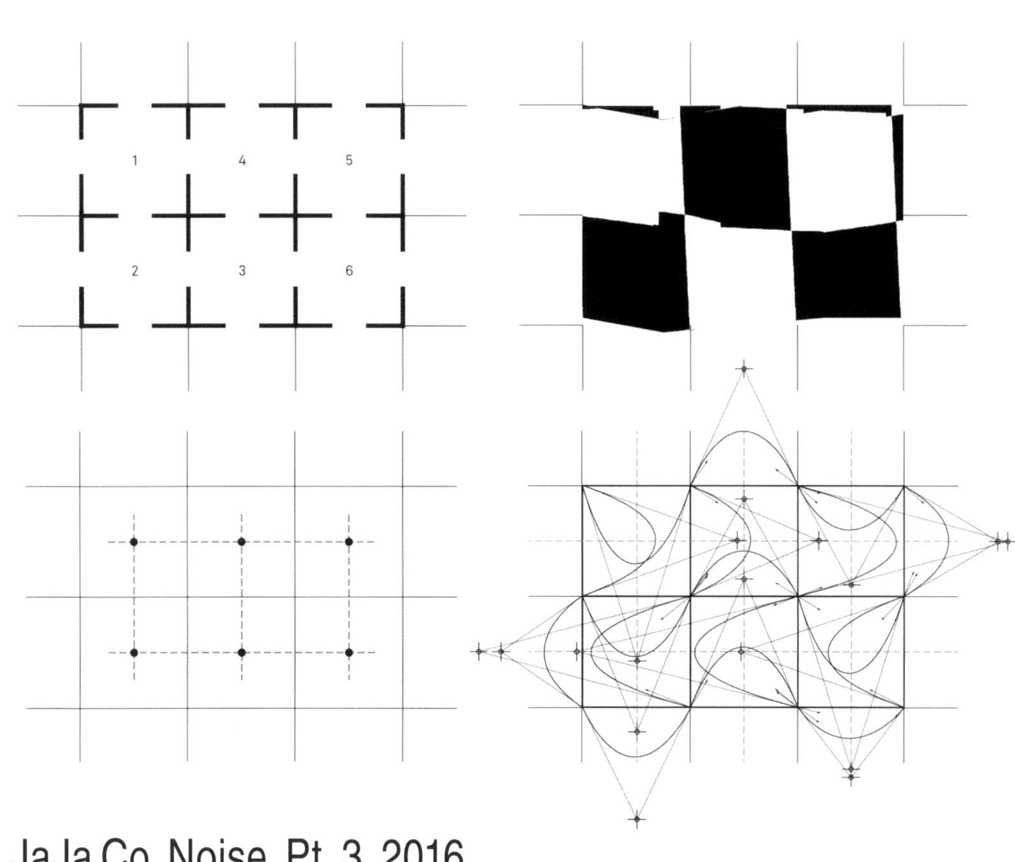

JaJa Co, Noise, Pt. 3, 2016

The projects in this cohort tend to be line drawings, layered and often transparent, and process oriented. No indication is given in any of the projects as to where the inscription is made (no site or even ground), of what materials, or for what purpose. The projects' common attribute is a cartography of forces, from paths to cuts, contours to sight lines. The revelation is the point of articulation between force and form—the piling up of traces to give the appearance of a fully formed object. But the trace as inscription is not a thing or an entity but a structuring principle that opens a space for architecture. Unlike a conventional drawing, its purpose is not to describe but rather to set out conditions of possibility. The "revealed original" is nowhere present but is always already a transcription of differentiating forces. As Derrida writes, "Trace as memory is not a pure breaching that might be reappropriated at any time as simple presence; it is rather the ungraspable and invisible difference between breaches." In other words, the revelation is the *field* of difference within the exertion of forces.

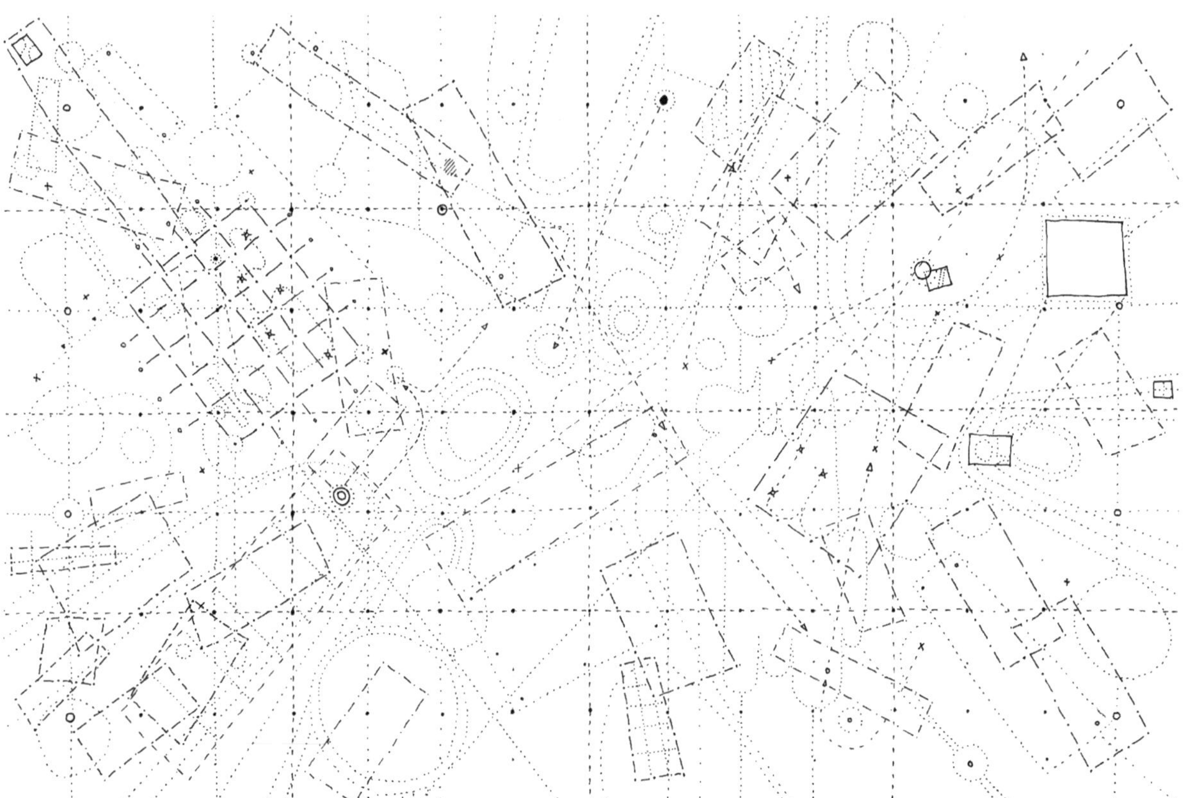

Bureau Spectacular, Ghosted Drawing Series, 2015

First Office, Possible Table, 2014

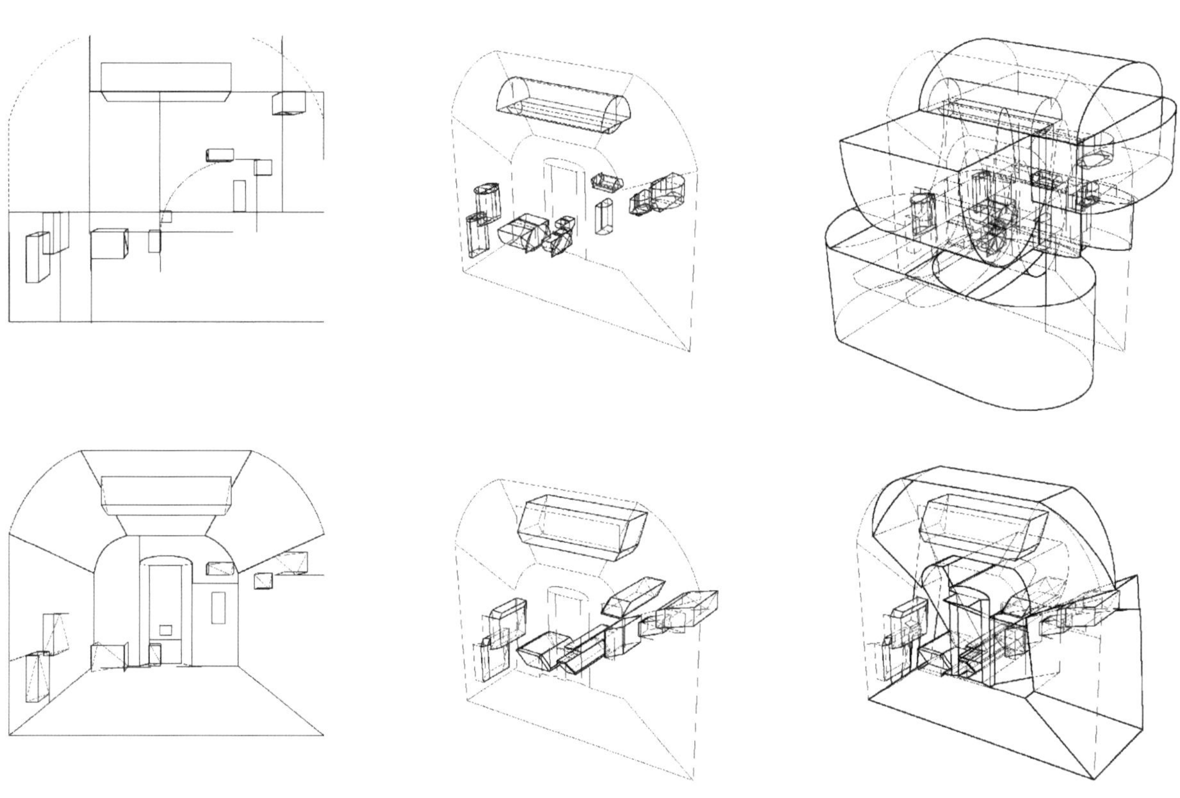

studioPM, Not-So-Still Life, 2018

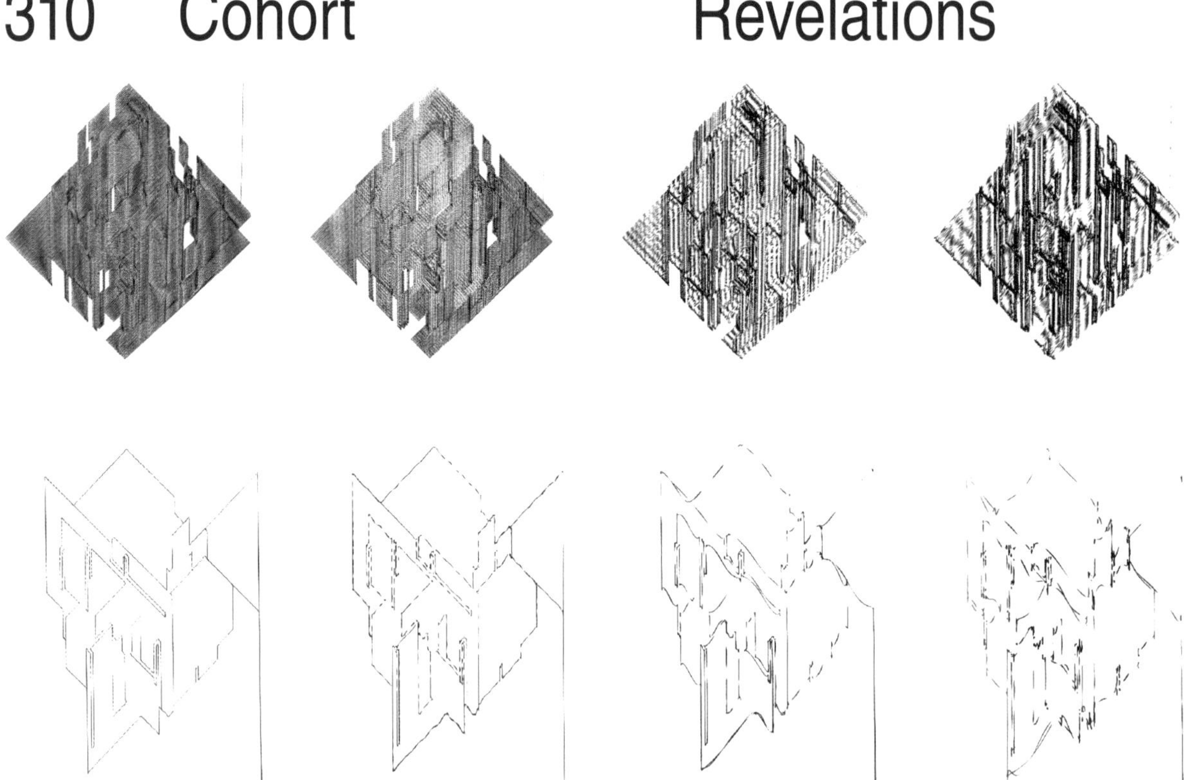

Erin Besler, Low Fidelity, 2012

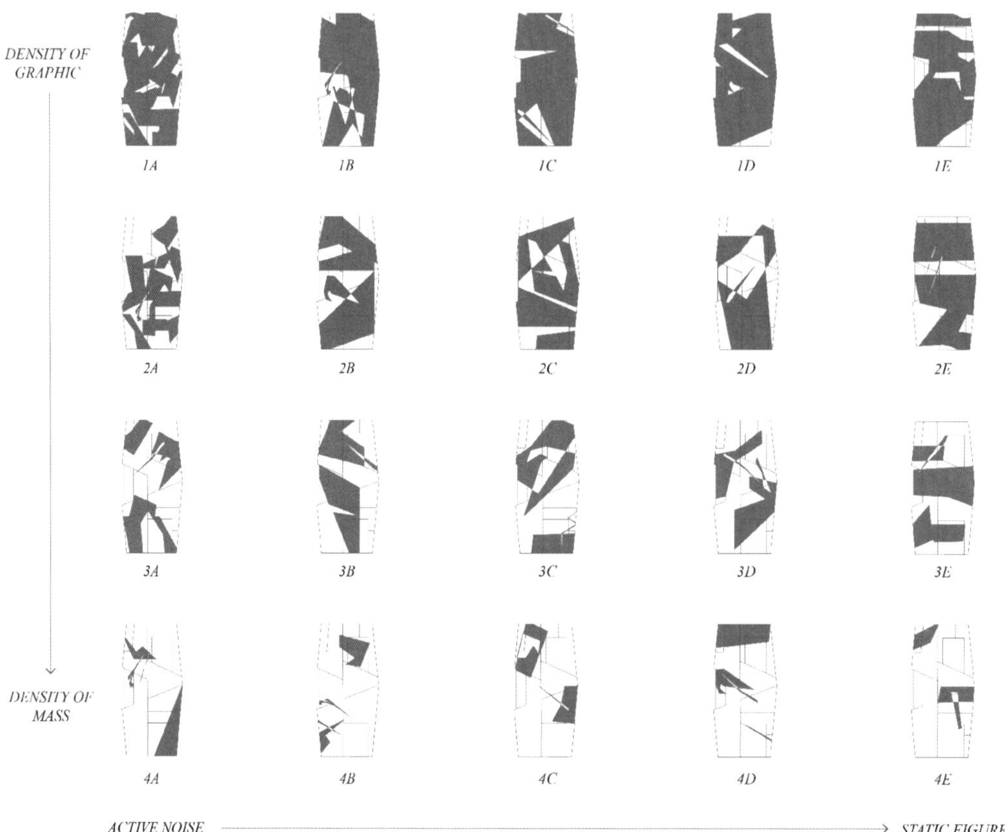

Viola Ago and Hans Tursack, Thick Skin, 2018

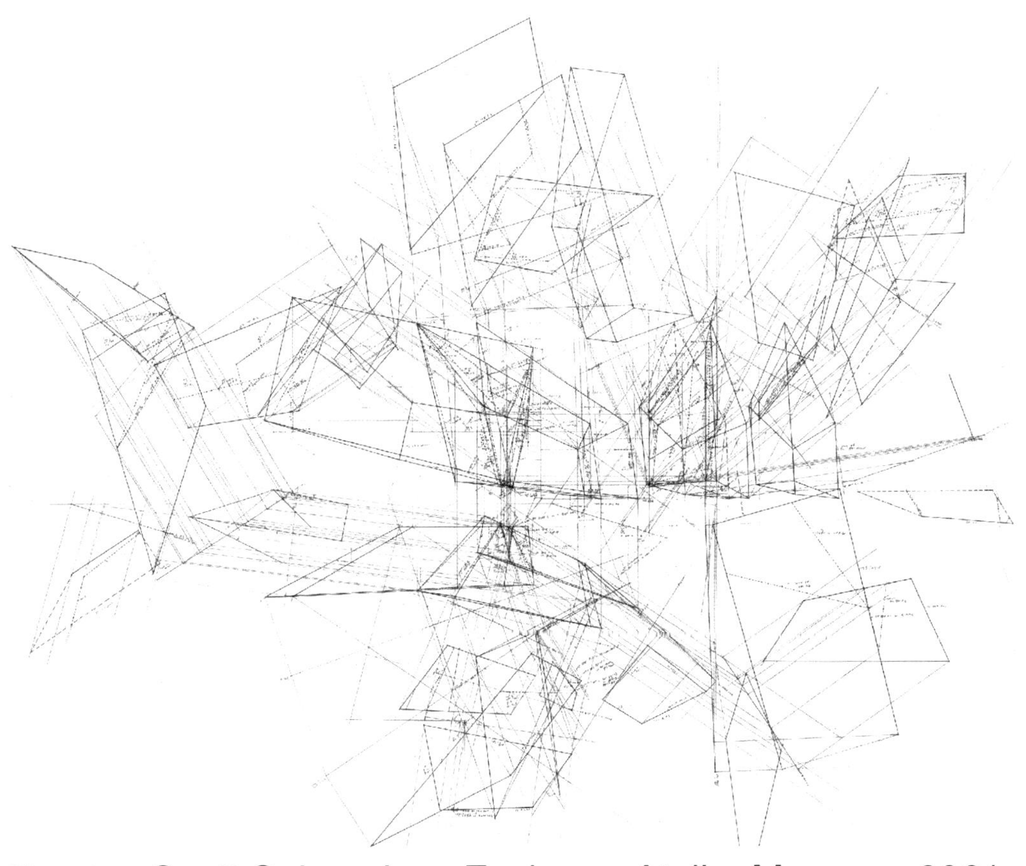

Preston Scott Cohen, Inc., Eyebeam Atelier Museum, 2001

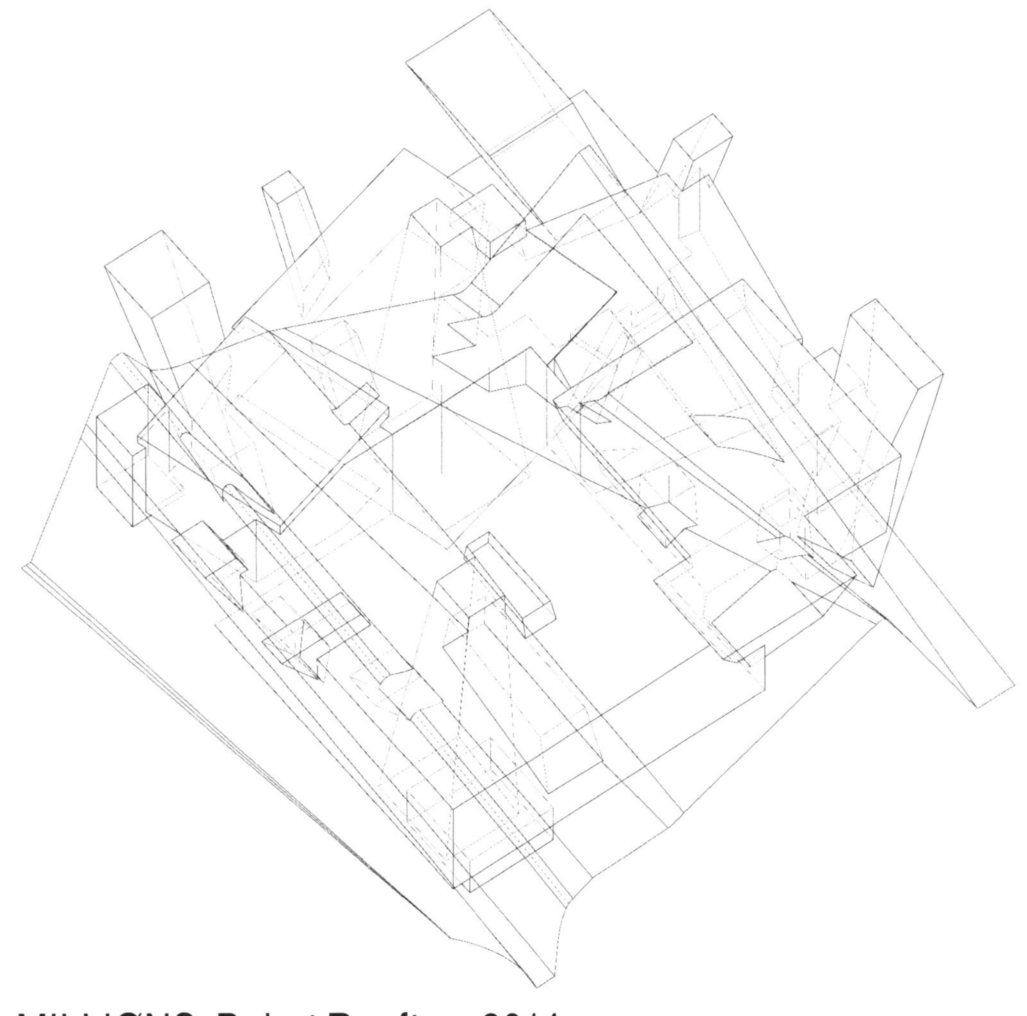

MILLIØNS, Beirut Rooftop, 2014

Substitution is one way to produce the simultaneous "collectedness" and "dispersal" of slack collections. A constellation of elements is called upon to discharge a list of tasks, and elements are substituted, like members of a team, in and out to execute the assignments. "Collectedness" in this cohort is therefore a temporary fitness between element and task: shapes are stacked in classical tripartite arrangements of base, piano nobile, and pediment; the planes of a stud-wall box are reconstituted as sheets, casts, or blocks; a tensegrity's lines of force are traced by escalators and hollow tubes. "Dispersal" is the possibility of rearrangement as the element-task pairings are cycled through. Some other pink shape takes a turn as pediment. A sheet wrinkles, hinting at the infinity of folded arrangements that could stand in for the stud wall. Escalators and tubes doubly trace the same line of force, such that neither holds the center.

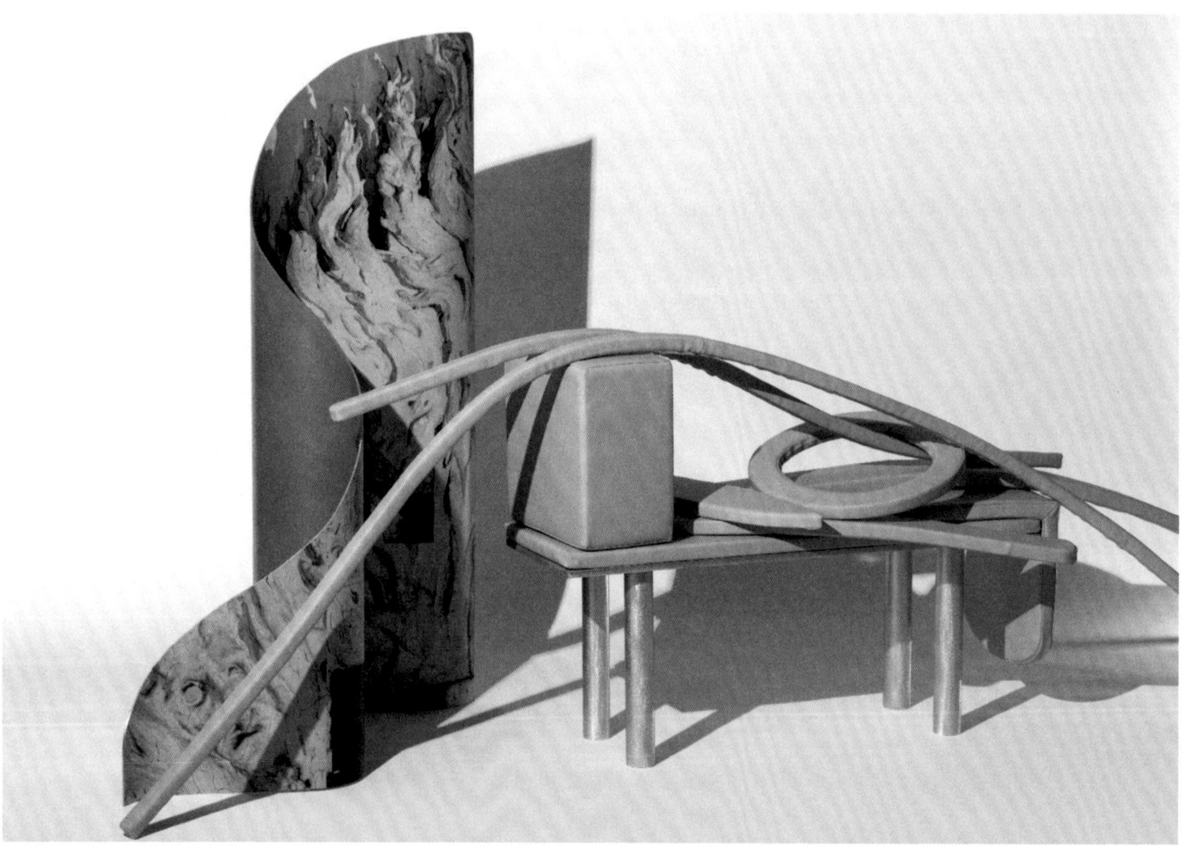

Andy and Dave, Wanna go there! (Partition), and Where is this? (Bench), 2018

Preston Scott Cohen, Inc., Eyebeam Atelier Museum, 2001

NEMESTUDIO, Our Junk, Their Ruin, 2018

The LADG, The Kid Gets out of the Picture, 2016

Lluís Alexandre Casanovas Blanco with María Luisa Blanco, Real Estate Boom House, Dynemaa Bobbin Lace Curtain Prototype #1, 2018

Welcome Projects, Retrospective City, 2014

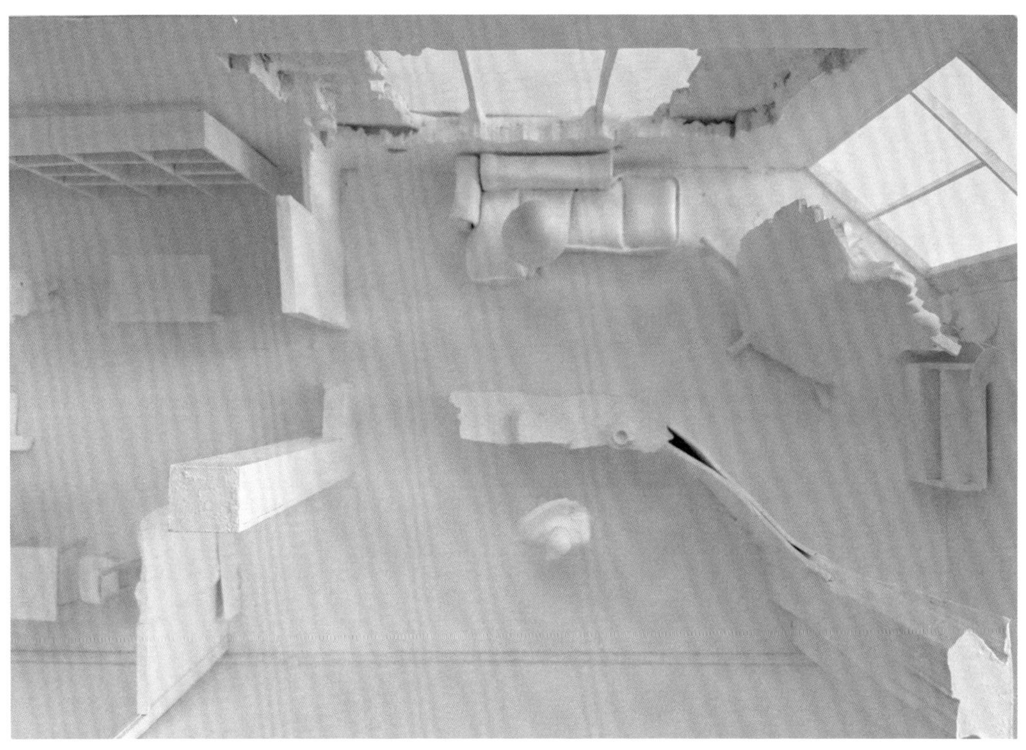

Descriptive Services, Drawing In-Painting, 2018

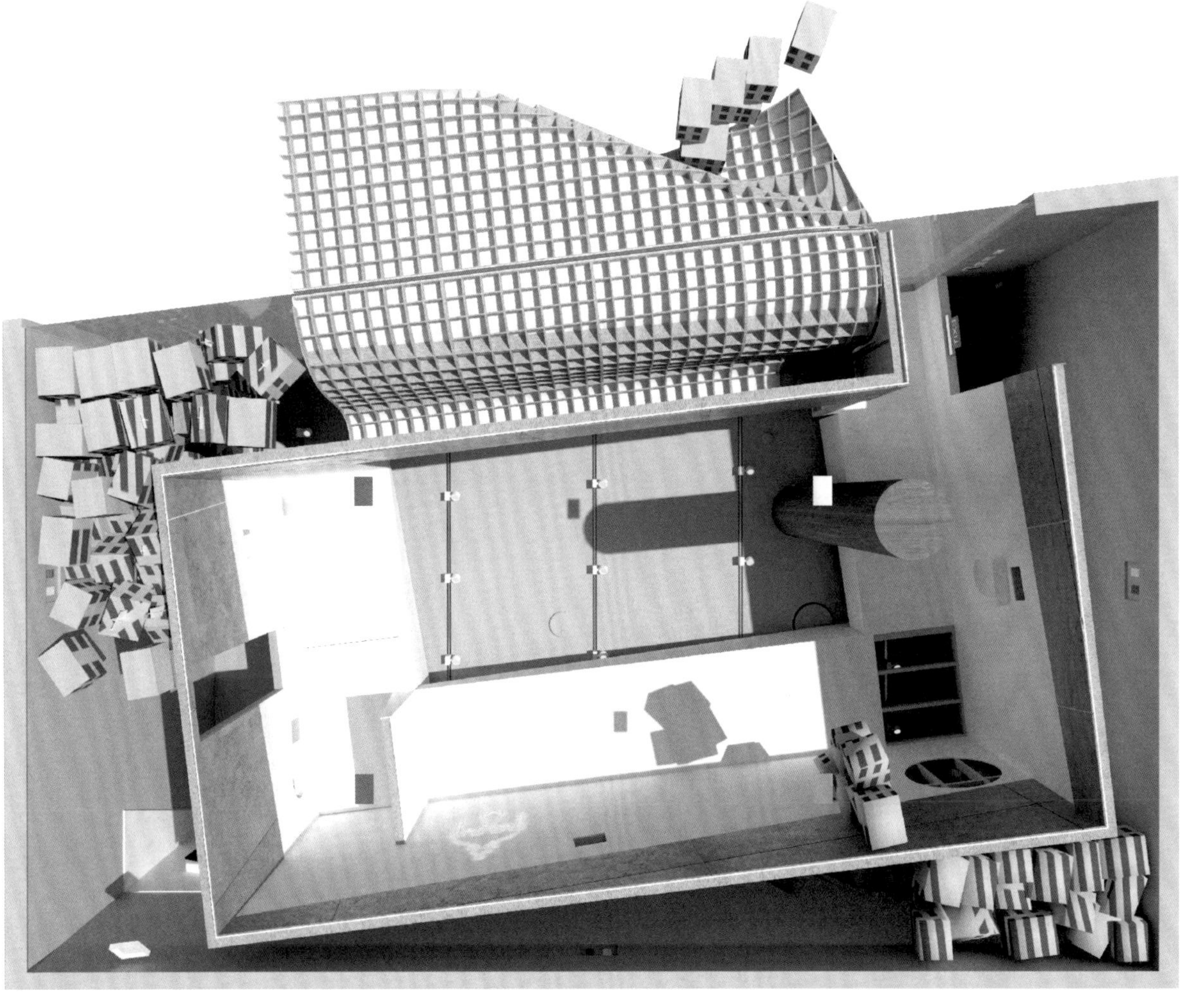

MR Studio, Teh Developed Srf, 2019

Archizoom's No-Stop City promised an egalitarian future with conveniences spread homogeneously across an unending plane, so long as one consented to being a passive consumer in a repeating landscape of beds, tents, toilets, and Ritz cracker boxes. This cohort offers a different kind of equivalence. Objects are distributed as givens at the opening of a scene. They are unevenly dispersed but available for use. This is not a full-fledged economy of objects that values one thing over another. It is instead a built-in tendency toward significance and collective understanding of how social and programmatic arrangements will work—a podium supports sitting or performing, a scaffold, storage or assembly. Traversing the field or conducting activities within it becomes tantamount to the first decisions of a cargo cult, assimilating new objects to established cultural patterns and in turn adjusting the understanding of both.

d.esk, Column & Canopy, 2016

stock-a-studio, neighbor neighbor, 2019

d.esk, Training Wheels, 2015

EXTENTS, SRFC_PLAY, 2017

stock-a-studio and EXTENTS, nude, 2018

Anthony Titus Studio, The Light in the Window is a Crack in the Sky, 2008

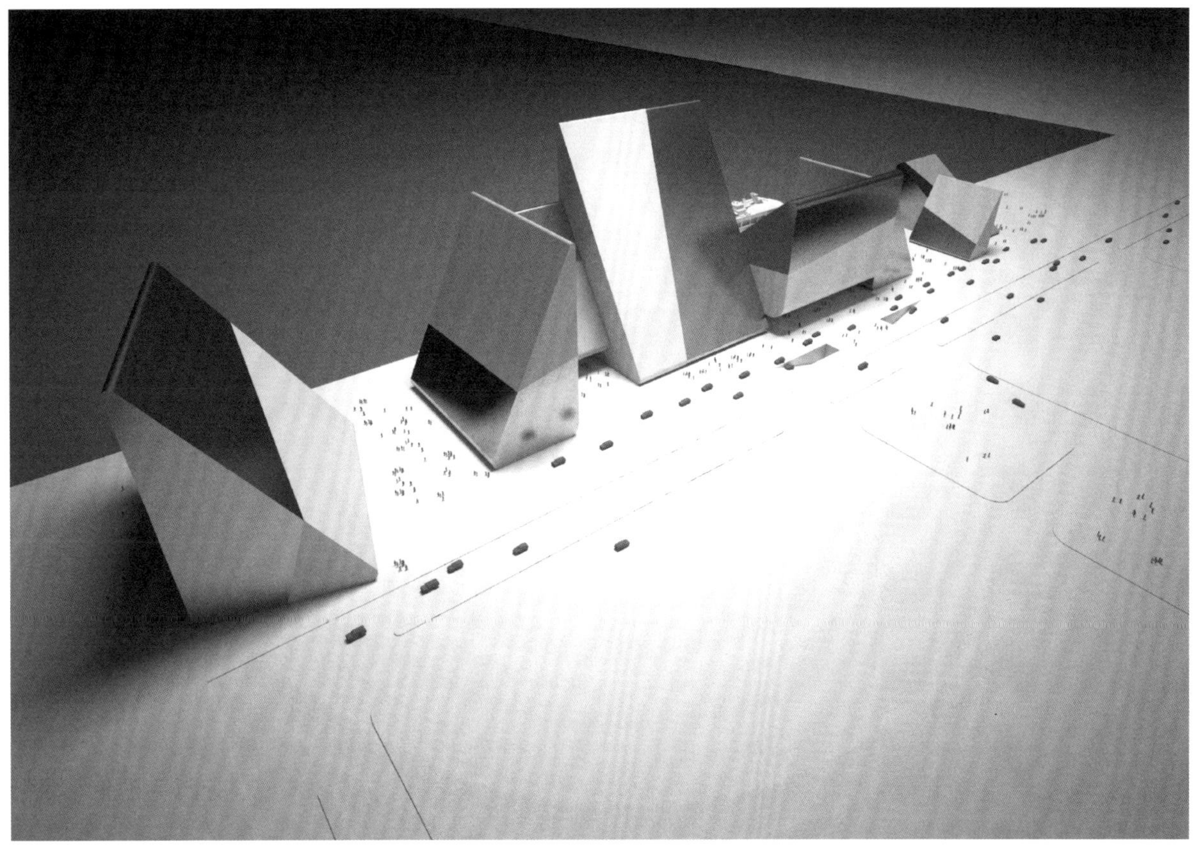

Paul Preissner Architects, Port of Kinmen Passenger Ferry Terminal, 2014

Curtis Roth, Decorating Villa Wolf, 2016

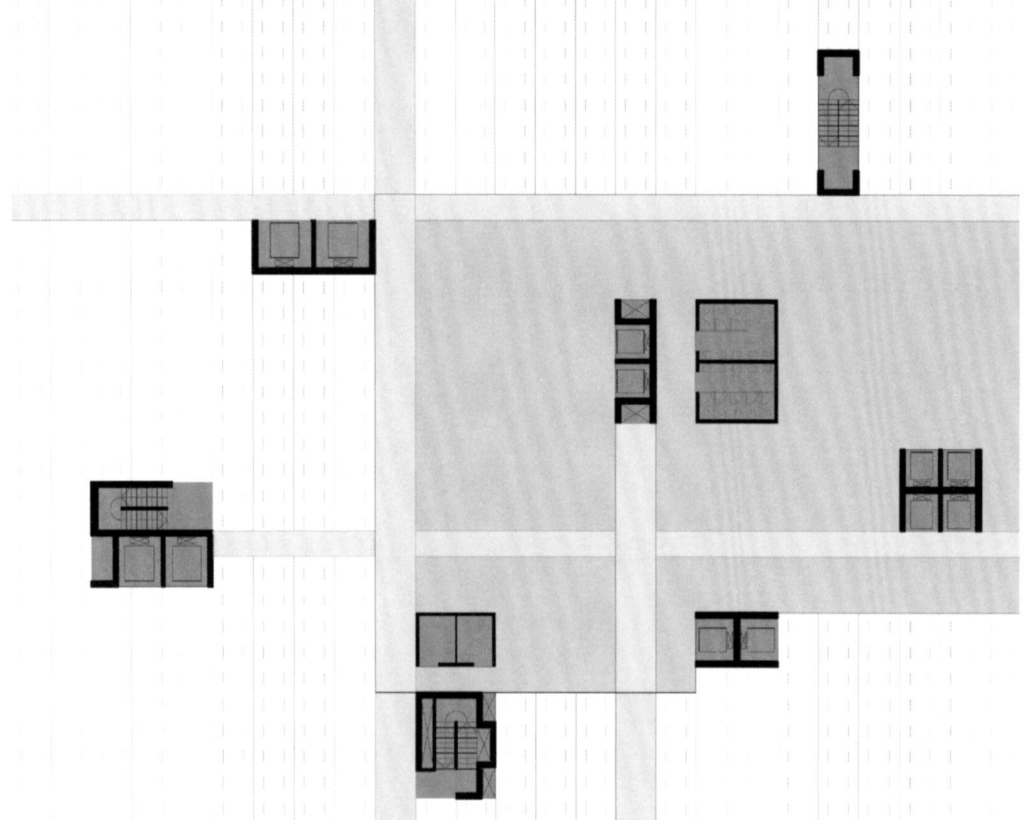

Ensamble Studio, Big Bang Tower, 2013

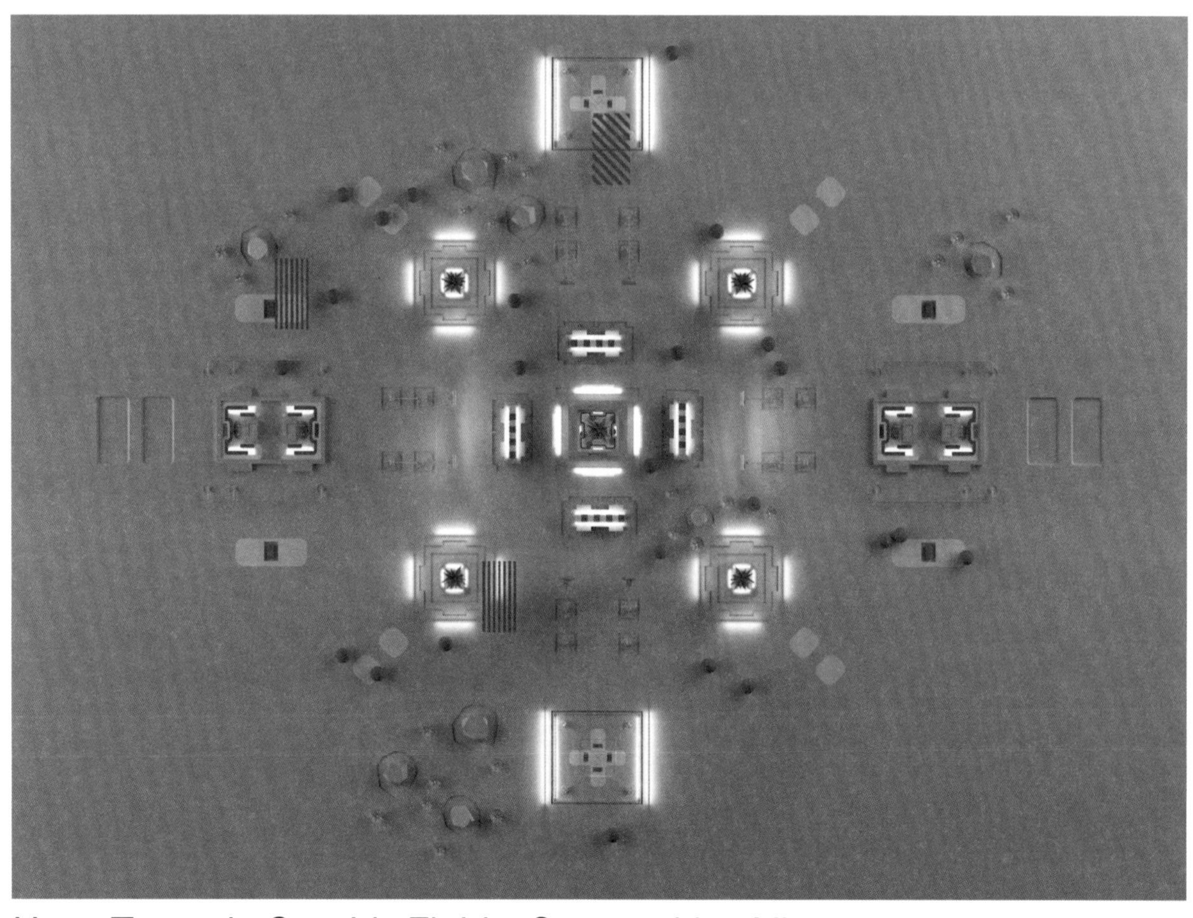

Hans Tursack, Graphic Fields, Composition VI, 2015

Say you want to image a rock and reproduce it. How will you capture it? Sense or measure it? Or rather, from which vantage will you approach it with a camera or scanner or photosensitive surface, and how will these registrations be reassembled? The nonorientable quality of rocks, along with their almost infinite complexity of detail, tends to multiply the means of measure and introduce the problem of how to put all the pieces back together. This is more than a problem of reassembly. The multiple vantages and planes of projection required to assess the size or composition of a rock are uncomfortably similar to the arbitrary vantages of a person trying to get a good view. This is to say images of rocks roll downhill to become pictures, with all the art-historical baggage of that term rooted in the individual viewing eye and representation on a flat plane. The descent from one category to another disrupts the indifference of rocks, their participation in live geologic processes, and their utility as building material. Architects in this cohort invent ways of getting back uphill. They improve picture-measures by folding them around blanks to make objects in the round, printing them on the fabric of beanbags to make them into furniture, or repeating a single measure in every plane of reassembly to make an entire world. Indifference, liveness, and utility are regained with effort.

Besler & Sons, Props, in progress

Ensamble Studio, Tabula Acustica, 2016

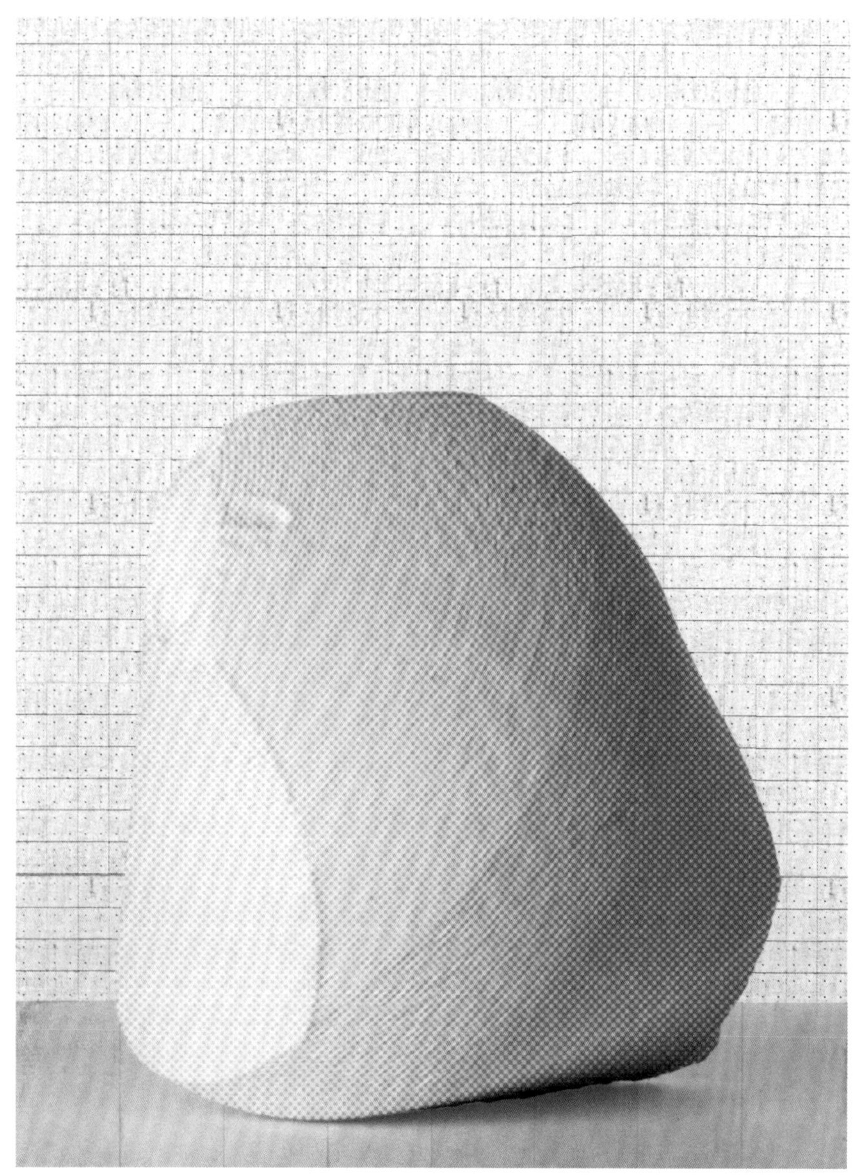

d.esk, Paperweight, 2013

stock-a-studio, all out of this one rock, 2017

Jaffer Kolb, Form in Form, 2015

Hume Coover Studio, Down by the River, 2015

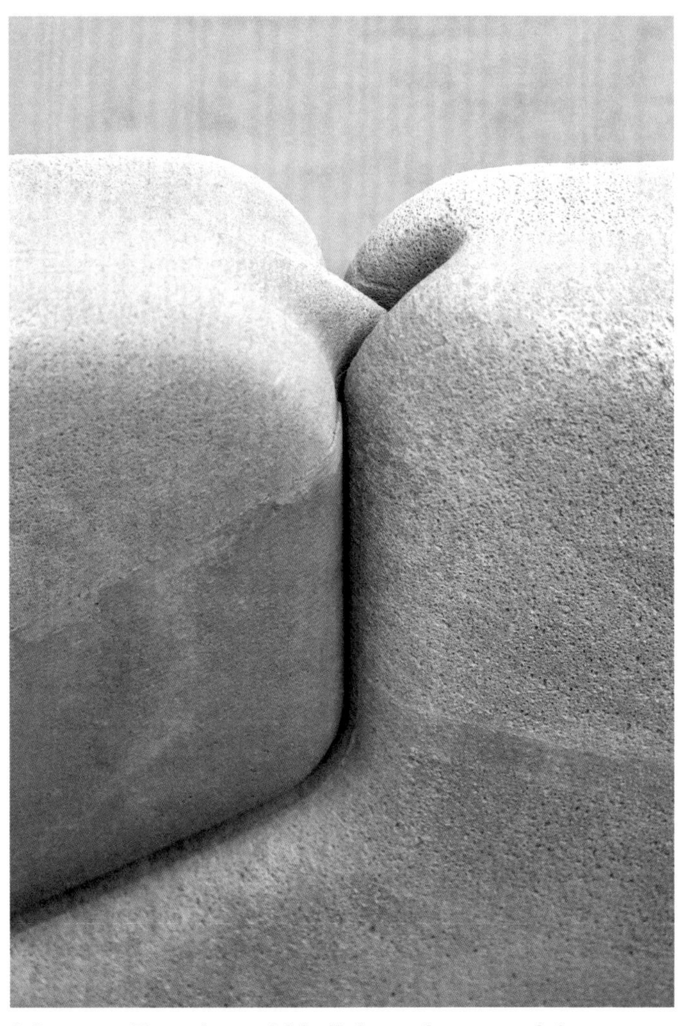

Matter Design, Walking Assembly, 2019

MOS, Rock, in progress

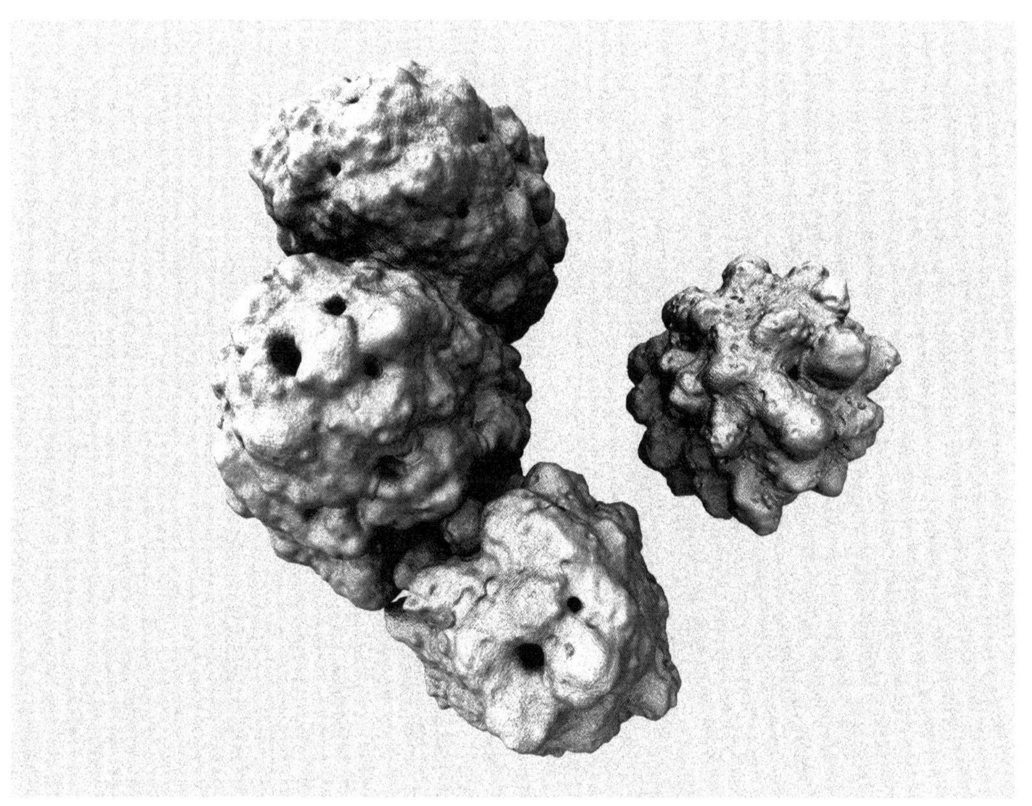

Adam Fure, Rocks, 2014

What is housing what? What original volume is being stacked *around*, and by what means? At modest scales, parts can be stacked in trabeated arrays that fairly imitate walls. The parts may be too discrete and individual to be mistaken for bricks, but the unruliness is confined to the level of symbolic decoration on an envelope that otherwise surrounds the building volume and separates inside from outside in the usual way. A little bigger, and niches become habitable nooks in a foamy, occupiable wrapper. Bigger still, and the in-betweens of assembly simply dissolve the binary of envelope and interior. Buildings become the space of assembled things and the thing-niches between them, such that space is never simply in or out but instead characterized by prepositions and static relations that apply equally to people and things: *on* a cantilever beam, *underneath* a stone counterweight. One more scale up, and the parts are enormous hollow volumes in the shape of familiar objects. Construction and occupation both split into literal and imaginative logics. On the one hand, the literal construction techniques are conventional enough and make for envelopes that sit politely at the outer limit of the building in the usual way, while on the other hand, in terms of the symbolic assembly of one huge part balanced on another, the building is a giant's superscaled play set.

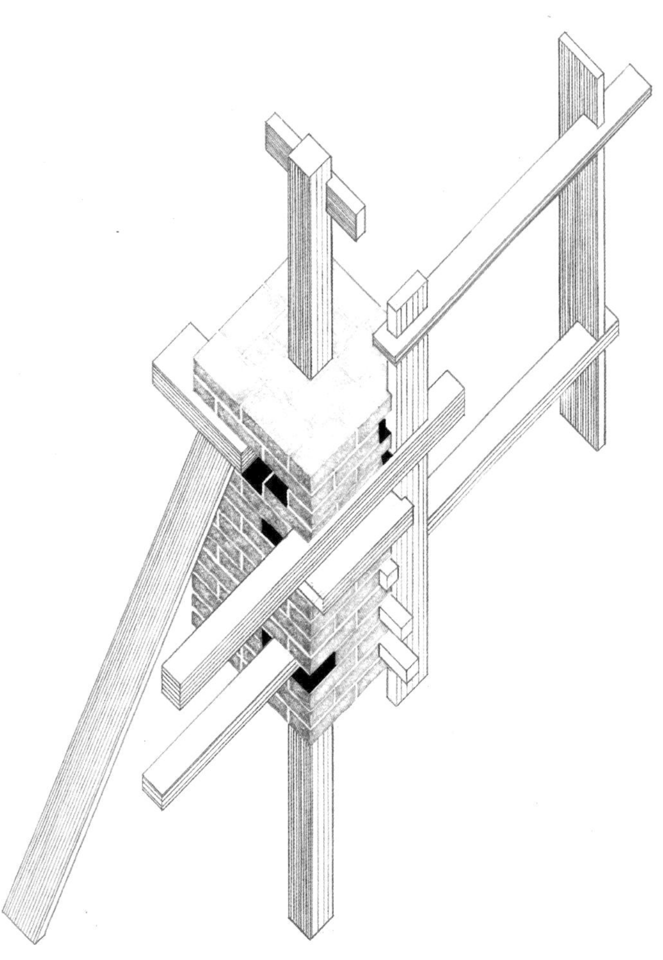

Owen Nichols, iffy architecture, 2018

OFFICE Kersten Geers David Van Severen, OFFICE 49: Water Tower, 2008

Ensamble Studio, Hemeroscopium House, 2008

Medium Office, Frame Tower, 2016

Paul Preissner Architects, Ring of Hope, 2017–

Paul Preissner Architects, Tripoli Special Economic Zone, 2019

LAMAS, Over Cast, 2015

The primary trait of first houses is that they exhibit of their making, but there are several ways to accomplish that theatrical display, each replete with specialized roles for architects and builders. First, a version we might call “tectonics” begins with the decomposition of buildings into elements, each one serving as evidence of a bygone craft culture. Gottfried Semper’s imagination of walls as weaving is the famous instance, but any pairing of elements with labor will do, so long as it conjures a complete economic and cultural unit that is doing something for the first time, organizing itself around the task of building. A second mode arrests or pauses a simulation, as though a single frame is selected from a film to stand in for an entire world of forces and materials that were in turn invented to generate a single construction. But rather than teleological stories of how buildings come to be, these are geysers of possibilities produced by synthetic laws, such that arresting and selecting just one is an essay on taste, wit, humor, and the audacity of ruling out everything else for just this one thing. And third, the theater of limiting construction to a set of “availables” shows what can be done with whatever’s on hand. Little slices through the life of a particular consumer or editor or professional shopper, they suspend for a moment the store-to-trash economic circulation of things to ask, what could these be?

Current Interests, Silver House Studio, in progress

First Office, Studio for Art, 2017

T+E+A+M, A Range Life, 2017

Mack Scogin Merrill Elam Architects, The Atlanta Pavilion, 2005

Toshiko Mori Architect, Thread Artists' Residency and Cultural Center, 2015

The LADG, The Kid Gets out of the Picture, 2016

The ziggurats in this cohort build a collective economics and raise it to the level of myth. Constant modules taken from a finite pool accrue stepwise from the ground, each level a bit smaller so as not to overburden or completely occupy the course below. The increment expends itself as it grows higher, creating a hierarchy of value by scarcity. The floor plate or play space or step is increasingly desirable, literally higher but also offered in ever more sparing amounts until whatever's on top is the last thing, the apotheotic thing, supported by an act of building that has completely exhausted itself in the ascent. As a point of comparison, parametric assemblies may continuously differentiate building components, but the effects of this customization are to stabilize and smooth, promising that architecture will modify itself to suit every individual whim. Ziggurats, by contrast, remain bluntly the same, staging a collective theater where ascent is measured against a diminishing schedule of resources.

MOS, Community Center No. 3 (Lali Gurans Orphanage), in progress

Pezo von Ellrichshausen, Mine Pavilion, 2014

PARA Project, Open Fort, 2009

Medium Office, Stack Villa 3, 2019

d.esk, Ziggurhut, 2018

The Open Workshop, Scaffoldia, 2016

Thom Moran, Tables and Chairs, 2010

PRODUCTORA, Pavilion on the Zocalo, 2014

Hollow unitary volumes convey the sense of an “inner, even secret life” that is a hallmark of objecthood’s animate qualities. Yet some ’liths stretch toward other formal strategies to achieve similar effects. They gamble on being able to retain the scene-making powers conferred by objecthood while at the same time multiplying in form and growing in number. Jesús Vassallo, Central Standard Office of design, CO-G, and Endemic Architecture ramify as a way of articulating mass so that a hollow volume seats, as if a head, the containment of inner secrets and shunts this life effect up or down to smaller branches. PRODUCTORA and OFFICE Kersten Geers David Van Severen make little crowds by multiplying blocks in twos and threes on plinths, emphasizing self-similarity within narrow limits of surface variation. Both strategies anticipate a scene onto which human participants might arrive. People are not merely able to stand alongside; they can stand in the manner of the building already beside itself. Image formats too are anticipated by buildings already linked to drawings and pictures of the self in a crowd.

PRODUCTORA, Aalto University Campus, 2012

OFFICE Kersten Geers David Van Severen, OFFICE 162: New NCCA, 2014

Farshid Moussavi Architecture, Folie Divine, 2017

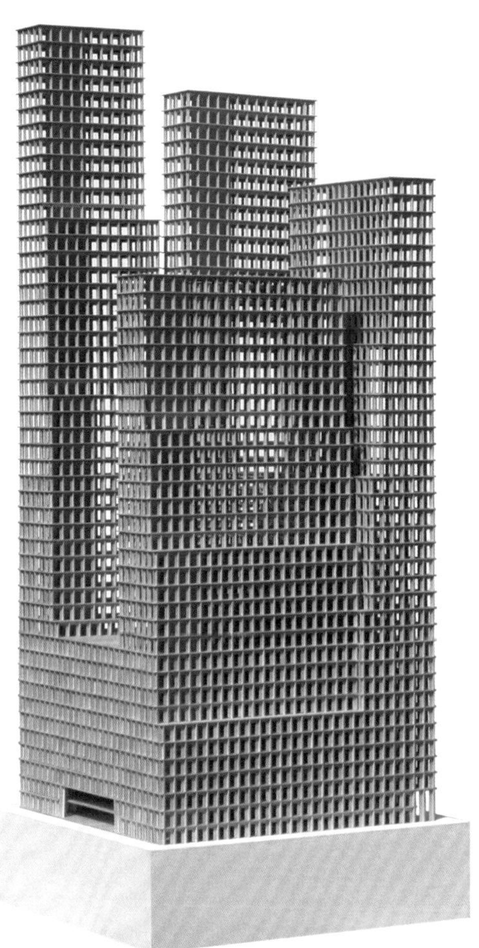

Jesús Vassallo, Timber Towers, 2015

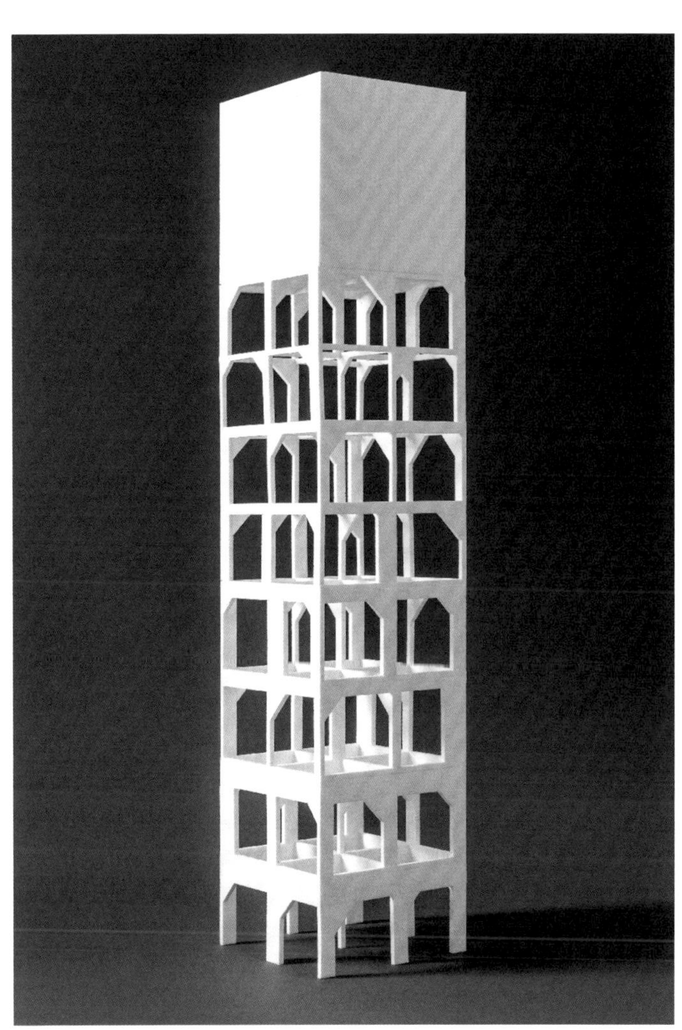

Jesús Vassallo, Water Towers, 2017

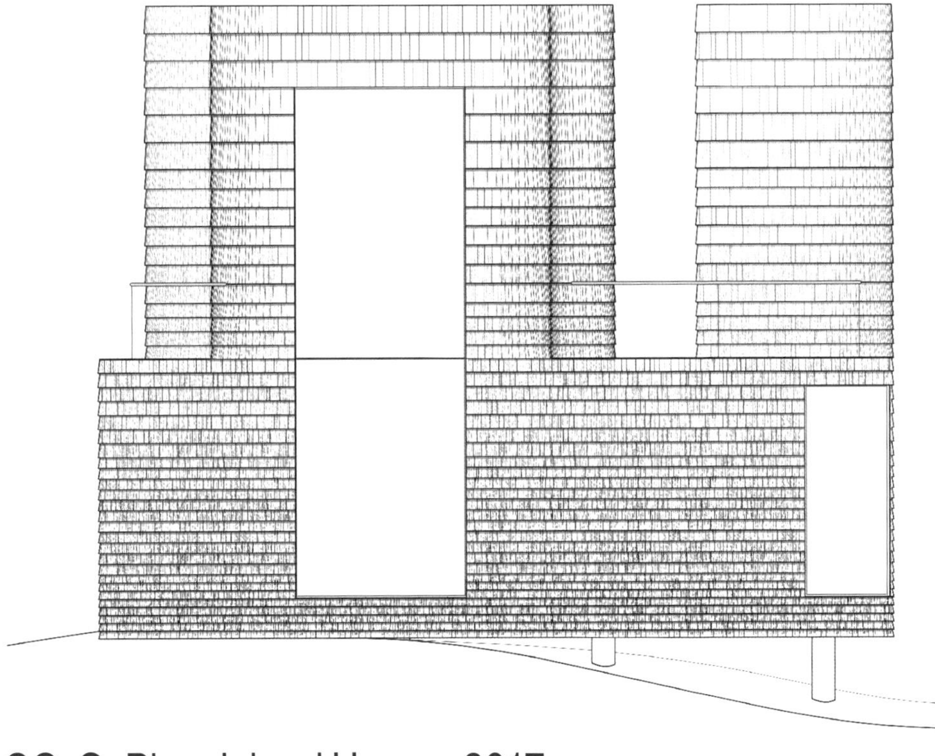

CO-G, Plum Island House, 2017

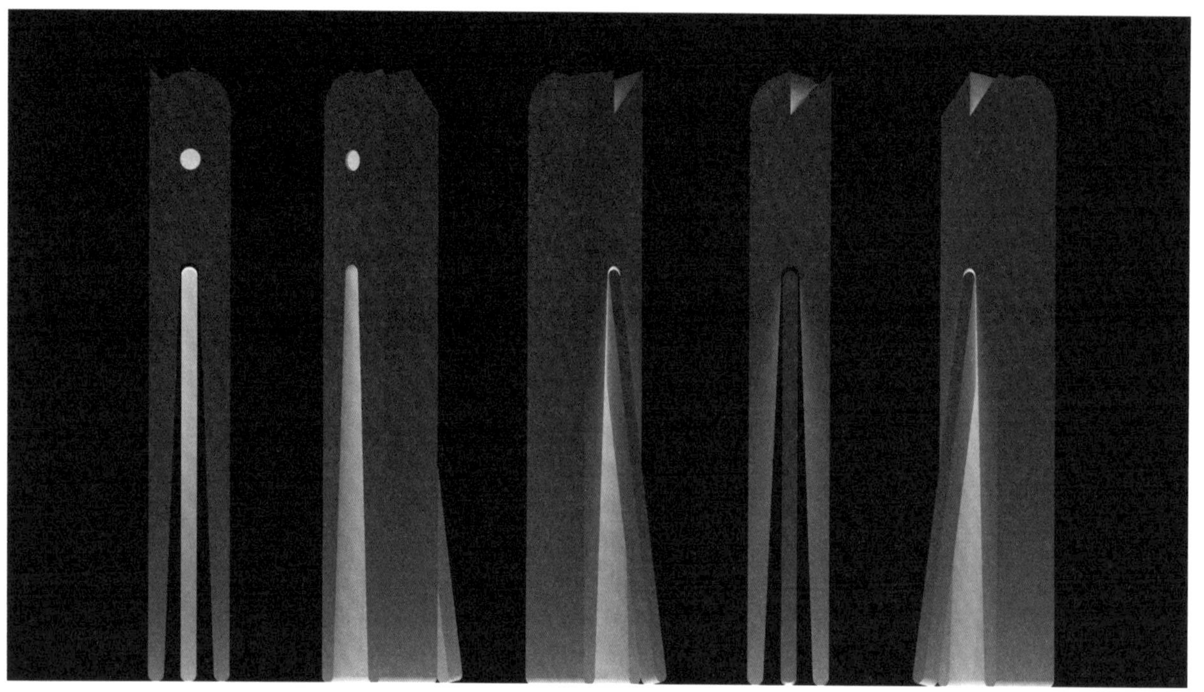

Central Standard Office of Design, The Cat that Ate the Canary, 2015

Endemic Architecture, San Francisco Music Hall, 2018

When a material object is worked formally to the point that it is forced to produce surface marks, seams, factures, or cuts, inscription takes place. To achieve a condition of the figural as inscription, however, requires a certain formal suturing and surface smoothing, for the figural eschews the fractured or the fragmented. This cohort, for example, favors the fusion of circles and squares, their extrusion into volumes or skins, and their repetition into sets of variations—a veritable architectural alphabet. The building material, on the other hand, seems inconsequential. The shape is everything. Other forces, meanwhile, are at work disrupting the shapes. And yet, the stochastic flows of energy vectors, digital shards, and points of perception and discourse that determine the architectural form seem to get fixed, as it were, when the figure asserts its shape as image while also getting twisted into anamorphosis in the process. The result is something like a pictographic script, spatialized letters, or what Freud called *Bilderschriften*—the glyphs in which dream content is presented. And as in a dream, there is just enough seemingly familiar information to make us think we might have access to some pictorial or symbolic meaning. But anamorphic figures lack meaning. They do not translate; they are glyphs without a code.

Pezo von Ellrichshausen, Bell Pavilion, 2017

Independent Architecture, Catamount Dormitory, 2016

EXTENTS, House UU, 2017

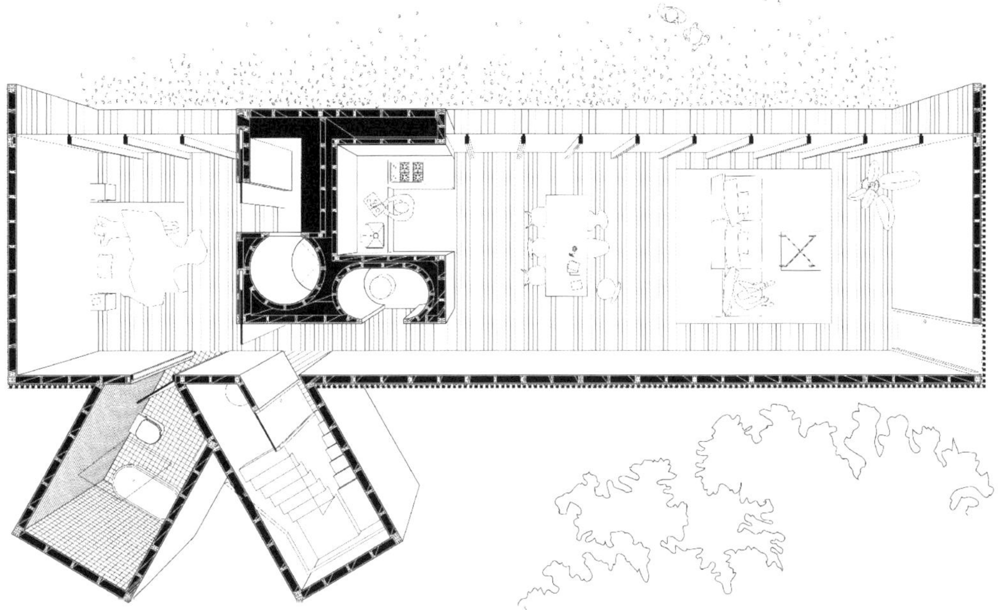

Only If, House 2, 2014

Höweler + Yoon, Shanghai Expo Park: Viewfinder Bridge, 2018

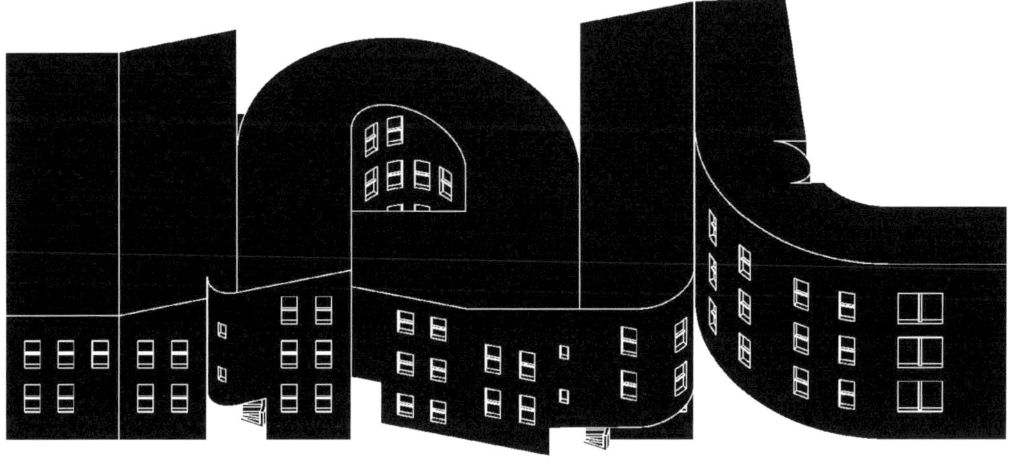

Studio Sean Canty, Irregular Infills, 2019

The cohort here leans toward an object that is without consciousness, an object that produces the uncanny effect of the "encountered original." The architectural object seems to have acquired a life of its own, but it is mindless, uncontrolled by any bodily command center. It is a remnant of some life substance that has refused the authoritative dignity bestowed by the Architectural Symbolic. What seems almost obscene about these creaturely objects is not that they are not human; it is rather the elevation of the *not quite* human to an architectural category (Vitruvian Man displaced by the Thing). Yet on the other hand, the inscription of the creaturely in architecture promises that out of a certain loss may come new experiences and programs. These creatures refuse transcendence and even elude any usefulness, all in order to produce a disquieting and disorienting but productive encounter. The creaturely neighbor remains an impenetrable, enigmatic alien. Far from serving a project of self-discipline and stable organization, it hystericizes the subject. Lacan: "The Thing has to be posited as exterior, as the prehistoric Other it is impossible to forget . . . something strange to me, although it is at the heart of me." And so the creaturely needs a viewer who is available, open. For the first encounter is the most adequate one; a second, more studied reading tends to sublate the raw impact of the encounter by forcing the Thing into a more comfortable frame of interpretation. But if the emotional impact of these projects is strong, it must be recognized that their subject position is determined more by architecture's present position in society than by any individual ambition of the architects.

d.esk, Slump Model, 2019

BairBalliet, No Middle Midrise, 2016

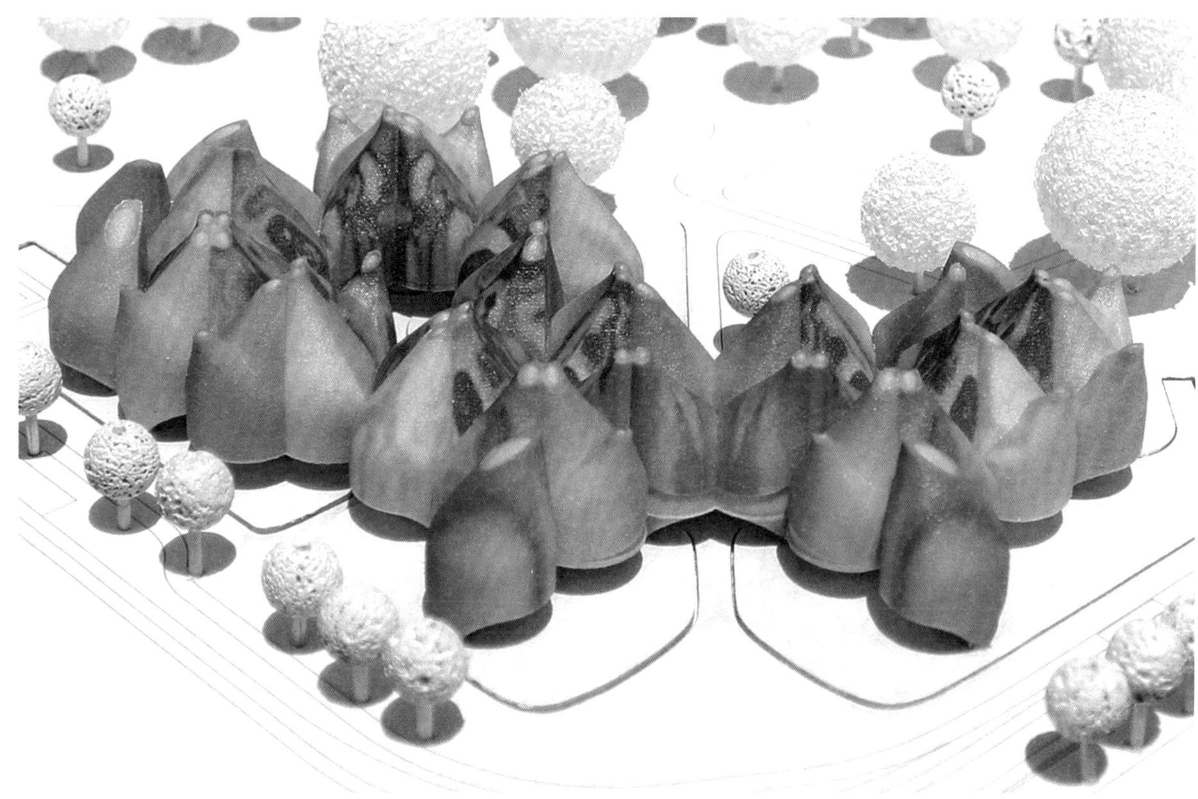

Young & Ayata, Bauhaus Museum Dessau, 2015

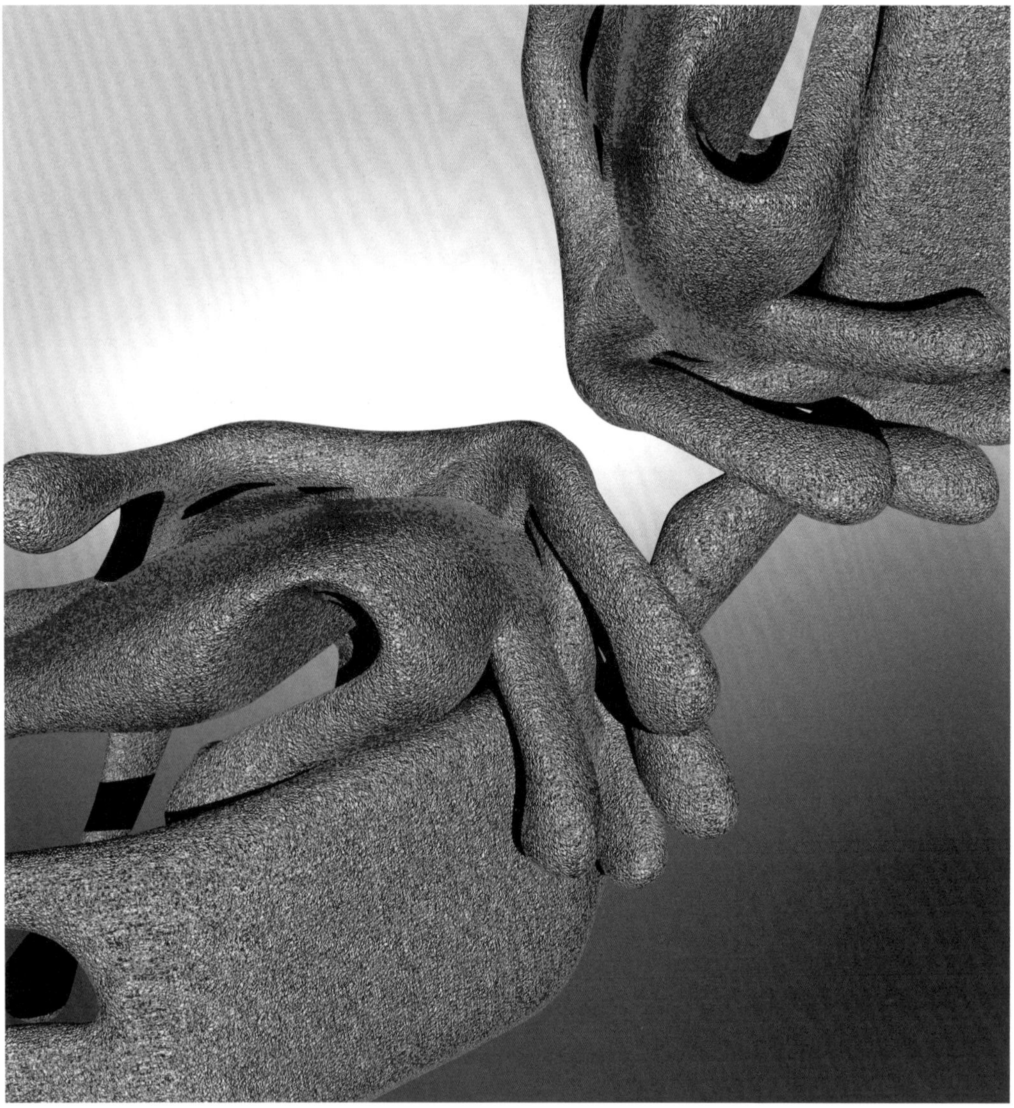

EADO, Inside Things, 2016

The Bittertang Farm, Buru Buru, 2014

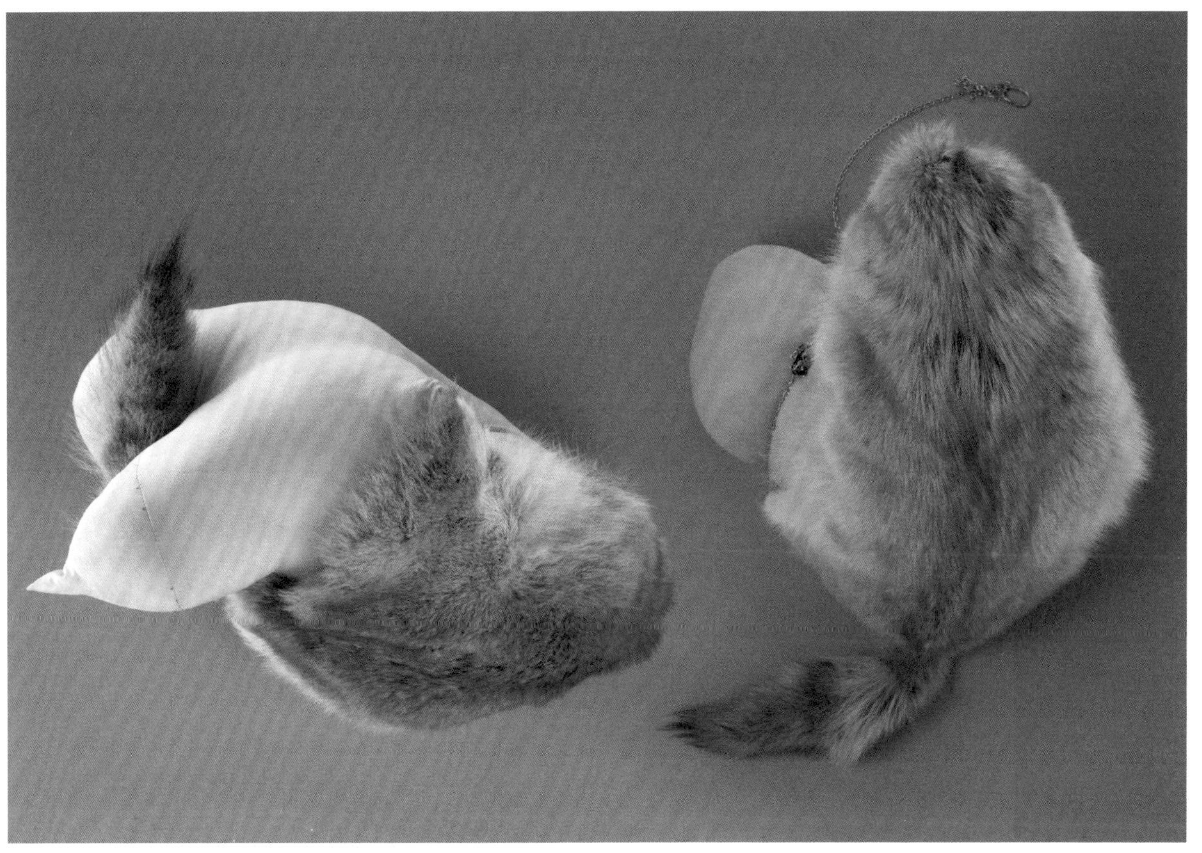

The LADG, Pillow Babies, 2014

The Bittertang Farm, Bessie, 2014

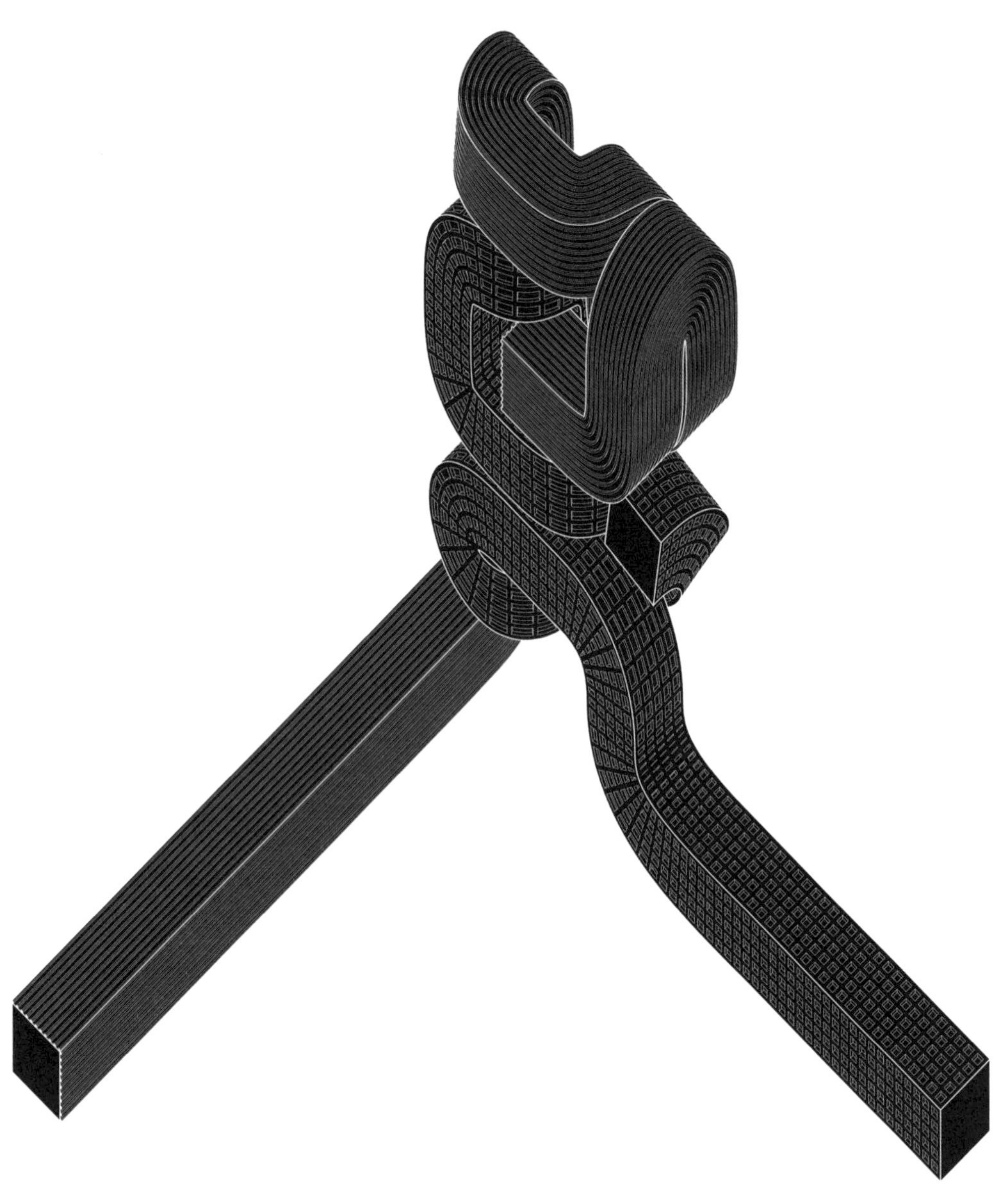

Outpost Office, Computerarchitektur No. 5, 2016

Marrikka Trotter

Blanks, Dents, Casts, and Other Forms of Negative Architecture

"On the Sixth, or Boeotian Order of Architecture," published pseudonymously in the *Knight's Quarterly* in 1824, mocked Sir John Soane's *oeuvre majeure* at the Bank of England for two seemingly bizarre formal moves. The first was Soane's decision to present a reduced, effaced facade at the lower level of the building—producing a sense of a mute, almost wiped blankness—while lining the majority of the building's ornamentation up along its skyline, like ornaments on a mantelpiece. To the authors of the "Boeotian Order," this had the effect of treating the bank's cornice line as if it were at street level—as if passersby had suddenly found themselves dropped into a trench. Behold, they sarcastically remarked, "the long lines of altars, acroteria, and vases, which are arranged, like the Street of the Tombs at Pompeii, on the summit of the Bank."[1] And indeed there is more than a passing resemblance between that archaeological site and the London roofline in question.

Soane's Dulwich Mausoleum (1817) presents an even more striking example of this treatment, with symbolic sarcophagi and vases situated above an indented high-water mark of sorts that Soane called a "retracted frieze." This tendency to *notch in* where ornament typically *protruded out* was the second idiosyncrasy seized upon by Soane's detractors. "Boeotian Order" describes Soane's deep horizontal grooves at the Bank of England as an unwelcome intrusion of planetary grandeur into the human realm of architectural design: "Is he a geologist? He dismisses the petty markings of the mason, and uses an interminable joint, which copies successfully the grand appearances of nature in the stratification of rocks."[2] The marked horizontal datums that characterize so much of Soane's work were thus more connected to the superimposed layers of the earth than the bricklayer's logic of building on top of it (and Soane was a bricklayer's son).

Soane's architecture of blanks and dents was composed in the context of a Western preoccupation with deep time, ruination, and the fleeting nature of the present civilizational moment. By the turn of the 19th century, the various earth sciences of the 1700s had been newly grouped under the term *geology*, and the Geological Society of London had been established. The historian of science Roy Porter noted the contemporaneous "dramatic surge of interest among higher ranks in society" in all things geohistorical—an intellectual event he links to the Grand Tour's heady mix of antiquarian tourism and volcanology.[3] There had been significant advances in paleontology alongside sensational discoveries like William Buckland's find of an "antediluvian" cache of bones in Kirkdale Cave, which was given much prominence in the popular press.[4] William Smith and other surveyors connected to the mining and canal-building industries had established the broad outlines of Britain's stratigraphic sequence, building up a picture of successive epochs characterized by unique layers of stone and fossils.[5]

In Britain, as in France, such developments were broadly framed by Baron Georges Cuvier's "catastrophist" model of earth's history.[6] Cuvier's pioneering investigations of fossil bones in both their stratigraphic and taxonometric contexts revealed striking evidence that different periods of the earth's past had supported unique biological systems of both flora and fauna, and that each populated episode was

George Bailey, "View of the Eastern Extremity of the North Front of the Bank of England."

“Street of the Tombs, Pompeii, Italy,” photocrom print, c. 1890–1900.

separated from the others by an obliterating natural disaster. Cuvier was also responsible for bringing the new concept of extinction into popular circulation. Unlike earlier theories of some kind of eternal cycle, which balanced life atop an enormous boil of inorganic material, Cuvier's paleontology literally sandwiched life into the sedimentary layers of earth's history. In his schema, plant life had preceded animal life, which had in turn preceded mankind; human bones were found only in the topmost layers of the earth's crust. There had been eras of unimaginable strangeness when beasts unlike anything humans had ever witnessed roamed a world devoid of Adamic creation. The history of the world could now be read in definite succession, from the first fossiliferous layers of rock to the detritus of the modern world. Early 18th-century theories of the earth, such as that of the "father of modern geology" James Hutton, had anticipated that human existence would continue indefinitely in the context of a self-renovating planet. In contrast, with Cuvier it was possible to imagine that humanity and all of its achievements would go down with their substrate, compressed into a thin line in the rock record.

There were reasons too to fear that such a fate was imminent: Soane and his contemporaries in Western Europe and North America experienced the "year without a summer" in 1816: a severe climate anomaly that was caused by the 1815 eruption of Mount Tambora in the Dutch East Indies (this remains the largest volcanic event in recorded human history). The huge cloud of volcanic ash and debris that Tambora ejected into the atmosphere partially blocked the sun's rays, creating a condition known as "volcanic winter" and producing severe agricultural shortages alongside the ominous experience of a cold and dark spring stretching into a cold and dark fall.[7] Hard on the heels of this event followed two great cholera pandemics (1817–1826 and 1829–1851), in which the disease spread from the Indian subcontinent to China, Indonesia, Hungary, Russia, and Germany before finally reaching the great metropolitan centers of Paris and London. Cholera's method of transmission was (then) unknown, and its choice of victims seemed frighteningly indiscriminate; Cuvier himself died of cholera in 1832, while the epidemic raged in Paris.[8] There was a general sense that time was progressing all too quickly—that the past, rushing forward to meet the future, threatened to eclipse the narrow window of a human present.

In this context, Soane's life is an example of the Romantic notion that the individual experience of the artistic genius was somehow a conduit for larger truths that would otherwise be difficult to notice or grasp.[9] Soane's bitter disappointment that his sons had failed to follow him into the profession of architecture—he had hoped for a dynasty—was compounded by deep grief at the death of his wife, Eliza, in 1815, and he projected his losses outward, into the larger circumstances of the world.[10] After Eliza's death, the frequency of Soane's newspaper clippings changed from sporadic, and largely concerned with client and professional matters, to daily or near daily, as he began to take a decisive interest in news items like extreme weather, catastrophic accidents, and natural disasters.[11] And beginning with the smallest snippets from the far-flung corners of India and Greece, he tracked the progress of the cholera epidemic meticulously, day by day, as it spread and neared and the newspapers fattened their coverage.

Soane also maintained a lifelong interest in geology following his Grand Tour (1778–1780), during which, as his

Sir John Soane, “Preliminary design for the Dulwich Mausoleum,” 1812.

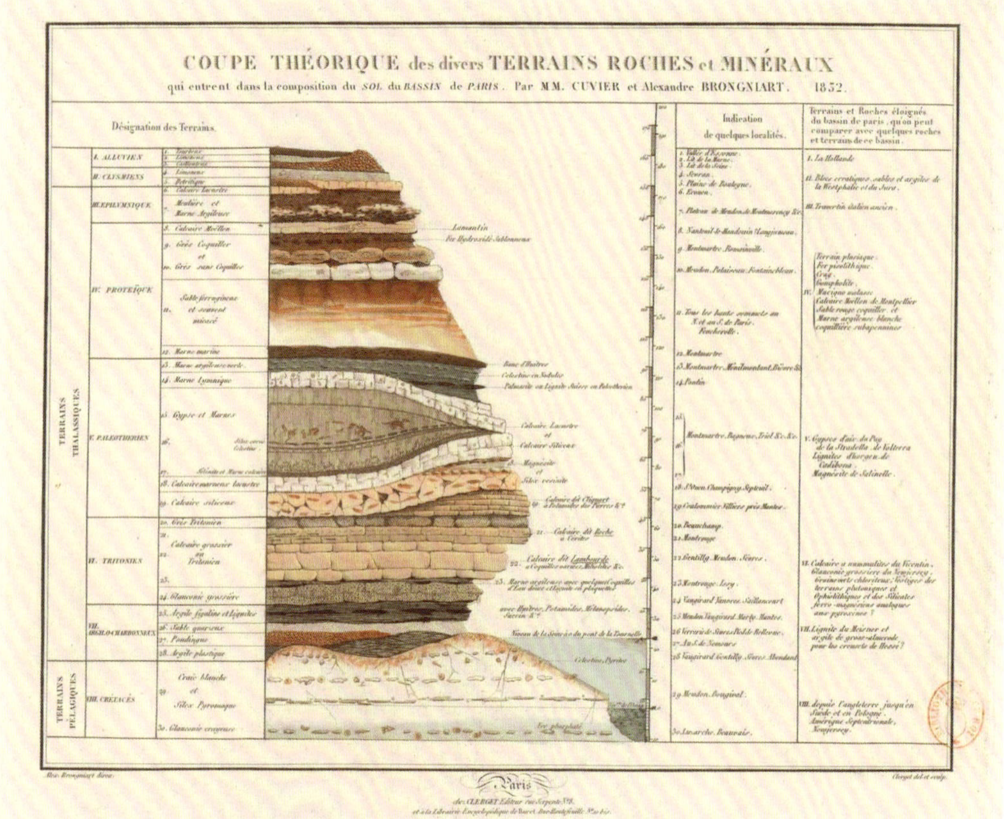

Georges Cuvier (1769–1832) and Alexandre Brongniart, "Coupe théorique de divers Terrains, Roches et Minéraux qui entrent dans la composition du Sol du Bassin de Paris. Par MM." Cuvier et Alexandre Brongniart, Éditeur scientifique, picture of coupe theorique, 1832.

surviving notebooks indicate, his curiosity about stratigraphy and volcanology occasionally outstripped his architectural pursuits.[12] He was particularly captivated by the intersections between the history of the earth and that of human civilization. Soane carefully noted the layers produced by superimposed lava flows and road surfaces to extrapolate their relative depositional ages, and paid attention to the rock upon which and from which buildings were erected.[13] As Soane's architectural career grew, he continued to follow developments in geological science, clipping news accounts of Buckland's Kirkdale discoveries and Gideon Mantell's fossil finds in the chalk near Lewes, saving a pamphlet advertising Mantell's geological museum, and collecting works on comparative anatomy and earth history.[14] Soane was particularly drawn to the discoveries and persona of Cuvier, keeping news items relating to him and his work and buying an English translation of *The Animal Kingdom*, Cuvier's most significant scientific work. Sometime between 1832 and 1835, Soane also acquired a bust of the scientist, which he displayed in his basement ante-room on a table inlaid with "various specimens of Marble and Granite."[15] There was, in fact, a deep affinity between the ways each man saw his own work. Both described themselves as antiquaries, collecting fragments of lost worlds.[16] If Cuvier's fossils were bones and shells, Soane's were bits of ornament, displayed in tight, intricate arrangements in his house museum at 13 Lincoln's Inn Fields. In both cases, the antiquarianism was linked to casts.

A cast is an index of the presence of a thing—a guarantee of its existence—and yet is only legible once the original is removed. It thus paradoxically stands in for precisely what it is not, filling the space in the lost object's stead. For Cuvier, not only were many fossils in fact mineral casts of long-vanished organic material, but, then as now, casts were circulating proxies for fragile paleontological materials that could not be easily handled or transported. In the context of architectural theory, the presence-absence dichotomy that casts so well embodied had come to the fore via a long-standing critique of baroque architecture, with its tendency to unify everything into a "moulded wall mass of pilasters and engaged columns," as the Abbé Jean-Louis de Cordemoy put it. The result was a lumpen "architecture in bas-relief."[17] An earlier generation of architects had responded with a return to the freestanding column and highly discrete ornamentation—most famously in the case of Jacques-Germain Soufflot's design for Saint-Geneviève in Paris—in an attempt to revivify a more authentic species of classicism.[18] For Soane no such reanimation of an extinct order of things seemed credible. Instead, he routinely suppressed and abstracted columns and elements of ornament, as if all that his own time could afford in the way of architectural articulation were faint, indented "sinkings," as Soane called them, like fingermarks in clay. This basic approach extended to Soane's massing as well. As John Summerson has shown, Soane used an extremely limited repertoire of forms over and over again, at varying scales and degrees of elaboration. Soane's Stock Office for the Bank of England—a complex and unprecedented spatial solution to an awkward problem—featured the shallow floating dome and central lantern that would be iterated throughout Soane's career.[19] At the Dulwich Mausoleum and the tomb Soane designed for Eliza, Soane's signature combination passes, as Summerson puts it, "from positive to negative": "You will notice that the inner surface of the dome becomes an outer surface; in fact, that the examples

Sir John Soane's Museum (formerly known as 13 Lincoln's Inn Fields and Soane House), interior dome, 1813.

Jacques-Germain Soufflot, section through Sainte-Geneviève facing high altar, 1757; engraving by Charpentier.

are modeled on a hypothetical 'cast' of the interior of the Stock Office dome, the lantern becoming (in the case of the Soane tomb) a solid cylindrical projection on the summit."[20] Once intuited, this sense that one is looking not at a piece of architecture itself but at its cast infects Soane's entire oeuvre. It is as if Soane were attempting to block out three-dimensional pockets of space for as-yet-unimagined alternatives while retaining "some faint glimmerings of architectural effect," as he put it.[21] In his words, it was futile to "blindly and servilely copy" the ancients, but it might be still possible to "catch the spirit of them" and "trace the springs whence we derive satisfaction from them."[22] Such traces, then, comprised a kind of *fort/da* compulsion to mark architecture's absence and its possible return at the same time—to register both its ghost and portent.

In this light, the strange mute bases that the authors of "Boeotian Order" found so objectionable come into clearer focus. In the new context of an old earth, the ground plane of London and its environs had to be understood as a temporary stratum in a depositional sequence that was still continuing. The Soanian encounter between building and subject is necessarily one of displacement in vertical space as well as in time, as if the present were always already an excavation of the future. Soane unsuccessfully sued the *Knight's Quarterly* and never established the true identities of its authors, whom he also intended to sue for libel, yet though he resented the criticism, his position was in sympathy with the geological analogy the piece contained.[23] In his description of the mock classical ruins he installed at his country house Pitzhanger Manor, Soane deployed a fictional third-person narrator to wonder if the ruins were created to "confuse the geologist and the antiquary."[24]

A sketch of these ruins in Soane's hand suggests a way to interpret this remark. While the broken column shafts on their bases to the left of the image appear to be resting on the current ground plane, the column capitals atop partial shafts on the right seem to sit on a deeper, and therefore earlier, level, which is indicated in pencil below. The image of antique architecture buried in the accumulated detritus of time would have been familiar to any Grand Tourist who had witnessed the dramatically silted-up ground of modern Rome in relation to its classical monuments. The presence of apparently equally ancient ruins on both the contemporary surface and an older stratum in Soane's drawing thus does in fact confuse any geological or antiquarian reading, in effect endowing architecture with powers of chronological destabilization.

Blankness over ornament, indentations over protrusions, casts over originals: all of these formal decisions constitute a type of negative architecture, where the *is* and *was* and *could be* is left to one side in favor of the *never-was* and the *not-yet*. This is not precisely the same negative as that of the critical project, with its ties to what K. Michael Hays calls "discontinuity and difference" and its most successful artifacts' shimmering, unsettled resistance to any fixed apprehension.[25] Rather, it is an architecture of stillness and muteness, of forms that are more adumbrated than inscrutable. With its crescendoing indications of impending extinction, our own moment seems more than a little analogous to Soane's. It is certainly not a coincidence that many of the practices represented in this volume are engaged in similar formal strategies; the bleakness of the present seems to ask for architectures that refuse their time. This is not to suggest that either Soane's architecture in 19th-century

Joseph Michael Gandy, “Interior View of the ‘Bank Stock Office,’” 1798.

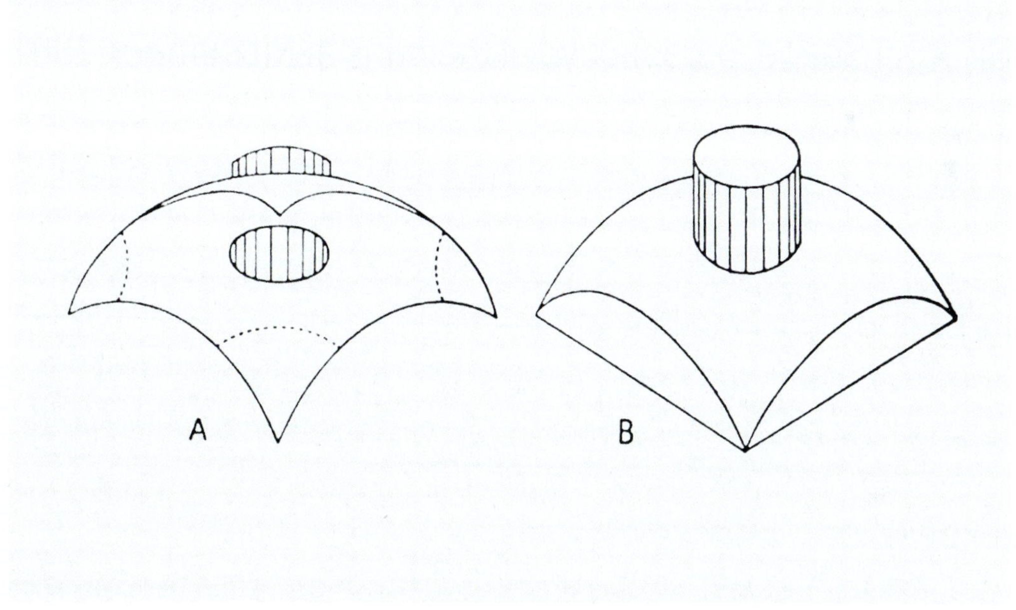

Sir John Summerson, diagram of how the lantern-dome motif in Soane’s oeuvre passes from positive to negative, from his *Sir John Soane: 1753–1837* (London: Art and Technics, 1952), 31.

Sir John Soane, perspective of the ruins at Pitzhanger, 1801.

Sir John Soane, main stair at Pitzhanger Manor with medallions.

England or the projects collected here are nostalgic, yearning for a return to some originary regime. Rather, they share a self-conscious quality that quashes any notion that there is some authenticity to which we might return.

Although it went unremarked upon in "Boeotian Order," one of the most consistent aspects of Soanean architecture is its palpable artifice, as if what one was confronting were less a building made of additive units of brick or stone and more a card stock simulacrum of one that has been scored, cut, and layered before being pasted or propped into place. At Pitzhanger, for example, an arrangement of three medallions is centered above an arched opening at the inside corner of a landing halfway up the main stair. Rather than accommodating the 90-degree turn of the wall, the third medallion simply maintains the spacing that would have existed on the flat drawing surface, producing the uncanny sense that the plaster-and-lath-over-brick construct in front of one's eyes is nothing more than a piece of embossed and folded paper. This same papery quality is also evident in much of the work seen here. As with the negative, this is not precisely the same as the cardboard architecture of Peter Eisenman's early work, with its humorless refusal of materiality, but rather a playful/mournful turn toward the materiality of cardboard or paper as such. In Soane's time, as now, I suspect this has less to do with any small-minded retreat into the insiderish workings of architectural representation and more to do with the difficulty of making work that inherently has to do with space and futurity in the context of a crisis of such great magnitude that its unfolding is experienced as a series of long-anticipated, inevitable events. What do you do at the end of history? It's not a bad idea to mock up space for another history to begin.

1 Oliver Medley and Reginald Holyoake [pseud.], "On the Sixth, or Boeotian Order of Architecture," *Knight's Quarterly* (1824): 458. The Boeotian Order authors were not Soane's only contemporaneous critics to pick up on the strange top-heaviness of his designs. Humphrey Repton accused Soane of "reversing or turning things topsy turvy—for instance the rustic storey such as we see at the bottom of buildings he placed at the top over the Corinthian entablature!" Humphrey Repton, *Memoir*, British Library, Add MS 62, 112, ff. 204–205; quoted in Gillian Darley, *John Soane: An Accidental Romantic* (New Haven: Yale University Press, 1999), 176. Philip Norris similarly mocked his "scrolls fix'd below, and pedestals above." Philip Norris, *Modern Goth: A Satire in Verse on Sir John Soane* (London, 1796).

2 "On the Sixth, or Boeotian Order of Architecture," 458–59. The "Ode on Dulwich College" these authors appended to their larger critique mocks that design's "*stepless* door, the *scored* wall / Pillars *sans* base or capital, / And curious antiques; / The chimney groups that fright the sweep, / And *acroteria* fifty deep, / And all my mighty freaks" (Ibid., 461–62). Here again the emphasis is on the overload of ornament at the top of the building and its absence lower down.

3 Roy Porter, *The Making of Geology: Earth Science in Britain, 1660–1815* (Cambridge: Cambridge University Press, 1977), 129, 131, 138–42.

4 Martin J. S. Rudwick, *Bursting the Limits of Time: The Reconstruction of Geohistory in the Age of Revolution* (Chicago: University of Chicago Press, 2005), 628–37.

5 Martin J. S. Rudwick, *Worlds Before Adam: The Reconstruction of Geohistory in the Age of Reform* (Chicago: University of Chicago Press, 2008), 35–37.

6 Porter, *The Making of Geology*, 157–69.

7 John Post, *The Last Great Subsistence Crisis in the Western World* (Baltimore: Johns Hopkins University Press, 1977).

8 See, for example, Pamela K. Gilbert, *Cholera and Nation: Doctoring the Social Body in Victorian England* (Albany: State University of New York Press, 2008). Literary figures like Lord Byron responded to the unusual weather with his poem "Darkness," which ominously describes "a dream, which was not all a dream," in which the sun is blotted out and all life on earth perishes. Lord Byron, "Darkness" (1816), in *The Prisoners of Chillon*, and *Other Poems* (Boston: Munroe & Francis, 1817), 18–20.

9 Adam White, "John Clare and Poetic 'Genius,'" *Authorship* 3, no. 2 (2014): 1–20; quoted in Darley, *John Soane*, 238–252.

10 Darley, *John Soane*, 228–36, 267–68.

11 See, for example, the clipped account of flooding at Plymouth Dock, January 6, 1817; the prognostication "Another Deluge Coming"; the speculations that a flood must have instigated early faith traditions, "Origin of Religious Worship," September 1820; the report of an earthquake at Comrie, April 15, 1822; and the account of the 1822 eruption of Mount Vesuvius in Soane's Press Clippings, 1805, etc., SM vol. NC/1. Soane's second volume of press cuttings contains articles on strong gales at Dover, December 30, 1821, floods in London and Lincolnshire in January 1822, and a violent tempest at Marseilles that

same month (Soane Press Clippings, 1822, SM vol. NC/3).

12 Soane traveled with Frederick Hervey, the Earl Bishop of Derry, who was a noted geological enthusiast in the circle of Sir William Hamilton, and likely also met the naturalist Thomas Bowdler. As Pierre de la Ruffinièredu Prey has noted, geology became a preoccupation for Soane at Paestum and throughout Calabria. Pierre de la Ruffinière du Prey, "John Soane's Architectural Education, 1753–80" (PhD diss., Princeton University, 1972), 180–81, 188, 206. Soane's notebooks indicate that he examined the bedrock of the Apennine mountains, stopped to examine the stratigraphy of a geological exposure in detail along the road between Veletri and Genzano, and at Paestum was as interested in the "petrified" composition of the stone from which they were shaped as he was in the famous ruins themselves. Soane, *Notes Italy & Italian Language*, &c, 1780, SM vol. 162, 162r, 162v; Soane, *Italian Sketches*, 1779, SM vol. 39, 61v, 31r (hereafter *Italian Sketches*). Not only did he complete the obligatory Grand Tour ascent of Mount Vesuvius—twice—but he also scaled Mount Etna and visited the volcanoes at Solfatara and Monte Nuovo. On Vesuvius and Etna, see du Prey, "Soane's Architectural Education," 214–15. For Monte Nuovo, see Soane, *Italian Sketches and Mema., 1778–1779*, SM vol. 164, 18–19 (hereafter *Italian Sketches and Mema.*). For Solfaterra, see Soane, *Italian Sketches and Mema.*, 51r.

13 See, for example, Soane, *Italian Sketches and Mema.*, 49r, 50v, 51v. At Catania Solfatara he noted the almost tidal advances and retreats of lava from Mt. Etna: as he noted in his travel notebook, this "Ancient Greek Town at the foot of Mount Etna has been (it is said) destroy'd & rebuilt 17 times, it is now a considerable town." Soane, *Italian Sketches and Mema.*, 15.

14 Soane's Press Clippings, NC/1: "1805, etc.": Notice from The Herald, November 7th 1821, of Gideon Mantell's fossil discoveries in the chalk near Lewes; NC/3: 62, account from *The Morning Herald*, March 3, account of organic remains uncovered in the Vale of Kirkdale by William Buckland; clipping of a newspaper's extract of a letter, undated, on advances in geology, including Buckland's discovery and George Bellas Greenough's geological map of England and Wales; report dated March 12, 1822, on Buckland's discovery of an "antediluvian den of hyenas." For Mantell's geological museum, see SM library reference number 6105, Sir John Soane Museum. Books included John Whitehurst's *Theory of the Earth*, Henry Brown's *Geology of Scripture*, and Granville Penn's *Comparative Estimate of the Mineral and Mosaical Geologies*.

15 SM library reference number 4573, Sir John Soane Museum. Peter Thornton and Helen Dorey, *A Miscellany of Objects from Sir John Soane's Museum* (London: Laurence King and Sir John Soane's Museum, 1992), 51; John Soane, *Description of the House and Museum on the North Side of Lincoln's Inn Fields . . .* (London: Levey, Robson, and Franklyn, 1836), 31.

16 Cuvier specifically associated his particular approach to comparative anatomy with antiquarianism. As he wrote in his

introduction to his *Recherches sur les ossemens fossiles de quadruped* (1812): "As an antiquary of a new order, I have been obliged to learn the art of deciphering and restoring these remains, of discovering and bringing together, in their primitive arrangement, the scattered and mutilated fragments of which they are composed, of reproducing, in all their original proportions and characters, the animals to which these fragments formerly belonged, and then of comparing them with those animals which still live on the surface of the earth. . . . That review has afforded me . . . a great body of rules and affinities . . . and the whole animal kingdom has been subjected to new laws in consequence." Georges Cuvier, *Essay on the Theory of the Earth*, trans. Robert Jameson, 3rd ed. (Edinburgh: William Blackwood, 1817), 1–2. These remarks are strikingly similar to Soane's description of his pedagogical aim to study "the precious fragments of antiquity . . . to discover the principles that directed the great artists of antiquity." Soane, "Royal Academy Lecture I," in David Watkin, *Sir John Soane: Enlightenment Thought and the Royal Academy Lectures* (Cambridge: Cambridge University Press, 1996), 499.

17 Abbé Jean-Louis de Cordemoy, quoted and discussed in Watkin, *Sir John Soane*, 141.

18 On the analytical underpinnings of Soufflot and his French contemporaries' use of freestanding columns, see Antoine Picon, "The Freestanding Column in Eighteenth-Century Religious Architecture," in *Things That Talk: Object Lessons from Art and Science*, ed. Lorraine Daston (New York: Zone Books, 2004), 67–99.

19 John Summerson, *Sir John Soane*, 1753–1837 (London: Art and Technics, 1952), 30–34.

20 Ibid., 31–32.

21 Soane, "Lecture X," in Watkin, *Sir John Soane*, 236. Summerson describes these elements collectively as "a substitute, a token order consisting of vertical strips in relief, in the places where columns of pilasters might be expected to occur." Summerson, *Sir John Soane*, 27.

22 John Soane, *Memoirs of the Professional Life of an Architect, between the Years 1768 and 1833* (London, 1834); quoted in the *Literary Gazette*, January 25, 1834, i.

23 See Darley's account of this unflattering episode in Darley, 278–79.

24 John Soane, "Description of Pitzhanger Manor-House and Domains . . . ," SM ref. no. 6605.

25 K. Michael Hays, "Critical Architecture: Between Culture and Form," *Perspecta* 21 (1984): 22–25.

Sylvia Lavin

Next Slide Please: Media History and the Archive of Everything Architectural

Like many others who teach in schools of architecture, I spent the final weeks of the 2020 Spring semester looking at screens, watching PowerPoint presentations of student design projects on Zoom turn into animated graphs of COVID-19 infection rates turn into body cams documenting dying and death, and iPhone videos of toppling monuments and public spaces, some alive with protest and others made macabre by maskless faces. On the one hand, this rapidly unfolding stream of images moving easily across a growing number platforms confirms shifts long since anticipated by some: close attention to reading architectural form, ritually performed during academic reviews of individual student design work, is being replaced by scanning operations seeking big data capable of warranting broad descriptions of economic and social structures.[1] On the other hand, the very same stream of images has also presented remarkable acts of visual information misdirection, revealing the extreme vulnerability of visible digital things to invisible forms of filtering and falsification and provoking a deepening awareness of all the images unseen, recordings not made, and photographs lost. The net result of the combined effects of long-established trends and sudden developments within architecture's media history is a field more dependent on images than ever and less confident in its capacity to manage them.

A recent contribution to what is, in effect, an emerging archive of everything architectural—one that offers a means of analyzing the surfeit of both data and doubt this archive is engendering—is the making available via online publication of all the public lectures given at the Architectural Association (AA) and the Southern California Institute of Architecture (SCI-Arc) since 1974.[2] In that

*The image pairs accompanying this essay rework a series of comparative pairs used by Colin Rowe in a 1976 lecture at the AA. In the grand finale of his talk, Rowe "holds a slide of Mondrian's *Victory Boogie-Woogie* on the left for a full seven minutes while asking for the 'next slide please' on the right," relentlessly comparing the painting, and judging it superior to, a series of artifacts, mostly plans, sampled from the sweep of architectural history. Here, Lavin puts these plans back into comparison with alternate views of themselves, beginning with *Victory Boogie-Woogie*, which is revealed at its edge to be not a painting in the strict sense, but a super low-relief agglomeration of pigment and tape. Like the Mondrian that moves from abstract composition to material-specific assembly, each of these new pairs open to readings both with and against Rowe's ahistorical interest in the figure-ground.

year, both schools initiated programs to record lectures using videotape. By the 1990s the schools were switching to digital recording methods, and in the 2010s each began the process of converting the original tapes into uploadable file formats. The combined archive went live in 2013, and the result constitutes a clearly extraordinary record, but of what, precisely, is less certain.[3] Does the fact that Peter Cook has been the most "popular" speaker at both institutions, having given a combined total of 29 lectures, constitute a salient piece of evidence? How do we think about the status in the field of persons like Carolyn Dry, an architect and US Navy researcher who was one of only three women to lecture as part of the "formal" series at SCI-Arc during the first 10 years of videotaped lectures?[4] Does her relative obscurity not only in design discourse but in current research on the histories of ecology and of representation relate to the fact that she argued that issues growing in importance to architecture, such as how oceans circulate or how solar winds affect the earth's geomagnetic field, could not be presented in the 2D static mediums used by architects?[5] Is it related to the fact that while SCI-Arc had more lectures on computation and ecology and more lectures by women than the AA, the AA had more lectures by historians and critics who had control over who entered the historical record and who did not? Such contrasts notwithstanding, there was more overlap between speakers at the two schools in the later years than in the early ones, as the field became less local and more homogeneous. The audience is rarely documented in the videos, so the demographic constitution of these events is not clear, but it is possible to say that of the 1,260 lectures examined here, seven were delivered by Black persons.[6] In other words, the archive—itself an astonishingly rich and heterogeneous visible thing and a painfully exposed visual bias—seems

Carolyn Dry, Self-Forming Port, drawing, 1983.

Carolyn Dry, Self-Forming Port, drawing, 1983.

simultaneously to consolidate the architectural discipline and to evaporate architecture altogether.

Despite generating this statistical quicksand, however, the archive does reveal some of the stable—not to say persistent or even recalcitrant—logics that are embedded within its own media history, a history that contains within it a parallel media history of architecture. When the lectures were first recorded using videotape in 1974, 100 percent of the presentations were made using slide transparencies. Both mechanical systems of reproduction were prone to glitches that slowed the pace of discourse: slides got stuck or mis-inserted, and video recordings were often interrupted when the tape needed to be changed. By 2004 at SCI-Arc and 2006 at the AA, 100 percent of the presentations were made using digital images, just as the recordings of the lectures were made using digital cameras.[7] Both formats permitted a continuous and speedy flow of high-resolution images.[8] This shift in apparatus coincided with a shift from a primarily side-by-side comparative mode to a one-at-a-time technique of analysis and presentation.[9] This development, furthermore, coincided with a transition from lectures that presented a large range but limited number of disparate materials to lectures that presented a proportionally larger number of images overall that were drawn from a narrower range of sources.[10] In other words, during the 1970s, standard operating procedure for a lecture at a school of architecture was to use a relatively small number of slow-moving slide images of historically and geographically divergent things to construct arguments based on the compare-and-contrast method of analysis. By the 2000s, the standard operating procedure was instead to use a relatively large number of convergent and rapidly shifting digital images, such as all the drawings made for a project or all projects made by one architect, to construct arguments based on a narrative sequence.

Piet Mondrian, *Victory Boogie-Woogie*, mixed media on canvas, 1943–1944.

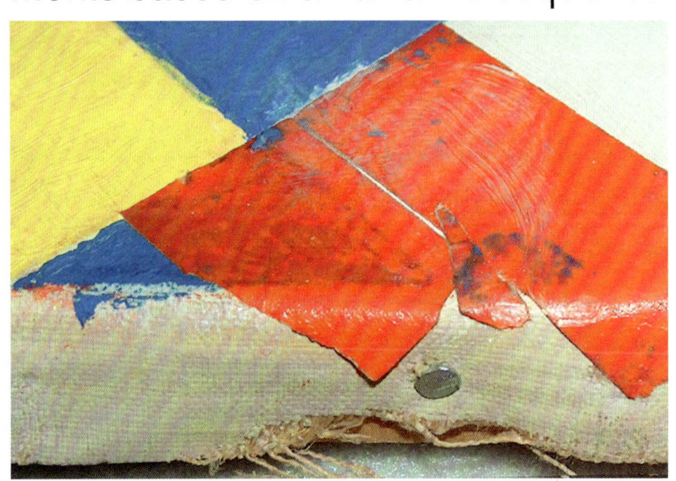

Piet Mondrian, *Victory Boogie-Woogie*, detail photograph, 1943–1944.

It is well known that the history of modern architecture was shaped by modes of organizing and using images, each of which conflated art historical methods, pedagogical devices, colonial practices, and technological instruments in various ways. But of all the apparatuses that were in circulation, the slide comparison is the most familiar to students of architectural criticism who learn that the history of modernism is a genealogy that links Heinrich Wölfflin, who is credited with establishing the method, to Colin Rowe, whose essay "The Mathematics of the Ideal Villa" he subtitled "Palladio and Le Corbusier *Compared*."[11] When Rowe first published the essay in 1947, the layout mimicked the side-by-side presentation of a projected lecture and intensified its principal effects in print form: two geographically and historically disparate architectural objects, La Rotonda and Savoye, are brought together in a visual juxtaposition. Neither building is presented with the goal of representing it fully. Instead, a limited number of images and a careful choice of words work together to delete differences and assert commonalities. Those points of convergence serve Rowe to suggest that because they are common to radically disparate things, they must be universal. Having thus achieved a virtually exclusive focus on matters of mathematics and proportion, Rowe uses their persistence to prove the existence of what he called architecture itself.[12] By 1976, when he gave a lecture at the AA, Rowe had honed this technique into a tour de force made of a handful of increasingly wild slide comparisons that cover everything from the Illinois Institute of Technology in Chicago to the Ducal Palace in Urbino, Italy, and

The Museum of Modern Art

RELEASE NO. 46

ITALY: THE NEW DOMESTIC LANDSCAPE — Counter Design as Postulation

Director: Emilio Ambasz

May 26, 1972 - September 11, 1972

Designer: Superstudio
Adolfo Natalini, Cristiano Toraldo di Francia, I. D. Roberto Magris, Piero Frassinelli, Alessandro Magris, Alessandro Poli

Patron: ANIC - Lanerossi, with the participation of Abet Print

Superstudio presents, in a larger dark area, a small cubic space made up of one-way mirrors on four sides. The public, which may walk around this cube, sees through the one-way mirror a space infinitely reflected. The space, symbolizing a benign environment void of any constructions presents, when one looks up, a continuing passage of clouds. Looking down, one sees the earth transformed into a continuous infrastructure of energy systems. Connected to that floor infrastructure emerge a number of tubes purporting to be life-supporting elements: air, heat, water, food, communications.

To the last is connected the only piece of equipment in the space, a television set. The TV presents a series of color images which describe Superstudio's philosophy, its conviction that we cannot arrive at the essence until we have divested ourselves of all elements of our present culture, designed objects included.

Statement by Superstudio

DESCRIPTION OF THE MICROEVENT/MICROENVIRONMENT

The proposed microevent is a critical reappraisal of the possibilities of life without objects. It is the reconsideration of the relations between the process of design and the environment through an alternative model of existence, rendered visible by a series of symbolic images.

The microenvironment is like a room with walls, the floor and ceiling are covered with black felt: thin luminescent lines make the corner angles stand out clearly.

A cube 180 cm. wide is placed in the center on a platform 40 cm. high. All the walls of the cube, except the one facing the entrance, are made of polarized mirror, so that the model inside becomes clearer and clearer as we move to the end of the room.

Such a model, repeated to infinity by the mirrors, is a square plate of checkered laminated plastic, with a little "machine" out of which come various terminals. One of the terminals is connected to a TV screen, which transmits a three-minute movie, a documentary on the model seen in various natural and work situations. The sound track gives information about the original concepts for the model.

(over)

Emilio Ambasz, Italy: The New Domestic Landscape, press release, 1972.

Superstudio, Gli Atti Fondamentali, Vita (Supersuperficie), Viaggio da A a B (A Journey from A to B), collage, 1971.

the city plan of Jaipur, India, and a discourse that ranges from modernism's neurotic object fixations and the passivity of the feminine to the iron curtain and the control of information, with a short discussion of *aboriginal* purity in between. This all builds to a grand finale during which Rowe holds a slide of Mondrian's *Victory Boogie-Woogie* on the left for a full seven minutes while asking for the "next slide please" on the right in increasingly rapid succession, until the painting emerges as victor of a series of negative comparisons and the dialectical resolution of all key conflicts of the 1970s.[13]

Rowe's double-barreled bravura reflects not only his long experience in exercising the slide comparison but also the fact that by the 1970s its biases were coming under fire. Critics like Vincent Scully who pressed comparativism to its extreme in pursuit of a universal definition of architecture were running afoul of students of indigenous architecture, for example, who resisted being captured by this image logic and subjected to the Anglo-European claims about architectural essentialism it facilitated.[14] Scully's famously melodramatic slide-driven teaching style, like Rowe's, also indicates the way in which the lecture hall had come to be conceived of as an extension of creative studio culture rather than regulated by the evidence-based character traditionally expected of an academic lecture. Under the guise of poetic license required by the exigencies of the lecture as performance, slides became not a means to see things objectively but things to be seen in themselves.[15] Wölfflin had already established that redesign—of, for example, Albrecht Dürer's *Knight, Death, and the Devil*—was a legitimate means to clarify an argument. Scully took his own slides of indigenous architecture, cutting and cropping anything that betrayed the naturalness he wanted to

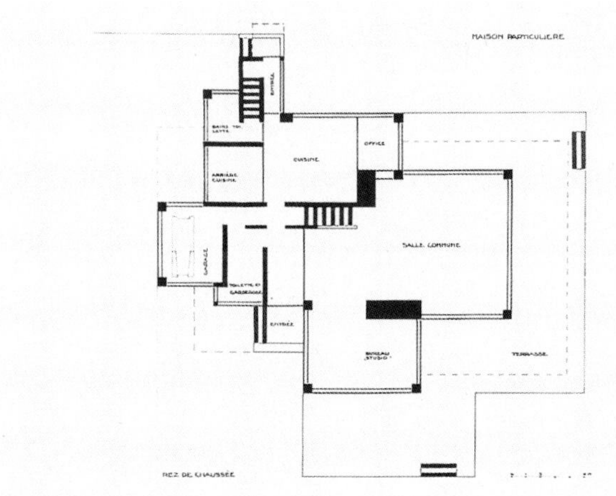

Theo van Doesburg and Cornelis van Eesteren, Maison Particulière, plan, 1923.

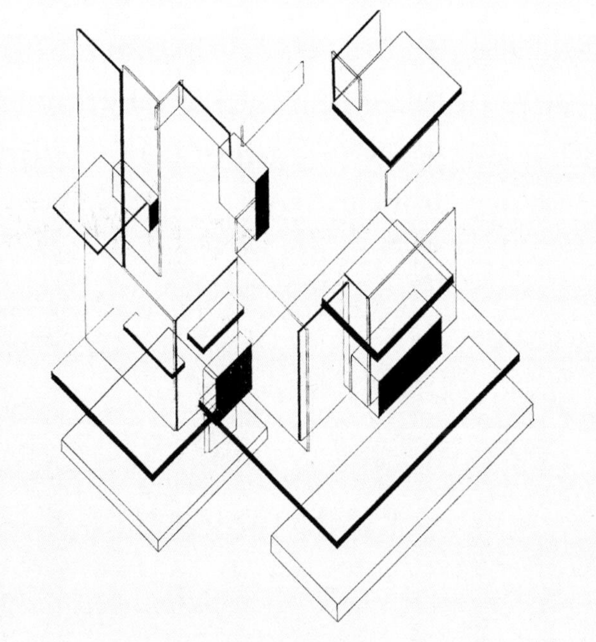

Theo van Doesburg and Cornelis van Eesteren, Architectural Analysis of the Maison Particulière, drawing, 1923.

emphasize, while Rudolf Wittkower, generally thought of as the link between Wölfflin and Rowe, fabricated the so-called 12th Palladian Villa. The side-by-side lecture as creative performance, in other words, used images that were doctored in unacknowledged ways as a fourth wall not to distinguish between the artifice of the performer and the actuality of the spectator but instead to protect the space of a weakening sense of architectural truth.

These "deceptions," in fact, were at least initially meant to pass unnoticed, so when Rowe at his AA lecture intentionally flipped his slide of the Place des Vosges around and upside down, because he said it looked better that way, he confirmed that everyone in the room was well aware that the slide lecture defaults were losing the capacity to construct persuasive reality effects. Indeed, although the projectionist at the AA assumed her slides would be shown side by side, Zaha Hadid in 1985 requested that the slides she brought in preloaded carousels be projected one at a time, thus declining to insert herself into this Wölfflinian lineage. She proceeded to show 115 slides, some without comment, but every single one an image of her own work.[16] In other words, long before PowerPoint and what has been called its cognitive and visual style became available, the architectural lecture had moved from the spatiotemporal breadth of comparative bivisibility to a monocular focus on a single architect.[17]

Although related to the emergence of the star-architect syndrome, the affordances of the single-source image stream are more numerous than this would suggest, and many of them rely on narrative rather than analysis.[18] For example, a common structure for such presentations was the walk-through, a technique that rejected the reduction of a complex object to a single image in favor of using a large number of images to simulate a phenomenological experience and to tie the speaker to the audience through parallel movement.[19] Even more common were presentations conceived as narratives that tracked an architect's oeuvre

Unknown author, Chateau Colbert de Villacerf, etching, 1856.

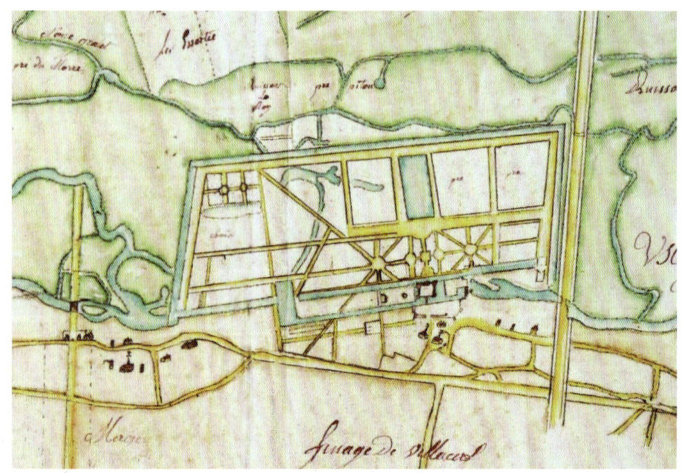

Unknown author, Chateau Colbert de Villacerf, plan, 1856.

or the unfolding of the design process.[20] Some used the technique to describe heroic confrontations with professional obstacles. In such cases, the narrative arc was typically resolved by the architect's mastery over economic or client villainy. Others used the momentum of narrative to make the development of a design appear to be propelled by an imminent formal logic, set into motion by the architect.[21] Across these differences, however, narrative emphasized the author in ways that, sometimes inadvertently, called attention to the architect as an embodied person rather than as a functional representation of an abstract discipline. Thus, Hadid began her 1987 lecture at the AA—which combined elements of the walk-through and the design process as narrative—by briefly describing how she had been offended when introduced at an event in New York as "the best ethnic architect—meaning I'm an Arab [and] I'm a woman."[22] Seven years later, the use of four rather than two carousels enabled her to offer more details about the design process of more projects and more comments about her made by men in the field with more detail: "Isn't it strange," she describes a journalist saying to her, "that you are an Arab and so successful. How did you get here? he asked, and I said by airplane. [*Audience laughs.*] He thought I had lived in a tentette [*sic*], in a sand place."[23]

If the slide comparison made small differences appear big and big differences appear inconsequential, the singular focus and narrative structure of the one-at-a-time performance emphasized distinguishing features of the architect as person and hence called attention to the structures that produce individuals. In fact, in 1972 Rowe had already recognized that deficiencies in the comparative method might trigger the dissolution of what he considered to be architecture by replacing the generality of mathematics with a disaggregated collection of persons conceived as singularities. While

Isamu Noguchi, Bollingen travels: Jantar Mantar observatory at Jaipur, Rajasthan, India, photograph, 1949.

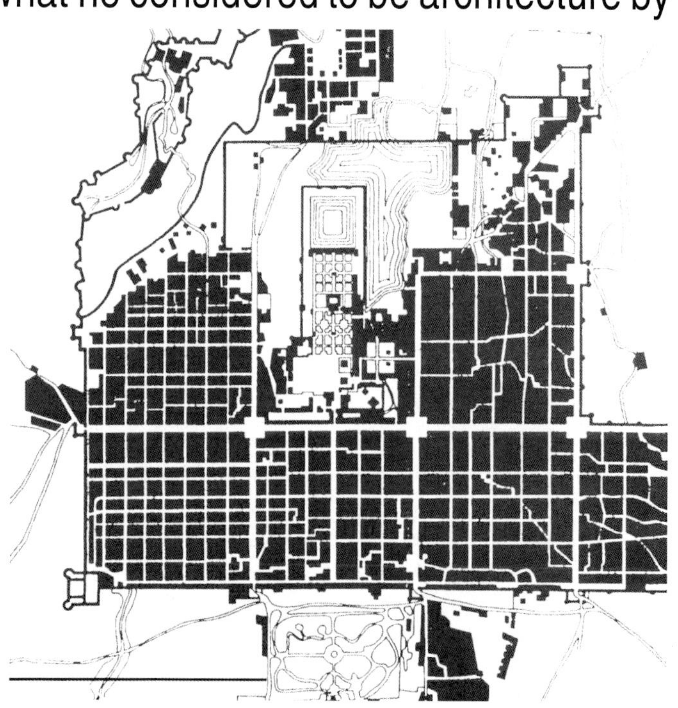

Wayne Copper, city plan, Jaipur, India, figure-ground drawing, 1967.

Kenneth Frampton used the comparative method to structure his essay "Frontality vs. Rotation," Rowe argued in his introduction to *Five Architects* that the architects did need not to be compared but rather protected, and offered them the sheltering umbrella of a cluster that sought to negotiate between the biases of the pair and atomization effects of the one-at-a-time.[24] This technique had appeared earlier in relation to architects working outside the territories and styles that were native, and hence well suited, to the slide comparison. On the West Coast, for example, Esther McCoy wrote *Five California Architects* in 1960 to describe a loose aggregation of architects that John Entenza, when he could not compare them in terms of style, suggested could instead be grouped by their collective contribution to having established a creative climate.[25] In 1976, Maurice Tuchman, senior curator at the Los Angeles County Museum of Art, described the contributors to the exhibition *California: 5 Footnotes to Modern Art History*, which included the group Environmental Communications, as sharing only their status as "neglected aspects of California art history."[26] Eventually, the cluster made its way to New York, where the 1988 exhibition *Deconstructivist Architecture* at the Museum of Modern Art deployed both the comparative and the cluster method, revealing the kind of admixture that often signals the emergence of a new paradigm altogether. The following year, Elizabeth Diller used 140 side-by-side slides but advanced them independently, exaggerating the performative dimension of the lecture not to reinforce but rather to call attention to the imminent breakdown of the comparative trope.[27]

Despite the many uncertainties about how best to manage our image world today, it is certain that the digitalization of all things and the emerging archive of everything architectural requires and makes possible more careful attention to domain-specific media histories. Architectural apparatuses and the visualities

Unknown Author, The Healing Baths at Wiesbaden, photograph of painting, 1936.

Wayne Copper, city plan, Wiesbaden, Germany, figure-ground drawing, 1967.

they established constructed a fourth wall that the lecture as performance interposed between architecture and everything else. That wall is now visible, which makes it possible to see that the slide comparison, along with the exclusions, biases, and universalisms it engendered, was fully obsolete by 2006, its use during the following decade a symptom of technical or intellectual laziness at best. Today, however, its very obsolescence could make the comparative method available to be put to work in ways that aim to de-essentialize this tool designed to essentialize. Unlike the cluster, the one-at-a-time, and the scan, which are still vying with each other and hence still bound to the contemporary, the anachronism of the side-by-side gives it the agility of the free agent, as well as its responsibilities.

Seizing this opportunity requires identifying and amplifying the productive features the comparison uniquely affords, which begins by rejecting its use as a nostalgic technique of historicism's seeking to recuperate the myth of architecture itself and instead deploying it as a device of disruption. The bivisibility of the comparison encourages close attention that could be used to undermine the broad generalities and post-truth ethics of advertising and branding logics that are well served by scanning; its doubleness could be set against the reification of the author, equally well served by the one-at-a-time. Its juxtapositionality can limit the way clustering continues the work of making small differences seem big. The comparison's greatest potential for the present moment, however, lies in its capacity to hold together difference, to connect things that have no historical common ground (though there may be a desire to make them appear to have one), as well as things that are firmly connected historically, despite a long history of efforts to imagine otherwise. Particularly in the era of the archive of everything architectural, which guarantees virtually infinite access to an infinity of images, the comparison's remarkably elastic and highly deliberate means of visual argument and analysis could maximize the forms of knowledge embedded within these media archaeologies and put them to work imagining new histories altogether.

1 During the final review season of 2020, which took place largely online because of the COVID-19 pandemic, it was widely noted that attentional issues associated with Zoom had led to reviews in which students presented work in collective formats and discussions focused on general trends rather than specific projects. This collectivization runs counter to the traditional emphasis on individual work that has structured most modern design education in the West and that some believe might remain an attribute of teaching in the future. On this history, see Mark Donchin and Gilbert Herbert, *The Collaborators: Interactions in the Architectural Design Process* (London: Ashgate, 2013). Before the pandemic, however, the shift in priority was already widely noted. For example, in framing their goals, the editors of this volume described the field in the following terms: "History and criticism have turned away from the analysis of visible form toward economic, social, and environmental processes." K. Michael Hays and Andrew Holder, email to the author, December 2, 2019. Even earlier, this shift was discussed as an emerging disciplinary paradigm in the context of the 2014 Venice Biennale, *Fundamentals*, curated by Rem Koolhaas.

2 The following discussion focuses on the period between 1974 and 2010 and is based on data extracted from lectures—796 at the AA and 464 at SCI-Arc—of approximately 60 minutes in duration, each given by a single person using images, and does not, unless otherwise noted, include data from round tables, symposia, panel discussions, or brief casual presentations of exhibitions or student work. I'd like to thank Zaid Kashef Alghata, who compiled this database, not only for his extraordinary effort and care in reviewing all the videos but also for his provocative comments and observations during our discussions about the material. I take responsibility for any errors. I have not attempted to ascertain if or how the videos are edited. My operating assumption has been that in the context of the "archive," the videos are unedited, although in the context of other publication platforms, such as social media channels, they are likely to have been edited. The AA lecture videos are available publicly on YouTube, https://www.youtube.com/user/AASchoolArchitecture; the SCI-Arc Media Archive is available publicly from the SCI-Arc Channel, https://channel.sciarc.edu/media-archive, and on YouTube, https://www.youtube.com/c/SCIArcMediaArchive.

3 The digitization of the SCI-Arc archive was funded by a grant from the Getty Foundation. On the history of the archive's formation, see Kevin McMahon, "Guerillas, Architects, and Cable TV: SCI-Arc's Videos in Context," in *A Confederacy of Heretics*, eds., Todd Gannon and Ewan Branda (Los Angeles: SCI-Arc Press/Getty Publications, 2013), 194–97. See also the following description from an unpublished document, "A Short History of Ray Kappe and SCI-Arc," written and informally circulated by Shelly Kappe: "Because the Kappes were interested in the potential of videotape, a video group was allowed to use an extra upstairs space in exchange for SCI-Arc using their cameras and equipment. Videotaping the Design Forum Public Lectures was begun immediately. SCI-Arc was the only school in the United States taping lectures at that time. Student cameramen did an excellent job as evidenced by the quality of the tapes that are now online. One of the most important students in charge of videotaping the lectures was Morton Neikrug. In the 1990s, when a budget wasn't provided to transfer tapes, in order to extend their life, Shelly Kappe coordinated a two weekend, Ray Kappe Home Tour, raising $10,000 to help save the Video Archive. . . . In 2012,

a $250,000 grant from the Getty Foundation funded the project to put the SCI-Arc Video Archive, 38 years of taped Design Forum Public Lectures, online so that it is now publicly accessible."

4 Between 1974 and 1984, the most intense decade of activism in support of what is called second-wave feminism, four women were invited to give a total of six solo lectures at SCI-Arc (Sheila Levrant de Bretteville, Susana Torre, Carolyn Dry, and Dolores Hayden). Although in 1980 Phyllis Birkby, best known for having founded the Women's School of Planning, gave a lecture on her individual work at an evening introducing new faculty to SCI-Arc, the evening's event was shared with Alberto Bertoli, who spoke first. That the faculty at SCI-Arc were well aware of the importance of the so-called women's issue during this 10 years is indicated by the fact that on February 24, 1976, the school hosted a "Women in Architecture" panel that included Ena Dubnoff, Claire Forest, Margo Heymann, Shelly Kappe, Lynn Paxton, Inga Rose, Mary Nastanero, and Margo Siegel. During the same 10 years, according to the video archive, two women gave full lectures at the AA, both in 1976. Denise Scott Brown spoke both alone and with Robert Venturi. However, neither of these presentations took place at the AA but rather at Art Net, a separate space developed by Peter Cook. Scott Brown's presentations there were part of a multispeaker, multiday event called "The Rally: Celebrating the Art and Wit of Architecture," which Cook organized in July 1976. Alison Smithson spoke at the AA with Peter Smithson on Sunday, April 4, 1976. She also gave a solo 17-minute presentation on October 31, 1975, at Art Net, during which she spoke about her exhibition on view in Cook's space.

5 Carolyn Dry was trained as an architect at the University of Pennsylvania. She later developed a "smart," self-healing form of cement with support from the National Science Foundation. On this material, see "Science Watch; Concrete Repairs Its Own Cracks," *New York Times*, September 22, 1992. She eventually joined the faculty at the University of Illinois and is founder and executive director of Natural Process Design. For her 1981 lecture at SCI-Arc, see Carolyn Dry, "Underwater Housing," January 1, 1981, SCI-Arc, digitized video, 1:23:29, SCI-Arc Channel, https://channel.sciarc.edu/browse/carolyn-dry-underwater-housing-1981.

6 At the AA the speakers were David Adjaye, Hanif Kara, and Ola Uduku (who spoke with a cocurator but during the evening series), and at SCI-Arc the speakers were Marc Cohen, Cornel West, Michaele Pride-Wells, and Stephen Slaughter. Shifting attitudes toward racial identity, poor record keeping, scholarly neglect, low-resolution images, and many other equally contingent factors make the number of lectures delivered by people of color both absolutely necessary to consider and exceedingly difficult to ascertain absolutely. A key factor in such archives is the choice of search terms, tags, and other metadata structures embedded in their information architecture: more search terms, particularly ones designed to improve the visibility of typically underrepresented persons and issues, would alter our understanding of the field. Expanding the database to include panel discussions, for example, would change the outcome, as would including nonacademic events that found their way into the archive. For example, a panel discussion on minorities in architecture took place at SCI-Arc on January 28, 1976, featuring two Black and two Latino men, Jack W. Haywood, Arthur Silvers, David Angelo, and Jesus Arguelles. However, these schools, as did most others, gave more time and hence more value to those who spoke alone, and the tabulations used here

reflect and reveal those priorities. Even allowing for a significant margin of error, the ratio between white and nonwhite speakers not only remains dismally unequal but demonstrates that institutions that have been regarded and that regard themselves as progressive have not been progressive in this regard.

7 The only exception is a 2008 lecture given by Greg Walsh, an early collaborator of Frank Gehry's. He used both digital images and slide transparencies.

8 A more narrowly technological analysis would study differences within slide and digital systems as well. For example, the slide carousel made large numbers of slides easier to manage and eventually allowed speakers to control the movement from slide to slide themselves. The introduction of video around 1997 also took place under varying conditions that altered the pace of the lecture. In addition, some speakers used multiple screens and multiple apparatuses. For the history of the slide in art and architectural history, from the point of view of visual culture, see Robert S. Nelson, "The Slide Lecture; or, the Work of Art 'History' in the Age of Mechanical Reproduction," *Critical Inquiry* 26, no. 3 (2000): 414–34; Jennifer F. Eisenhauer, "Next Slide Please: The Magical, Scientific, and Corporate Discourses of Visual Projection Technologies," *Studies in Art Education* 47, no. 3 (2006): 198–214; Allan T. Kohl, "Revisioning Art History: How a Century of Change in Imaging Technologies Helped to Shape a Discipline," *Visual Resources Association Bulletin* 39, no. 1 (2012): 1–13; Catalina Mejía Moreno, "The 'Corporeality" of the Image in Walter Gropius' Monumentale Kunst und Industriebau Lecture," *Intermédialités*, no. 24–25 (Fall 2014–Spring 2015), https://doi.org/10.7202/1034165ar.

9 At SCI-Arc, 207 slide lectures were side by side while only 12 lectures using digital images were side by side. At the AA, 282 slide lectures were side by side while only 31 digital lectures were side by side.

10 For example, Bernard Tschumi used 50 slides in his 1978 lecture and 165 digital images in 2010.

11 My emphasis. See Colin Rowe, "The Mathematics of the Ideal Villa: Palladio and Le Corbusier Compared," *Architectural Review* 103 (March 1947): 101–4. There is a substantial literature on this genealogy. For some recent contributions that focus particularly on Rowe and comparitivism, see Roy Kozlovsky, "Pairing Le Corbusier and the Affordances of Comparisons for Architectural History," *Journal of Architecture* 24, no. 4 (2019): 549–70; Braden R. Engel, "Ambichronous Historiography: Colin Rowe and the Teaching of Architectural History," *Journal of Art Historiography*, no. 14 (June 2016), https://arthistoriography.files.wordpress.com/2016/05/engel.pdf; and Raúl Martínez, "The Methodological Approaches of Colin Rowe: The Multifaceted, Intellectual Connoisseur at La Tourette," *Architectural Research Quarterly* 22, no. 3 (September 2018): 205–13.

12 On Rowe and the concept of architecture itself, see my *Architecture Itself and Other Postmodernist Myths* (Leipzig: Spector, 2018).

13 Rowe's lecture, delivered December 18, 1976, anticipates the argument of and uses many of the same images as *Collage City*, coauthored with Fred Koetter and first published in 1978. The lecture, however, relies less on the restrained vocabulary of figure-ground than the book and instead uses a more unwieldy set of analytic terms, some Freudian, others philological, and still others patrician, if not paternalistic. See Colin Rowe, "Inside Out: Outside In?" December 18, 1976, Architectural Association, YouTube video, 58:35, posted by AA School of Architecture, March 25, 2014, https://youtu.be/Ipec8Juluz8.

14 See, for example, the review of Vincent Scully's 1989 *Pueblo: Mountain, Village, Dance* by J. C. H. King, *RAIN*, no. 17 (December 1976): 8–9. The reviews of the second edition become even more biting. On Scully's photographs, see Albert Narath, "The Historiography of Mud: Vincent Scully, Ralph Knowles and the Image of Ecology," *Journal of Architecture* 21, no. 8 (2016): 1312–35.

15 Although slides were already important to and deployed by the Eameses at midcentury, slides became a distinct medium widely used by architects during the 1970s. Some well-known examples include the many projected slides used as primary elements both outside and inside buildings at the Osaka Expo of 1970, the work of Environmental Communications in Los Angeles, which was almost exclusively slide based, and the use of slides exclusively in the architectural section of the exhibition *Contemporanea: Incontri internazionali d'arte*, at the Parcheggio di Villa Borghese, Rome, in 1973–74.

16 The lecture focused on her work for the International Bauausstellung Berlin. See Zaha Hadid, "Berlin 750, Part 2," moderated by Pascal Schöning, May 8, 1987, Architectural Association, YouTube video, 51:09, posted by AA School of Architecture, March 27, 2015, https://youtu.be/AX-MPDikQ7o.

17 The term *bivisibility* is developed by Whitney Davis in his essay, "Bivisibility: Why Art History Is Comparative," in *Comparativism in Art History*, ed. Jaś Elsner (London: Routledge, 2017), 42–59. He defines bivisibility as the way in which things made to be used visually are simultaneously framed by the expectations of a historically situated visual culture and also fully visible outside those expectations. Davis argues that a specific type of comparativism, one that enables the historian "analytically to inhabit the diversity and variety of others we can never actually become," is the best means of addressing this impossibility (56). On PowerPoint, see Edward Tufte, *The Cognitive Style of PowerPoint: Pitching Out Corrupts Within* (Cheshire, CT: Graphics Press, 2003).

18 The difference between presentations by architects and presentations by historians, theorists, and critics bears further analysis in the context of comparativism and other visual rhetorics, since it would be natural to assume that historians were more likely to be comparative than architects by virtue of training and because of different objectives motivating the giving of lectures. Yet while historians moved away from the slide comparison somewhat later than architects did (for example, Charles Jencks, Robert Maxwell, and Andrew Benjamin were among the last to use slide transparencies in the comparative mode), many were also early adopters of the one-at-a-time mode (Robin Evans, for example), and still others, like Reyner Banham, went back and forth. Conversely, many architects used the side-by-side format, including Hans Hollein, Ron Herron, and Diane Lewis; Ben van Berkel and Kazuyo Sejima did so until well into the 2000s.

19 For example, Tod Williams and Billie Tsien, when presenting a series of residential projects, began with images of the site, showing movement around the house, through the entry, and into the interior, where they walk though various spaces and conclude with details. The narrative is structured around phrases such as "here we are on the bridge" (14:49). The commentary also focuses on phenomenological issues such as light and shade, contact between the body and the architecture via handrails, and views both within the house and of the photographer's vantage point. See Tod Williams and Billie Tsien, lecture, November 4, 1987, SCI-Arc, digitized video, 1:25:29, SCI-Arc Channel, https://channel.

sciarc.edu/browse/tod-williams-billie-tsien-november-4-1987. The link between the number of slides and the capacity to portray architectural experience was made in 1972 by Patricia Sloane, a painter who was concerned with poor color in slide reproductions. She wrote, "Slides of architecture are even more unsatisfactory than those of sculpture, and for similar reasons. No student can be expected to get an adequate idea of Chartres Cathedral from three slides of it. Thirty to fifty should be available." Patricia Sloane, "Color Slides for Teaching Art history," *Art Journal* 31, no. 3 (Spring 1972): 276–80.

20 César Pelli, for example, presented a series of projects in chronological order linked by the phrase "and also I designed." See César Pelli, lecture (part 1 of 2), March 5, 1975, SCI-Arc, digitized video, 31:10, SCI-Arc Channel, https://channel.sciarc.edu/browse/cesar-pelli-march-5-1975-part-1-of-2.

21 This way of describing form is closely linked to the use of moving images, an association that began at the Bauhaus and continues through the early use of film and animation by Peter Eisenman.

22 The introduction was made by Peter Eisenman, who after noting her "ethnic" nature continued, according to Hadid, "If only you were Jewish, you would fit all the bills" (Hadid, "Berlin 750," AA lecture, 1:40). This aspect of her discourse, however, was important even without a specific person to whom bias could be attributed. For example, in 1985 Hadid told her audience at SCI-Arc, "People thought I was an Arab and therefore I had no culture. But I am Iraqi, and we are the cradle of civilization" (3:18). Zaha Hadid, lecture, February 21, 1985, SCI-Arc, digitized video, 1:00:19, SCI-Arc Channel, https://channel.sciarc.edu/browse/zaha-hadid-february-21-1985.

23 See Zaha Hadid, John Dennys Memorial Lecture, June 1, 1996, Architectural Association, YouTube video, 1:15:50, posted by AA School of Architecture, April 30, 2015, https://youtu.be/W6hUlTk8E1U.

24 Colin Rowe, introduction to *Five Architects: Eisenman, Graves, Gwathmey, Hejduk, Meier* (New York: Wittenborn, 1972), 8.

25 John Entenza, foreword to *Five California Architects*, by Esther McCoy (New York: Reinhold, 1960), vi.

26 Maurice Tuchman, foreword to *California: 5 Footnotes to Modern Art History*, ed. Stephanie Barron (Los Angeles: Los Angeles County Museum of Art, 1977), 8.

27 The careful design of the lecture as performance, with the slides as both performer and backdrop, is announced from the outset of Diller's lecture, when she requests that projectionist "level" the two projectors, allowing her to use them as a single image in two parts. See Elizabeth Diller, lecture, October 25, 1989, SCI-Arc, digitized video, 56:12, SCI-Arc Channel, https://channel.sciarc.edu/browse/elizabeth-diller-october-25-1989.
The first digital presentation in the video archive is dated 1985, three years before *Deconstructivist Architecture*, which, though certainly not MoMA's first showing of digitally born material, was still among the first in this design context.
With regard to the lectures, digitally based presentations were initially about digital technology. For example, Jerry Wilhelm gave a presentation at SCI-Arc in 1985 using 95 slides and five animations as he discussed "Really Universal Computer Aided Production." In 1998 at SCI-Arc Alan Sondheim used a continuous digital scroll to present "The Geography of the Internet," while at the AA Bernard Cache showed slides of screenshots of his computer to present digitally produced ornament.

Labyrinths
Eidetic Houses
Booleans
Superimpositions
Revelations
Slack Collections
Scatters, Remnants
Dirt, Earth, and Rocks
Trabeated Stacks
First Houses
Seven Wonders
Monoliths
Anamorphic Figures
The Creaturely

In each of the projects presented in this pair, continuous surfaces are produced by digital algorithms and with complete indifference to site or program (in stark contrast to the graphite-on-paper techniques of Pezo von Ellrichshausen and the programmatic realism of Endemic Architecture and OFFICE Kersten Geers David Van Severen). In Outpost Office's Computerarchitektur No. 4, differences between inside and outside and room and corridor are collapsed into a plane that extends in all directions, featuring figures that can, in principle, be extruded and layered. And yet the form of the labyrinth is as unpredictable as it is relentless, because the maze-generation algorithm used makes optimal choices

Outpost Office, Computerarchitektur No. 4, 2016

locally and at each step in the replication process. A hypothetical Theseus may never encounter the same configuration twice but will nevertheless succumb to a deadening sameness. Mobilizing the same potential for endlessness, Young & Ayata's LIMA-MALI-AMIL-ILAM appropriates and repeats a small set of familiar plans to create rooms, but the local symmetries and figure/poché combinations are always different. "The ultimate hope," the architect writes of the drawings for this project, "is that they draw the viewer into a close attention rather than a close reading." In both cases, a shallow extrusion of lines gives the plans a low relief and deceptively simple sense of realism.

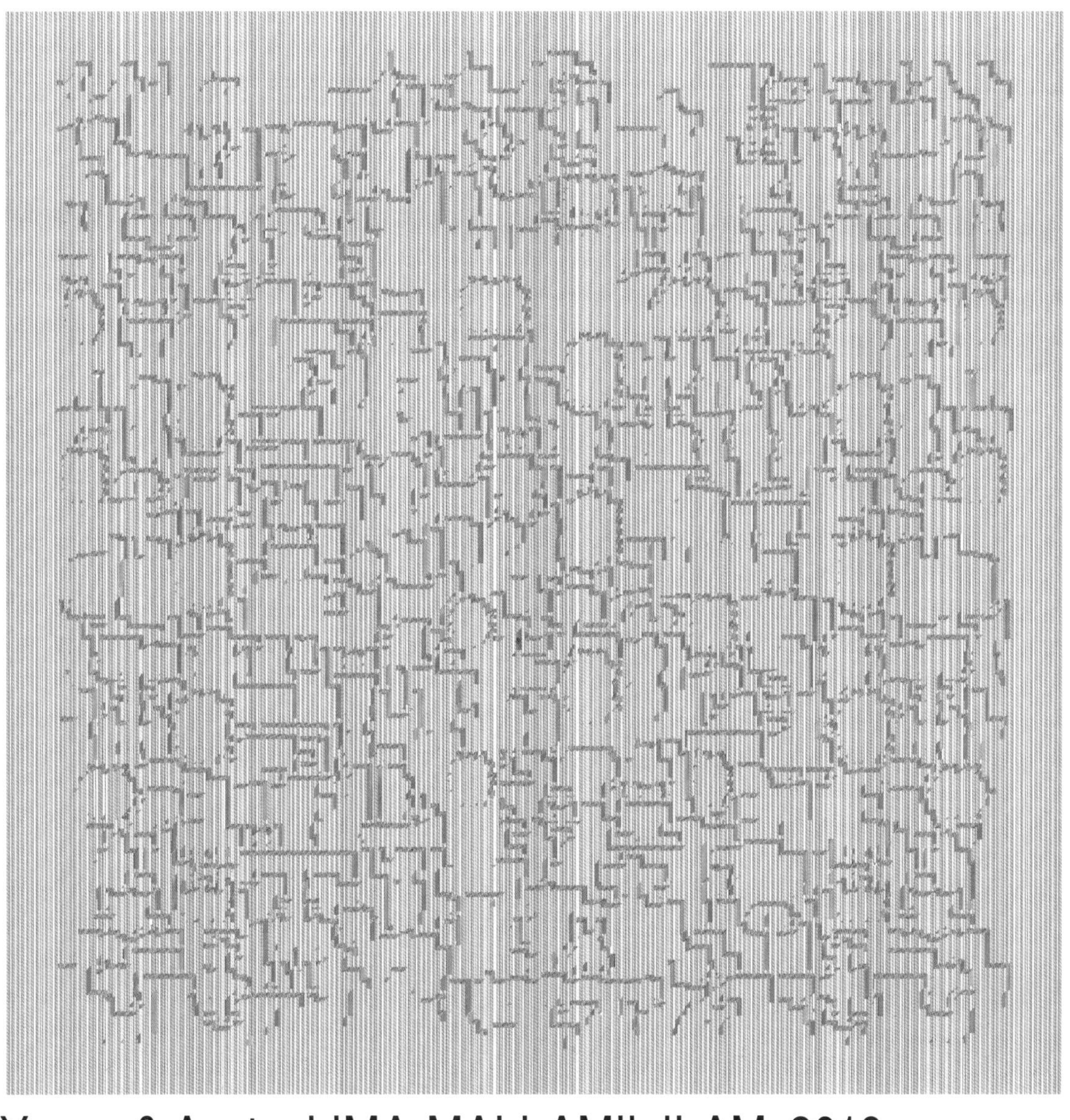

Young & Ayata, LIMA-MALI-AMIL-ILAM, 2016

Studio Sean Canty's Janus House and MOS's House No. 10 both set familiar pitched roof masses in orbit around courtyards, with volumes protruding outward in plan from empty centers. Each of these protrusions is a kind of eidetic unit in that it exhibits the crystalline sharpness of being right there, exactly as expected. When gathered into a constellation in one house, though, it is no longer possible to accept any one instance of the eidetic as ineluctable, however *expected* it might be. And so, as a category of recollection, the whole collection moves from imaged to imagined, gaining a quality of the fantastic. In the Janus duplex scheme, the courtyard is cut equally into the two halves of the house, and also

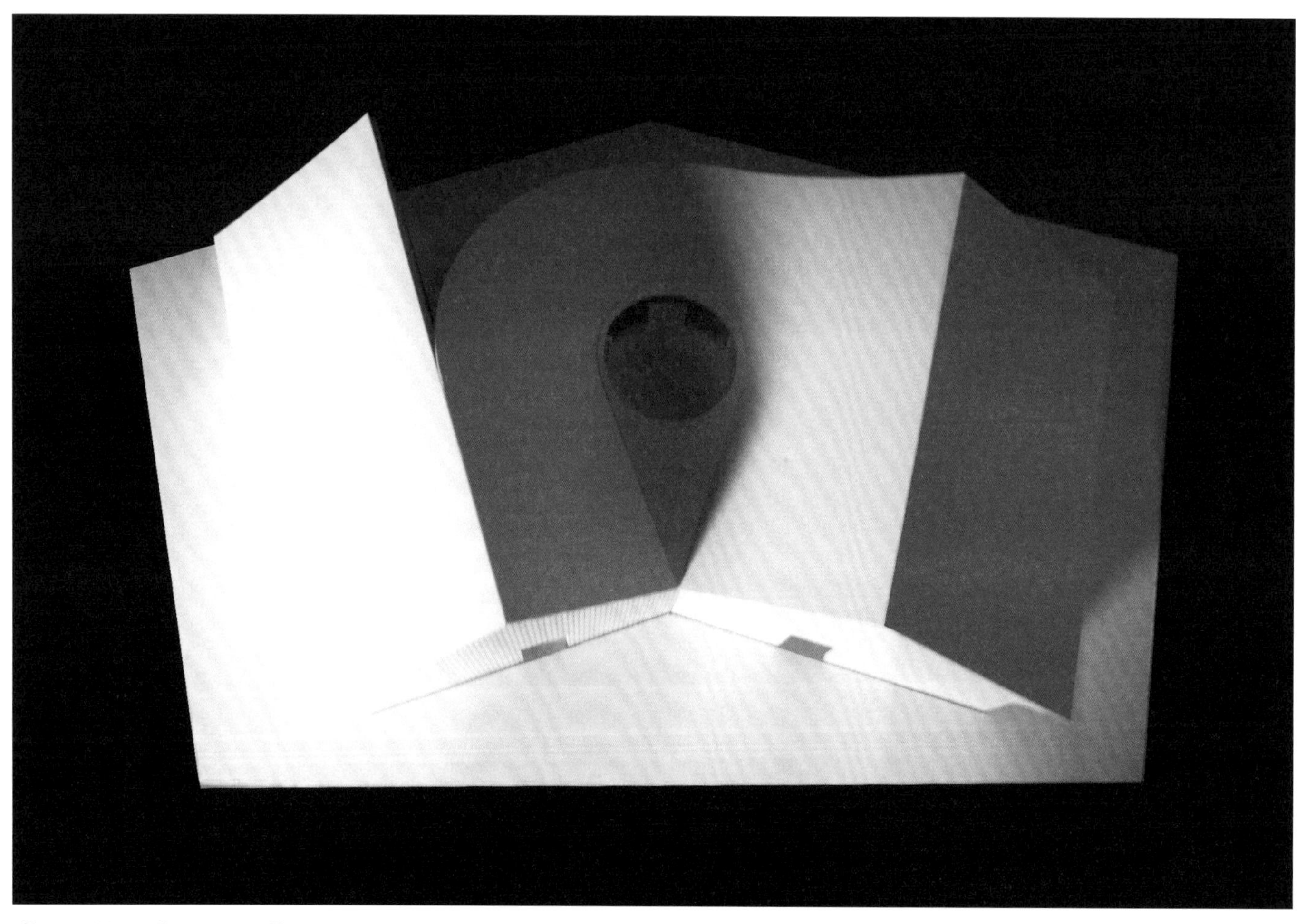

Studio Sean Canty, Janus House, 2019

apprehended equally, such that the machinery of the house might cause a neighbor to be mistaken for someone who belongs in the dining room. House No. 10, by contrast, is nearly as visible to itself from the inside as it is to others from the outside. It is almost the reverse of the Janus scheme, redesignating the constitution of a family as something looser, more distant, like house members or neighbors: logo-like cuts in the masses made by the excavation of the courtyard mean that entering and exiting happen literally under a billboard, as though the center of the house were not merely an outside, but an outside unfamiliar enough to need signage: sleep here.

MOS, House No. 10 (House with Courtyard), 2015–18

Johnston Marklee's Vault House and Höweler + Yoon's Lithos Wellness Center both use Boolean arithmetic to excavate curved voids from a seemingly solid block, but there the similarities end. At Lithos the "voids" are conceived as part of a set that extends from the surrounding city—or, more exactly, the city's landscape—into the building. As the Boolean operation is realized in the componentry of constructive systems, it continues working between building and landscape to find points of identity between the two. The laminar buildup of stairs from the landscape is mirrored by a striated ceiling descending from above, as though the wooden finish of the floor plates continued downward in a jigsaw stack. Vault House instead uses the two sides of the Boolean operation to wedge apart entirely different genres of technology and habitation. Its carved-out vaults furnish just the basics for getting in, looking out, and being in

Johnston Marklee, Vault House, 2013

a room—all in homogeneous white plaster. Glass, shading, handrails, storage compartments, recessed lighting, and all the other devices that refine and screen elemental habitation are placed at the extreme edges of the house, where vaults pierce the wall system. Cut into slots in the wall cavity, perpendicular to the direction of the extruded vaults, these refinements rise, lower, and intercede like a layering of technical garments. The profiles of the vaults are visible at these moments of penetration through the wall. It is as though the full sophistication of the vault's symbolic form—replete with graduated vaults, hanging abutments, and baseball-stitch intersections between crossing cylinders—has been aligned with technological capacity at the outer limits of the envelope. Inside these sophistications, stretched taut in a tent-like surround, fantasies of an uncomplicated existence can flourish undisturbed.

Höweler + Yoon, Lithos Wellness Center, 2021

Reading JaJa Co's Hat to Home; or, Dome to Domus, project from the vantage of the circle turns the inscribed arc into an engine: bars of closets and toilets spin off tangentially, and walls pivot around the center. Reading from the square makes the circle a lucky coincidence in a tenuous array of fragments that barely come to touch in the thickness of glass. Switching vantages between the two superimposed figures

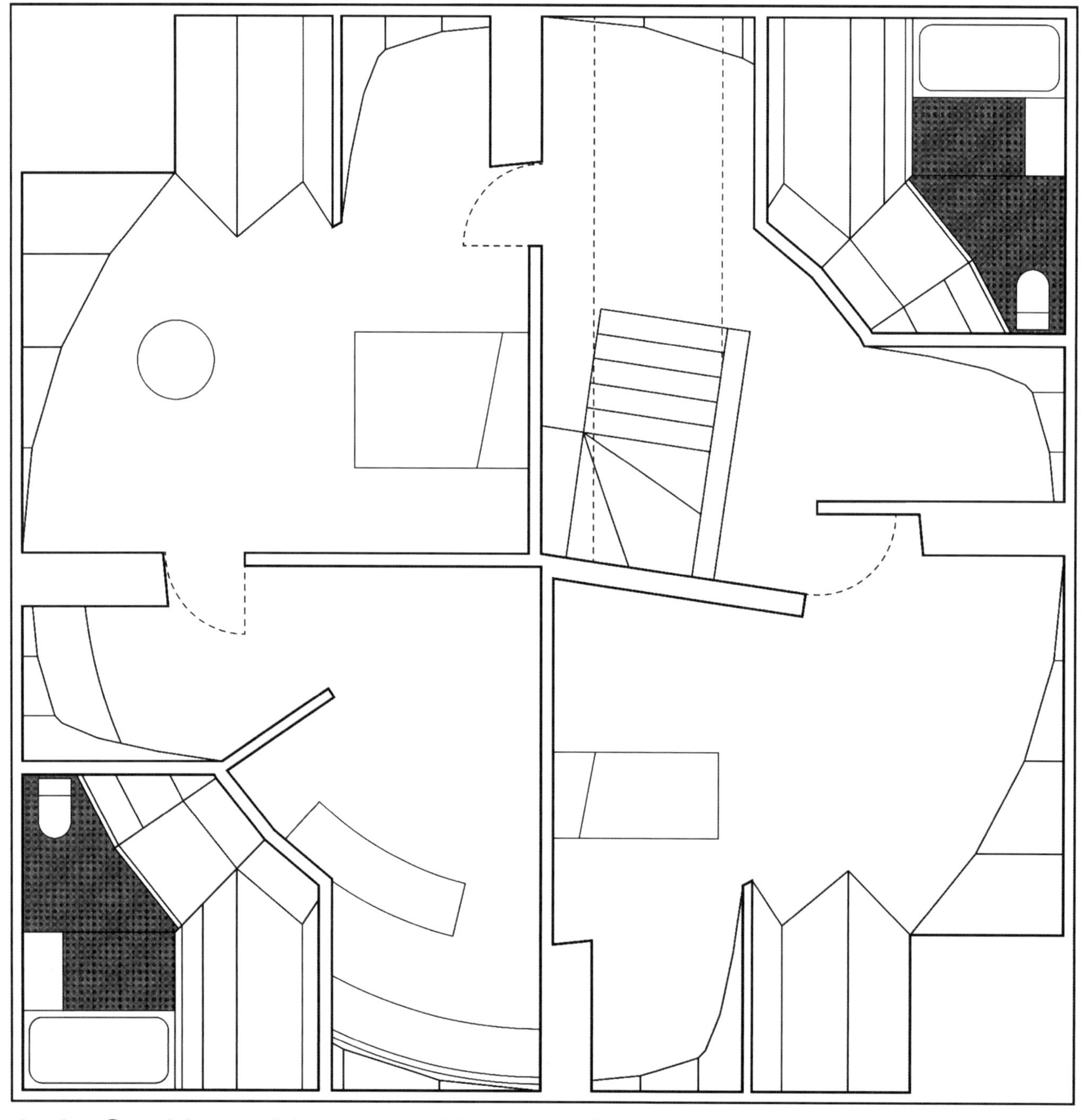

JaJa Co, Hat to Home; or, Dome to Domus, 2014

reverses hierarchy, order, and implied motion. In Paul Preissner's Yeoui Naru Ferry Terminal, a grid, a roof, three radiating piers, and a plinth all describe the same edge, but by different geometric means. The grid truncates, the roof approximates, the piers graze tangentially, the plinth congeals: from each we can see the others implying a volume of a lobby that exists completely in none of them.

Paul Preissner Architects, Yeoui Naru Ferry Terminal, 2017

MALL's drawing for Domestic Hats constructs a mnemonic system using transcriptions of relations between forces (tectonic, programmatic, social, and economic) appropriated from vernacular houses of the American South, themselves already translated and repeated several times, enabling the emergence of a figural field—a deferred figural effect grounded in social reality. The drawing traces all the cuts made in the foam models, and from them the ghost of the dollhouse emerges. In d.esk's Slump Model we find revealed the cohabitation

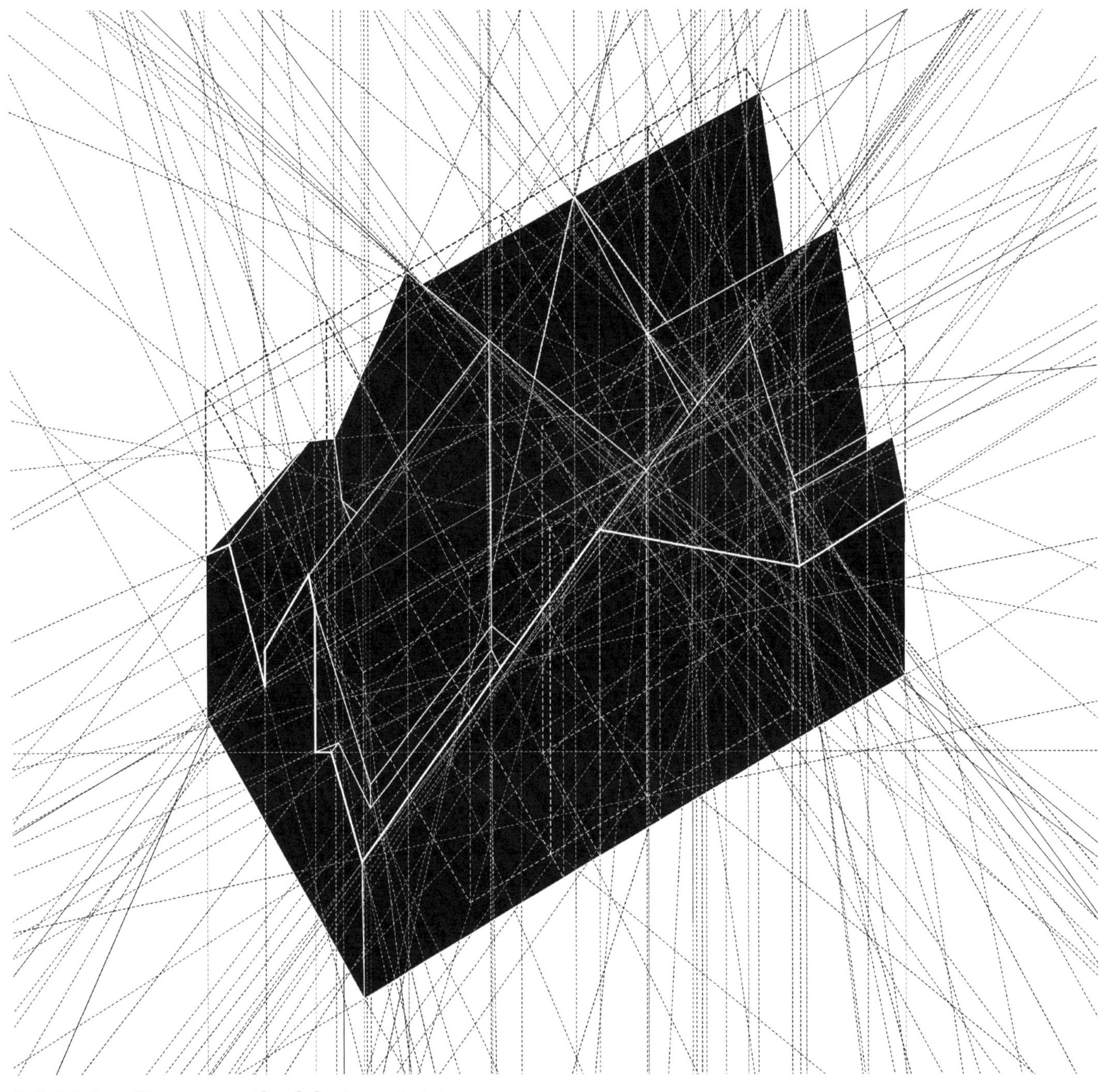

MALL, Domestic Hats, 2014

of two scales and two tectonics—not of those between two rigorously organized entities but rather two contingent forms of collapse traced in two kinds of line. But even in the one-to-two construction, what d.esk calls “the villa” is never actually present as such; what appears is but a weave of traces—drawn lines, metal rods, crumpled paper, strips of tape—that marks the contour between inside and outside. The villa is designed to fail, to withdraw, and yet it is in that very withdrawal that multiple possible habitations are revealed.

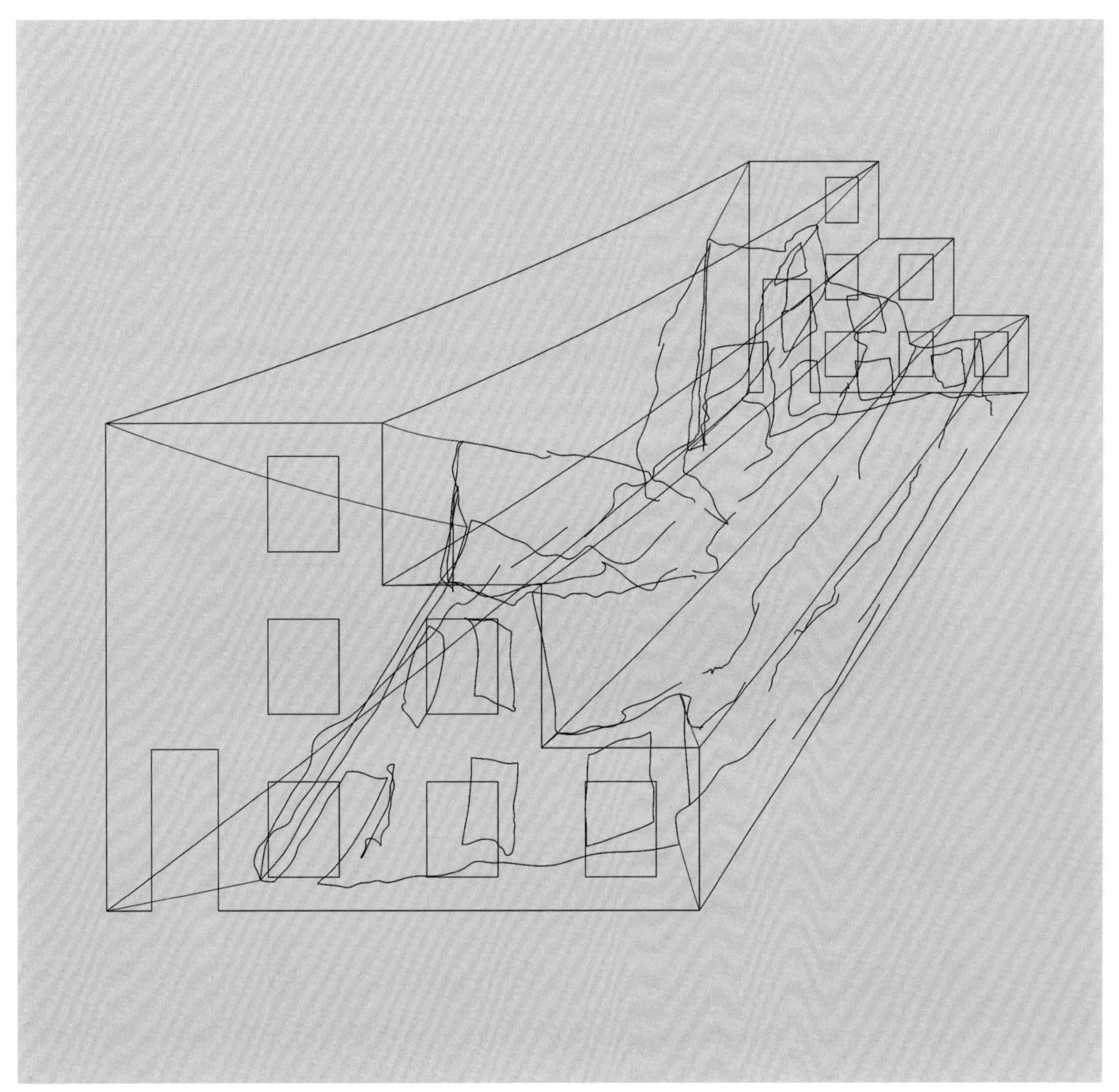

d.esk, Slump Model, 2019

Exercise is the putative reason for gathering at Common Accounts' Refresh, Renew Pavilion, and stock-a-studio's [a kit of these some parts] x budget gym], but neither project is much concerned with providing a good place to work out. The gym theme instead sets a catalog of parts for construction, then provides an impulse for arranging and assembling them. Gym is not necessarily the outcome but rather the material and the means. Refresh, Renew, plays a game of substitution, working backward from the mass of a temple and inscribing it with parts borrowed from gyms. A gridded workout floor separates the structure from the ground like a plinth, lending it a certain aloofness. The steel tubing of the gym apparatus becomes an array of columns of various orders, supporting an entablature of exercise balls. The blackness of the balls is the decorative theme of the frieze, but it leaks down to spangle the

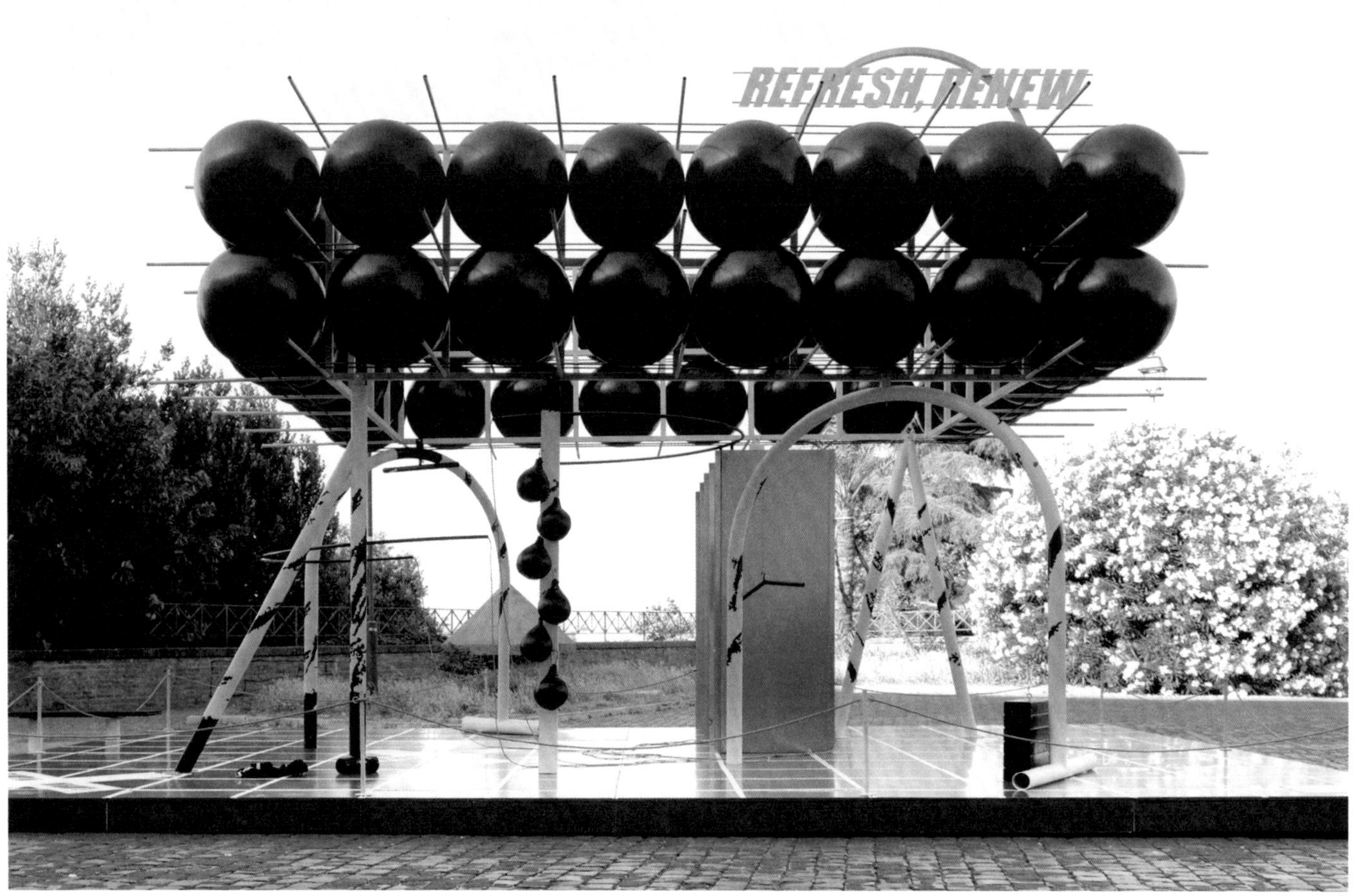

Common Accounts, Refresh, Renew Pavilion, 2019

columns as appliqué and thus becomes a general motif. Then, [a kit of these some parts] does not begin with the image of any particular whole. It instead mines adjacencies between parts to produce its effects. The straps, pads, and lashings that hold the thing together are also the workout apparatus, giving each relationship between parts double duty as a structural joint and an activity station. And adjacency is not only physical but decorative, affirmed by the speckly surface treatments of concrete, galvanized steel, foam, and spray paint that create visual fits across spatial gaps. This insistence on maintaining the fitness of optical adjacency extends to the site. How can the construction "fit" against the arbitrariness of the surrounding environment? Stickers of printed water resolve the problem. From every vantage it's speckles against speckles and water against water.

stock-a-studio, [a kit of these some parts] x budget gym], 2019

The problem with scatters is how to end them. Edges must be consistent with the god-like action that initiates a scene from above, while at the same time giving architects the latitude to work on circumscribed sites. Curtis Roth's Instrument 3: The Mesh borrows facades from the Villa Savoye to make houses of cards, as though these have been flattened to sheets and scattered by some deity no longer on the premises. The houses are grouped as episodes or isolated as little islands, evoking Le Corbusier's fantasies of ground-level traffic swooping along drives and through *portes cocheres*. The island groupings allow the site plan a free-ranging logic of

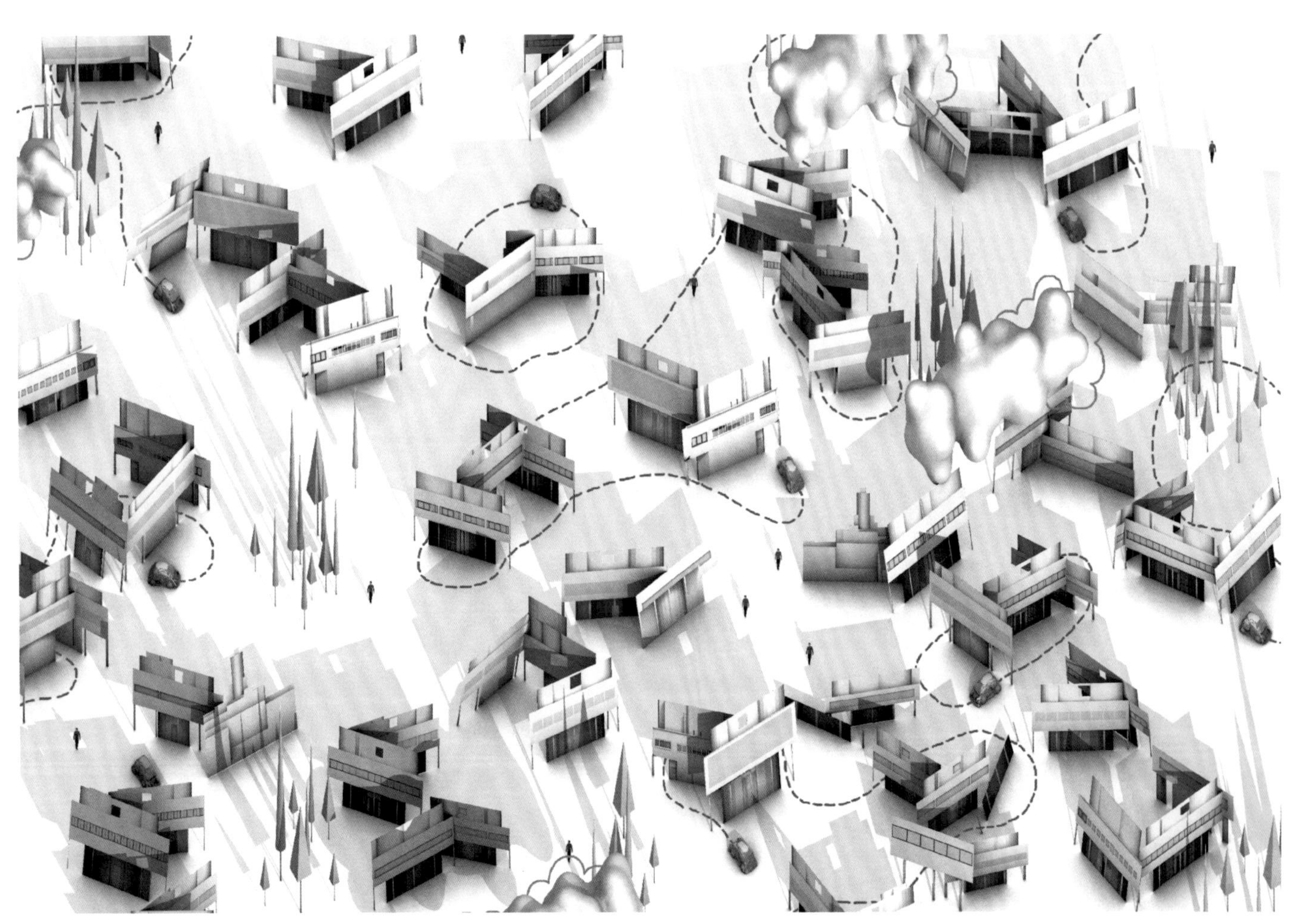

Curtis Roth, Instrument 3: The Mesh, 2016

distribution in tightly packed clusters, while the vehicular motion around and through them reconnects to a larger archipelago. Hans Tursack's Composition VIII uses a pyramidal assembly to satisfy both the necessity for compactness on a defined patch of ground and the arbitrary scattering that sets the scene. The kit-model joinery of its construction looks designed to receive the objects around it, such that the radiating bands of knickknacks can be read as componentry unfolded from the elevations of a larger original. The looseness of construction material is held in close orbit by the eminent possibility of use.

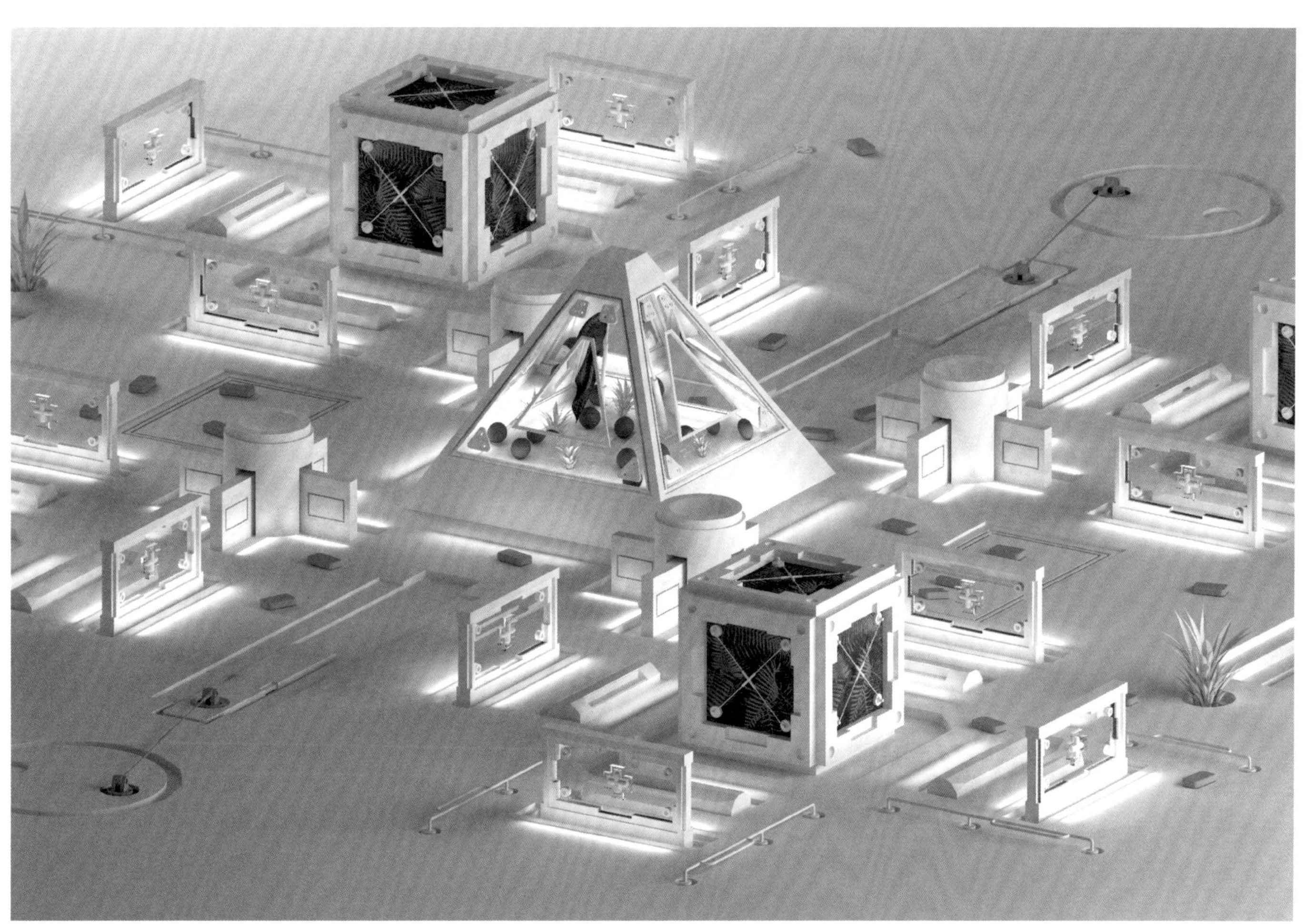

Hans Tursack, Graphic Fields, Composition VIII, 2015

The indices of rock-making become the rudiments of organization for Ensamble Studio's Truffle. The crenellations left behind by hay bales distribute shelves, seats, and a hearth. The horizontally striped elevation—formal residue of digging equipment—squatly reiterates an almost classical three-part facade order. Familiar house traits find new positions and affordances on unfamiliar surfaces, but always inevitably, deferentially, acceding to the spots where they're offered a fit, because of course the shape of the rock, once cast, could be no other way. The remapping accommodates the manufactured facts. Facture is separated from architectural use in the tilt-up casts of 10 Casts by Descriptive Services. Cast horizontally and tipped vertically, the reoriented slabs prop up walls and support a string

Ensamble Studio, The Truffle, 2010

of pipes. Here program, use, and building componentry are not mapped onto some obdurate given like the notion of a rock, as in the Truffle. Instead, they collaborate with the rock to make an interior. Plumbing, walls, props, and cast surfaces are all freely specified and located, constrained only insofar as they all must cooperate to stand up and make walls. Precarity locks them into position. The threat of collapse is not only the temporal possibility that someday the construction will end up in pieces on the floor but also the collapse of category. The flat white surfaces on the reverse of the plaster casts are only walls in their present position, at the mercy of the grey slab's top-heaviness. If they fall, they are not recoverable as parts of a wall waiting to be reassembled in some evident arrangement.

Descriptive Services, 10 Casts, 2016

What it means to occupy is doubled and split across two scales in both MALL's Best Sandwiches (later used as the formal basis for the firm's Office Stack building proposal), and Farshid Moussavi Architecture's Folie Divine, an apartment building. Despite their programmatic differences, at the small scale the two buildings are similar insofar as the office worker or resident or spends time on a horizontal slab, mostly inside a wrapper made of windows and walls. Distinctions between the buildings at this scale are in the handling of apertures and opaque surfaces in the hands of the designer—technologies that belong to the author and affect the occupant only passively. At the scale of the gigantic, though, another set of technologies comes into play that is more volatile and distributed across larger segments of the building's audience. Despite their huge size, the design of both buildings invites them to be read as assemblies of huge parts that are subject to rearrangements and redesign: Folie Divine's thick floor slabs and Best Sandwiches' chunky volumes

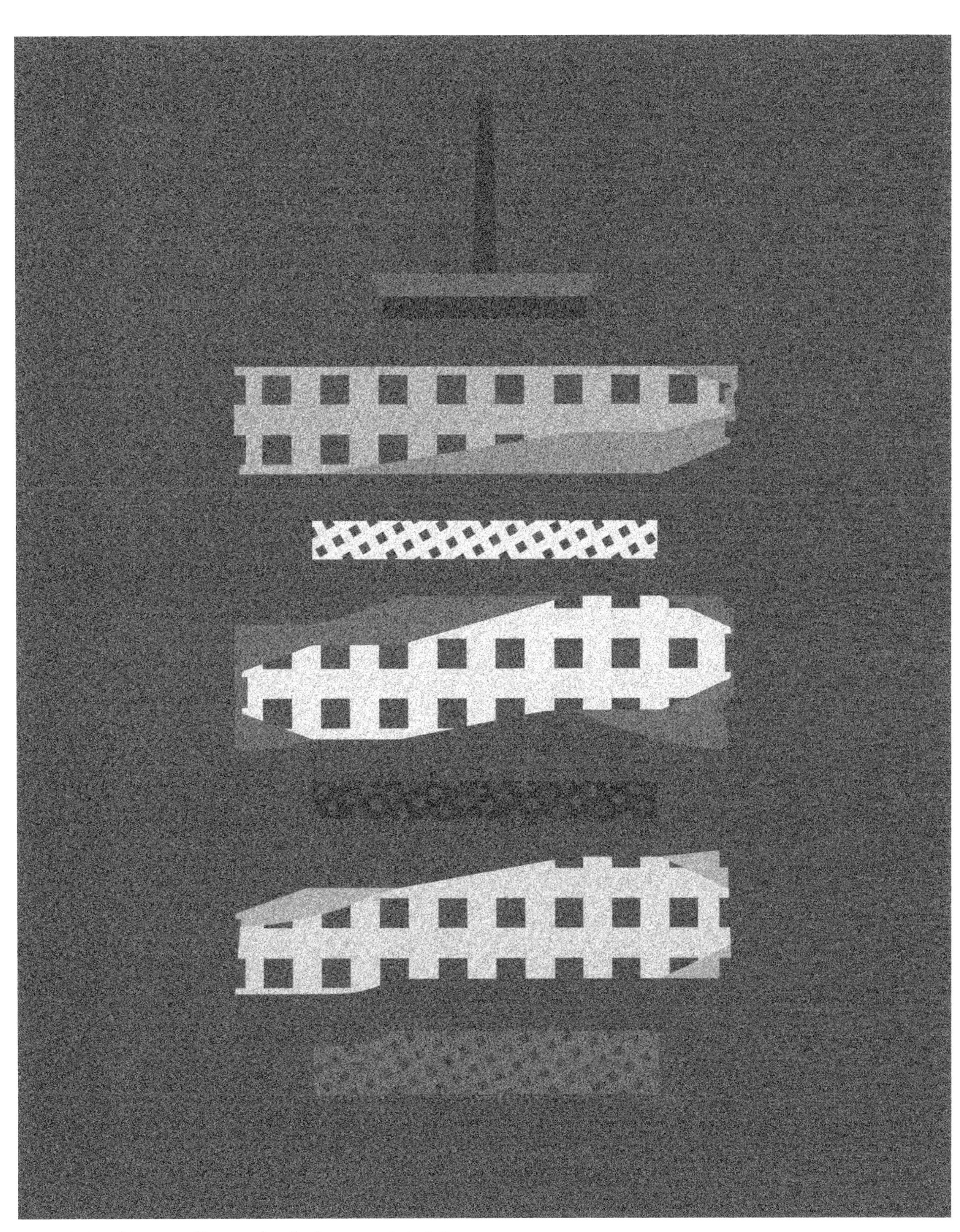

MALL, Best Sandwiches, 2016

are both semigeneric components stacked shakily so as to emphasize a provisional arrangement. The mental operations that allow occupants (and designers) to think of alternative possibilities and arrangements for these masses could be called technologies of imagination, and this is where the two buildings diverge. Mentally assembling another Folie Divine would require technologies of imaginative specification. One must select and procure parts that are the work of experts and the products of precision machining. Another Best Sandwiches, on the other hand, would require technologies of imaginative fantasy—allegorical drawings or collages that make architecture as easy as making a sandwich. At stake between the two is the definition of a democratic practice that distributes agency between architect and audience: in one, an easily imaginable architecture that stipulates a need for experts and precise technique; in the other, an apparently guileless technique that requires expert media capable of transporting an audience to fantasy.

Farshid Moussavi Architecture, Folie Divine, 2017

If a house is the first, it is always do-it-yourself. There is no template to pattern it after, just a hollowness to enclose. Under these lights with a vacuum of example but a clear task to be done, the house can emerge from the labor or forms embedded in the building materials around us so that construction is a long, sighing *of course* at the naturalness of that way of dwelling in that assemblage. Current Interests' Silver House Studio is an ineffable arrangement of labor that permits otherwise unthinkable material choices. *Of course* silver baffles would blanket a frame. Material aligns with trade labor so that the steel crew hands off the jobsite to the wall insulation team. The completeness of the house, the scope of what is to be done,

Current Interests, Silver House Studio, in progress

coincides with this schedule of tasks so that the house is finished when the trades depart the scene. Alternatively, the architect can refuse entanglements of labor and choose instead to scavenge for formal analogies between available materials and architectural elements, as d.esk does in Colossal Paper. Layered depositions of a 3D print furnish a coursing pattern, a leaning sheet creates a roof, and a heightfield of Maxime du Camp's photograph of the Great Sphinx decorates the center. In this way of working, the house stops at just barely enough. More could be done, more cognates could be found between available stuff and parts of the house, but habitation is now thinkable, and the rest is for the second house.

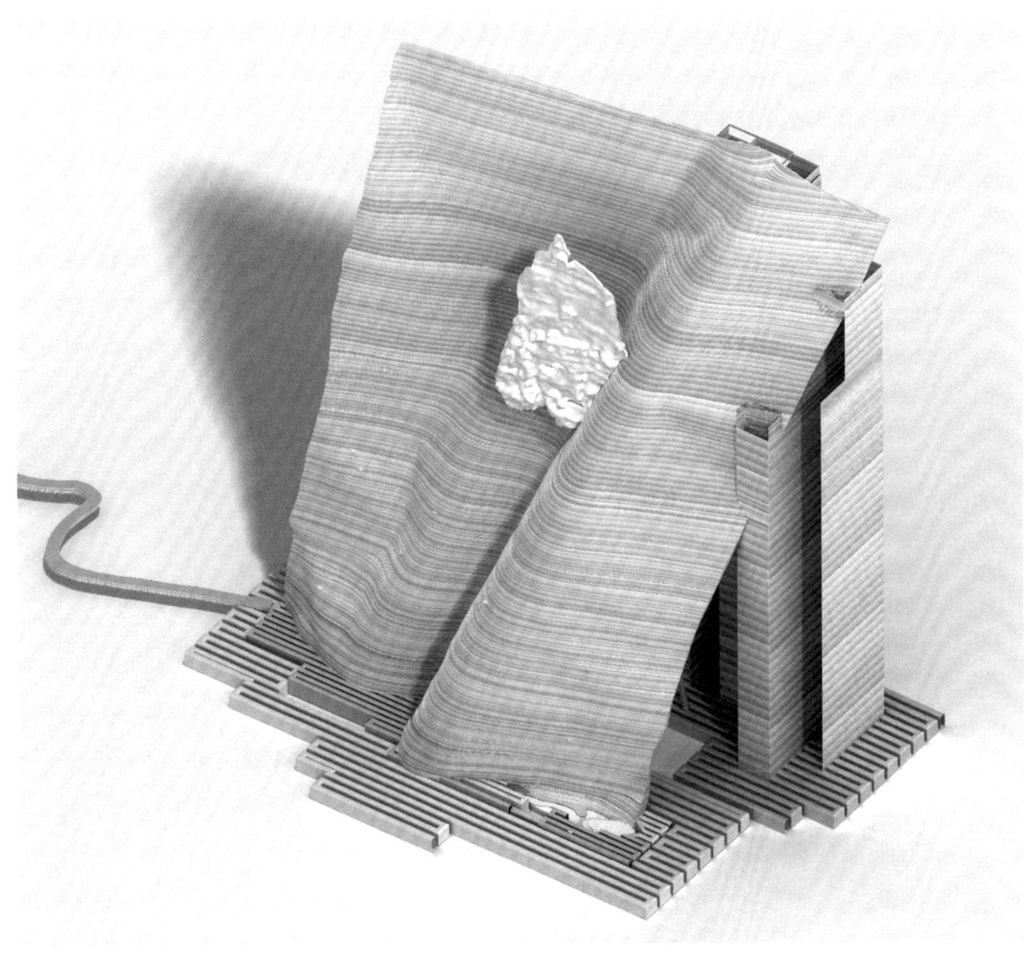

d.esk, Colossal Paper, 2019

How to mark the earth so as to make it intelligible to people? And of all things, how to make the earth comprehensible as a monument, as though its eons of geologic accretion and obliteration, when taken in as a view, represent some human endeavor? One way to solve this problem is to make the earth complicit in manufacturing a structure. The hollow shells of cube, a hemisphere, and a cone rest atop excavations in NEMESTUDIO's Museum of Lost Volumes, so that each becomes a familiar shape when seen

NEMESTUDIO, Museum of Lost Volumes, 2015

in the vivisection of a wall placard. It is a reverse extraction, injecting an image into the planet's crust. Design Earth injects too, but only invisibly, to support a cenotaph in their Trash Peaks series. It is the miracle of a planetary sphere made comprehensibly miniature for a moment, lodged in a divot on the surface of this vastly larger thing, which, despite being big to the point of near invisibility, is present as an actor on the scene because of the way it affords physical support.

Design Earth, Trash Peaks, 2017

At the extremes of repetitive composition, monoliths become villages without people. They both set the scene and occupy it. The trick is to multiply hollowness while still retaining it as a secret reserve, withholding it from occupation. The cubic frames of Jesús Vassallo's Water Towers limn the edges of blocks that exist only as stage spikes to locate the choreography of otherwise

Jesús Vassallo, Water Towers, 2017

independent units: standing on standing. Endemic Architecture bundles turrets incised with monumental arches that similarly separate the effect of hollowness from the requirements of shelter. Somewhere in the thicket of legs there may be an envelope, but it exists only to provide the shelter that the building itself refuses to furnish.

Endemic Architecture, San Francisco Music Hall, 2018

While WOJR's studies probe the symbolic deep structure of architecture, those of Matter Design move between gravity and the medial imaginary. These differences give the projects access to different kinds of productive machinery. WOJR's Étude imagines that architecture's anthropomorphism is a modular, always compatible part-to-part: the universe of expression is anything that can happen to a Lego. Matter Design's Walking Assembly at first looks

WOJR, Études, 2015

stereotomic, but the blocks are each self-contained figures formed to clasp and grasp their neighbors. This model of expression is anything that can happen between a bag of sand and a hug. Both projects set themselves away from the ground—WOJR's on little feet so the characters can go find the setting where they're understood; Matter Design's on rockers so they can wobble just enough to find their place in a stair.

Matter Design, Walking Assembly, 2019

Franz Kafka wrote of a being called Odradek: “One is tempted to believe that the creature once had some sort of intelligible shape and is now only a broken-down remnant. Yet this does not seem to be the case; at least there is no sign of it; nowhere is there an unfinished or unbroken surface to suggest anything of the kind; the whole thing looks senseless enough, but in its own way perfectly finished.” The same could be believed of our creaturely pair. Odradek is a figure of distortion, and like our pair it arrives from the remnants of commodity culture. Yet it is also a motif of hope, if not transcendence. Theodor Adorno: “Odradek is indeed so dialectical that it can also properly be said of it that almost nothing has made everything well again.”

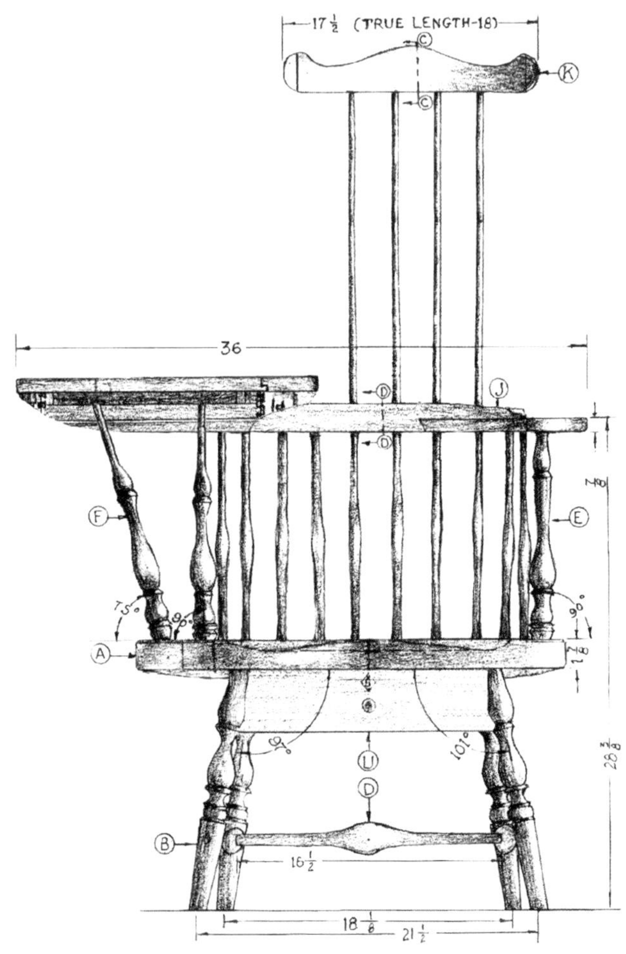

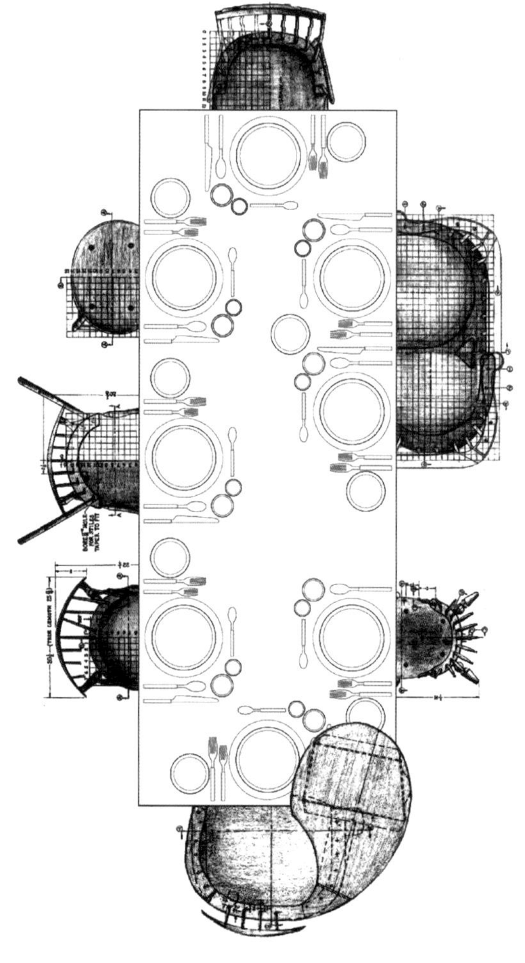

Norman Kelley, Wrong Chairs, 2014

“Almost nothing” is but a slight adjustment to what we already have: Norman Kelly’s Wrong Chairs and the Bittertang Farm’s Workout Bench have the appearance of derelict commodities (a displaced section of the leg of a vintage chair, pantyhose slouching below the knees), but they are also things inscribed (one skeletal, one fleshy), and thus they do not stay the same; rather, they *live on*. Encounters with them are liminal, “in the cavity between what things claim to be and what they are.” They live in corridors and hallways, under staircases, and in attics. They have life and they are alive, but with the discordance that comes from the reassignment of consumer detritus to a primordial stew, out of which might walk new beings.

The Bittertang Farm, Workout Bench, 2016

Edward Eigen

Cotton Mather Engraved and Ungraved

> It is the Desire of *Immortality* inwrought into the very Nature of Man that produced the Invention of *Epitaphs*, and while some will ascribe the Invention unto the Scholars of *Linus*, who so signified their Affection to their slain Master, others will that it may be ascend as high as the *Great Stone* of Abel, mentioned in the first Book of *Samuel*, which they'll tell us, was Erected as a Memorial to *Abel*, by his Father *Adam*, with that Inscription upon it, *Here was shed the Blood of the Righteous Abel*.
> — Cotton Mather, *Magnalia Christi Americana* (1702)

Finished reading the epigraph? That such a "massy" block of text precedes these brief comments on inscriptions and epitaphs seems to ignore the lesson offered in the preface to an early literary work of American identity formation: "Good Reader: As large Gates to small Edifices, so are long Prefaces to little Bookes." Published anonymously by Edward Johnson, a worldly woodworker who arrived in Salem in 1630, the not-so-little and very knotty *Wonder-Working Providence* (1654) was a prophetic account of the effort "to re-build the most glorious Edifice of Mount Sion in a Wildernesse."[1] The Congregational minister Cotton Mather, singular author of the still more compendious and portentous *Magnalia Christi Americana: or, the Ecclesiastical History of New-England* (1702), had littler reason and certainly demonstrated less inclination than Johnson to presume the (inherent) *goodness* of his readers. Mather admitted that his work of seven "books" collected in two volumes was written in a "*Style* Embellished with too much of *Ornament*," among many other faults, not the least of which was its proud pedantry.[2] The slights of critics ("Zoilian outrages," in Mather's learned yet roiling diction) were not the only insults this devourer of books was meant to endure. Mather, whose vast literary output includes "De Tristibus; or, The Cure of Melancholy," was assailed on all sides, or as he would have it, "exposed unto the buffetings and outrages of Azazel" (with reference to the Levitical scapegoat).[3] In this expulsion ritual was typologically foretold the scene, setting, and motive of Mather's epochal history of the New World, a "waste and howling wilderness" in which mortal dangers everywhere lay in wait.

Mather's "Puritan Baroque"[4] masterpiece begins, inevitably, with the Puritans' arrival on the "*American Strand*."[5] In an introductory passage that recalls the opening lines of the *Aeneid*—"first from the shores of Troy"—Mather shadows a covenanted people "flying from the deprivations of Europe" and alighting upon a foreordained western shore. Beyond lie "Indian Wildernesses" that Divine Providence had "irradiated" for and by the Puritans' arrival. Before his untidy work is done, Mather amasses and then wanderingly leads his reader through chamber upon chamber of scriptural allusion, historical chronicle, prose invention, and partially misremembered Greek, Latin, and Hebrew quotations. If a witting guide to this labyrinth is wanted, the self-described "library cormorant" Susan Howe has provided one luminous red (and read) thread through Mather's volumes' worth of circular prophecy. Patience and fortitude![6] But it is the end of things written, the afterword, that stands out so distinctly as a significant marker, and a marker of significance, in the *Magnalia*, here regarded as an ichnology of an unsettling New World. A sort of exquisite corpse, or rather a paradigmatic exercise in "auto-American-biography,"[7] the *Magnalia* is syncopated and punctuated by invented epitaphs of exemplary

Puritans. It is well to recall that *exemplum* once referred to a clearing in the woods, the axe work of excision defining forms and boundaries, making place for the light, the dark, and the umbrageous.[8] An exercise in literary if not literal stone rubbing, this essay looks upon these remains, inscriptions of Mather's own invention that appear and endure only in print. In this context, the desire for immortality is seen to be pardonably overwrought, and the erection of monuments such as the *Great Stone* of Abel merely stumbling stones toward the recognition of less literary lives cruelly uncommemorated. The name of one them, Onesimus, Cotton Mather's slave, serves as linguistic token of the misuse of human kindness.

But then it should be asked, what kinds of readers are there besides Johnson's good readers? For one, the prefatory poem to the *Magnalia*, written by the Salem preacher Nicholas Noyes, is addressed "To the Candid Reader." Not without present significance, *candor* comes from the Latin *candidus*, a dazzling whiteness that appears in sacred texts to describe robes of glory and divine light; it signifies that which is pure and unblemished, and by extension speech that is frank and guileless.[9] And who are these readers, even if they were unlettered? In Mather's *The Negro Christianized* (1706), a tract addressed to slaves and servants, rote catechism serves as the first step toward literacy in "the Sacred Scriptures, *which make Wise unto Salvation*" (2 Timothy 3:15). In now attempting a very partial reading of the *Magnalia*, the question is, what becomes of those for whom no epitaph was written? Our proof text is subepitaphic—indeed, an epithet that served immemorially, or at least since the Apostolic Age, as a name in place of a duly given proper name. In a word, Onesimus, who by rights should have been inscribed on

Boston's Ebenezer Stone (about which more below), another monument of Mather's massy imagination.

About the epigraph above. The invention of the epitaph, however its genealogy be inscribed, presumes a "desire for immortality" that is "inwrought" in the "nature of man." Like a preface, the epitaph presumes on the good graces and also the candor of the reader. Whatever his race—in virtue of his very name, *ha-adam*, man is of the dust of earth and constitutively red (with shame)—the desire to speak beyond the grave is an intrinsic, indeed graven, character trait and the most human of all faults. In part because of Mather's own self-diagnosed flaws as a writer, which he equally celebrated as a sort of stylistic *felix culpa*, the *Magnalia* has been described as "the most revealing unread book of American literature."[10] That readerly neglect is arguably for the better. "It will not be so much a Surprise unto me," Mather lamented, "if I should live to see our *Church-History* vexed with *Aniemad-versions* of Calumnious Writers."[11] Thus Mather anxiously anticipated his own troubled literary posterity. Through ruses of anonymity, pseudonymity, and other para-authorial jests scattered like salt throughout his text, Mather attempted to disarm animadverters, both named and unnamed, of their pointed critical asterisks and obeli (daggers).

Among the more obscure of these ruses is one whose decryption depends on the legible appearance of the printed word (once the proper page and line of text was spotted). Suitably enough, it is buried in a reference to a recondite volume on ancient shape-shifting theonyms: "Thus I would have tried whether I could not have Anagrammatized my name into concealment," Mather declares, "or I would have referr'd it to be found in the second Chapter of the second Syntagm of *Selden de Diis Syris*."[12] Obliquely directed to John Selden's

Magnalia Chriſti Americana:

OR, THE

Eccleſiaſtical Hiſtory

OF

NEW-ENGLAND,

FROM

Its Firſt Planting in the Year 1620. unto the Year of our LORD, 1698.

In Seven BOOKS.

I. Antiquities: In Seven Chapters. With an Appendix.
II. Containing the Lives of the Governours, and Names of the Magiſtrates of *New-England:* In Thirteen Chapters. With an Appendix.
III. The Lives of Sixty Famous Divines, by whoſe Miniſtry the Churches of *New-England* have been Planted and Continued.
IV. An Account of the Univerſity of *Cambridge* in *New-England*; in Two Parts. The Firſt contains the Laws, the Benefactors, and Viciſſitudes of *Harvard College*; with Remarks upon it. The Second Part contains the Lives of ſome Eminent Perſons Educated in it.
V. Acts and Monuments of the Faith and Order in the Churches of *New-England*, paſſed in their Synods; with Hiſtorical Remarks upon thoſe Venerable Aſſemblies; and a great Variety of Church-Caſes occurring, and reſolved by the Synods of thoſe Churches: In Four Parts.
VI. A Faithful Record of many Illuſtrious, Wonderful Providences, both of Mercies and Judgments, on divers Perſons in *New-England:* In Eight Chapters.
VII. *The Wars of the Lord.* Being an Hiſtory of the Manifold Afflictions and Diſturbances of the Churches in *New-England*, from their Various Adverſaries, and the Wonderful Methods and Mercies of God in their Deliverance: In Six Chapters: To which is ſubjoined, An Appendix of Remarkable Occurrences which *New-England* had in the Wars with the *Indian* Salvages, from the Year 1688, to the Year 1698.

By the Reverend and Learned *COTTON MATHER*, M. A.
And Paſtor of the North Church in *Boſton*, *New-England*.

LONDON:
Printed for *Thomas Parkhurſt*, at the *Bible* and *Three Crowns* in *Cheapſide*. MDCCII.

Cotton Mather, *Magnalia Christi Americana, or, The ecclesiastical history of New-England*, 1702.

appointed by Washington Consul to China, and that he died in 1794. Between this shaft and the Grant family tomb is a stone a few inches in height and so sunk in the ground that it almost escapes notice. It bears the name of Goodeth (Judith ?) Copp, who died on the 25th of May, 1670, at the age of 75 years. She was the wife of William Copp, for whom the Hill was named. While this memorial of her former existence still remains, and seems able to defy the elements for centuries, that which records the decease of her husband has disappeared, although stones sacred to the memory of other members of the Copp family can be seen in different places in the cemetery.

The most noted tomb in the ground, and the one almost invariably the first inquired for by people from other States and even from Europe, is that of Reverend Cotton Mather. It is near the Charter Street gate, and is a simple vault of brick upon which rests a heavy slab of brown stone into which two separate squares of slate have been set — one of recent date and the other bearing marks of age, with the following inscription, which is almost illegible:

THE MATHER TOMB.

THE REVEREND DOCTORS
INCREASE, COTTON,
& SAMUEL MATHER
were intered in this Vault.
'Tis the Tomb of our Father's
MATHER — CROCKER'S
I DIED Augt 27th 1723 Æ 84
C DIED FEB 13th 1727 Æ 65
S DIED June 27th 1785 Æ 79

In addition to these clergymen, the vault contains the remains of many of their descendants. (Cotton Mather was three times married; by his first two wives he had fifteen children). It was last opened about fifteen years ago, when one of the Crocker family was deposited under its arch; the relics of these ancient worthies were found mingled in great confusion. There

Edward MacDonald, *Old Copp's Hill and Burial Ground*, with historical sketches, 1891.

study of Syrian deities, the reader would find in the entry for Astarte (the Phoenician "mother of the gods") the following passage: "*Mader* enim sive *Mather*" (Mather's name was sometimes spelled Madder, which variation colored or rather spotted its meaning in other ways).[13] Could it be that Mather wished to align himself with Jeremiah, the prophet who raged against the worship of Astarte in the cities of Judah and the streets of Jerusalem? Indeed, Perry Miller, a crucial interpreter of the oratorical form that structured Puritan spiritual and civic sentiment, memorably labeled the *Magnalia* "a colossal jeremiad."[14] But in these preliminaries the author of New England's providential history was not preaching the imminence of communal retribution visited on a covenanted people by a vengeful god. Rather he was attending to the lonelier and decidedly more human desire to circumvent the disfavor of his own critics.

In attaching and detaching his proper name to and from his great tome/tomb, Mather inscribes an auto-epitaph that anticipates something worse than death: the wrath of hostile readers. He finally commits himself to posterity in an act of humiliation and redemption—a confession: "Whereas now I freely confess, 'tis Cotton Mather that has written all these things; *Me, me, ad sum qui scripsi; tu me convertite Ferrum*" (Me—here I am, I wrote it—turn your swords on me).[15] One Virgilian scholar suggests that the marked repetition (*Me, me*) of the line from the *Aeneid* serves the purpose of "keeping an agreeable picture a moment longer before the mind."[16] But for a reader attuned to the off-beat cadence and rhythm of Mather's text there are to be heard symptoms of distress, an embattled politics of the self. In this authorial "auto-machia," as Sacvan Bercovitch diagnoses it, "every gesture of I-ness contains its own counter-gesture."[17] Mather's is a running gag of authorial self-denial, filled with repetitions and hesitations, assertions and refusals, building up or bowing down to the recognition that the final word will be left to be said or read by others who live after the author himself is no longer present to settle the Mather.

But Mather's historical reputation was ultimately bound more than anything to his role in a notorious episode in the sociology of texts, the witchcraft trials vividly described in the *Magnalia*. In May 1692 Mather advised the Court of Oyer and Terminer on how to evaluate evidence—largely immaterial in nature—of the "Devil's book." This was the codex in which the spiritually afflicted, "under the Command of that *Blackman* as they called him" (that is to say the devil), damnably inscribed their signatures.[18] As dramatized in Herman Melville's story, "The Apple-Tree Table; Or, Original Spiritual Manifestations," Mather's account of the witch trials made for "doleful, ghostly, ghastly" reading.[19]

How, then, are the watchwords of unhastened mortality to be written and read? "It needs scarcely be said," William Wordsworth observed, "that an Epitaph presupposes a Monument, upon which it is to be engraven."[20] Note, "practiced reader,"[21] the quietly emphatic *scarcely*. There is an internal consistency to the poet's apophasis. Wordsworth—who was eulogistically said not only to have put man and nature on "talking terms" but also to have "filled this common earth of ours with angel presences to haunt and help mankind"[22]—was evidently moved to communicate that which could almost have been left unsaid, that almost unsaid stroke itself resting on a presupposition. Thus too the monument awaits the epitaph, while the epitaph answers to a desire of perpetuation, which is possible (in written form) only when "nations," the collective authors of monuments, first learn the "use of letters."[23] (Below, by invoking the name of Onesimus, we will refer to use of still living but socially dead persons.)

As Wordsworth explains in rough, anthropological terms, "Nations have wished that certain external signs should point out the places where their Dead are interred. Among savage Tribes unacquainted with letters, this has mostly been done either by rude stones placed near the Graves, or by Mounds of earth raised over them."[24] Rudeness presents its own challenge to the reader. "Some things are remarkable and curious for their elegance, richness, shape, and magnificence, and some others for their simplicity, and remote Antiquity," observed the eminent Cornish antiquarian William Borlase in his landmark study of rude stone monuments. "If the Reader is of that turn, as to be delighted only with the former kind, I can promise him but little pleasure in the ensuing Treatise."[25] But the study of epitaphs is guided not only by a pleasure principle but also beyond it, to a restless contemplation on desire and loss. Where Wordsworth and Mather meet, in the vestibule that is our epigraph, is with their mutual reading of John Weever's monumental 900-page tome, *Ancient Funerall Monuments*, which sets forth Linus as the progenitor of epitaphal inscriptions.[26] The identity of the legendary Theban poet is derived from the word for ritual lamentation, *ailinon* (alas, for Linus). His is the very name of threnody, just as Onesimus nominally bore the stigma of servitude, which for Mather was also a sign of possible salvation.

As we read to the end of the epigraph, Mather "ascends" to ever higher textual witnesses commemorating the source of the epitaph form. But here, instead of conversing with the dead, which is one purpose served by this reverential sort of inscription, Mather ends up in dialogue with himself, losing and then finding himself again within the textual wildernesses of the *Magnalia* itself. Let us follow him between the unruly lines.

One wary critic, referring to an "imaginative writer" (Mather), observed that there was no "ground for his theory" that the Great Stone of Abel was "a monument to the memory of the first martyr." For indeed, after having "vainly sought for any authorization of it," either in Samuel or "elsewhere in Scripture," the critic could find no mention of this primordial monument.[27] Elsewhere within the *Magnalia*, Mather comes to the same conclusion, recognizing the faulty grounds for his own reading of 1 Samuel 6:18. The problem, one of translation, had been addressed by John Edwards in his *Discourse Concerning the Authority, Stile, and Perfection of the Books of the Old and New Testament* (1695), where the English Calvinistic divine parses the finely pointed distinction between the Great Stone of Abel (Hebrew: *Eben Gedolah*) and the "stone of mourning" (Abel Hagedolah). Edwards writes, "If then I should assert that this is the *Tombstone* which *Adam* erected in Memory of his murder'd Son *Abel*, and so was the first Funeral Monument in the World, I am sure there is none can disprove it. But because there is no certainty of this, and it may be *Abel* in this Place is no more than *Ebel*, *luctus* (as that Hebrew Word signifies), and so related to the remarkable Occasion of *Mourning* which we read of *v.* 19, therefore I shall dismiss it, and propound that which is plain, certain, and undeniable."[28] Thus, on the second reading, Mather recognized that the "names" of the stone he identifies as the origins of the epitaph "differ in the Original."[29] Difference matters internally to words read properly and otherwise, but so too does context. *Luctus*, which signifies mourning, organizes the meaning of the *Magnalia*'s concluding book, "Decennium Luctuosum," which spells out

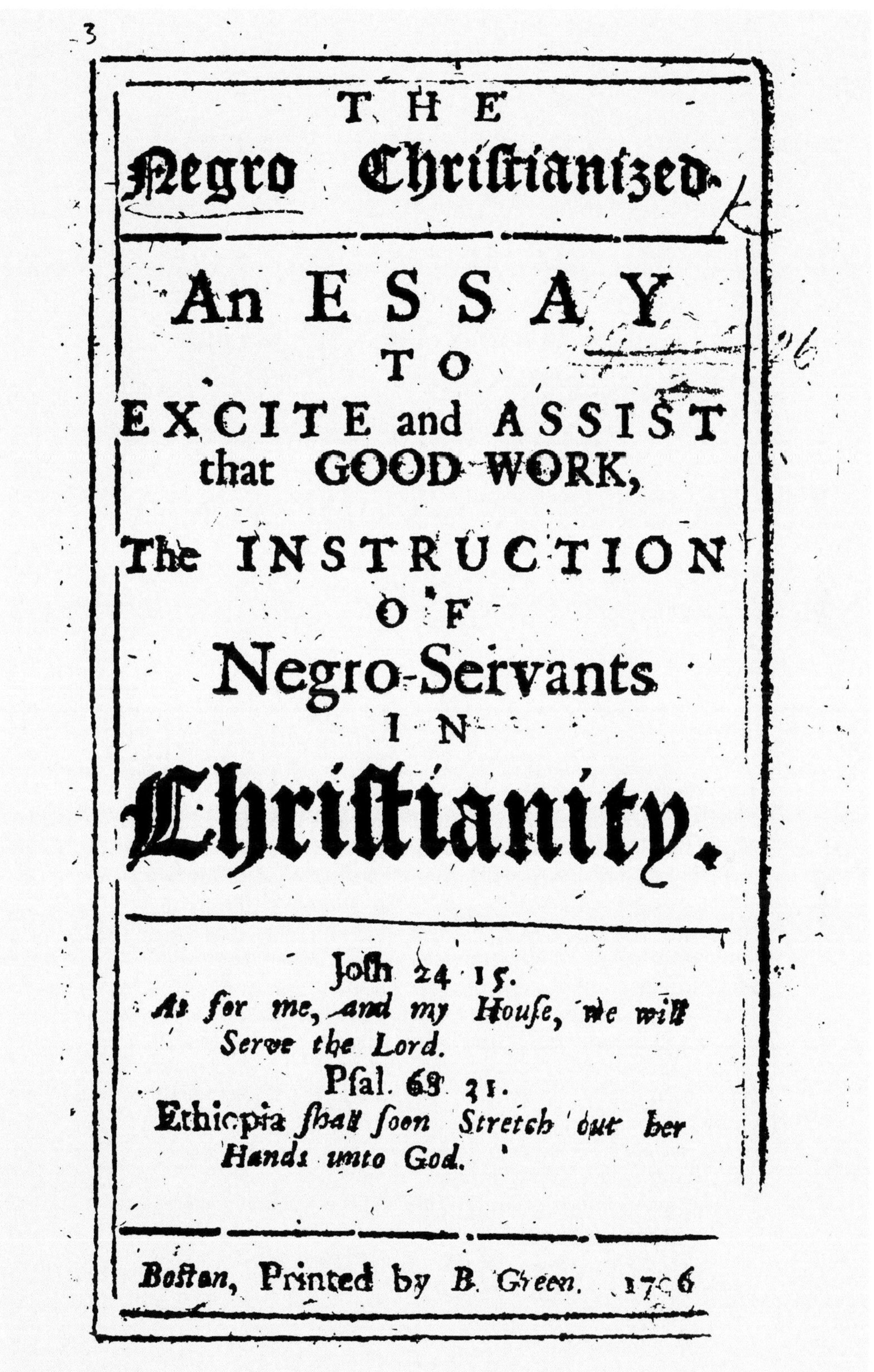
THE
Negro Christianized.

An ESSAY
TO
EXCITE and ASSIST
that GOOD WORK,
The INSTRUCTION
OF
Negro-Servants
IN
Christianity.

Josh. 24. 15.
As for me, and my House, we will Serve the Lord.
Psal. 68. 31.
Ethiopia *shall soon Stretch out her Hands unto God.*

Boston, Printed by *B. Green.* 1706

Cotton Mather, *The Negro Christianized: An Essay to Excite and Assist the Good Work*, 1706.

PL. IX.

RUDE STONE-MONUMENTS.

BOOK III.

CHAP. I.

Of Rude Stone-Monuments in general.

SOME things are remarkable and curious for their elegance, richneſs, ſhape, and magnificence, and ſome others for their ſimplicity, and remote Antiquity. If the Reader is of that turn, as to be delighted only with the former kind of Monuments, I can promiſe him but little pleaſure in the enſuing Treatiſe; but if he has a juſt regard for the firſt ages and cuſtoms of mankind, and is willing to enquire into the original of thoſe Monuments, which are diſperſed not only in thoſe Iſlands of Britain, but in moſt other nations, and certainly preceded all the improvements of art, imagery, and fancy, he may not loſe his labour wholly, nor miſs of entertainment. He may here ſee the ſame Monuments in Aſia, and at home at his own doors; the ſame in Egypt, and the Weſternmoſt parts of Britain; and may perhaps diſcover the intent and deſign of them, ſet forth in other hiſtories, better than we can expect from the hiſtory of our own country.

The precariouſneſs of human life, and the uncertainty of worldly affairs, taught people very ſoon after the Creation to endeavour by ſome memorials to perpetuate the remembrance of thoſe perſons and events, which had been of importance in their time.

Religion

William Borlase, *Antiquities, Historical and Monumental, of the County of Cornwall*, 1769.

the decade-long war in which the godly exiles were pitted against indigenous peoples ("savages") alien to salvation. The strife ensued, Mather wrote, in spite of the efforts of John Eliot, so-called Apostle to the Indians, to rescue (salvage) the savages "out of their worse than *Egyptian* Darkness."[30] In whatever form, but especially when formless and yet animate darkness was perceived as the mortal enemy. And so it was as a bright glade in a menacing forest that Harvard College, "truly a *Sion-College*," was founded for the "rising generation" of "Criolians," as Mather referred to American-born persons of European ancestry.[31] Without this "nursery," Mather rued, "for such Men among our selves *Darkness must have soon covered the Land, and Gross Darkness the People*."[32] These men among ourselves notably included his father, Increase Mather, who between 1685 and 1701 served Harvard as acting president, then as rector, and finally as president. Disappointed in his own great expectation to assume its presidency, Cotton Mather regarded Harvard as a family institution that came with hereditary rights, obligations, and attendant disappointments.

Delivery from danger, from death, from darkness—for there can be no reading in the dark, though there is much fearfully written about the dark—was the occasion for the other source of epitaphs discussed by Mather. "Now from the *Stones* of *Abel*," he writes, "we will a little gather what we should wish to write upon the *Stones* of our *Ebenezer*."[33] Mather develops the significance of this word-made monument in the chapter "Boston, the Chief Town of New-England and of the English America," which concludes the *Magnalia*'s first book, "Antiquities; or, A Field prepar'd for Considerable Things to be Acted Thereupon." In the "primordial" wilderness, all was yet to be settled and concluded according to the unseen plan of Providence. Ever fascinated with proper names, Mather notes, "Little was *this* expected by them that settled the Town, when for a while Boston was proverbially called Lost Town, for the mean and sad Circumstances of it."[34] Many were the setbacks and fatal discouragements suffered by the emigrants—famine, smallpox, fire, war—in sum forming a syllabus of supplications and prayers answered. "May the Changes, and especially the Judgments that have come upon the Town, direct us what *help* to petition from the *God of our Salvations*."[35] The circuit of sacred communication was materialized in the Ebenezer (Hebrew: *'eben*, "stone" + *'ezer*, "help"), mentioned in 1 Samuel 7:12.[36] Yet while Mather imaginatively ascribed an epitaph to the Great Stone of Abel, borrowing Matthew 23:35 for the purpose—for recall, a monument awaits an inscription, and thus one must be provided—he was still uncertain about what words awaited the Ebenezer. "I know not whether any thing might be *Writ* upon it," Mather explains, "but I am sure there is one thing to be now *Read* upon it, by our selves, in the Text we find it Namely, thus much, *That a People whom the God of Heaven hath remarkably helped in their Distresses, ought greatly and gratefully to acknowledge what* help of *Heaven they have received*."[37] What help of heaven did Cotton Mather receive? Was it in the form of a person such as *ourselves*, or someone or something else of a different nature? Are some among us not truly ourselves?

Enter Onesimus. "This Day, a surprising Thing befel me," Mather wrote in his diary entry for October 13, 1706, a day he had set aside for "solemn THANKSGIVINGS to God, for his many marvelous Favours to me; especially in my *Ministry*, and in my *Family*."[38] That this "thing" (a human person) *befell* Mather no doubt reflects the belief of Protestant divines in unexpected occurrences as sources of "extra-biblical revelation," in this notable instance confirming Mather's righteous conduct.[39] By Mather's own account, "Some Gentlemen of our Church, understanding (without any Application of mine to them for such a Thing), that I wanted a *good Servant* at the expense of between forty and fifty Pounds, purchased for me, a very likely *Slave* . . . and this Day they presented him unto me."[40] A gift from his congregation, this "young Man, who is a *Negro* of a promising Aspect and Temper," seemed to Mather, ever a reader of signs and tokens, "to be a mighty Smile of Heaven upon my family."[41] No application necessary.

To adopt for a moment the catechistic form Mather developed in his tract *The Negro Christianized*: Q. What help did Mather receive? A. Precisely the help he had wished for, a good servant costing between forty and fifty pounds, even if he had not *explicitly* asked for it (the helping human person) to be provided by his congregation. His prayers, *scarcely* having been spoken, were directly answered. Let us follow with another more pointed Q&A, which appears in the *Biblia Americana*, Mather's enormous manuscript compilation of Bible commentary, which characteristically ranges across scholarly, speculative, apologetic, and practical inquiries.[42]

> Q. The *Curse* upon *Cham* [Ham], does it not Justify our Enslaving the Negros, wherever we can find them?
>
> A. The whole Family of *Cham* was not concern'd in that *Curse*. None but Canaan, the youngest Son of *Cham*, is mentioned; and he is Thrice mentioned. The *Negroes* are not the posterity of *Canaan*.[43]

In his ecumenical history of the Curse of Ham (ecumenical because it has produced a legacy of shame among all the Abrahamic religions), David M. Goldenberg examines not only the interpretive crux of the dreadfully fraught Bible story—why is it that while Ham sinned by disrespecting his father, Noah, it was Ham's son Canaan who bore the bane of judgment?—but also how the curse historically took shape through successive, lethally misconstrued reinterpretations of scripture. The identification of Black Africans with slavery by writers in the Near East and Roman worlds, a product of then-prevailing social realities, fostered the mistaken assumption that "Ham" itself referred to blackness. Thus arose expressions such as *banu ham* (Arabic) and *bnei ham* (Hebrew) in which "Sons of Ham" was used as a synonym for "Black African."[44] Yet the mention of sons and thereby of fathers speaks to the animating generational fatality identified by Harvard sociologist Orlando Patterson—the "natal alienation" that constitutes slavery. "Not only was the slave denied all claims on, and obligations to, his parents and living blood relations but, by extension, all such claims and obligations on his more remote ancestors and his descendants. He was truly a genealogical isolate."[45] There was no pretext for nor postscript to his solitary being in the world; he had no hereditary claim on (written) history.

It was left to Mather to give his servant—the desired yet surprising *thing* that befell him—a proper name. Cotton Mather's own name memorializes and perpetuates the fame of his eminent forebears John Cotton (epitaph: "Whose highest praise it is that he was the first man in New-England") and Richard Mather, who were but the foremost fraction of the "happy *Decemvirate*" of Mathers, spiritual leaders of that "great Number of *Voluntary Exiles*" on their errand into the wilderness. Mather writes of his slave's christening, "I putt upon him ye name of *Onesimus*; and I resolved, with ye help of ye Lord, that I would use the best Endeavours to make him a servant of Christ; and also be more serviceable than

30 Book I.

The BOSTONIAN EBENEZER.

SOME

Hiſtorical Remarks

On the State of

BOSTON,

The *Chief Town* of *New-England*, and of the *Engliſh* AMERICA.

With Some

Agreeable Methods

FOR

Preſerving and Promoting the *Good State* of THAT, as well as any *other Town* in the like Circumſtances.

Humbly Offered by a Native *of* BOSTON.

Ezek. 48. 35. *The Name of the City from that Day ſhall be,* THE LORD IS THERE.

Urbs Metropolis, ut ſit maximæ Auctoritatis, conſtituatur præcipuum pietatis Exemplum & Sacrarium. Aphor. Polit.

The Hiſtory of *BOSTON*, Related and Improved.

At Boſton *Lecture*, 7. d. 2. m. 1698.

REmarkable and Memorable was the Time, when an *Army* of Terrible *Deſtroyers* was coming againſt one of the *Chief Towns* in the Land of *Iſrael.* God reſcued the *Town* from the Irreſiſtible Fury and Approach of thoſe *Deſtroyers*, by an immediate Hand of Heaven upon them. Upon that Miraculous Reſcue of the *Town*, and of the whole Country, whoſe Fate was much enwrapped in it, there follow'd that Action of the Prophet *SAMUEL*, which is this Day to be, with ſome Imitation, Repeated in the midſt of thee, O *BOSTON*, *Thou Helped of the Lord*.

1 SAM.

Cotton Mather, *The Bostonian Ebenezer*, 1698.

Otto Elliger, Stone of Ebenezer, from David Martin, *History of the Old and New Testaments*, engraving, 1707.

ever to a flock, which laide me under such Obligations."[46] This line from Mather's diary—and what it describes is indeed a life sentence for Onesimus—accounts for the preacher's further liberation to conduct the work of salvation, and in so doing canceling his obligation to his flock. Not "Cotton" nor "Mather" but rather the name "Onesimus," from the Greek *onesis* ("use," "profit," or "advantage"), articulates the terms of the exchange, which took place on a day set aside for Thanksgiving. Onesimus was to be used up without concern for what remained of him.

The prototypical Onesimus, a fugitive slave, appears in a supplication written to his owner, Philemon, by Paul; for this purpose, Paul, who usually dictated his letters to a scribe, took the stylus into his own hand. Paul was as a father to both these souls, having converted Philemon at Ephesus and baptized Onesimus when he and Saul/Paul—himself reborn by conversion—met as fellow prisoners. "I beseech thee for my son Onesimus," Paul wrote, "whom I have begotten in my bonds" (Philemon 1:10). John Calvin observes in his *Commentaries on the Epistles*, "Here it is of importance to consider how deep is [Paul's] condescension, when he gives the name of 'son' to a slave, and a runaway, and a thief."[47] But in recommending charitable terms for Onesimus's return, Paul explains that he was to be received into Philemon's house, "not now as a servant, but above a servant, even as a brother beloved, specially to me" (Philemon 1:16). Paul's stern but affective letter is structured by the language of kinship, real and fictive. But what of the lapses of brotherhood, said to stem from the Curse of Ham, that left the structure of slavery cruelly unchanged?

In her searching study of Mather's household, considered as an "experiment in Christian slaveholding," Kathryn

S. Koo asks more pointedly, "What might literacy have signified to Onesimus?"[48] The absence of any record of his own thoughts on the matter makes it impossible to assess Onesimus's response to the education that was "imposed" upon him.[49] Rather than form an argument from absence, scrutiny turns to the absence of literacy itself, an imposed silence that impeded the slave's self-possession. For his part, Mather saw Onesimus as amply spoken for in scripture. In *The Negro Christianized* he comments on Paul's letter to Philemon: "*Onesimus* was doubtless a *Slave*: but this poor *Slave*, on whose behalf a great Apostle of God was more than a little concerned; yea, one Book in our Bible was Written on his behalf! When he was *Christianized*, it was presently said unto his *Master*, Philem. II. *In time past he was unprofitable to thee, but now he will be profitable*."[50] The slave is not a prophet, for he does not speak in his own special words about the salvation of his people, but is made to be profitable by those who speak on his behalf so that he might enter into Christian communion.

Was this "Book in *our* Bible" all that was written for or about the "poor slave"?[51] Having entered into the bonds of Christian fellowship, was he not also worthy of an epitaph? What lesson—*lesson* itself being a sort of readerly act—might it offer to those historically fated to illiteracy? The first requisite of this special form of address, according to Wordsworth, was that "it should speak, in a tone which shall sink into the heart, the general language of humanity as connected with the subject of death."[52] But what of those who pass through life in a natal state of social death, beholden by an unforgivable mortgage to those who speak on their behalf? The problem of Onesimus, or generically those of his kind and inborn condition, is not addressed by Wordsworth's second requirement for the epitaph. As a "species of composition," Wordsworth explains, the epitaph must excite in the "Reader's mind" a "distinct and clear conception" of the individual whose "death is deplored and whose memory is to be preserved."[53] As was earlier stated, there is no record of what Onesimus himself made of the education imposed on him, but if Mather's *The Negro Christianized* speaks on his behalf, it does not do so with the intention of deploring his living death. Can a proper epigraph be written for one such as Onesimus, known only by the epithet conferred on him? As one astute reader of Wordsworth asks, is the required "common or universal feeling of humanity"—which can be rewritten as "universal feeling *for* [common?] humanity"—something that "exists in the human mind from the start"? Does it inhere "primarily in the epitaph itself," or it is "aroused in the reader as a result of his reading the epitaph"?[54] There must be mutual sympathy and recognition of kind hearts and kindred spirits to complete a circuit of communication beyond the grave. The epitaph is not meant for just anyone, and some bodies are not so much excommunicated as compelled to accept lessons that might have no specific meaning for them.

The written terms on which Mather and Onesimus terminated their relationship, which is to say by which the latter was released from servitude to the former, are spelled out in a memo preserved at the American Antiquarian Society. Yet before he left Mather's household, Onesimus had to provide for his own replacement. The memo stipulates that Onesimus was to be released only in consideration of "having advanced a Summ, toward the purchase of a Negro-Lad, who may serve many occasions of my Family in his Room."[55] Onesimus was thus replaced by Obadiah, whose name means "servant of Yahweh."[56] The chain of servitude in Mather's home remained unbroken. Onesimus's notional "room" would continue to be occupied. The transcribed version of the memo reproduced in the published edition of Mather's diary omits the crossed-out lines in which Mather's thoughts on his servant's welfare undergo an ungenerous revision. The corrections, overwriting, and marginal annotations are "more revealing" than what Mather let stand, offering a "rare glimpse of Mather at work, revising and rethinking the ties of kinship upon which Christianized slavery rested."[57] A comparison might be drawn to the composition of Paul's epistle to Philemon in which the Apostle indicates, "I Paul have written this with mine own hand" (Philemon 1:19). Strikingly, the plea on behalf of Onesimus is his autograph. The unasked question, however, is, what sort of epigraph should have appeared on the Boston Ebenezer to commemorate the thanks owed to Onesimus by Mather and indeed the City of Boston for his role in delivering them from the smallpox epidemic of 1721–1722? The memo marks out the limits of Mather's concern for his soon-to-be-former slave: "~~and I now stand obliged to provide for him in case of Sickness or Lameness~~."[58] With respect to moral accountancy, Mather "literally cancels out" the obligations that he at first considered himself under as Onesimus's former master.[59]

What the stricken lines evidence is a failure to apply the Golden Rule. The problem here, of course, is not to do with the humble and humbling ruler, the instrument of the strict writing master. For no such straightening tool was needed for Mather to belie out the precepts of *Bonifacius* (1710), his tract of Puritan charity that later counted among its avid readers Benjamin Franklin. The handwritten evidence cancels, in the rational manner of a ledger book, that moral sentiment that was meant to be engraved in the hearts, if not also the minds, of men. This irreproachable form of writing is elaborated in Mather's *A Man of Reason* (1718). Here the discussion was not of blackness (still less Blackness) but of relative obscurity, or rather the way in which, "by our Fall from GOD, the strength of *Reason* is much impaired in us; the Eye of *Reason* is darkened."[60] Consolation was to be had and guidance provided by the certainty that there were "many things in *Scriptures* which are, *Above Reason*." Even amid the moral chiaroscuro between gloom and glory, the "*Word of GOD*, & the *Book of Truth*" remained legible, even and especially when reason would cavil at the lesson. For Mather the truest challenge and remedy to the faultiness of carnal reason appeared in a single line, indeed a "Rule" from scripture that might serve to "rectify" mankind: "*For a Man to do unto others, as he would own it reasonable for others to do unto him*." Mather placed special emphasis on the manner in which this precept was delivered and materialized. "Our Saviour has Honoured & Confirmed this *Rule* with His own Royal Stamp upon it," and so it was "engraved by the Hand of GOD, upon the *Reason* of Mankind."[61] Reasonable, rational, *and* charitable? The test was whether mankind of a (darkly perceived) different kin could still be treated with kindness. In his cancellation of the terms of care owed to Onesimus, Mather failed.

This dilemma can be translated directly to Mather's conception of the Boston Ebenezer Stone (help stone), an imaginary monument based on a literary biblical prototype. "I know not whether any thing might be *Writ* upon it," Mather speculated. But among the acts of deliverance for which Boston had truly to be thankful was surely Onesimus's communication of a remedy for smallpox, which is recorded in a number of Mather's "lost works."[62] The editor of these writings was well aware that readers might not welcome the prospect of undiscovered "composures" from Mather's "tireless pen," except that this was not a "new batch of funeral sermons," the occasion for many of Mather's epitaphs, but rather unpublished tracts and letters on variolous inoculation. One in a series of communications headed "Curiosa Americana," a letter to Dr. John Woodward, secretary of the Royal Society in London, contains Mather's description of how knowledge about vaccination was communicated to him by Onesimus:

> I do assure you, that many months before I mett with any Intimations of treating y^e *Small-Pox*, with ye Method of Inoculation, any where in *Europe*; I had from a Servant of my own an Account of its being practiced in *Africa*. Enquiring of my Negro-man *Onesimus*, who is a pretty Intelligent Fellow, Whether he ever had y^e *Small-Pox*; he answered, both, *Yes*, and, *No*; and then told me, that he had undergone an Operation, which had given him something of y^e *Small-Pox*, & would forever praeserve him from it; adding, That it was often used among y^e *Guramantese*."[63]

In a passing reference to the letter Perry Miller notes, "(He [Mather] so strove to get Onesimus's story accurately that he tried to imitate the dialect orthographically.)"[64] Thus in Miller's once-canonical account of the Puritan mind, Onesimus is only heard from (literally) within a pair of spanceling parentheses. Mather, for his part, uses parentheses when addressing the supposition that the "Wretched *Negroes*" are "the offspring of Cham (which yet is not so very certain)."[65] Parentheses, often and typically used to interpose a space and time apart, a room as it were, within a sentence, here serve to defer judgment indefinitely. And this when Mather's

Abel being Dead yet ſpeaketh;

OR, THE

LIFE & DEATH

Of that deſervedly Famous Man of GOD,

Mr John Cotton,

Late TEACHER of the Church of

CHRIST, at *BOSTON* in

NEW-ENGLAND.

By *JOHN NORTON*, Teacher of the ſame Church.

Heb.13.7. *Remember them which have the rule over you, who have ſpoken unto you the word of God; whoſe faith follow, conſidering the end of their converſation.*

LONDON,

Printed by *Tho. Newcomb* for *Lodowick Lloyd*, and are to be ſold at his Shop next the *Caſtle-Tavern* in *Cornhill*. 1658.

John Norton, *Abel Being Dead yet Speaketh*, 1658.

A Man of Reason.

A Brief ESSAY
to demonstrate,
That all MEN should hearken to
REASON;
AND,
What a World of EVIL would be prevented in the World, if Men would once become so REASONABLE.

Nam et Communis Intelligentia nobis Res notas efficit, ea quæ in Animis nostris inchoavit, ut Honesta in Virtute Ponantur, in Vitiis Turpia.
Cic.

BOSTON: in *N. E.*
Printed for John Edwards, on the South Side of the Town-House in King-Street
1718.

Cotton Mather, *A Man of Reason*, 1718.

"pretense" of having transcribed Onesimus's speech was to provide a "sign of scientific immediacy in the written form of his record."[66]

How effective was Mather's striving to "get" Onesimus correctly by means of orthography? His very mention of the "Guramantese" can be viewed as a form of "dysgraphia," or what the poet Christina Sharpe diagnoses as the "inability of language to cohere around the bodies and suffering" of a people irreparably separated from their place and language of origin.[67] The demonym is Mather's spelling of "Coromantee," as Akan-speaking people from West Africa (now Ghana) were then known. But a more incisive record of the remembered practice of Onesimus's people was written on his own skin. For Mather, the necessary proof of inoculation was "imprinted on him [Onesimus] physically."[68] As Mather related the incident to John Woodward, "He described the Operation to me, and shew'd me in his Arm the Scar, which it had left upon him."[69] The evidence Onesimus bore on his own body was deployed by Mather in arguing for a campaign of vaccination during the Boston smallpox epidemic. But Mather imagined no corresponding lithic inscription; it was never suggested that Onesimus's name be commemorated on the Boston Ebenezer as the living medium of an answered prayer.

Like the life-preserving scars on Onesimus's arm from the operation performed by fellow-caring Guramantese people, which at once affirmed and denied ("*Yes*, and, *No*") his exposure to so mortal a contagion, the lesson of Mather's *The Negro Christianized* at once affirmed and denied the relation between salvific grace and the promise of freedom in this dark and menacing world. Here it is not the case that the written record, when published in its entirety, reveals a change of mind, a canceled line of handwritten text; rather, it is the natural friability of the written record that proves resistant to legibility. The textual suppositions provided by the good and candid reader in the face of lacunae bring to the surface patterns of intention that the document, in its original, uncompromised state, might not warrant or guarantee. But there is no going back, just as with epitaphs, if properly written, there can be left remaining nothing more to say. The interpretive crux is to be found in historian Lorenzo Johnston Greene's examination of the petition made by ministers, prompted by Mather's Christianizing efforts, for a law stating that baptism did not alter a slave's status: "It is Desired That y^{e} wel-knowne $Discouragem^{t}$ upon y^{e} endeavours of many masters [to†] Christianize their slaues, may be removed by a Law which may take away all pre [text†] to Release from just servitude, by receiuing of Baptisme."[70] As indicated in the footnote to this passage, from the published edition of *The Acts and Resolves, Public and Private, of the Province of the Massachusetts*, the obelus indicates "Manuscript mutilated." What is missing is the pretext to a release from suffering, which baptism alone, a cleansing of sins, was not to be. Christianizing converted slaves into "knowing and willing *Servants* of God."[71] And servants to other men they remained. Onesimus was his name.

And what of Mather's own efforts at (authorial) self-mastery? The last place to look is with his autographic epitaph, as if inscribed on the mantelpiece at the core of the many-atticked house that is the *Magnalia*. The textual edifice was itself a literary foreplan of exemplary selfhood, until at long last the pile crumbled from internal contradiction and what might be regarded as restrictive zoning when applied to the broad spectrum and hues of meaningful American experience. Employing a bit of verbal magic, Mather was at pains to save himself. "The more Stones they throw at this Book," Mather wrote in anticipatory defiance of his critics, "there will . . . be the more Proofs, that it is a Tree which hath good Fruits growing upon it."[72] Here Mather seems to have had in mind "The stone which the builders rejected has become the chief cornerstone" (Psalms 118:22), but what he despairs of are ejected stones, rude words, that heap up in reproach. He will turn it to right. "But I will build my self a Monument with them, whereon shall be inscribed that Clause in the Epitaph of the Martyr *Stephen*: Excepit lapides, cui petra Christus erat" (He died by stoning, but his rock was Christ).[73] But even while making a literary, if not also a lithographic, martyr of himself, Mather had another exemplum in mind, in the figure of the doomed scholar, dissident priest, and biblical translator John Wyckliffe. "Perhaps the *Epitaph*, which the old *Monks* bestow'd upon *Wickliff*, will be rather endeavour'd for me, (*If I am thought worth one!*)"[74] That concluding parenthetical self-assessment is a fine specimen of "Matherese," characterized by gestures of belligerent courtesy, self-flattering modesty, and denigrating compliments.[75] Mather thus disparages Wycliffe's monkish disparagers while at the same time implicitly asking his (good?) reader to endorse the flattering comparison of himself to the doomed reformer. But as Thomas Fuller observed, while Wycliffe earned a vile epitaph, he still "had *no Tombe*."[76] According to a decree issued by the Council of Constance, what remained of Wycliffe's mortal remains were "ungraved," cast from his—as it happens, temporary—resting place in the Lutterworth churchyard, burned, and the ashes dumped into the nearby River Swift. But the epitaph endures in print, its final line reading, "at his death despaired like *Cain*, and stricken by the horrible Judgements of God, breathed forth his wicked Soul to the dark mansion of the black Divell."[77]

Cain. Dark mansions. The black devil. Surely this is not what Wordsworth had in mind when he wrote, quoting Samuel Johnson, that an epitaph "is indeed commonly panegyrical; because we are seldom distinguished with a Stone but by our Friends."[78] Let us conclude by dispensing with the stone while attending to the voice of the dead, once, still, and always among us, including that of Abel. The lesson comes from Mather's biography of Rev. John Norton, his grandfather Richard Mather's appointed successor as minister of St. Botolph's Church, Boston. (Norton's epitaph: "If you need to ask who he was, you ought not to know.")[79] Mather writes that Norton did "the part of a surviving Brother for Mr. *Cotton*, in raising up, or at least keeping up the Name of that Great Man, by publishing a most elegant Account of his *Life*."[80] This he did in the hauntingly titled *Abel Being Dead Yet Speaketh; or, The Life & Death of that Deservedly Famous Man of God, Mr. John Cotton* (1658). Drawing on Paul's Epistle to the Hebrews 11:4, a fixture of eulogistic sermons, Norton observed, "by Faith *Abel* being dead many thousand years since, yet speaketh, and will speak whilst time shall be no more. That the living speak, is no wonder: but that the dead speak, is more than miraculous."[81] How is this miracle to be accomplished?

In and by loving brotherhood. Norton writes, "He is a true friend, who continueth the memory of his deceased friend, not only in love to them, but also in love to ourselves, thereby easing in part our loss, and saving so much of our own lives."[82] Here is a different calculus of charity and obligation and grace than that which attended Mather's dealing with Onesimus. "He may the better be heard," Norton explains, for we are talking about speaking with the dead, "who reckoned his Friend one half of himself: when *Moses* intimates a Friend to be as our own Soul."[83] As if to finally settle what was owed to him, which might not be entirely different from the question of who is owned by whom, Mather includes in his lengthy biography lines from the elegy written to Norton by the preacher Thomas Shepard (himself a "relentless searcher of souls, and acute divider between the states of grace and reprobation"[84]):

Of a more *Heavenly* Strain, his Notions were,
More pure, Sublime, Scholastical, and clear.
More like th' Apostles *Paul* and *John*, I wist,
Was this our *Orthodox Evangelist*.[85]

In the *Magnalia*'s consistent Johannine imagery, Norton is favorably compared to the Apostle in virtue of the saint's own words, "*He was a Burning and a Shining Light*" (John 5:35).[86] Indeed, let there be light, so long as it does not cast certain *things* in permanent shadow. But here, candid reader, simply as an addendum to these notes on epitaphs, let us conclude with a reading from Paul on brotherly feeling and its absence. With respect to the Great Stone of Abel, the first monument to be misread by Mather, Paul writes, "By faith Abel offered unto God a more excellent sacrifice than Cain, by which he obtained witness, that he was righteous, God testifying of his gifts: and by it he being dead, yet speaketh" (Hebrews 11:4). Righteous testimony endures; it is the articulation of breath, spirit itself. But with respect to brother love, in *The Negro Christianized* Mather refers to the most forbidding of inscriptions: "One Table of the *Ten Commandments*, has this for the Sum of it; *Thou shalt Love thy Neighbour as thy self*. Man, Thy *Negro* is thy *Neighbour*. T'were an Ignorance, unworthy of a *Man*, to imagine otherwise. Yea, if thou dost grant, *That God hath made of one Blood, all Nations of men*, he is thy *Brother* too."[87]

What is the epitaph for the ungraven, not for a specific individual, but for a diasporic people, not flying from the deprivations of Europe, but wrested from their native lands and delivered from the hold into the suffering of the *American Strand*? For them the epitaphist must look elsewhere, to cryptic language. Inspired by Nicolas Abraham and Maria Torok's reckoning with the project of mourning "after Auschwitz," the literary scholar Simon Gikandi deploys the epigraph as a bulwark against oblivion. His is not massy and vermiculated like the block of text prepending this essay but is rather like a troubled body of water. The lines are from Derek Walcott's "The Sea Is History": "Where are your monuments, your battles, martyrs? / Where is your tribal memory?" Then, following the paired, hectoring question marks, which insinuate that there is nothing left to be said, it continues: "Sirs, / In that gray vault. The sea. The sea / Has locked them up. The sea is History."[88] Like a stone awaiting its epitaph, this unvigiled vault is a place, is in a state of suspension, lying somewhere beneath the wake of history.[89]

Afterword

Ignorance is the enemy. Let us no longer dedicate to it monuments inscribed with the epitaph: *Here was shed the Blood of* [fill in the blank].

1 Edward Johnson, *The Wonder-Working Providence of Sions Saviour, in New England* (London: Nath. Brooke, 1654), 26. The book's London publisher gave it the second title *A History of New-England from the English Planting in the Yeere 1628, until the Yeere 1652*.

2 Cotton Mather, "A General Introduction," in *Magnalia Christi Americana: or, the Ecclesiastical History of New-England* (London: Thomas Parkhurst, 1702), §5.

3 Ibid., bk. 4, 66.

4 Austin Warren, "Grandfather Mather and His Wonder Book," *Sewanee Review* 72, no. 1 (1964): 112.

5 Mather, "General Introduction," *Magnalia Christi*, §5.

6 Susan Howe, *The Birth-Mark: Unsettling the Wilderness in American Literary History* (1993; New York: New Directions, 2015), 30–36.

7 Sacvan Bercovitch, *The Puritan Origins of the American Self* (New Haven: Yale University Press, 1975), 136.

8 John D. Lyons, *Exemplum: The Rhetoric of Example in Early Modern France and Italy* (Princeton, NJ: Princeton University Press, 2014), 3.

9 For the poem by Nicholas Noyes, see Mather, *Magnalia Christi*, bk. 4, 154. On notions of candor, see Stuart M. McManus, "A New Renaissance Source on Colour: Umberto Decembrio's 'De Candore,'" *Journal of the Warburg and Courtauld Institutes* 76 (2013): 279.

10 Leo Marx, "The Puritan Origins of the American Self, by Sacvan Bercovitch," *New York Times Book Review*, February 1, 1976, 21.

11 Mather, "General Introduction," *Magnalia Christi*, §6.

12 Ibid.

13 "Mylittae certè nimiùm congruit forsan Persarum Mitra. *Mader* enim sive *Mather* (unde facile Mitra deflectitur) Persice." John Selden, *De Diis Syris Syntagmata duo* (London: Guilielmus Stansbeins, 1617), 165. See also Jan Stievermann, *Prophecy, Piety, and the Problem of Historicity: Interpreting the Hebrew Scriptures in Cotton Mather's Biblia Americana* (Tübingen: Mohr Siebeck, 2016), 162.

14 Perry Miller, *The New England Mind: From Colony to Province* (Cambridge, MA: Belknap Press, 1953), 33.

15 Mather has tinkered with Virgil's text, which originally read: "Me, me, adsum qui feci, in me convertite ferrum," *Aeniad* 9.427.

16 James Henry, *Aeneidea; or, Critical, Exegetical, and Aesthetical Remarks on the Aeneis, vol. 2* (Dublin: Dublin University Press, 1878), 806.

17 Savcan Bercovitch, *The Puritan Origins of the American Self* (New Haven, CT: Yale University Press, 1975), 18.

18 Ibid., bk. 2, 60; Christopher Trigg, "The Devil's Book at Salem," *Early American Literature* 49, no. 1 (2014): 37.

19 Herman Melville, "The Apple-Tree Table; Or, Original Spiritual Manifestations," *Putnam's Monthly Magazine* 7, no. 41 (May 1856): 467.

20 William Wordsworth, "Essay on Epitaphs," *The Friend* 25 (February 22, 1810): 403.

21 Ibid.

22 "Wordsworth: An Address by Canon Rawnsley," in *A Reminiscence of Wordsworth Day, Cockermouth, April*

7th, 1896 (Cockermouth, UK: Brash Bros., 1896), 48.

23 Wordsworth, "Essay on Epitaphs," 403.

24 Ibid.

25 William Borlase, *Antiquities, Historical and Monumental, of the County of Cornwall*, 2nd ed. (London: W. Bowyer and J. Nichols, 1769), 158.

26 John Weever, *Ancient Funerall Monuments within the United Monarchie of Great Britaine, Ireland, and the Islands Adjacent* (London: Thomas Harper, 1631), 9; cited in Wordsworth, "Essay on Epitaphs," 403.

27 "Burial Customs and Obitual Lore," *National Quarterly Review* 4, no. 7 (December 1861): 69.

28 John Edwards, *A Discourse Concerning the Authority, Stile, and Perfection of the Books of the Old and New Testament*, vol. 3 (London: J. D. for Jonathan Robinson, 1695), 279. The problem emerges from a significative shift in the text, noted by the medieval French commentator Rashi (Shlomo Yitzchaki), between the words *abel* (for the martyr Abel) and *avel* (for mourning), both used in reference to the stone. The author is indebted to Leo Edison Eigen for patiently leading him through this linguistic maze.

29 Mather, *Magnalia Christi*, bk. 1, 37.

30 Ibid., bk. 3, 199.

31 Mather derived the term *Criolian* from Thomas Thorowgood's *Iewes in America* (1650), which held that the American Indians were the Lost Tribes of Israel, a thesis rich in millenarian expectation. John Canup, "Cotton Mather and 'Criolian Degeneracy,'" *Journal of Early American Literature* 24, no. 1 (1989): 28.

32 Mather, *Magnalia Christi*, bk. 4, 126.

33 Ibid., bk. 1, 37.

34 Ibid., bk. 1, 31.

35 Ibid., bk. 1, 37.

36 Ibid. "Then Samuel *took a Stone, and set it up, . . . and called the Name of it*, Ebenezer, saying, Hitherto the Lord hath Helped us" (1 Samuel 7:12).

37 Mather, *Magnalia Christi*, bk. 1, 31.

38 *Diary of Cotton Mather*, 13d. 10m. 1706/7, Massachusetts Historical Society Collections, ser. 7, vol. 7 (Norwood, MA: Plimpton, 1911), 578.

39 Michael Witmore, *Culture of Accidents: Unexpected Knowledges in Early Modern England* (Palo Alto, CA: Stanford University Press, 2002), 90.

40 *Diary of Cotton Mather*, 579. See also Henry W. Haynes, "Cotton Mather and His Slaves," in *Proceedings of the American Antiquarian Society*, n.s., vol. 6 (Worcester, MA: Chas. Hamilton, 1890), 191–95.

41 *Diary of Cotton Mather*, 579.

42 Jan Stievermann, "Cotton Mather and 'Biblia Americana'—America's First Bible Commentary: General Introduction," in *Cotton Mather and Biblia Americana—America's First Bible Commentary: Essays in Reappraisal*, ed. Jan Stievermann and Reiner Smolinski (Tübingen: Mohr Siebeck, 2010), 11.

43 Cotton Mather, *Biblia Americana: America's First Bible Commentary; A Synoptic Commentary on the Old and New Testaments*, vol. 1, *Genesis*, ed. Reiner Smolinski (Tübingen: Mohr Siebeck, 2010), 672. The author gratefully acknowledges Reiner Smolinski's generous assistance in explaining Mather's method (or lack thereof) of source citation.

44 David M. Goldenberg, *The Curse of Ham: Race and Slavery in Early Judaism, Christianity, and Islam* (Princeton, NJ: Princeton University Press, 2003), 166–67.
45 Orlando Patterson, *Slavery and Social Death: A Comparative Study* (Cambridge, MA: Harvard University Press, 1982), 5.
46 *Diary of Cotton Mather*, 579. See also Elisabeth Ceppi, *Invisible Masters: Gender, Race, and the Economy of Service in Early New England* (Hanover, NH: Dartmouth College Press, 2018), 147–50.
47 John Calvin, *Commentaries on the Epistles to Timothy, Titus, and Philemon*, trans. William Pringle (Edinburgh: Calvin Translation Society, 1856), 353.
48 Kathryn S. Koo, "Strangers in the House of God: Cotton Mather, Onesimus, and an Experiment in Christian Slaveholding," in *Proceedings of the American Antiquarian Society*, vol. 117, pt. 1 (Worcester, MA: American Antiquarian Society, 2007), 162.
49 Ibid.
50 Cotton Mather, *The Negro Christianized: An Essay to Excite and Assist the Good Work, the Instruction of Negro-Servants in Christianity* (Boston: B. Green, 1706), 22.
51 Emphasis added.
52 Wordsworth, "Essay on Epitaphs," 411.
53 Ibid.
54 Herbert Lindenberger, *On Wordsworth's Prelude* (Princeton, NJ: Princeton University Press, 1963), 26–27.
55 *Diary of Cotton Mather*, October 1, 1717, 447.
56 Ibid.
57 Koo, "Strangers in the House of God," 168.
58 Ibid.
59 Ibid.
60 Cotton Mather, *A Man of Reason* (Boston, printed for John Edwards, 1718), 15.
61 Ibid., 17.
62 G. L. Kittredge, "Some Lost Works of Cotton Mather," *Proceedings of the Massachusetts Historical Society* 45 (1911–1912): 418.
63 Mather to Woodward, July 12, 1716, quoted in Kittredge, "Some Lost Works of Cotton Mather," 422.
64 Miller, *The New England Mind*, 346.
65 Mather, *The Negro Christianized*, 2.
66 Carla Mulford, "New Science and the Question of Identity," in Carla Mulford and David S. Shields, eds., *Finding Colonial Americas: Essays Honoring J. A. Leo Lemay* (Newark, NJ: University of Delaware Press, 2001), 91.
67 Christina Sharpe, *In the Wake: On Blackness and Being* (Durham, NC: Duke University Press, 2016), 96.
68 Margo Minardi, "The Boston Inoculation Controversy of 1721–1722: An Incident in the History of Race," *William and Mary Quarterly* 61, no. 1 (2004): 56.
69 Mather to Woodward, July 12, 1716, 422, quoted in Minardi, "Boston Inoculation Controversy," 56.
70 "Memorials of the ministers presented to the Governor and the General Assembly of the Province of the Massachusetts Bay, Boston, May 30, 1694," in *The Acts and Resolves, Public and Private, of the Province of the Massachusetts Bay*, vol. 7, appendix, vol. 2 (Boston: Wright & Potter, 1892), 537; Lorenzo Johnston Greene, *The Negro in Colonial New England* (1942; New York: Atheneum, 1968), 267.
71 David Whitford, "A Calvinist Heritage to the 'Curse of Ham': Assessing the Accuracy of a Claim about Racial Subordination,"

Church History and Religious Culture 90, no. 1 (2010): 37.

72 Mather, "General Introduction," *Magnalia Christi*, §6.

73 Ibid.

74 Ibid.

75 Kenneth Silverman, *The Life and Times of Cotton Mather* (New York: Harper & Row, 1984), 255.

76 Thomas Fuller, *The Church-History of Britain* (London: John Williams, 1655), 171.

77 Ibid., 171–72. The full epitaph reads, "The Divels Instrument, Churches Enemie, Peoples confusion, Hereticks Idol, Hypocrites Mirror, Schisms Broacher, hatreds sower, lyes forger, flatteries sinke, who at his death despaired like Cain, and stricken by the horrible Judgments of God, breathed forth his wicked Soul to the dark mansion of the black Divell." Fuller appends one of the witticisms for which he was evidently well esteemed: "Surley *He* with whose Name this Epitaph beginneth and endeth, was with the maker clean thorow the contrivance thereof."

78 Wordsworth, "Essay on Epitaphs," 402.

79 "Quis fuerat, Ultra si quæras, Dignus es qui Nescias." Mather, *Magnalia Christi*, bk. 3, 41.

80 Ibid., bk. 3, 37.

81 John Norton, *Abel Being Dead Yet Speaketh; or, The Life & Death of that Deservedly Famous Man of God, Mr. John Cotton* (London: Tho. Newcomb for Lodowick Lloyd, 1658), 3.

82 Ibid., 4.

83 Ibid.

84 Miller, *The New England Mind*, 3.

85 Mather, *Magnalia Christi*, bk. 3, 38.

86 Ibid., bk. 3, 32.

87 Mather, *The Negro Christianized*, 5.

88 Simon Gikandi, preface to *Slavery and the Culture of Taste* (Princeton, NJ: Princeton University Press, 2011), ix; Nicolas Abraham and Maria Torok, "Mourning or Melancholia: Introjection versus Incorporation," in *The Shell and the Kernel: Renewals of Psychoanalysis*, vol. 1, ed. and trans. Nicholas T. Rand (Chicago: University of Chicago Press, 1994), 125–39.

89 On the question of literary/historical wake work, see Sharpe, *In the Wake*.

453 Project

JaJa Co
Studio Sean Canty
Erin Besler
MILLIØNS
T+E+A+M
Ensamble Studio
MALL
First Office
The LADG
PARA Project
Marshall Brown Projects
BairBalliet

JaJa Co
Scoring, Building, 2020
Finishing

“Scoring, Building” was an event and a pavilion. It won a competition put on by the Los Angeles art and architecture nonprofit Materials & Applications. The installation took place from January 18 to February 29, 2020, at the Mackey Apartments.

The project excessively adhered to the rules. By excessive I mean to a degree beyond a functional limit. Any element that could be doubled or tripled was doubled or tripled, as long as the allotted space could hold it or the materials could bear it. The pavilion’s textural, organizational, and perceptual effects all proceeded from this excess. By rules I mean instruction. Instructions for building a room in a gap on the site were repeated identically four times, one room inside the other, to make an enfilade. The instructions were written using typical Type V construction details, but activities like cutting, fastening, framing, and tilting were given more time for iteration. The construction documents were wordier than most, sampling language from standards organizations, trade associations, and product installation guides. The drawings used notational marks to show how the instructions came together.

On long walls, the builder followed instructions to cut a window every third stud bay, and on short walls, a door every second bay. The stud spacing was modified from typical framing standards to follow a syncopated meter—3, 1, 3, 1—instead of 1, 1, 1, 1, 1, 1, 1, 1. In combination, the pattern set up two deep doors and two deep windows. The mudding instructions established a different kind of texture. The builders filled gaps between drywall panels with gypsum paste according to material specifications, but scraped down dried spackle with their knives several times. This is traditionally done only once before switching to sandpaper, but scraping repeatedly produced smooth walls with less dust.

A schedule set a rhythm for the appearance of formal and material effects. Typical project management schedules could not create evenly paced work patterns, so we chose a less common type. Location-based scheduling, used in repetitive building projects like the Empire State Building, organizes work by continuous speeds instead of the more prevalent activity-based scheduling that prioritizes continuous tasks. Work is arranged as a function of time and distance, which makes location-based schedules spatial. In effect, the timeline was a sequencer that arranged material deliveries, payments, room making, and color changes.

All the materials were off-the-shelf products, but time-sensitive items were substituted in as much as possible to amplify and further control the effects choreographed by the schedule. There were four colors of construction chalk coded by level of permanence: violet, blue, orange, and green. Violet is level 0 because it dusts off while orange is level 2 because it stays put. Whereas some of the pavilion's materials use color to show how they resist weathering, others signaled construction timing. Pink spackle belongs in a category of Dry Indicator materials because it turns white when it dries, indicating that it is time to scrape it down and paint.

We found a site only after we won the competition, so the most difficult part of the process was not the timing or budgeting but figuring out how big the pavilion would be. Without a site up front, a proportional system was created to form a series of rooms and awnings. Relying on material installation guides became useful at this point because they rarely reference dimensions. An eight-foot square is listed as two gypsum panel products for commercial reasons. Thus, the building's footprint was found by laying down studs and panels, and all the rooms were derived as percentages from this

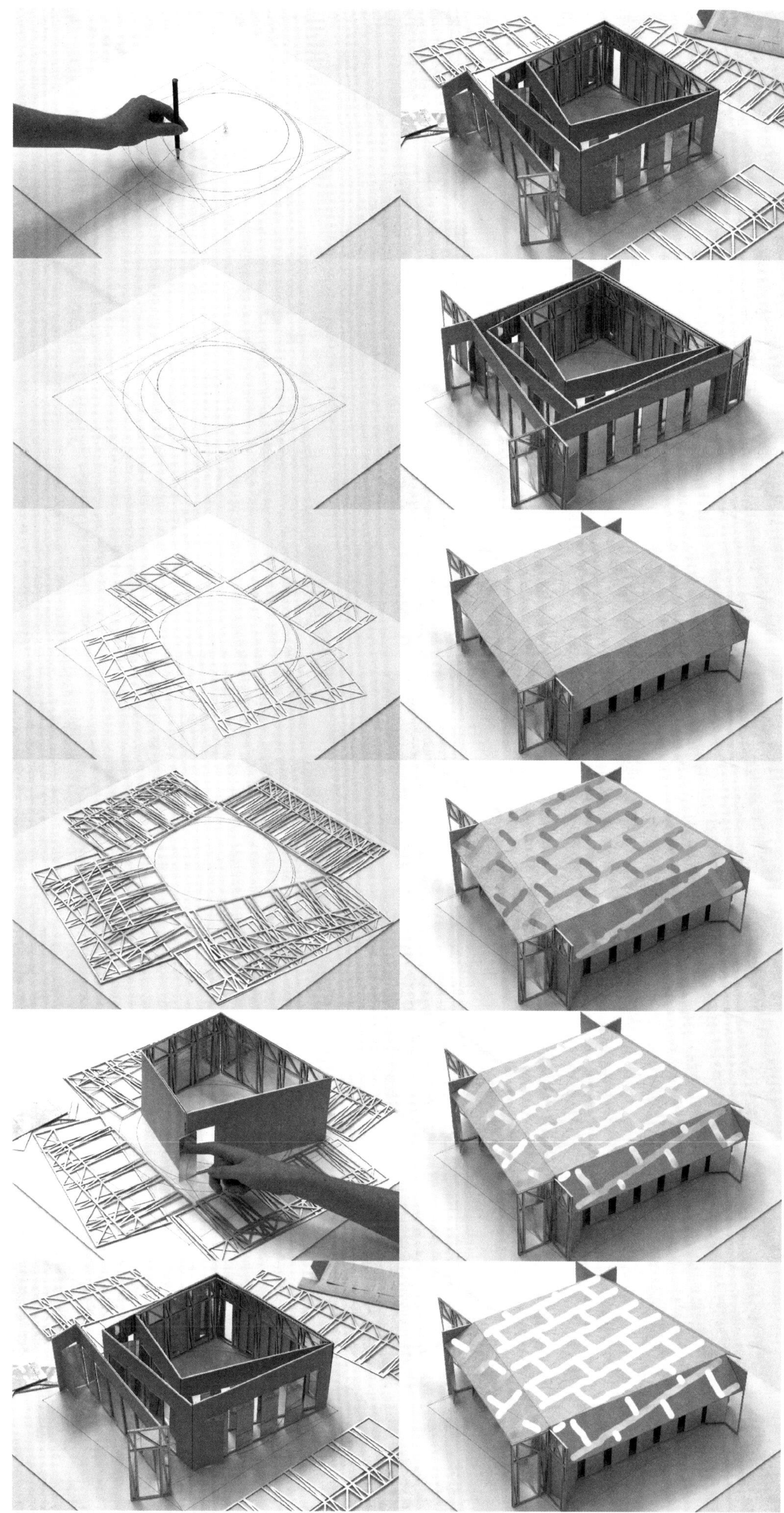

CD PROTRAK NS 25
WWW.CD-PATENTS.COM INTER
SI G40 WWW.CD-PATEN

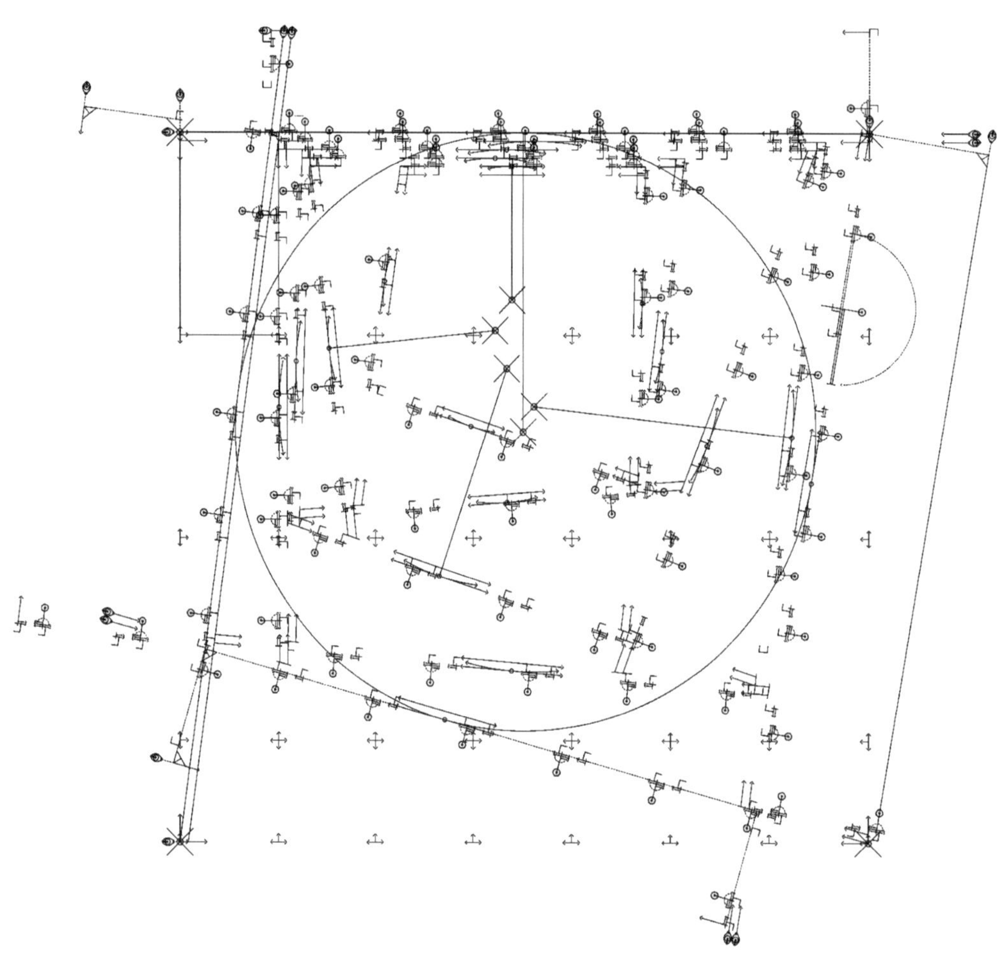

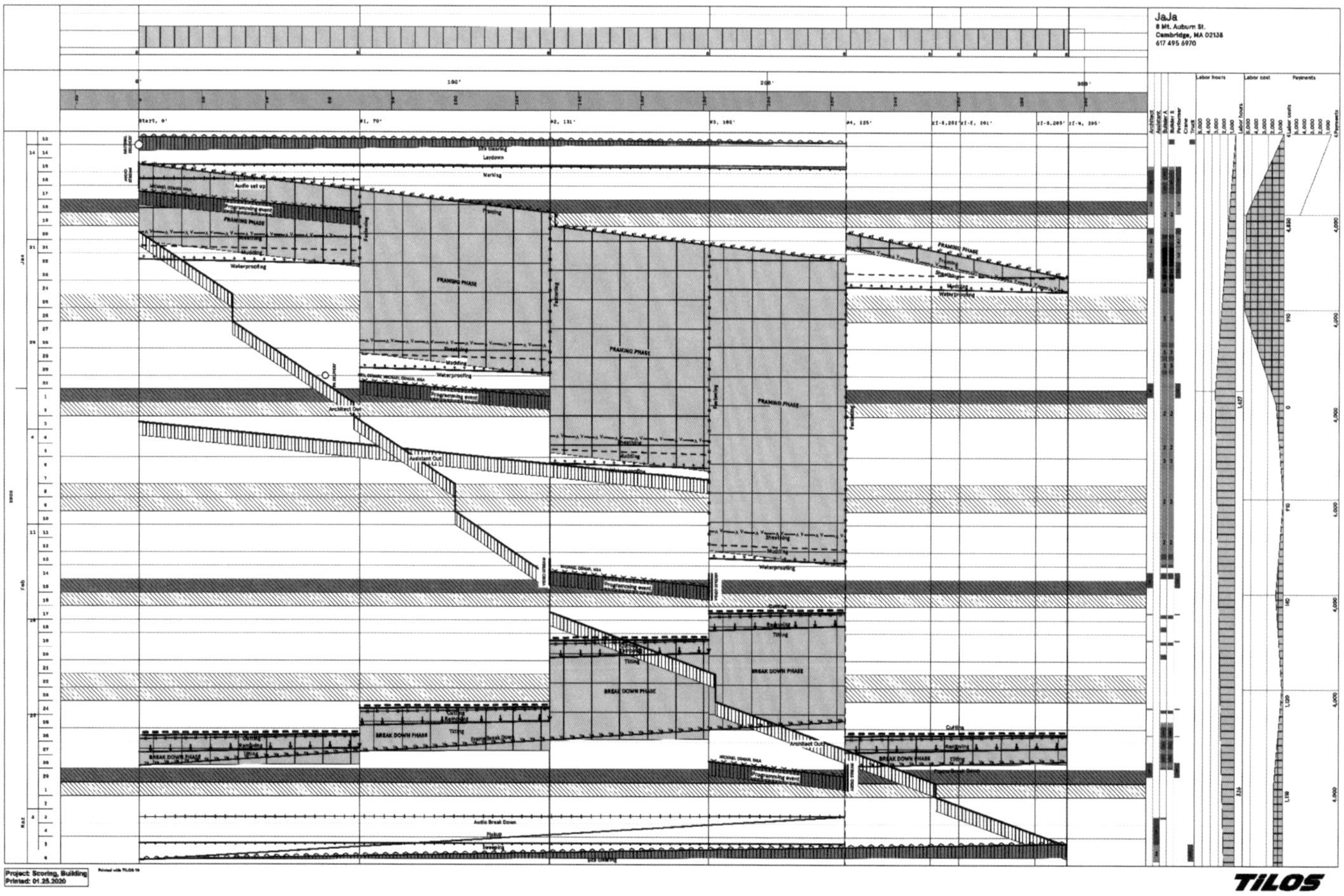

JaJa
8 Mt. Auburn St.
Cambridge, MA 02138
617 495 6970

Labor hours

Labor cost

Payments

Project: Scoring, Building
Printed: 01.25.2020

TILOS

figure by snapping chalk lines. Though the instructions were precise, there was some built-in indeterminacy. A system of drawing circles tangent to two non-parallel lines meant that the circles, used to dimension an inward offset, could be any size. Doors and windows jostled in place from lines askew. Rooms were built from the outside in, so their footprints would eventually make inscribing diagonals and circles impossible. This signaled to the builders when to stop.

"Scoring, Building" was a pavilion, but more so, it was an event. Its six-week schedule explored color and form through overlapping notational systems. To see how a builder's repertoire could engage design, industry rules were repeated excessively. Extra time was given for working materials beyond their intended use. Off-the-shelf products made building according to the instructions possible.

Building construction is a performance between materials and people, but its movements are rarely considered as design. Rather, efficiency determines coordination. The rush to finish overlooks the potential for a construction process to operate compositionally. When typical building acts are included as part of architectural aesthetics, construction choreography becomes interdependent to its physical form.

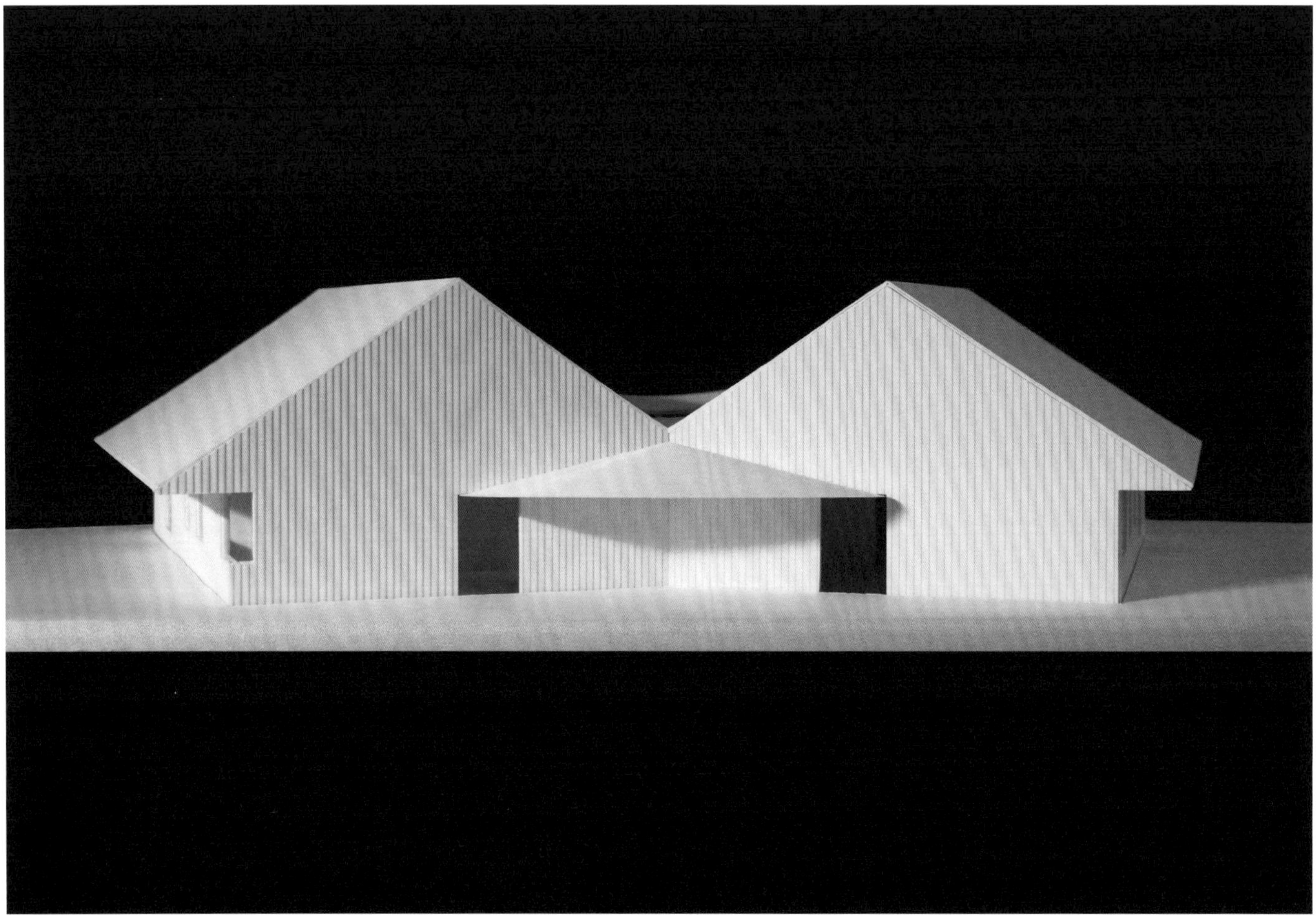

Studio Sean Canty
Janus House, 2019
Conjoined Domesticities

Janus House is a curious departure from a surrounding neighborhood of prairie houses, gambrel houses, cape houses, and farmhouses. Modestly sized on a generous plot, the defining compositional unit of the house is doubled along its front and tripled around the back. This formal problem sets up a problem of basic arithmetic in contrast to its neighbors, which are easily countable, lot by lot, as singular dwellings. Janus House's front elevation conceals the relationship of exterior expression to interior domestic space through a cast of doubles: two gables, two doors, and two of all the required pieces of domestic equipment. The house's roof plan reveals a double of two cones—one elliptical and one circular—that conjoin the residences. Each pairing shares formal, spatial, material, and organizational properties with relative degrees of sameness and difference. Instead of articulating its dual residences with the obvious legibility that characterizes the rest of the neighborhood, Janus House renders its paired components with medium resolution.[1] Moments of geometric symmetry in elevation are contrasted with programmatic differences in plan. Ornamental adornment is muted in service of the house's formal vocabulary. The constant doubling is neither fully articulated as two houses nor entirely sublimated within a monolithic block.

Kinship

Twinning is not new to the canon of architecture, but it still holds some novelty. Identical twins appear in John Hedjuk's Tegel housing while WOJR's Twins: Houses in Five Parts is characterized by fraternal twins: two separate houses share shapes in plan but manifest different formal expressions in elevation. Perhaps the most famous exploration of twinning is the two churches at the Piazza del Popolo. Commissioned by Pope Alexander VIII, the churches were designed and developed by a series of architects from Carlo Rainaldi to Carlo Fontana and finally Gian Lorenzo Bernini. These twins are both the backdrop of the piazza and the monumental entry to the Campo Marzio beyond. Similarities in their exterior form belie differences in plan. One church is driven by a circular plan with a centralized axis; the other has an elliptical plan that is near axial. These formal distinctions are a consequence of the contingencies of site and program. The elliptical plan of the first church creates a stronger relationship to the piazza, while the circular plan of the second church foregrounds a more internal orientation.

The plan of Janus House arrives at its composition by merging key traits of two recognizable housing types in a single volume: the axiality of a dogtrot house and the centrality of a courtyard typology. The house's twin logic is established through the transformation of the dogtrot, an ordinary American housing type. Inherently symmetrical in plan, a dogtrot house is characterized by two gabled wings, separated by a covered open space. In Janus House, this organization is signaled but immediately altered. There is no open breezeway between the two house fronts. Instead the gabled volumes pinch together, first compressing the formerly open space to zero, then replacing it with a shared projecting conical awning as though interior and outdoor spaces were collapsed by a compressive force. The sublimation of this typological feature in geometric plasticity is the first in a set of baroque techniques applied to American house forms: exaggerating and contorting primitive forms (which emphasize the parts within the whole) and restrained introversion (which conceals the relationship of interior spaces).[2] Historically, these sensibilities drew attention to the baroque orchestration of mass and volume, as well as the play between light and shadow.

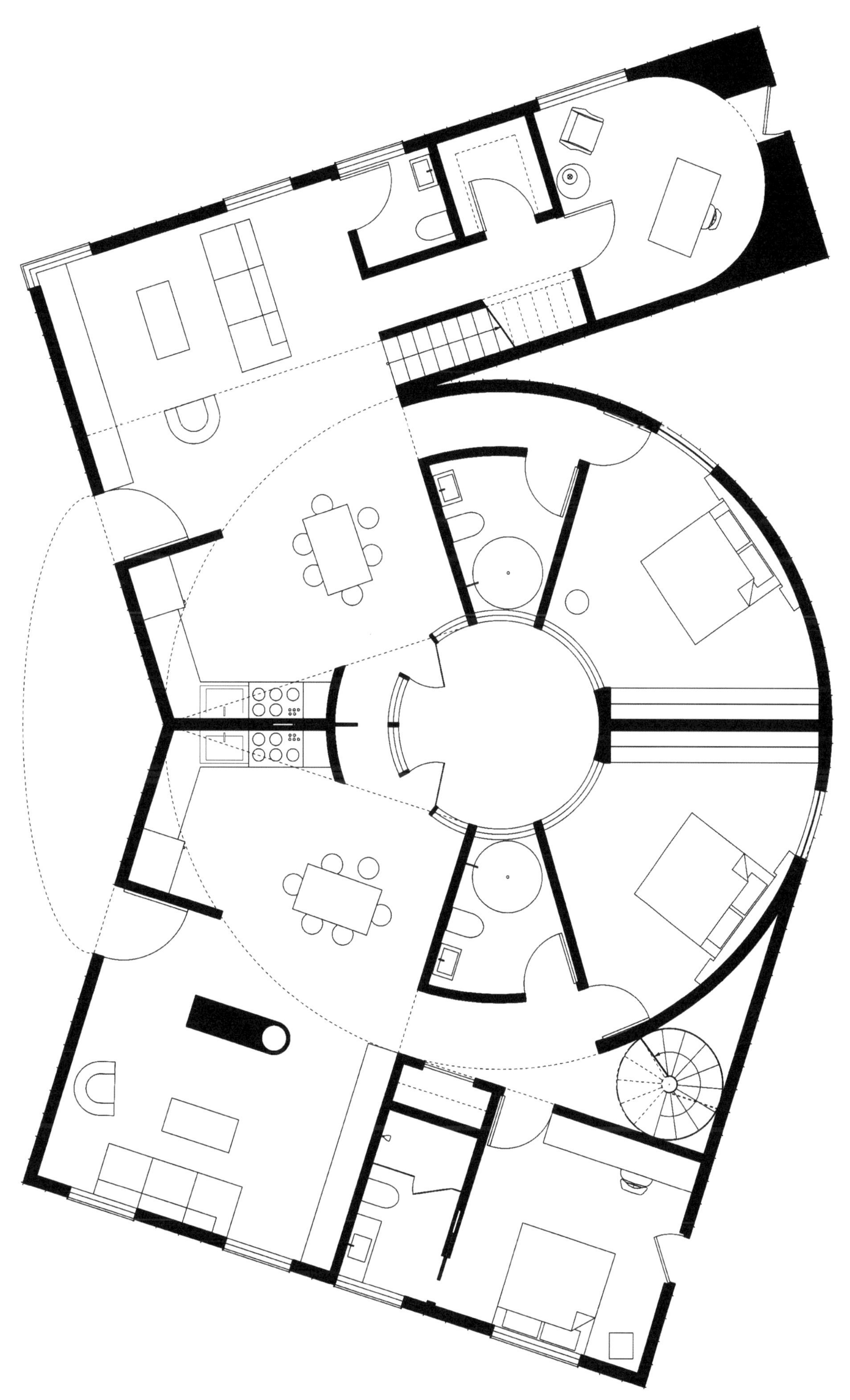

The didactic parity of the dogtrot plan is complicated by the insertion of a circular courtyard, which introduces a richness into the experience of the house's interior spaces. In tandem with the exteriorized dogtrot at the front awning, the circular courtyard reads as an almost-execution of a literal through-way, caught at the end of an acute angle in plan. Together, both typologies enable a mixture of organizational gestures in plan between center and edge. Interior rooms are arranged either linearly, radially, or with a blend between these two dominant orders. Movement and views in these spaces are centrally oriented. The composite organization of these interior spaces also extends to the ordering of light. The interior courtyard spatializes the sun's path throughout the day by admitting southern and northern light to illuminate the most private and public functions of the house. A cadence of square windows on the east, west, and north facades frames views of the surrounding lot, while pulling in morning and afternoon sunlight.

In elevation, the dogtrot's traditional gabled wings remain clearly articulated at the front, while these forms pull apart at the back. This formal play builds on the project's twin logic to spawn a triplet of forms: full gable, drum, and half gable. Each form acts a foil to the other while joined by an underlying kinship.

A Non-Traditional Family

The continuous surface of Janus House allows the house to be read as both a unified form and multiple discrete forms depending on the vantage point. The house outlines spaces of varying depths and qualities, while oscillating between flatness and depth, between surface and mass, and between center and periphery. These oscillations are created by a family of geometries: material vernacular, figural perimeter, and constant center. Transparency is exchanged for material gloss and sheen on the exterior facade. The interior courtyard is glazed and porous, dematerializing the boundary between house one and house two where both become one: an idea of shared occupation.

Although the same footprint is given to each house, subtle distinctions in use imbue the plan with functional specificity. One residence prioritizes leisure and work with a small office and mezzanine study that give the space an airy loft-like feeling. A freestanding fireplace reorients the living room in this residence by obscuring the kitchen, dining, and courtyard beyond. The second residence is oriented toward accommodating a small family or guests with the addition of a second bedroom and bathroom. In the common areas, the fireplace is replaced with a loft space over the living room that prioritizes more solitary workspace. Diagonal sight lines allow visibility between the residences within these shared living areas.

In these spaces, Janus House's invitation to close readings of geometry moves easily back into the language of type and familiar domesticities, which appear both conjoined and distinct analogous to the form. The house asks plainly, can my home be your home too?

1 Michael Meredith, "44 Low-Resolution Houses," in *44 Low-Resolution Houses* (Princeton, NJ: Princeton University School of Architecture, 2018), iii–vi.

2 Paul Zucker, "Space and Movement in High Baroque City Planning," *Journal of the Society of Architectural Historians* 14, no. 1 (1955): 8–13.

Erin Besler
Low Fidelity, 2018
Infinite Transformations

> “In spite of its having Greek shepherds’ names (Polystyrene, Phenoplast, Polyvinyl, Polyethylene), plastic . . . is an essentially alchemical substance . . . more than a substance, plastic is the very idea of its infinite transformation . . . it is less an object than the trace of a movement.”
> — Roland Barthes, “Plastic,” *Mythologies*

In an era measured by “quickbites,” TikTok, and the constant churn of Instagram Stories, three-and-a-half minutes is an eternity, totally unsuitable for sustaining anybody’s attention. But in the summer of 2012 a video of this length seemed short and teasingly playful, even casual, situated in a moment when the term “viral” was still tinged with excitement and promise.

Conversations at the time seemed stubbornly focused on high-fidelity reproduction and the tools that were supposedly capable of producing it. The “shop” of the architecture school expanded to include various new experts and machines, and the studio became inundated with shoptalk: higher-resolution screens, more memory, faster processors, more gigabits, more gigabytes, more megahertz, more DPI. . . . These benchmarks were said to offer proof that precision, veracity, and authenticity itself could be better achieved with ever-advancing technologies.

But after witnessing the introduction of multiple new capacities and new standards of technological optimization, exhaustion set in. Projects that made use of these sophisticated tools, whether in their design, production, or fabrication, seemed to be aimed at smoothing over gaps between architectural transformations and eliminating differences across architectural mediums. I was interested in the gaps, in reproducing the differences, and in reproducing a lot of them. Turning to a recent historical moment of overproduction made sense: Peter Eisenman served obligingly (albeit unknowingly at the time) as a model for machinic production, serial process, and transformations in motion. It began with delaminating a series of his drawings into a set number of layers. This seemed obvious at the time. Pulling the drawings apart was, in a sense, a way to turn one thing into many. The layers were then encoded as tool paths for an industrial robot arm. And then, using the supposedly exacting control that is synonymous with robotic precision, in particular the control of speed, path, and motion, the project became an adaptable means to produce exponentially more multiples. I used this work space as a means to overproduce and designed a system in which drawings on paper—or, more precisely, constructions made out of layers of paper and sheets of adhesive vinyl—confronted issues of material thickness as they were projected through matter into models, thereby further confounding the distinction between two- and three-dimensional presentation.

Paper Becomes Plastic

Polystyrene is a relatively low-cost, lightweight, utilitarian, and ubiquitous material. The more commonly used term, "foam," really speaks to its prosaicness. But it's still surprisingly well suited for exhibition display. In a lot of ways, it's an ideal three-dimensional analog to the flatness of paper—appearing to be even more object-like, material, immanent. The exposed surface has a noisy regularity. It's largely forgiving of the scuffs that packing, storage, and transportation so often inflict on material objects. It's pliable, but its extrusions hold together in tension. It's plastic in composition and conception. Foam is a three-dimensional blank page on which a robotically controlled hot wire can move drawings into models.

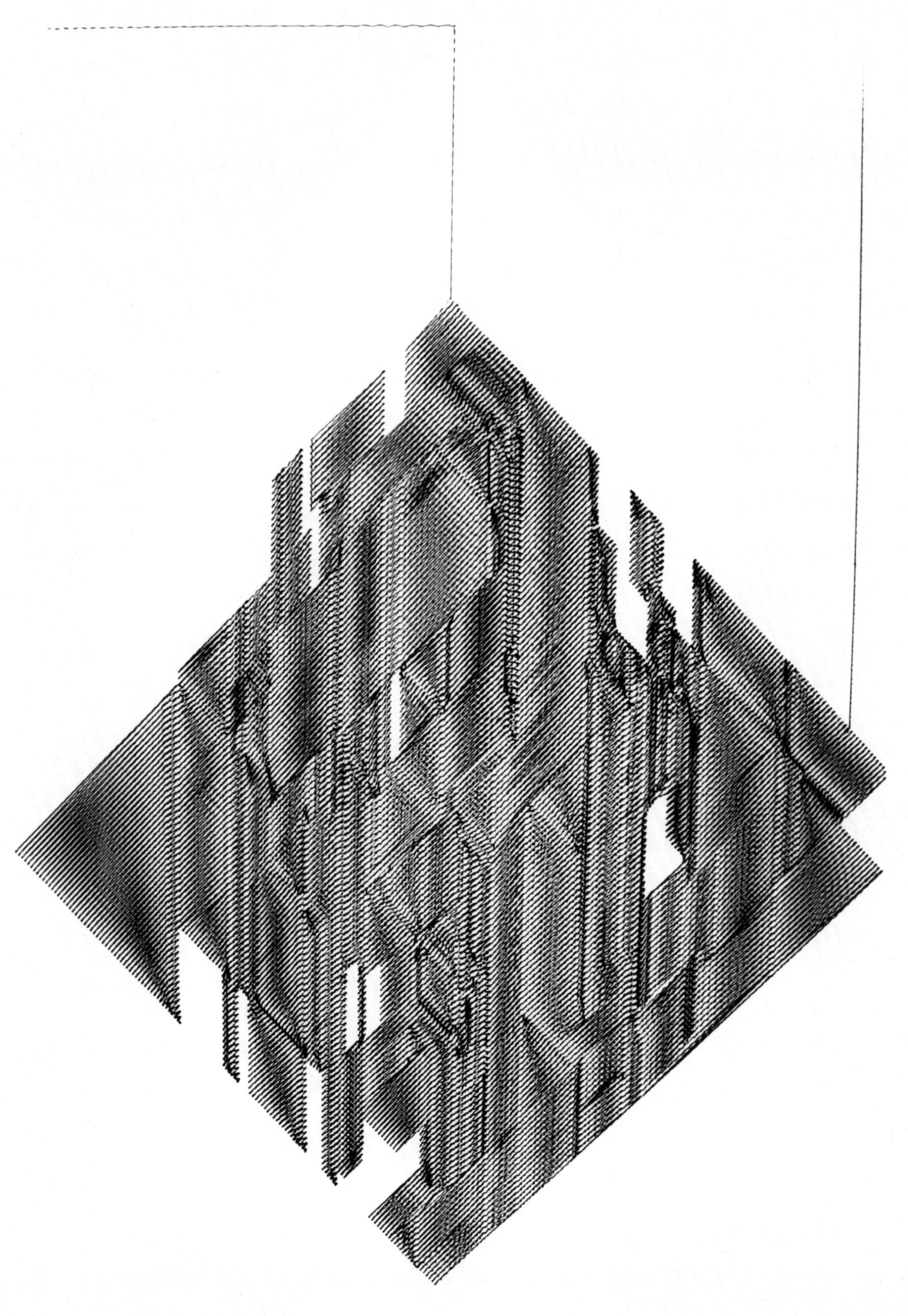

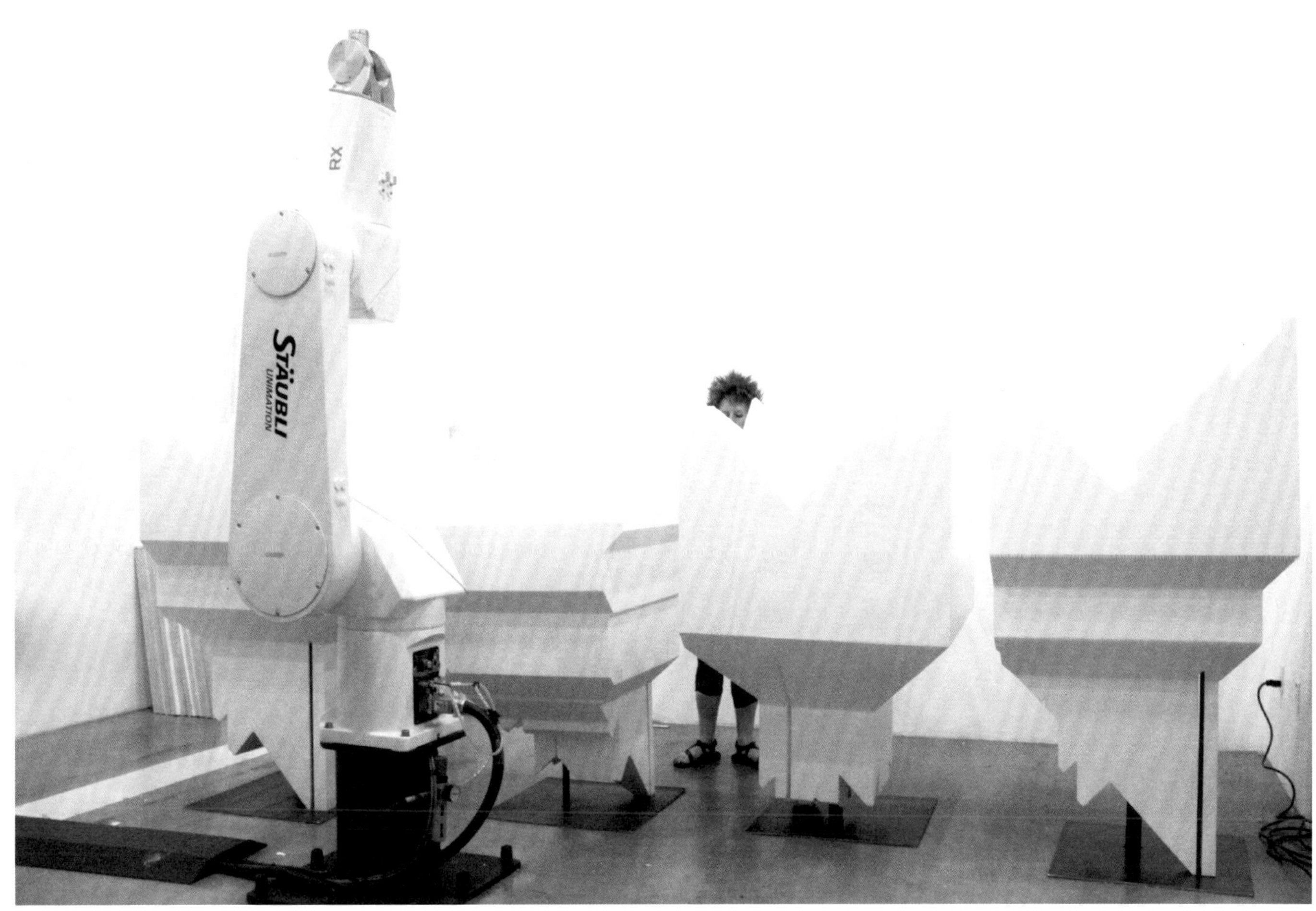

If a wire turned drawings into models, it probably shouldn't have come as a surprise that a pen would be an effective way to turn drawings into more drawings. Somehow it seemed counterintuitive, even beneath the dignity of the industrial robot arm to attach to its extremity an everyday Sharpie marker or a Tombow pen. But the markers and pens captured a dimension in the process that the foam had not. For all of the promise and expectation of machinic precision, things wobbled. It was within this chance opportunity, which seemed to escape the confines of control, where tools reacted and inscribed something in the process that brought the project into its next phase: scripting a three-and-a-half minute video.

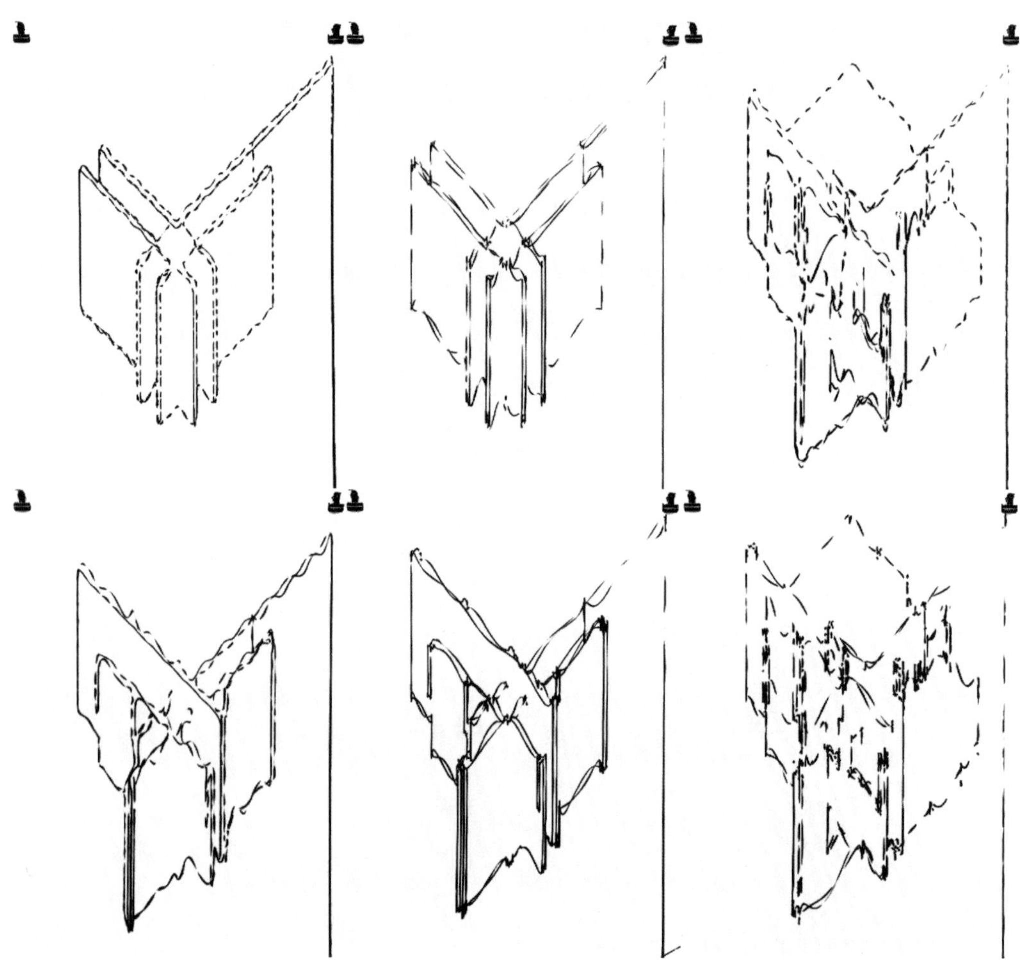

Script for a video called *Low Fidelity*

This is House VI. Here is the architect Peter Eisenman.

These are the transformations for House VI. There are fourteen. They are not drawings in the conventional sense. They are two-dimensional objects. Comprised of layered, colored paper, Zipatone, etc., the objects have thickness.

They form part of the permanent collection of the Museum of Modern Art in New York.

Jeffrey Kipnis says of House VI that "Eisenman proposed that one could detach design from the mind-numbing convention of service and instead transform a finite set of elements according to" some generative something-or-other.

Eisenman says: "House VI also looks like a model. It is a model in that it 'represents' a series of transformational diagrams."

This is a short video about Erin Besler's thesis, Low Fidelity, the process of which is its own reality.

These are drawings of the drawings of the transformations of House VI.

The conceptual space of the layers has been unpacked into separate objects.

These are low-fidelity pens.

Their tips are mangled and broken.

In all there are forty-two drawings in the series of the drawings of the fourteen transformations of House VI: fourteen drawings of objects, fourteen drawings of black, fourteen drawings of white.

This is one-pound virgin expanded polystyrene, known colloquially as "foam."

This is a hot wire cutter. It's Erin's hot wire cutter. The hot wire cutter is powered by a BK Precision 80-volt variable power supply.

These are the translations of the drawings
into three-dimensional objects.
There are forty-eight three-dimensional objects in the series.
Eight are the extrusion of the drawing through itself.
Four of them are over five feet tall.
Thirty-four are the projected representation
of the axonometric object.
Six are represented through the deposition of
the material of the drawing in layers.
This is Erin's desk.
These are the translations of the drawings
into two-dimensional objects.
There are four-hundred and twelve two-
dimensional translations in the series.
Two-hundred and six are created by connecting
end-points, the most simple way to create a line.
Some are created by interpolating through a series
of points, akin to the modern B-Spline.
This thesis consumed over one-million, one-hundred and one
thousand, six-hundred and one cubic inches of foam.
Half of this foam was recycled. Thank you Universal Foam.
This is a five-minute and nineteen-second two-
dimensional translation in six seconds.
This is an eight-minute and thirty-seven second two-
dimensional translation in two seconds.
This is a one-minute and one-second two-
dimensional translation in four seconds.
These are Erin's thesis books. There are four of them.
There are over one-thousand two-hundred objects in this thesis.
This was a short video about the objects in
Erin Besler's thesis, Low Fidelity.

MILLIØNS
Bathing, Again, 2018
A Loose Collection

What does it mean to *organize a gathering*, a collective experience? Not under the guise of a rigid social order, but instead by *rendering*—by *delivering*, or *handing over*—a kind of loose collection of the organic and the inorganic? Our interest in collectivity was and remains layered and difficult to articulate. It is a *sensibility* around lived life. We are drawn to the *possibility of collective form in our time*—form that is itself both *collected*, and also a platform, or material substrate, for social collectivity. Is it possible for these two kinds of "collection" to exceed metaphorical relations? A significant amount of our work simply posits that possibility as a kind of open, insistent question.

We identify two clear points of entry onto that question. The first is material (or *environmental*, if you like): certain lived activities, when shared, simply produce a smaller carbon footprint than when those same activities are pursued individually. This we accept, within bounds, as a kind of quasi-objective condition. Second: while the emphasis on individualism in modern life has undoubtedly fueled important liberation movements, by *disentangling* the individual from the collective, it has also intensified conditions of spatial isolation, with an almost maniacal precision. Today it can be said that the ideal building block for neoliberalism—its most fundamental genetic unit, so to speak—is the *aphrogenic* individual, completely spatially isolated, connected to lived life only by utilities and a media cable. Those critical of this fact confront a naive but productive question: how can architecture *disassemble* the conditions of modern loneliness?

Bathing

Bathing was a social activity for thousands of years—and still is for many cultures. In Roman bathing culture, for example, the average

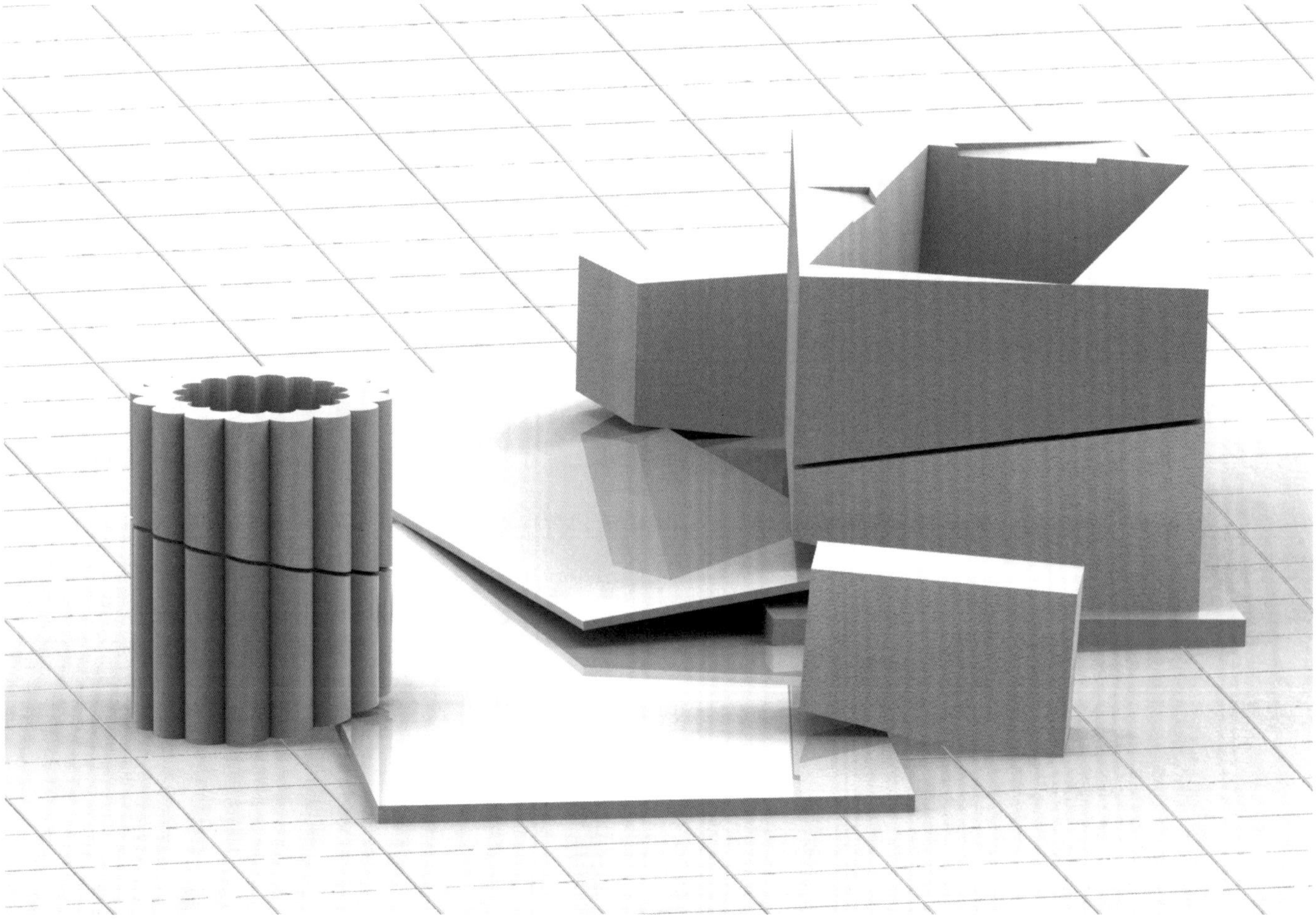

working day ended at noon, and the remainder of the day was spent at the bathhouse socializing, exercising, cleaning, conversing, eating, even engaging in political debates. We're not nostalgic for that time—it contained so many terrible inequalities—but we can nonetheless borrow certain ideas and revitalize them in our time.

The well-documented history of pre-modern bathing testifies its transformations during just the past 150 years. It wasn't until the late 19th century that the bathroom became thought of as a separate, efficient space in the home. Prior to that, there was always a kind of spaciousness to the bathing arrangements. In the Victorian home, for example, the bathroom was the same size as many other rooms. Despite its spaciousness, however, the 19th-century English bathroom represented a drastic privatization of bathing culture. If the public bath was still quite common in European culture in the 18th and 19th centuries, it disappeared rapidly from British life in the 20th century.

But it was in America, where no widespread culture of public bathing existed, that the private bath cell achieved its purest form. The "compact bathroom," as it was known, was largely the result of one crucial development in early 20th-century America: the aligning of all fixtures along a single "wet wall," which was far more spatially efficient, and cheaper to build and rent out, than the "dignified distances" retained by English bathrooms. Coupled with the invention of the built-in, one-sided cast bathtub—which set the normative dimensional width of the standard residential bathroom—the wet wall was a technical revolution in the history of hygiene. It inaugurated a period of intensive cellularization and individuation that, in our time, has culminated in a severe *desocialization* of a once-social activity.

So, by the outset of the 21st century, *bathing*—which once meant entering into an extended social period of conversation, relaxation, enjoyment, and semi-collective self-care—had been reduced, under the pressures of 20th-century rationalism and industrialization, into a private and individualized routine, and to the twin functions of efficiency and hygiene: a single station in the self-care cycle of the isolated apartment dweller.

Bathing, Again

We wanted from the beginning to completely destabilize this modern conception of bathing. Very early on we decided the set would be a kind of loose but flexible arrangement of pieces that can be scalable to fit large space, smaller space, outdoor or indoor spaces, in a living room or a bedroom, etc.—anywhere that a simple plumbing point can be located. Once the routines around bathing are opened up, any arrangement scenario becomes possible. Part of what we are interested in is rethinking how day-to-day isolated practices can merge with one another and produce entirely new cycles of life.

We were already investigating bathing cultures, mostly in other parts of the world—Ottoman baths in particular, but also Roman, Turkish, Korean—when we received the project prompt. We also happened to be visiting Villa Savoye at nearly the exact moment we received this commission, so of course the master bathroom there was also on our mind—the way it sits essentially in the bedroom itself, with very little demarcation. That was also an important precedent for us, but we wanted to ask if might be possible to radicalize that condition even further.

So, our conception of the work was much more a *furnishing of bathing* than simply the design of bathing fixtures. Once you dispense with spatial efficiency as a mandate, and once you dispense of the notion that routines have to be efficient, or that they'd have to take place at a specific time of the day, a freedom is established, and all the old principles that welded life to this very narrow conception of space and form quickly dissolve.

In the early conceptual images, we wanted to show the entire set (including the bathtub, which was not included in the gallery show), and the way all these elements relate to one another and to sub-collectives of bathers. Many of these images are the opposite of the typical client-facing rendering—just quick images that were made along the way, to show ourselves certain ideas.

There are of course also special technical challenges for any bathing furniture, so we spent time researching the kinds of materials and finishes that would be suitable. The washbasin is sealed in a marine polymer primer and finished with an iridescent automobile paint, so it's watertight but also retains its thermal properties.

A very important dimension for us: how to deal with a sanitary legacy of modernity that immediately associates whiteness with cleanliness? We wanted to undermine that, but in subtle ways. The washbasin finish is extremely difficult to photograph, because its iridescence really requires movement—you have to move around it to see the colors beneath the surface. The organization itself, which appears completely disheveled, or haphazard, relies on precise tolerances and sympathies between numerical-material processes (specifically CNC and 3D silica deposition). We wanted the "roundness," or "in-the-roundness," to be destabilizing, unfamiliar, but of course the angles of incidence among a series of very heavy elements—the washbasin alone is over 800 pounds— had to be very carefully prefigured through computational processes. Near-tangencies and adjacencies had to be very carefully calibrated prior to installation, or the entire composition would have spun progressively off-axis into a misaligned mess. In any case, all of these were decisions aimed at moving the ritual of bathing in some different direction.

The relationship between architectural form and communal life is one entry point onto a possible *new counterculture in architecture*. This counterculture cannot be the one that emerged around social housing projects in the 1930s, or around social dissent in the 1960s. It has to emerge out of contemporary realities—realities that are at once social, geometric, and energetic. By looking at the habits and routines of our daily lives—the basic necessities like eating, bathing, sleeping, etc.—can we discover in these almost primordial activities ways of first disassembling, and then *recollecting* modern lives?

T+E+A+M
Detroit Reassembly Plant, 2016
Building Material, Building Media

Among the most heavily mediated icons of Detroit's post-industrial decline, the Packard Plant is a crumbling complex of reinforced concrete and brick buildings. It was designed by Albert Kahn and built during the first decades of the 20th century, and the site originally housed the assembly line for the Packard Motor Car Company. Detroit Reassembly Plant is T+E+A+M's proposal for building with and upon the entropic remains of this industrial ruin to produce a counterimage to that of disuse and abandonment so commonly associated with Detroit's modern history.

Rather than conceiving of this transformation as delineating a clear "before" and "after," the project extends the temporal frame with which we define the lifespan of a building and its component materials. We recover, sort, and recombine parts of the building as found—from the scale of a multistory structural frame down to bits of rubble—into a range of forms further characterized by texture, color, and structural logic. Arranged scenographically on the site, the new architectural forms collapse into image, arresting the building's material instability through visual media.

Material, Structure, Image

A pile assumes a geometric form when its aggregate components come to rest. Sand, gravel, fill, rocks—granular materials with self-similar masses and shapes—will settle under the interplay of gravity, friction, and compression. The resulting incline of the pile is referred to as the angle of repose, the slope at which material reaches a state of rest or equilibrium. What the pile looks like (its color, texture, shape) and how it behaves structurally derive from the intrinsic qualities of each material rather than being imposed by design. Engineering a building or a landscape is often a matter of overcoming a material's natural angle of repose. Adding tensile support defends a compressive structure against failure—falling, spreading, slumping, tipping, or otherwise seeking equilibrium. The scale and geometric relationship of the parts also impart strength and stability to the whole, as the Romans demonstrated to the world by perfecting the rounded arch.

Like the pile, the Roman arch combines image, structure, and materiality into a single architectural form. Since arches can support weight beyond their own, they can gang together into arcades, stack up into towers, punctuate load-bearing walls. The wide availability of compressive materials, such as stone and Roman brick, powered a proliferation of arches across Roman buildings and infrastructure, such that the arch became the architectural image of the Roman Empire.

Reassembly

The Pantheon's massive dome, a three-dimensional descendant of the arch, grows thicker toward its base to counteract forces pushing outward. The composition of the concrete changes throughout, while presenting a smooth surface at the coffered interior of the dome. Within the thickness of the dome's base are fragments of pottery and chunks of broken masonry. Roman garbage gains a new use as cheap aggregate, hidden from view so as not to take away from the dome's smooth monolithic appearance.

In Detroit Reassembly Plant, new and reused materials visually coincide in surprising ways. Rather than bury them within the thickness of a wall, we collect and sort the found materials according to both their structural and visual potential. The sheer excess of concrete and brick available on the Packard Plant site allows for an inverted material economy where the open efficiency of the regular

concrete frame give way to massive and chunky forms that take advantage of the vast resource at hand. While Detroit Reassembly Plant is a speculative project, these forms and tectonics developed from a material process tested at one-to-one scale. The literal fragments of the deteriorating brick and reinforced concrete structure become an aggregate for casting. Different techniques for casting the waste aggregates with plastic yield a range of forms, whose spatial and formal qualities transcend those of the pile alone.

While several architectural types comprise the reconfigured landscape of Detroit Reassembly Plant, they can be roughly categorized into two approaches to piling:

1. Unformed piles, where gravity acts on an aggregation of consistently sized granules of material.
2. Formed piles, where plasticity has been introduced through another material recovered from an abundant waste stream: polymer plastic.

Unformed piles grow throughout the site as demolition materials are collected and sorted alongside plastics gathered from regional sources. Introducing topographic change in an otherwise flat site, unformed piles help establish a scenography that joins foreground and background. However, unformed piles are not just ornamental; they are volumetric, meeting the scale of building and landscape. Their loose materiality keeps them provisional. Unformed piles lay in wait, holding the potential for becoming formed piles.

Formed piles take the shape of formwork. Heated plastic serves as a binding medium to unify the aggregate and provides tensile strength, enabling megaliths that are sometimes asymmetric, attenuated, or slumped in ways a purely compressive structure could not be. Conic shells, mega-masonry blocks, and thin-walled domes proliferate throughout the Detroit Reassembly Plant's site. Some stand alone, and some join with remaining portions of Kahn's

reinforced concrete structure to produce interiors for the plant's new program and to frame large urban plazas between.

These formal types repeat, stack, and array into an immersive scenography, proliferating the chunky materiality from highly textured foregrounds to blended backgrounds. Where ancient Rome tucked its garbage-aggregate away from view, here the large-scale aggregates of reused brick and concrete define the project's image.

Entropy and Media

Detroit Reassembly Plant approaches construction as a twofold act: temporarily arresting material processes that are in dialogue with environmental and economic forces; and reassembling those aggregates and parts into forms and spaces characterized by the material reality of the site. All is in service of an architectural experience that moves across thresholds of novelty and recognition. What appears at a distance to be a grey-toned profile reveals itself, upon closer inspection, to be an irregular dome with highly textured surfaces. At an even closer range, the textured surfaces resolve into variously sized fragments a hundred-year-old floor slab captured in re-melted HDPE. Old materials in new configurations retain links to material histories and make connections to present conditions, opening up alternate associations through new images. The materiality and scenographic nature of Detroit Reassembly Plant anticipates the building's reduction to image once again. Understood as another snapshot within a continuing process of material and cultural change, the project fosters a feedback between building as material and building as media.

Ensamble Studio Hemeroscopium House, 2008 *Balancing Act*

Act 1: The Factory

Factories are not typical places where architects look for inspiration, but this is where we find it. Hemeroscopium House is born from a fortuitous encounter (and most likely some latent curiosity too): a "cemetery" of beams. We come across this residual place in a precast concrete factory in Madrid. It was not part of the official visit itinerary but absorbs our memory of the trip. In this yard, huge prestressed beams rest on the ground, discarded, after showing signs of failure during the fabrication process. They seem fully functional despite being called waste, and we wonder whether we can "borrow" them. There is no urgency for us to build our house, nor a requirement to use this technology. But somehow these two previously disconnected dots start a line of thought.

Act 2: The Technology

The decision to use large-scale prestressed elements is neither capricious nor completely rational. They comprise the civil engineering works that give mobility to our city, populating its urban landscape: bridges, viaducts, retention walls, water channels. . . . But what if a beam at the scale of a highway became a full wall at the scale of a house? It is intriguing to speculate about the architectural implications of such translation: decontextualizing infrastructural elements to construct a domestic space.

Act 3: The Catalog

The opportunistic approach to recycling waste material from the factory in order to build a house economically seems a win-win situation at first but turns out to be an impossibility after weeks of negotiation. Liability. The idea is triggered anyway.

In prefabrication, molds are expensive tools unless there is enough volume produced of the molded element, which is not the case for our single-family house. It soon becomes clear that the range of options is limited to the factory's most basic catalog of products—that is, to reusing existing formwork. The challenge becomes how to build a nonstandard building using standard parts.

Act 4: The Design

The plot is located in the suburbs of Madrid, slightly elevated with admirable distant views. We want a house that is both intimate and open—transparent, because we like being together even when we are not. We use physical models as means to investigate and simultaneously play, seeking the magical positioning for the given parts to delineate spaces and access views. When this balance is set, engineering follows. Everything has to be precisely decided and choreographed beforehand to minimize the chance of contingencies during construction. At this point we know we will be the building contractors, or the house might never happen.

Act 5: The Assembly

The kit arrives from the factory. In helicoidal sequence, parts are assembled one after another, threading interdependencies: first, slabs are placed on the ground and an I-beam forms a massive wall; next, a U-beam covers a passageway; next, an I-beam makes both a lintel for the lower floor and a wall for the upper; next, an inverted U-beam traces a flying pool; next, a Vierendeel truss defines a floor-to-ceiling window and more slabs build the second floor; next, a Warren truss delimits a terrace; next, an I-beam completes the roof and cantilevers, supporting the last set of slabs. All sit in partial balance. A 20-ton granite rock comes last, counterbalancing the whole. The house takes 120 days to be fabricated off-site and seven to be assembled on-site. This difference comes as a revelation.

Act 6: Ambiguity

The pool element deserves a special mention. It is a one-lane swimming pool. But is it allowed to fly? It is also a cantilevered beam. But is it a structural or a landscape element? Reading it as one or the other has dramatically different implications for zoning law. The ambiguity is nerve-wracking for the building inspector and one of our neighbors, but we find it amusing and productive. In the end, we swim in the sky.

Act 7: The Assembled

Once the structure is assembled, architecture appears. Space is formed, views framed. Programs unfold in sequence with the articulated skeleton that defines surfaces and boundaries, spiraling around a central space. This is the social space that naturally congregates communal life in the house. This is also the environmental

space that provides shade and humidity, which channels wind and shelters outdoor life. The courtyard house typology is revisited here, where intimacy and openness are made compatible, where interior spaces look inwardly at each other while sometimes extending our views to the horizon. Despite the heavy weight of the concrete members, their long spans, tangential joints, and asymmetric supports, they make the space flow and the house float. Another happy contradiction.

Act 8: Multiple Hats

Assuming the role of the architect, the client, and the contractor is both a tactical move and a necessity to ensure the freedom needed to explore the unknown. We come to think of the house as our test ground, one essential experiment within a lifelong research project. Working in such a manner is liberating: we design the brief and the project, set the priorities, and assume full responsibility. And we digest the result. Over time, we celebrate the successes and identify the mistakes. We learn from both, passing the acquired knowledge to projects to come. Ideas travel and theories formulate, freed from the body that first gave them shape.

MALL
Office Stack, 2018
Psst!

Pssst!

I have recently become obsessed with superlatives, "best culture," and how pop might once again shift architecture's forms and relation to contemporaneity. Combine "best" with any other noun, and a plethora of lifestyle and shopping sites populate our screens with endless lists of opinions: best bed linens, best nail design, best shower curtain, and best donut shop, to name a few. If contemporary culture is preoccupied with sorting through what to consume and how to label it, architects can boldly reinscribe these pop tendencies back into the architectural project. This is the starting point for Best Sandwiches, a project made entirely out of the very best BLTs, sloppy joes, hamburgers, grilled cheese, and club sandwiches all collected, sorted, hoarded, and stockpiled from Philadelphia to Milwaukee and Atlanta to New Orleans. First examining color and form then probing apertures and profiles, these food-like buildings represent a collection of architectural sandwiches. Placed on ceramic plates (thin podiums) and scattered onto a picnic blanket (blue and white checkered ground), Best Sandwiches's representational agenda mixes food photography with still-life painting, rendered with a spectrum of colors that look even better on-screen.

Oops!

At some point, the summer picnic soiree ended and the sandwich analogy extended to disciplinary expertise: As Best Sandwiches transitioned into Office Stack, a 22-story office tower located in the American South, there was a seriousness inserted into the project. Rather than concentrating on our post-picnic-party blues, focus shifted to a set of analytical exercises around the open office floor plan, circulation optioneering, and net/gross area calculations. The mid-rise office tower is a typology that thrives on stackable, leasable floors that are efficient, repetitive, and generate the greatest amount of income per square foot. In most cases, extrusion of the interior floor plate is synonymous with extrusion of the tower's exterior form. In Office Stack, other motivations are at play, namely the idea to start and stop the described "floor plate extrusion" in section. Imaginary lines chart out precisely where one building stops and the next one starts, generating a teetering stack effect of the whole. These lines, a slice-and-dice technique of sorts, become physical gaps and produce in-between spaces signaling a significant change of architectural tectonic between one massing layer to the next. Shared exterior amenity space for office tenants creates an alibi for those gaps while other programmed outdoor space is carved into slabs to break up a larger block. Corners are eroded, scooped out, and contain indentations at varying depths until our next meeting with our structural engineer (Oops!, again), yet all floors recognize the extents of the larger perimeter bounding box. Meaning: it is all neatly packed.

Phew!

Let's be clear: the project is a bespoke stack, not a pile. Stacks are neat and orderly. Tidy stacks resemble English tea or club sandwiches, while piles are more messy or melty, like a grilled cheese or open-faced turkey, if a sandwich at all. Office Stack is analogous to a BLT, where the separate legibilities of bacon, lettuce, and tomato are all pronounced and shapely. These sandwich layers are held together by two pieces of toasted bread creating an overall five-layer massing. Layered as five mini-towers, the ambition of this project is to divide a tower into discrete chunks denying the reading of one architecture in favor of many. From the east the building is a monolith; from the south an expressed diagonal stair stringer on

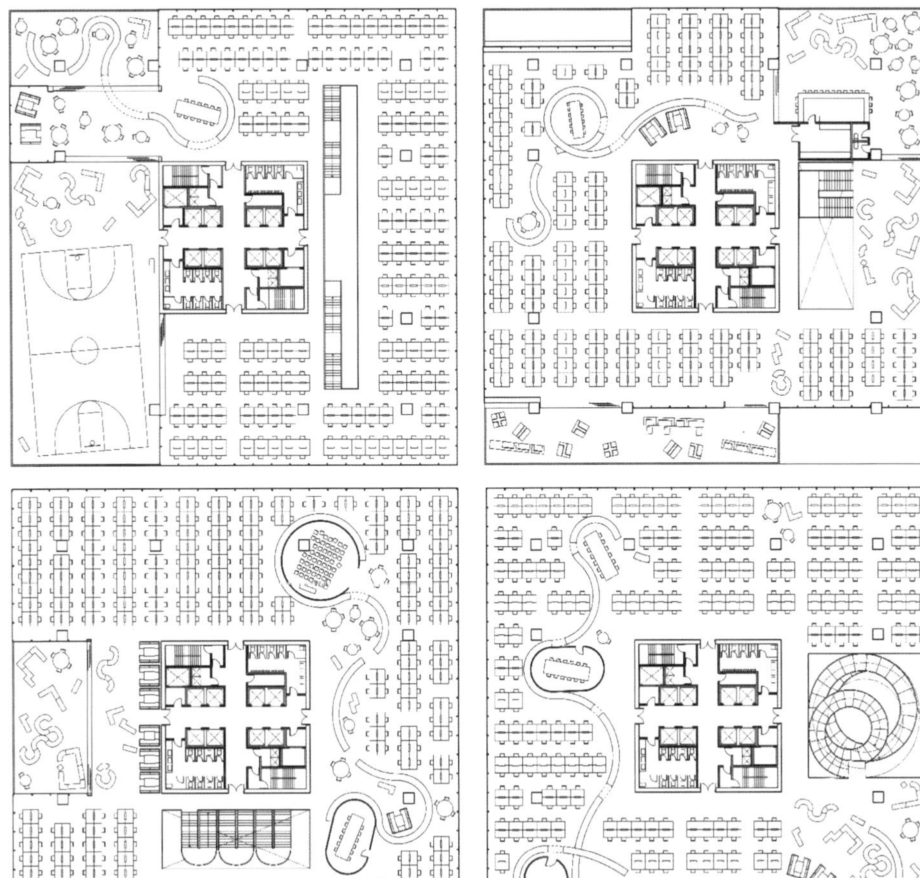

the facade joins two otherwise disconnected blocks of floors; and at the top, pitched housings for mechanical equipment make a village of enormous houses on top of a five-story building.

Ah-ha!

Pink frit makes everything look better. Architectural elements within each sandwich stack treat architecture as a set of graphic operations that can be found in the treatment of facade patterns, plan logic, expressed stairs, and lighting design. This made-to-order logic within each sandwich stack allows for a range of possibilities for office tenants. There are four cardinal elevations, typical of most towers, but within each face of Office Stack there are multiple elevational figures. This dizzying array of apertures, grids, punches, and profiles challenges the traditional curtain-wall facade. A pink frit consumes 50 percent of the glass facade wallpapering over floor-to-ceiling height glass, exaggerating views with a soft glow. Pink is all part of the plan in our superlative strategy for making architecture: “Ah-ha! Let’s add even more.” It is a kind of pop-inspired decision-making to casually flip through our collection of architecture and select the very best.

First Office
Battleship House, 2020
In a Shrunken Field: A Postconceptual Position

Paint tone, brush width, and canvas support were some of the attributes of what the Russian avant-gardists called the *faktura* of painting: its material practice and manufacture.[1] Even a slight difference in two white hues could produce an "irrational" gap of space, wrote Kazimir Malevich, without recourse to the calculated technique of perspective.[2] Following the concept of faktura, other modern painters and their critics collapsed these material specificities onto the flat plane of painting—the supporting framework unique to their medium. The labor of painting, its "operations and works," thus began to define a limited and focused discourse through media.[3] While parallel arguments were made for sculpture, sound, poetry, and film to define clear boundaries among the arts, architecture was initially excluded, or perhaps self-excluded, from this modern overhaul. It seemed to emerge as an impossible medium, too multifaceted to conform to any single set of techniques. The field's diverse and changing forms of labor and material practices resulted in often contradictory forms of material support. So, while the arts entered the postwar period with a conscious effort toward self-purification, architecture avoided the encounter with its own modernity, with a few late exceptions.[4]

Yet Craig Dworkin's close reading of multiple nearly blank artworks links two seemingly distinct artistic movements to one another: medium specificity and conceptualism. In writing that "the most conceptual works are always caught up in the most material specifics," Dworkin showed the supporting material necessary to present nearly blank formats with extreme self-awareness.[5] Similarly, Rosalind Krauss reads abstract grids into windows, thereby materializing the conceptualized canvas into a mundane object of building construction. Her psychoanalytic reading of mullions as geometric lines, however, could also be understood in reverse: within her claim that behind every grid, there lies a window, is the possibility that within every window there must also necessarily be a conceptual grid.[6] And so we cannot unsee the infinitely flat matrix of lines, made visible by two closed window panes, bisected by horizontal mullions, or that same mechanism revealing the conceptual structure of deep perspectival space when the vectors of the mullions converge on a single vanishing point. Krauss's conceptual analysis of Casper David Friedrich's *painter's window* lurks in the frames, panes, and mullions of every window in general.

Whereas medium specificity seems to have been unfit for architectural appropriation, "conceptual architecture" was hypothesized in 1970 in an issue of *Design Quarterly* put together by John Margolies. In his letter to participants, Margolies wrote that he was "not interested in the traditional magazine format of ordered text and pictures," soliciting from the authors "a more *general* and less *specific* type of communication."[7] In this context, Peter Eisenman's erased essay, "Notes on Conceptual Architecture," may have simply been one application of those guidelines: specific text was left out, and only the general format of the page, including its marginal support, remained.[8] Beyond its apparent obedience to the editorial directive, this act of publishing a series of nearly blank pages may have appeared quite ordinary in 1970. By that time, the art world had grown accustomed to such forms of redaction with Robert Rauschenberg's *Erased De Kooning Drawing* from 1953, John Cage's *4'33"* of silence composed in 1952, and Jean Cocteau's depiction of the blank poetry book titled *Nudisme* in his film *Orpheus* from 1949.[9] What made this particular submission peculiar was that it finally made its appearance in the rather conservative and professional field of architecture.[10]

In all of these examples, the conceptual position produced a distance of writers from their voices, bringing them into a *structuralist* mode of production. These acts represent variations on Roland Barthes's tantalizing description of writing, after the "Death of the Author":

> Having buried the Author, the modern scriptor can thus no longer believe, as according to the pathetic view of his predecessors, that this hand is too slow for his thought or passion and that consequently, making a law of necessity, he must emphasize this delay and indefinitely 'polish' his form. For him, on the contrary, the hand, cut off from any voice, borne by a pure gesture of inscription (and not of expression), traces a field without origin—or which, at least, has no one origin than language itself, language which ceaselessly calls into question all origins.[11]

The term "scriptor," defined to mean a mere typist or copyist, replaces the word "author" as the hand extends not "thought or passion" but a "gesture of inscription."[12] The act of writing does not seek to produce meaning, but records the vast technicality of "language" without origin, rendering the act of writing as a sort of cultural reflex. With this dire observation, a scrivener—as we have been told about the incipient automation of architecture—might just prefer not to do it.[13] We've often wondered why library copies of the *DQ* issue haven't received cheeky pencil scribbles from other readers qua writers, as they filled in an old game of "mad libs" left behind by other scriptors.

How could this conceptual-historical-structuralist act, whatever you want to call it, have not produced heightened forms of self-awareness or in-depth discussions on specifying techniques in designing buildings? The action of publishing these nearly blank pages in 1970 made any future acts of building blank surfaces, scrutinizing subfloors, designing data sheets, and formulating formats of architectural production as inevitable reenactments. So, we might be alone in this view. "Reading is nothing more than a *referendum*," wrote Barthes in arguing against the passive consumption of text. Perhaps we can extend his statement to reading buildings' floor plans and facades, as we reject a current trend to train an army of formal analysts as mere consumers.[14]

The function of a "blank form" is its capacity to reveal general categories to be filled in with specific content. In fact, we can simply use *blank* as a noun rather than an adjective here. A blank is simply a document, an empty *form-ulaire* waiting to be filled in by its reader-writer.[15] We see our projects as resulting from our inscriptions of content into blanks such as these; in our documentation, paint swatches, expansion gaps, contraction joints, screw drive types, and wainscoting could be the content of an otherwise blank form. As we fill out forms, we feel like we are certifying or making things more certain, specifying the generalities, or simply writing. If in 1970, redaction was the general form of writing—the first conceptual position—then filling in the blanks in 2020, fifty years later, is the specific form of writing—or what we are now calling the *postconceptual position*. That is, to produce a "writerly" project in architecture, we work on specifying the technicalities—formats, materials, sizes, colors, ducts, mullions, and hinges—of architecture's blank forms.

We would like to give one example of a blank in architecture that we have attempted to fill in with the specificities of our own time and place. This blank form comes from the photographs of the 19th-century natural historian Eugène Trutat, who documented a series of megalithic monuments, often referred to as dolmens. We have adopted these six-thousand-year-old rude stone structures as the potential generality from which specific residential projects can be produced. One of these prehistoric specimens, the Dolmen de Vaour in the Tarn region of France, has especially captured our attention because of its particular posture. The first step of formal analysis would be to redact its specificity—but much of this work has already been done, simply erased by the passage of time, loss of memory, erosion, accident, and by this architecture's existence antecedent to human writing. Still, it is relatively similar to other dolmens. Several stones form the perimeter of its nearly rectangular interior; these vertical supports are called orthostates. One orthostate is long, forming a sort-of wall-like enclosure, while the others are chunky and can almost be read as truncated columns. All vertical stones are set in from the perimeter, allowing a rather large horizontal slab to appear to float above them. This capstone appears to have broken into two unequal parts. The stones are rude, not hewn, and they are rough and textured, blending in with the grey landscape beyond. The low contrast between the monument and its

surroundings inspires us to use a tentative tone in our description. “Relatively similar,” “nearly rectangular,” “sort-of wall-like,” and “rather large” are ways of generalizing, of constructing a precedent through informal analysis. To imagine this primitive hut as a model for residential construction would require specifying what this description has left out from the mundane reality of very specific building stuff.[16]

The Battleship House—a two-bedroom backyard dwelling on the property of a historic home adjacent to the University of Virginia campus—inscribes the informal arrangement of the dolmen’s orthostates into the domestic interior. Its plan is not defined through the composition of rooms—the living spaces—as it would be done in a traditional project, but rather through the specification of the infrastructural cores—the mechanical walls, normally tucked away inside the walls. These cores are arranged at will, depending on site and circumstance, not unlike the ships in the gridded sea in a game of Battleship. Hence, we gave the house its name: Battleship. Kitchen counters, a powder room, a pantry or a large closet, two bathrooms, two Murphy beds, and the sofa for the living room are all developed as freestanding elements, allowing for the spaces to occupy the air among them. In this way, hallways are created simply by the gap between two things; rooms are defined by the leftover space between three things; doors are inserted for privacy purposes between two or three other things. At times, these internal ships stop short of the ceiling, exposing a slit for cove lighting. At other times, the reveals in the flashing offer similarly expanded gaps on the exterior, splintering the siding at the seams. But we call this project Battleship for yet another reason: the color “battleship grey” covers the building’s every detail. The surplus of this tone following World War II made the color choice ubiquitous, and it can still be specified for nearly every product—duct, paint, screw, or pane—such that the details of an entire house could conform to the same mute palette.

Although the house is now on hold, we brought a full-scale, but contracted, version of it into the SCI-Arc Gallery in Los Angeles for the exhibition *Rude forms among us*. The shrunken Battleship was shown alongside the photographs by Trutat, on loan from the Muséum de Toulouse, courtesy of the Head of the Photo Library and Curatorial Assistant, Frédérique Gaillard. Squeezing this awkwardly large construction into the gallery required precise measurement. The gallery walls only approximated 90-degree corners, while the floor deviated from its level condition by an incline of two inches in both axes of rotation. While measuring out the space that inexplicably seemed to elude him, master builder Austin Anderson spotted the contraction joints in the concrete floor. A normal + (plus) clearly marked the surface. This datum point became the (0, 0) coordinate for construction—the reference from which all future measurements would radiate outward. Measuring from this point, we taped out the floor and laid down the sill plates, shimming and bolting into the solid concrete floor. Of course, this house would not be made of stone. The material selected was a SIP (Structural Insulated Panel) that is composed of two sheets of OSB (Oriented Strand Board) that form a sort of ice cream sandwich filled with EPS (Expanded Polystyrene). Every panel was tied together by lumber splines that measured either four or eight inches deep and spanned the full height of the 10-foot wall or the full span of the 16-foot roof. The blocks were laid out as placeholders, eventually to be filled in with stuff: running water, electrical conduit, copper flashing, domestic appliances. Following the awkward capstone of the Dolmen de Vaour, this house's roof was similarly broken. We scored and folded the SIPs as though we were handling giant sheets of foam core. Only one thin paper layer, in this case, specified as a strand-board sheet, would clad a continuous surface of the underside of the roof, while the scored seams of the SIPs above burst open exposing the stark stupidity of the foam

94
WILL
CONSTRUCTION

within. Using a paint gun, we clad these surfaces evenly in high gloss "forest black" paint, diluted two-to-one with water. As a result, the strand boards' appearance shifted with light conditions, ranging from a rough velvet to a reflective smooth texture, approximating a stony finish.

Working in a gallery, we are constantly reminded of the walls, the limits of the room. In Trutat's photographs, the dolmen is located in the landscape—the horizon divides the picture into two equal halves: the upper half filled by sky and the lower half filled by earth. By contrast, the gallery's corners—where the white walls meet the grey floor—are too low to enact the illusion of air meeting ground. Taping out a line 38″ above the ground level, we delineated a new horizontal line as the backdrop to the house. The walls were then painted in two tones: the upper half clad in matte "mountain air"—a pinkish hue of dark white; and the lower half finished in glossy "SCI-Arc special"—a greenish hue of light grey. While the upper paint illuminated the interior air with soft warmth, the lower paint reflected the dirty texture and greenish tone miming the polished high sheen of the concrete floor. The addition of wainscoting to the gallery, thus, transformed an interior into a modeled landscape, extending the illusion of the ground beyond the limits of the room. We have, thus, adapted to the shrunken field of architecture.[17]

So, it was this dark house that you bumped into when you backed up to look at the photographs. And if only for a moment, the fleeting present and the infinite past synced up. Here, without too many explanations, we happened upon a *rude form* that brought us to a time at some remove from our own. Whether the megaliths entered our contemporary consciousness or we moved closer to the Stone Age was not all that important. What was important in these spaces was to feel a slight release from the present, to feel at ease and at home here and then.

1 See Yve-Alain Bois, "Malevitch, le carré, le degré zero" [Malevich, The Square, The Degree Zero], *Macula* 1 (1976); Benjamin Buchloh, "From Faktura to Factography," *October* 30 (Autumn 1984); and Maria Gough, "Faktura: The Making of the Russian Avant-Garde," *Res: Anthropology and Aesthetics* 36 (Autumn 1999) for an in-depth discussion and historical evolution of the term *faktura*.

2 El Lissitzky defines Malevich's construction of parallel space as "irrational" in "A. and Pangeometry," in Sophie Lissitzky-Küppers, *El Lissitzky: Life, Letters, Texts* (London: Thames and Hudson, 1968), 350.

3 Clement Greenberg, "Modernist Painting," *Art and Literature in Paris* (Spring 1965).

4 Sylvia Lavin, "Architecture Beside Itself," *Everything All at Once: The Software, Videos, and Architecture of MOS*, ed. Michael Meredith and Hilary Sample (New York: Princeton Architectural Press, 2012), 86.

5 Craig Dworkin, *No Medium* (Cambridge, MA, and London: MIT Press, 2013), 25.

6 Rosalind Krauss, "Grids," *October* 9 (Summer 1979): 58.

7 John S. Margolies's letter to participants, re: *Design Quarterly* 78/79—a special double issue on "conceptual architecture."

8 Peter Eisenman, "Notes on Conceptual Architecture: Towards a Definition," *Design Quarterly* 78/79 (Minneapolis: Walker Art Center, 1970): 1–5.

9 For more on blank artforms, read Craig Dworkin "On Nothing" as well as the Nothing archive.

10 In writing about the "notes," Mark Jarzombek reminds us of the labor required on the part of the architect to use the historiographic apparatus of the footnote to construct this first conceptual position. "Arbeit ohne Opus," as Jarzombek would call it, takes full advantage of Margolies's promise that he would not "tamper" with the formats and ideas and print the submitted materials precisely as they were laid out by their authors. Eisenman does the work to research and buttress the potentiality of a masterpiece, to lay out on the page his thinking process as it relates to a sequence of writings past, producing minimal material for publication. The project of reference was notably termed conceptual, though Jarzombek also categorized it as "historical." See Mark Jarzombek, "A Conceptual Introduction to Architecture," *Log* 15 (Winter 2009): 89–98.

11 Roland Barthes, "The Death of the Author," *Image–Music–Text* (New York: Hill and Wang, 1977), 146.

12 A definition in the *Oxford English* Dictionary for "scriptor," is a writer, especially a scribe, a copyist.

13 Edward Eigen often invokes "Bartleby, the Scrivener" by Herman Melville; some post-structural French writers have probably written similar things, but we love Edward and understand what *he* is saying.

14 Roland Barthes, *S-Z: An Essay* (New York: Hill and Wang, 1970), 4

15 One definition of "blank," in the *OED* is "[a] document, 'paper,' or 'form' with spaces left blank to be filled up at the pleasure of the person to whom it is given (e.g., a blank charter), or as the event may determine; a blank form." Take as an example "a death certificate," a ubiquitous bureaucratic blank that someday will be filled out on all of our behalf. On this pro forma sheet, there are discrete spaces left open for the name of the deceased, the age, the address, and the sex—all relatively easy, although increasingly nuanced, facts identifying a person. Lower, there are larger gaps that span the length of a sentence or even a paragraph, for identifying the possible causes of death. Sometimes, these can be picked from a pull-down menu of a number of identified and codified diseases and organ failures, but at other moments,

a narrative may be filled in; some evidence and poetic license may even replace the simple notion of a numerical fact in this data sheet.

16 We can probably trace our notion of a blank to something like the primitive hut, but with some important distinctions. The primitive hut was first described by Marc-Antoine Laugier in 1753, who, in the frontispiece to his *Essay on Architecture*, depicted four trees with intertwining branches that formed a shelter in the forest. Walking into the clearing, the architect—allegorically represented by a wandering putto—encountered this inspirational structure that would in turn guide his classical sensibility of stone construction that seemingly emerged from the syntax of wooden parts. Needless to say, rude stone monuments offer no such grand narrative. But they are neither a myth nor a drawing; they are real stone structures that exist in the landscapes of every continent.

17 In another essay, "Sculpture in the Expanded Field," (*October*, 1979) Krauss describes sculpture in relationship to "not architecture" and "not landscape," producing an expanded field along the axes of the semiotic square. We take architects' fascination with this diagram to mean its reverse: in order to participate in the institutional culture of the museum, we have allowed buildings to contract into a shrunken field by squeezing into the tight spaces of the galleries. For a similar and earlier critique of this phenomenon, see Sylvia Lavin's article "Vanishing Point: The Contemporary Pavilion" in *Artforum* 51, no. 2 (October 2012).

The LADG
House in Los Angeles 1, 2016
On Offering

They requested an almost unthinkable transposition. Two artists, he a figurative painter and she a photographer, asked us to relocate their working studio from the light industrial district just east of Downtown Los Angeles to the suburban hillsides further north. This was not a request for swap of lifestyle signifiers, trading the loft-style for the mien of the semi-detached garage. The studio was not a "studio" meant to flatter a taste for open plans and collected furniture, but something like a small warehouse: messed with art-in-progress; trussed ceiling; kitchen and bathroom lodged in a clearly added box. The suburb they had in mind was a similarly unforgiving, authentic example of its species: a patch of Los Angeles City proper, platted in the nineteen-aughts; chaotically steep streets delivering cars to small garages; backyards; room-filled stucco boxes, each defended against its neighbors by moats of fences and five-foot strips of side yard grass. What possible isomorphism could permit us to think the transformation of one into the other? And what motive could we invent for why?

Something about the logic of possessing territory had gotten stuck. Inside the loft, projects could proceed via a rhythm of surges. Maybe first the spreading to claim a spot, then after a while a retreat, leaving patches of loft to go feral before they were reclaimed by some other activity or thing. Outside, though, was another story, and this was making it difficult to maintain a long-held analogy between inside and outside underpinning the imaginative fantasy of living there. Space outside was no longer a fungible, dynamic thing, exchanged between programs in cycles of use and abandonment. This shift was in part a consequence of Skid Row, just a few blocks away. For a long time this had been no big deal—a quirk of the place or not-unpleasant daily tug of attention to the abjection of the real. But the exertions of force between the City and the 4,000-some people experiencing homelessness over time began conforming to martial patterns of entrenchment. Brutal clean-out attempts were met with bigger, more permanent street encampments. Add to this the creep of real estate speculation ever-eastward from downtown, which, block-by-block, engaged in its own conversion of itinerant "just being" to patterns of holding, defending, and dominating. Each extreme of the economic spectrum was digging in.

In the grand myth of American property, suburbs are also the place where you go to stake out, dig in, and defend. Our project would be to bend architecture back against this imagination of how physical stuff abets entrenched inhabitation—to unstick the two.

The lot was an island with a few existing buildings. Local irregularities in the steep hillside bent the street in a wide arc, which in turn made a bulge in the end of the block too fat, too deep to be carved into pie slices accessible from the street. The result was a kind of donut hole in the repeating fabric of the surround, ringed by the fences and back edges of nine neighboring yards, accessed via a narrow 150-foot drive flanked on both sides by flowering bushes and trees. Entering from the street had the cinematic effect of an allée, building anticipation for a sight, but delivering repetition instead of epiphany. At the top: a few small white stucco buildings in a mid-century ranch style, mostly identical to hundreds of others in the surrounding neighborhood.

We considered the possibility of acting out. Maybe the ranch houses could serve as the foil for some radical insertion. This was tempting. The acres of neutral stucco facades were the modernist infant's dream of tabula rasa tilted up vertically into a scenographic backdrop, theoretically capable of absorbing almost without limit

the differences between it and whatever new thing we might build. But the neighborhood impressed us with two intelligences. First, because so much had been built for so little, both in the economy of dollars and in that of material accumulation. Ranch houses are not made of much, but they do a lot. Second, because the general scheme of a ranch house, pitched roofs doing their best to loosely follow a rambling collection of walls below, seemed readily available to do exactly the opposite of what they had promised their original owners. Instead of securely claiming a patch of land as the possession of a family, the shambolic roof–wall relation could just as easily be incidental, or even antagonistic to the real enclosure and fixing of territory. Cliff May, arguably the inventor of the modern ranch home, understood this. A fantastically prolific designer and marketer, he authored more than a thousand custom homes and upward of 18,000 tract buildings, generating demand for his work

with a near-constant presence in *Sunset* magazine over a 20-year span. It's a "home with a garden in every room," he would be quoted in an article accompanying pictures of a new construction. Or, "it's only one acre but it's a whole kingdom," or "we make science do our work." Each of these veers exhilaratingly close to a class of speech called the semantically reversible sentence, where nouns can shuffle positions without changing the meaning of the statement. It's not quite true of May, but thinking of these slight modifications projected for us an alternate future of the ranch, where "gardens have rooms in every home" and "a whole kingdom is only one acre" where "we make work do our science." In this version of the suburbs, spatial proprieties fragment, activities leak across zones, and productive labor mixes indiscriminately with analytic or reflective pursuits. This was the kind of reversibility that would allow us to add to the existing house all the un-suburban things the clients were leaving behind with the studio: a darkroom, a place to paint, and an event space masquerading as a parking spot.

We resolved to make these things with the equipment offered by the ranch house. The reversals we had in mind all seemed achievable with slight intensifications to the original. The kit of components could remain the same, but each would be "agnosticized" to loosen determinate relationships to the envelope and mute signals ordinating "in" from "out."

The plans of ranch homes are packed with L-, Z-, and I- shaped walls that efficiently lock rooms and closets in relation to each other. We arranged six of these along the front third of the site, positioning them to stand alone without collectively implying any singular or preferentially bounded interior. Without this relationship between perimeter shape and envelope, the walls bracket and bound potential rooms in all directions so that the yard is as much subdivided into a series of compartments as the spots underneath roofs. The number of "places" on the site increases, and these are linked by gaps—alternately filled with windows, doors, passages, and stairs—to make a grammar of connections like simple machines. The studio is joined to the courtyard by a vestibule that, while open, requires a 180-degree turn to pass from one to the other. A diagonal opening smooths the connection of the courtyard to the patio of the existing house.

Each wall-figure is inflated at one end to make rooms out of the hollow stud walls. These too are a product of the desire to make every component of the ranch a potential space-generating device, but in this case the intensification separates instead of connects. The inflation reiterates the separation of its interior-like atmosphere trapped in a balloon. Each is treated as an event that terminates the wall-figure with a sharp, discrete punctuation of program. Just one thing—a closet, an equipment shed, an outdoor shower, a bathroom, canvas storage, a darkroom—set afloat at figure's end. The wall surface hugs tightly to the program of each cavity to make a surreal acceptance of whatever might be offered from activities on the inside. A hand reaching in the bathroom vanity to grab a tube of toothpaste is suspended in a white box cantilevered over a patch of courtyard near a garden spigot. Finished canvases stacked in a storage closet protrude into the rear yard, seen as a blank white volume from the frame of a strip window just inches to the right.

Two roofs sit atop the collection of wall figures, skewed slightly from the existing house to face the approach from the drive. These are the firmest designations of place and program: studio and carport/event space. But the roofs are too big and spill over on all sides with deep projecting eaves. The painting studio and carport perimeters are not lines of enclosure at all, but constellations of niches that ring the edges of both indoor and outdoor rooms. The roof-to-enclosure relation is so tenuous that the drip chains running

from the gutters to the collection cisterns look like tension cables struggling to hold the buoyant assembly in a fixed position. There is no front or back to the compound. There are no mannered systems of propriety that suggest the right activity in the right place at the right time. These have been replaced by a system of linkages and openings that recommend approaches of different kinds—slow strolls, concealed approaches, hurried walks. Everything juts out to offer a spot or a surface or room. It makes these offers to itself. It makes these offers to the identically stuccoed back facades of its neighbors. Walls keep their long historical identification with powers of exclusion and delineation, but they float free of each other and all the other apparatuses that would signal what's being excluded and to which side. Instead they radiate these powers in all directions. Most spaces are rooms. Most rooms are available. Almost everything is outside. The inside-like-outside analogy that sustained an imagination of loft life is replaced with an offer made to the suburbs.

PARA Project
Pioneertown House, 2018
Proximities

Scene

Pioneertown, California, was originally built in the 1940s as a live-in motion-picture set for actors; now, it functions more as a pilgrimage scene for Angelenos. The seemingly alien landscape of the Mojave Desert—with its big boulder piles and yucca palms—makes for a quick foreign escape from the urbanity of Los Angeles. The particular site for this house is a 5-acre boulder-filled parcel, owned by a West Hollywood art-dealing couple who want a weekend spot and artist studio. There is an existing 1950s homestead on the property: a modest masonry cabin, just a hole, about 20 square feet. Directly adjacent to the site's most impressive boulders, this humble house is both too small for the client and architecturally unequipped to partner up with the rock. The little thing is overwhelmed.

Survey

How to help this little house articulate itself? Not as house-as-rock, or rock-as-house, but to better stand apart through self-description. To insist that architecture is not like a rock, but that architecture is like architecture, and in this case pairs up with a rock. Perhaps the house could use some self-reflection before the coupling.

Problem

The problem is the homestead's role in the comparative act between a geological thing and architectural things, between (found) object and (constructed) room. To better substantiate the pairing, we need more comparative acts within the architectural half of this diptych. We need more reflection within the architecture itself. We need more rooms here. We need more house.

Plan

Pioneertown House is a new house around this old house. It experiments with the particular and idiosyncratic proximities of more familiar architectural pieces—rooms, courts, closets, counters, bookcases, beds—where the manner in which these fragments approach each other matters as much or more than the things themselves. Its organization insists on making room for reflection between its architectural parts.

Pilgrimage

A pilgrimage of domestic fragments enters the scene. All are actors. All gather around the homestead—within certain proximities. Each fragment struggles to find a form of likeness and nearness to the others; as if recognizing a fundamental discordance, each piece keeps its distance (they're close enough). It's still a little awkward. As one seems to describe the other, pairs seem arranged. Ambiguities arise. Orientation and artifice are in play.

Proximities

In plan, the homestead's partner seems to be the bedroom. They're exactly the same proportion and both are made of masonry block. In section, though, the ground of the homestead is removed to form an equal volume below itself. This new den seems to be the homestead's other couple: it's a diptych. But the dirt that made the den composes the new bedroom blocks, sharing something of themselves. These two doppelgangers, the bedroom and den, both make breaks in the forecourt's wall. Along one side, the forecourt's interior seems continuous with the exterior of the bedroom. To access the den, a spiral stair scrolls from the same fractured forecourt face.

This large U-shaped forecourt, open to the sky, separates carport from residence. Both the forecourt and the newly coupled homestead share a vertical orientation, and both enjoy certain denied relationships to the site. On the blunt side, the forecourt's vanity

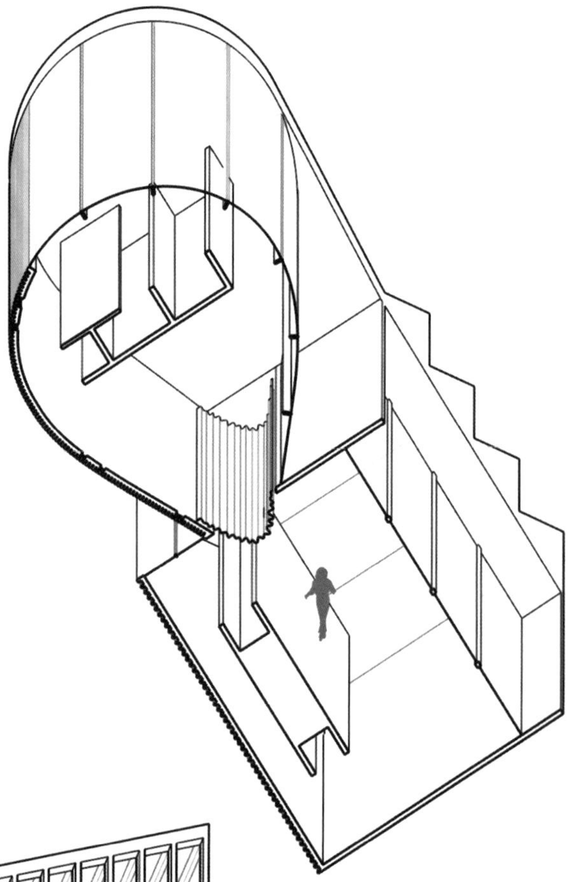

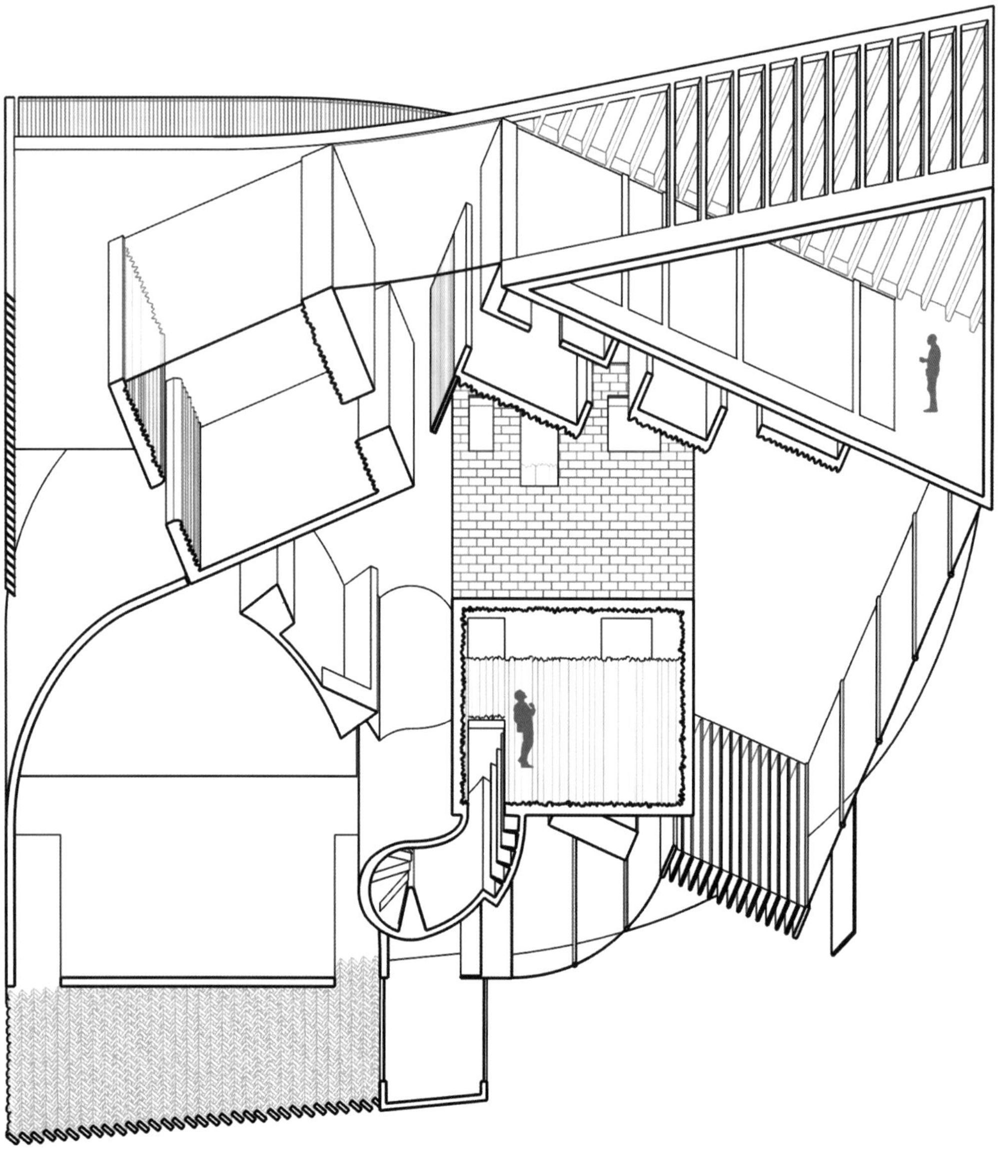

mirrors itself, projecting an egg-shaped void outward into the landscape. Here the top of the boulder pile can be seen reflected too, but the court replaces its base. The homestead's ceiling is exchanged for a large wedge-shaped light monitor. Coupled with the den below, its old interior is now exteriorized. The old object, now a void.

The foyer, kitchen, dining, and bedroom all maintain quasi-cardinal horizontal relations around the old homestead. Its former exteriority is now interiorized, as though the four square walls of the homestead elevation still marked important directions. The most private spaces—bedroom, bathroom, study, daybed—are closest to the rock. Each almost abut and open toward the boulder's northern face. Here the surface of the rock acts as each room's fourth wall.

On the boulder's east side is a small studio, a kind of phantom limb. Separated from the homestead by the new house, this little one maintains its distance altogether, around the rock, insisting

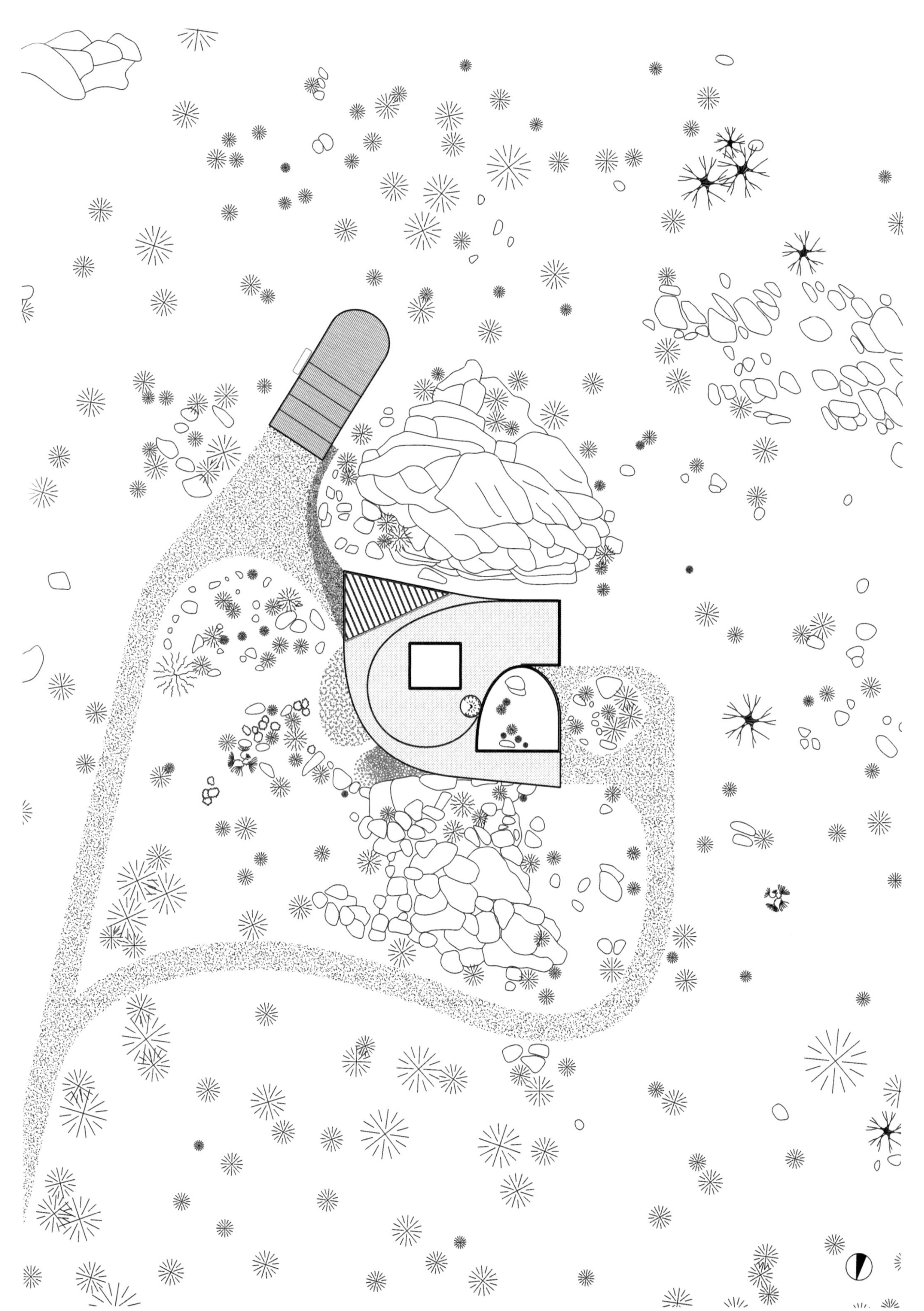

on room for reflection between architectural things at the scale of the site too.

The scene is now an arrangement of the homestead's approximations. We understand differences between pairings precisely because they share the stage. And where the realm for understanding is between things, each one becomes the context for its other. A composition of nearness that holds things apart.

The homestead seems a little more itself with its newfound proximities. Finally, intimacy with the boulder.

Postscript

Influences and points of departure include Mary Miss's *Decoys*, John Hejduk's House 1, Louis Kahn's Fisher House (and his Dominican-Motherhouse-plan struggle in the late 1960s). Anachronistically, Andrew Zago's 1980s thesis project, Schizophrenic Space. Equally influential, though perhaps less evident, are Toyo Ito's White U, and Kazuo Shinohara's Uncompleted House.

Marshall Brown Projects
Ziggurat, 2016
How to Build a Collage

Collage remains an unconventional form of architectural representation despite its consistent and often conspicuous presence since the beginning of modernism. Collage was formative in the work of Mies van der Rohe, Eileen Grey, Superstudio, Rem Koolhaas, Craig Hodgetts, Carme Pinós, Enric Miralles, and many others. Since its inception, my practice has also been engaged in a productive struggle with collage. And to my frustration, architectural literature has relatively little to say about collage methods, its possible conventions, or its instrumental value in the production of architecture.[1] Collage leverages indeterminacy and is highly effective in the critical moments where concepts and forms first take shape.

In 2016 I chose a single collage from my production as source material for Ziggurat, a garden folly for the Arts Club of Chicago. The referent collage fuses elements from Peter Eisenman's Koizumi Sangyo Corporation Headquarters, Frank Gehry's Schnabel House, and Zaha Hadid's Rosenthal Center for Contemporary Art. From concept through construction, Ziggurat is a demonstration of collage as a generative technique as well as a conceptual framework in architecture. The source collage was selected from a series titled *Chimera*, and it is composed of architectural photography cut directly from journals and assembled by hand with glue—an autonomous exercise in collage-making freed from the usual constraints of architecture. Each collage from the series incorporates a minimum of three image fragments cut from photographs of different buildings. Pieces never overlap, which necessitates the search for alignments and obsessive construction of seams. The edges of every fragment are carefully designed and cut to fit with their intended counterparts, like pieces of reverse-engineered puzzles. The identity of

the architectural samples matters less than their potential for productive unions. Collages made this way produce a double reading. Because of variations in coloration, scale, or viewpoint, the heterogeneous effect of collage is still strongly present. However, the alignments and seams work together to create disorienting visual tension between fragmentation and synthesis. Like the mythical lion-goat-dragon for which they are named, the *Chimeras* are both one and many.

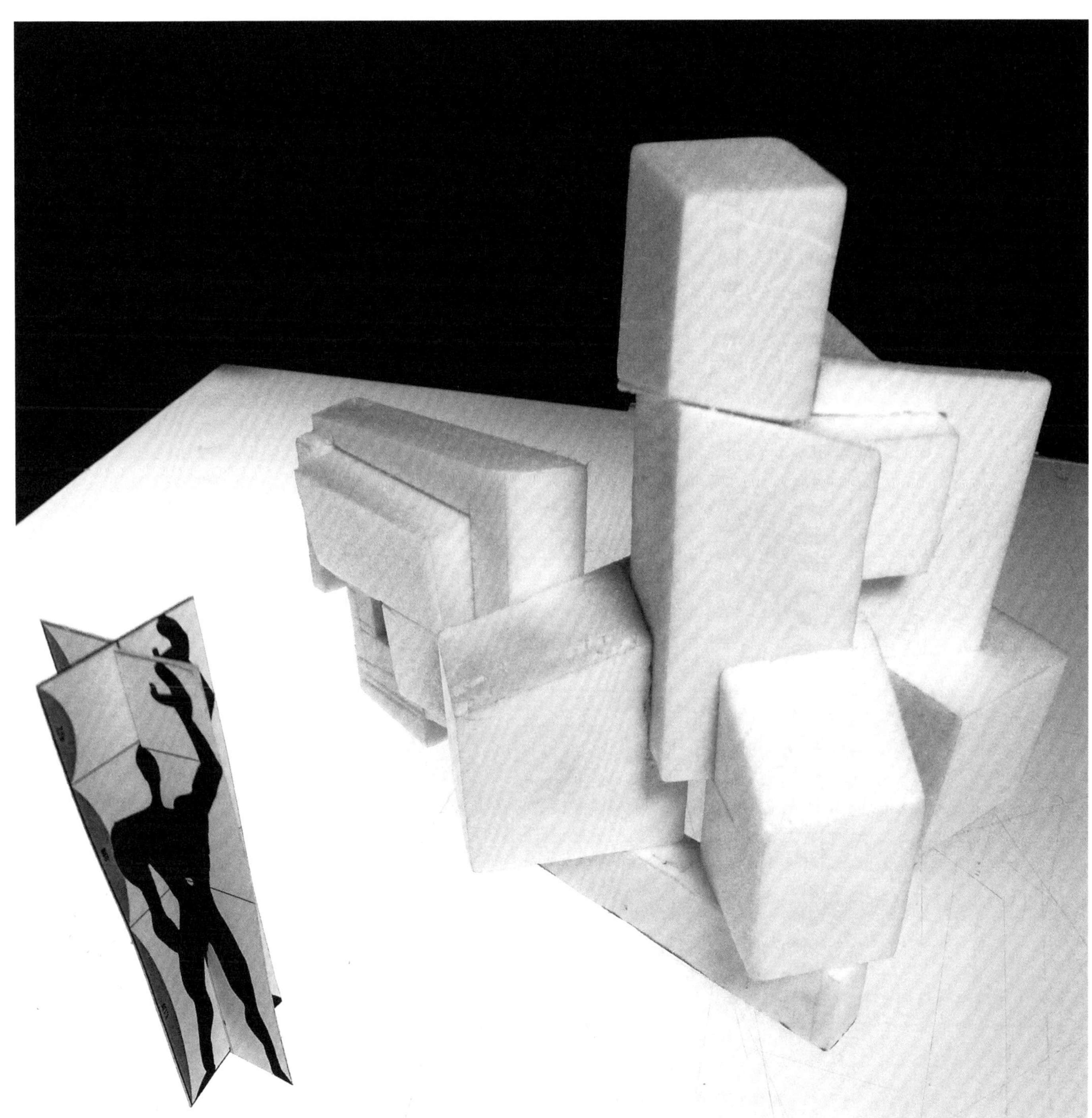

Unlike other uses of collage in architecture that emphasize disjunction, collision, or quotation, my practice uses it to synthesize disparate elements into new architectural wholes. Elsewhere I have articulated a theorem of creative miscegenation, which states that the legibility of architectural configurations is engendered by their promiscuous associations among a generalized discursive field.[2] A work of architecture cannot be understood outside the broader field of which it is a part, and the work is not constrained by its precedents but instead creates a new set of relations between them and itself.

Building a collage requires several translations. The first is scalar. Ziggurat needed to be as large as possible but still fit within a narrow garden site, resulting in a structure approximately 10 feet tall and 12 feet in diameter. Ziggurat is not large, but still somehow cuts a monumental figure, thus pointing to the second translation—from a two-dimensional composition to a three-dimensional form. Whatever architecture we imagine existing behind the collage must be discovered by extrapolation or inference. For Ziggurat this is accomplished by moving directly from collage to model. The drawings serve only for developing the surface articulations and as instructions for the fabricators, which leads to the third and final translation into a material manifestation and method of construction.

One might expect this building to employ a mix of materials chosen from its referents, given that it springs from a collage. Instead, the sources are subsumed by deploying one surface material throughout the entire built form. Though the referent buildings are still recognizable within the collage, Ziggurat's continuous aluminum cladding unifies the built assemblage as an independent architectural identity. Half-inch-thick aluminum foam panels are supported by framing secured to an aluminum I-beam foundation. Of course, this building, like any other, negotiates the circumstances of its site, economics, and construction with higher conceptual and aesthetic aspirations. The aluminum foam provides lightness and durability, but more importantly, its expression (for lack of a better term) oscillates between artificial and elemental. Half-inch open joints run continuously around the corners, paradoxically unifying the panels into volumes. The rough and porous surfaces begin to resemble stone blocks, making Ziggurat appear deceptively massive. The articulation of seams critically informs the structural design

and construction process as well.[3] Since the original commission was a temporary installation, the design is segmented into eight structurally independent sections that allowed for quick demounting at the original site in Chicago and easy reassembly at its current home, the Crystal Bridges Museum of American Art.

Architecture and collage are both fundamentally charged with fusing disparate elements into synthetic figures. And in both cases, this alchemy is produced through the manipulation of seams. The seams created between two pieces of paper in a collage are not lines, but gaps. If one magnifies a collage, the seams become fissures. Seams create the space for conceptual connections by holding entirely unrelated things ever so slightly apart. Architects should be uniquely able to recognize the significance of seams since collage-making is analogous to the assemblage of architecture itself. Architectural seams allow us to assemble aluminum panels, I-beams, wood, and bolts into something significantly more than the collected parts. Collage, though a two-dimensional medium, works similarly. As architectonics is an art of joining, so is collage.

1 The most notable exception is Ben Nicholson's 1990 essay, "Collage Making" in his book *Appliance House* (Chicago: Chicago Institute for Architecture and Urbanism, 1990). Only very recently has there been a spate of books on collage in architecture, including *Montage and the Metropolis* by Martino Stierli (2019); *Mies van der Rohe: Montage, Collage*, edited by Andreas Beitin, Wolf Eiermann, and Brigitte Franzen (2017); *Collage and Architecture* by Jennifer A. E. Shields (2013); and *Graphic Assembly* by Craig Buckley (2018).

2 For a further articulation of the theorem of creative miscegenation, see Marshall Brown, "Creative Miscegenation in Architecture, A Theorem," in *Authorship: Discourse, a Series on Architecture*, edited by Monica Ponce de Leon (Princeton, NJ: Princeton University Press, 2019), 113–25.

3 Ziggurat was engineered, fabricated, and installed by Navillus Woodworks of Chicago.

BairBalliet
The Next Port of Call, 2016
Part & Parcel

The idiom "part and parcel" refers to a basic or essential part. Both words, essentially carrying the same meaning, can be traced back to the 16th century to describe the exchange of property among characters of nobility such as kings, lords, and barons. Excessive language tended to breed within these legal documents that served to emphasize the exchange of power as parts were parceled. The redundancies found in legal doublets such as these are thought to have been motivated by profit, as clerks and solicitors were paid per word when drawing up conveyances, or, alternatively, they originated in the transition of language for legal purpose. Still in use today, the phrase suggests a productive *more*—more territory filled with more parts. It exceeds the technical definition to include more design, more form, more character, and more qualities.

The Next Port of Call works to move a technical operation into a realm where qualities and character appear. The project is a set of partial relationships that design building mass and volume as well as the attributes of the space in between. The collection offers an alternative to architecture's more ubiquitous "part-to-whole" problem. Here, excess is a tactic to negotiate an expansive parcel in a vast city. The result is a site full of characters roaming vacant terrain; at times standing alone, at other times huddling together, and sometimes squatting in existing buildings.

Parcels

The whole of the project, the entire "parcel," is developed by allusion but never achieved. Designed interruptions divide space, resisting a full reading of the parcel while offering insights into the whole. Some parts are left out, leaving gaps in otherwise continuous forms. Across the site, architecture is understood as a series of incomplete objects.

They are physically dispersed yet connected by implied geometries that create volumes and foster temporal programs activated by the everyday subject as they commute to work, recreate, and mingle.

The project is situated on a vast 26-acre parcel between the Detroit River to the south and a mix of light industrial and residential to the north. The scene includes a hulking one million square feet of late 1950s modernism, a United States Post Office and Distribution Center, the Detroit River, and a park that spans between them. The post office sits atop a plinth functioning as both backdrop and proscenium. The plinth is a stage for viewing the river, even though it barricades access from the neighborhood to the park and river. The Next Port of Call reimagines the site through a series of building-scale nip/tucks: excavations and recompositions that both address the site's impenetrability as well as offer new ways of occupation.

The site, like many others in Detroit, reveals a striking relationship between the built and unbuilt city. The balance between these two, engendered by high vacancy rates, heightens one's depth of field and produces two unique ways of relating to buildings. First, buildings are experienced in the round. All elevations are exposed, making relationships like front, back, and side ambivalent to the moving subject. Second, subjects look through or between buildings, always expanding the immediate context with fuller views of the city beyond.

The Next Port of Call looks for ways to preserve these unusual experiences through zoning. The project develops a strategy of multiplicity, situating buildings to highlight the spaces in between as much as the buildings themselves. The interstitial zones are frequently neglected or simply leftover: interior courts, porticoes, and plazas that enhance civic life are placed in direct dialogue with building mass. These two elements—solid and void—populate the park in an orchestrated yet casual composition.

Parts

In a "part and parcel" relationship, parts operate like the parcel but at the finer scale of individual building forms. The DNA of the building forms can be genetically traced throughout the various buildings, though their quantities and proportions offer reduplicates as opposed to exact copies. The term *chimera* has come to describe any mythical or fictional creature with defined portions taken from various animals: a thing composed of disparate parts. Chimeras are useful for producing imaginary figments that simultaneously come loaded with references to other known creatures. Similarly, the Next Port of Call builds a recombinant formal taxonomy, one more specific to parts of a body as opposed to a body of parts. This taxonomy is composed of architectural elements that have historically challenged one's perception of dimensional bigness and visual depth: plinths (as mass relates to ground), parapets (as mass relates to sky) and partial walls (as mass relates to void). Respectively, these three elemental types are architecture's feet, midsection, and head. In the Next Port of Call, buildings are designed to offer contrasting qualities: rooted at the base or standing on tiptoes, upright or slouched into their neighbor. They overreach to contribute to the skyline or dip down to lie low on the horizon.

The curvaceous forms lean on interpretations of iconic Detroit profiles of various scales and types. They are arranged on planimetric circles of different sizes and distances from one another. The forms are sliced, sheared, and dissected, offering visual "ins" through and between parts. Using techniques such as the multiplication of serial profiles, removal of mass to reveal hidden profiles, and reorientation of self-similar profiles, new relationships to fronts emerge. While designed in-the-round, each part exhibits spatial qualities in moments of disruption, where two-dimensional profiles and surface edges produce planar breaks in an otherwise three-dimensional

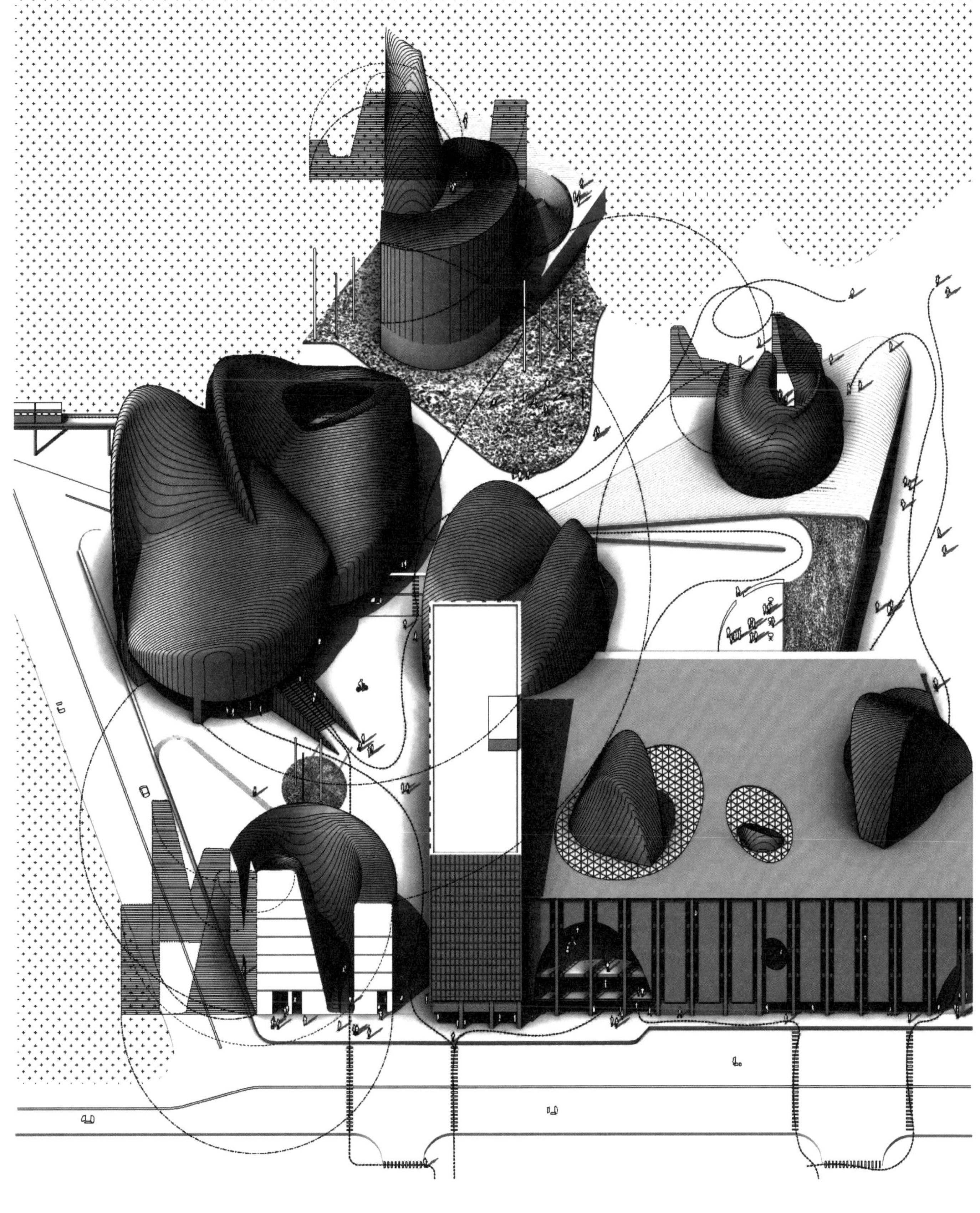

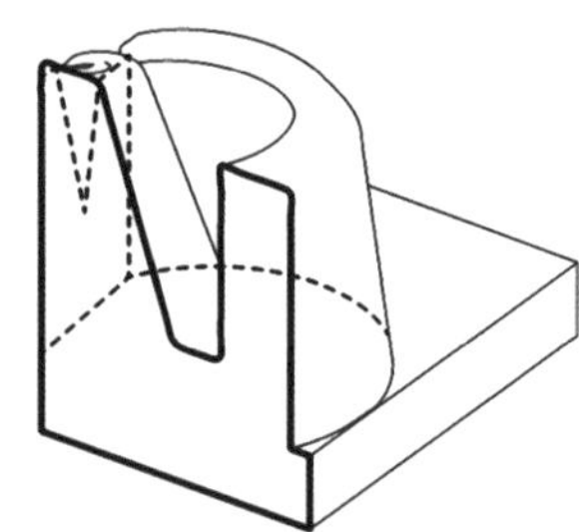
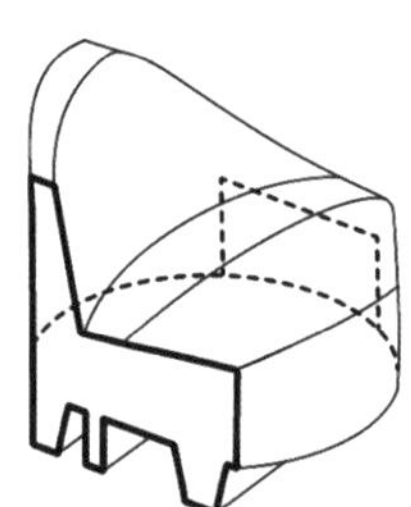
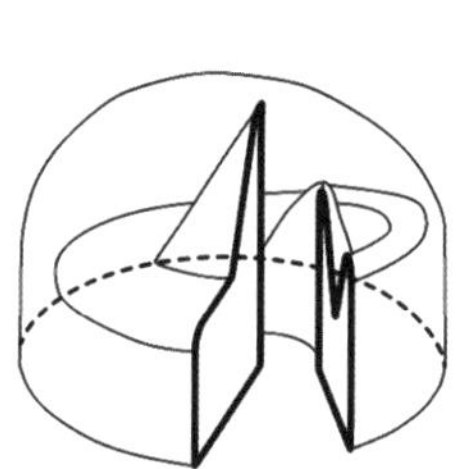
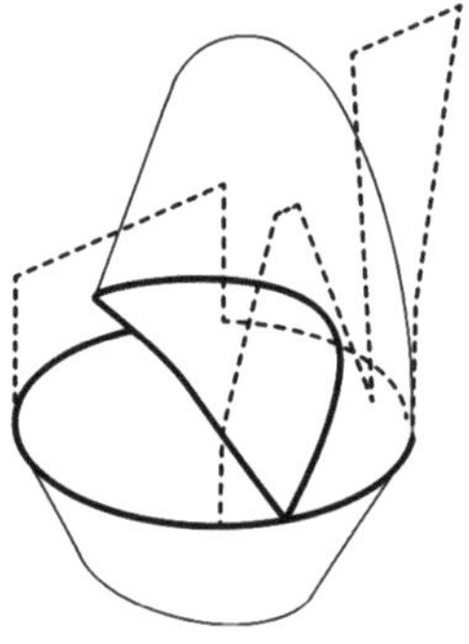

1 2 3 4

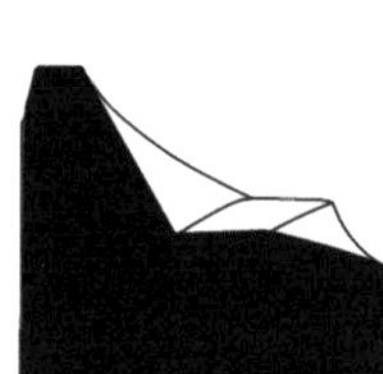

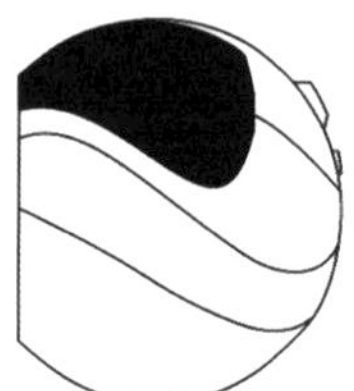

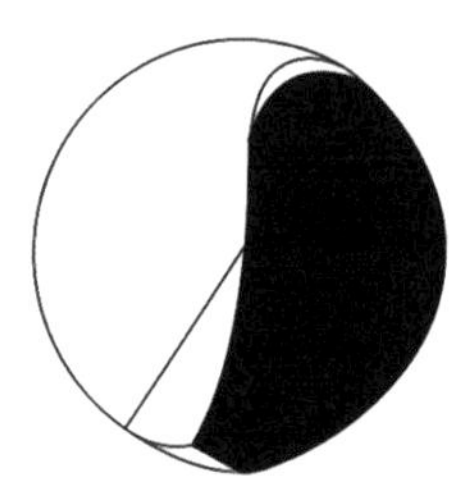

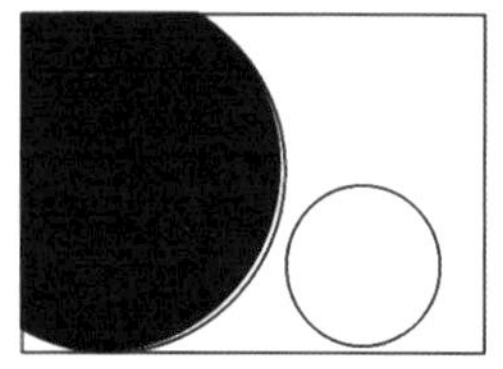
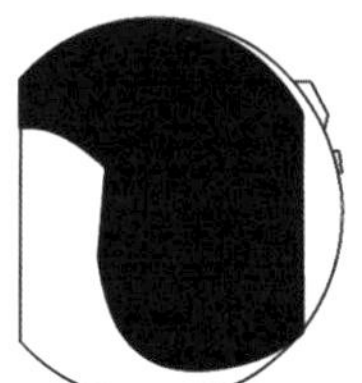

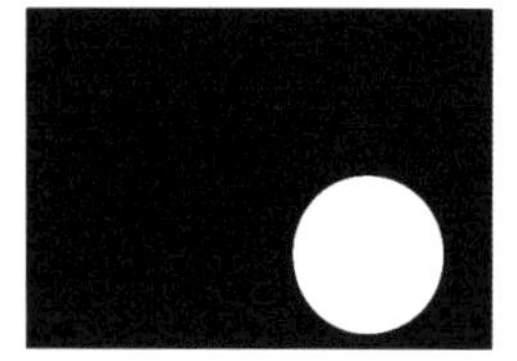

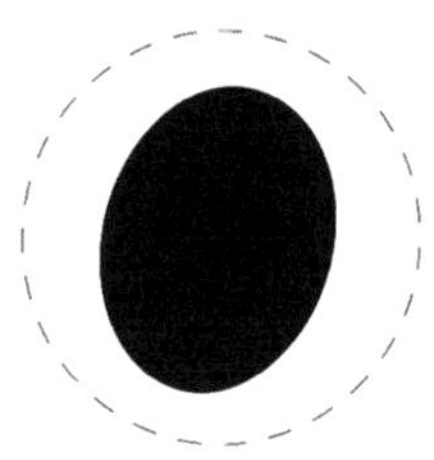

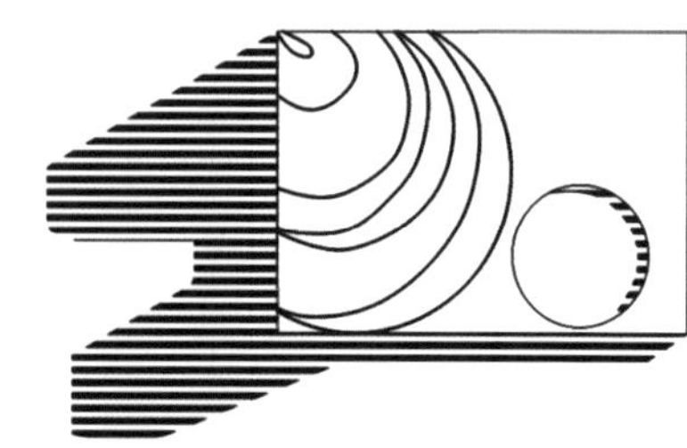

circular sequence. The Rail Hub is a rotund building that links the parcel to the broader urban context, physically as a tethered 14th stop to the Detroit People Mover and visually as it doubles in plan and stretches in elevation to accommodate multiple scenarios. The subtractive cuts in the mass for through circulation and extrusion/pivoting of building mass are paired with more nuanced formal traits such as the thinning of walls to diminish an otherwise imposing mass. These disruptions expose the building section to the exterior implying spatial continuity between buildings despite their physical separation. In a shift from exterior to interior, bulbous inserts reveal volumetric cuts into the existing post office building and the underlying geometry of their construction.

The Next Port of Call expands the architectural imagination at both the scale of the parcel and the part. It establishes design tactics and then exploits them in order to produce genetic mutations among the cast of characters. Always reproducing, though not replicating, the buildings participate in a larger choreography where common features suggest familial resemblance but are fraternal in their multiplicity. The project optimistically fills out the next urban frontier through partiality, offering an alternative to material densification in service of amplification of parts and an implied wholeness of the parcel.

Phillip Denny
Field Notes on the Creaturely (from the Monstrous to the Cute)

Like Bigfoot, the mysterious creature of American folklore, creaturely architecture appears once in a generation before quickly retreating deep into the woods of discourse. Sightings are rare but memorable, each time disturbing the dearly held belief that there are no monsters lurking in the dark thicket beyond the rustic hut. Always occupying a marginal position, the creature's remoteness is both reassuring and menacing. It has never been convincingly captured by theory. Sustained description of the creature is exceedingly difficult for two reasons: first, because it never sticks around for long; and second, because each time it surfaces, it seems to have changed shape.[1]

Mack Scogin and Merrill Elam Architects' 1999 design for a science center in Wolfsburg, Germany, is one such sighting. The proposed building appeared as a stylobate (or perhaps Kubrick's monolith) held aloft on spindly tendrils. Like the tripod from *War of the Worlds*, it was an extraterrestrial being stalking the earth's surface. Where the platform typically functions as a sturdy base for the colonnade in classical architecture, Wolfsburg's organizational logic is apparently alien, a confluence of parts whose purposes are not wholly understood. Scogin and Elam, for their part, admitted there was much about the thing that they did not know: "What we know is that the building is large and that it is of the fantastic," they wrote in a brief text. It was "a big discovery of the City of Wolfsburg."[2] The architects subjected it to careful examination, documenting its anatomy as if it were an exciting find in the wild. According to their careful measurements, the Wolfsburg Creature was big indeed, slightly taller than the

Statue of Liberty in New York Harbor (151 feet, 1 inch, from toe to torch; or 305 feet, 1 inch, pedestal included) but somewhat shorter than the Great Pyramid of Giza (455 feet from ground to apex). Scogin and Elam's recourse to discovery and limited knowledge evinces a desire to claim the tenuous space between form making and form finding, the familiar and the fantastic, the authored and the found.

Greg Lynn explored neighboring discursive territory—albeit channeled through the terms of biomorphism and aided by then-new digital modelling software—when he referred to the 40,000-some "eggs" of his 1997 Embryological House project as a "brood." (A nest of eggs was even shown as if under an incubator, à la *Jurassic Park*, in the 2003 exhibition *Greg Lynn: Intricate Surface* at the MAK Vienna.) What would hatch was to be a departure from architecture's known quantities, such as the trabeated system and the accompanying intellectual tradition of the *tektonik*.[3] In their theorizing, Lynn and his fellow travelers frequently made use of potent biological notions of speciation, evolution, and differentiation, and even with the benefit of roughly two decades of historical distance, this work still tends to be discussed in those terms. One researcher at the Canadian Centre for Architecture in Montreal noted that while each egg was unique, they all bore "a certain family resemblance to each other."[4] Lynn, like Scogin and Elam before him, rigorously documented the slight deviations of the eggs' spline geometry in a series of painstaking descriptive drawings. To some of his critics, the work would seem to have done little more than inaugurate a novel formal language of the "blob"; for Lynn, the eggs suggested the possibility of moving the biological from the realm of metaphor toward a literal, functional paradigm for architecture. To him, the ovoid geometries of the Embryological

Samuel Wale, Frontispiece of Marc-Antoine Laugier, *Essai sur l'architecture*, engraving, 1755.

Mack Scogin Merrill Elam Architects, Wolfsburg Science Center Invited Competition, physical model, 1999.

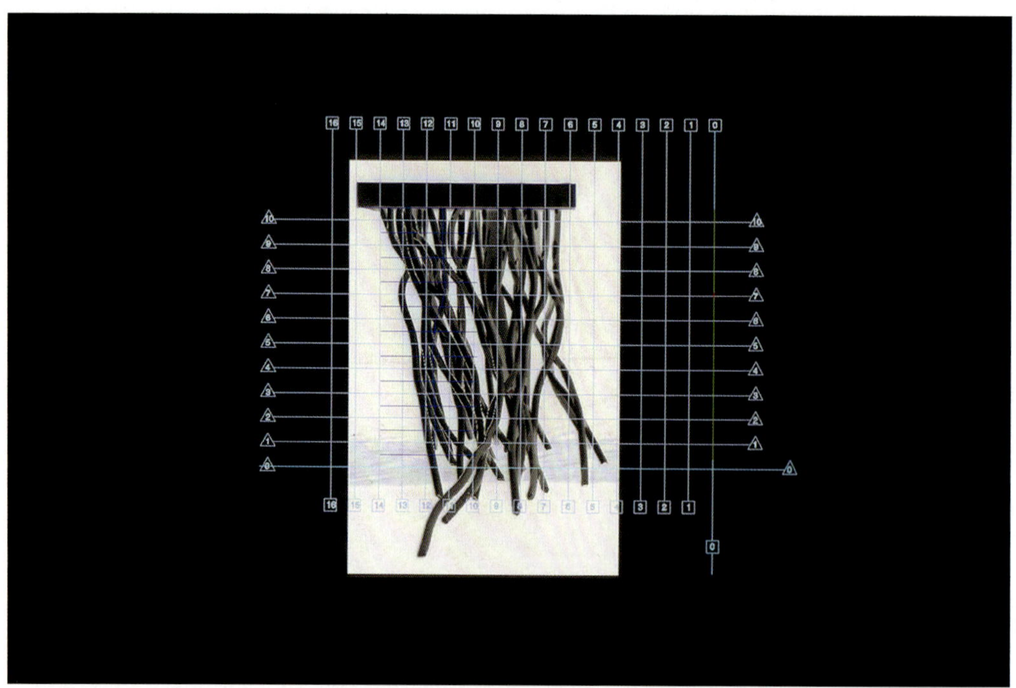

Mack Scogin Merrill Elam Architects, Wolfsburg Science Center Invited Competition, drawing, 1999.

House posited a revised configuration of buildings' environmental metabolism: "The egg initially exhibits a high degree of simplicity and radial symmetry. As it unfolds in an open relationship with its environment, it breaks symmetry, differentiates, and becomes more complex and heterogeneous because of its feedback with exigencies and constraints outside of its control."[5]

A predisposition to the creaturely is a robust through line in Lynn's work and writing. It is a project that has evolved over decades, but which first took its mature form around 1991, in a competition convened by Stanley Tigerman to reimagine several of Chicago's landmarks. On that occasion, Lynn conjured the Sears (now Willis) Tower's monstrous doppelgänger, supine and spineless—in a word, "stranded." It was a pile of Lovecraftian tentacles spilled along the city's downtown riverfront, like the Kraken dredged up from the murky depths of Lake Michigan. Lynn observed how it seemed to make itself at home in its surrounds, "entangling its monolithic mass with local contextual forces."[6] Like an octopus squeezing into the most improbable crannies, or a creature building a nest, its parts "accommodate[d] themselves to the multiple and often discontinuous borders of the site," Lynn noted. Contrary to the landmark skyscraper's singular stiffness, "the differentiated Sears Tower proliferates."

That same year, across the prairie in Ames, Iowa, architect and theorist Jennifer Bloomer summoned up what she called Tabbles of Bower, an assemblage comprising 13 parts, among them "cowslab," "cowhide," "tabby columns," and "ribs."[7] In a lengthy essay detailing the intellectual origins and material development of the project from beef to building, Bloomer wrote "the cowslab constitutes the floor of the construction. It is a two-and-a-half-inch-thick concrete slab in the shape of two cows placed nose-to-nose." In a few grainy photographs of the thing, we see the cowhide levitating above the slab, held aloft by four so-called tabby columns as a sort of bovine baldachin. "It appears, complete and full-blown, at the end of an uncertain period of gestation," Bloomer observed. As a bricolage of collected animal parts, Tabbles of Bower uncomfortably appropriated unconventional materials as familiar architectural elements—that is, as columns and slabs. Where biology never transcended its status as a metaphor, albeit a powerful one, guiding Greg Lynn's digital project, Bloomer's gestating Bower grew, in a literal sense, out of its organic materials.

Bessie, a creature belonging to the architects of the Bittertang Farm since 2014, could be considered a direct descendant of Bloomer's Bower, but only in part. According to Bittertang, Bessie comprises the reconfigured components, "from hoof to ear," of twelve cows and eight goats.[8] Bessie resembles a rat king, a tangle of bodies, a structure convened from assembled parts—or disassembled parts, as the case may be. Bessie is a remix, the product of parts reorganized according to a logic other than that of their source materials. The creature demonstrates the tectonic possibilities of bones, sinew, and skins. The Bittertang farmers explain that a cow's "bones typically carry 1000 pounds. Their lightness and strength would make them an ideal architectural component, however the problem is that bones are short and within an animal rely on various liquids, ligaments, and sinew to connect together multiple bones." The architects of the Bittertang Farm circumvented the problem by cutting and joining bony segments to the necessary lengths. Tibias became osseous columns, slenderer than any extant order. Pelts became furry floors. Udders and other membranes

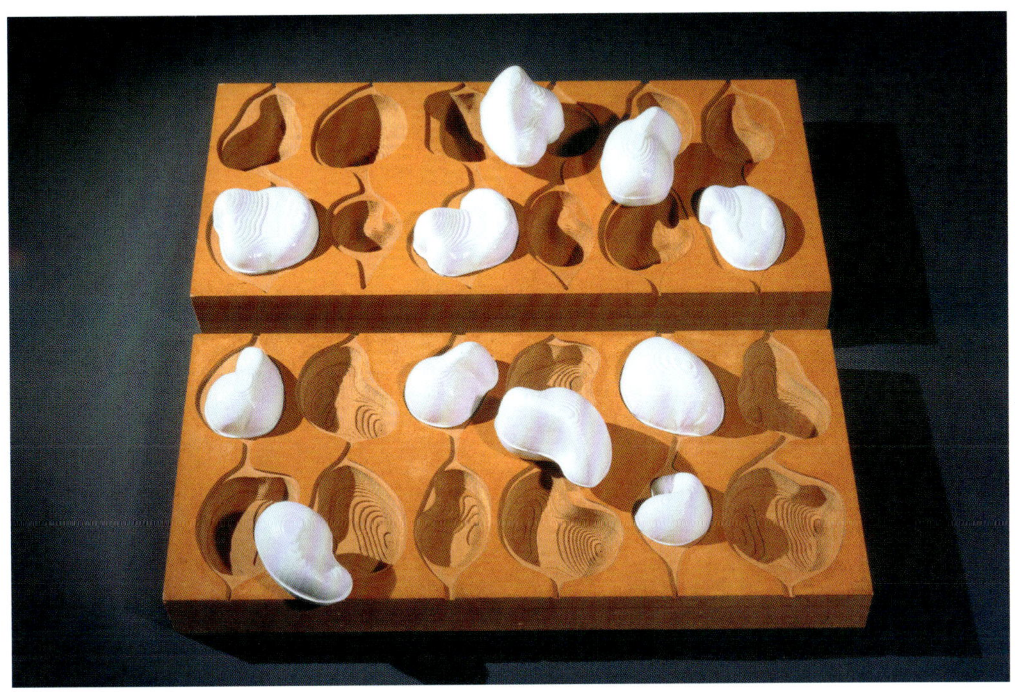

Greg Lynn, “Eggs” or “Brood” from Embryological House, physical model, 2001.

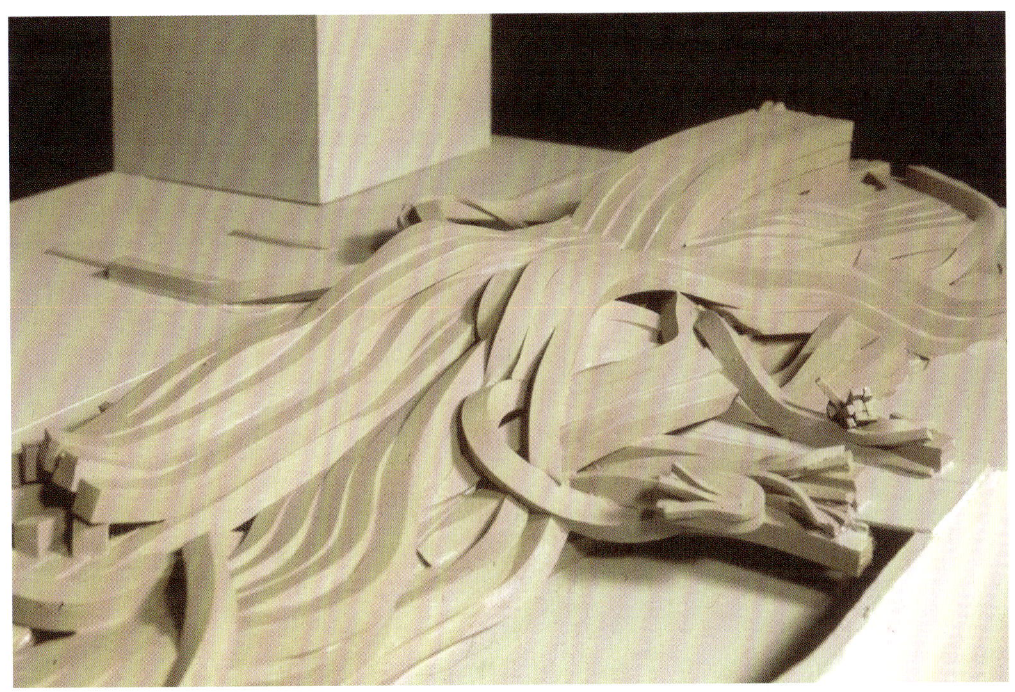

Greg Lynn, Stranded Sears Tower, physical model, 1992.

Jennifer Bloomer, Abodes of Theory and Flesh: Tabbles of Bower, photograph, 1992.

The Bittertang Farm, Bessie: Animal as Building Block, rendering, 2014.

were filled with air as a fleshy form of pneumatic architecture, "inflated to create giant engorged cows," or a buoyant herd.

Bittertang generously forwarded a similar though markedly smaller specimen to Cambridge, Massachusetts, in 2018. Assembled from Cornish hens, but also named Bessie, it demonstrated the technique's singular problems with scale. Where modern construction tends to meet challenges of size with techniques of modular standardization, Bessie's scalability uniquely depends on the availability of appropriately scaled materials; it depends, that is, on finding right-sized animals. Substituting Cornish hens for cows brings with it a raft of wicked problems that swapping, say, bricks for concrete masonry units does not. Moreover, Bessie and the hens unhouse our habituated expectations of architecture's objecthood. Although we have always assumed that "meatspace" referred to a real, existing world experienced by our fleshy bodies, the Bittertang creatures literalize the term in unsettling fashion, instead offering meaty architecture for us meaty beings.[9]

Another group of creatures was shown in Los Angeles in 2016, collected by architect Ellie Abrons of EADO. Her Inside Things were bulbous multicolor forms shown in specially designed, cuboid habitats. Mostly resting in corners or slowly spilling out of their pens like viscous ooze, the creatures at least appear to be docile. According to Abrons, "The parts allude to something familiar—figures imbued with vitality that walk the line between living things and not living things." At points, the Things sweetly mimed some of the features of their human keepers and curious visitors. Several of the forms were dotted with vaguely developed orifices, and some other blobs embraced one another, enlacing fingerly protrusions in a gesture uncannily resembling clasped human hands. Elsewhere, the Things had seemingly chewed through the walls of their habitats, revealing terrifying polypoidal mouths.

The attractive outsides of Abrons's Inside Things bear a striking resemblance to Andrew Holder's Pillow Babies, a litter of almost two hundred unruly runts born in 2013 that quickly proved to be too much for their bachelor father to handle alone. Like sausages stuffed and tied by hand, the Babies revealed only the outer surface of a hidden inside, chock-full of stuffing, or rather packed with potential. As Holder reported, "each pillow is a baby that hasn't become anything in particular." Like Abrons's Things, the Babies are loosely suggestive, voluptuous bodies, borderline unseemly, although, as Holder observes, "the seam is the only definite line in each object."[11] Like Lynn's eggs, these nylon-skinned objects explore the anexact, indeterminate relations between geometry and form, with the added difference that Holder greets the unformed things as "Babies," developing beings that will grow in ways that never fail to surprise their parents.

These latest reported appearances suggest that the creature is venturing out into the open with increasing frequency, welcomed in from the woods by rugged young architects such as Holder and Abrons, among others. But whether Things or Babies, these recent appearances suggest a late modulation of the creaturely, a decisive turn that has seen a category once perceived as monstrous, threatening, and necessarily marginal become, in a word, cute.

What does it mean that architecture's creatures have suddenly become adorable? The literary critic and cultural theorist Sianne Ngai identifies cuteness as both a minor aesthetic category—especially so if held up against the vaunted sublime and the beautiful—and yet terribly consequential.[12]

The Bittertang Farm, Bessie: Animal as Building Block, physical model, 2017.

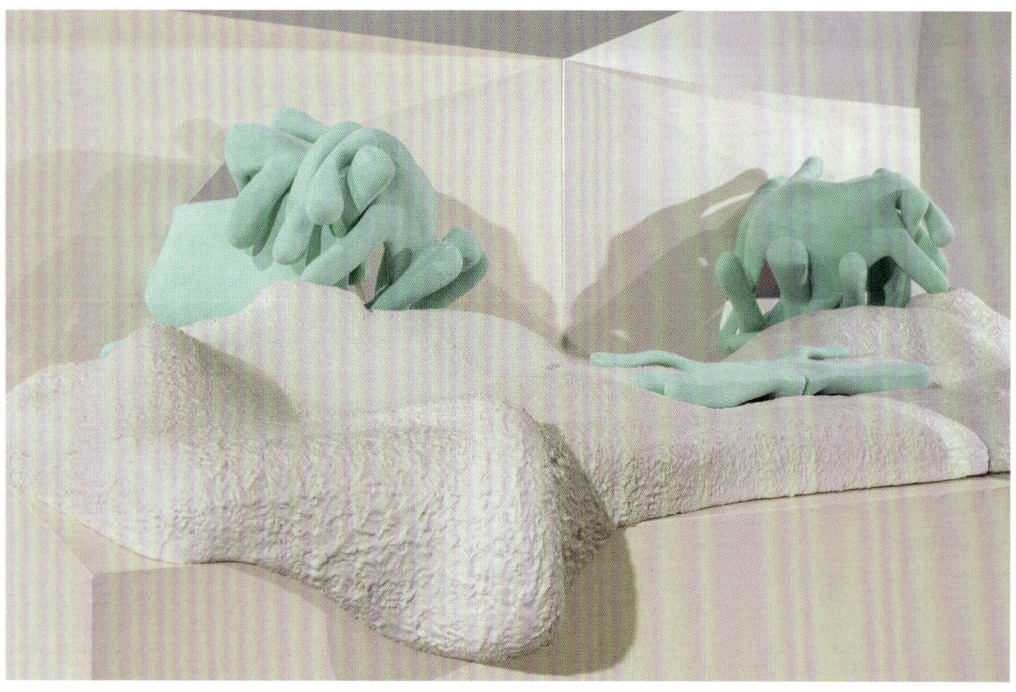

EADO, Inside Things, physical model, 2016.

EADO, Inside Things, physical model, 2016.

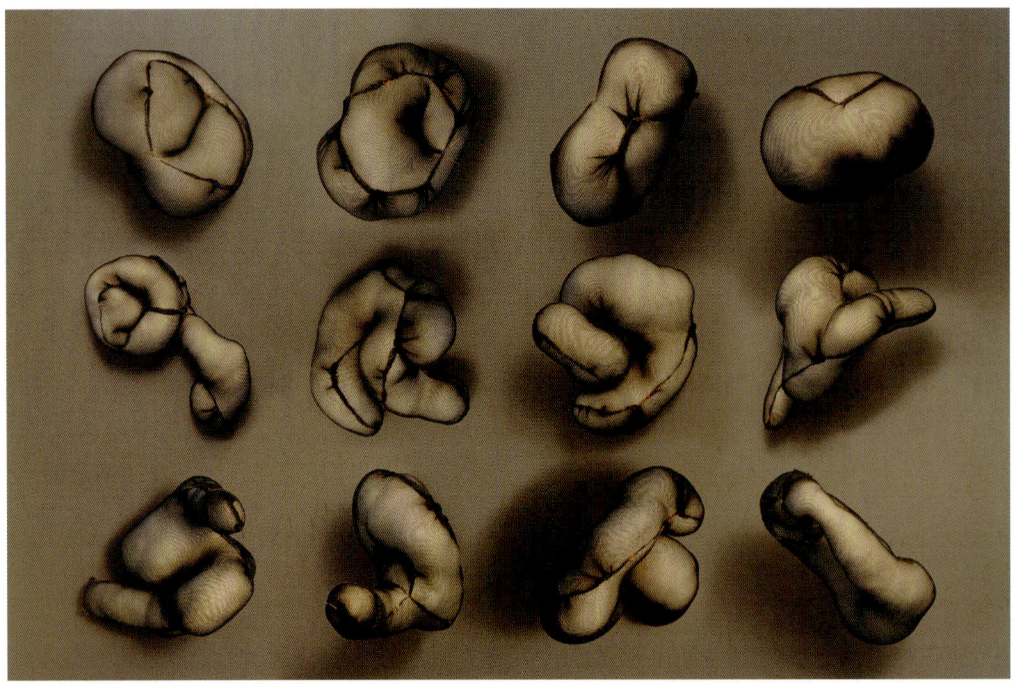

The LADG, Pillow Babies, physical models, 2013.

Where the proud sublimes of Kant and Burke are rare and awe-inducing experiences, judgments of cuteness are quotidian, routine, even banal. But for exactly that reason, cuteness is an integral part of our contemporary aesthetic repertoire to a degree that the ambivalent terror of the sublime simply is not. For Ngai, cuteness registers the vulnerability of a thing, a differential "asymmetry of power," and more specifically the subject's "sense of power" over the object.[13] Insofar as the cute object presents itself as vulnerable, it exerts an affective demand for tender care, a call for tenderness issued to its subject. But the cute is no less ambivalent than the sublime is (or can be) both wonderful and terrible; to call something cute, after all, can be to judge it either positively or negatively, to compliment or to belittle.

The cute creature has distinct advantages over its frightening predecessors. Where the monsters have been banished to a safe distance on the periphery, we tend to invite the cute in and draw it closer to us. As Ngai claims, cuteness is "an aesthetic about our desire to fondle things 'close at hand.'"[14] The bulbous forms and furry hides of Abrons's and Holder's cute objects beckon us toward them, and they reward our gentle touch. "Cuteness is a response to the 'unformed' look of infants, to the amorphous and bloblike as opposed to the articulated or well defined," Ngai writes. "Indeed, the more malleable or easily deformable the cute object appears, the cuter it will seem."[15]

The significance of the recent turn to cuteness might be that it suddenly makes a discourse of the creaturely possible. Whereas the monstrous always required the diligent maintenance of extreme distance—monsters needed to be banished to the periphery to remain "real," after all—cuteness demands intimacy and immediacy.[16] Monstrous creatures were transgressive yet suspect, insofar as confirming the creature's presence meant crossing the outer threshold of architecture and plausibility, moving outward toward a margin labeled "here there be monsters," and warily leaving a center incapable of admitting their existence. While the monsters were all-too-successfully held at bay, cute creatures have recently come inside without our invitation; where the monster needed remote reaches in which to lurk out of sight, the cute is already at home with us.

What lessons, finally, might these cute creatures teach us? Many, myself included, have tended to address the creaturely in terms of semblance. But cuteness helps us to realize that the creature's potential in architecture was never in *looking* like a thing so much as in *acting* like a thing.[17] Creatures, whether monstrous or cute, place demands upon us; they produce affects, and they thereby enact effects. They exercise "thing-power," the name the philosopher Jane Bennett has given to "the ability of man-made items to exceed their status as objects and to manifest traces of independence or aliveness."[18] Thing-power baffles the subject-object paradigm. Further, it suggests that architectural things may intersect with, and even become coextensive to, our own human interests and scheming, but also that they exist independently of and even indifferently to us. These creatures, whether monstrous or cute, disturb the anthropocentricity of our building, and they rattle the assured sovereignty of architecture's claim to administer an ontological divide between the human and nonhuman. But rather than representing a looming threat, they register the possibility of enacting an alternative distribution of relations across the human/nonhuman divide, such that these paradigms might someday fail to hold, released from the strong gravitational pull of the anthropocentric. Coming to terms with architecture's thing-power may mean finally cultivating unprecedented and productive kinships with what Lynn called "multiplicitous and inorganic bodies." It also means admitting the tenuousness and lightness of our own bodies' entanglements with the world and acknowledging the lively power inherent in architecture's obdurate materiality. But first of all, it means seeing the creaturely side of architecture.

1 The author extends his thanks to K. Michael Hays and Andrew Holder for the invitation to take up this expedition. Reports and reflections on the creaturely appear only haphazardly in architecture's recent scholarly literature, but, save for this project, there has been heretofore no attempt to draw these references together.

2 Wolfsburg Science Center Invited Competition project description, Mack Scogin Merrill Elam Architects website, http://msmearch.com/type/museums-and-galleries/wolfsburg-science-center-invited-competition.

3 Kenneth Frampton, *Studies in Tectonic Culture: The Poetics of Construction in Nineteenth and Twentieth Century Architecture* (Cambridge, MA: MIT Press, 1995).

4 Howard Shubert, "Embryological House," in *Origins of the Digital*, Canadian Centre for Architecture, April 2009, https://www.cca.qc.ca/en/articles/issues/4/origins-of-the-digital/5/embryological-house.

5 Greg Lynn, "The Renewed Novelty of Symmetry," *Assemblage* 26 (April 1995): 14.

6 Greg Lynn, "Multiplicitous and Inorganic Bodies," in *Folds, Bodies, and Blobs: Collected Essays* (Brussels: La Lettre Volée, 1998), 33–62.

7 Jennifer Bloomer, "Abodes of Theory and Flesh: Tabbles of Bower," *Assemblage* 17 (April 1992): 6–29.

8 Bessie: Animal as a Building Block (2014) project description, the Bittertang Farm website, http://www.bittertang.com/Cows/index.htm.

9 I would be remiss not to acknowledge Mitchell Joachim and Maria Aiolova's path-breaking meatspace research, particularly the fully organic "In Vitro Meat Habitat" of 2008, a "victimless shelter" grown from "3D printed, extruded pig cells to form real organic dwellings." See Terreform, "In Vitro Meat Habitat" (2008) project description, http://www.terreform.org/projects_habitat_meat.html.

10 Inside Things (2016) project description, EADO website, https://www.ellieabrons.com/Inside-Things.

11 Andrew Holder, "The Ramifications of Pillow Baby," *Pidgin* 21 (2016): 2–13.

12 Sianne Ngai, *Our Aesthetic Categories: Cute, Zany, Interesting* (Cambridge, MA: Harvard University Press, 2012).

13 Ibid., 11.

14 Ibid., 27.

15 Ibid., 30.

16 As recently as 2008, Catherine Ingraham unambiguously declared, "I do not think monstrosity is, at this point, possible in architecture." Ingraham, "Nothing Will Come of Nothing," *Perspecta* 40, "Monster" (2008): 202–7.

17 See Claus Benjamin Freyinger and Andrew Holder's reflections on the limits of semblance in "Looking Like Things; or, Negative Similarity" in *Possible Mediums*, ed. Kelly Bair, Kristy Balliet, Adam Fure, and Kyle Miller (Barcelona: Actar, 2017), 159–61.

18 Jane Bennett, *Vibrant Matter: A Political Ecology of Things* (Durham, NC: Duke University Press, 2009), xvi.

K. Michael Hays

Architecture's Inscriptions: Reading Symptoms and Enjoyments

A millennial ethos in architecture has produced modifications in the object that deviate from long-standing problematics. Complex animated surfaces—ornamental draperies and wrappers, as well as structural skins and ribbons—have challenged the dominance of tectonic frames and geometrically organized facades. Modulated arrays of corpuscles, tiles, shingles, and facets, together with stochastically stacked, twisted, and punctured volumes, have replaced compositional continuity and hierarchies of parts. New types of organization have emerged as well: scatters of digitally sampled building fragments, superimpositions and loosely curated collections of shapes, Boolean cutouts and Rhino-torqued volumes. At the same time, on the other side of the formal spectrum, new archaisms have appeared: primitive huts and first houses, labyrinths and mazes, megaliths at once precisely shaped and loosely piled, geological formations, recycled materials, recycled parts. And then there's the fascination with rocks. These, and other, diverse modifications in the *object* have been accompanied by a complex but singular change in the *subject*: the demise of the architecture discipline's authoritative structures and master signifiers, or what I will call the Architectural Symbolic.[1] Throughout history the symbolic authority of architecture has been derived variously, from antiquity, nature, reason, epochal will, technology, and, from the 1960s until recently, language itself (wherein architecture's universal grammar and contingent particulars are reconciled as a kind of speech). In the late 20th century, architecture developed the theory of the sign to its fullest, and with it came the understanding of architecture as a specific kind of production whose primary task is the construction of cultural meaning and knowledge. This is what was meant by the autonomy of architecture in the 1970s and '80s.[2] Since the mid-1990s, however, many architects and scholars have become skeptical, cynical even, about the relevance of any kind of symbolic superstructure or set of master codes that might sustain architecture as a distinct medium, practice, and conception. Thus rejecting disciplinary structures and histories, they have chosen instead to focus on the phenomenality of experience or else to pursue an overly empiricist approach to studying technologies and techniques of design. Even thoughtful readings of architecture through phenomenology, like those following Graham

Harman's object-oriented ontology, end up treating architecture merely as an illustration or metaphor for philosophy; and even thoughtful critiques of symptomatic reading, like those of the Aggregate Architectural History Collaborative, reduce architecture to the economies and technics of control, leaving nothing of its mysteries or aspirations. Countering both of these tendencies, this book presents an array of contemporary practices that, we suggest, together instaurate a collective research project that seeks to reconceptualize and work through the reconstitution of the architectural *subject* after the demise of the architectural Symbolic. Architectural inscription defines this project, and it appears in these practices as highly varied organizations of material marks designed not to usher in immediate references or direct meanings but rather to enact a displacement of these by what perhaps precedes figuration: the event or encounter, the mnemonic trace, a network of signification, and a material support *presupposed* by the act of inscription that then brings the figural into being. Architecture takes its place in a space opened up for it. The inaugural act of opening up that space is *inscription*—a material figure of anteriority and spacing. Here I will speak of an architectural materiality that is anterior to the architectural phenomenon but no less real for that. To insist on the materiality of architecture in a general way is not very profound. It is well known that architecture is the art practice most burdened with the stuff of the world—gravity and weather, laws and fashions, sensations and experiences. Attention to the manifest sensory properties of materials—the rhythm and connection of the units of assembly, the representational effects of color, texture, sound, and smell—often yields potent and memorable images, which should be counted among architecture's fundamental achievements. My point here is more particular: that architecture's materiality simultaneously operates as a latent form—a regulating trace or a differential of the image-figure—and a disarticulating force; that architectural inscriptions, to borrow words from T. J. Clark, "do *not* analogize or open onto 'sensations' or 'phenomena': that they posit a lack or failure of any such opening or analogy; and that they do so precisely in their material individuality as marks—their atomized facticity, their separateness."[3] Clark was speaking of the "uncontrollable power" of Cézanne's brushstrokes, "the wedges and commas of color that go to build his pictures."[4] We will isolate architectural signifiers of equal power and articulate inscription as a double order—at once a diagram or operator that gives rise to new architectures and performances *and* an overdetermined network of historical iterations and traces. The materiality of inscription exhibits the *work* of architecture beneath its phenomenal presentation, the transformation of its latent form into a manifest image. It therefore has a historical, dialogical, and social character, as well as the power to constrain and interrupt.

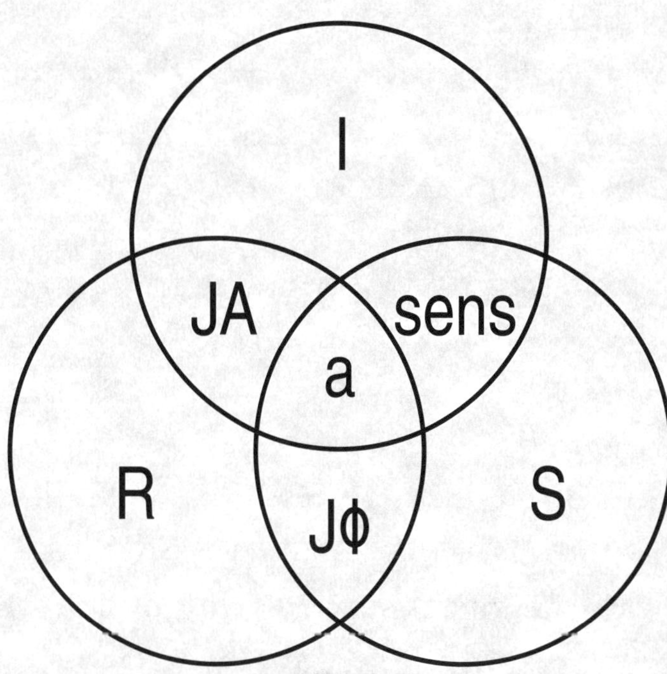

Jacques Lacan, RSI as Borromean knot with modes of jouissance.

It is within that dynamic field that our best thinking about materiality, figure, and their workings will take place. Here I approach the question of inscriptions as a series of modifications in the architectural subject by way of Jacques Lacan's model of the RSI (Real, Symbolic, Imaginary). Represented by the Borromean knot, the RSI offers us a topology of subject formation and a map of the functioning of the psyche: each ring of the knot is one of the three registers of experience—the orders of the Real, the Symbolic, and the Imaginary—and the *objet a*, the very semblance of Being, appears at the intersection of the three. Lacan assigns to the knot of the RSI the function of the "plus-one," emphasizing that it is the very materiality of the knot that produces a surplus of signification in which its isolated elements cohere.[5] Speaking of the limits of signification, Lacan remarks that "I have found nothing better to represent this limit than the Borromean knot. To represent it, you should clearly understand that it is not a matter of figure, or a representation, it is a matter of positing that it is the Real that is at stake, that this limit is conceivable only in terms of ek-sistence."[6] Which is to say, the topographics of the subject is a matter of Being, the construction of an ontology. And for us, in architecture, the stakes are equally high: knotting the architectural Symbolic together with the Real and the Imaginary enables us to generate new forms of architectural signification. My use of Lacan's framework in this context is no arbitrary choice. For it turns out that the evolution of his thinking in the 1970s precisely scans the history of architecture's own deflation of the Symbolic and the research that followed it. As a preliminary example of this historical and thematic parallel, consider Aldo Rossi's 1971 project for the San Cataldo Cemetery, Modena, in comparison with Peter Eisenman's 1978 project for the Cannaregio district in Venice (which was no doubt, in part, a response to Rossi). Rossi makes a structuralist analogy: the individual tombs are to the entire cemetery as individual houses are to the city. The conic communal grave and the cubic die that is the sanctuary for the war dead are similarly analogous to the monuments and "permanences" of the city: homologies between systems of difference. Eisenman's project begins with a curiously absent object of desire, Le Corbusier's unrealized

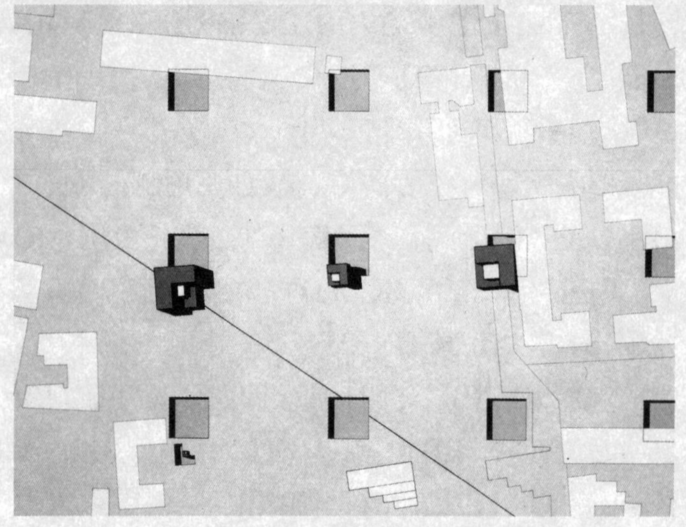

Peter Eisenman, project for Cannaregio, plan, 1978.

hospital project of 1965. Eisenman abstracts the hospital's gridded diagram and folds it over onto the irregular fabric of the adjacent site, where it is pressed into the Venetian *fondamento* as a series of holes, which may be understood as "potential sites for future houses or potential sites for future graves."[7] The two projects, both allegories of the deflation of symbolic authority (the morphology of the European city and Le Corbusier's formal language) can be compared according to the characteristics of Lacan's Imaginary (for Rossi) and Symbolic (for Eisenman): Modena involves the relations of parts and fragments, while Cannaregio concerns itself with a totalizing system; Modena constructs images and scenes of encounters with its part-objects, Cannaregio imposes codes and order on the site as datum; Rossi's objects are syntagmatic substitutions or reiterations of type, Eisenman's are mere traces and replications of other objects (Le Corbusier's and Eisenman's own). But the most striking commonality is the crushing negativity figured in both projects: in the bleached-blank surfaces and haunting shadows of Modena's Imaginary and in the empty repetitions of Eisenman's gridded Symbolic. Across the presumed axis of meaning constructed between the Imaginary and Symbolic, one encounters not meaning but its fading. The authority and certainty of Architecture are lost from the beginning in these projects, and all mere architectural objects are but attempts to fill the emptiness of that loss.[8] Beginning around 1974, Lacan began to develop the diagram of just this sort of system of signification, one comprising a lack in the Symbolic, along with the symptom and the particular enjoyment he called *jouissance*. Early in his constructions of the psychic topographics (from about 1960 to 1972), Lacan held that it was the infrastructural interaction between the Imaginary and the Symbolic—with the Real positioned as an outside beyond symbolization—that determined the entire structured field of subject formation. The Imaginary-Symbolic axis delineates the domain of meaning: where the Symbolic provides the signifiers and combinatory rules of the language, the Imaginary projects (as if in a mirror) shimmering visions and compensatory fantasies. The Real constantly enacts and disrupts exchanges with the other two domains by way of the overdetermined materiality of the symptom. Over the course of the seminars, Lacan develops his idea of the symptom from what at first appears as a kind of signifying particulate into a dynamic entity that seems more gelatinous, or perhaps, following the theory of quantum physics, is in many places at the same time. In his twenty-second seminar, on the RSI (1974–1975), Lacan remarks that the symptom is that which does not cease to write itself; it is a mobile operator that distributes *jouissance*. It is "the way in which the subject derives *jouissance* from the unconscious insofar as the unconscious determines the subject."[9] Lacan gives a formula for the symptom, *f(x)*, where *f* is the *jouissance* function and x is any element of the Real that finds its way through to the status of signifier, any condensation of the unconscious that can be perceived.[10] It is a decisive move in the trajectory of Lacan's thought: *jouissance* takes an element of the unconscious, one of its signifiers, removes it from its endless process of ciphering and transforms it into an element outside meaning—a glyph, a letter, an ornament. In the symptom, the signifier is made into nothing more, though nothing less, than a mark. The symptom does not, as in Sigmund Freud's system, call out for interpretation by mapping its effects onto the symbolic language of the Other. Rather, the symptom encapsulates a kernel of the material excess that eludes language and meaning but nevertheless motors the interaction of the orders in the RSI. This understanding of the symptom relative to the RSI allows for an important shift in Lacan's thought from 1972 to 1976, from a primary attention to the symptom as a signifier more or less isolated in the Symbolic, to the alliance of the symptom to the Real, and the designation of the symptom as a mobile trace of the subject's *jouissance*, all of which culminates in the introduction of the *sinthome* in 1975, a concept to which we will return.[11] The history of architecture's relation to the Symbolic and to its various accompanying hegemonies, hierarchies, and power structures cannot be undone. The deflation and delegitimation of traditional disciplinary orders have most often been accompanied by a negation of the Symbolic that is based on the assumption that any expansive or progressive architecture seeking to shatter the status quo through the discipline itself would be intrinsically inassimilable to its Symbolic register. There are, then, only two alternatives: to retreat from the Symbolic register, with its concern for shared codes and regulating parameters, to a pre-Symbolic Imaginary register of mood, atmosphere, fantasy, and affect; or to launch destructive

Aldo Rossi and Gianni Braghieri, Cemetery of San Cataldo, Modena, plan, 1971.

indictments from an extra-Symbolic and rebellious Real. In either case, the assumption is that any uncompromised, ideologically correct, and ethical architecture is one that cuts all ties to the Symbolic. This cutting loose from the Symbolic has the dramatic effect of disentangling all three rings of the chain—the disintegration of the subject of architecture itself. One could cede that, at times, pace Lacan, this static logic might nevertheless constitute viable options; after all, a discipline need not last forever. The problem with dismissing the Symbolic, however, arises from the fact that, despite some constitutive deficiencies, the Symbolic is also the site of all social support, adjudications of historical injustices and inequities, and articulations of relationships between the self and the Other.[12] Moreover, the bits of the Real in the Symbolic (conveyed by one mode of *jouissance*) deconstruct any division between the phenomena of empirical reality and that which lies beyond our representational systems, just as the Real in the Imaginary confounds the presentation of boundaries between inside and outside and emphasizes the materiality and corporeality of architecture, as well as its social function. And most fundamentally, according to the logic of the Borromean knot, any interrelation of any two of its registers is, as I say, unthinkable without the involvement of the third. Indeed, what the RSI offers most emphatically is a way of modeling the constitutive imbrication of the three registers, as well as the resultant excess of psychic energy. To say it another way, in the RSI we have a topological modeling of the subject's consistency that yields a robust materialism, which accounts for architecture's effects primarily through the instances and concepts of symptom and enjoyment. I emphasize this as an alternative to models of architecture based on speech and communication, resemblances, and precedents, which have dominated architectural theory since the 1960s, as well as to the more recent post-hermeneutics of the technical a priori, which insist that to proceed with a properly material analysis of architecture, we must focus on and reconstruct the apparatus of production of both the object perceived and the context of its subjective perception and that these together exhaust the interpretation. The model of speech treats the symptom as arising when symbolic communication breaks down; it is a malady to be fixed by clear references and conventional meanings. The analysis of technics regards the symptom as a metaphor for underlying forces, which must be excavated as the ontic operational causes of an existing condition. Both these positions betray a "belief" in the symptom.[13] Belief in the symptom is a belief that the symptom has meaning, which can in principle be known even if actual explanation falls short; it locates *jouissance* only in the Other of the Symbolic. In contrast, the model of the RSI suggested here holds not a belief in the symptom but an exhortation to enjoy it.[14] The model of the RSI enables us to see how the

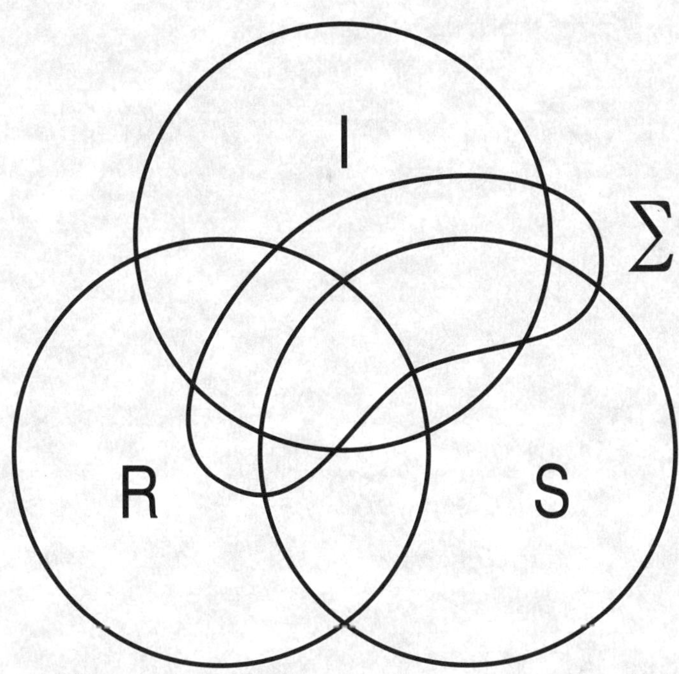

Jacque Lacan, RSI with the fourth ring of the sinthome.

production of art (architecture was the first art for Lacan) functions as a reknotting, for it is such productions that constitute a newly invented fourth ring—a novel creation, not a replacement for a broken Symbolic—that provides the subject with a singular consistency and *jouissance*. The RSI, though it consists of three rings, becomes fourfold, with the symptom transformed in Lacan's later thinking into a fourth register. This is the *sinthome*, "situated at the place where the knot slips [where the Symbolic breaks], where there is a lapsus in the knot."[15] The *sinthome*, in its relation to *jouissance* and the Real, is a radical expansion of the symptom and its signifiers in the Symbolic. The new ring (∑ in the diagram) weaves into and engages the RSI, giving the subject a new consistency. The *sinthome* is the inscription of the creative plus-one of Lacan's knot—a vitalizing incursion of the Real into the subject's Symbolic regime, which also supplies the materialization of the body image in the Imaginary. Whereas Lacan's earlier version of the symptom searches incessantly for a signifier to make itself meaningful (and for architecture, we can think again of the ceaseless typological substitutions of Rossi and topographical repetitions of Eisenman), the *sinthome* forms a material support that exists both before and after the signifier. It is beyond analysis (in the psychoanalytic sense) but before speech. It does not eradicate symbolic structures but instead reanimates them, overwhelming meaning with enjoyment. Far from a psychoanalytic abstraction, this function is, for Lacan, inherent in art and writing. Throughout the RSI seminar, he speaks of a mode of "writing in an untamed way," a mode of inscription intimately related to the Real that binds the three registers together.[16] And in his final, twenty-third seminar, on the *sinthome*, he uses the work of James Joyce—in particular *Finnegan's Wake*, for its singularity as a system of signification and an object, its materiality of sound and resistance to interpretation, and its production of *jouissance* across all registers of the RSI—as his primary example of the *sinthome*. Joyce used his art to supplement a lacking and abusive father, a failing symbolic authority, and to establish a consistency of self. But the production of art generally is not, for Lacan, merely an example of the *sinthome*; rather, art making is what directly instantiates the *sinthome* in the reorganization of the subject after the demise of the Symbolic. The enjoyment granted by the *sinthome*, then, is not that generated by a recognizable referent or a communicable meaning of the type that so excited the architecture of postmodernism but instead one that emerges from a material nexus of *jouissance* and signification—a kind of mnemographics, the force of which precedes and destabilizes meaning, producing the inscription's overabundance. The *sinthome* as inscription is the very mark of the subject's Being. It was, of course, Jacques Derrida and Paul de Man who joined Lacan in emphatically identifying, analyzing, and asserting inscription as a precondition of signification. Derrida spoke of "inscription *in general*, in order to make it quite clear that it is not simply the notation of a prepared speech representing itself, but inscription within speech and inscription as *habitation* always already situated."[17] With the notion of "situated habitation"—of *in*-habiting space—Derrida moved beyond particular and already prepared spaces and their representation (the ontic realm of spaces) to the question and operations of spacing *as such* in different disciplines, including architecture.[18] De Man's effort, likewise, was to rethink the materiality of the signifier, or "the letter," the self-referential and self-identical mark from which a new aesthetic can emerge. He uses the word *letter* in Lacan's sense of a socially inscribed mark, an element of the Real. While "phenomenality," for De Man, is the normative aesthetic to which we constantly return, the materiality of the letter jams any aesthetic transparency and, through its sheer refusal of reference, creates forms that diagram alternative histories to those already programmed by the present. Developing these notions, we will come to understand that architecture as inscription is architecture before speech, just as the *sinthome* as inscription is the spacing out of the social Symbolic (not its undoing) and inscription as habitation is a spacing out of what constitutes the possibility of inhabitation itself. "*Inscription in general*," explains Rodolphe Gasché,

> is the name for a *possibility* that all speech must presuppose—that marks all speech—before it can be linked to incision, engraving, drawing, the letter—in short, to writing in the common sense of the term. Without inscription *in general*, without an *instituted trace*, without arche-writing or proto-writing affecting speech as the possibility of its notation whether or not that possibility is ever actualized, no actual notation would be possible. . . . The possibility of inscription is thus a necessary possibility, one that must always be possible.[19]

Habitation is the space of inscription in general, a disruptive act of in-habiting, the spacing out of space from within.[20] Thought generally, inscription is the material support for habitation and signification. No mere question of writing, then, inscription is the mark of the relationship between matter and signification. And in this, architecture becomes the inaugural instant of habitation, and thus an absolutely central subject of consideration. Of crucial importance is the fact that in Lacan's system, architecture, as the inaugural work of art, is organized around a constitutive spatial absence, emptiness. Lacan defines architecture itself in terms of the Thing; architecture is the drapery around the primordial void, housing the unrepresentable Thing. As he explains in the seventh seminar (1959–1960), "We see the link forged between the temple, as a construction around emptiness that designates the place of the Thing, to the figuration of emptiness on the walls [through painting] of this emptiness itself."[21] Considering a primordial vase (not unlike Heidegger's) "as an object made to represent the existence of the emptiness at the center of the real that is called the Thing," Lacan posited that "this emptiness as represented in the representation presents itself as a *nihil*, as nothing. And that is why the potter, just like you to whom I am speaking, creates the vase with his hand around this emptiness, creates it, just like the mythical creator, *ex nihilo,* starting with a hole."[22] Though the Thing can never be captured by the signifier, the thread of the *sinthome* encircles the Thing repeatedly, incessantly, wrapping the emptiness in its skeins. The singular insistence of this drive demands the diversity of the new and persists as an impetus for creation. Derrida too found it necessary to theorize emptiness. In his essays of the 1960s and 1970s he set forth many of the interrelations that would come to define poststructuralism and organize theoretical discourse in architecture for the next three decades. These include the complex interactions between form and meaning, between structure and supplement, the ontic and the ontological, speech and inscription, all of which continue to concern us today. Derrida's early essays (before he began to use the term *deconstruction*) introduce the now familiar conceptual assemblage of emptiness, excess, and deferral, which Derrida first formulates as the "essential nothing," the "*pure absence*—not the absence of this or that, but the absence of everything in which all presence is announced."[23] Emptiness, Derrida argues, must be anterior to any existence or any oeuvre; it is that which can be continuously added to, that which can contain excess. Such is the precondition for the "pure text," the "book about nothing" that Gustave Flaubert dreamed of—"a book without exterior attachments, which would be held together by the inner force of its style . . . a book which would have almost no subject"—indeed, a text analogous to the object of autonomy and disciplinary specificity sought by our architectural predecessors.[24] The theorist or critic cannot approach a work about nothing directly. While the determinate emptiness must be acknowledged "as that which constitutes the specificity of object" around which critical discourse circles, this emptiness is not knowable as such.[25] We can conceive nothingness only as Lacan did architecture: as a kind of drapery wrapped around the void of becoming, the pure *à venir.* "This nothing *itself,*" writes Derrida, "is determined by disappearing. It is the transition to the determination of the work as the disguising of its origin. But the origin is possible and conceivable only in disguise" (*sous le travestissement*).[26] The relationship of the disguise to passage, the *transition* to the determination of the work, is the crux. A formalist-structuralist account of a work (which is the main target of Derrida's critique) relies on geometry, diagram, and a totality that is always concrete. Schematized and spatialized, its field is divested of its forces: "Meaning is rethought as form; and structure is the *formal* unity of form and meaning."[27] In contrast, the determination of the work about nothing must actualize the excess of possibilities veiled in the said transition to the work's determination (its becoming), and it must do so first by losing its origin, leaving structure as but a ghostly trace: "Thus, the relief and design of structures appears more clearly when content, which is the living energy of meaning, is neutralized. Somewhat like the architecture of an uninhabited or deserted city, reduced to its skeleton by some catastrophe of nature or art. A city no longer inhabited, not simply left behind, but haunted by meaning and culture. This state of being haunted, which keeps the city from returning to nature, is perhaps the general mode of presence or absence of the thing itself in pure language."[28] Here Derrida shifts his notion of spacing toward a marking of the inhabitation of the site by prefigural mnemonic systems out of which epistemic and aesthetic frames emerge—the skeleton as diagram of historical forces, for example. The essential nothing, as has been said, cannot be apprehended as such; nothing is not an idea, nor an object, but a haunting. After reflecting on creative writing and the endemic absence of a beginning idea—that is, "the consciousness of having something to say as the consciousness of nothing"—Derrida declares that this perception of the not-quite-nothingness, like a haunting vacancy, is the very condition from which all expression arises and proceeds:

> It is the consciousness of nothing, upon which all consciousness of something enriches itself, takes on meaning and shape. And upon whose basis all speech can be brought forth. For the thought of the thing as *what* it *is* has already been confused with the experience of pure speech; and this experience has been confused with experience *itself.* Now, does not pure speech require inscription, somewhat in the manner that Leibnizian essence requires existence and pushes on towards the world like power towards the act?[29]

The term *pure speech* (*pure parole*) should be understood as applying to all forms of expression, not just the spoken word. And the phrases "pushes on" (*se presse*) and "power" endow pure speech with a vector and force. It is inscription that articulates the actualization of the virtual force and form of expression—the force and signification that structuralism lacks. As inscription disguises its origin, its letters are perceptible only as material marks of a voice forever lost, its force disseminated from the emptiness. But inscription is also pure possibility. Derrida is aware of a certain anguish that accompanies not the writer but the transition itself, the passage, an anguish toward actualizing the virtuality of *pure parole.* For pure speech is also "a kind of autonomous overassemblage of meanings, a power of pure equivocality," and many media may supply the surface for inscription.[30]

"It need scarcely be said, that an Epitaph presupposes a Monument, upon which it is to be engraven." So wrote Wordsworth, who saw in inscription something both commonplace and profound. As Wordsworth scholar Cynthia Chase argues, "Monument" here is "flatly literal" and indeterminant. On it the inscription performs rather than describes; it presents "an *indeterminably meaningful* mark, rather than a meaning or a sign."[31] The materiality of the inscription does not refer to or mean anything beyond what the mark itself already manifests; its material power is the antithesis of verbal presence. The monument is presupposed because the inscription must find the material support of a system of signification, not a referent. It is that system that is presupposed. The monument—its surface, its matter—is nothing more or less than the anteriority of that system, pure and necessary. "All positing is presupposing of already existent signification."[32] "It does something very different," writes De Man. "Unlike the here and now of speech, the here and now of the inscription is neither false nor misleading." Rather, the here and now of inscription "is undeniable as well as totally blank."[33] Inscription is the actualization of virtual force and the condition of sense in architecture. In the architecture presented in this book, inscriptions appear variously: an irruption of excessive signification; a brute and mute materialism; a withdrawal into the archaic or into primal, earthy elements; simple, halting primary shapes; staccato repetitions; and random arrays of remnants and fragments. Our first examples:

The Truffle, by Ensamble Studio, is among the most radical of recent experimental projects—radical in the sense of roots and beginnings, inherent and fundamental. It is radical insofar as it forces us straight to the question, *Architecture: is it happening?* In an essay on the subject of the sublime in art, Jean-François Lyotard argues that this is the question of the sublime: *Arrive-t-il? Is it happening?* The sublime is not an object; it is an event, it is the now of the event. The happening is a coming into appearance, a thing coming into itself. The architecture that we see is happening, now. The event of the sublime arrives before it is identified by cognition; it is anterior to any conceptual frame adequate to its understanding. Our first encounter with the Truffle is a similarly raw event, an affective experience of being unable to account for this thing we had expected to scan as an architectural object. *Is this it? Is architecture happening?* The question marks a failure to conceptualize the nature of what only later will have made itself known. As Lyotard writes,

> That it happens "precedes," so to speak, the question pertaining to what happens. Or rather, the question precedes itself, because "that it happens" is the question relevant as event, and it "then" pertains to the event that has just happened. The event happens as a question mark "before" happening as a question. *It happens* is rather "in the first place" *is it happening, is this it, is it possible?* Only "then" is any mark determined by the questioning: is this or that happening, is it this or something else, is it possible that this or that?[34]

With the Truffle, the feeling of surprise and wonder that we have encountered an object somehow meaningful is disturbed by the attendant anxiety that, even having committed ourselves to an occurrence of significance, nothing will come to pass. Thus does the sublime implicate the question of Being itself. The first encounter with the earth-laden lump is not a positive judgment of the type, *This is beautiful*. It is rather a suspension of judgment and a suspension of time—*Is it happening?*—that threatens us with formlessness and ontological dislocation. And yet to leave that question open is architecture's only chance to assert itself, to found itself in the very self-asking of the question, *Architecture: is it happening?* Architecture is the art of the beginning of Being. The Truffle puts the viewer directly in touch with the beginning of things: earth and air, hydration and heat, metabolic and ecological processes, encounters of matter. Because form is suppressed, we are more attentive to materials. The focus on the determinant role of base material is an architectural critique both of idealist intentionality and the mechanical empiricism of data-driven parametricism. It puts forward a conception of materiality as brute, contingent, and obdurate. Here matter bypasses tropological or typological organization (phenomenality) and goes directly into the *jouissance* of sensation and affect. Thus we have constructed a radical rift between an architecture of the representational (notwithstanding the metaphorical title, the Truffle) and an inscription of the material. Form in this case derives from the tug of gravity and push of hydrostatic pressure, the exchange of heat between two materials, the contingency of the way hay and dirt fall into place. The "thinginess" of the architectural object comes from these immanent conditions and can no longer be interpreted as self-contained but rather is always in dynamic relation with what is outside its own limits. (We may think of Hegel's understanding of the brute exigencies and externality of architecture at its historical beginning.[35]) How, from within this flat and rude order of being, does it happen that architecture comes into appearance? Ensamble Studio explains:

> The Truffle is a piece of nature built with earth, full of air. A space within a stone that sits on the ground and blends with the territory. It camouflages, by emulating the processes of mineral formation in its structure, and integrates with the natural environment, complying with its laws. *To build it, we made a hole* in the ground, piling up on its perimeter the topsoil removed, and we obtained a retaining dike without mechanical consistency. Then, we materialized the air building a volume with hay bales and flooded the space between the earth and the built air to solidify it. The poured mass concrete wrapped the air and protected itself with the ground. Time passed and we removed the earth discovering an amorphous mass. The earth and the concrete exchanged their properties. The land provided the concrete with its texture and color, its form and its essence, and concrete gave the earth its strength and internal structure. *But what we had created was not yet architecture*, we had fabricated a stone. *We made a few cuts* using quarry machinery to explore its core and discovered its mass inside built with hay, now compressed by the hydrostatic pressure exerted by concrete on the flimsy vegetable structure. To empty the interior, the calf Paulina arrived, and enjoyed the 50 cubic meters of the nicest food, from which she nourished for a year until she left her habitat, already as an adult and weighing 300 kilograms. She had eaten the interior volume, and space appeared for the first time, restoring the architectural condition of the truffle after having been a shelter for the animal and the vegetable mass for a long time.[36]

It is an extraordinary, almost biblical story of creation—of *that it happens*, of how it is that architecture comes into appearance, into being. In the beginning was a hole. In Lacan's reading of Heidegger, the hole is required for any act of creation. In his essay "The Thing," Heidegger uses the primordial pot to explore Being, non-Being, and creation ex nihilo. The pot does not originate in the forming of its clay surround; rather, as we have seen, it is the bringing forth of the void that will hold the fullness subsequently enacted. Lacan develops this image of the clay pot (he calls it a vase) enclosing the hole to describe the empty latency that is the beginning of architecture, the first art. "To put it briefly, primitive architecture can be defined as something organized around emptiness . . . and it is the true meaning of all architecture."[37] He takes note of the primitive marks on the walls of a cavern and from there, architecture, which leads to the invention of perspective and anamorphosis:

> From that point on one is entangled in a knot which seems to flee increasingly from the meaning of this emptiness. And I believe the Baroque return to the play of forms, to all manner of devices, including anamorphosis, is an effort to restore the true meaning of artistic inquiry; artists use the discovery of the property of lines to make something emerge that is precisely there where one has lost one's bearings or, strictly speaking, nowhere. . . . You introduce the idea of the Thing and the Non-Thing. It is, if you like, true that the Thing is also the Non-Thing.[38]

The Thing that came before nothing and is nothing but inscription stands in a long line of architecture, from the hieroglyphs on Hegel's pyramid to the lines of Brunelleschi's perspective to the Baroque's vectors. Ensamble Studio's hut comes last in this lineage yet seems to reach back to something even more archaic. In each case, a hole is marked at the center. The hole is the same hole that enables the knot at the center of the RSI to exist. "But what we had created was not yet architecture," Ensamble Studio recognizes. Emptiness cannot become architecture until the hole is made perceivable *as holed*. In order to produce an experience of the construction as something other than concrete wrapped around air and hay, to begin to frame a Symbolic domain, to close in on its legibility and understanding *as architecture*, some element must, paradoxically, be excluded—cut out, subtracted, removed. The vertical cut across the concrete rock, which creates a planar face and an aperture opening up the interior, is the inscription that allows difference to arise and individuation of other architectural elements to appear. Once the cut is made, the plane becomes a facade; once one surface is a facade, other surfaces become walls whose character can be judged (stacked, layered, or merely floated); once vertical surfaces become walls—once, that is, they have been constructed as elevations of a constructed object—then the object may also be seen as sitting on a base. Kant's enormously suggestive notion of purposiveness without purpose is brought to mind as the lump begins to shine (*erscheinen*), if not with beauty (certainly not) then nevertheless with the sense that it is the earth itself that has been brought to life. Before the cut, what has come into being as a theoretical object was not distinguishable from its site, nor its parts differentiated from one another. In psychoanalytic terms, it was in the domain of a pure Imaginary, the partitioned and spectacularized register of identification and immanence—pre-Symbolic, before the signifier, filled with babble, muttering, and rumbling. Architecture does not appear without the signifying cut, nor is the site brought forth but by the interruption of this singular mark. The cut as signifier organizes the materials into a state that has both absences and presences. Differentiations (not plenitudes) can thus be assigned; a code can be ciphered. This move toward the Symbolic (toward architecture's rules and regulations) strengthens the Imaginary. Indeed, the overlap of the Imaginary and the Symbolic produces a site of *jouis-sens*, of meaning and memory swallowed up by enjoyment.[39] The cut is the necessary artifice, the setting up of relations of difference that vibrate and animate traditional Symbolic structures. It is an instance of Heidegger's worlding of the earth, the nexus of immanence and exteriority that characterizes the Thing itself. At a different register, Johnston Marklee's Vault House begins with an irreducible architectural unit—the vaulted volume—and develops it into an array of variations stacked, layered, and intersecting inside a rectangular solid. The design involves Boolean operations of packing and subtracting, sliding, passing through, and spinning round to manipulate the vault unit as a way of testing and extending the range of possible elementary sensations hidden in ordinary perception of this ubiquitous architectural figure. At the same time, the ninety-degree rotations in plan, elevation, and section erase from the figures all their functional, constructional, and even perceptual associations. This effect is supported and enhanced by the suppression of frames for apertures and the use of an elastomeric, cementitious wrapper to cover all enclosing surfaces, interior and exterior, thus eliminating the need for any tectonic expression in joints, trims, or textures and rendering the entire "carved" volume scaleless. The vault as volume becomes vault as epigraph, and the vault as signifier becomes almost indistinguishable from the material support of the medium as the hylomorphic separations between figure and medium, ornament and structure, form and matter, all start to collapse, assuring that all we will find on the other side of this signifier is another signifier. The proliferation of vault variations is understood less as an expression of some precoded typology (like a digitally produced version of a vaulted shotgun house, say) and more as a particular, repeated signifier that gives the project its formal consistency while remaining external to phenomenal appearance and empty of any historical, semantic residue. Nevertheless, among the elementary sensations effected by these procedures are the myriad changing views through the house, overlapping and layered contours, the lifting and floating of the vaulted base, light penetrating from unseen wells, and vaulted contours framed against the sky. But these *petites sensations* constitute nothing less than the dematerialization of the phenomenal object, allowing the more radical materiality of the signifier itself to be revealed in its nonphenomenal, unrepresentable, Real dimension.[40] As stylistically opposed as they are, what the Truffle and the Vault House have in common is a search for the preconditions of architectural signification, whether by digging them out from some rudimentary process of making or by digitally capturing a basic architectural algorithm, marking it, and then multiplying and varying it so as to fix what inevitably remains, in both projects, an indeterminate ground. Neither project claims any immediacy of reference or historical precedent that presumes to encode referential meaning. Yet both conjure a certain anteriority, a notion of a preexisting virtual diagram from which architecture emerges. In each, inscription actualizes this diagram in a particular way, revealing the material conditions of possibility for architecture as a system of signification. If in the Truffle, inscription takes the form of a material mark, which is the singular act of cutting and the resultant material signifier, then the vault of the Vault House seems to be a different kind of signifier operating in two distinct modes. On the one hand, there is an almost fanciful array of transformed, shuffled vaults, some flattened against the elevation, others stacked, layered, and extruded in section, all twisted and intersecting to striking visual effect. A formal motif repeats across different instances in the series of vaults, and as the items in the series form a combinatory, the array interacts with the physical context of the project to produce complex views and other contextual effects. These repeated, interrelated signifiers in the series are different from the singular and irreducible signifier, vault, which we might think of as a kind of unary mark or originary signifier that begins and oversees the whole process. While this irreducible element does not, in the first instance, signify anything, it seems wrong to call it an "empty signifier," for it replicates the form of vault, complicates it by pushing it through digital transformations, and implicates the existing context and all its contingencies. These various foldings constitute a spacing in Derrida's sense of the instituted trace of an inhabiting force; the freestanding vault forms are inscribed as traces. But the unary trace is different. It is a protosignifier, a pre-Symbolic mark identical only to itself—a virtuality that is a material potential, a singular condition of possibility, and the stopping point of the combinatory.[41] Lacan makes it clear early in his work that "it is first of all the materiality of the signifier that I have emphasized, that materiality is *singular* in many ways, the first of which is not to allow of partition."[42] We might also think of the singular signifier as a kind of fixity or indivisible kernel that exists before, behind, and beyond the project—something out of our perceptual reach that nevertheless anchors and negates (indeed, anchors by negating) the inevitable dialectical slippages of meaning and incessant substitution of relational signifiers. This unary signifier is a kind of stoppage, existing as a material mark, a spacing, a constitutive kernel of unmeaning—an inscription. In his study of Lacan's status of the Real, Tom Eyers draws a cogent distinction not explicitly made by Lacan between what he calls the "signifier-in-relation," designating the familiar linguistic formulation of meaning, and the "signifier-in-isolation," which exists as a material mark that withdraws from relational meaning. The latter Eyers links especially to the Real, even as it has a particular relation to each register of the RSI:

> In the Imaginary, the withdrawn [isolated] signifier serves to support the movements of primary narcissism; in the Symbolic, the signifier-in-isolation forms the material underside of the signifier-in-relation; and the Real, as the domain of materiality and of the body, functions as the store from which the materiality of the signifier-in-isolation draws. Thus, it is as a signifier-in-isolation that the *sinthome* forms the fourth of the Borromean rings, serving, in its very meaningless insistence, to hold the subject together.[43]

The signifier-in-relation is defined purely by its relations to other signifiers, which operate differentially to produce meaning. The signifier-in-isolation, as a unary trait or glyph isolated from networks of relational meaning, has multiple instantiations, which culminate in the *sinthome*.[44] It is a powerful distinction, and it encapsulates much of what I have proposed thus far about the status of the cut in the Truffle and the vault of the Vault House, our first two examples of architectural inscription. The concept of the signifier-in-relation is familiar to architecture from the linguistics-based theories of the 1970s concerning meaning and representation; it follows the Saussurean axiom that in language there are no positive terms, only relations and differences of signifiers. The signifier-in-relation is associated with the scenes and encounters of the Imaginary and the rules and logics of the Symbolic and inaugurates all the consequences of what we understand by the production of meaning—the authority of precedent, the persistence of type, the sign as signifier and signified unit, the power of representation. But to reduce architecture to the production of sense at the level of linguistic expression (the speaking voice) is to miss the more fundamental, material inscription of which speech is but an epiphenomenon. The other sort of signifier we have considered, the signifier-in-isolation, does not accede merely to the epistemological sedimentations and relational logics of the Symbolic or to the anxious panoply of Imaginary effects (though it touches these too). It is withdrawn from relations of signification and persists through the Real, which provides the subject with consistency even as it dislocates and disrupts meaning. To be clear, I do not want to attribute to inscription the same status of some pure geometrical element or formal type, though certain aspects of these generative notions do come to mind. Nor do I want it understood as Graham Harman's withdrawn object; inscription is not a way out of architecture.[45] An architectural inscription is better thought of as an outline of architecture, a diagram, a contour against a necessary background but where the background is integral to its figure. Architectural inscription can make powerful but previously indiscernible disciplinary latencies appear, anamorphically as it were, at the edges. In this characterization, there is an invocation of a field and the mark, a topographics of the virtual, a spacing that places us between the sensible and the intelligible. It is not the shape of a thing but a diagram of matter and signification. It is the Real in view. Eyers declares that "when language is conceived in these terms, it should be understood less as the extra-material 'representation' of matter and more as the very 'thing' of human experience itself, as mysterious and insistent as any previous theorization of matter."[46] Substitute "architecture" for "language" and I am making that same claim. Much follows from this claim. Architecture encloses the emptiness where the Thing appears, the void that generates the sublime event. But the sublime is not a magnificent conceptual formulation; it is rather what De Man calls "the prosaic materiality" of the inscription that enacts the sublime. This primary function of architecture can be understood through the mechanism of the RSI. Though the Real, home of the Thing, is strictly unrepresentable, even inaccessible, it nevertheless can be woven into the Imaginary and the Symbolic by the architectural inscription as *sinthome*. Architecture's own elements, understood as glyphs, traits, and *objets a* become singular bits of the Real that vibrate with vitality.[47] I am suggesting that the immanent pleasures of the sensorium brought about by the Truffle and the almost mathematical transcendence of form in the Vault House generate powerful affects that are singularly architectural. Lacan begins to bring it to a point for us in the seventh seminar. Before his analysis of the potter and the vase, before his discussion of the origin of the work of architecture as enclosing the Thing, he tells the story of a collection of matchboxes in the home of the surrealist poet Jacques Prévert. We can read the story and, for the matchbox, substitute the vault:

> The match boxes appeared as follows: they were all the same and were laid out in an extremely agreeable way that involved each one being so close to the one next to it that the little drawer was slightly displaced. As a result, they were all threaded together so as to form a continuous ribbon that ran along the mantelpiece, climbed the wall, extended to the molding, and climbed down again next to the door. I don't say that it went on to infinity, but it was extremely satisfying from an ornamental point of view. . . . This arrangement demonstrated that a match box isn't simply something that has a certain utility, that it isn't even a type in the Platonic sense, an abstract match box, that the match box all by itself is a thing with all its coherence of being. The wholly gratuitous,

> proliferating, superfluous, and quasi-absurd character of this collection pointed to its thingness as match box. Thus the collector found his motive in this form of apprehension that concerns less the match box than the Thing that subsists in a match box.[48]

In a strikingly architectural framing of the question (a prosaic box enclosing the primordial void), Lacan asserts that the point of Prévert's effort is neither function nor typology but *thingness*, and furthermore that it concerns "*the Thing* that subsists in a matchbox," the same Thing that is produced and enclosed by the original work of architecture. The effort reveals "that a box of matches is not simply an object, but that, in the form of an *Erscheinung*, as it appeared in its truly imposing multiplicity, it may be a Thing."[49] The matchbox, and so the vault, prosaic though it is but understood now as a signifier-in-isolation, is thus a trace of the Real, which conveys a specific *jouissance*, one at the intersection of the Symbolic and the Real. This *jouissance* is perhaps best understood as the necessity of the signifier to repeat but at the same time to withdraw from meaningful, fully cognizable relations. Consider another example:

> A quick drive around neighborhoods such as Peachtree Hills, Cabbagetown, and Midtown demonstrates stylistic differences in the domestic architecture of Atlanta. Arguably the single most common element of these houses is the roof. Whether located in English Avenue, Old Fourth Ward, or Ansley Park, shared rooflines crisscross neighborhood boundaries. Ordinary and simplistic, yet highly repetitive, gable and hip roofs dominate the scene while butterfly and mansard roofs represent a rarer species. Dormers, A-frame, and shed roofs are combined to make a complex system of functional rooftops with countless variations.
>
> These copy-paste forms not only populate the housing stock but represent house figures and house shapes widely accepted by the public.[50]

In the project Domestic Hats, Jennifer Bonner of MALL reads the roofs of Atlanta's neighborhoods as symptoms of particular domesticities. The roofs of Cabbagetown, for example, top the shotgun houses and simple cottages of the former mill village, while the roofs of wealthy neighborhoods like Buckhead are often ostentatiously complex. Domestic Hats appropriates parts of roofs (dormers, hips, crickets, gables, etc.) and merges them, irrespective of their originating contexts, through Boolean operations. What results is not a building like the Truffle or the Vault House, but a series of models, which, as Stan Allen reminds us, are "not constructed: they are output, that is to say, monolithic and singular." Moreover, these models are "insistently object-like" and yet retain "the conceptual power of the scientific model, that is to say, the ability to figure and fix future forms and patterns."[51]

The resulting signifier—let's just call it "hat"—is a reinscription of an inscription (insofar as the original symptoms are themselves inscriptions), which causes a certain disconnection and isolation of the signifier, abstracting it away from any regime of meaning or possibility of interpretation. And yet something of the symptom remains, insofar as hat is a signifier that, as Lacan says, "does not cease to write itself," that returns incessantly and inexorably. It is evident most obviously in the obsessive repetition of the hats but also in their ungainly size and lack of detail in the foam models, which give them a slightly untoward presence. Rather than constrain the roof to its "proper" role of enhancing a determinate plan through dormers and ridges, the hat overtakes the entire project, including all the volumetric twists and strains; any plan or even sectional characteristic is formed completely by the modelling of the hat.[52] But in the end, the ultimate, inescapably symptomatic object is the large aggregated lump that results from fusing heaps of wirecutter waste and presenting the results as the remainder of the entire project, the final hat. Except that it will not go through our perceptual apparatus as such, as hat; it might well have been litter (or a letter).[53] As signifier-in-isolation, it just remains, thing-like. In the symptom, the signifier is tied to *jouissance*, as we have seen—*f(x)* being the mechanism, the *only* mechanism, by which the symptom can be deciphered. *Jouissance* is a corporeal energy; it cannot be formalized as a phenomenon, yet it echoes in the perceiver as a kind of anxious, even painful otherness attending to the pleasure of the symptom. The binding of the signifier to *jouissance* inevitably alters the signifier, removing it from the chain of endless substitutions, couplings, and decouplings. Think again of the matchbox story. The investment of *jouissance* transforms the signifier from an ordinary element of differentiation belonging to a structure of relation into a singular, self-identical, vibrating glyph from the Real—a signifier-in-isolation. In Bonner's project, hat is neither a signifier that has a referent in an actual roof nor even a signifier-in-relation that produces a typology of roofs but rather a symptomal inscription beyond any tectonic, stylistic, or typological sense. Indeed, it should be understood as that which is fundamentally anterior to reference and outside of sense. Hat does not function meaningfully in accordance with the rules that govern the production of meaning. Instead, it functions materially. It is in this way that architectural inscription, understood through the concept of the signifier-in-isolation, can be seen as constituting a piece of the architectural Real. I have presented the vault and the roof as signifiers isolated in their material element, modulated by *jouissance*, and moving through their Symbolic-Imaginary support toward contact with the Real, the ever-renewed source of possibilities for architecture. In this system, the vault and the roof are self-identical glyphs (analogous to the triglyphs in the antique system of ordination)

—irreducible inscriptions, between the sensible and the intelligible, supporting the emergence of new forms and significations. This is the working of the architectural *sinthome* in the era of the deflated Symbolic. In this system, the grid is the perfect figure of the architectural Symbolic. The grid announces and insists on architectural authority and autonomy, establishing a distinct spatial order and a differential across the contexts over which it is laid. And yet it is almost infinitely accommodating of the otherness of all the external fragments that it appropriates, incorporates, and temporarily unites. It exhibits both a hegemonic, territorializing power and a sublimatory capacity. To begin a project with a grid, then to formally disrupt it by adding, subtracting, or otherwise transforming it, and finally to follow through on some of the possible implications of the transformation—this is a classic formal exercise in architecture. What is new about Noise, Pt. 3, a project by Michelle Chang of JaJa Co, is the nature of the disruption to the grid. Using Perlin noise, Chang propagates an array of points across a two-by-three grid, allowing each point to be the locus of a gradient force. Combined, the points create what Chang calls "a web of modulating intensities that give the effect of a continuous, irregular field."[54] The geometric grid is crumpled by this virtual, flowing field, twisted out shape as if by a storm of corrosive synthetic dust. Following this, an image or simulation of a plan diagram is produced from this aleatoric transformational process—this is the first stage of Chang's inscription. Insofar as the distorting virtual noise is produced by a procedural texture—that is, a graphic effect generated by a mathematical algorithm rather than some sort of stored image or precoded software—Chang's plan diagrams for Noise, Pt. 3, are, strictly speaking, not conventional architectural drawings but mathematized data storage formats, transformed into nonsignifying marks—glyphs from the digital unconscious.[55] Simply by virtue of the sheer amount of data transformation involved, they are different in kind both from the "naturally" randomized patterns of wall- and window-like elements of the Truffle and from the digitally merged volumes of the Vault House. But more important is the fact that the diagrams store microspatial accidents and stochastic patterns, rather than a fixed figure like a vault. What appear in Chang's "drawings" as walls and apertures are, in fact, a different kind of signifier: traces of the signal-to-noise ratio, as it were, that summarize a myriad of overtone fluctuations emanating from the original grid. Yet they encode nothing and are encoded by no one. The designing subject is effectively eliminated during this preliminary stage of the process, producing an instructional, operational image—indeed, an architectural "plan," but one with, as yet, no architectural intention. Friedrich Kittler argues, with regard to sound, that "ever since the invention of the phonograph there has been writing without a subject."[56] The apparatus of phonography captures background and bodily noise regardless of signification—the materiality of the voice rather than the content of the message. And yet the destruction of the subject in sound recording paradoxically occurs *through* the body, or as Kittler calls it, following Lacan, the "bodily real," a body without Imaginary fullness or Symbolic completeness. While the parts of this morcellated body interact with the space, the ambient noise in the room, and the recording device itself, its very corporeal presence produces its own grunts and stutters that are highly specific but uncontrollable. "The phonograph stores indices rather than poems. And these indices speak precisely to the extent that their sender cannot manipulate them."[57] Analogously, Chang's aleatory architecture is radically embedded in the machinery of its own production and engulfed by noise, such that the very materiality of the originating architectural "body" (the grid) and its reinscription assure the dissolution of conventional architectural meaning and inaugurate a new interpretive process. Kittler aligns the materiality of noise with the Lacanian Real, which, I want to suggest, is also entirely compatible with De Man's difficult concept of the materiality of inscription. Without venturing into the complications of De Man's concept-defining disagreements with Michael Riffaterre's semiotic method of reading poetry (which, De Man argues, misses the fact that inscription "undoes the distinction between reference and signification on which all semiotic systems . . . depend"), we can nevertheless take a look at the evidence for De Man's claims about inscription itself.[58] For De Man, a descriptive reading of the structure of meaning in a poem is faulty because it rests on the assumption that reality is a "determined, stable principle."[59] While such a reading may even dispense with referentiality, it still assumes the phenomenal existence of the poem's signifying elements and their availability to cognitive capture. According to Riffaterre's reading of Victor Hugo's poem "Écrit sur la vitre d'une fenêtre flamande," for example, the ringing of bells evokes images of a dancer descending the "invisible cristal" stair of time while the very surface of the Flemish windowpane on which the poem is supposedly written becomes a phenomenalized metaphor for the linking of mind and sense. Such imagery, for De Man, makes a semiotic approach to the poem "highly effective as a descriptive discipline, but at the cost of understanding."[60] Ultimately, what eludes Riffaterre in Hugo's poem is just what its title indicates: that the letters themselves are "written on the glass of a Flemish window," which De Man calls "the materiality of an inscription."[61] The marks do not function as signs; they may be significant but of what is indeterminate. Unlike speech, "the prosaic materiality of the letter" is a "here and now" that is "undeniable as well as totally blank."[62] It is in the Real, beyond both the visible and the legible—a virtual "there and then" that is actualized in the "here and now" of a reading performance. But there is more. De Man's materiality of inscription comes with a certain kind of performative power, a way of seeing that he calls "*material* vision" (the emphasis being his).[63] He draws an example from Kant's discussion of the sublime that involves a sighting of the heavens and the ocean. Kant instructs that we must be able to find the sublime "as the poets do it"—that is, to find it "merely by what appears to the eye" (*was der Augenschein zeigt*).[64] De Man excerpts the following passage from Kant's reflections:

> If then we call the sight of the starry heaven *sublime*, we must not place at the basis of our judgment concepts of worlds inhabited by rational beings, and regard the bright points, with which we see the space above us filled, as their suns moving in circles purposively fixed with reference to them; but we must regard it, just as we see it, as a distant, all-embracing vault.[65]

Material vision is "the only word that comes to mind," writes De Man, as he translates *Augenschein*. He insists that this vision is performative, though not phenomenal or metaphorical, or even mindful, and is based on Kant's radical "formal materialism." De Man: "In the same way and to the same extent that this vision is purely material, devoid of any reflexive or intellectual complication, it is also purely formal, devoid of any semantic depth and reducible to the formal mathematization or geometrization of pure optics."[66] His allusion to the geometry of pure opticality is an important abstraction. Kant's poets see neither shelter nor dwelling, neither type nor trope; their architectonic perception is of a "flat third-person world." Starry heaven and ocean as a vault and floor are a priori, before any understanding. But *Augenschhein* is not a metamorphosis of the vault into something significant; the poet "does not see prior to dwelling, but merely sees."[67] "A pre-seeing seeing," J. Hillis Miller calls it, "a tautological eye eyeing."[68] But De Man goes further, raising the question of "how this materiality is then to be understood in linguistic terms."[69] He answers with what he, following Lacan, calls the "letter," which very much resembles what Eyers calls Lacan's signifier-in-isolation. As De Man helpfully explicates, "The play of the letter and the syllable, the way of saying . . . as opposed to what is being said . . . as meaning-producing tropes are replaced by the fragmentation of sentences and propositions into discrete words, or the fragmentation of words into syllables and finally letters."[70] It is this operation of the letter that Lacan sees occurring in *jouissance*: the dissolution of the poem into letters. De Man calls it many things, but his most powerful expression is "the undoing of cognition and its replacement by the uncontrollable power of the letter as inscription."[71] Is this not precisely what happens in Chang's shattering of the grid into senseless glyphs? While it would be incorrect to identify Kant's architectonic in Chang's project, or in any of the others we have considered here, nevertheless whatever it is that happens in and happens *as* Kant's *Augenschein*, it happens in each of these works. In his analysis of De Man's essay on Kant, Andrzej Warminski cogently concludes that "what the poets do is not even so much to *see* according to the *Augenschein* as to read an inscription, dismembered sentences, words, syllables, letters—like the illegible letter (or all too interpretable hieroglyph?) of the arching line of the sky on top of the straight or squiggly line of the ocean."[72] Or, one might add, like the twisted and crumpled lines of the architectural grid. To read the line of the sky or the ocean as "illegible letter" is to insist on the excessive, disarticulating and rearticulating power of the *sinthome*. Similarly, the very unrecognizability and recalcitrance of Chang's new image-grid, as *sinthome*, becomes potential for a more fully developed material. What material vision registers is the failure of representation and its displacement by the purely formal materiality of the architectural signifiers, the architectonics of the *sinthome*. This distorted grid, which is the first processual phase of Noise, Pt. 3, comprises layers of inscription on different media, from the digitally imposed texturing of the grid to the image of an architectural drawing. The process follows the same logic as De Man's argument, from the mathematization and geometrization of the letter to its dismemberment into squiggly lines. But the processes of the project do not stop there. Having ripped the plan from space and time and folded it into a self-enclosed world all its own, Chang then reinscribes the previously inscribed forms in a second-level, cross-media operation of specifically architectural design. The already processed glyph assemblages further twist and combine into a functional domestic apparatus complete with cooking counters, baths, fireplaces, and a beautifully wrought stair. Design reterritorializes noise; it presents the unsymbolizable as architecture, which, again, is the vocation of the *sinthome*. This is an important distinction. With Noise, Pt. 3, Chang does not construct symbolic architecture but rather presents the unsymbolizable as architecture, as the Thing of the void. Architecture has transcended the meaning of its elements as walls, windows, roofs, and vaults are broken apart and scattered across the object. It has found that the privation of reference leads inevitably, if paradoxically, to an assertion of excess and potential, to Derrida's famous "overabundance" of the signifier or De Man's "uncontrollable power of the letter."[73] Finally, it is in the mode of reading demanded by such an object, in the *Augenschien* or *material* vision, that the object "has been raised to the dignity of the Thing"—not as representation (for there is no signifier for the Thing) but as the very thing of experience itself, recalcitrant and mysterious but nevertheless as insistent as the poets' encounter with the all-embracing vault. Let me try to say this another way. Though "glitch" is an already domesticated term for a malfunction (noise in the system), it is nevertheless helpful to borrow a conceptual point from glitch aesthetics: "A glitch can be understood as *the residue of an impossibility*—an indicator that the void of the Real threatening our imaginary fantasy has once again been kept at bay."[74] This issue should be familiar by now. The Real shatters meaning. So it would be easy to try to install the glitch in the register of the Real, as a failure of legibility. But a glitch is not a failed moment of data registration; it is rather a proper registration of "improper" data, the impasse of formalization brought about when software is unable to treat disrupted data or noise in any other than the "correct" way—that is, to produce it in all its perversely coded distortions. Something like this happens with the aleatory data of Noise, Pt. 3, is forced through the final media transfer into a functioning building. For data can be processed as building only in the forms that the medium of building already has available for data. And that processing will inevitably be disruptive—not simply glitchy but also, I am suggesting, creative and enabling. Perhaps the most satisfying, if nevertheless startling, of these final moments of inscription in Noise, Pt. 3, are the cracks and tears produced by the misalignments of the lower and upper floors of the house. Walls pull away from one another, window heads are clipped and rotated out of alignment, the door is nothing but a gaping remnant. Misshapen gridlines in plan produce protrusions and jagged edges in three dimensions—all incised tracks of architecture struggling with digital noise. At the same time, the horizontal line between the lower and upper floors functions as a datum against which these accidents are registered. The enjoyment that each inscription grants is a *jouissance* intrinsic to architecture, having to do with an intelligence and a competence that is specifically architectural. One can be open to new enjoyments in architecture only if one is always already enjoying the system within which architecture occurs. Such is the work of the architectural *sinthome* as it reaches into the architecturalization of the Real.

So where does this leave us? In these four recent works of experimental architecture there are so many striking commonalities, along with significant differences, that one cannot escape the temptation to try to sort out the tendencies into a system. First, in every case, the notion of the signified has dwindled from its traditional status as a carrier of meaning, giving way to a singular signifier as a mark in a material matrix. In the Truffle, this is most apparent in the cut (the paradigmatic inscription) and its result: the cleft face and opening of the concrete, which enter into and produce the combinatory assemblage that is the architectural object. It is also true of the Vault House and Domestic Hats, which obliterate reference through formal operations that repeat and transform a single element, vault or roof. In the latter cases, however, the inscription persists apart from the networks of relations (including site and program) that would render it conducive to meaning; it is the signifier-in-isolation. Moreover, in every case, the respective inscriptions that trigger the event of architecture's appearance (cut, vault, hat, and the scattered remnants of a grid) are sustainable only if, prior to the event, a specific material diagram of signification is presupposed—an architectural RSI, if you will, anterior to the mark. Think back to Wordsworth, whom I will paraphrase: an inscription presupposes a material support and a system of signification, upon which it is inscribed. Or perhaps better, in the words of the editors of the book *Material Events*, "Whatever *inscription* designates, it conjures sheer anteriority. It does not deliver us to any immediacy of reference, to any historical narrative that presumes to encode such, but to mnemonic programs that appear to precede and legislate these."[75] Here, then, with what are usually taken as fixed narratives and memories rendered virtual (anterior), are also the differences in the ways the projects actualize the virtual. First, in the Truffle, the materiality of the cut is raw and immanent—its past seems archaic but its future opens onto explorations of the technics of suspension, preparatory to the possibility of an event. While the vault and roof, though certainly producing corporeal effects, transcend what can be embodied, even as they demand a way of seeing that De Man called "*material* vision," a way of registering the materiality of just what the eye sees *prior to* phenomenality or cognition. And furthermore, we saw that Domestic Hats contains something inscrutable beyond the formal composition: a surplus mood or resonance, a hauntedness that is particular and distinctive yet held just out of our perceptual reach. In Noise, Pt. 3, by contrast, the signifier is so disrupted by aleatoric graphic interference that the jittery materiality of the signifier-in-isolation threatens any putative transcendence of its indeterminate signification. At the same time, Noise, Pt. 3 has little of the Truffle's earthy immanence, even though, like Truffle, its stochastic processes determine its form. The noise-infected grid is not so much a geometrical presence as a kind of protosignifier, or even the absence of the very possibility of substantive presence—all of which results in a buzzing swarm of signifiers detached from any relations, remnants and scatters arranged only according to their sheer materiality. And finally, in all four works, materiality appears as event (again invoking the virtual)—a shift, in De Man's words, "from trope to performance" that is punctual and irreversible, a happening, "an *occurrence*, which has the materiality of something that actually happens, that actually occurs. And there, the thought of material occurrence, something that occurs materially, that leaves a trace on the world, that does something to the world as such."[76] Let me propose, then, that we can discern some preliminary patterns in the tendencies exhibited across these projects by plotting them along an axis of signification that ranges between the two differential terms of *immanent processes* and *transcendent form*. This doubled formulation, itself already a kind of pseudo-chiastic structure, is a fundamental dialectic within architecture, operative in theory at least since Hegel's argument that architecture is the art of the external because it proclaims its own externality as a way of transcending that externality.[77] Moreover, in the context of our consideration of the RSI, this axis of signification gives us a first piece to begin to construct a semiotic square of the sort developed by Lacan's contemporary A. J. Greimas to analyze relationships among positions in a discursive field. The semiotic square begins with a binary opposition of two "contraries" along a "complex" axis. In our case these are immanent processes (*S*) and transcendent form (-*S*). Across from that axis, each term is negated by a "contradictory" ($\bar{S}$ and -$\bar{S}$ placed diagonally opposite it along a second, "neutral" axis (which we will soon come to in our own examples). The semiotic square logically exhausts the possibilities of opposition, but Greimas insists that it also goes beyond binarity and pure logic to account for signification. By inserting the Greimas diagram into our analysis of the RSI, we can elicit "entanglements" from the square. For example, Greimas himself suggests that Lacan's Imaginary and Symbolic can be related to the complex axis, with the symptom in the third position and the Real in the fourth along the neutral axis, thus thwarting the illusory closure of the "elementary structure of signification."[78] I will not strictly follow his suggestion in what follows. Nevertheless, combined with the RSI, the semiotic square will help us arrive at a preliminary and tentative cartography of the field of architectural inscriptions comprised by this volume, which I have taken the four projects to represent. In our first position of the diagram (*S*), immanent processes, the viewer's experience takes place within particular, contingent, and materially determined limits and operations. In its contrary (-*S*), transcendent form, the viewer stands back from the immediate object and her own intimate and practical relation to it and sees in the project an iterative formal structure. It seems to me that while none of our examples fits exactly into either of these two generic categories, the Truffle tends toward immanent processes and the Vault House toward transcendent form. And in general, as we pull out and look at the larger field of projects *Inscriptions* presents, we can see operational signifiers like cut, cast, pour, pile, and stack as more immanent and Boolean operations performed on geometric forms and patterns, as well as primordial typologies and abstract shapes, as having a degree of transcendence. If we arrange the Truffle and the Vault House somewhere along this immanent processes–transcendent form axis, other features come into play. First, the Imaginary and Symbolic registers of Lacan's RSI appear to align, not precisely but resonantly, with these two categories, as we might expect based on Greimas's suggestion. For example, the Truffle manifests the initial binary organizations characteristic of the Imaginary, such as inside/outside and subject/other, in the uneasiness of our first encounter with the project, in the uncertainty we feel about the identity of such an *objet trouvé*. And as we have noted, there is a particular corporeal *jouis-sens* at work in the Truffle, a kind of *jouissance* that occurs in the Borromean knot at the intersection of the Imaginary and the Symbolic.[79] The Vault House, meanwhile, lands closer to the Symbolic, insofar as it moves away from the signifier-in-relation associated with the Imaginary and toward the withdrawn signifier, the unary signifier that anticipates the Symbolic even as it remains outside of it. The mode of *jouissance* produced here is what Lacan indicated in his diagram of the RSI with the symbol $J\Phi$, marking the *jouissance* at the intersection of the Symbolic and the Real—the *jouissance* of the signifier and ordination, which tames the Real and yet is also stimulated by it. On the other hand, Domestic Hats, while employing operations similar to the Vault House, seems to move even further away from the Symbolic, perhaps toward the haunting uncanniness of the Real, or else the other way, toward the scenes and fantasies of the domestic Imaginary. And finally, Noise, Pt. 3 should surely be placed in opposition to both immanent processes and transcendent form, for it is the simultaneous incorporation and negation of both terms. And so a third category begins to cohere, a structural inversion of the first two, something closer to the Real, involving the undoing of cognition by the uncontrollable power of inscription—a process enacted and revealed by both Domestic Hats and Noise, Pt. 3. Let us name this third position ($\bar{S}$) *aleatoric revelations*. Of course, aleatoric processes have been used in art practices for some time, especially in music and cinema, and it should not be surprising that a number of projects published in this volume could be booked in this category. In architecture, Peter Eisenman's early house projects of the 1960s and 1970s are among the first experiments in the inscription of complex transformational processes onto the architectural object itself. It is interesting to recall that, in the series of houses, what Eisenman was searching for was an antifoundationalist, posthumanist formalism, learning directly first from structuralism, and later from deconstruction, as well as psychoanalysis. Erin Besler's project Low Fidelity treats Eisenman's House VI as a historical document and formal resource, just as Eisenman had begun with the villas of Palladio and Le Corbusier. Besler's own interests lie in the material discrepancies and degradations that occur in translations across media. Beginning with Eisenman's axonometrics for House VI—which are not drawings, in fact, but layers of colored paper and adhesive vinyl on mylar—Besler records and translates the representations through various two-dimensional and three-dimensional modeling processes. The inability of the modeling processes to reproduce them with complete fidelity (failing to account for variations in paper thickness, for example) produces distortions and deviations that are amplified in each successive step of translation. The process of deterioration is striking. An array of mysterious partial objects is the result. The most surprising effect is that the objects take on a "life" of their own, their mutations becoming disturbingly malformed. In order to constitute itself, each new object (a translation of a transformation of an appropriated original—a kind of doubled inscription) must detach itself from its origin in House VI to become a completely new "organ without a body," as it were, outside its former host, a misshapen part-object.[80] Whatever is lost of the original object (House VI) in the processes, the low-fidelity translations also generate a surplus, which clings to the new part-objects like a digital deformity. The objects, then, can be understood theoretically as so many *objets a*, representatives of the surplus, standing in for the lost bits of House VI, obdurate remainders left undigested by the translation process. If we thus take House VI as an object reduced to a signifier in a failing Symbolic, then these mutant *objets a* are operators of a *jouissance* threaded directly through the Real on account of an impasse of formalization—remains of a body now detached that still somehow vibrate with an uncanny echo of life. All this now leads us to a wholly new category, beyond aleatoric revelations (one I might have discussed early in this paper with regard to the Thing, but at the time seemed superfluous). What we have explored merely as an example of stochastic decay and degradation of representation now appears to take up a position of its own, one that appears rather precisely, in the Greimasian system, as a "contradictory" of transcendent form (at least insofar as we have been obliged to speak of bodies and deformities) and as a "complementary" of immanent processes (insofar as it involves direct transformations of matter). What I have in mind is a fourth register ($-\bar{S}$, which I will call *the creaturely*. Bringing this category into our Borromean knot, we can define it, first, as comprising objects whose entire effectivity consists in a surplus *jouissance*, designated by Lacan as *JA*, and, second, as having evaded any encounter with authorized symbolization. Recall that the *jouissance* of the signifier ($J\Phi$, at the intersection of the Real and the Symbolic) "enjoys" the *objet a* as an attempt, made through ceaseless repetition, to plug the lack in the Symbolic. The Other *jouissance* (*JA*, at the intersection of the Real and the Imaginary) also enjoys the *objet a*, but it develops its own separate and singular symbolic register from the lack itself, beyond the authoritative Symbolic's signifier, outside of language itself. It is another way of inhabiting the knot, suggested by the fact that, in later iterations of the knot, Lacan wedges the *objet a* into the central space that binds all three registers of the RSI, indicating that it is the kernel that produces the surplus enjoyment, the *plus-de-jouir*. As such, the *objet a* interrupts the possibility of a unified or continuous *jouissance* and modulates (at least) three different modes of *jouissance*. This makes the Other *jouissance* (*JA*) a more singular and limited kind of *jouissance*, one that fundamentally involves a certain kind of corporeality (insofar as the fiction of the whole body is strongly related to the Imaginary) yet lies outside the organization by the Symbolic—a body without organization, or an organ with substance but without body symbolization. By placing the *objet a* at the center of the knot, Lacan announced a new phase in his conception of the RSI. Whereas previously the body was brought into being between the Imaginary (mirror stage) and the Symbolic (signifier), now the body of the Real is understood in a topological sense, as an organism with an insatiable and circling drive, rather than a linear but never-fulfilled desire. The *a* in the center represents a primordial form, a pure *objet a*. The production of Other *jouissance*, inflected by the *objet a*, also involves an encounter and a scene, which are characteristics of the Imaginary, now shot through with a *jouissance* written on the body in proximity to the Thing, in the very place where we find the *Erscheinung* of the Thing. Each of these attributes is a feature of the category of the creaturely. In this way, Lacan's leitmotiv of creation ex nihilo takes on a new valance, for now the creaturely object is the architecture in which the Thing subsists. The creaturely introduces a kind of mimetic surplus whose proximity to the human body produces anxiety because the inscription of the body seems both symptomatic (a reflex of contemporary "bare life" and the urgent need to imagine alternatives) and autonomous (beyond human control, produced from spontaneous surplus). It is a golem arrived unsummoned. Yet it is the relation between the creaturely and the more general domain of nonhuman things that produces an openness to transience and discontinuity—an openness to the imaginaries of other art practices, to performance and installation—and an immersion in experimentation. At the same time, in the projects shown in this collection, it seems that prehistorical, preverbal, preoedipal architectural creatures have been exhumed from the most primitive and originary recesses of the architectural psyche. Ellie Abrons's digital biomorphs and anamorphs, like those in the project Inside Things, provide an example. As she describes, their "parts seem too big for their wholes, forms don't quite fit together, and proto-figures combine to produce objects whose outsides don't quite reveal their insides. . . . The parts allude to something familiar—figures imbued with vitality that walk the line between living things and not living things."[81] The type of vision needed here—a vision trained in the creaturely—is a version of De Man's *material* vision, in which all things are just there and all relations flat. And yet Abrons's images for Inside Things are produced through elaborate digital character rigging and texture mapping—techniques of animation and artifice. Looking at one of the little things, one expects that at any moment it will throb or tighten up if touched. It lives beyond the negation of its Symbolic order; one cannot simply adjust expectations to accommodate what is seen. What is thereby viewed is the Other *jouissance* (*JA*)—*jouissance* materialized as thick flesh. But the creaturely can also be other than fleshy. Digital processing is often employed by practices experimenting in biomorphing and anamorphing, but Norman Kelley's Wrong Chairs series draws from a very different métier: wood crafting of the eighteenth and nineteenth centuries. At first, however, the chairs seem badly crafted, mismeasured, and missing parts. Or is it our vision that is a little off? If we were to close one eye and see them as anamorphoses, would things click into alignment? Theirs is a truly uncanny domesticity, negating any residue of a repeatable type in the category of transcendent form while at the same time opposing aleatoric processes with a singular figure. That is their thingness. What is more, the precision and detail of the drawings are akin to the *choisisme* of Alain Robbe-Grillet. Documenting and describing things, rather than interpreting and explaining them, gives the things an autonomy and life of their own.[82] The creaturely as Thing returns us to the distinction between the signifier-in-relation and the signifier-in-isolation, inasmuch as the Thing is modeled on the *objet a*—the filler of the void, the signifier in the Real—but in a highly ambiguous way. The Thing is the object of sublimation, which is produced when a not-quite-ordinary object (a string of matchboxes, say, a set of chairs) is incarnated as a replacement, an *objet a*, for the lost object of desire (the radically absent figure of the Other) and thus expanding the contours of the Imaginary and populating its field with alternative imaginary schemes. The texture mapped onto Abrons's biomorphs has the desiring affect of skin, the protuberances like fingers. These parts of the image connect with other signifiers, some even familiar (a glove, perhaps, a child's stuffed animal, an embryonic still life), and conjure a certain kind of figure. If the *objet a* here appears to follow the logic of the signifier-in-relation and desire, then it is nevertheless also true that there is nothing apparent in the cavities inside these things to support any sort of life-form or a mimesis thereof; indeed, the character rigging works (it produces fleshy wrinkles and folds), but it's not really biological—the creature's insides are geological.[83] Our encounter with the creature starts to loop, repeating itself as the scopic drive is triggered. Then the Thing threatens the subject with its own dissolution, signifiers scatter, and the signifier-in-isolation returns, now as the *objet a* of the Real and the drive.[84] The Thing prevents the realization of any of our putative imaginaries, and thus we can only repeat our encounter. Lacan writes that "it is necessary to ground this repetition first of all in the very split that occurs in the subject in relation to the encounter. This split . . . enables us to apprehend the Real, in its dialectical effects, as originally unwelcome. It is precisely through this that the Real finds itself, in the subject, to a very great degree the accomplice of the drive."[85] The ambiguity of the Thing is structural. Lacan's early concept of the Thing as residing in the emptiness of the Real comes from his reading of a passage from Freud's account of the subject's first coming into consciousness in the "primary perceptive," or *Nebenmensch*, complex. The subject learns to think, Freud maintains, in relation to its perceptions of a nearby fellow creature (probably not its parents, perhaps another child). This *Nebenmensch* is "the adjoining person" that stands between the subject and its primary maternal object. The complex of perceptions divides reality into the representable world of cognition and the unrepresentable, unassimilable element that Freud calls *das Ding*, the Thing. It is worth quoting at length:

> Let us suppose that the object which furnishes the perception resembles the subject—a *Nebenmensch*. If so, the theoretical interest is also explained by the fact that such an object was simultaneously the first satisfying object and further the first hostile object. . . . Then the perceptual complexes proceeding from this *Nebenmensch* will in part be new and noncomparable—its traits [*seine Züge*], for instance, in the visual sphere. But other perceptions—for example, those of the movements of its hands—will coincide in the subject with memories of quite similar visual impressions of his own, of his own body, which are associated with memories of movements experienced by the subject. Other perceptions of the object too—for instance, when it screams—will awaken the memory of his [the subject's] own screaming and at the same time of his own experiences of pain. Thus the *Komplex des Nebenmenschen* falls into two components, one of which makes an impression by its constant structure and stays together as a *thing* [*durch konstantes Gefüge imponiert, als Ding beisammenbleibt*], while the other can be understood by the activity of memory—that is, can be traced back to information from [the subject's] own body.[86]

Lacan glosses the two components of the *Nebenmensch* complex thus: first, *das Ding* is the structure that "affirms itself through an unchanging apparatus [*un appareil constant*], which remains together as a *thing*" but is also alien, "*entfremdet*, something strange to me, although it is at the heart of me"; and second, *die Vorstellung* is the system of figures or signifiers through which the *Nebenmensch* can be represented and remembered. Lacan stresses that *das Ding*, this particular doubled object (or frame of an object, an object thus set up), is the primary object on which is grounded all possible subject-object relations and, equally, the unassimilable empty site that remains when entry into the Symbolic is complete:

"*Das Ding* is at the center only in the sense that it is excluded. That is to say, in reality *das Ding* has to be posited as exterior, as the pre-historic Other that is impossible to forget."[87] The space of the Thing (which, recall, is also the empty void of originary architecture) is the space that is most familiar and, at the same time, most alienated. Lacan calls this condition "extimacy," to name that which is most intimate to the subject even as it lies definitively beyond the subject's grasp. Lacan also uses Freud's phrase *einziger Zug* to form his related concept of the unary trait, the singular inscription or mark that, when incessantly repeated, becomes a trace of the Real. To encounter the Thing is to experience, within the most familiar interior, the uncanny proximity of the unrepresentable exterior, which is nothing less than a bit of the Real at the very center of Symbolic order. With this last point—that the Thing divides between the intimate psychic interior and an exterior at the edge of the Real—we must now come finally to the question of the social, for it is precisely the encounter with the Thing that is both architecture's fundamental fantasy (the disciplinary machinery that constitutes and guarantees architecture's ongoing coherence) and its figure of the political unconscious—the scene where architecture's inscriptions and the social Symbolic contract find their common diagram. Recall our introduction of the architectural Thing as a veil around emptiness (veiled so that we are obliged "to encircle it or bypass it in order to conceive it"). It is because of the primordial emptiness that we are compelled to create, to domesticate the void. But at the same time, "the Thing is that which in the Real suffers from the signifier"; it is itself marked by the dynamics of social signification. The Thing "suffers" insofar as it carries the traumatic remainder that cannot be properly assimilated into the Symbolic. We can think of that remainder as the *objet a* encysted inside the Thing, as it were, and of that entire assemblage as the work of architecture.[88] And finally, the Thing is "veiled," dissimulated, in disguise; "it is by nature, in the refinding of the object, represented by something else." The Thing as lost object is a kind of *Nachträglichkeit*—it is constituted as lost in its very refinding. "It is thus refound without our knowing, except through the refinding, that it was ever lost."[89] All of which seems to me to be the precise conditions under which the houses in Amanda Williams's Color(ed) Theory series were first found, and which I will now consider as my example of the workings of the social dimension, not to say the politics, of architectural inscription. The houses in and around Chicago's Englewood neighborhood were slated for demolition. Williams:

> These are structures that can't be saved, that are not going to be rehabbed, that are not even good enough for people to squat in, in a certain sense. I didn't ask anyone's permission to paint the houses. I was terrified by what might happen.

> The practice of discriminatory housing lending created this landscape to begin with. That trauma that comes after years and years and years of disinvestment, of being lied to, of not really having control over how your environment gets shaped, or your ability to own your environment. These were fully intact blocks and neighborhoods, and so *to know what isn't there, is as important as noting what is there.*[90]

The houses found by Williams are a symptom of the social life of a particular community. The image of each house follows a unary trait that both instantiates and limits a particular affective range and a pattern of use repeated across all the houses. But what is important for my argument is that, whatever Williams saw in the houses as found objects, there was also something missing—a constitutive absence or emptiness that required the veil of the Thing. Williams and trusted friends and family painted the houses in different monochromatic hues. Color is the disguise of the Thing, the inscription that constructs the houses as architecture but also emphasizes that the houses should be treated individually, as singular moments, that they enter into architecture not as a typology but one by one, as an indeterminate or incompletable series. Color plays an originating role, rather like that of the cut in the Truffle: it constitutes architecture not as an inert object but as an act and an event. Color raises the object to the "dignity of the Thing," Lacan's definition of the enactment of sublimation's open-ended energy.[91] Importantly, the colors are not coded programmatically; they have no empirical value, or better, any differences that may exist in their value are indiscernible. Their selection is thus a pure choice and, as such, is effectively indistinguishable from an aleatoric process. Coated with color, any message or "speech" that the houses might emit is "interdicted" (a readerly response Lacan makes much of in his consideration of Joyce) in a way not unlike the bluntly muted foam models of Bonner's Domestic Hats. Perspectival vision and even tectonic representation are

Amanda Williams, Color(ed) Theory Series, *Pink Oil Moisturizer*, 2014–2016.

destroyed by color. Upon encountering any one of the houses, our first impression is that the act of inscription that brings the house into architecture also flattens it and erases reference and meaning, confounds it. And yet something of this Thing remains. "To know what isn't there, is as important as noting what is there." Architecture's fundamental fantasy is put in place to enable the architectural subject to enjoy its coherence in the Symbolic. But part of the architectural Symbolic is, to repeat, hegemonic, elite, and exclusionary; historically, the architectural Symbolic has admitted few works by people of color. These are among the signifiers suffered by this colored Thing, sanctioned as it is by the architectural Symbolic but on the edge of the Real. It is here too that the Imaginary comes to the fore in a way different from the other projects we have seen. For in this case, fantasies of the wholeness of identity (an architectural identity contaminated by the white imaginary)—the machinations of the mirror stage—are inherently contradictory and misleading, coming as they do imbricated with aggressiveness, dominance, hostility to otherness, and even hateful, racist bigotry.[92] The disruptive intrusion of the Thing constitutes the place from which ethical and political potentials that are explicitly racial can arise out of trauma; the color of the Thing both covers over its traumatic history and allows its entry into the domain of architecture. There is mystery in the metonymy of Williams's colors, "for the relationship to the Real as it is renewed in art at that moment makes the object appear purified; it involves a renewal of its dignity by means of which these imaginary insertions are, one might say, repetitively restated."[93] What happens on a second take—as we regard the project obliquely, anamorphically, encircling or bypassing it "in order to conceive it"—is that the Real, fraught with architecture's difficult history of racism, irrupts in the Imaginary and the Symbolic and utterly undoes the coherence of the RSI. When your eye lands on the shattered steps of the pink house, you experience the upsetting proto-*jouissance* Roland Barthes theorized as the photographic punctum, "that accident which pricks me (but also bruises me, is poignant to me)."[94] But when you realize that the color of the house is that of Luster's Pink Oil Moisturizer, a common beauty product familiar especially to older generations of Black women, the tightening in your chest and throat is the return in the Real of what has been refused in the Imaginary-Symbolic axis. It is the Other *jouissance* (*JA*), the *jouissance* beyond the signifier inasmuch as it does not directly engage the Symbolic. But the Symbolic is engaged nonetheless, along with the Imaginary. For the house as Thing threatens to subvert not only the social Symbolic order, by marking its institutional racism, but also the hegemonic fantasies of the Imaginary, by populating its scenes with an affective history of bigotry. Though the Symbolic initially finds the houses, as a racialized symptom, to be unassimilable to its paternalistic signifying system, Williams's Color(ed) Theory project has flipped the symptom, spinning it into the fourth ring, which, rather than acting as an impediment to the conjoining of the three registers of the RSI, now becomes the singular thread of their coherence—the *sinthome*. The Real, as manifest in the Other *jouissance* (*JA*) at the intersection of the Imaginary and the Real, is now encountered as the Symbolic's internal limit. The relations between the Real, the Symbolic, and the Imaginary have been changed by the house as Thing. The result is that the politics of race, woven into the strands of the *sinthome*, can be conveyed to the viewer *because* those politics have been inscribed as architecture in Williams's project, not in spite of their inscription. To say it a different way, the Real as the realm of the ethical exceeds and disrupts the aesthetics of the Symbolic and the Imaginary, and yet it is only through the Symbolic and Imaginary that we can gain access to the Real. We apprehend the ethical and political through architecture's inscription. But the politics of race have been inscribed in a particular way, and we must make one final move to grasp it. I have held onto an unsolvable contradiction throughout this essay, and I must now call it out. The particular event of architecture (what I earlier argued followed the *Arrive-t-il?*) cannot be enacted except by thinking Architecture ("as such," capital A), the presupposed whole anterior system of signification that supports the event; but to think Architecture is to fail to think the particularity of any event of architecture. In order to understand more fully how Williams's colored houses intervene in the Symbolic order, we must make use of Lacan's difficult concept of the *pas-tout*, a complement of the Other *jouissance* (*JA*), which subverts the Symbolic and touches the Real.[95] Let us begin with a Symbolic structure defined by the conventional logic of exception. It comprises two contradictory statements: First, *all* architecture is subject to the signifier—meaning that all architecture is marked and legitimated by the authority of the architectural Symbolic. And yet logically a constitutive exception can always be found. Hence, the second statement: there is *at least one example* of architecture that is *not* subject to the signifier. A primitive hut or an archetype, for example, may be seen as not being subject to a signifier, playing the role analogous to that of the primal father in social systems. As Antoine Picon suggests, "The archetype points toward a prearchitectural necessity. Because of this, it appears as primitive and above all simple, insofar as it is supposed to predate any architectural operation."[96] This position of the archetype is a structural necessity of the logic of exception—the law and its necessary transgression. The exception grounds the rule. It constitutes the limits and guarantees the integrity of each particular instance of the set "architecture." But this determination of the Symbolic *thereby* is opened up to the possibility of a politics of identification that produces racialized and gendered fantasies of disciplinary unity and wholeness—a limited All with the need for a constitutive exception, in which accepted examples must fit the homogeneity and totality of the predetermined set. Color(ed) Theory requires a different sort of determination of the Symbolic, different from what is effectively the paternalistic and phallic determination of the first; it requires a "not-All" in which every example will be an exception. In his twentieth seminar (1972–1973) Lacan gives us the structure of an alternative Symbolic in which each event of architecture, in its singularity, must also be counted as subject to the signifier of the Symbolic, though no totality can attest to such identity. What results is a system so decentered that its disciplinary signifier and that signifier's transgression (conveyed by *JA*, the Other *jouissance*) become one and the same. This counter Symbolic is *pas-tout*—"not-All"—with the following alternative formulation: First, there is *no* architecture that is *not* subject to the signifier; and second, *not-All* (*pas tout*) architecture is subject to the signifier. Now, logically (quite like the logic of Greimas's square), these two assertions are inversions of the first two assertions with which we began. Together the new assertions generate, on the one hand, a law (all architecture answers to the Symbolic) and, on the other, its more individuated contrary (something is exempt, which is an architecture that is *pas tout*). But Lacan does not follow logic; for him, the two formulations (the two pairs of statements) are the conceptualization of two distinct registers of psychic formation, two different possible relations of the Symbolic and the Real. In the second formulation, unlike the first, there is no claim of a universality grounded in a constitutive exception and no guarantee of totality. If there is no exception that remains, unmarked, outside the Symbolic, then the Symbolic itself is what is not whole or complete. And while there is no architecture that does not suffer the signifier, architecture is *not-all* inside the Symbolic. There is an architecture that touches the Real, and everything about it is nonpermanent, nonuniversal: not-All. Within this schema, Color(ed) Theory can insist that the vernacular houses be inscribed in that architectural Symbolic, not left hanging delegitimated in the social Imaginary. And with their entry into the Symbolic, the houses bring their irreducible contingency and particularity. But they do *not* constitute a "minor architecture."[97] Instead, this position within the Symbolic refuses the boundaries set by presumably unmarked universals and thus cannot be appropriated as an essentialist notion of a unified category of architecture. It recognizes no exception—whether archetypal or its opposite, the vernacular. So whereas the first way of entering the domain of architecture promises totalization according to the Symbolic, the synecdochal, and the transcendental, the second way—the way of the *sinthome* and the Other *jouissance* (*JA*)—touches the Real, embracing the contingent, the metonymic, and the immanent sublime. Architectural inscription offers the resources for allowing us to pass from identity politics to a political economy of the Thing, a figure located no longer in a field totalized by a disciplinary Symbolic but in a theoretically infinite series of possible encounters, without limit and without totalization, a field without the stability of the marginal or the minor.

1 Throughout this essay I follow the theoretical convention wherein the subject is *not* an individual person but rather, first and foremost, the complex articulation of a symbolic production. Following the Lacanian poststructuralist tradition—which has offered this decisive subject construction based on material heterogeneity, rather than unity—architecture itself can be treated as the subject, and I will do so here.

2 The concept of autonomy has of late become fraught with literal mindedness. The argument for autonomy was never an argument for disengagement or withdrawal but rather an attempt, against a dominant empiricist functionalism, to account for architecture as a mode of knowledge through a critical disciplinarity. Massimo Scolari put it concisely in his article for the 15th Triennale of Architecture in 1973: "Architecture is a cognitive process that in and of itself, in the acknowledgment of its own autonomy, is today necessitating a refounding of the discipline; that refuses interdisciplinary solutions to its own crisis; that does not pursue and immerse itself in political, economic, social, and technological events only to mask its own creative and formal sterility, but rather desires to understand them so as to be able to intervene in them with lucidity—not to determine them, but not to be subordinate to them either." Massimo Scolari, "The New Architecture and the Avant-Garde," in *Architecture Theory since 1968*, ed. K. Michael Hays (Cambridge, MA: MIT Press, 1998), 131.

3 T. J. Clark, "Phenomenality and Materiality in Cézanne," in *Material Events: Paul de Man and the Afterlife of Theory*, ed. Barbara Cohen, Tom Cohen, J. Hillis Miller, and Andrzej Warminski (Minneapolis: University of Minnesota Press, 2001), 102.

4 Ibid., 93.

5 The nature of Lacan's materiality (the anterior materiality of the Real) is integral to the precise configuration of the knot: if you cut any one of the three rings, the whole is undone; all the rings become separate. Alain Badiou describes this as a distinction between the algebra of a chain (wherein cutting one ring leaves the others connected) and the topology of the knot. "The One of the Borromean knot is that of a consistency that affects the whole. It is a One of adherence, the collective property of the terms, whereas the One of the chain prescribes the places of the connection, which have a separating function. What is it that makes the knot into 'something else'? It is because the One does not have the same assignation therein as in the algebraic order. The One of numbers is sustained by the zero in order to repeat itself by addition. The One of the knot holds together the terms of the series." Lacan's materialist subject thus "manages to think the structural law of the empty place as the punctual anchoring of the excess over the place." Alain Badiou, *A Theory of the Subject* (New York: Continuum, 2009), 227, 261.

6 Jacques Lacan, lesson of April 15, 1975, *The Seminar of Jacques Lacan*, book 22, *RSI, 1974–1975*, translated unofficially by Cormac Gallagher from unpublished French transcripts, http://www.lacaninireland.com/web/wp-content/uploads/2010/06/RSI-Complete-With-Diagrams.pdf, PDF p. 155 (hereafter cited as Seminar 22). The use of Heidegger's term "ek-sistence" here indicates that the limits are ontological not merely epistemological.

7 Peter Eisenman, "Three Texts for Venice," *Domus*, no. 611 (November 1980): 9. The three texts—"The Emptiness of the Future" (modernism), "The Emptiness of the Present" (contextualism), and "The Emptiness of the Past" (postmodernism)—anticipate Eisenman's definitive declaration of the demise of the Symbolic in his "The End of the Classical: The End of

the Beginning, the End of the End," *Perspecta* 21 (1984): 155–73.

8 For a full account of these two projects in a Lacanian interpretive framework, see my *Architecture's Desire: Reading the Late Avant-Garde* (Cambridge, MA: MIT Press, 2010).

9 Lacan, Seminar 22, 98. I have modified the translation based on Jacques-Alain Miller's reading of the RSI seminar in his essay "The Sinthome, a Mixture of Symptom and Fantasy," in *The Later Lacan: An Introduction*, ed. Véronique Voruz and Bogdan Wolf (Albany: State University of New York Press, 2007), 71. In the RSI, the zones of overlap of the three registers delineate three modes of *jouissance*: *jouissance* of sensation (between I and S), *jouissance* of the signifier (between S and R), and the other *jouissance* (between R and I). The central zone of the knot can be understood as representing either the symptom or the *objet a*. *Jouissance* is a pleasurable dissatisfaction experienced by the body, and it thrives on never reaching its goal. Inscription, in these terms, is thus a way of inciting and organizing *jouissance*.

10 This is one of many of Lacan's mathemes we will encounter in the course of my argument. It is important to point out that, while I will try to specify the character of my own use of each of these mathemes, Lacan refused to define them, treating them as, indeed, inscriptions with no stable meaning but rather enormous generative power.

11 The term *sinthome* is from an old French spelling of the modern homophone *symptôme*. Lacan employs a different word to signal related but different constellations of concepts. He relates the use of *sinthome* particularly to his thinking about art. Importantly, the *sinthome* names a singular approach to art, not a generic category.

12 See Mari Ruti, *The Singularity of Being: Lacan and the Immortal Within* (New York: Fordham University Press, 2012), especially her discussion of Alain Badiou and Lacanian ethics in chapter 4, "The Possibility of the Impossible," 83–101.

13 This is inference on my part. I know of no one in either camp who actually makes reference to the topic of the symptom. What Bernhard Siegert does call for is "a reconceptualization of ontology, which one could call 'operative ontologies,' that asks for the concrete ontic operations and practices that produce first of all ontological distinctions—among many others, also those between image and picture, or figure and ground, or active and passive, or message and medium, subject and object, man and animal and so on. These ontic operations are called cultural techniques." Bernhard Siegert, "After the Media: The Textility of Cultural Techniques," in *Media Theory and Cultural Technologies: In Memoriam Friedrich Kittler*, ed. Maria Teresa Cruz (Newcastle upon Tyne: Cambridge Scholars Publishing, 2017), 4. It is interesting that both Siegert and Friedrich Kittler make use of Lacan's categories of the RSI. As far as I am aware, however, none of their followers in architecture have tried to develop this dimension of their work. See Friedrich Kittler, *Gramophone, Film, Typewriter*, trans. Geoffrey Winthrop-Young and Michael Wutz (Palo Alto, CA: Stanford University Press, 1999); and Bernhard Siegert, "Doors: On the Materiality of the Symbolic," *Grey Room* 47 (Spring 2012): 6–23.

14 Here I am referring to Slavoj Žižek, *Enjoy Your Symptom: Jacques Lacan in Hollywood and Out* (New York: Routledge, 2001).

15 Jacques Lacan, *Le séminaire de Jacques Lacan*, book 23, *Le sinthome, 1975–1976*, ed. Jacques-Alain Miller (Paris: Éditions du Seuil, 1999), 79. Translation mine.

16 Lacan, lesson of January 21, 1975, Seminar 22, 59–60.

17 Jacques Derrida, *Of Grammatology*, trans. Gayatri Chakravorty Spivak (1967;

Baltimore: Johns Hopkins University Press, 1974), 290.

18 "Spacing is a concept which . . . carries the meaning of a productive, positive, generative force. Like *dissemination*, like *différance*, it carries along with it a genetic motif: it is not only the interval, the space constituted between two things (which is the usual sense of spacing), but also spacing, the operation, or in any event, the movement of setting aside." Jacques Derrida, "Positions: Interview with Jean-Louis Houdebine and Guy Scarpetta," in *Positions*, trans. Alan Bass (Chicago: University of Chicago Press, 1981), 106n42. As an example of spacing in architecture, Derrida cites Bernard Tschumi's 1982 project for Parc de la Villette, Paris.

19 Rodolphe Gasché, *The Tain of the Mirror: Derrida and the Philosophy of Reflection* (Cambridge, MA: Harvard University Press, 1986), 157.

20 Peggy Kamuf argues that habitation is the spacing of *différance* from within: "By emphasizing that deconstructive movements inhabit *in a certain way*, however, Derrida is announcing something like an *awakening* of the action that habitually slumbers passively unaware in this state called habitation or inhabiting. If indeed everyone always inhabits—and who could deny that?—then the question is *how* one inhabits there where one finds oneself and that *in which* one is already inscribed. For, that habitation is indeed another name for inscription and thus for différance is what we will have come to understand many pages later in *Of Grammatology*." Peggy Kamuf, "A Certain Way of Inhabiting," in *Reading Derrida's Of Grammatology*, ed. Sean Gaston and Ian Maclachlan (London: Continuum, 2011), 37.

21 Jacques Lacan, *The Seminar of Jacques Lacan*, ed. Jacques-Alain Miller, book 7, *The Ethics of Psychoanalysis, 1959–1960*, trans. Dennis Porter (London: Tavistock/Routledge, 1992), 140 (hereafter cited as Seminar 7).

22 Ibid., 121.

23 Jacques Derrida, "Force and Signification," in *Writing and Difference*, trans. Alan Bass (1967; Chicago: University of Chicago Press, 1978), 8.

24 Gustave Flaubert, *The Letters of Gustave Flaubert, 1830–1857*, ed. and trans. Francis Steegmuller (Cambridge, MA: Harvard University Press, 1980), 154.

25 Derrida, "Force and Signification," 8.

26 Ibid., 8.

27 Ibid., 5.

28 Ibid., 5. Peter Eisenman begins his introduction to the 1982 English translation of Aldo Rossi's *Architecture of the City* with this excerpt. The passage facilitates a shift of Rossi's theory of the city toward poststructuralism and psychoanalysis and gives Eisenman a way to assimilate Rossi's aphoristic mention of skeletons and fractures to his own rhetoric of the unhappy consciousness.

29 Derrida, "Force and Signification," 8–9. In a footnote to the term *inscription*, Derrida declares that pure speech is constituted by the requirement of inscription, that it is "a kind of privileged representation of inscription."

30 Ibid., 9. The original French reads "une sort de sur-compossibilité autonome," referring to the concept of compossibility from Leibniz, which emphasizes the excess of signifying possibilities before the inaugural instant of inscription. See Christopher Johnson's analysis of Derrida's essay in "The Passion of Inscription," chapter 1 of his *System and Writing in the Philosophy of Jacques Derrida* (Cambridge: Cambridge University Press, 1993).

31 Cynthia Chase, "Monument and Inscription: Wordsworth's 'Lines,'" *Diacritics* 17, no. 4 (Winter 1987): 75.

32 Ibid., 75.

33 Paul de Man, "Hypogram and Inscription:

Michael Riffaterre's Poetics of Reading," *Diacritics* 12, no. 4 (Winter 1981): 28.

34 Jean-François Lyotard, "The Sublime and the Avant-Garde," in *The Inhuman: Reflections on Time*, trans. Geoffrey Bennington and Rachel Bowlby (1988; Palo Alto, CA: Stanford University Press, 1991), 90.

35 G. W. F. Hegel, *Aesthetics: Lectures on Fine Art*, trans. T. M. Knox (Oxford: Clarendon, 1975), 83ff.

36 The Truffle (2010) project description, Ensamble Studio website, https://www.ensamble.info/thetruffle. Italics mine.

37 Lacan, Seminar 7, 135–36.

38 Ibid., 136.

39 Note that this mode of *jouissance*, *jouis-sens*, appears in the trefoil knot at the overlap between the Imaginary and the Symbolic. It may seem here that I contradict myself when I speak of the lack of meaning *and* the enjoyment of meaning. But the inscription of this type *jouissance* is meaningless in the sense that it does not open onto any particular signification. It is also enjoyment-in-meaning itself (*jouis-sens*) insofar as inscription is the production of signification, the activity that prepares signification.

40 Lyotard sees the work of Paul Cézanne as an investigation of elementary sensations that would rid perception of its prejudices. These *petites sensations* (Cézanne's term) "constitute the entire pictorial existence of an object . . . without consideration of history of 'subject,' of line, of space, even of light." Jean-François Lyotard, "The Sublime and the Avant-Garde," trans. Lisa Liebmann, *Artforum* 22, no. 8 (April 1984): 41.

41 The Borromean knot as inscription supports a single signifier, the signifier One (S1), which is a support for the interrelations of subsequent signifiers. Lacan is characteristically cryptic. The one of the unary trait is the one of repetition. It is a mark that becomes one by being remarked.

42 Jacques Lacan, "Seminar on 'The Purloined Letter,'" in *Écrits*, trans. Bruce Fink (1966; New York: W. W. Norton, 2006), 16.

43 Tom Eyers, *Lacan and the Concept of the 'Real'* (London: Palgrave Macmillan, 2012), 153. Lacan describes two movements of the mirror phase. The first is that of the corporeal image, or primary narcissism, which is prior and resistant to symbolization; the second is that of the relation to the other, or secondary narcissism, which depends on such symbolization.

44 It is part of the power of Eyers's typology, but also part of its risk, that it bundles diverse instances and avatars of the signifier-in-isolation, including the unary trait, the letter, and most notably the *objet a*, as well as the *sinthome* itself. The risk is the reduction of the varying functionality of these Lacanian concepts; the power is the coherence of a scheme for Lacan's complex yet consistent development of ideas over decades and an ability to link the different domains represented by the RSI.

45 See Graham Harman, *The Quadruple Object* (Winchester: Zero Books, 2011). See also the excellent explication of Harman's consequences for architecture in Bryan Norwood, "Metaphors for Nothing," *Log* 33 (Winter 2015): 107–19.

46 Eyers, *Lacan and the Concept of the 'Real'*, 128.

47 As early as 1966, Lacan referred to the singularity of "the letter," a piece of the Real, and the "latent vitalism in its notion of the whole." Lacan, *Écrits*, 16.

48 Lacan, Seminar 7, 114.

49 Ibid.

50 Domestic Hats (2014) project description, MALL website, https://jenniferbonner.com/03-Domestic-Hats.

51 Stan Allen, "Pattern Recognition: Scanning *Inscriptions*," in this volume.

52 Bonner's recent interest in buildings made of letters of the alphabet confirms the

tendency. On the letter as a nonreferential assemblage, see Jacques Lacan, *The Seminar of Jacques Lacan*, Encore book 20, *On Feminine Sexuality: The Limits of Love and Knowledge, 1972–1973*, ed. Jacques-Alain Miller, trans. Bruce Fink (New York: W. W. Norton, 1999), 46ff. An architecture made of letters is a reinscription of an inscription, a material marking or tracing that does not in itself mean anything but nevertheless sets up a very precise architectural pattern. The extraordinary designs of Johann David Steingruber's *Architectural Alphabet* (1773) appear often in Bonner's teaching.

53 In the lecture "Lituraterre" of Seminar 18, Lacan plays on puns like *letter/litter*, *literal/littoral*, and *literature/litura-terre*. Lesson of May 12, 1971, *The Seminar of Jacques Lacan*, book 18, *On a Discourse That Might Not Be a Semblance, 1971*, translated unofficially by Cormac Gallagher from unpublished French transcripts, http://www.lacaninireland.com/web/wp-content/uploads/2010/06/Book-18-On-a-discourse-that-might-not-be-a-semblance.pdf, PDF p. 126.

54 Michelle Chang, "Turning a Banana Inside Out," *Plat*, October 6, 2019, https://www.platjournal.com/articles/turning-a-banana-inside-out.

55 On the shift from drawing to image, see John May, *Signal. Image. Architecture.* (New York: Columbia Books on Architecture and the City, 2019).

56 Kittler, *Gramophone, Film, Typewriter*, 83.

57 Ibid.

58 De Man, "Hypogram and Inscription," 34.

59 Ibid., 26.

60 Ibid., 19.

61 Ibid., 34.

62 Ibid., 28.

63 Paul de Man, "Phenomenality and Materiality in Kant," in *Aesthetic Ideology*, ed. Andrzej Warminski (Minneapolis: University of Minnesota Press, 1996), 82.

64 A more literal translation would be "merely by what the appearance-to-the-eyes presents," or perhaps "merely by what meets the eye."

65 Immanuel Kant, *Critique of Judgment*, trans. J. H. Bernard (New York: Hafner, 1951), quoted in De Man, "Phenomenality and Materiality in Kant," 82.

66 De Man, "Phenomenality and Materiality in Kant," 82–83.

67 Ibid., 81.

68 J. Hillis Miller, "Paul de Man as Allergen," in *Material Events*, 192.

69 De Man, "Phenomenality and Materiality in Kant," 82.

70 Ibid., 89.

71 De Man, "Hypogram and Inscription," 25.

72 Andrzej Warminski, "'As the Poets Do It': On the Material Sublime," in *Material Events*, 21.

73 Derrida, "Force and Signification," 290; and De Man, "Hypogram and Inscription," 25.

74 Hugh S. Manon, "Resolution, Truncation, Glitch," in *Cinematic Cuts: Theorizing Film Endings*, ed. Sheila Kunkle (Albany: State University of New York Press, 2016), 34.

75 Tom Cohen, J. Hillis Miller, and Barbara Cohen, "A 'Materiality without Matter'?" in *Material Events*, viii.

76 De Man, "Kant and Schiller," in *Aesthetic Ideology*, 132.

77 Hegel, *Aesthetics*, 1:83–85.

78 A. J. Greimas and François Rastier, "The Interaction of Semiotic Constraints," *Yale French Studies* 41 (1968): 86–105. "Entanglements" is Greimas's word for the metonymic complexity that can result from the square. The two most fruitful uses of the semiotic square, which I follow here, are Rosalind Krauss, "Sculpture in the Expanded Field," *October* 8 (Spring 1979): 30–44; and Fredric Jameson, "Constraints of the Postmodern," in *The Seeds of Time* (New York: Columbia University Press, 1994), 129–205.

79 Historically, in architecture this *jouissance* might include caryatids, gothic monsters, and fanciful baroque ornaments. It is a kind

of "overhearing" (*je ouïr sens*), as in sensing meanings other than the literal.

80 The term *part-object* goes back to Freud, who referred to the breast and the feces as examples of part-objects. Lacan's conceptualization of the part-object is quite loose and changes with the development, around 1963–1964, of the concept of *objet a* as the object cause of desire. Now an object becomes a part-object by virtue of the fact that the subject takes it for the object cause of desire, *objet a*. A particular kind of part-object operates as what Lacan, in Seminar 11, calls the "lamella." See Jacques Lacan, *The Seminar of Jacques Lacan*, book 11, *The Four Fundamental Concepts of Psychoanalysis* (1963–1964), ed. Jacques-Alain Miller, trans. Alan Sheridan (New York: W. W. Norton, 1979), 197 (hereafter cited as Seminar 11). A lamella has a life force, but no substantive body. A helpful and amusingly vivid example is given by Lilian Munk Rösing in her book *Pixar with Lacan* (London: Bloomsbury, 2017). In *Toy Story 3*, Mr. Potato Head is transformed into Mr. Tortilla Head by detaching his part-objects (nose, ears, eyes, etc.) from his potato body and reattaching them to a tortilla. "The interesting thing about this idea is that it turns the partial objects into that which constitutes subjects. The partial objects are not just attributes to Mr. Potato Head's bodily substance, rather they seem to be the substance themselves, ready to occupy any convenient body" (40). "Organ without a body" is a favorite phrase of Slavoj Žižek's that crosses Lacan's lamella with Deleuze and Guattari's recording apparatus, the body without organs.

81 Inside Things (2016) project description, EADO website, https://www.ellieabrons.com/Inside-Things.

82 It is here that the influence of John Hejduk and his particular involvement with the Thing must be noted. A plaque bearing Robbe-Grillet's remark about the work of Kafka famously hung in Hejduk's office: "The hallucinatory effect derives from the extraordinary clarity and not from mystery or mist. Nothing is more fantastic ultimately than precision." John Hejduk, *Mask of Medusa* (New York: Rizzoli, 1985), 39.

83 In her essay in this volume, Catherine Ingraham points out that figuration from the outside is different from the figural from the inside: "Figuration becomes allied with appearances, whereas the figural represents psychic and physical forces." See Ingraham, "Sites of Inscriptions," in this volume.

84 Both desire and drive seek the Thing. Desire is the constant connection and reconnection of signifiers in an endless search for an impossible object that will bring satisfaction. But the object obtained is never the thing that is desired. The drive achieves enjoyment in the very *failing* to get the object. As desire begins to divest itself of the realization of the object, it moves toward emancipation in the drive.

85 Lacan, Seminar 11, 69.

86 Sigmund Freud, *The Standard Edition of the Complete Psychological Works of Sigmund Freud*, trans. James Strachey et al. (London: Vintage, 2001), 1:331. Translation modified.

87 Lacan, Seminar 11, 69. *Appareil constant* is Lacan's translation of Freud's *konstantes Gefüge*, which conveys an almost machine-like character of the Thing.

88 For a justification of this construction, see Lacan's comments in lesson 14, March 12, 1969, Jacques Lacan, *The Seminar of Jacques Lacan*, book 16, *From an Other to the Other, 1968–1969*, translated unofficially by Cormac Gallagher from unpublished French transcripts, http://www.lacaninireland.com/web/wp-content/uploads/2010/06/Book-16-from-an-Other-to-the-other.pdf, PDF pp. 210–27.

89 Lacan, Seminar 7, 118.

90 Amanda Williams, "Color(ed) Theory Suite,

2014–2016," *Radical Acts* exhibition, Museum of Modern Art, https://www.moma.org/audio/playlist/290/3760. Italics mine.

91 Lacan, Seminar 7, 112.

92 It is worth recalling too that Frantz Fanon's explicit engagement with Lacan on what we would now call the white imaginary is through the mechanism of the mirror stage in the Imaginary register. See Frantz Fanon, *Black Skin, White Masks*, trans. Richard Philcox (1952; New York: Grove Press, 2008).

93 Lacan, Seminar 7, 141.

94 Roland Barthes, *Camera Lucida: Reflections on Photography*, trans. Richard Howard (New York: Hill and Wang, 1981), 27.

95 Lacan, Seminar 20.

96 Picon, "Archetype, Ornament, and the Subversion of Architectural Categories," in this volume. Picon also notes the inherent contradiction: the archetype "always already belongs to the architectural realm, despite its claim to be anterior to it. Another way to put it would be to observe that an archetype is not actually an object, but a relation between a virtual object—the diagram—and a built one, or to be still more accurate, it is an operator that connects the two. Its highly subversive mode of existence (epitomizing the desire for a foundation and ultimately disproving its very possibility) finds a counterpoint in the equally subversive power, albeit in the opposite direction, of the traditional architectural ornament."

97 For a well-argued construction of a feminist minor architecture, see Karen Burns, "Becomings: Architecture, Feminism, Deleuze—Before and After the Fold," in *Deleuze and Architecture*, ed. Hélène Frichot and Stephen Loo (Edinburgh: Edinburgh University Press, 2013), 15–39.

Credits

Andrew Holder

5 First Office (top). Eugène Trutat (bottom).

7 First Office (top). Ensamble Studio (bottom).

8 JaJa Co (top). Paul Preissner Architects (bottom).

9 Institut de France, Paris (top). Courtesy Wellcome Collection (bottom).

11 Current Interests.

12 JaJa Co (top). FreelandBuck (bottom).

13 d.esk (top). Medium Office (bottom).

16 Medium Office.

17 Rudolf Schulze (top). Bibliothèque Nationale de France (bottom).

18 Medium Office (top). Hans Koesters (top). Anthony Titus Studio (bottom).

19 MIRACLES Architecture; photo by Kyle Reich (top). Illustration by Mindy Seu (bottom).

20 Photo by Justin Knight, courtesy Harvard GSD.

21 Preston Scott Cohen, Inc. (top). Andrew Holder (bottom).

22 Photo by Justin Knight, courtesy Harvard GSD (top). Exhibition design by Mindy Seu and Adam Strobel.

23 Exhibition design by Mindy Seu and Adam Strobel (bottom).

Catherine Ingraham

121 Mack Scogin Merrill Elam Architects.

122 Mack Scogin Merrill Elam Architects (top). Mack Scogin Merrill Elam Architects, photo © Timothy Hursley (bottom).

Stan Allen

122 Artstor, access provided by Harvard University.

135 Miriam Mibao.

138 Erin Besler (top). formlessfinder (bottom).

139 T+E+A+M (top). Kyle Reynolds, is-office (bottom).

140 Victoria & Albert Museum of Childhood.

141 OFFICE Kersten Geers David Van Severen (top). Hans Tursack (bottom).

143 Thomas Ruff, Artists Rights Society (top). Christ & Gantenbein; photo by Justin Knight, courtesy Harvard GSD (bottom).

144 Stan Allen (top). First Office (bottom).

Antoine Picon

271 DOME / MIT Library collections.

272 d.esk; courtesy David Eskenazi.

273 Artstor / Avery Library Architectural Plans and Sections, Columbia University.

274 Jesús Vassallo.

Lucia Allais

279 Lucia Allais.

281 Melissa Cheung, *Columbia Daily Spectator*.

282 Harvard Fine Arts Library, Digital Images & Slides Collection.

283 Artists Rights Society.

285 Photo by Justin Knight, courtesy Harvard GSD.

Marrikka Trotter

351 Sir John Soane's Museum, London, SM 12.10.2; photographed by Hugh Kelly.

352 Photocrom Print Collection, United States Library of Congress, LCCN2001700923.

355 Sir John Soane's Museum, London, SM (66) 65/4/45; photographed by Hugh Kelly.

356 BnF Gallica.

359 Sir John Soane's Museum, London; photo by Gareth Gardner.

360 Archives Nationales, Paris.

363 Sir John Soane's Museum, London, SM 11.4.1; photographed by Hugh Kelly (top). Sir John Summerson (bottom).

364 Sir John Soane's Museum, London, ADD7.

365 Photo by Will Pryce for *Country Life*; courtesy Future Publishing Limited.

Sylvia Lavin

372 Carolyn Dry.

374 The Museum of Modern Art, New York (left). © Superstudio. Photo: Cristiano Toraldo di Francia, Archivio Toraldo di Francia, Filottrano (right).

373 Artstor.

375 Artstor.

376 Archives dépatementales de l'Aube; courtesy Wikimedia Commons.

377 Isamu Noguchi, 1949 (left). The Noguchi Museum Archive. © INFGM / ARS. Wayne Copper; *Cornell Journal of Architecture* (right).
378 Artstor (left). Wayne Copper; Cornell University Department of Architecture (right).

Edward Eigen
421 Image courtesy Gale Primary Sources; printed for T. Parkhurst.
422 Hathi Trust Digital Library.
427 Harvard University Library, sourced from the British Library.
428 Gale Primary Sources, sourced from the British Library.
433 ProQuest, access provided by Harvard University.
434 Emory Candler School of Theology, Pitts Theology Library.
441 Sabin Americana: History of the Americas; printed for T. Newcomb for L. Lloyd.
442 Eighteenth Century Collections Online; printed for John Edwards, on the south side of the Townhouse in King Street.

Phillip Denny
521 Image courtesy Gale, Harvard Library.
552 Mack Scogin Merrill Elam Architects.
555 Greg Lynn.
556 The MIT Press (top). The Bittertang Farm (bottom).
559 The Bittertang Farm; photo by Justin Knight, courtesy Harvard GSD (top). EADO; photo by Joshua White Photography, courtesy SCI-Arc (bottom).
560 EADO; photo by Joshua White Photography, courtesy SCI-Arc (top). The LADG (bottom).

K. Michael Hays
568 Peter Eisenman Architects, courtesy Canadian Centre for Architecture.
569 Aldo Rossi, courtesy the Museum of Modern Art, New York.
598 Amanda Williams.

All project images © their authors unless otherwise specified. Supplemental credits below.

Category
154 New Affiliates, Tunbridge Winter Cabin: Photo by Michael Vahrenwald / ESTO. Ultramoderne, Escape: Commissioned by Storefront for Art and Architecture for "Souvenirs: New New York Icons," 2017.
155 JaJa Co, Scoring, Building: Photo by Tag Christof.
157 Höweler + Yoon, Collier Memorial: Photo by Iwan Baan.
160 WOJR, Dwelling: Image by Alexis Nicolas Basso. Architecture Office, House in House: Image by Thomas Kim. Studio Offshore, Lakeshore Hut: Image © 2016 Alexander Eisenschmidt. Bureau Spectacular, Inside Outside Between Beyond: Photo by Injee Unshin.
161 WOJR, House of the Woodland: Image by D-Render.
162 French 2D, Outlier Lofts: Photo by John Horner Photography. Tom de Paor, Aill Breac: Photo by N. Carvalho. MALL, Domestic Hats: Photo by Caitlin Peterson.
164 LAMAS, Townships Farmhouse: Photo by Stéphane Groleau / Laetitia Boudaud.
165 Besler & Sons, Roof Deck at MoMA PS1: Photo by Walker Olesen.
166 Now Here, 1/2 House: Photo by Joshua White Photography.
168 Studio Anna Heringer, Traunstein Forum Internat: Photo by Stefano Mori.
169 Höweler + Yoon, Lithos Wellness Center: Rendering by Luxigon.
172 FreelandBuck, Stack House: Photo by Eric Staudenmaier.
173 FreelandBuck, Hungry Man Production Offices: Photo by Eric Staudenmaier. Ajay Manthripragada, Page House and Gallery: Photo by Naho Kubota. nARCHITECTS, NY State Equal Rights Heritage Center: Photo by James Ewing.
175 JaJa Co, Scoring, Building: Photo by Tag Christof.

Credits

177 JaJa Co, Scoring, Building: Photo by Tag Christof.
180 SpinaGu, Thick: Photo by Joshua White Photography.
181 MALL, Haus Gables: Image by NAARO.
182 New Affiliates, Tunbridge Winter Cabin: Photo by Michael Vahrenwald / ESTO. Fievre + Jones, Bywater Artist Residence I: Photo by Eric Staudenmaier.
183 BairBalliet, Loud Lines: Photo by Malvin Bunata.
186 Kristy Balliet, Beyond Volume: Photo by Phil Arnold.
188 Kristy Balliet, Beyond Volume: Photo by Phil Arnold. MIRACLES Architecture, Poppy Red: Photo by Kyle Reich.
189 Viola Ago and Hans Tursack, Understorey: Images by Hadley Fruits and Jeffrey Halstead.
190 Fievre + Jones, Bywater Artist Residence I: Photo by Eric Staudenmaier.
196 Architecture Office, Parti Wall: Photo by Jamie Young. Lluís Alexandre Casanovas Blanco with María Luisa Blanc, Real Estate Boom House: Photo by Pol Rebaque. Kyle May, Extent: Photo by Daniel Schwartz.
200 Hans Tursack, Graphic Fields, Composition VII: Photo by Brilliant Graphics.
209 Adam Fure, Rocks: Image by Vergil Design Visualization.
216 Amélia e Rodrigo, Building Stories: Photo by José Hevia.
220 MALL, BLT: Photo by Adam DeTour. Ultramoderne, Escape: Commissioned by Storefront for Art and Architecture for *Souvenirs: New New York Icons*, 2017.
222 Ultramoderne, Framework: Finalist for the Philadelphia Contemporary Museum (invited competition).
224 Christ & Gantenbein, Zurich University Hospital USZ: Photo by Stefano Graziani.
226 Adam Fure, the Force of Things: Photo by Marina Levitskaya.
227 Toshiko Mori Architect, Thread Artists' Residency and Cultural Center: Photo by Jordan MacTavish. Studio Anna Heringer, Three Bamboo Hostels: Photo by Jenny Ji.
230 PRODUCTORA, Housing Prototype in Apan: Photo by Jaime Navarro.
231 MoDusArchitects, Mountain Lodge: Photo by Oliver Jaist.
234 Studio Anna Heringer, METI School: Photo by Kurt Hoerbst.
238 Pezo von Ellrichshausen, Crux Pavilion: Photo by Diana Quintela.
239 Tom de Paor, 4am: Photo by Alice Clancy. PRODUCTORA, Pavilion on the Zocalo: Photo by Luis Gallardo.
245 Farshid Moussavi Architecture, Folie Divine: Photo by Paul Phung. Ultramoderne, Southlight: Photo by Naho Kubota.
247 Ensamble Studio, Towers of Landscape: Photo by Bettina Cohen.
248 Jesús Vassallo, Water Towers: Photo by Nash Baker.
249 Paul Preissner Architects, Five Rooms: Photo by Tom Harris.
250 is-office, Crowns: Photo by Nick Zukauskas.
251 MAIO, 110 Rooms: Photo by José Hevia.
252 SpinaGu, Thick: Photo by Joshua White Photography.
254 Ania Jaworska, Gated Area: Photo by Travis Roozee. Johnston Marklee, View House: Photo by Gustavo Frittegotto, Sergio Pirrone, Diego Arraigada.
255 Independent Architecture, Catamount Dormitory: Photo by James Florio.
256 Höweler + Yoon, Shanghai Expo Park Viewfinder Bridge: Rendering by Squared Design Lab.
257 Pezo von Ellrichshausen, Bell Pavilion: Photo and fabrication by Studio Radish.
258 BairBalliet, Loud Lines: Photo by Malvin Bunata. Kristy Balliet, Elbows: Photo by Phil Arnold. Ania Jaworska, Set / Unit 3: Courtesy Volume Gallery.
259 Ania Jaworska, Set / Unit 6: Courtesy Volume Gallery. Kristy Balliet, Elbows: Photo by Phil Arnold.

Credits

260 BairBalliet, No Middle Midrise: Photo by Malvin Bunata.
261 SPORTS, City Thread: Photo by Justin Harris.
262 SPORTS, Myth: Photo by Wallo Villacorta.
263 The Bittertang Farm, Brood of Fluffy: Photo by Justin Knight, courtesy Harvard GSD.
265 SPORTS, Myth: Photo by Wallo Villacorta. Kristy Balliet, Block: Photo by Phil Arnold. Studio Anna Heringer, Kindergarten: Photo by Margarethe Holzer.
267 Kristy Balliet, Inverted Icon: Photo by Phil Arnold.

Cohort

292 Ultramoderne, Southlight: Photo by Naho Kubota.
294 Architecture Office, House in House: Image by Nephew LA. Independent Architecture, Motherhouse: Photo by James Florio.
295 LAMAS, Townships Farmhouse: Photo by Stéphane Groleau / Laetitia Boudaud.
297 PARA Project, Crawford Attic Writing Room: Photo by Justin Knight, courtesy Harvard GSD.
300 WOJR, House of Horns (bottom): Visualization by D Render.
306 Fievre + Jones, Bywater Artist Residence I: Photo by Eric Staudenmaier. Ultramoderne, Four Corners: Video credit to Noah Klersfeld.
312 Andy and Dave, Wanna go there! and Where is this?: Photo by David Brandon Geeting.
314 Lluís Alexandre Casanovas Blanco with María Luisa Blanc, Real Estate Boom House: Photo by Pol Rebaque. Welcome Projects, Retrospective City: Photo by Tom Bonner.
325 Adam Fure, Rocks: Image by Vergil Design Visualization.
331 First Office, Studio for Art: Photo by Stephen Barling.
336 PRODUCTORA, Pavilion on the Zocalo: Photo by Luis Gallardo.
338 Farshid Moussavi Architecture, Folie Divine: Photo by Paul Phung.
339 Jesús Vassallo, Water Towers: Photo by Nash Baker.
342 Independent Architecture, Catamount Dormitory: Photo by James Florio.
345 BairBalliet, No Middle Midrise: Photo by Malvin Bunata.

Pair

399 Hans Tursack, Graphic Fields, Composition VII: Photo by Brilliant Graphics.
401 Descriptive Services, 10 Casts: Photo by Victoria Singleton.
410 Jesús Vassallo, Water Towers: Photo by Nash Baker.

Project

454 JaJa Co, Scoring, Building: Photo by Tag Christof.
458–59 JaJa Co, Scoring, Building: Photo by Tag Christof.
477–83 MILLIØNS, Bathing, Again: Furniture set commissioned by Friedman Benda Gallery, New York, and CHAMBER.
498 MALL, Office Stack: Rendering by Glen Marquardt.
503–17 First Office, Battleship House: Photography by Marten Elder; additional support for the exhibition was provided by the Graham Foundation for Advanced Studies in the Fine Arts.
542 BairBalliet, The Next Port of Call: Photo by Spencer G. McNeil.

Colophon

The editors would like to acknowledge the support of the Harvard University Graduate School of Design, particularly Sarah M. Whiting and Mohsen Mostafavi, who, as Deans of the School, offered patient counsel during the project's long gestation from exhibition to book. Chelsea Spencer and Marielle Suba were not only incisive editors but helped to clarify our purpose and expand our ambition. Mindy Seu, Adam Strobel, Evan Orf, and Christina Shivers were essential to the design and curation of the 2018 show at the Druker Design Gallery, which would not have been possible without the efforts of Ken Stewart, Dan Borelli, David Zimmerman-Stewart, and the ever-resourceful GSD exhibitions staff. David Solomon deserves special thanks for his early work wrangling the contents of the exhibition into the more compact format of a book proposal.

Additionally, Andrew would like to thank Claus Benjamin Freyinger, Michelle Chang, Sean Canty, John McMorrough, Andrew Atwood, and of course K. Michael Hays for the constant encouragement and clear-eyed critique they delivered in equal measure, along with the rare gift of having them as both friends and colleagues. And Michael would like to thank Marrikka Trotter, Bryan Norwood, and of course Andrew Holder for their strategic advice in early stages of the project.

Library of Congress
Cataloging-in-Publication Data
Names: Hays, K. Michael, editor.
Holder, Andrew, editor.
Title: Inscriptions : architecture before speech
K. Michael Hays, Andrew Holder.
Description: Cambridge, MA: Harvard
University Graduate School of
Design, [2021]
Identifiers: LCCN 2021010260
ISBN 978-1-934510-79-7 (hardcover)
Subjects: LCSH: Architecture--Philosophy.
Architecture, Modern--21st century--
Philosophy.
Classification: LCC NA2500 .I553 2021
DDC 720.1--dc23
LC record available at https://lccn.loc.gov/2021010260

Inscriptions: Architecture Before Speech
K. Michael Hays and Andrew Holder

Designer: Studio Lin
Copyeditor: Chelsea Spencer
Proofreading and editorial support: Taylor Davey
Separations: Colour & Books
Printer: Fine Books, the Netherlands
Distributor: Harvard University Press

Published by the Harvard University
Graduate School of Design

Dean and Josep Lluís Sert Professor of
Architecture: Sarah M. Whiting
Assistant Dean and Director of Communications
and Public Programs: Ken Stewart
Associate Editor: Marielle Suba
Publications Manager: Meghan Sandberg

ISBN 978-1-934510-79-7

Harvard University
Graduate School of Design
48 Quincy Street
Cambridge, MA 02138
gsd.harvard.edu